HDRA ENCYCLOPEDIA OF
organic
GARDENING

the organic
organisation

HDRA ENCYCLOPEDIA OF
organic
GARDENING

THE HENRY DOUBLEDAY RESEARCH ASSOCIATION

Editor-in-chief Pauline Pears

A Dorling Kindersley Book

LONDON, NEW YORK, MUNICH,
MELBOURNE, DELHI

Project editor Louise Abbott
Senior art editor Stephen Josland
Art editor Alison Lotinga
Photography Peter Anderson
Illustrations Marian Hill

Managing editor Anna Kruger
Managing art editor Lee Griffiths

DTP design Louise Waller
Media resources Romaine Werblow
Picture research Samantha Nunn
Production controller Ruth Charlton

FIRST PUBLISHED IN GREAT BRITAIN
IN 2001 BY DORLING KINDERSLEY LIMITED,
80 STRAND, LONDON WC2R 0RL
A PENGUIN COMPANY

A CIP CATALOGUE RECORD FOR THIS
BOOK IS AVAILABLE FROM
THE BRITISH LIBRARY.
ISBN 07513 33816 HARDBACK
ISBN 4053 08915 PAPERBACK

COLOUR REPRODUCTION BY
COLOURSCAN, SINGAPORE
PRINTED AND BOUND IN CHINA
BY TOPPAN PRINTING CO. LTD.

THIS BOOK IS PRINTED ON PAPER FROM
SUSTAINABLY MANAGED FORESTS.

SEE OUR COMPLETE CATALOGUE AT
www.dk.com

the organic
organisation

HDRA is a charity and Europe's largest organic membership organisation. It is dedicated to researching and promoting organic gardening, horticulture and food. Membership is open to all who want to support organic growing

HDRA showcases its work and provides practical support for organic gardeners at three sites: at Ryton Organic Gardens in Warwickshire; Yalding Organic Gardens in Kent; and the Organic Kitchen Garden at Audley End, an English Heritage property. All these sites are open to the public for ideas, inspiration and enjoyment.

HDRA's information and education departments provide organic gardening and related advice to members, the media, industry and statutory bodies. We also run campaigns such as Organic Gardening for Schools, sponsored by Duchy Originals, and Organic Food For All, sponsored by KETTLE® Organic Chips, to encourage young people and novice gardeners to grow their own vegetables organically.

In our research department, we support councils and waste management and composting initiatives; we run a service for commercial landscapers and undertake research on organic farms. We have also developed professional organic horticultural standards for landscaping, and for garden plants and products. Accredited products will carry the HDRA logo (above).

As well as supporting gardeners and organic farmers in the UK, HDRA is also active internationally, working to improve small-scale organic farming in developing countries.

All of this work is made possible thanks to our members, supporters and donors

Dr Susan Kay-Williams

Chief Executive, HDRA

For further information, contact:
HDRA, the organic organisation
Ryton Organic Gardens, Coventry CV8 3LG
Tel: 024 7630 3517
Fax: 024 7663 9229
Email: enquiry@hdra.org.uk,
Visit us at www.hdra.org.uk

Registered charity no: 298104

THE EDITOR-IN-CHIEF

Pauline Pears MSc
An expert in organic vegetable growing and composting, with 25 years' experience working in the organic movement. Ran HDRA's Information and Education department for many years; now a Senior Horticultural Advisor with HDRA. Author, trainer and broadcaster.

THE CONTRIBUTORS

Kathleen Askew Sustainable landscape gardener and garden designer. Awards include a Gold Medal garden at the Chelsea Flower Show.

Anna Corbett Organic gardening specialist with a particular interest in growing herbs and vegetables. Writer, author and teacher.

Sally Cunningham HDRA deputy head gardener, a biker with a lifelong passion for plants and anything classed as natural history. Also paints, keeps hens and an allotment.

Patsy Dyer HDRA Advisor and garden designer. Has worked in Botanical Gardens in America and the UK.

Alan Gear Chief Executive, HDRA. A well-known figure on the organic scene. Regularly writes, broadcasts and lectures on organic gardening, farming and food.

Jackie Gear Executive Director, HDRA. Organic gardening and food writer, respected for her creative energy, and forthright views on all things organic.

Dr Isabelle Van Groeningen Garden consultant; co-designer of HDRA's Paradise garden and the award-winning "Go Organic" garden at Hampton Court 2000.

Andrew Miller BA DipLA MLI Chartered landscape architect; co-designer of HDRA's Paradise garden and the award-winning "Go Organic" garden at Hampton Court 2000.

Adam Pasco Editor, BBC Gardeners' World Magazine. Passionate gardener, enthusiastic composter and qualified horticulturist, with a growing interest in organic gardening.

Bernard Salt Writer with 60 years' practical experience in organic gardening.

Colin Shaw MA Freelance writer, photographer and lecturer. Enjoys applying technical solutions to gardening problems. Pioneered Square Foot gardening in the UK.

Bob Sherman BA MIoH Organic gardener for 25 years. Head of Horticulture at HDRA; Vice Chairman of the RHS Fruit Group.

Owen Smith Founder of "Future Foods". A botanist with a special interest in unusual edible plants and sustainable food production.

Janet Walker Plant lover and experienced vegetable grower, fascinated by the life cycle of plant pests and diseases. Past member of HDRA's Advisory team.

John Walker Writer, author and Permaculture designer committed to developing sustainable gardening techniques. Grows his own food in a small urban garden.

Dr Martin Warnes Runs Pestwatch, advising and training growers and retailers on garden pest control and promoting sustainable pest management.

For full contributor credits see p.416

Contents

Organic gardening: an introduction

ORGANIC METHODS ALLOW YOU TO CREATE ANY GARDEN YOU
WANT; THE METHODS ARE PRACTICAL, AND EFFECTIVE

PUT SIMPLY, ORGANIC GARDENING is an environmentally friendly, people-friendly style of gardening. Organic gardening methods can be used by everyone, to create and maintain almost any shape, size and style of garden, in any location, from a city centre to a rural idyll.

Organic gardening gives you the chance to create the garden you want, safe in the knowledge that you are also "doing your bit" to protect the wider environment.

From food to flowers

The organic movement really started in the middle of the 20th century, when forward-thinking, visionary individuals such as Lawrence D. Hills and Lady Eve Balfour began to question the direction that farming and food production, and in its wake, gardening, was taking. Their concern was, in particular, for healthy food production, and it is in the area of food production that organic growing is most advanced. But organic methods are not just for the fruit and vegetable patch. They can be applied to all areas of the garden, from lawns to shrubberies and windowsills. Interest is now growing in managing public parks, sports pitches, bowling greens and even car parks organically.

The future is organic

The last decade has seen a phenomenal rise in interest in all things organic. The organic movement – for a long time an energetic, committed, active, but relatively small group of enthusiasts – has really come of age. Organic food is widely available both in major supermarket chains and in more specialist shops throughout Europe, governments are supporting organic farming and research, and more and more people are turning to organic methods of gardening. Every time there is another food scare, or the dangers of another pesticide come to light, more people turn to eating, and growing, organically.

The bigger picture (facing page)
Organic methods are used today to create and maintain every sort and style of garden, however large or small. They are no longer confined to the kitchen garden or vegetable patch.

Pots and troughs (left)
No growing space is so tiny that organic principles cannot be applied, even plants in pots.

The development of the organic movement

Work in progress
HDRA looks to the past and to modern science to find organic techniques for the future. Above: trialling slug repellents. Below: the restored vine-house at Audley End.

Although artificial fertilisers were invented 150 years ago, they did not gain widespread acceptance until the mid-1940s, in the years following World War II. For a long time, farmers were suspicious of "artificial manure", believing that only proper "muck" put "heart" into the soil. Modern pesticides, many of which were developed as nerve poisons during the war years, have a similarly short history. Prior to 1950, the number of chemicals that were used by farmers against pests was surprisingly limited. Nevertheless, it would be wrong to think of farming at the turn of the century as being the same as the organic growing that is practised today. The fundamentals may not have changed much, but the modern, improved techniques, equipment and plant varieties used by today's organic farmers would have astonished their Victorian forebears.

Organic pioneers

The post-war years in the UK were marked by a huge drive by the government to increase agricultural production. Most farmers jumped aboard the chemical bandwagon, spurred on by subsidies and other incentives. As a result, crop yields, aided by improvements in plant breeding, rose sharply. On the face of it the new policy was an unqualified success, and yet, even in the beginning, a small number of voices were raised in protest.

Their essential concern was that, by abandoning the use of animal manure in favour of artificial nutrients, the very health of the soil was being imperilled. An impoverished soil, it was argued, produces unhealthy plants which undermine, rather than enhance, the health of people and livestock.

Lady Eve Balfour, one of the chief exponents of this theory, founded the Soil Association in 1945 in order to highlight the vital relationship between the health of soil, plants, animals and man. This marked the start of the "Organic Movement" in Britain.

Going so markedly against the advice of government, and of virtually every academic and research establishment in the land, it took a brave soul to stand out against the orthodoxy of the day. In general, it was the farmers who noticed the deterioration of their soil, or who suffered pesticide mishaps, so it was they who rallied to the organic cause in those early years.

In gardens of the time, too, the desire to be "modern" persuaded many people to switch to ready-bagged fertilisers and "miracle" products like DDT. But here, also, a tiny minority stood their ground – amongst them Lawrence D. Hills, who was one of the founding members of the Soil Association. In 1958 he set up an organisation for organic gardeners and called it the Henry Doubleday Research Association, or "HDRA – the organic organisation", as it is better known today. He named it after a Victorian, Essex-based Quaker and experimental horticulturist, whose work and philosophy he greatly admired.

The movement grows

During the 1960s, a backlash against the use of pesticides began, fuelled by Rachel Carson's revelations in her hard-hitting book *Silent Spring*, which highlighted the harmful environmental consequences of these chemicals. This gained pace with the public's increasing environmental awareness during the 1970s and 1980s. Organic food began to go on sale at about this time, though only in small specialist shops. During the final decade of the 20th century, a series of food scares, including BSE (Bovine spongiform encepalopathy, or Mad Cow Disease) and the issue of genetic modification (GM) (see also p.294), produced an explosion in demand. Now, in the new millennium, the outlook for organic production could not be brighter. Some even predict that, at current rates of growth, organic farming will have all but replaced conventional agriculture within the next 25 years. Organic gardening has likewise shown a massive increase in practitioners. HDRA, one of the leading UK organic organisations, has seen a tenfold rise in membership in the last 15 years.

So today, who says what is organic?

If food is to be marketed as "organic", the consumer needs to have confidence that it really has been grown organically. To maintain consumer confidence it is now, in many countries, illegal to sell produce as organic unless it carries a recognised organic symbol, which confirms that it has been grown to an approved set of organic standards. These standards – the practical application of the basic organic principles – cover every aspect of growing, storing and processing food, including soil management, animal welfare, and pest and weed control. In the UK the Soil Association is the largest certifying body, and its symbol the most widely used.

There are, at the time of writing, no legal standards governing amenity horticulture – parks, public gardens, golf courses, car parks and so on – but these are on the agenda. Organic gardeners know that it is perfectly possible to manage the entire garden – including roses, lawns, shrubberies and flower borders – without using chemical fertilisers and sprays. So why should the same not apply to public gardens and parks, school grounds and the like? In some countries, such as Germany, Denmark and Switzerland, such initiatives are already underway. In the UK, HDRA is working with others involved in the horticultural industry to frame a set of organic standards for amenity horticulture and landscaping.

Gardeners can choose to work to HDRA's Organic Guidelines for Gardeners (see p.397), which are adapted from the standards for commercial growing. The information provided in this book is based on those guidelines. Gardening, on whatever scale, obviously includes many aspects, such as lawns and patios, that do not concern farmers. HDRA Guidelines cover some of these non-food areas; other are under consideration.

Related systems

The fundamental principles of organic growing are also at the heart of the growing systems used by two other "movements" – Biodynamics and Permaculture. Biodynamic methods, used by farmers and gardeners alike, are based on the teachings of Rudolf Steiner, an Austrian radical philosopher working in the 1920s. Permaculture is an interdisciplinary ecological design philosophy developed by Australian Bill Mollison in the late 20th century. Both Biodynamics and Permaculture provide, for some people, a philosophy for life.

Organic gardening products

One area of gardening where it would be helpful to have legally recognised standards is that of garden products – fertilisers, composts and pesticides, for instance. Currently an item can be labelled as organic as long as it is of living origin, this being a dictionary definition of the word. This means that manure from battery chicken houses, for example, can be sold as "organic manure" although it is not acceptable for use in an organic garden.

Increasingly, however, gardening products are carrying an HDRA or other organic symbol, or a statement that they are suitable for use in an organic garden. If not, buy from an organic organisation, or check with the supplier before buying. The HDRA Guidelines and the relevant chapters in this book will help you to ask the right questions.

There is an increasing range of organic – and so-called organic – gardening products available. See page 19 for more information.

RELATED SYSTEMS

Biodynamic agriculture
Biodynamic thinking recognises a spiritual dimension to life, enlarging the basis of science to include the cosmic and what is beyond the sense-perceptible. It has a holistic world-view that, for example, sees the influence of planetary rhythms on the growth of plants and animals as of equal importance to a purely chemical analysis.

It is the regeneration of the forces that work through the soil to the plants, aided by "enlivened" compost or manure, that is the central aim of Biodynamics and which makes it conspicuously different to other organic systems. When crops are harvested from the land it is not only their substance that is removed but also the forces and vitality that make them worth eating. To give back this vitality, biodynamic gardeners use special therapeutic preparations for the soil, plants, compost and manure. Biodynamic produce carries the Demeter symbol.

Permaculture
Permaculture is an ecological design system which helps find solutions to the many problems facing us – both locally and globally.

Permaculture tackles how to grow food, build houses and create communities while minimising the environmental impact. It encourages us to be resourceful and self-reliant. By thinking carefully about the way we use our resources, it is possible to get much more out of life by using less. We can be more productive for less effort, reaping benefits for our environment and ourselves, for now and for generations to come. This is the essence of Permaculture – the design of an ecologically sound, sustainable way of living – in households, gardens, communities and businesses.

What can organics offer you?

The organic way has so much to offer you, your family and your wider environment.

Healthy eating

Organically grown produce can never be guaranteed as pesticide-free – our world is too polluted to claim that – but it is grown without recourse to the arsenal of pesticides that may be used in conventional growing. Deaths from pesticide poisoning in the western world are few, but we have really no idea about the cumulative, chronic effects of the cocktail of low levels of pesticides that we all consume in and on conventionally grown food. Babies and young children, with their low body weight, are particularly at risk. Pesticides are even found in breast milk.

By growing your own organic fruit, herbs and vegetables, you can be sure your food is as healthy – and as fresh – as it can be. You can enjoy a much wider range of varieties than you could find in the shops, too. What is more, analysis shows that organically grown food tends to be nutritionally superior in respect of vital ingredients such as vitamin C.

And it is not just food that can contain pesticide residues. Cut flowers, often imported from countries where pesticide use is less strictly controlled, may have been sprayed with substances that have been banned in other countries – so growing your own makes sense.

Healthy gardening

By gardening organically you can avoid using any pesticides at all. You, your children, and visiting wildlife can enjoy the garden environment in safety.

Healthy wildlife

Wildlife has inevitably suffered, both in numbers and species range, as the environment has become progressively degraded. It is alarming to find that once-common species of bird such as hedge sparrows, song thrushes and skylarks are now quite rare in the UK. Countless lesser-known species maintain only a precarious existence.

Not surprisingly, wildlife flourishes on organic farms and in organic gardens, and it is to be hoped that as more farmers and gardeners abandon chemicals, the steady decline of wildlife will be reversed. Scientific studies have shown that organic farms support a greater number, and diversity, of wild creatures than most conventionally managed farmland. In spite of the relatively small area of land devoted to gardens in comparison with farmland, it is still significant. Even a modestly sized organic garden can attract a diverse and plentiful wildlife community. In fact, one of the great pleasures of gardening organically is enjoying the birds, butterflies and other smaller creatures that inhabit your garden with you. With diversity comes balance, so pests are less of a problem where wildlife flourishes.

Reaping the rewards
Organic gardening creates a healthy environment and food for your family. Growing your own fresh, healthy crops will allow you to rediscover the seasonal pleasures of harvesting, and also to grow lesser-known, even traditionally local varieties of fruits and vegetables. Not only beautiful border plants but good-looking cutting flowers for the house can be managed entirely using organic methods.

Healthy environment

Environmental pollution is an increasingly common factor in modern life. Waste disposal sites and incinerators, designed to dispose of the ever-increasing mountains of rubbish, do not make pleasant neighbours. Organic gardening encourages reuse and recycling of items often thrown away or burned, helping to reduce the waste mountain.

It is hard to overestimate the damage to the environment that has been wrought by agricultural intensification during the last half-century. Precious landscape features, such as hedgerows, wildflower-rich meadows and country ponds, have been destroyed on a massive scale. Overuse of fertilisers has polluted lakes and rivers, in many cases choking them almost to death through the proliferation of algal blooms and waterweeds. Pesticides are everywhere in the environment, on land, in the sea and even at the North and South Poles, where they accumulate in the body fat of creatures such as seals, penguins and polar bears.

Organic farming and gardening, which do not rely on artificial inputs, cause little pollution. They preserve and enhance landscape features which make habitats for the wildlife that is vital for pest control. It is little wonder that scientific comparisons consistently rate organic growing as the most sustainable there is.

Healthy "pocket"

The hidden costs of conventional agriculture are huge. In the UK alone, the annual costs of cleaning up drinking water to reduce the pesticide content to an "acceptable" level are in the region of £120 million a year. Removing nitrates costs another £16 million. These costs are paid, of course, by the end user. No wonder water companies support organic growing.

Organic gardening methods can cut your costs. Making compost and leafmould, for example, can eliminate the need to purchase soil improvers and fertilisers, and you can save considerable amounts of money on organic produce by growing your own.

Healthy future

The idea that we do not inherit the earth from our ancestors, but borrow it from our children, is a compelling one. Organic methods help us to fulfil this philosophy.

Worldwide, pressures are to intensify food production, increasing reliance on chemical inputs and the rapidly declining range of crops and cultivars bred to respond to those inputs. Genetic modification (GM) is the latest, and most worrying, embodiment of this trend, which is the antithesis of organic growing. These developments deny local knowledge, traditional expertise, sustainability, diversity and devolution of power and control. Industrial agriculturalists may protest that theirs is the only way to feed the world, but many would take issue with this. The organic movement offers a healthy, sustainable alternative view of the future.

Best of both worlds
Growing plants to attract wildlife may bring an appreciation of the gentle beauty of wild and native plants, but organic gardening is not all nostalgia. It uses the best of traditional methods (especially those that, like the "no-dig" potatoes below left, save on labour) but also searches for ways to use and recycle today's materials.

So what is organic gardening?

Organic gardening is not just a matter of replacing chemicals such as artificial fertilisers and pesticides with more natural products, as it is often simplistically described. There is a great deal more to it than that, in both theory and practice.

Basic principles

The organic approach recognises the marvellous complexity of our living world; the detailed and intricate ways in which all living organisms are interconnected. It aims to work within this delicate framework, in harmony with nature.

Feeding the soil

Conventional fertilisers are generally soluble, their ingredients directly available to plants. The organic way, on the other hand, relies on soil-living creatures to make food available to plants.

Unbelievable as it may sound, a single teaspoonful of fertile soil can contain more bacteria and fungi than the number of people living on the planet. These micro-organisms, which are invisible to the naked eye, break down compost, manure and other organic materials that are added to the soil, to provide a steady supply of nutrients for plants to take up. Their activities also help to improve soil structure. Soil fed in this way tends to produce healthier plants that are better able to withstand attack from pests and diseases, or have a much better chance of recovery.

Incentives and benefits
Organic methods can be applied to the whole garden, not just food crops; it is nurturing the soil that is essential. Recycling helps to prevent unnecessary waste, and other, natural cycles can be used to advantage: if you grow plants to benefit wildlife, the wildlife will in turn help to control pests.

Natural pest control

All creatures, whatever their size, risk attack by pests and diseases. They are part of a great food chain. In the words of Jonathan Swift: "... a flea has smaller fleas that on him prey, and these have smaller fleas to bite 'em, and so proceed *ad infinitum*".

So, ladybird beetles prey on greenfly, song thrushes eat snails, and toads devour slugs. It is nature's way. As an organic gardener you can capitalise on the situation by creating the right conditions to attract these unpaid pest controllers – the gardener's friends. There are other strategies in the organic cupboard too – barriers and traps, pest- and disease-resisting plant varieties, companion planting and crop rotation. These are just some of the techniques which alone, or in combination, provide realistic alternatives to the use of pesticides.

Managing weeds

Weeds can be a valuable resource as a compost ingredient or food for wildlife, but they can also smother plants, compete for food and water and spoil the appearance of a path or border. There are currently no organic weedkilling sprays, but there are plenty of effective alternatives, both for clearing weedy ground and for keeping weeds under control. You just need to choose the one that suits the circumstances. Options include hoeing, mulching, cultivations, hand-weeding and the use of heat in the form of a flame or infra-red burner.

Conservation and the environment

By taking a holistic approach to the use of finite resources and by minimising impact on the environment, organic growing makes a positive contribution towards creating a sustainable future for all life on earth. This means recycling and reusing, instead of dumping or burning or buying in new; providing habitats where wildlife can flourish; and avoiding the use of non-reusable resources. It also involves choosing locally available materials, rather than those transported over long distances.

Welfare considerations

Animal welfare is an important element of organic farming. There is no place in the organic philosophy for factory farming, such as battery and broiler hen houses or intensive piggeries. As a logical extension, organic gardeners do not use by-products – such as manures – from intensive agriculture. There is concern for people too – the standards governing the trade in organic food are increasingly coming together with those concerned with "fair trade", to provide better livelihoods for those employed in farming, particularly in developing countries.

"Animal-free" gardening

The use of animal manures is an integral part of most organic farming systems, but it is quite possible to garden without using any products of animal origin if you prefer. Garden compost, leguminous green manures, leafmould and plant-based fertilisers are all "animal-free" organic gardening ingredients.

ORGANIC GARDENING "DO'S"

Do:
• Manage the whole garden organically – edible crops, ornamentals, lawns and paths.
• Make the garden wildlife-friendly, encouraging wildlife to control pests.
• Learn to distinguish pests from predators.
• Play to your garden's strengths, capitalising on its particular characteristics.
• Make soil care a priority.
• Make compost and leafmould to feed the soil.
• Reuse and recycle, to cut down the use of finite resources and reduce disposal problems such as landfill.
• Use organically grown seeds where possible.
• Consider the environmental implications when choosing materials for hard landscaping, fencing, soil improving and so forth.
• Collect rainwater, and reduce the need for watering by improving soil and growing appropriate plants.
• Make local sources your first choice.
• Use traditional methods where appropriate.
• Make use of the latest scientific findings where acceptable organically.
• Stop using artificial fertilisers.
• Give up smoking bonfires.
• Control weeds without herbicides.
• Avoid the use of pesticides and preservative-treated wood.
• Say no to genetically modified cultivars.
• Recognise the value of genetic diversity and the preservation of threatened cultivars.

Materials and methods
Using both traditional methods and equipment and the latest and best "high-tech" materials fits in with the organic ethos, provided that sustainability is always kept in view; why use imported timber, for example, when a local industry may be able to supply materials such as the hop poles seen below in a Kentish garden.

Preserving heritage vegetables

Diversity is a keystone of organic growing, and freedom of choice something that all gardeners appreciate, particularly when it comes to plant choice. HDRA's Heritage Seed Library (HSL) helps to maintain both within the vegetable kingdom.

Genetic loss

Over the years vegetable cultivars come and go from seed catalogues, as fashions, plant breeding and growing methods advance and change. Cultivars are also lost when the last member of a family dies and no-one takes on a particular vegetable that has been maintained in the family for generations. Every time this happens, a piece of our genetic heritage is lost. In the late 1970s, new EC regulations accelerated the loss of cultivars. The regulations were devised to encourage breeding of new cultivars; the introduction of plant patenting allowed breeders greater profit from their work. The regulations were also intended to help sort out the problem of synonyms, where one cultivar might be on sale under several names. One outcome of the new regulations was that it became illegal, in Europe, to sell seed of any cultivar that was not included in a national or EC list. In order to add a cultivar to the list, it has to be tested, to see if it is a unique variety, and to make sure that it breeds true. The trouble is that it can cost hundreds of pounds to have each variety tested and registered. Whilst this is not a problem for cultivars with high-volume sales that can absorb the increased cost, those that sell in small amounts cannot justify registration fees.

Seed library founded

It was in response to this legislation that HDRA founded the HSL. Its initial aim was to save as many as possible of the cultivars that did not make it on to the original lists, before they disappeared for good. And, unlike the many collections in official "gene banks", the aim was to keep them in cultivation – by making seed available to HSL members to grow. They are encouraged to save seed for their own use, and for others.

Another essential aspect of the HSL is its "heirloom" cultivars – which would never otherwise be available to the general public. Unlike modern cultivars, bred to meet the requirements of supermarket selling, heirlooms have been lovingly saved over the generations, maintained for their garden worth. When an heirloom is offered to the collection it often comes with valuable anecdotal information that gives each its own history. Because none of these cultivars are F1 hybrids (see p.314), gardeners can continue to save seed, while maintaining the integrity of the particular cultivar.

Genetic heritage

The HSL, which is open to anyone who cares to join (see *Resources*, p.402, for details), contains around 700 varieties, or "accessions", at present. Not all will grow prize-winning crops, though some do. They are not all chosen for their flavour – though many are very tasty. They are not all unusual in their appearance – though some certainly are. What they all have in common is that sale of their seed is illegal, yet the genes they contain are part of our genetic heritage, a valuable resource that may be of vital importance to plant breeders and gardeners, now and in the future.

Growing for seed
When grown for seed, crops such as this giant leek, 'Colossal', may need to be isolated in an insect-proof cage when in flower to keep the cultivar true. This prevents cross-pollination with other leek cultivars.

HERITAGE HIGHLIGHTS

The varieties pictured and described here are taken from the many that feature in the HDRA Heritage Seed Library's catalogues. The selection may vary from year to year depending on seed availability.

Pea 'Salmon-flowered'
An extremely pretty pea (far left) whose flowers and pods cluster at the top of the plant. When grown up a wigwam the flowers form a crown at the top. Plants produce a good crop and the peas themselves are tasty.

Leek 'Babington'
Not a true leek but a species on its own, found growing in the wild in the UK, where it may be a relic of early cultivation in monasteries. The flowerheads form bulbils, giving them a rather extraterrestrial appearance (left). These, and bulbils formed at the bottom of the plant, are used for propagation. It is used rather like garlic – the green shoots are cut for eating, while bulbs, which can be strongly flavoured, can be lifted and stored.

Early outdoor tomato 'Standpoint'
A heavy-cropping, early cultivar (left) that withstands bad weather well. Produces a profusion of golfball-sized fruit. Originally introduced by the University of Idaho.

Climbing French bean 'Cherokee Trail of Tears'
The Cherokee nation was forced out of its homeland in the 1830s on a march that became known as the Trail of Tears. They took their most precious possessions with them, including, naturally, their seeds. One of those was this climbing bean (far left). The small, black shiny seeds, produced in purple pods, are usually dried for winter use.

Going organic

As this book will show, "going organic" is not simply a question of changing your brand of spray or fertiliser (though you may well do this). It involves a change of approach, treating the garden as a complete entity where natural systems are promoted and allowed to thrive. You will start developing long-term strategies for maintaining soil fertility and managing pests and diseases.

Getting started

The best way to go organic is to take the plunge – to start using organic methods, and give up chemical methods, in every area of the garden at once. This book is full of practical advice to help in the "conversion" process, whether you are starting with a blank plot, clearing a weedy patch or converting an existing garden.

In this book, the chapter *Soil and Soil Care* helps you to get to know your soil, and learn how to get the best from it. *Weeds and Weed Control* gives advice on clearing a weedy plot, as well as keeping weeds under control. Prevention is the most effective strategy when dealing with pests and diseases. *Plant Health* and *Features for Wildlife* are both full of hints and tips. Organic methods do not stop at the edge of the flower bed – they are used for lawns too (see *Lawns and Lawn Care*). It is also important to "think organic" in relation to hard landscaping (see *The Garden Framework*) and in the greenhouse (*Gardening Under Cover*).

HDRA's Organic Guidelines for Gardeners (p.397) list techniques and materials suitable for use in an organic garden. These are divided up into three categories – Best Practice, Acceptable and Qualified Acceptance. When starting out you may find that you are mainly using techniques in the second and third categories, advancing to "Best Practice" as you, and your garden, adjust to organic methods.

How long does it take?

Commercial growers converting to organic methods are required to go through a "conversion period", commonly two years. During this period the land is managed organically, but produce cannot yet be sold as organic. Depending on past management, you may find that your garden goes through a "conversion period" while it is adapting to the change; or everything may flourish from the start!

Outside help

If you are new to organics, or simply need some advice or new ideas, there are organisations that can help. HDRA – the organic organisation, based in the UK (see p.402), runs a free organic gardening advice service for its members. It also runs organic gardens on three sites in England that are open to the public. Twice a year, HDRA members across the UK also open their gardens, providing a welcome chance to see a diverse range of organic gardens and to talk with other organic gardeners.

Local organic gardening groups can be found all over the country. A list of local groups, gardening advice, fact sheets and more is available from HDRA, or on its website at www.hdra.org.uk.

Revamp problem areas

There may be areas of your garden that you are not able, for whatever reason, to manage effectively organically. A common example is weed control on paths, drives and patios. With some thought, it should be possible to redesign these areas to make organic management a more practical option.

Dispose of unwanted pesticides

If the garden shed is full of pesticides and herbicides not suitable for an organic garden, dispose of these safely. Your local council should be able to advise.

Change the way you shop

Organic gardening products are available in some garden shops. Specialist mail order catalogues usually supply a greater range. In an ideal world, anything you use in an organic garden would itself have been grown or produced organically. Unfortunately this is not yet possible; although the range is growing, at times you will have to use conventionally grown seed, for example, or manures from animals not raised organically. Suggestions for alternative options are given opposite where appropriate. To conform to the organic principles of sustainability, always try to reuse and recycle waste materials from your own garden and locality in preference to buying in.

THE ORGANIC GARDEN SHOP

	Item	Organic choice	Notes	Other options
Plants and seeds	Seeds and sets	Organically grown vegetable and herb seed, onion sets and garlic bulbs. Also some flower seeds	Must carry a recognised organic symbol. Recent development; range still limited but expanding fast	If organic seed is not available in the cultivar you want, use untreated seed (see p.314) or save your own. Do not use genetically modified cultivars
	Transplants	Organically grown vegetable "plug" plants; also some wild flowers	Must carry a recognised organic symbol	Raise your own
	Bulbs	Organically grown bulbs	Limited range from few sources. Must carry a recognised organic symbol. Never buy bulbs taken from the wild	
	Potato tubers	Organically grown seed potatoes. Select pest- and disease-resistant cultivars where appropriate	Reasonable range available. Must carry a recognised organic symbol	If organic seed potatoes are not available in the cultivar you want, use conventional ones, or grow micropropagated plants, then save your own tubers
	Herbaceous plants, shrubs, fruit trees and bushes	A limited range, and supply, of organically grown plants is available, from specialist shops and nurseries	Must carry a recognised organic symbol	Raise your own from seed and cuttings
	Herb plants	A good range is available	Must show a recognised organic symbol	
Pots and growing media	Pots and trays	Biodegradable compressed paper and coir	Do not use peat pots; reuse plastic pots	Make your own paper pots for plant raising; recycle household items
	Growing bags	Available containing organic growing media	Avoid those containing peat	Grow in soil or large pots
	Growing media	Organic seed, multipurpose and potting composts are available	Avoid those containing peat	Make your own using organic ingredients
	Moisture retainer	Seaweed-based products		
Soil fertility	Soil improvers	Composted animal manures and plant wastes. Wide range from low- to high-fertility materials	Buy products that have some form of organic approval if available. Do not buy products that originate from intensive farming systems	Make your own from recycled garden waste, composted manure, autumn leaves and so on
	Green manure seeds	Not commonly available as organically grown as yet		Conventionally grown, or save your own
	Fertilisers	A wide range of plant-, animal- and mineral-based products. Some from organic sources	Buy products that have some form of organic approval if available. Do not use chicken manure pellets from intensive farming systems	Use other means of improving soil fertility
	Liquid feeds	A range of plant-, animal- and mineral-based products. Some from organic sources	For container plants, baskets etc – buy products that have some form of organic approval if available	Make your own from comfrey or nettle leaves
Compost-making	Compost bins	Wood or recycled plastic	Check out wood preservatives that may have been used	Make your own, or use a simple covered heap
	Compost activators	Bacterial and herbal		Grass mowings or comfrey leaves
	Worm compost bins	Wood, recycled plastic, compressed paper		Make your own or convert a plastic dustbin
Weed control	Loose mulches	Biodegradable mulches, occasionally of organic origin	Buy products that have some form of organic approval if available	Shredded garden prunings
	Mulch membranes	Biodegradable and synthetic mulches		Cardboard and newspaper
	Flame weeders	Gas- and paraffin-powered		
Pest control	Pesticides	All those permitted for use in an organic garden are available	See p.103 for acceptable products	
	Barriers and traps	Fleece, slug traps, grease bands etc		Improvise some with household materials
	Biological controls	Good range but mostly mail order only		
	Wildlife habitats	Boxes for birds, lacewings, hedgehogs and other predators		Make your own

Organic by design

A GARDEN CAN BE CREATED AND MANAGED ORGANICALLY WHETHER ITS SHAPE, SIZE AND DESIGN

WHETHER YOU ARE REVAMPING an existing garden or starting a new one from scratch, it pays to think organic from the very start. An organic garden relies on careful planning, as much as the actual gardening, to be successful. Within reason, whatever the design you have planned for your garden, you can make it organic – whether you have several rural acres or a tiny urban plot.

Find a comfortable seat, sit back, relax and take your time to develop your plans. Discuss ideas with those who will use the garden. Always consider the maintenance implications, and be realistic when deciding how much time you will want to spend working in the garden. Now is the time to build in low, or high, maintenance features. Plan in solutions and design out potential problems.

With the help of a scaled plan drawing of the existing garden, a sharp pencil and a rubber, you can gradually work out a suitable master plan, incorporating all the elements you require. Make lots of copies of the basic plan, or use a tracing paper overlay, so that you can try out all sorts of options.

When faced by a major overhaul of your garden, work out the complete plan before you embark on any work. Then decide on an order of priority. If time, courage or financial restraints mean that you cannot take on the whole garden in one season, phase the work over several years, completing one area at a time. This is better for morale than having a half-finished garden which drags on for years, giving little pleasure but much frustration.

Site assessment

When taking on a new garden it pays to take your time to familiarise yourself with the site.

• **A closer examination** of the soil and the existing vegetation will give you vital clues about soil condition and fertility; whether there are particularly wet or compacted areas, for example. (See *Soils and Soil Care*, pp.33–37, for further information on soil assessment.)

• **Observe the position** of the sun throughout the day, remembering that the winter sun may not make it over the top of trees or buildings. Identify suntraps and, equally important, likely frost pockets: low areas where frost gets trapped and the winter sun cannot reach to thaw it. Note the prevailing wind direction to see where windbreaks may be helpful. Some areas may be cold and exposed, whilst other parts can be sheltered pockets, with quite a different microclimate. Mark all these aspects, and the direction of North, on your plan.

• **Consider the relationship** between your garden and its surroundings. Are there unsightly buildings or objects that need screening, or have one's attention drawn away from them? Are there views of trees or buildings which could add to the pleasure in your garden? You can create a focal point by "borrowing" from the surrounding landscape, and give an illusion that your garden is larger than it is in reality.

• **Assess existing vegetation** for wildlife potential.

• **Watch out** for cables, pipes and drains, and make a note of where they are. If you are likely to need access to them at any time, avoid laying hard surfaces or planting big trees and shrubs over them.

• **When taking on** an existing garden it can be very hard to imagine it looking any different from what is there already. It is always worth living with a garden that is new to you for a year before making major changes. You may find that boring shrubs burst into unexpected glory, bare patches erupt with an explosion of spring bulbs and oddly positioned trees actually provide just the right amount of shade. Do not be afraid to contemplate removing existing elements to introduce new, better ones. If you do not like a plant, or it is not performing well enough because of old age or disease, take it out.

Before creating permanent paths, watch where you and your family walk. It is against human nature to go the long way round on a path if there is an easy short cut. To allow for these "desire lines", you may need to change the location of your paths, or make the short cuts inaccessible.

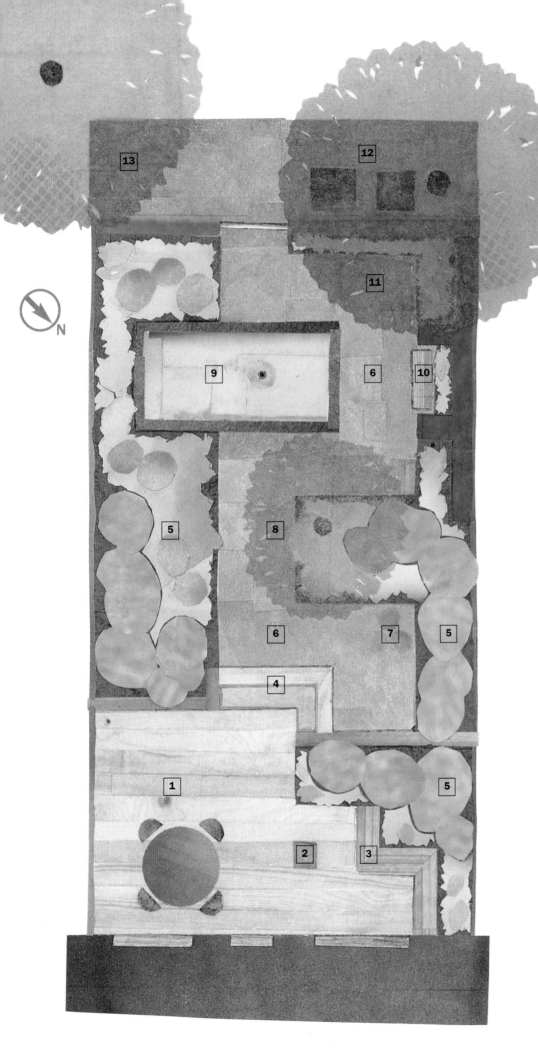

SMART TOWN GARDEN

An elegant but low-maintenance design for a busy working couple who want somewhere to relax and entertain friends.

1 Decking and patio furniture of green oak or Western red cedar. All wood from renewable sources

2 Sculpture – look for interesting pieces using local, natural or recycled materials rather than mass-produced ornaments

3 Timber seating for party guests

4 Wide timber steps, with low retaining wall of green oak either side

5 Low-maintenance planting of native species shrubs to attract and give shelter to wildlife

6 Paths of broken slate (by-product of slate quarrying) laid over weed-suppressing geotextile

7 Frost-proof terracotta pots (renewable material)

8 Ornamental spring-flowering tree to support wildlife, especially birds – allies in controlling garden pests

9 Solar-powered fountain in shallow formal pool – the garden's focal point. Water encourages birds into the garden to bathe and drink and forms a habitat for other creatures

10 Secluded timber bench, enclosed by formal clipped hedging

11 Planting of hostas and ferns which are tolerant of dry shade under tree

12 Recycling area for compost bin and leafmould cage, screened by clipped hedge. The hedge will provide a nesting place for birds

13 Storage area for additional garden furniture and for woody prunings until a shredder is hired

Planning considerations

A garden should be considered an extension of the house, providing you with open-air rooms which can be used for both work and play. While much attention is given to the functional, yet decorative, layout of a house, that of the garden tends to be ignored. The same level of thought can be put into the layout and furnishing of a garden. Compile yourself a wish list, including all the elements you must have – the basics like washing lines and compost heaps – as well as those you would like to have. Remember to include organic essentials (see list of Design Elements, p.26). Once you start planning, you will see how much fits into the space.

Living spaces

As well as looking good, a garden should remain practical. Make a separate list of the functional elements and give these priority. Fresh herbs are best positioned near the kitchen door (as long as the site is a sunny one), as is a generous seating area if you like to take your main meals outdoors. On the other hand, a relaxing area, with comfortable chairs and a small table where you can enjoy afternoon tea or have an evening drink, should be removed from the house so that you can look back across the garden. Or put them in a secluded garden "room", surrounded by scented flowers. Somewhere quiet and private gives you the chance to have a peaceful afternoon sleep, while at the opposite end of the garden, space could be provided for children to kick a ball about safely.

If you have small children, the play area should be sited within view of the patio or kitchen window so that you can keep an eye on them, whereas when they are older they prefer an element of secrecy, and you may prefer to have them out of sight.

Suburban orchard

Designs can often be based on existing features. This garden has been planned for a couple whose children have left home. They want to grow a few vegetables and give the garden an "orchardy" feel by making more of some beautiful old apple trees.

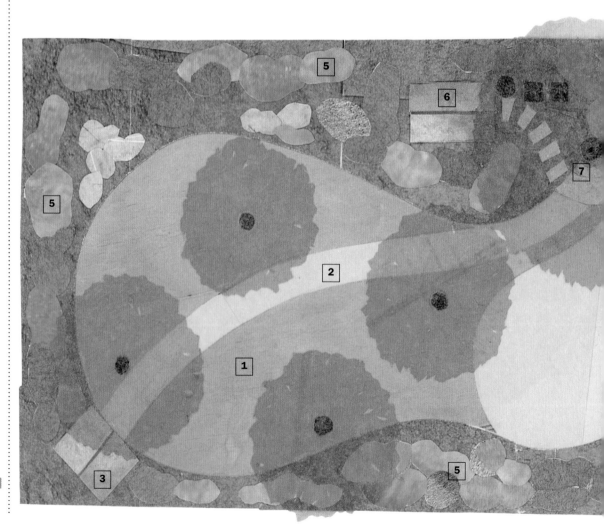

Productive areas

Nothing tastes better than home-grown vegetables and fruit. You may want, and have room for, a separate vegetable garden. If not, vegetables – and fruit and herbs – can be incorporated into the flower borders. Where space is an issue, and growing food a high priority, give some thought as to how you can create a vegetable area which, even in the depths of winter, will still look good. The easiest way to achieve this is by creating a crisp layout with edged beds. This way the bed margins will always stay defined, giving the garden a tidy look at all times of year. Espalier-grown fruit trees or arches can provide height. Although yielding less than free-standing trees, trained fruit takes up less space and can make a decorative screen. To add a decorative and colourful note, the beds could be edged with herbs or annual flowers which will be beneficial as they attract predatory insects. (See *Growing Fruit*, p.237, and *Growing Vegetables*, p.293.)

Compost and other organic recycling

Somewhere to recycle green garden waste – weeds, old plants, autumn leaves, kitchen scraps and so on – is an essential in any organic garden. In most cases, this means a compost heap, or heaps. Resist the temptation to site your compost heap in an out-of-the-way, inaccessible spot at the end of the garden. Compost bins can come in a range of designs and sizes to suit all gardens, so it is not always essential to hide them. It may be more practical to have several dotted around a larger garden, rather than one permanent site. An area to stack, temporarily, material for composting and shredding can be invaluable. A worm compost bin used to recycle kitchen scraps is best located in a sheltered spot near the kitchen door. Leafmould heaps can usually be accommodated somewhere in amongst trees and shrubs, as they require little attention. In a small garden, stuff autumn leaves into black plastic sacks, to store out of sight while turning to leafmould.

KEY TO THE SUBURBAN ORCHARD

1 Wildflower area beneath apple trees will attract pollinating insects. Care is taken when mowing these meadow areas not to damage the tree trunks or bark
2 Mown path leads to gazebo. Having short and and long grass creates habitats for a diversity of creatures, from thrushes (short grass) to amphibians (long grass)
3 Sedum roof on timber gazebo provides an additional wildlife habitat
4 Vegetables to be grown within flower borders. Ornamentals "camouflage" the vegetables, making them less vulnerable to some pests
5 Native species shrubs to support wildlife
6 Shed with insect-sheltering sedum roof and water butt to collect and store rainwater
7 Circular wooden seat under tree
8 Flowers grown amongst vegetables, for cutting and to attract beneficial insects
9 Arches, over rolled gravel path (heavily rolled surface helps to control weeds), support climbing vegetables as well as ornamental climbers
10 Lawn, managed organically
11 Green oak decking with pergola
12 Pond (in former toddlers' sand pit) uses rainwater from roof and has overflow pipe to garden
13 Bench on paved terrace. Mortared joints eliminate weeds in paving
14 Low hedge separates terrace from rest of garden
15 Urn/vase creates focal point

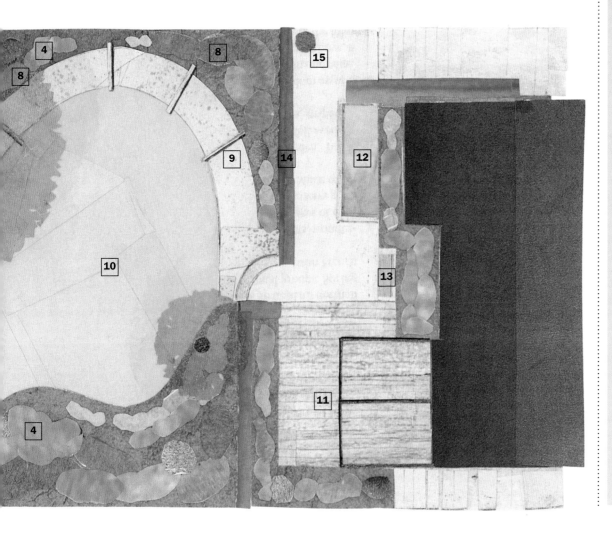

Greenhouses and cold frames

If you are keen to grow food or exotic plants, or to do more out-of-season gardening, a greenhouse is a wonderful addition to a garden. It is a tie, however, requiring regular attention. (See *Gardening Under Cover*, p.218, for advice on locating a greenhouse). More economical to buy, but less visually appealing, is a polythene tunnel. A cold frame can be useful for growing some early crops, or as a hardening-off area. Place it away from frost pockets, in a sunny position. If none of these is possible, a small heated propagator positioned on a north-facing windowsill will be useful for rooting cuttings and raising seeds.

Plant selection

In a natural environment, plants are never artificially fed, mulched or watered. They obtain all the necessary nutrition and moisture from their surroundings. Rainfall provides the moisture, and nutrients are supplied by soil organisms, which decompose vegetation and animal remains. The plants that survive and thrive are adapted to that particular environment. If the conditions change, the vegetation pattern will adapt itself accordingly. By choosing the right plants for the growing environments in your garden, and by selecting plants which fit the available space, you will find gardening becomes easier and relatively trouble-free. It will cut down on watering, feeding, staking and pest and disease control, as well as pruning.

Wildlife

Native wildlife is your friend in the garden. Apart from keeping you company, the local fauna performs a vital function in the garden. Provide suitable board and lodging and, in return, these creatures, from

Traditional back garden
Most designs have to cater to an assortment of needs. This is a practical family garden for growing a small range of edibles as well as ornamentals, hanging out the washing, and giving the children their own "private" space.

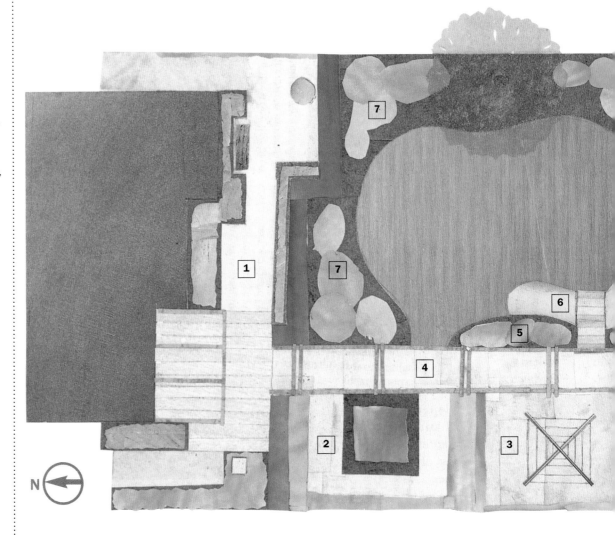

microbes to birds, will help you to keep the garden thriving, free from pests and diseases.

Thickets, shrubberies, mixed hedgerows, dead wood, ponds and scrubby growth all help to provide shelter and habitats for these useful creatures. Planting fruiting trees and shrubs such as hollies, hawthorns, rowans, crab apples and shrub roses will not only provide a colourful touch for the garden in autumn and winter, they will also provide a vital food source for these creatures. Annual and perennial flowers are useful to attract nectar-feeding insects into the garden. Some hybridised forms, particularly with double flowers, are sterile and will be of no value to nectar-feeding insects, neither will they set seed, depriving birds and mammals of food.

Water is always welcomed by wildlife. A pond (see *Gardening for Wildlife*, pp.198–201), situated in a quiet corner of the garden, can become home to many beneficial creatures. Site it in the vicinity of shrubs and trees and some long grass to extend the habitat variety. If an informal pond is not an option, consider some other form of water feature such as a small fountain, flow form (see p.71), cascade or even a simple bird bath.

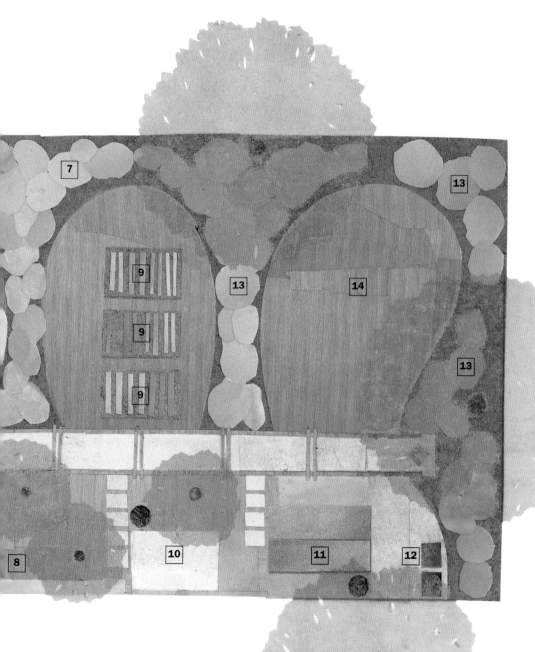

KEY TO THE TRADITIONAL BACK GARDEN

1 Easy-maintenance sitting area, part-decked with green oak, part-paved. Mortared joints keep out weeds. Wooden pergola over decking clad with climbers provides welcome shade, as the area is south-facing. In family gardens, ensure that children, whether sitting with you or in their own play areas, have some sort of protection from hot sun

2 Herb garden to provide culinary essentials and also attract beneficial insects

3 Washing line screened by trellis and space-saving espalier and fan-trained fruit trees

4 Path of natural broken slate (by-product of slate industry) laid over geotextile to control weeds

5 Bog garden makes best use of a badly drained "problem" area

6 Small pond provides habitat for pest-controlling creatures such as frogs and drinking and bathing water for birds

7 Vegetables and flowers for cutting combined in ornamental borders

8 Trained fruit trees around soft fruit bushes

9 Raised beds for easy-to-reach vegetables. These give improved drainage and avoid compaction caused by treading on soil

10 Greenhouse, for propagation and a few specialist plants, has water butt to collect rainwater for use on vegetables

11 Shed for storing tools and toys; sedum roof and water butt

12 Recycling area for making soil improvers – compost and leafmould – and stacking manure

13 Planting of native, shade-tolerant species, mainly shrubs, to support wildlife

14 Secluded play area for older children

Design elements

Even when you are not aiming for a formal style of garden, it pays to create a good structural layout – the bones of the garden. This will ensure that it looks attractive in winter as well as summer. Some of Britain's most famous gardens, such as Sissinghurst and Hidcote, are highly structured, consisting of a sequence of garden rooms, all laid out in simple but nonetheless strict geometric patterns. It is the opulent mass of flowers breaking out of their boundaries that takes away the linearity during the summer months. Once winter returns, the crisp straight lines of paths and hedges provide a totally different, but equally attractive, picture.

Paths and seating areas

Hard surface areas – paths, terraces and patios – are an expensive, but long-lasting, investment. The choice of material you use should be influenced by the style of the house, the cost, local availability and the environmental impact of the production of that material (see *The Garden Framework*, p.129, for more information). Options include real, or reconstituted, stone paving slabs, engineering bricks, timber planks, gravel or slate chippings.

Screens and windbreaks

A screen may be created in a garden to provide privacy, shelter, a visual barrier, noise absorption or to keep animals in (or out). A decorative reason for screening is to create spaces or garden rooms, which are part of the intrigue in a garden. Rather than taking in the whole garden in one glance, it is often much nicer to leave some of the garden to your imagination, and just give an enticing glimpse of things to come.

Screening for privacy requires a solid, preferably quick, answer. A brick or stone wall is instant and long-lasting, but expensive. It provides an attractive background to planting, and is ideal for climbers and trained plants. It can also create shelter, providing a special microclimate in the garden, but it is not the best choice as a windbreak. Timber fencing is a quick and affordable solution but is often treated with preservatives, and has a restricted lifespan. A hedge is in many ways an attractive option. Although it will take some years to establish, a hedge is cheap, long-lasting if well maintained, absorbs noise and pollution, and if well chosen, adds wildlife interest to the garden. It is also the most effective windbreak.

If a screen is to act as a windbreak, it should be around 50 per cent permeable to be effective. A solid wall or fence deflects the wind upwards, causing turbulence on the other side. A hedge, living fence or fedge (see p.140) or slatted fence will slow down the air as it passes through.

Internal screens do not need to be opaque; it can be more interesting to create a net-curtain effect, arresting the eye at that point, yet allowing a glimpse of the garden beyond.

Design principles

• **Focus** Focal points, which draw the eye, are an important design feature. A specimen tree, statue or sculptural plant may be used.
• **Scale** Plants and features should be of a scale that suits the garden. Avoid too many large trees and shrubs in small gardens; select small- to medium-sized ones. In larger gardens use bolder groups.
• **Unity** Elements in the garden, including hard landscaping and the house itself, should relate harmoniously to one another.
• **Rhythm** It is pleasing to have a repetition of elements. Plants may be repeated in a border, or the pattern in paving repeated along its length.
• **Contrast** Contrast in colour, texture and pattern can be achieved both in planting and hard landscaping.

ENVIRONMENTALLY SOUND CONSTRUCTION MATERIALS

First choice for materials should be those that make the least impact on the environment.
• Recycled or waste materials: re-use old bricks, paving slabs and stone, available from reclamation yards. Certain quarrying processes produce by-products such as small slate chippings, ideal for surfacing paths. Plastics, such as polystyrene, are recycled into imitation timber products, which will not decompose.
• Timber: try to use native timbers, preferably naturally resistant hardwoods rather than those treated with preservatives (see *The Garden Framework*, p.130–131, for more details).

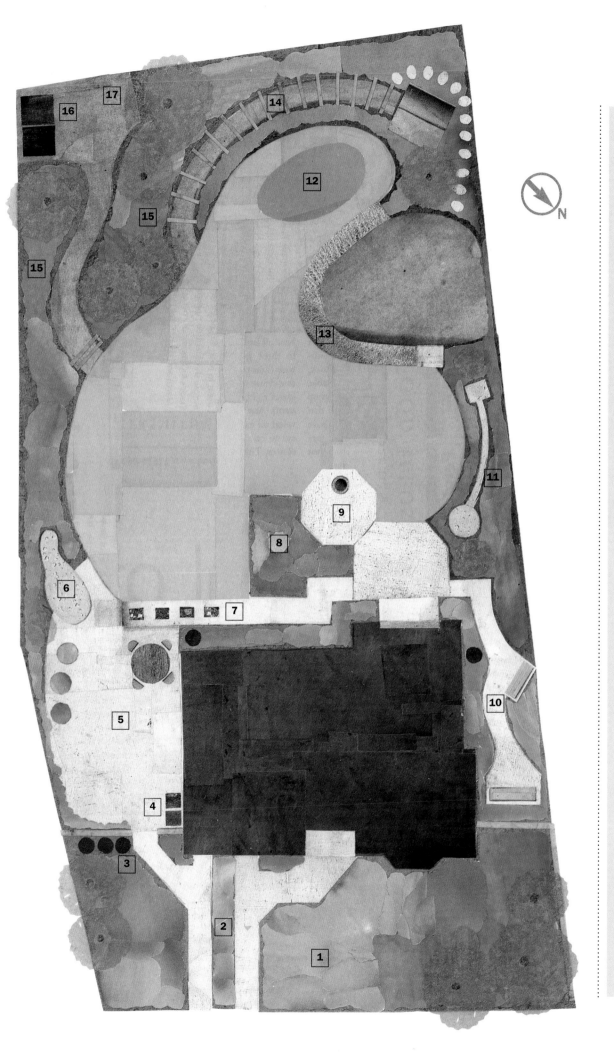

FAMILY PLOT

A family with two children want a garden that will be fun as well as a place to foster their interest in wildlife.

1 Low-maintenance dense planting in front garden gives good weed control

2 Driveway of gravel, stone chippings or crushed brick aggregate laid on compacted rubble base over weed-suppressing geotextile. Mat-forming plants in centre

3 Recycling bins for storing paper, glass and metal

4 Worm bins for providing high-nutrient compost

5 Sitting area. Herbs in planting pockets in paving of reclaimed stone or brick. Tubs for salads and edible flowers to be chosen and planted by children

6 Small pond to support wildlife, covered with secure metal grid while children are small

7 Mosaic slabs, made by family, set into path

8 Bird table to encourage birds to visit and nest in garden

9 Barbecue and bench on patio of reclaimed stone or brick

10 Secret garden with benches. Planted with ferns which will enjoy the shade

11 Shallow rill, for paper boat races, connects reservoir and pebble fountain

12 Wildflower meadow with longer grass, set within lawn, to attract beneficial insects and other creatures

13 Lavender "moat" separates children's play area from lawn. Play area has floor of play-grade chipped bark with log-pile edging

14 Living-willow tunnel, with floor of deep, weed-suppressing chipped bark, to children's den

15 Planting of small native trees and shrubs to support wildlife

16 Compost/leafmould bins

17 Logs to give haven to beetles, frogs and toads (good pest-controllers) and to grow shiitake mushrooms

KEY TO THE EDIBLE PARADISE

1 Diverse food plants including hazelnuts, mulberries, wild strawberries, Japanese wineberries, blackberries and sunflowers
2 Meadow containing edible leaves such as sorrel, dandelion and salad burnet. Close-mown margins control their spread and give access
3 Raised beds for salads and edible flowers
4 Paved area using reclaimed timber
5 Solar glasshouse provides natural warmth for tender crops and solar-heated hot tub

6 Composting toilet
7 Worm compost bins, outside log and vegetable store
8 Butts store water from all roofs
9 Paths of reclaimed brick and crushed brick aggregates; planting pockets for herbs
10 Lavender, thyme, monarda and origanum to attract beneficial insects
11 Hedge of *Rosa eglanteria* and *R. rugosa*, providing fruits for humans and birds
12 Chicken house. Adjoining orchard doubles as chicken run
13 Soft fruit; peach trained against sunny wall

14 Shady area. Leafmould and compost bins, logs to grow mushrooms, ivy for nesting birds
15 Vegetable beds allowing for 4-year rotation (see p.303)
16 Greenhouse and cold frames; toolshed. Area surfaced with bark mulch
17 Pool, with gentle slope for wildlife access; leads into bog garden
18 Comfrey for making liquid feed
19 Patio of log rounds, grooved for nonslip surface and infilled with fine crushed brick aggregate
20 Lawn

Edible paradise
This plan shows a highly productive plot for food-loving gardener-cooks who want to grow unusual crops as well as more conventional fruit and vegetables.

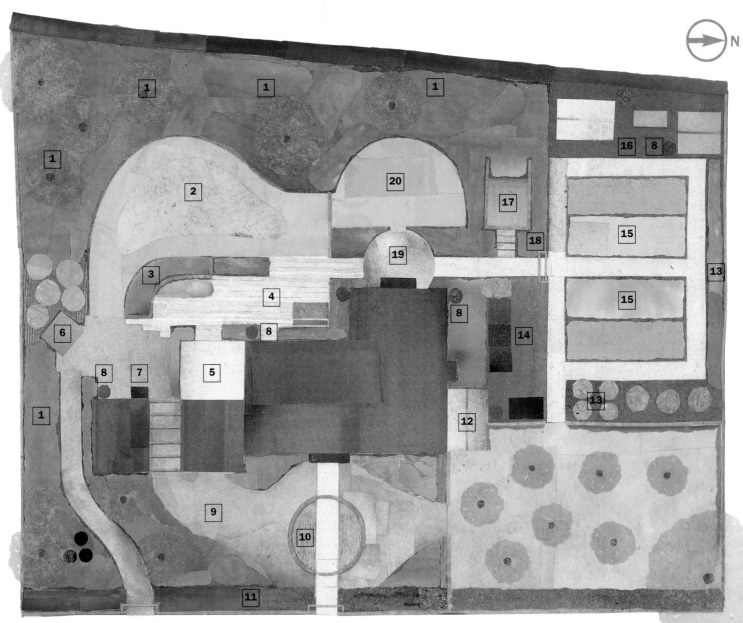

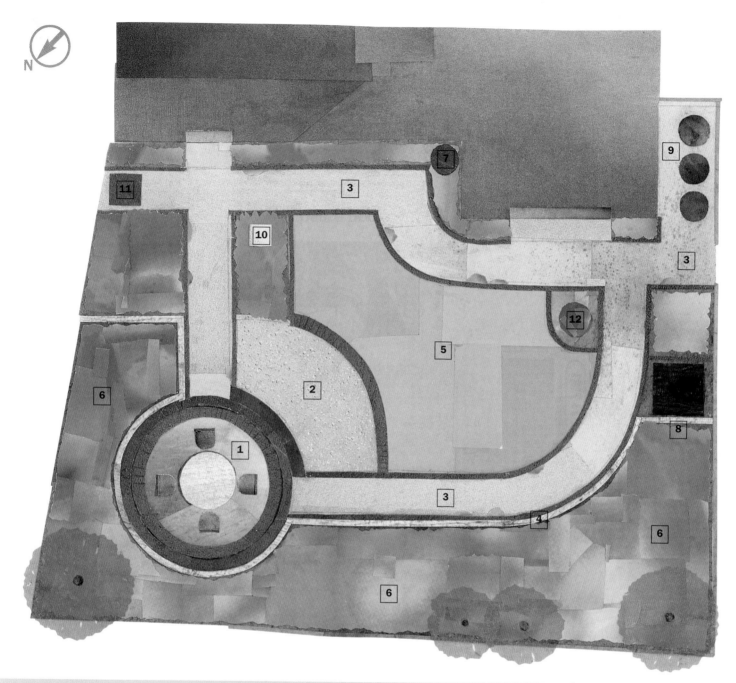

KEY TO THE CITY GARDEN

1 Patio, with table and chairs for outdoor eating, uses only natural materials – reclaimed bricks encircle paving of broken tiles

2 Pond attracts wildlife such as pest-controlling birds, insects and amphibians. Has gentle slope on flowerbed side to give creatures easy access and exit

3 Retaining wall, needed after levelling slope, constructed from heavy, vertical, reclaimed timber beams

4 Paths of crushed slate (by-product of slate industry) are edged with brick. They contain pockets for carpeting plants to enliven the slate's dark tones

5 Small flowery lawn contains spring bulbs, daisies and clover, which will help increase wildlife diversity. Requires little mowing or maintenance

6 Low-maintenance, all-year-interest planting of shrubs will also provide food and shelter for birds and other creatures

7 Water butt collects rainwater from house roof for use on plants in pot and topping up pond

8 Compost box

9 Household recycling bins for paper, glass, metal

10 Bird table attracts pest-controlling birds

11 Worm compost bin for recycling kitchen waste

12 Terracotta pot (focal point) can be used for herbs or salad plants

City garden

A garden on a small sloping site has been designed to provide relaxation and refreshment in an urban surrounding.

The basics

KEY ORGANIC TECHNIQUES FOR A GREENER GARDEN

Soil and soil care

THE SOIL IS A LIVING ENVIRONMENT, WITH AS MUCH
INFLUENCE ON PLANTS AS THE ENVIRONMENT ABOVE GROUND

TO AN ORGANIC GARDENER, the soil is the most important aspect of the garden. Building and maintaining a fertile, healthy soil must be the first priority. Much can be done to improve poor soils, but before work begins it is important to find out more about your soil type, its "texture" and its "structure". Soil texture or type depends on the physical location and the geology of the area. Soil structure is determined by previous cultivations – how the soil has been managed, if at all, in the past. Both texture and structure have an effect on soil chemistry – whether it is more acid or alkaline. This in turn will determine which plants are likely to be growing well, and the amount of life in the soil.

What is soil?

Soil is often just taken for granted – treated like dirt. Although it may look lifeless, the soil is a complete underground living environment, teeming with life. It supports plants and provides them with the food and water they need. The soil environment is just as important to plants as the environment above ground.

Understanding the particular characteristics of the soil in your garden will help you to get the best from it, and to look after it effectively. The type of soil, and its past history of cultivation, will influence what you can grow, how and when (or if) you should cultivate it, how easy it will be to work, its nutrient- and water-holding capacity, how freely it drains and how quickly it warms up in the spring.

Getting to know a soil

As you garden, you will gradually get to know your soil as you cultivate, sow, plant and weed, and notice which plants thrive and which are less successful. If you are just getting to know a new garden or plot, however, take a close look at the soil right at the start. Pick up a handful and feel it to get an idea of the texture (see overleaf); dig a hole and look at the "soil profile" to find out more about the structure, or send a sample for analysis (see p.37) to measure the pH and identify nutrient imbalances.

Soil structure

The fertility of a soil is not simply a question of the quantity of plant foods that it contains – it is the sum of all the features that are necessary for plant growth. The structure of the soil – the way it is put together – is just as important. A heavy clay soil, for example, can be rich in plant foods, but grow poor plants, because it is too heavy and waterlogged for adequate root growth. Simply improving its structure, allowing more air into the soil by adding bulky organic matter, can make a dramatic difference. Light sandy soils may be poor in nutrients, but the simple addition of a low-fertility soil improver such as leafmould, which increases the soil's ability to hold on to food and water, can again make a dramatic improvement.

Unlike soil type, soil structure is something that the gardener can alter. This chapter describes how to understand and improve soil structure, and, just as importantly, how to avoid destroying it.

**Get to know your soil
(facing page)**
The simplest activities such as walking and digging in your garden, and breaking a clod of soil down in your hand when both wet and dry, will tell you a lot about your soil. The more you garden and grow plants the more you will learn, almost without being aware of it.

SOIL STRUCTURE INDICATORS

Good structure	Poor structure
• Plant roots penetrate deeply.	• Plants are shallow-rooting.
• Sweet, earthy smell.	• Unpleasant smell.
• Water does not sit long in the bottom of a hole after rain.	• Water sits in holes or on the surface (below), or drains through immediately.
• The soil is relatively easy to dig.	• Soil sticky or in hard lumps, or very dry.
• No hard "pan" – compacted layer – in the topsoil.	• Few worms.
• Lots of worm channels.	• Compacted layer in topsoil.
• Top layers of soil crumbly and friable when both wet and dry.	• Surface layer slumps when wet, and dries out to a crust.

What's in a soil?

Around half the volume of soil is made up of mineral particles from weathered rocks, organic matter and living organisms; the other half is water and air. Together these ingredients form an effective medium to support plant growth. Plant foods are supplied by mineral particles and the breakdown of organic matter. The chemical composition of the soil also determines its pH – its acidity or alkalinity. This will affect what plants you can grow, and possibly also the availability of certain nutrients.

Soil type

Over millions of years rocks are weathered down into small particles, which form the basic ingredient of almost all soils. The size and chemical composition of the particles depends on the rock they came from and determines the type of soil you have. There are three types of weathered rock particle that make up soil: sand, silt and clay.

The proportion of the different particles found in a soil determine its type – what name it is given – and how it behaves and should be managed. Most soils contain a mixture of all three particle types. If they are in roughly equal proportions, the soil is called a loam. If one type begins to predominate, then it will be called a sandy, silt or clay loam – and the soil will begin to take on the characteristics of that particular particle type. It is not always easy to work out exactly what type of soil you have, particularly in a garden where different soils may have been brought in. However, handling a sample of moist soil, rubbing it between your fingers, rolling it into a "sausage", can give you some indication of the predominating particle types (see *Appearance and feel* in the table below). Take a handful of soil and add water to it. Work the soil in your hand until it is evenly moist and take out any stones or lumps.

• **Clay soils** Soils where clay particles predominate tend to be dense, sticky and heavy to work. The tiny clay particles settle together, with little room for air.

• **Sandy soils** At the other extreme, soils with a high sand content tend to be dry. The relatively large spaces between sandy soil particles are too big to hold water, so it drains through quickly, taking plant nutrients with it.

• **Silt soils** Fall somewhere between clay and sand.

• **Peat soils** These form where wet, acid conditions prevented full decomposition of organic matter. They are rich in organic matter and may be very

Soil type

All soils, except peaty ones, are rock-based, and their differing particle sizes, although they may seem minimal to us, are criticial to their different textures. If a particle of clay were enlarged until it was as big as one of sand, then the grain of sand, similarly enlarged, would be a boulder as tall as a person.

WHAT TYPE IS YOUR SOIL?

Soil type	Appearance and feel	Advantages	Disadvantages
Peaty soils and soils very rich in organic matter	Black or very dark, feels spongy; will not maintain any shape, cannot be rolled into a ball	Easy to work, makes a good seedbed	Can be very dry in summer and wet in winter; peat only suitable for acid-loving plants
Clay soils	Sticky, heavy feel; holds together well in a ball; can be rolled into a "sausage" shape: the higher the clay content, the thinner the sausage	Can be rich in plant nutrients and water	Roots may find it difficult to penetrate the soil to reach nutrients and water
Sandy soils	Feels gritty, makes a rasping sound when rubbed between the fingers. A light sand will not stick together or form a ball; a sandy loam is slightly more cohesive	Sandy soils warm up quickly and are easy to cultivate	Usually low in nutrients; water drains away rapidly, often washing out nutrients with it
Silty soils	Soapy, very silky feel; makes a squeaky sound when rubbed, leaving fingers dirty	Reasonably moisture-retentive and nutrient-rich	Compacts easily, so can be heavy to work
Chalky (calcareous) soils	Shallow, with lumps of white chalk or flint; high pH, free-draining	Some plants will only thrive in chalky soil	High demand for food and water. Lumps and flints may make planting difficult

acid and infertile, but can be fertile and productive.
• **Chalky soils** These tend to be alkaline and
free-draining. They formed over limestone.

Air and water

Air and water are vital for soil-living creatures, and
for effective root and plant growth. Air and water are
found in the spaces, or pores, between soil particles.
Larger pores between sand particles or soil crumbs
contain air, but they are usually too large to hold on
to water. Medium-sized pores hold water that roots
can take up. A soil that contains a good mixture of
both pore sizes can be described as well-drained and
moisture-retentive. In a waterlogged soil, water will
have replaced air in larger pores, making it difficult
for plants and creatures to survive.

Soil life

Soil teems with many different kinds of life – from
microscopic bacteria and fungi to more noticeable
creatures such as earthworms, beetles, slugs and
insect larvae. Many of these creatures are responsible
for recycling organic matter, breaking it down so
that the nutrients it contains are once again available
to plants. Their activities also build soil structure.

Some soil-living organisms can be plant pests,
and others may cause disease – but most do
no harm, or are positively beneficial. As in the
environment above ground, the more diverse and
active the community, the less likely it is that one
particular organism will get out of hand. Problems

are less likely to arise in a soil with a good structure
and rich in organic matter, which encourages a
diverse and active micro-flora and fauna.

Worms are the most obvious and well-known
creatures found in soil. They are sometimes seen on
the surface of the soil and are unearthed when soil
is cultivated. They help process organic matter by
dragging it down into the soil before eating it. Their
tunnels serve to aerate the soil and help it to drain;
their casts provide a source of nutrients, and they
help to form soil crumbs (see right).

Useful micro-organisms

There are many microscopic organisms living in the
soil. Despite their size, or lack of it, they perform
functions vital to soil health. They include bacteria
which can take up nitrogen from the air (nitrogen-
fixing), and beneficial mycorrhizal fungi.

Nitrogen-fixing bacteria exist in a symbiotic
relationship with the plant, living in nodules on the
roots. Mycorrhizal fungi live by attaching themselves
to the roots of plants. They work in harmony with
the plant by helping it to absorb more water and
nutrients; in return the plant provides food for the
fungi. The surface area of the fungi is very much
greater than the area of the roots, so the fungi
effectively extend the feeding area of the plant.
Mycorrhizal fungi are fragile and are very sensitive
to fungicides. They prefer soil that is not disturbed
so thrive in "no-dig" gardens and those with a
high organic content to the soil.

SOIL CRUMBS

The various types of mineral
particles in a soil aggregate
together, with organic matter,
to form what are called soil
"crumbs", a few millimetres in
diameter. The network of pores
between the crumbs holds air
and water, and this is where
roots grow and soil creatures
live. Where soil structure is
good, these crumbs do not
break down easily – and can
survive battering by rain and
cultivation. Where structure
is poor, the crumbs easily
collapse. A common example
of this collapse is a hard crust,
or "cap", which forms at
the surface when a poor soil
dries out.

WHAT PLANT NUTRIENTS DO

Different nutrients are needed for different aspects of plant growth. Among the major nutrients, or "macronutrients", nitrogen fuels the growth of leaves and shoots, while magnesium is important in the production of chlorophyll, the pigment that makes leaves green (magnesium deficiency shown far right). Phosphorus is important in the growth of roots; potassium is vital to flowering and fruiting, and "hardens" growth, increasing resistance to pests, diseases and frost.

CHEMICAL SYMBOLS

Plant nutrients are commonly referred to by their chemical symbols – usually one or two letters – especially in the world of synthetic fertilisers, where the "N:P:K" ratio is a prominent aspect of labelling. However, organic gardeners may also find it useful to learn this convenient "shorthand".

Macronutrients
Nitrogen (N)
Phosphorus (P)
Potassium (K)
Magnesium (Mg)
Calcium (Ca)
Sulphur (S)

Micronutrients, or trace elements
Iron (Fe)
Manganese (Mn)
Copper (Cu)
Zinc (Zn)
Boron (B)
Molybdenum (Mb)

Symbols may also appear together to indicate chemical compounds – usually simply a common or more manageable form in which the nutrient can be applied. For example, rock phosphate may be written as P_2O_5, potash as K_2O and limestone, or calcium carbonate as $CaCO_3$.

Organic matter

Organic matter is the term used to describe the dead and decomposing remains of living things, such as plant debris, animal remains and manures. It is a crucial part of the soil, providing food for soil-living creatures; for plants in particular, it is a major source of nitrogen. Without it, soil would be just sterile rock dust.

Organic matter is continually being broken down by soil creatures, and by natural oxidation. In nature it is replenished in the natural cycles of life and death. Humus is the final product in the breakdown of organic matter. It acts as a valuable reservoir of water and plant nutrients, and it helps to form stable soil crumbs.

In short, organic matter:
- Feeds soil-living creatures;
- Encourages a diverse flora and fauna in the soil;
- Improves the physical structure of the soil;
- Supplies plant foods;
- Absorbs water;
- Holds on to plant foods;
- Buffers soil against pH changes.

Plant nutrients

Plant foods are supplied by the breakdown of mineral particles and organic matter. Soil contains a wide range of nutrients that are required, in larger (macronutrients) or smaller amounts (micronutrients or trace elements), for healthy plant growth. Most nutrients required for plant growth come from the basic mineral particles that make up the soil

skeleton. They are also found in organic matter. Nitrogen is only found in living (or decaying) tissue, so bulky organic matter is a major source.

The complete range of plant foods can be found in most soils. Depending on what you are growing, you may need to augment the levels of nitrogen, phosphorus, potassium and possibly magnesium – the nutrients that plants use in greatest amounts. Other minerals can occasionally be lacking, causing plant mineral deficiencies, which result in a variety of symptoms (see pp.88-89).

However, deficiency symptoms in plants are not always due to a shortage of a particular nutrient in the soil. An excess of one nutrient – caused by adding too much fertiliser, for example – can alter the chemistry of the soil to make other nutrients unavailable to plants. Poor structure, water shortage and an unsuitable pH can also prevent plants from obtaining the nutrients that they need. Some nutrients, including nitrogen, are easily washed out of the soil.

There is generally no need to be concerned about the precise levels of plant foods in your soil. Using organic methods of soil management, you should be able to provide plants with a good balanced diet. In a new garden, however, or where plants are failing for no obvious reason, a soil analysis may be of use, to highlight any particular deficiency or imbalance that may exist. Ideally, use a soil analysis service designed for organic growers; this will indicate the potential of the soil, not simply the nutrients currently available.

Soil chemistry

An important characteristic of soil is its level of alkalinity or acidity, known as the pH. The pH scale runs from 1, extremely acidic, to 14, extremely alkaline. The range found in most soils is 4–8, with the majority of plants growing in the range 5.5–7.5. Ornamentals tend to tolerate quite a wide pH range, although some, such as many rhododendrons and heathers, will only grow on more acid soils, while others can tolerate a high pH. Vegetables prefer a pH in the range 6.5–7, fruit 6–6.5 (see those chapters for more details). The calcium level in the soil controls pH. Calcium can be washed out of the soil, especially if free-draining, making the soil more acid.

What effects does pH have?

The pH of a soil governs the availability of nutrients to plants. In very acid soils, plant foods may be washed out, or dissolve in the soil water at toxic levels. At the other end of the scale, plant foods may be locked up in the soil, unavailable to plants. Plants that can grow in more extreme pHs have adapted to deal with these problems.

Soil pH also has an effect on the diversity, and activity, of the soil life. Certain diseases, such as potato scab, are more troublesome on alkaline soils, while clubroot is much less so. Leatherjackets and wireworms are more common in acid conditions, but earthworms dislike acid soils.

Why test the pH?

An initial pH test when you take over a new garden (see below) can help you to choose the appropriate plants for the site. Always test the pH before adding lime to the soil, for example in the vegetable plot. Excessive liming can lock up certain nutrients, making them unavailable to plants.

LEARNING MORE ABOUT YOUR SOIL

Soil profiles

A good way to learn more about the structure of your soil is to dig a hole and have a look at what is known as the "soil profile". This will involve a fair amount of digging, but can tell you a lot, and it may save disappointment in the future.

Dig a hole at least 1m x 1m (3ft x 3ft) and 1m (3ft) or so deep. Clean up one vertical face of the hole and see what you can see.

The soil is likely to show two, or sometimes three, distinct layers:
• The upper layer, called topsoil, will be the darkest in colour, with the top few centimetres being darker still if the soil has been well looked after. This is where most organic matter and soil life is concentrated. The topsoil layer can be from 5 to 60cm (2–24in) deep. Its depth and composition depend on the geographical location and past soil management. You might even find quite wide variations in different parts of your garden.
• Topsoil ends where there is a distinct colour change to the subsoil. Deep roots will penetrate the subsoil layer to find water; it will contain little else in the way of organic matter. The state of the subsoil will affect how the soil drains.
• On particularly shallow soils you may also see a third layer, the parent bedrock.

Taking a soil sample

If you are going to send soil for analysis to test for nutrient levels, or measure the pH (see right), it is important to take a representative sample, otherwise the results will be meaningless. Only a small quantity of soil is required for analysis, but it must be representative of the thousands of kilos of soil in your garden.

If you are sending a sample for analysis, contact the testing service first to find out the quantity of soil required.

Do:
• Take soil to a depth of 15cm (6in).
• Take separate samples from distinct areas or plots that have been treated differently.
• Take soil from at least 10 places in each plot, distributed randomly over the area. Put the soil into a clean plastic bucket and mix it thoroughly, using a trowel or other implement. Take the final sample for analysis from this.

Don't:
• Sample soil that has been recently limed or manured, or from near compost heaps, bonfires or hedges.
• Just take one trowelful of soil.
• Touch samples with your hands.

Measuring pH

There are several ways to measure pH:

Meters
Buy a simple pH meter, consisting of a probe inserted into the soil that displays a readout almost immediately. It may not be very accurate, but will give you a rough and ready reading, with the advantage that you can take spot-readings at various points in the garden.

Kits
The easiest and cheapest pH testing kits use a liquid colour change to indicate pH. These are a little more involved than the simple probe or meter, but can give reasonably accurate results. Take samples from various parts of the garden.

Analysis
For an accurate reading, send a sample to a soil analysis laboratory, preferably one that provides a service for organic growers. It is important that the sample, or samples, are representative of the garden (see left).

Indicator plants

Look at the plants already growing in your garden and in the surrounding area. These "indicator plants" may be able to tell you a lot about soil chemistry. Be aware, though, that plants that thrive in extreme soil types are also usually just as happy on more average soils, so take a good look around to see if you can get a broad picture. One other note of caution: if you have moved into a newly built home where a garden area has been created from scratch, remember that it is common practice for developers to import topsoil (often unfortunately to cover a multitude of sins), and this may not match the soil in the locality.

• **Heavy clay/wet soil** Coltsfoot, horsetail (mare's tail).

• **Peaty/acidic soil** Corn spurrey, azaleas, rhododendrons, blueberry, corydalis, meconopsis. Blue hydrangeas retain their colour only on acid soils.

• **Sandy, dry soil** Rock roses (*Cistus*).

• **Chalky soil** Ceanothus, hibiscus, rosemary, scabious, beech, clematis. Grapevines also thrive on chalk.

Managing soil organically

How you treat your soil depends on the soil type, how it has been managed in the past, and what is growing, or will be growing, in it. If drought-loving plants are chosen for a poor, free-draining soil, for example, it will need little attention. A wild flower meadow, which needs a low-nutrient soil to flourish, will soon be taken over by other species if you start to feed it. On the other hand, a compacted clay soil in the garden of a newly built house will need considerable effort to improve it. Shrubs growing in loamy soil will need no more than the occasional organic mulch, while a vegetable plot should have a planned programme to maintain its performance.

The organic approach

The organic approach to soil care is a combination of good horticultural practice and the use, as needed, of bulky organic materials such as composts, animal manures and green manures, supplemented with organic fertilisers (natural products of animal, plant or mineral origin). Organic inputs are often recycled

Working from paths
Narrow beds are an ideal solution for heavy soils; raising the beds enables plenty of organic matter to be added, and working from paths avoids compacting the ground by treading on it.

PRINCIPLES OF ORGANIC SOIL CARE

• **Feed the soil** Bulky organic soil improvers feed the soil-living creatures that build soil structure and fertility.
• **Walk with care** A compacted soil is airless, difficult for roots to penetrate, and a poor environment for soil-living creatures.
• **Dig only when necessary** Digging has its uses, but it can destroy soil structure.
• **Keep it covered** A covering of plants, or a mulch, protects the soil structure.
• **Take care with plant nutrients** More problems are caused by over-fertilising than under-fertilising. The performance of your plants should be your guide.
• **Check the pH before you lime** Liming unnecessarily can make nutrients unavailable.

---

waste products. As well as benefiting the soil, their use helps to avoid the pollution that their disposal – in landfill sites or a bonfire – would cause. Organic gardeners, following nature's example, recycle plant and animal wastes, feeding the soil, rather than feeding plants directly. Soil-living creatures break down bulky organic materials in the soil. In the process, structure is improved, and foods are made available to plants. A biologically active soil is a healthy place to grow.

Bulky soil improvers

Bulky organic materials (see p.40), being of living origin, contain a wide range of essential plant foods and trace elements, as compared with the "quick-fix" fast-food diet of artificial fertilisers with their readily soluble, limited selection of plant foods – which do nothing for the soil life or soil structure. They may be dug into the soil, or spread over it as a mulch (see opposite). Plants fed on an organic diet are less attractive to certain pests and diseases; organic composts can help to control soil-borne pests and diseases.

Avoiding soil compaction

Compaction occurs when soils are walked on regularly, or cultivated, in wet conditions. It is a particular problem on heavy soils. Avoid it by creating paths or growing on beds that are narrow enough to be worked on from surrounding paths. Regular use of a mechanical cultivator can also cause a compacted layer or "pan" below the soil surface.

Digging and cultivating

Dig only when necessary, keeping it to a minimum. Digging is essential to break up hard and compacted ground, but regular digging increases the rate that organic matter, that essential component of a good soil, breaks down. Digging can encourage weeds too; every time you turn the soil over a new batch of weed seeds is brought to the surface to germinate.

Dig only when soil conditions are right, especially if your soil is heavy. It should not be so wet that it sticks to your spade, nor so dry that you have to break up huge clods.

It is quite possible to garden without regular digging. The chapter *Growing Vegetables* gives information on the no-dig system (see p.326).

Covering the soil with mulches

Regular mulching with an organic soil improver will do wonders for the structure of the vital surface layers of the soil – so emerging seedlings and water will penetrate it more easily. It will also help to keep the soil moist. Mulches insulate the soil from rapid changes in temperature and moisture. For this reason it is important not to mulch a dry soil until it has been soaked through by the rain. Wait until the soil has warmed up before mulching young plants. (Mulching a cold soil will keep it cool, slowing growth, making young plants more susceptible to

pest damage). As an added bonus, mulches suppress weeds (see pp.76–77) and attract beetles, centipedes and other pest-eating creatures, which enjoy the dark, moist conditions created. Keep mulches away from the base of most plants, particularly those with woody stems, to avoid encouraging stem rots.

Living mulches or green manures

Green manures (see pp.56–57) are grown to cover bare soil – over winter, for example, or between widely spaced plants. They are specific plants grown to protect and build soil structure, and to prevent nutrients being washed out of the soil. Leguminous green manures can be a useful source of nitrogen, which bacteria living in nodules on their roots take up from the air. These "nitrogen-fixers" can be valuable when growing vegetables, particularly if you do not want to use animal manures.

Altering soil chemistry

Organic fertilisers can be used, where necessary, to supply additional nutrients to the soil. Other mineral-based compounds can be used to change the pH of the soil; most commonly to raise it (increase alkalinity) by adding lime (see p.61).

Distributing weight
When ground is wet, working from a board will spread your weight and protect the soil structure, especially on clay and silty soils.

DIGGING TO BREAK UP COMPACTION

- Divide the area to be dug in half, lengthways.
- Take out a trench of soil, one spade deep – or as deep as the topsoil if this is less than one spade deep.
- Loosen the soil in the bottom of the trench with a fork. Stab the tines in vertically and move the fork gently back and forth.
- Dig the next trench, throwing the soil forward to fill in the first trench.
- Continue to the end of the plot, then turn round and come back the other way.
- Fill in the final trench with the soil taken from your first trench.

Bulky organic soil improvers

Bulky materials of living origin maintain and improve soil structure – helping light soils to hold on to food and water, and heavy soils to drain more effectively. They may also supply plant foods, released as they are broken down by soil-living creatures. The table opposite lists a range of bulky organic soil improvers. Each has a "fertility rating" as a guide to the nutrient value of each, especially their nitrogen content. These can only be a broad indication, as the exact nutrient content of this type of material can vary quite widely, depending on the basic ingredients, and how it has been stored. Remember that there is often no need to use a nutrient-rich material. Low-fertility soil improvers can be extremely effective in maintaining soil fertility, despite their low nutrient value.

Many materials, such as kitchen and garden waste and animal manures, are usually composted before use to stabilise the plant foods they contain, and to make them easier to apply.

Sources of organic soil improvers

Recycling, one of the basic tenets of organic growing, reduces the need to bring in outside inputs, and also cuts down on the volume of "waste" to be disposed of. It is rarely possible to be totally self-sufficient in a garden situation, but all bulky organic materials from the house and garden should be recycled for use in the garden. These can be augmented with supplies brought in from other appropriate sources in the locality.

Proprietary soil improvers, such as composted manures and plant wastes, can be purchased if you are unable to make enough of your own. Where possible, choose a product that has some form of accreditation from HDRA, or another organic certifying body. When in doubt, check with the supplier for the source of the ingredients. The word "organic" is not sufficient on its own; it may simply mean that the ingredients are "of living origin", not that they are appropriate for an organic garden.

Applying organic matter to the soil

All soil improvers can be applied as a mulch. Most can also be dug into the soil. Keep them in the top 15–20cm (6–8in) or so, where the main feeding

---

MAXIMUM YEARLY APPLICATION RATES

- **High-fertility soil improvers** – up to one full builder's wheelbarrow (50 litres) per 5sq m (11 gal/50sq ft). This makes an evenly spread layer approximately 5mm (¼in) deep.
- **Medium-fertility soil improvers** – up to two full builder's wheelbarrows (100 litres) per 5sq m (22 gal/50sq ft), making an evenly spread layer approximately 1cm (½in) deep.
- **Low-fertility soil improvers** can be applied in greater quantities, and more frequently if needed. As mulches, use a 15cm (6in) layer of lightweight materials such as bark and straw; up to 10cm (4in) for heavier materials, and those such as leafmould that pack down densely.

Bulky organic soil improvers
Below, from left to right: manure and other waste from a chicken run; cow manure with straw beddding (see also p.58); seaweed; spent mushroom compost; hop waste; leafmould; garden compost; municipal shreddings at a green waste composting site.

SOME ORGANIC SOIL IMPROVERS

Material	Fertility rating *	Mulch	Dig in	Notes
Bark, fine grade	Low	•	•	See Weeds and Weed Control, pp.76–77
Compost, garden	Medium	•	•	See pp.42–49
Compost, green waste	Low	•	•	Compost from large-scale composting plants, recycling green waste; a good source of potassium; little nitrogen
Compost, worm (mostly from vegetable waste)	High	•	•	See pp.52–55
Hay	Medium	•		Apply as a mulch only
Leafmould	Low	•	•	Composted autumn leaves
Manures, animal	Medium to high	•	•	Should be well-rotted before use; source from non-intensive or organic farms
Spent mushroom compost	Medium	•	•	Tends to be alkaline. Source from organic growers to avoid pesticide contamination
Proprietary products – composted manures, plant wastes and food wastes	Variable	•	•	Bagged materials available to purchase
Prunings, shredded green	Low to medium	•		Compost before use (see pp.42–49)
Prunings, shredded woody	Low	•		Apply as a mulch around trees, shrubs and perennial plants only; compost before use (see pp.42–49)
Straw	Low	•		Source from an organic farm if possible
Wood chips and coarse bark	Low	•		Apply as a mulch around trees, shrubs and perennial plants only

* This relates to the nutrient content of the material, particularly nitrogen

roots of plants are at work and where good structure is most critical. Apply medium- and high-fertility materials in the spring and summer only; their goodness will be wasted if applied over winter when plant growth is minimal. As for application rates, the maxim "if some is good, more must be better" does not apply when adding nutrient-rich materials to the soil. Too much nitrogen, for example, encourages leafy growth rather than fruits and flowers. Any excess may just be wasted, washed out of the soil and into our water supplies. Let the performance of your plants be your guide.

Making garden compost

A compost heap is both a recycling facility for kitchen and garden waste, and a small processing plant, producing a first-class, medium-fertility soil improver – garden compost. No garden should be without one – or two, or three…

Making compost is often seen as a complex art, but in fact it is not that difficult. Anyone can learn to do it. The actual process of converting waste to compost is carried out by naturally occurring creatures, from worms to microbes, that appear as if by magic. All you have to do is to supply a suitable mixture of ingredients, and let them get on with it.

Where to make compost

You can make compost in a simple covered heap at the bottom of the garden, but a compost box or bin (see pp.46–47) looks neater and can be easier to manage. Your compost heap or bin should be sited on bare earth or grass, not on a hard surface such as paving slabs. It can be in sun or shade; what is important is that it is accessible, with plenty of room around it for adding, removing and turning material.

The size of the heap or bin will depend on how much material you generate. Larger heaps are better, but choose a size that suits you. If you have a large garden, you may well need more than one bin. If you do not generate much garden waste, but want to compost kitchen scraps, consider a high-fibre heap (see overleaf) or a worm bin (see p.50).

What goes on a compost heap?

The main ingredients in a garden heap are likely to be weeds, mowings and other green waste, plus fruit and vegetable scraps from the kitchen. Other items, such as strawy manure, can be brought in to augment supplies. Anything once alive will compost, but some items are best avoided for health or practical reasons.

"Greens" and "browns"

The key to making good compost is to use a mixture of types of ingredients. Young, sappy materials, such as grass mowings, rot quickly to a smelly sludge; these are known as "greens". They need to be mixed with tougher, dry items like old

The finished product
Garden compost is a rich, dark soil-like material, and has a pleasant earthy smell when mature.

A home for a heap
A compost bin can be tucked into a corner of the ornamental garden, or take centre stage in the vegetable plot.

What to compost (right)

*A huge variety of organic waste can be recycled onto the compost heap. Large quantities of items marked * are best dealt with in heaps of their own. Other miscellaneous compostable items include wood ash and eggshells. However, do **not** add:*
- *Meat and fish scraps*
- *Glass and tins*
- *Dog faeces*
- *Used cat litter*
- *Disposable nappies*
- *Coal and coke ash*
- *Plastics*
- *Synthetic fibres*

To be composted:

From left to right: general household waste; old straw; weeds; spent bedding plants; soft hedge clippings; dead cut flowers; bedding from rabbit and hamster cages; grass clippings, opened up with the addition of some crumpled sheets of newspaper.

INGREDIENTS FOR THE COMPOST HEAP

"Greens" – quick to rot	Intermediate	"Browns" – slow to rot
Comfrey leaves	Fruit and vegetable scraps	Old straw
Grass mowings	Bracken	Tough vegetable stems
Poultry manure (without bedding)	Rhubarb leaves	Herbaceous stems
Young weeds and plants	Tea and coffee grounds	Old bedding plants
Nettles	Tea bags	Autumn leaves*
	Vegetable plant remains	Woody prunings*
	Strawy animal manures	Tough and evergreen hedge clippings*
	Cut flowers	Cardboard tubes, egg boxes, paper bags
	Soft hedge clippings	and similar paper items, crumpled up
	Herbivore pet bedding	Newspaper
	Perennial weeds*	

bedding plants – "browns", which are slow to rot on their own. "Browns" add the necessary fibre to give the compost a good structure.

Many compostable items themselves contain a good balance of "green" and "brown". When you have been making compost for a while you will get a feel for the right mixture. If the contents of your compost heap tend to be wet and smelly, mix in more "browns"; if they are dry, bring in the "greens".

The only other ingredients needed are air and water. Mix materials that tend to slump and exclude air, such as grass mowings, with more open items to ensure a supply of air. Water dry items, or mix them with the moister "greens".

High-fibre composting

A research project by the Centre for Alternative Technology in Wales has identified that one of the main problems in composting, especially for those with smaller gardens, is a lack of "brown" materials to balance the "greens", which tend to be predominately kitchen waste. To address this problem, they have developed the "high-fibre" composting technique, which uses waste paper and packaging – kitchen paper, paper bags, cardboard cartons and tubes, for example – to provide the balance of ingredients required. These are crumpled up before being added to the heap. Roughly equal volumes of kitchen waste and paper products are added as they become available. The composting process is slow, but requires no further attention.

Compost activators

"Greens", which are quick to rot, will activate a heap; in other words, will get it started. There are various types of activator on the market said to speed up the composting process, but a mixed heap should compost perfectly adequately without.

Chopping and shredding
Mashing and chopping up tough material will help it compost down. A sharp spade can be used to chop most items, including tough brassica stems. A mechanical shredder will make short work of woody hedge prunings, for example, which can then be composted or used as a mulch.

Composting weeds and diseased material

To avoid the risk of spreading troublesome weeds, compost them before they seed. Put perennial roots in a black plastic sack, mixed with some grass mowings, and leave to rot for a year. When dead, add to the compost heap.

The biological activity in a compost heap is so great that it can break down many plant diseases. Any heat produced will help the process. Even so, it is probably wise not to add plants infected with very persistent diseases such as clubroot and white rot. Foliage infected with potato blight can be safely composted, except in countries where the tough overwintering sexual spores are found.

Hedge clippings and woody prunings

Add soft young clippings – from a regularly pruned hedge, for example – to the compost heap. Tougher prunings in any quantity, including evergreen hedge clippings, are best composted separately, preferably after shredding. Heap them up or put them in a compost bin, and water well. Mix with a "green" material, or water with a nitrogen-rich liquid feed, such as nettle or comfrey liquid (see pp.206–207), to speed up the process. Use after six months or more as a mulch on established shrubs and trees.

Recycling woody waste

Tough and chunky material will compost much more quickly if chopped up into smaller pieces. A sharp spade will chop all but the woody items. For these, use a powered shredder. Hire a shredder for occasional use or buy the most powerful one you can afford. Try out a range – some are much quieter and easier to use than others.

It is important to wear adequate safety protection when using a shredder. Never use it in a confined

A SIMPLE BIN

This compost cage is simple and cheap to make. It is also an excellent way to recycle cardboard boxes.

Hammer four posts well into the ground in a square formation, and unroll chicken wire around the posts on the inner and the outer sides, stapling or nailing it in place (**1**). Be sure when you trim it to size to turn over any sharp edges. Slide cardboard down between the two layers (**2**) for insulation. You can leave the front open for easy access (**3**), or make a hinged fourth side, like a gate, that will keep the heap neat. Cover the heap with old carpet or similar (**4**).

Compost bins
Fom left to right:
• Four posts, some wire netting and a slatted wooden front make a simple, economic bin.
• A sectional or beehive wooden box (see also facing page, above) makes filling and removing the compost simple.
• A traditional wooden "New Zealand" box. Two of these side by side is ideal. One bay is filled while the other is maturing. Removable slats are taken out to get at the compost.
• Recycled plastic containers are compact, and usually have no base; simply lift them off the ground to get at the compost.

space, particularly when shredding plants such as laurel and hellebore, which contain toxins.

If you have space, woody items can just be stacked in an out-of-the-way corner and left to decay over a period of years. They will make a valuable wildlife habitat (see also p.190). Some may be suitable for use around the garden, as plant supports, for example. Your local waste disposal site may recycle woody items if you cannot. Avoid bonfires, which cause pollution and nuisance, unless you have diseased woody plants to dispose of.

Compost bins

Compost bins can be purchased or homemade, preferably from recycled or reused materials. As long as it fulfils the basic criteria listed, the design choice is yours. Choose one that suits your needs and garden. Place it in an accessible spot, directly onto bare ground. It can have a fixed site or, depending on the model, it can be moved to different parts of the garden between batches.

Once you have started making compost, you may find that two or more containers are needed,

A BEEHIVE BOX

One of the easiest wooden bins to construct, the beehive type has the advantage of looking neat in a garden setting. It can be painted and stained; some people make smart wooden lids to complete the effect. The wooden layers are all built the same way, with the battens that hold them together standing proud (**1**) so each will fit securely on top of the one below. The bin can be built up at the same rate as you add the compost (**2,3**), up to a height of 1m (3ft) or so. As the contents decompose the compost will sink, and layers can be removed to start a new heap. Turning the compost is easy with this type of bin, provided that the piece of ground next to it is left clear: simply take off the layers and restack them next to the heap, turning the compost into the "new" bin as you go (**4**).

although it is possible to get by with just one. Once maturing, compost can be covered with carpet or a plastic sheet, freeing up the bin that it was in.

Making compost

• Collect a mixed batch of "greens" and "browns" suitable for composting, as much as you can find.
• Add it to the compost bin, spreading it out to the edges. Firm down gently and water if dry.
• Continue to add to the bin as and when material becomes available. If you add kitchen waste on its

---

WHAT MAKES A GOOD COMPOST BIN?
• Solid sides.
• Open base.
• Wide top opening for easy filling.
• Rainproof lid or cover that does not blow away.
• Minimum volume of 300 litres (66 gal), or 75cm x 75cm x 1m (30in x 30in x 39in).
• Removable side, or lift-off container, to access compost.

The composting process
If you fill a bin gradually, the bottom layers will be the first to decompose (right), generating heat that will rise through the heap and be lost from an unlidded bin or uncovered heap. The heat is valuable to the composting process, so cover the heap to keep it in. A cover will also conserve moisture, while keeping out the rain. You can add extra insulation by making or buying a compost "duvet" – a padded plastic pad (far right).

own, mix it in with what is already in the bin.
• You may never fill the bin completely, as everything decreases in volume as it decays.
• After 6–12 months, or sooner if the bin is almost full, stop adding any more.
• Leave it to finish composting, and start a new one, which can be used in the meantime.
• Alternatively, check progress. Remove any compost that has formed in the lower layers. Replace the uncomposted material in the bin, adjusting the mixture if it is too wet or dry. Continue to add to this heap.

Hot tips for quicker compost

• **Fill the compost bin in one go** with a good mixture of materials. The heap should get quite hot, speeding the process and killing weed seeds.
• **Turn the heap.** Remove everything from the bin, mix it all up, and replace it in the container. Turning a "hot" heap that has cooled will reactivate it; this can usually be repeated once or twice. Turning a slow heap now and again gives you an opportunity to see how it is working, and to adjust the mixture if necessary.
• **Chop up** tough and bulky items with a spade or shredder.

How long does it take?

Compost is ready to use when it looks like a dark soil (as shown on p.42), and none of the original ingredients are recognisable – apart from the odd twig, eggshell or corn cob. It can be ready to use in as little as 12 weeks in summer, if you follow the "hot tips" above, but it can also take up to a year or more. Both quick and slow compost can be equally valuable.

Using compost

Garden compost can be classified as a medium-fertility soil improver. Apply it where required at a rate of up to two full builder's wheelbarrows (100 litres) per 5sq m (22 gal/50sq ft). This is a layer of approximately 1cm (½in) thick spread out evenly over the ground. Apply compost in spring or summer as a mulch, or dig it into the top 20cm (8in) of the soil.

TRENCH COMPOSTING

Another way to recycle kitchen and vegetable waste is to bury it in a trench or pit, and then grow peas, beans, courgettes or pumpkins on top of it. It is an effective way of providing a source of nutrients and moisture exactly where it is required.

In the autumn, dig a trench or pit, one spade deep. For peas and beans, dig it one spade wide, and as long as the row. Make a pit around 1m x 1m (3ft x 3ft) for each cucurbit plant. Gradually fill with vegetable scraps and kitchen waste, covering each addition with soil. When full, cover with the rest of the soil and leave it for a couple of months.

Sow or plant into the trench at the appropriate time for the crop, after the soil has settled.

Making leafmould

When leaves fall from trees in the autumn, they decay on the ground to form a rich, dark material called leafmould, which is an excellent soil conditioner. Making leafmould in your garden is easy to do. All you need is a supply of autumn leaves, and a simple container to stop them blowing away. Throwing leaves out with the rubbish, or burning them, is a waste of a very valuable resource.

Which leaves to use?

Any leaves fallen from deciduous trees and shrubs can be collected in autumn to make leafmould. Do not use evergreens, such as laurel and holly. Leaves of some species take longer than others to decay, but all rot down eventually. To supplement supplies, collect leaves from quiet streets or, with permission, from parks and cemeteries. Leaves from busy roadsides can be polluted with oil and vehicle emissions. Local authorities may be prepared to deliver a supply. Never collect leaves or leafmould from woodland. An easy way to collect up leaves from a lawn is to run the mower over them. The grass and chopped leaf mixture collected by the mower will rot down easily. Alternatively, mow without the collection box on the mower. The chopped leaves will soon be taken down into the lawn.

Making the leafmould

Collect fallen leaves in the autumn, preferably after rain so they are wet. If the leaves are dry, soak them well with water. Stuff the leaves into a container or stack them in a corner. Leave them to decay.

Simple leafmould containers can be made with netting and posts, or bought. There is no need for a lid or solid sides, nor is size critical – just big enough to hold your supply of leaves. Smaller quantities can be stuffed into plastic bags. Make a few air holes with a garden fork when the bags are full, and tie the top loosely. An even simpler method is to just pile the leaves in a sheltered corner and wait.

A leafmould heap may heat up slightly, but the process is generally slow and cold. It can take anything from nine months to two or more years to make a useable batch, depending on the tree species, and the particular use. The panel opposite suggests ways to use your leafmould.

LEAFMOULD AGEING

1 Freshly collected leaves in autumn.
2 The following autumn – rough, year-old leafmould makes an excellent mulch.
3 Two-year-old leafmould is much finer and can be used as a soil improver or an ingredient in growing media (see pp.116–117).

Leafmould containers
The simplest cages are made from four wooden stakes driven into the ground wrapped with chicken wire or clematis netting. A cage full of leaves decreases in volume dramatically as they decay to form leafmould.

USING LEAVES AND LEAFMOULD

Leafmould can generally be used as a low-fertility soil improver (see pp.40–41) and a moisture-retaining mulch after one year. It should be darker and more crumbly than the newly fallen leaves, but does not have to be fully rotted. For a finer product, for use in seed and potting mixes or as a top-dressing for lawns, leave it to decay for another year, or even two if the leaves are very slow to rot.

Apply leafmould in a layer up to 10cm (4in) thick, leaving it as a surface mulch or lightly forking it in if required. It can be applied to any plants at any time of year.

• Leafmould is particularly valuable as a winter cover for bare soil, especially where small seeds, such as carrots, are to be sown. Newly fallen leaves can also be used for winter cover, raking them off in the spring before sowing.

• Leafmould also makes a good moisture-retentive mulch, applied once the soil has warmed up in the spring.

• Protect the crowns of tender plants such as penstemons with a blanket of leafmould or newly fallen leaves, held down with conifer prunings. It will keep off frost in the winter, and help to retain moisture in the summer.

• To make a more nutrient-rich material for use in a potting mix, add comfrey leaves to one-year-old-leafmould (see also p.207) and allow them to decay together for a few months.

• Two-year-old leafmould can be mixed with loam and sand to make a top-dressing mix for a lawn (see p.179).

Worm composting

Certain types of earthworm, found naturally in piles of leaves and in manure and compost heaps, specialise in decomposing plant wastes. Colonies of these worms can be housed in a container and fed kitchen and garden waste, which they will convert into a rich manure known as worm compost – a high-fertility soil improver.

A worm compost system can be kept working all year round. It is a good alternative to a traditional compost heap when the main material available for composting is kitchen scraps and vegetable waste. It cannot cope with large volumes of material at once.

Worms for a worm bin
Brandling worms have a characteristic red-and-yellow banding. Their eggs are borne in tiny, lemon-shaped cocoons.

The worms and worm bins

The common-or-garden earthworms seen in soil are not suitable for use in worm composting bins. Brandling worms (*Eisenia foetida*) are the type most commonly used. They are very efficient recyclers of organic waste and will reproduce quickly in the confines of the bin. It is a good idea to start a worm bin with at least 1,000 worms – about 500g (18oz) in weight. They can be extracted from a maturing compost heap, a manure stack or another worm bin, or they can be purchased by mail order. The dark,

moist conditions that worms need to live in can be provided by keeping them in a plastic bin or a wooden box of some form. Worm bins can be purchased, or you can make your own – or adapt existing containers such as wooden crates or boxes (see facing page), or a plastic dustbin (see below). As worms like to feed near the surface, the most effective bins have a relatively large surface area. Good drainage is vital, as kitchen waste can produce a lot of moisture, and the worms will drown if conditions are too wet. If there is no reason to move your worm bin, there is no need for it to have a base; it can simply be set directly on to the soil. There is no need for the container to be "worm-proof"; the worms will stay put if the conditions are right for them.

Where to keep a worm bin

Worms work best at temperatures between 12 and 25°C (50–77°F). They will survive considerably lower temperatures, but the rate at which they produce compost will slow down. Keep a worm bin where temperatures do not fluctuate widely – out of direct sunlight in summer. Bring the bin into a shed

Dustbin worm bin
Cross-section through a plastic dustbin converted into a worm composting bin (see method, far right).

MAKING A WORM BIN FROM A DUSTBIN

1 Drill two rings of holes all around the bin, one 10–15cm (4–6in) from the bottom, the other 7.5–10cm (3–4in) below the rim.
2 To create a drainage reservoir so that the worms do not drown in accumulated liquid, fill the base of the bin with a layer of gravel approximately 15cm (6in) deep. This also stabilises the bin with its weight.
3 Cut a circle of plywood to fit over the gravel and drill holes in it – or use a perforated disc of heavy-duty polythene.
4 Add a 15–30cm (6–12in) layer of damp bedding material. This can be strips of newspaper, shredded cardboard, old compost or leafmould; it must not be raw, uncomposted material.
5 Add the worms.
6 Add a thin layer of suitable food (see facing page), spread loosely over half of the surface.
7 Cover the food with a layer of damp newspaper. Replace the lid of the bin.

or warm greenhouse in winter, or insulate it well before the cold weather starts. A worm bin with an integral drainage sump can be kept indoors, in a shed or porch for example, and moved out in the summer. Other bins may need to be set on bare soil to absorb any excess liquid produced.

Feeding the worms

A worm compost bin is, typically, used to process kitchen and vegetable scraps, which are usually available "little and often". This suits the worms, which cannot process large quantities at once. Remember that they are, in effect, livestock, with limited appetites! Excess food will "go off" before they can process it – resulting in an unpleasant smell. The worms will not process putrefying food, and may well die. A worm bin can also be used to process garden waste if it is added in small quantities. A sprinkling of ground limestone (see p.61) every month will help to keep conditions in the bin sweet.

How much your worm bin can process in a week depends on the temperature and the number of worms. Add no more than 3–4 litres (5–7 pints) of suitable food at a time. Start slowly, and build up the feeding gradually. It is important to judge what is happening before adding any more. Chop up

larger items to speed up the process. A worm bin will survive many weeks without food being added. Do not be tempted to add lots of extra food before you go away on holiday.

Common problems

A worm compost system that is working well does not smell. If a worm bin begins to smell unpleasant, and the food you add is not being processed, this is a

---

WHAT CAN I PUT IN MY WORM BIN?

Yes	No
• Vegetable peelings	• Large amounts of citrus peel
• Vegetable crop waste	• Dairy products
• Egg shells	• Meat and fish
• Fruit peelings	• Cat/dog faeces
• Cooked leftovers	• Bought flowers
• Shredded paper	• Plastic, glass, tins and other items not of living origin
• Paper bags	
• Coffee grounds	
• Tea leaves	
• Onion skins	
• Egg boxes	
• Kitchen paper	

WOODEN WORM BIN

This homemade worm bin is useful where quantities of waste are very small and space is limited. It consists of two wooden boxes from which the bases have been removed, one within the other, with a thick layer of straw packed between the two as insulation – this helps avoid extreme fluctuations of temperature, and in cold weather, will ensure that the worms keep on doing their work. The box needs a sturdy lid. Polythene around the inner sides of the inner box keeps moisture in, as well as helping to keep the worms warm. Add small amounts of food to the existing compost in a different spot each time, and cover it with damp newspaper to keep it moist.

Additional visitors
Small white, thread-like enchytraid worms may appear in large numbers in a worm bin. They are quite harmless, but can be a sign that the contents of the bin are rather acid. They are not young compost worms.

Extracting the worms
When the finished worm compost is spread out on the ground, the worms will automatically move to gather in the cooler, damper conditions under the sheet of wet newspaper. This worm-rich compost can then be gathered up and returned to the bin.

sure sign that something is wrong. The two main causes are overfeeding, and excess moisture, which may be the result of poor drainage or overfeeding. If there are still some live worms in the compost, stop feeding for a while. Mix in moisture-absorbing materials, such as newspaper, egg boxes, paper towels and cardboard tubes. Add a sprinkling of limestone and clear any drainage holes.

If on investigation you cannot see any active worms at all, you will have to assume that they are dead. Clear out the bin and start again.

Tiny black fruit flies may appear in a worm bin, especially in summer. They are not a health hazard, but can be annoying. Burying waste as you add it may cut down their numbers. Alternatively, they can be caught in a homemade trap. Never use pesticides on a worm compost bin.

Removing the compost

After a few months of regular feeding, the worms will have begun to produce a rich, dark compost in the bottom of the bin. To remove a small amount, scrape back the top layer of uneaten material and worms and take what you need.

If you want to remove larger quantities of compost, first scoop off the top layer of semi-decomposed food and worms and set this aside, and then replace this material when you have emptied out the compost.

Extracting the worms

You may find that the compost is full of worms. These should be extracted if you are to use the compost in growing media, or you may just want them to put back into your worm bin. On a dry, sunny day, spread the compost out on a hard surface, in a layer no more than 5cm (2in) deep. Place a layer of wet newspaper, several sheets thick, over one-third to a half of the compost. Go away and do something else for several hours. The worms will hide under the newspaper and can be shovelled up in the damp compost below. By repeating the process, you can collect nearly all of the worms.

Using worm compost

Worm compost made from vegetable waste is a high-fertility soil improver (see also p.41), with a fine crumbly texture. It tends to be richer than garden compost, and the plant foods it contains are more readily available. It is rich in humus, and has good water-holding capacity. These qualities, and the fact that it tends to be available in relatively small quantities, mean that it is usually used more like a concentrated fertiliser than a bulky organic compost (see opposite, below for some suggestions).

Worm liquid

Vegetable waste has a very high moisture content. Water will tend to accumulate in plastic worm bins,

Collecting liquid
This proprietary worm bin has a tap at the base to drain off liquid rich in nutrients. Put the bin on bricks so that you can get a collecting vessel under it.

Mountains of food
Gross feeders such as young melon and squash plants enjoy the richness of worm compost in their compost mix.

and the worms may drown unless adequate drainage is provided. If there is a reservoir at the bottom of the bin, the liquid can be drained off through a standard water butt tap. This liquid contains some plant foods, which can be recycled by watering it onto the compost heap. It may also be used to feed container-grown plants (diluted in at least 10 parts by volume of water) but the results are likely to be variable.

WAYS TO USE WORM COMPOST
• Apply as a top-dressing to greedy feeders such as marrows and other fruiting vegetable crops during the growing season.
• Apply as a top-dressing for patio pots or house plants – if necessary, remove the top 2cm (1in) of the potting mix (see also *Container Gardening*, p.203), and replace with worm compost. Water as usual.
• Add to a proprietary potting mix to enrich it and improve its water-holding capacity – for hanging baskets, for example.
• Use as an ingredient in homemade potting composts and other growing media (see right, and also pp.114–117).

POTTING MIX WITH WORM COMPOST

This is a rich potting mix, suitable for tomatoes, aubergines and hanging baskets, for example. Mix together:

• One or two 9-litre (2 gal) buckets of worm compost.
• One bucket of sharp sand or horticultural grit.
• Three buckets of well-rotted leafmould, or other peat alternative.
• 75g (2½oz) ground limestone (see p.61).

Green manures

Green manures are plants grown to improve the soil, rather than for food or ornament. Their beneficial characteristics include nitrogen-fixing, dense foliage for weed suppression, and extensive or penetrative roots, ideal for opening up heavy soils and improving light soils.

Why grow green manures?

• **To add plant foods** Clovers and related green manures absorb nitrogen from the air and fix it in nodules on their roots. It becomes available to plants when the green manure is dug in. Some root down to extract minerals from deep in the soil, bringing them up for subsequent shallow-rooted plants.

• **To protect soil** Green manures protect soil from compaction by heavy rain, particularly important on heavy clay. Green manures also mop up plant foods from the soil, so they are not washed out by rain.

• **To improve structure** Grazing rye, with its very extensive fine root system, improves heavy soil by opening up the structure; on lighter soils, the roots bind with soil particles, helping them to hold water.

• **To smother weeds** Green manures germinate quickly and grow rapidly, smothering weed seedlings. (See *Weeds and Weed Control*, p.76.)

• **To control pests** Frogs, beetles and other natural predators appreciate the cool, damp cover provided by a green manure. Some insects can be confused by the presence of a green manure crop planted between food crops. (See *Plant Health*, p.95.)

• **To "rest" your soil** To give your soil a rest, sow a longer-term green manure and leave it to grow for a whole season. This will help soil recover from constant cultivation and improve fertility and structure with little effort.

Choosing a green manure

The specific green manure you choose will depend on what you want to achieve, how long the ground needs to be covered, what was there before, what you will be planting next, the time of year and the type of soil you have. At first, the list of possibilities seems long and confusing, but if you apply some simple rules you can choose the best plant for your situation. These are the questions you need to ask when choosing which green manure to use:

• **How does the green manure fit into my crop rotation?** (See *Growing Vegetables*, p.302.)

• **When do I want to sow?** Choose hardy varieties to overwinter.

• **How long do I want the green manure to grow for?** Some mature more quickly than others.

• **What I am going to plant next?** Grazing rye can inhibit seed germination for several weeks after it has been incorporated, so it is best not grown before sowing small seeds.

• **What variety suits the garden soil best?**

• **Is nitrogen-fixing required?**

Armed with this information, you can choose a suitable green manure from the table opposite. Whichever one you use the principle is the same – the seeds are sown, the plant grows and at a certain

Green manures
Below, from left to right: phacelia, which if allowed to flower is a magnet for beneficial insects; alfalfa, also known as lucerne; clover; grazing rye.

Digging in a green manure
Green manure plants need to decompose rapidly once incorporated into the soil. Younger plants will rot down more rapidly, so dig them in before growth begins to toughen up – before flower buds appear, ideally. If you leave the plants to flower (which mustard, far left, can do after just a few weeks) you run the additional risk of seed forming and ripening.

point it is incorporated back into the soil. Dig the plants into the top 10–15cm (6–8in) of soil, chopping them up with a sharp spade as you do so.

When to dig in

Digging in is best done some weeks before you want to use the ground. Early spring is usually a good time when green manures have been used over winter. Allow anything from a week to a month or more for the foliage to decompose and the soil to settle before using the ground again. The younger the plants and the warmer the soil, the quicker the turnaround can be.

No-dig green manures

If you are using the "no-dig" technique (see p.326), you can still grow green manures. Instead of digging in the plants, simply cut them down and leave the foliage on the surface to decompose; you can plant through this layer, treating it exactly as a mulch, or move it to one side to sow seeds. Alternatively, cut, remove and compost the crop.

Perennial green manures and grazing rye may re-grow after cutting down. It may be possible to hoe off regrowth. Alternatively, kill it off with a light-excluding mulch, or a crop of potatoes grown under straw (see *Growing Vegetables*, p.327).

CHOOSING GREEN MANURES

Green manure	Sowing time	Growing period	Soil type	Nitrogen-fixer?
Alfalfa (ha) *Medicago sativa*	Late spring–midsummer	1 year +	Avoid acid or wet soils	Yes**
Buckwheat (hha) *Fagopyrum esculentum*	Late spring–late summer	1–3 months	Thrives on poor soils	No
Beans, field (ha) *Vicia faba*	Autumn–early winter	Over winter	Prefers heavy soil	Yes
Clover, crimson (ha) *Trifolium incarnatum*	Early spring–late summer	2–3 months; may overwinter	Prefers lighter soil	Yes
Clover, Essex red (hp) *Trifolium pratense*	Spring–late summer	3–18 months	Good loam	Yes
Fenugreek (hha) *Trigonella foenum-graecum*	Early spring–late summer	2–3 months	Well-drained	Yes **
Lupin (ha) *Lupinus angustifolius*	Early spring–midsummer	2–4 months	Light, acid soils	Yes
Mustard (hha) *Sinapis alba*	Early spring–late summer	1–2 months	Most	No
Phacelia (ha/hha) *Phacelia tanacetifolia*	Early spring–late summer	1–3 months; may overwinter	Most	No
Rye, Hungarian grazing * (ha) *Secale cereale*	Late summer–early winter	Over winter	Most	No
Tares, winter (ha) *Vicia sativa*	Spring/late summer–early autumn	2–3 months; overwinter	Avoid acid and dry soils	Yes
Trefoil (hb) *Medicago lupulina*	Spring–late summer	3 months +	Will stand light dry soils, pref. not acid	Yes

(ha) hardy annual; **(hha)** half hardy annual; **(hp)** hardy perennial; **(hb)** hardy biennial
* Will inhibit germination of small seeds for a few weeks after digging in.   ** Nitrogen-fixer only in soils that contain suitable bacteria

FARMYARD MANURE WITH BEDDING

Straw is a traditional animal bedding material, which rots down to make a useful soil improver when mixed with animal manures. However, some livestock, especially horses, are bedded on wood shavings, which although fine for the animals are not as ideal for the gardener. Wood shavings are very slow to break down and can actually rob the soil of nitrogen, rather than contributing to fertility, if they are not very well composted before use. To avoid such a risk, mix shavings-based manures with grass mowings, poultry manure or other high-nitrogen material and leave to rot for a year or two. If in doubt, use it only on perennial plants where the soil will not be cultivated – for example, in a shrub border.

Animal manures

Animal manures, from chickens and other poultry, cattle, horses and goats, are a traditional source of soil fertility in an organic garden. They are most valuable when composted with some form of bedding material. The resulting medium- to high-fertility soil improver provides bulk, to build soil structure, and nutrients, which are made available to plants as the manures decompose in the soil.

Urine is the main source of the plant nutrients, particularly nitrogen and potassium, in manures. It is soaked up by bedding (see facing page). These nutrients are easily washed out of fresh manures if not stored under cover. With birds, the urine is in fact the dab of white on the droppings, so the manure itself can be very rich.

Sourcing manure

Most organic farmers recycle their manures on the farm. Any other manure is likely to be polluted with residues of veterinary products used to treat the animals. If manure from an organic farm is not available, try to source it from "free range" and less intensive livestock units. Never use manures from intensive "factory" farms. It is easy to find local stables keen to give away their manure, but do remember that horses are wormed regularly, and the mixtures used contain pesticides, which remain for two or more weeks in the manure. Check with the stables when its horses were last dosed for worms.

Storing manure

Animal manures should be composted or well-rotted before use. This is to stabilise their nutrients, which might otherwise be washed out by the rain, and avoid any risk of damage to plants. Manures can be added to a compost heap, or if mixed with bedding they can be stacked up as a separate manure heap. If poultry manure has no bedding material with it, add it to the compost heap or mix it with straw to stack.

MAKING A MANURE HEAP

• Stack the manure in a position where it can remain undisturbed for several months.
• If the bedding is dry, soak it well.
• Tread down the material.
• Cover with a waterproof sheet.
• Leave for three months if from an organic source, otherwise six months to allow for any unwanted pollutants to break down. If based on wood shavings, at least a year will be needed (see facing page).

Chicken cycle
Manure from the pens of these free-range chickens will be rich in nitrogen, and should be used sparingly.

USING MANURE

Well-rotted manure can be dug into the soil or spread over it (right) as a mulch, especially if it contains plenty of straw. Don't let it touch living plant stems.

A sack or mesh bag of manure can be soaked in water (far right, suspended in a rainwater butt) to make manure "tea", which can be used as a liquid feed, but as the analysis of the liquid can be so variable, it is difficult to give precise instructions for its use. Apply it occasionally in place of water to plants that need a boost.

Buying ready-rotted manure

Proprietary brands of composted manures are also available. Where possible, choose a product that has a symbol or logo, or some other form of accreditation from an organic certifying body. When in doubt, check with the supplier for the source of the raw ingredients. The word "organic" is not sufficient recommendation on its own; this may simply mean that the ingredients are "of living origin", not that they are appropriate for use in an organic garden (see also p.11).

Other manure-based products

Chicken manure pellets, available as a proprietary product, are a highly concentrated source of nutrients and should be regarded as a fertiliser rather than a manure (see facing page for more information). Again, check labelling carefully to ensure that the product is suitable for an organically managed garden. Farmyard manure is also used as the basis of some proprietary liquid feeds, usually with the addition of trace elements.

Using animal manures

Well-rotted manures improve soil structure and water-holding capacity, and supply nitrogen, potassium and other plant foods. Their nutrient content will vary with the proportion of manure and urine to straw or other bedding, and if they have been stored under cover (nitrogen and potassium are easily washed out in the rain). However, they should be medium- to high-fertility soil improvers. Apply at a rate of one or two wheelbarrow loads (50–100 litres) per 5sq m (11–22 gal/50sq ft).

The main use for manures is in the vegetable garden, on hungry crops such as potatoes, courgettes and marrows, pumpkins and squashes, tomatoes and brassicas. They also make a good top-dressing for roses that are pruned hard every year, and for herbaceous plants, applied every two or three years. Manures can be used more widely on poor soils, but should not be applied where root crops such as carrots are to grow, or plants that prefer a poor, dry soil. Well-rotted manure can also be used in potting mixes (see pp.114–117).

When handling manures and other animal-based products, keep cuts covered, wash your hands under running water before handling food and keep anti-tetanus protection up to date.

Alternatives to manure

For those who wish to avoid animal products, remember that it is not essential to use manure in an organic garden. Soil fertility can be equally well maintained using other soil improvers, fertilisers and green manures described in this chapter.

Adding fertilisers and altering soil pH

Organic fertilisers are products of plant, animal or mineral origin. The nutrients they contain are generally released slowly over a period of time, as the fertiliser is broken down by microorganisms. This slow-release feeding is generally much better for plants than the quick fix of chemical fertilisers, avoiding the fast, sappy growth that can cause plants to be more susceptible to insect attack and late-spring frosts. Some organic fertilisers, such as pelleted chicken manure, blood fish and bone, seaweed meal, and the compound mixtures, supply a range of plant foods. Others, such as rock phosphate, are more specific. As these products are all of natural origin, they will also tend to contain a range of minor and trace elements as well.

It is sensible to follow basic hygiene rules when applying any fertiliser, especially the animal-based products. Wear gloves and wash your hands after application. Always follow the instructions, and do not be tempted to add extra, "just for luck".

Where specific mineral deficiency symptoms occur on plants (see p.89), the cause may not be a simple shortage of that mineral. The *A–Z of Plant Problems*, p.367, has more details. The solution should be to deal with the cause rather than symptoms, but for short-term relief more soluble mineral sources can be used. The major ones are Epsom salts (magnesium), borax (boron) and seaweed with iron (iron). Wood ash is a good natural source of potash, but as it is very soluble it is generally best recycled through the compost heap.

Altering the pH of the soil

If you need to raise the pH of your soil, that is to make it more alkaline, use ground limestone (calcium carbonate) or dolomitic limestone (calcium magnesium carbonate). These slow-acting limestones are gentler on the soil than slaked or hydrated lime. They are usually applied in autumn, to allow them to act on the soil before the next growing season, but it can take a year for the full effect to develop. The rate used will depend on the pH change required. As a general rule, add 200g/sq m (7oz/sq yd) annually until you reach the desired pH. Dolomitic limestone is the preferred choice where magnesium levels tend to be low.

Making a soil more acidic is much more difficult. Composted pine needles can have some effect, and sulphur chips (a natural-mined product) can slowly make a soil slightly more acid, but where the soil is basically alkaline, you are better advised simply to grow plants that suit the soil.

ORGANIC FERTILISERS

Fertiliser	Major nutrients	Function	Use
Bonemeal	P_2O_5 20%	Promotes strong root growth	As a base dressing before planting shrubs, fruit and other perennials
Blood, fish and bone	N 3.5%; P_2O_5 8%	General fertiliser for leaf and root growth	Apply in spring and early summer
Hoof and horn	N 12%	Slow-release supply of nitrogen, where strong growth is required	Apply in spring and early summer as required
Pelletised chicken manure	Approx: N 5%; P_2O_5 3%; K_2O 3%	High nitrogen source	Annual vegetable beds; base dressing on poor soils
Seaweed meal	N 2%; K_2O 2.7%	Helps build up humus levels in soil	Annual beds; fruit trees and bushes; lawns and turf
Phosphate, rock	P_2O_5 27%	To correct a phosphate deficiency	Good non-animal alternative to bone meal
Potash, organic garden (plant source)	K_2O 20%	Supplies potash, released over one season	Fruit and vegetables
Ground limestone	Calcium carbonate	Raises pH; supplies calcium	Use where an increase in pH is required
Dolomitic limestone	Calcium magnesium carbonate	Raises pH; supplies calcium and magnesium	Use where an increase in pH is required
Gypsum	Calcium sulphate: S 13%; Ca 16%	Supplies calcium without altering pH	A gypsum:dolomitic limestone mix (80:20) can be used to help lighten heavy clay soils

See p.36 for key to chemical symbols. Mixed organic fertilisers for specific uses, such as on vegetables or lawns, are also available.

Water and watering

WITH SENSIBLE WATERING STRATEGIES AND GOOD CHOICE OF
PLANTS, ORGANIC GARDENERS CAN CUT BACK ON WATER USE

EVERY LIVING THING needs water – without it, life
cannot exist. Plants need water so that the vital
processes of photosynthesis, respiration and
absorption of nutrients can occur. In other
words, they need water to grow, flower and fruit.

Being an organic gardener means being aware
of the resources used in the garden, and the wider
implications of their use – and this includes water.
Water conservation, storage and recycling are
essential organic gardening strategies. Organic
methods of soil care and management, careful plant
choice, and correct timing and appropriate delivery
of water help to minimise use of this valuable
resource, and avoid problems of drought – and of
overwatering.

A shortage of water affects plants in a number of
ways, depending on the type of plant, and the extent
of the shortage. Even before plants show obvious
signs of drought stress, such as wilting, their growth
and performance may be reduced. As with most
resources, not only too little but also too much
water presents plants with problems (see overleaf).

Problems caused by water shortage

• Leafy vegetable crops such as spinach and cabbage
will be much less productive. Plant vigour in general
will be lower, giving smaller, slower-growing plants.
Flowers may drop and fruits may be reduced in
both size and quality.

• Some plants will "bolt" (flower prematurely) if they
fail to receive enough water. Annuals will flower for
a very short period only before dying.

• Trees and shrubs will shed their leaves in a severe
drought; shoots and even branches may die and
snap off. Herbaceous perennials will wilt, lose their
leaves and eventually die back to ground level.

• A shortage of water can result in nutrient
deficiencies or imbalances, because the plants are
unable to absorb what they need through their
roots. In very dry climates the buildup of various
salt deposits in the soil due to high evaporation
exacerbates this tendency.

• Plants become more susceptible to disease and
pest attack when water is short. Powdery mildew, for
example, is much more common on roses, grape

WATER CONSERVATION

On a global scale, fresh water
is a scarce resource. Although
our planet has vast reserves
of water, approximately 94%
of it, located in the oceans,
is unsuitable for irrigation
purposes. The remaining 6%
is fresh water, but is mostly
held either as ice and snow
in glaciers and polar ice
caps (nearly 2%), or deep
underground within rock
strata (4%). Very little is easily
accessible for human use.
Rivers, for example, contain
0.00008% of the earth's water.
Areas of high rainfall are also
localised in occurrence and
global warming may alter
the existing patterns of
precipitation. Our current
levels of use for domestic,
industrial and agricultural
purposes both deplete water
reserves and contaminate them
and cannot be sustained in the
long term. The cost of cleaning
up water to drinking standards
is high – so it is wasteful to
squander it on our gardens.

The construction of large
dams for irrigation and
hydroelectric purposes have
radically altered or destroyed
whole ecosystems. As our
demand for fresh water
increases globally, we must
develop much more prudent
and equitable strategies for its
use. Responsible use – reducing
consumption, and recycling –
by organic gardeners is part of
this process.

Domestic water use accounts
for some 65% of the total water
used by humanity, so it is clear
that any savings made at home,
and in the garden, are worth
pursuing.

The arid approach
*Desert gardens demand good water
conservation and thoughtful planting –
strategies useful to all organic growers.*

FACTORS THAT INCREASE WATER LOSS FROM PLANTS

Sunshine
Bright sunshine causes more water loss than cloudy days.

Temperature
The hotter plants are, the more water they lose.

Humidity (lack of)
Plants lose water more quickly if the air is dry.

Winds
Strong winds increase the rate of water loss through leaves.

vines, soft fruit and many other plants when the soil is dry. Potato scab is also worse on dry soils. Blossom end rot is a disorder of tomatoes and peppers caused by water shortage (see also *Plant Health*, p.88). Stressed plants are also favourites of pests such as aphids and whitefly.

Excess water

An overly wet soil or growing medium will also affect plant growth. A wet soil warms up much more slowly in the spring; growth is slow, and young plants are more likely to succumb to pest and disease attack. When the pore spaces are filled with water, oxygen is driven out of the soil, creating "anaerobic" conditions. This can lead to the death of roots through oxygen deficiency.

There are several symptoms associated with excess water. Root diseases may become more common, and sickly, yellow, drooping foliage is often indicative of overwatered or poorly drained plants whose roots have rotted. Very moist conditions also allow slugs and snails to feed and breed at increased rates. Some plants, including camellias and pelargoniums, develop oedema, where watery blisters develop on the leaves. These blisters may become corky or burst.

Problems caused by excess watering

• Washes nutrients away.
• Wastes water – a valuable resource.
• Damages soil structure if applied by sprinkler, causing capping (see p.109) and puddling the surface.
• Encourages leafy growth at the expense of flowers.
• Encourages shallow rooting – making plants more susceptible to water shortages.
• Provides ideal conditions for slugs and snails.
• Root diseases may be more common.
• Becomes expensive if water is metered.
• Reduces flavour of fruit crops.

Soils with too much water

Poorly drained soils can be improved by installing a drainage system, which usually takes the form of perforated pipes buried below the soil surface. This is a major undertaking and it is worth trying to improve the soil structure first (see pp.38–41). The easiest option is to accept the soil as it is and convert the area into a bog garden, which will provide a great deal of beauty and interest.

HOW TO WATER LESS

There is a whole range of techniques that can be employed in the garden to reduce the need for watering – saving a great deal of time, and water.

• Choose plants that suit the soil and climate. Where water is scarce, attractive ornamental plantings can be made using succulents and drought-resistant perennials, grasses and shrubs.
• Increase the soil's water-holding capacity or, in the case of heavy clay, increase the availablity of the water to your plants by incorporating bulky organic soil improvers (see p.41). Applied as a mulch they will improve the structure of the soil at the surface, allowing rain to be absorbed more effectively and reducing run-off and puddle formation.
• Dig, where appropriate, to break up compacted ground, to encourage extensive plant rooting.
• Do not dig soil in dry weather, as this increases the rate at which it dries out.
• Mulch the soil surface (see *Weeds and Weed Control*, pp.76–77) with low-fertility soil improvers (see p.41) such as leafmould, bark chippings or other bulky material to help cut moisture loss and reduce weed growth. Make sure that the soil is moist before applying a mulch. You want the mulch to keep moisture in, rather than out. If the ground is dry, water thoroughly before laying down the mulch. In dry climates, a mulch of rocks and gravel will often trap and condense moisture and direct it to the soil surface.
• Remove weeds. Weeds will compete with plants for scarce water supplies.
• Where a tree or shrub has been planted into grass, keep a 1m (3ft) square around it grass-free (preferably mulched) for at least two years.
• Shelter plants from drying winds by building, or growing, windbreaks to protect them. Hot dry winds can increase water loss dramatically.
• When making new lawns, sow drought-tolerant grass types (see p.183). Allow grass to grow longer – up to 7.5cm (3in) – in dry weather. Grass that is not mown too frequently develops deeper roots and is more drought-resistant.
• Shade young seedlings in hot weather.
• Use seep- and soaker hose irrigation systems rather than overhead sprinklers.

CHOOSING DROUGHT-RESISTANT PLANTS

Plants that cope well with water shortage often have grey foliage (for example, eucalyptus). It may also be covered in hairs, or felted, like santolina and lavender. Leaves may be reduced to thin needles; think of pines in coastal districts, where winds are strong and drying. Alternatively, leaves and stems may be fleshy and succulent, storing reserves of water; sedums and sempervivums are good examples, as are cacti, which also protect their water reserves with tough skins, spines and prickles.

Drought-resistant plant choices for the garden include:

Trees and shrubs
Arbutus; atriplex; caryopteris; *Castanea* (sweet chestnut); cistus (rock or sun roses); cytisus (broom); elaeagnus; eucalyptus; hebes; lavender; olearia; phlomis (Jerusalem sage); pines; oaks; *Rhus* (sumach); rosemary; santolina (cotton lavender); tamarisk; gorse.

Perennials
Achilleas (yarrows); agapanthus; alliums; crambe; *Cynara* (artichokes and cardoons); dianthus (pinks); eryngiums, including sea holly (pictured); euphorbias (spurges); gypsophila; *Iberis* (candytuft); *Kniphofia* (red hot pokers); lychnis; oenothera (evening primroses); osteospermums; penstemons; perovskia; sedums; sempervivums (houseleeks); *Stachys* (lamb's ears); verbascums; yuccas.

Using water well

A plant's requirement for water varies depending on the stage it is at in its life cycle. Seedlings, which have a small root system, are very susceptible to water shortage, and may not recover if they dry out. Newly planted trees and shrubs, especially bare root transplants, will need additional watering in dry conditions for a year or two, but once established most will survive without.

Some plants have a critical period when water is essential if they are to perform to your requirements. Peas and beans, for example, need a good water supply to encourage flowering and seed set, but not until the flowers start to form. A camellia may drop all its flower buds in the spring if it has been short of water in the previous early autumn.

The type of plant can govern its water needs. Drought-resistant plants, adapted to surviving extremely dry conditions, positively thrive where water is short, and may fail if the soil is too wet.

The location of the plant also has a bearing on its watering requirements. Plants in containers, for example, rely on you, the gardener, for their supply.

MAKING BEST USE OF WATER

- Give priority to seedlings, transplants and newly planted specimens.
- Water in the early morning.
- Apply water directly to soil, not plants.
- Soak ground well; do not just wet the surface.
- Water at critical growth stages.
- Do not water plants that do not need it.
- Use a soaker hose rather than a sprinkler.
- Use a timer to control supply.
- Do not water lawns.

Plants in "rain shadow" locations – such as next to a house, wall or fence, where the soil receives less rain – are more likely to be short of water.

When to water

The most effective time to water is in the early morning or in the evening, when the air and soil are cool, and less water will be lost by evaporation.

PLANTS IN CONTAINERS

Plants in pots, tubs, seed trays, baskets and other containers need careful watering. They should never dry out completely, but neither should the growing medium be waterlogged. Supply water as it is needed rather than sticking to a routine. In hot dry weather, when plants are growing vigorously, a hanging basket, or a tomato plant in a large pot for example, may need to be watered twice a day. A slow-growing houseplant may need watering no more than once over the winter.

If a pot has dried out, water applied from above may simply run through without wetting the compost. Where possible, sit the tray or pot in a container of water, leaving it until the surface of the growing medium is moist. Remove and allow to drain well. A very dry pot may need total immersion in a bucket of water.

WATERING CROPS IN DRY WEATHER

All vegetable crops need regular watering in the early stages, as seedlings and young plants. The least thirsty vegetable crops to grow, once established, are: beetroot, sprouting broccoli, Brussels sprouts, winter cabbage, spring cabbage, carrots, leeks, winter cauliflower, onions, parsnips, radishes, swede and turnips. Critical times for watering other crops – only, of course, if the weather is dry – are:

While flowering
Peas and all types of beans; continue as pods start to form
Potatoes
Sweetcorn

While fruiting
Peas and beans
Sweetcorn, as cobs swell
Courgettes and marrows
Tomatoes

All the time
Leafy vegetables, such as lettuce and spinach. Summer cabbage

---

Avoid watering slug-susceptible plants in the evening, though; watering leaves a film of moisture on plants and soil, creating ideal conditions for slugs and snails.

Water shortage is not the only cause of wilting. Root rots, wilt diseases and root-eating pests such as vine weevil are also possible

How much water?

It is not easy to advise on how much water you should apply, and how often, as this depends on the plants you are growing, the temperature and a host of other factors. The golden rule is to give plants an occasional thorough soaking every so often rather than little and often. During dry weather 11 litres per sq m (2 gal per sq yd) on row crops should be sufficient to moisten the root zone successfully.

Once you have watered a plant or a bed, check the soil to make sure that the water has penetrated down to the roots. A wet soil surface may hide a dry soil beneath. Water again if necessary.

Watering vegetables

Vegetables respond to watering in different ways, depending on the crop, and its growth stage. Water encourages vegetative (leaf and shoot) growth, which is useful for leafy crops, but can delay cropping of peas, beans and tomatoes, and may reduce flavour. More leafy growth does not necessarily mean higher yields of root crops. Where time, and water, is short, water only those plants that will benefit, at the key stages that will give maximum response (see above).

Methods of applying water

You can deliver water to plants in many ways, ranging from the most basic to very high-tech. It depends on your budget, the time you have available and how much water you have. Water is best directed to the plant's roots, avoiding soaking the

Methods of watering
Always direct water at plant roots, either with a hose or spray (below left), or by filling reservoirs sunk into the soil, such as porous clay pots, open lengths of pipe, or plastic bottles upended with the lids loosened. The clay pots between the lettuces (below right), have been given lids to reduce evaporation, a traditional method known as "pitcher irrigation". Porous seep- and soaker hose, laid between plants (bottom) or just below the soil, is one of the most valuable modern contributions to water conservation.

leaves, flowers and stems where it may encourage disease. Sprinklers are one of the least efficient ways of watering and should be avoided where possible, as much of the water is blown away or evaporates before it reaches the plants. In dry climates, where watering is an essential and often daily task, it makes good sense to avoid surface evaporation by directing the water below ground level to the plant roots using seephose irrigation (see below).

Hand systems

Water can simply be applied with a watering can or hose. This has the advantages of allowing you to give individual plants water when they need it, and in the correct quantity. The disadvantage is that this can take up a lot of time, and plants can die if you

are absent. Hoses fitted with a trigger-operated mechanism reduce the water wasted as you move between plants. Water delicate seedlings with a fine rose to avoid damaging them. If they are in a seed tray or pot, stand it in a tray of water until the compost is moist, rather than watering from above.

You can increase the efficiency of hand-watering by directing the water below ground to where the roots are. This reduces evaporation and keeps the surface dry, which helps to prevent weed growth. Traditionally an unglazed pot is buried next to a plant, into which water is poured. This seeps out gradually. Other possibilities include a large funnel, or an inverted plastic drinks bottle with the base cut off, and the cap loosely secured so that water can escape. For trees and shrubs, a piece of perforated agricultural drainage pipe laid with one end at root level and the other at the surface works well.

Irrigation systems

Elaborate, gravity-fed irrigation channels are found in many parts of the world. The same principles can be adapted to garden-scale operations if you have a suitable water source and sloping site.

"Seep-" or "soaker" hose irrigation is more practical for most sites where there are rows of plants with the same water requirements. Water passes along porous or "leaky" pipes, soaking into the surrounding soil through small holes. If the pipes are buried below the surface, or under a loose mulch or weedproof membrane (see *Weeds and Weed Control*, pp.76–77), evaporation is virtually nil, ensuring that the plants get to use all the water. The water supply is turned on only for as long as is necessary to water the plants, then switched off – or an automatic timer can be fitted.

For more widely spaced plants, trickle irrigation, where individual drippers are fitted at specified locations along a pipe, is more appropriate. This sort of system can also be used for a series of hanging baskets or planters.

A basic system that can be used in a greenhouse or for houseplants uses a series of wicks connected to a central reservoir. Water is drawn along the wicks by capillary action to the soil in the pots, thus maintaining moisture levels. All you need to do is top up the reservoir regularly.

What water to use?

Water used to irrigate a garden can be obtained from a number of sources. There is little need to use drinking-quality water on garden plants and crops.

Mains water

Mains water is clean, usually available whenever you want it, and supplied at high pressure. The provision of this service, however, may come at an unnecessary cost – both financial and environmental. The chlorine in tap water may harm your soil's microbe population and damage sensitive plants. Tap water may also have a high pH, making it unsuitable for use on lime-hating plants.

Rainwater

Rainwater is generally of good quality, free from contaminants, and has a relatively low pH, making it suitable for use on all types of plants. Surprisingly large volumes can easily be harvested from roofs via the guttering and downpipes and stored in water butts, tanks and ponds. To work out how much water you are likely to be able to collect, you need to know your roof area and average rainfall in your region. By multiplying these you can calculate the likely volume of water your roof will yield. Bear in mind that there will be some inefficiencies – so a figure of about 75 per cent of the total is realistic.

Store as great a volume as you can. The supply from a single water butt will not last long in dry weather. A container with a tight-fitting, light-excluding cover is preferable, to reduce evaporation, to help to discourage mosquitoes and leaves and other detritus from accumulating, to prevent algae from growing, and to keep children out. If your tank or butt is situated above the garden, you may be able to allow gravity to do the work of moving the water, using a hose attached to the tap. If not, a small pump may be needed, or simply use a watering can.

River, springs and wells

If you are lucky enough to have one in your garden, water from clean natural sources such as wells, lakes, springs and rivers is perfectly suitable for use in the garden. Check with your local water authority that you have permission to extract water, and what restrictions or charges are in operation. Excessive use

WATER STORAGE RECEPTACLES

Storage container	Pros	Cons
Water butt, plastic	Relatively cheap, many sizes; reused/recycled butts available	Damaged by UV (sunlight)
Water butt, wood	Attractive	Heavy, often leaks if not kept full
Tank, steel	Durable	Unattractive, will rust
Tank, concrete	Durable, suitable for underground use	Expensive to construct
Tank, ferro-cement	Durable, fairly cheap, design and shape can be customised	Need to be fairly skilled to construct

The grey way
Waste water can be diverted from a household sink or bath before it disappears down the drain. It should not be stored like rainwater, however, nor should it be used on food plants. An overflow is helpful to direct excess water down a drain, rather than soaking the surrounding ground.

of natural supplies could cause them to run out, threatening the local ecology, so be reasonable in your usage. You may also need to pump or filter the water before using it in irrigation pipes. Be aware of the possibility of contamination by agrochemicals in intensively farmed areas.

Grey water

Grey water is the term used for domestic waste water, excluding sewage. As the volumes produced are quite large, grey water can be valuable for garden use as

long as it is handled correctly, and it is not too contaminated with soaps, detergents, fats and grease. Waste water from dishwashers is unsuitable; the detergents they use can harm plants. Water from the bath or shower (avoid bubble bath and oils, and other perfumed gels and soaps if you can), and that used for washing vegetables is most suitable. It can simply be transported in a washing-up bowl, or siphoned from the bath. Waste pipes can be fitted with a diverter, to collect the water before it goes down the drain.

Grey water, with the exception of that which has simply been used to wash vegetables, should not be used on plants for eating. Nor is it suitable for use on acid-loving plants. Rotate grey water applications around the garden to avoid potential buildup of harmful substances. Bath or shower water is likely to contain bacteria, some of which could be potentially harmful to health, so it should not be stored – use it immediately. It can be run through a straw filter or a reed bed before use if greater purity is required.

A reed bed is a large, more long-term project which will take some time to establish (see opposite). To make a simple straw filter, fill a well-perforated bucket with straw, and allow your grey water to flow through it before directing it on to permanent plantings. Empty the bucket onto the compost heap at regular intervals and renew the straw.

Drains and downpipes
Rain is a free source of clean water, and collecting and storing it in a water butt, pond, tank or trough is an excellent method of water conservation.

Reed beds for purification

One of the best ways of cleaning up grey water is through a reed bed system, where the water flows through a gravel-filled trough or tank containing reeds and other water plants. The vast numbers of bacteria living on the roots of the reeds break down the waste materials in the water into a form that is safe for plants to use. Their numbers are especially high because the reeds are able to transport oxygen down to their roots via their hollow stems. The grey water leaves the reed bed in a fit state for irrigating the whole garden, including vegetables.

Reed beds do not work as efficiently at low temperatures, so if you live in a cold climate it may be necessary to divert your grey water back into the mains drainage system during the winter. Plumbing in a separate pipe with a valve that can be opened and shut will allow you to direct the water to the reed bed or down into the sewer at will. A "surge tank" large enough to hold all the water leaving the house at one time allows the water to flow at a controlled rate into the reed bed via another valve.

Types of reed bed

There are two basic types of reed bed, horizontal and vertical. In horizontal reed beds, the waste water enters at one end of a waterproof trough and flows through it in a horizontal direction, whereas in vertical beds it pours into the centre of the trough and flows downwards to the bottom before leaving. Vertical systems are now more popular as they take up less space and are believed to be more efficient.

In the vertical reed bed, the base of the trough contains about 50cm (20in) of coarse gravel, with a 20cm (8in) layer of pea gravel on top. The reeds are planted into this, spacing them about 50cm (20in) apart. The most commonly used species is common reed (*Phragmites australis*), but others that are locally common in your region could also be used. A rough guide to the size of the trough is 1.5–3 square metres (1.5–3 sq yds) for each person in the household. Beds need to be rested at frequent intervals, so it is a good idea to have several small ones that can be used alternately. The processed water can be collected or allowed to trickle away into the ground.

Using flowforms

A recently developed method of further improving the quality of the water that leaves a reed bed is the "flowform". This consists of a series of stepped bowls into which the water flows. The design of the cascade makes the water flow in a figure-of-eight pattern as it progresses downwards. This oxygenates it and is believed by some to further enhance its qualities on other, more subtle levels. A flowform is certainly a beautiful addition to the garden, and to the purification process.

Water diverter
A homemade device allows water from the downpipe to be diverted into a collecting pipe, or in times of surplus simply to drain away normally.

FLOWFORMS

The rhythmic oscillation of water passing through a flowform is fascinating to watch and soothing to hear, as well as being an effective means of oxygenating water. Though all flowforms consist basically of a pattern of interlocking pools, various designs are available. Moisture-loving plants such as ferns will thrive in the cool, moist atmosphere created by the cascading water. The rims of the shallow pools will become favourite perching spots for garden birds.

Weeds and weed control

"IS THIS A WEED?" IS A COMMON QUESTION ASKED BY NOVICE GARDENERS. THE ANSWER IS, "IT DEPENDS"

Whether a plant is a weed or not simply depends on the identity of the particular plant, on where it is growing, and the effect it is likely to have on the plants around it. Simply put, a weed is an invasive plant, growing where you do not want it. A weed can be an annual, a biennial, a herbaceous or shrubby perennial, or even a tree species. This chapter introduces you to the way that weeds work – how and why they are so efficient – and the range of organic methods that you can employ to clear weeds, and keep them under control.

The aim in an organic garden is not to eradicate every weed, but to keep them at an acceptable level appropriate to the situation. Plants that can be weeds can also make a positive contribution to a garden – in which case they are no longer weeds!

What makes a weed?

Plants that become weeds are aggressive colonisers, the invaders of the plant world. Some are wild plants, others are plants that were deliberately introduced into gardens. Japanese knotweed (*Reynoutria japonica*), for example, was introduced into British gardens in 1825, as "a plant of sterling merit". It is now Britain's most troublesome weed, almost impossible to eradicate, and it is illegal to plant it.

We can still, unwittingly, plant potential weeds today. Russian vine (*Fallopia baldschuanica*), for example, is a useful fast-growing creeper that can cover an ugly fence or garden shed in a few months; but in a few years it can overwhelm a full-sized tree. Yellow archangel (*Lamium galeobdelon*) and periwinkle (*Vinca major*) give quick ground cover, but can soon take over the whole border.

PRINCIPLES OF ORGANIC WEED CONTROL

• Know your weeds. Knowing how a weed survives and reproduces helps in choosing the most effective method of dealing with it.
• Design out problem areas; design in effective weed prevention.
• Take time to clear perennial weeds effectively before any permanent planting – even if this could take a year or more.
• Choose methods to suit the time and energy that you have available.
• When clearing ground, be realistic. Do not clear more than you are able to keep weed-free.
• Never leave soil bare: plant it, cover it, or sow a green manure.
• Mulches can both prevent and eradicate weeds – for little effort.

Take up the hoe (facing page)
A hoe can be a particularly effective tool for controlling weeds at varying stages of growth.

WEEDS IN THE GARDEN

Positive attributes

Weeds can be:
• Attractive – such as field pansy and scarlet pimpernel;
• Edible – like chickweed, fat hen, nettles, ground elder;
• Food and shelter for birds, for example teasel, thistles, ivy;
• Food for beneficial insects (such as cow parsley) and host to creatures that will eat pests;
• Attractive to butterflies (dandelion);
• Useful additions to the compost heap: deep-rooted weeds such as dandelions can bring up potassium and phosphorus for other plants.

Negative attributes

Weeds can:
• Spoil the appearance of beds and borders;
• Overwhelm other plants, smothering them with vigorous growth;
• Compete for soil moisture and nutrients;
• Reduce yields of fruit and vegetables;
• Make harvesting more difficult;
• Act as host plants for pests and diseases.

How weeds work

Knowing how weeds reproduce, spread and survive adverse conditions can help you to develop an effective weed management and control strategy.

Weeds use a variety of techniques to achieve their aim: survival and invasion.

• **Annuals and biennials** Annual weeds grow, set seed and die in the space of a year. Some may produce several generations in one year. Seed is their mechanism for spread and survival. Some weeds can even set seed after they have been hoed off when in flower. Annual weeds are most common in regularly disturbed ground such as vegetable plots and annual borders.

Biennials flower in their second year and spread as seed. They are more common in perennial and shrub beds and plantings, where ground is not disturbed every year.

• **Perennial survival** Perennial weeds make use of a range of mechanisms for their long-term survival and spread. This can include both seed and vegetative means, such as runners, stolons, rhizomes and long, deep "tap" roots.

INVASION TECHNIQUES

• **Quick turnaround** Groundsel can grow and produce seed in as little as five weeks.
• **Regeneration from roots** A 10mm (½in) section of Japanese knotweed root is said to be able to regrow. Tap roots of dandelion and dock can resprout after the plant is cut down.
• **Rapid, smothering growth** Cleavers can clamber 1.2m (4ft) over other plants; a single chickweed plant can cover 1sq m (10sq ft).
• **Effective seed distribution** When ripe, hairy bittercress seedpods will fling the seeds 1m (3ft) or more as you touch the plant.
• **Rapid vegetative spread** Field bindweed can spread over 25sq m (250sq ft) in one season; one creeping buttercup plant can colonise up to 4sq m (40sq ft) in one year.
• **Reproduction in adverse conditions** Groundsel survives to -9°C (16°F) and can flower in any month of the year.
• **Long-term survival of seed** Poppy seed can survive 80–100 years, docks 50 or more.
• **Huge quantities of seed** Rosebay willow-herb can produce 80,000 seeds on one plant.

HOW WEEDS SPREAD

1 Seeds
Often produced in huge quantities, seeds are spread by wind, water, animals and mechanical propulsion.

2 Runners and stolons
Runners are creeping stems which grow along the ground. Buds along them produce plantlets which root quickly. Stolons are stems which arch over and produce roots at the tip, even before touching the soil.

3 Roots and rhizomes
Tough, fleshy, tap roots can regrow after cutting or dying back. Even chopped-up pieces of tap root may also regrow, as can small chopped or broken-up sections of the rootlike, underground creeping stems known as rhizomes.

4 Bulbs and bulbils
Bulbs, bulbils or tubers that break off easily when the plant is dug up or pulled out will easily produce a new plant. Cultivation simply spreads them.

Weed prevention

Prevention is always better than cure where weeds are concerned, and making simple adjustments to the way you garden, or adopting new techniques, can greatly reduce the chances of weeds getting a toehold among your plants.

Closer planting, for example, not only makes displays look good more quickly, it also cuts down on space where weeds can grow. Removing intermediate plants at a later date will prevent overcrowding. In the same way, close, evenly spaced vegetables (see p.316) will soon cover the ground and smother out weeds.

Simply cutting down on digging can reduce weed problems. Turning over the soil encourages the germination of thousands of weed seeds from the soil's "weed bank" by exposing them to the light. There is no need to dig soil on a regular basis even when growing vegetables (see also p.326).

Rethink your watering techniques. A hose or sprinkler wets a large area of soil, encouraging weed germination. Instead, use a drip or seep irrigation system, or water into sunken pots.

Crop rotation

Vegetable crops tend to be associated with weeds that have a similar life cycle. Crops also differ in their ability to compete with weeds, and in how easy it is to weed between plants. Potatoes and squashes, for example, compete well and are also easy to weed; other crops, such as onions, are poor competitors and are less easy to weed. Using a crop rotation (see p.301) which alternates different crops can help you to keep weeds under control in a vegetable plot.

Stale seedbed

A stale seedbed is one that is prepared two to three weeks in advance of sowing, to allow a flush of weeds to germinate. Hoe or flame these off (see p.78), then sow or plant as usual. This technique is useful when broadcast sowing – as with grass for a lawn – where weed control would be difficult, or when direct-sowing slow-germinating crops such as carrots or parsnips. A variation on this technique is to mulch ground with black plastic before sowing. Research has shown that covering soil with a black plastic mulch for four to eight weeks, then removing it before sowing or planting vegetables, can reduce annual weeds and increase yields significantly.

A quick start

Using transplants rather than sowing direct gives plants a head start over any weeds, and also allows time for a stale seedbed to be used. Also, if you are concerned about distinguishing between seeds you have sown and weed seedlings, using transplants helps to avoid confusion.

> ## The most effective time to weed carrots is four weeks after half the crop has come up

Preventing path weeds

Weeds in a path, patio or other hard surface may grow up from below, or blow in as seeds. Effective ground preparation and weed-proof membranes laid beneath the chosen surface can stop weeds growing up from below. To prevent seedling weeds getting a hold in paving, point the joints between bricks or slabs (see p.132). Regular brushing with a stiff brush can also be effective. Use a high-pressure hose to remove algae from a path or patio. Frequent walking over gravel is a good way of keeping weeds down. If large areas of hard surface are unused and weedy, consider converting them to some other use.

Cover the ground

One of the most formidable weapons that the organic gardener can deploy to prevent weeds is mulching to exclude light from the soil, effectively stifling their growth (see overleaf).

Weeds rapidly colonise bare ground. Seeds already in the soil will germinate, and others will move in from outside. Keeping the soil covered, with a mulch or growing plants, will keep the weeds at bay. Mulches can be used in almost any location, including paths. Simply choose the appropriate material(s) for the job – with an appearance that suits the location and an appropriate lifespan.

NATURAL WEED KILLERS

Some plants inhibit the growth of others by producing toxic substances, either when growing or decaying. This effect, known as allelopathy, is often selective, working against some species and not others. It is particularly effective in preventing the germination of annual broad-leaved weeds. Buckwheat, an excellent smother crop, is thought to produce allelopathic chemicals. Grazing rye is another weed-smothering green manure. When it is dug into the soil, or cut and left as a mulch, it releases chemicals as it decomposes that inhibit the germination of small seeds for a few weeks. It is, however, quite safe to plant young plants into, or through, the decomposing foliage, taking advantage of its weed-suppressing capacity.

Mulches for weed control

Effective mulches
Below, from left to right: a living mulch of thyme grown as ground-cover; clover, a green manure, covering the ground beneath sweetcorn plants; coarse bark chippings; lawn clippings spread over layers of newspaper; rotted straw; ornamental bark; cardboard – a mulch membrane – around crops; synthetic landscape fabric in the fruit garden.

Weed-controlling mulches come in two forms – loose mulches, such as wood or bark chippings, and mulch membranes: sheets of material such as cardboard or synthetic landscape fabric. They can be biodegradable or synthetic. As with all areas of organic gardening, the first choice should be a recycled biodegradable material such as cardboard or wood chips, but for longer term, low-maintenance control, synthetic materials may be the most effective option.

Living mulches

Living mulches may be ornamental – permanent plantings of ground-cover shrubs and perennials – or functional – the so-called green manures, or smother crops, which are used to cover ground temporarily and improve the soil.

Effective ground-cover plants are tough, rapidly spreading ornamentals that will compete successfully with weeds for food, water and light (see also *Woody Plants and Climbers*, p.147). Ground-cover plants are particularly useful for weed control in areas where access is difficult.

Green manures (see pp.56–57), such as buckwheat, grazing rye and *Phacelia*, make good weed-preventing smother crops (living mulches). Grow them where ground is to be left bare for a few months or more – over the winter months, for example, or when you have prepared a plot but are not yet ready to plant it up. They can also be sown between widely spaced shrubs. Vigorous, fast-growing annual flowers such as *Limnanthes douglasii* and candytuft can be used in the same way.

Trefoil, a low-growing green manure that tolerates some shade, can be sown between rows of sweetcorn. Sow trefoil, broadcast, when the corn is around 15cm (6in) high. When the corn is cut down at the end of the season, the trefoil can be left to protect the ground over winter.

Loose mulches

On weed-free ground, a loose mulch, 10cm (4in) deep, will provide effective weed control. Any weeds that may appear are easily removed. You can reduce the depth of mulch needed, and hence the cost, by spreading it over a mulch membrane (see opposite for details). A mulch membrane will also stop gravel, glass chips or similar materials from working into the soil.

Mulch membranes

Mulch membranes can be used to clear weeds from open ground and beds, as long as there are no woody weeds present. They are also used to prevent weeds from growing on ground that has been cleared. Holes can be cut to allow planting through the membrane as appropriate. Membranes are usually covered with a loose mulch, to hold them in place, extend their lifespan and improve their appearance. A mulch membrane must be permeable, to allow air and water into the soil, unless it is only to be kept in place for a few months.

MULCHES FOR WEED CONTROL

Loose mulches

Composted bark products (P; B)
Attractive, dark-coloured mulch.

Wood chips (P; B)
Forest waste, or chipped scrap wood, composted before sale.
Available in stained colours. Lower cost than bark.
Apply a high-nitrogen fertiliser before mulching young plants.

Coarse grade municipal compost (P; B)
Recycled green waste. Quicker to degrade than bark or wood
chips.

Shredded prunings (P; B)
Home-produced or from a tree contractor. Compost for a few
months before use, or use fresh on paths.

Straw and hay (A; B)
Informal appearance. Should last for a season. Use a layer 15cm
(6in) thick. Hay will feed plants as it decays, but may produce its
own crop of seedling weeds.

Gravel and slate waste (P)
Good around plants that like dry, hot conditions.

Leafmould (A; B)
A home-made, short-term mulch. Best used over a membrane.

Glass chips (P)
For something different! Range of colours, made from recycled
glass. No sharp edges. Only for use over a mulch membrane.

Cocoa shells (A)
Waste product of the chocolate industry. Apply in a layer at least
5cm (2in) deep. Water lightly after application to moisten
surface. Higher in nitrogen than wood-based mulches.

Membranes

Newspaper (A; B)
No-cost option for a single season. Lay opened-out newspapers,
at least 8 sheets thick, around and between existing plants. Top
with grass mowings or leafmould to keep in place.

Cardboard (A; B)
No-cost option for a single season. Lay on soil, overlapping well
to prevent weeds growing through. Keep in place with straw or
hay. Vigorous plants such as pumpkins can be planted through
the cardboard.

Paper mulch (A; B)
Sturdy paper in a roll, for use on annual vegetable beds.

Synthetic spun fabric (P)
Long-term weed control; cover with loose mulch to protect from
light.

Woven plastic (P)
Medium-term weed control. Cover with loose mulch to extend life.

Coir matting (P; B)
3–5 year lifespan; no need to cover it. Hold in place with wire
staples or fixing pegs.

Black polythene sheeting (400–600 gauge)
Suitable only as a ground-clearing mulch (see also p.79). Do not
cover ground for more than a few months without removing the
polythene to allow air and water into the soil. Hold in place by
burying edges in the ground or weighting with heavy items such
as wooden planks or car tyres.

PLANTING THROUGH A MULCH MEMBRANE

1 Clear the ground, or cut down existing vegetation.

2 Add any soil improvers required, bearing in mind the lifespan of the mulch.

3 Level the ground if necessary.

4 Spread the membrane over the soil. Spade the edges 25–30cm (10-12in) into the soil, fix with wire staples or hold the edges down with heavy planks, bricks or the like.

5 Set the plants out in their proposed positions.

6 With a sharp knife, cut crosses in the membrane where each plant is to go.

7 Plant your plants, and water them in.

8 Top with 5cm (2in) of loose mulch.

Perennial weeds may grow up around the planting cut. Cut them off with a knife or scissors.

A Single season mulches for annual or perennial beds   P Mulches for perennial beds only   B Biodegradable, the preferred choice

Weed control and clearance

Preventative measures can never be rigorous enough to eliminate the need for some weeding. Hoeing and hand-weeding can be a relaxing and satisfying occupation. The key is to do the weeding when the weeds are small. Only when you put it off does it become a chore. Hand-clearing neglected ground (see opposite) can be a long job, but here again, knowing your weeds will help. Overleaf are some tried and tested strategies that can be used to beat some of the most persistent perennial weeds, using the general techniques that are outlined here.

Hand-weeding

Hand-weeding is the only really "selective" organic method of weed control, allowing you to remove the real weeds and retain self-sown ornamentals and other "weeds" that you would like to keep. Use a hand fork or weeding hoe to loosen weeds when necessary; even annual weeds can regrow if the top breaks off as you are trying to pull the whole plant out. Hand-weeding is easiest after a good rainstorm, and on uncompacted soil, such as in beds that are never walked on and those that are well mulched.

Paths and patios can also be hand-weeded. There is a range of tools available to help extract weeds from cracks between paving slabs.

Hoeing

Once you have learned the art, hoeing can be a quick and effective method of keeping ground, and gravel paths, weed free. Hoeing works best against seedling weeds (annual and perennial), but it can also be quite effective in removing the tops of perennial weeds, though regular hoeing over a period of years will be needed to kill them completely.

Hoes come in many shapes and sizes, suitable for large or restricted areas, and for use standing up or kneeling. If you can, try a hoe before buying to see that it suits you and the handle is the correct length.

Thermal weeding

Modern thermal weeders kill weeds with a short blast of heat, lasting no more than a few seconds. The plants do not burn, they simply wilt and die. The heat may be applied as a flame, hot air, infrared radiation from a heated grid, or a combination of these. The main use in the organic garden is on hard surfaces – paths, drives and patios. Seedling weeds are easily killed with a single pass. More established annuals and biennials may need anything from three to six treatments. Perennials weeds will be gradually weakened, and may eventually die. Thermal treatment should also kill weed seeds on the ground.

TIPS FOR EFFECTIVE HOEING

- Choose a hoe that you find easy to use.
- Keep the hoe sharp
- Cut plants off just where the stem joins the root.
- Hoe regularly, when weeds are small.
- Hoe on a dry day.
- Collect up the weeds if rain is likely.
- Leave sufficient space between crop rows to allow for easy hoeing.

Clearing weed-infested ground

Weeds rapidly colonise bare ground, either newly created by building developments or where a garden or allotment has fallen into disuse. At first there will probably be a mixture of annual and perennial weeds, but if the land continues to be neglected, perennials will soon dominate. However daunting the task may look, overgrown land can be cleared without using herbicides, using one, or a combination, of the methods below.

Cutting down

Simply cutting down weeds can be a quick short-term solution to a weed problem, preventing seeding and spreading. Repeated cutting can, eventually, clear even persistent perennial weeds over a period of years. The most effective time to cut, to weaken the roots of perennials and avoid seeding, is when flower buds are just beginning to show. Scything is the most peaceful method, and can be quick and effective – but of course needs skill. The alternative is an electric- or petrol-powered line trimmer.

Digging or forking over

Forking the ground over, removing weeds and roots, is a relatively quick, but physically challenging, way to clear ground of many perennials. Breaking up the ground first with a spade or a digging hoe will ease the work, as will covering the ground with a mulch membrane for a few weeks or more before starting. This method is good for weeds with tap roots such as dandelions and docks, and can be effective against couch grass and ground elder if you are diligent.

Never strip off the top layer of soil together with the weed roots. You will be removing the most fertile soil from the area.

Mechanical cultivation

A mechanical cultivator (rotavator) can be useful when clearing a large area of ground, but it does have its drawbacks. Using a cultivator can be hard work if the ground is thick with perennial weeds and grasses. If perennial weeds are present, they will be chopped up into many pieces; each portion of root or rhizome may regrow, potentially increasing the problem manyfold. Cultivate in late spring or early summer when the soil is dry and weeds are growing well. Leave the ground until it is "greening up" with weed regrowth, then cultivate again. Repeat as necessary. If you can only cultivate once, it may be possible to hoe off the regrowth, otherwise choose another method. It is much more difficult and time-consuming to dig out hundreds of chopped-up pieces of root than it is whole plants. Lightweight mechanical cultivators can be used for weed control between row crops.

Clearing ground without digging

A light-excluding mulch membrane will stop weeds growing, and will, in time, kill them. If you want to convert an area of lawn into a vegetable or flower bed, mulch it in the spring and it will be clear by the autumn, if not before. Persistent perennials may take a couple of years or more to die. Vigorous annual plants, such as squashes and sunflowers, can be planted through the mulch, though perennial weeds may grow up through the holes cut for the plants. Mulching is most effective during the season when weeds are actively growing.

Grassing down

Where there is a severe perennial weed problem such as ground elder or horsetail, put the ground down to grass – either sowing seed or laying turf. Regular mowing for two or three years should solve the problem. A rather extreme measure, perhaps, but worth it in the long run.

KNOW YOUR ROOTS

1 Some weeds, particularly annuals such as groundsel, bittercress and chickweed, have shallow, fibrous roots that are easily removed.

2 Weeds with spreading, creeping roots such as creeping thistle, bindweed and couch grass need to have the soil around their roots well loosened so that every piece of root can be removed.

3 The long tap roots of weeds such as dandelion and dock must be removed in their entirety to prevent regrowth.

Forking out
For weeds such as creeping thistle, loosen the soil all around the root area in order to pull out the entire root run.

PERENNIAL WEED PROFILES

◁ Field bindweed

Convolvulus arvensis (see also Hedge Bindweed, facing page, bottom right)

Survival and spread

An extensive network of roots and rhizomes, which can give rise to new plants. Roots can reach a depth of 10m (30ft). Rarely seeds; more in dry years.

Control

• Hoe frequently over a period of years.
• Fork out early infestations, removing every piece. Probably not worth trying where well established.
• Cover with membrane for 2+ years.

◁ Lesser celandine

Ranunculus ficaria

Survival and spread

An attractive plant that flowers in early spring. Spreads rapidly when disturbed. One form produces bulbils in the angles of the leaves; the other form seeds. Both produce root tubers.

Control

• Mulch membrane.
• Do not dig – tubers and bulbils easily detach from plant.

Blackberry/bramble ▷

Rubus fruticosus

Survival and spread

A prickly, fast-growing woody weed. Spreads by stolons and seed.

Control

• Dig out young plants as soon as seen.
• Cut back established plants regularly. Dig out where practicable.

Creeping buttercup ▷

Ranunculus repens

Survival and spread

Common on moist soils and lawns. Spreads by runners; new plants form and root at intervals in late spring and early summer. Also seeds.

Control

• Hoe when small.
• Established plants are hard to pull out by hand. Dig them out or cover with a mulch membrane for a year or two.

◁ Couch grass

Elymus (Agropyron) repens

Survival and spread

Has shallow, creeping, tough white rhizomes, often thought of as roots. Rhizome tips are very sharp – can grow through potatoes. Rarely seeds.

Control

• Hoeing regularly in late summer reduces production of new rhizomes.
• Fork over soil, removing all rhizomes.
• Cover with mulch membrane for 2–3 years.

◁ Dandelion

Taraxacum officinale

Survival and spread

Plants can regenerate from any part of the substantial tap root. Seeds freely, early spring to autumn.

Control

• Cut down before seeding.
• Dig out.
• Cover with mulch membrane for 2–3 years.

Dock ▷

Rumex spp.

Survival and spread

Plants can regenerate from top 15cm (6in) of the tap root. Seeds prolifically.

Control

• Hoe off seedlings.
• Cut down plants before seeding.
• Dig out established plants.
• Cover with mulch membrane for 2–3 years.

Ground elder ▷

Aegopodium podagraria

Survival and spread

White, underground creeping stems just under the surface. New leaves produced at every node. Few seeds.

Control

• Persistent regular hoeing.
• On small areas dig out plants, including every bit of root.
• Grass down and mow for a few years.
• Cover with mulch membrane for at least 2–3 years.

◁ Horsetail
Equisetum arvense
Survival and spread
Extensive, creeping black underground stems which can penetrate 2m (6ft) or more down into the soil.
Control
• May be smothered out by vigorous plant growth.
• Persistent hoeing.
• Cover with mulch membrane for several years.

◁ Japanese knotweed
Reynoutria japonica
Survival and spread
Spreads by stout rhizomes that can extend to 7m (22ft) and go 2m (6ft) or more deep and even grow under tarmac. Tiny fragments can regrow. Some spread by seed.
Control
• Cut down every 2 weeks through growing season, for 10 years or more.
• Pull up stems from base when mature in early and midsummer, for at least 5 years.

Stinging nettle ▷
Urtica dioica
Survival and spread
A valuable plant for wildlife, and for making a liquid plant food. The stems, purplish at first, creep along the soil surface. They become erect and green in spring. Seeds abundantly.
Control
• Fork out, or undercut with spade.
• Cover with mulch membrane for 2–3 years.

Enchanter's nightshade ▷
Circaea lutetiana
Survival and spread
Spreads by shallow, creeping, brittle white rhizomes. Also seeds.
Control
• Dig out very carefully; rhizomes break easily.
• Do not leave to seed.
• Cover with mulch membrane for several years.

◁ Oxalis, pink-flowered
Oxalis corymbosa, O. latifolia
(cultivated forms can also be invasive)
Survival and spread
Numerous, very persistent bulbils – easily spread and long-living. Pinkish-brown, shallow underground tubers.
Control
• Cover with mulch membrane or grass down for several years.
• Do not dig or hoe; cultivation just spreads the problem.

◁ Perennial sow-thistle
Sonchus arvensis
Survival and spread
Creeping roots grow new shoots – even from small fragments. Main roots grow deep – down to 60cm (2ft) – and extensively. Also seeds.
Control
• Do not allow to seed.
• Regular, persistent hoeing for several years.
• Cover with mulch membrane.
• Smother out (see Creeping thistle).

Creeping thistle ▷
Cirsium arvense
Survival and spread
Aerial shoots develop from white, creeping, brittle, horizontal roots. Stout fleshy tap root. Few seeds.
Control
• Hoe off young plants.
• Cover with mulch membrane.
• With a dense stand, allow plants to grow large. Before they flower, cut down. Repeat. Cultivate ground and sow a vigorous medium-term green manure crop such as tares or crimson clover.

Hedge bindweed ▷
Calystegia (Convolvulus) sepium
Survival and spread
Spreads by white, brittle creeping underground stems. Rarely seeds.
Control
• Hoe frequently over a period of years.
• Fork out early infestations, removing every piece. Probably not worth trying where well established.
• Cover with mulch membrane for several years.

CHOOSING WEED-CONTROL MULCHES AND TECHNIQUES TO SUIT THE SITUATION

	Cardboard	Coir matting	Newspaper	Tree mats	Synthetic permeable membranes	Black plastic sheeting	Ornamental bark or wood chips	Leafmould	Cocoa shells	Municipal compost (coarse grade)
Clearing rough ground	•				•	•				
Annual vegetables	•		•					•		
Annual flowers								•	•	
Shrubs	•	•	•	•	•		•	•	•	•
Herbaceous perennials					•		•	•	•	•
New plantings	•	•	•		•		•	•	•	•
Fruit trees and bushes	•		•					•	•	•
Trees	•	•	•	•	•		•	•	•	•
Paving/tarmac					•					
Gravel paths					•					
Ground not in use	•				•		•	•		

See pp.76–77 for advice on using mulches effectively; pp.78–79 for other techniques

Gravel	Slate waste	Glass chips	Cutting down	Ground-cover plants (ornamental)	Green manure crops	Hand-weeding	Hoeing	Digging/ forking	Rotavating/ cultivating	Stale seedbed	Thermal weeding
			•		•	•		•	•		
			•		•	•	•			•	
						•	•				
•	•	•		•	•	•		•			
•	•					•		•			
•	•	•		•	•	•					
						•	•	•			
•	•	•		•		•	•	•			
						•	•				•
				•							•
	•	•	•	•	•	•		•			

Plant health

USE ORGANIC METHODS OF SOIL AND GARDEN MANAGEMENT
TO PROTECT YOUR PLANTS THE NATURAL WAY

IT IS ONLY RECENT GENERATIONS that have come to rely on artificial chemical inputs for pest and disease control, and in doing so many gardeners have forgotten that it is possible to produce good food and maintain beautiful gardens without pesticides. In this chapter the nature of plant pests and diseases will be described, along with the extensive range of methods, both ancient and modern, that organic gardeners can use to maintain a healthy garden and keep pest and disease problems at acceptable levels.

A natural balance

Organic gardening emphasises soil health and the link between a healthy soil, healthy plants and our own health. A healthy soil leads to healthy plant growth in a stable and sustainable environment. Natural environments, or ecosystems, usually contain a diversity of plant and animal species, including plant pests and the causal agents of plant disease; all

the organisms live in balance with each other (or in equilibrium). In organic gardens we try to emulate this balance of species and the ecological stability that results. Although gardens are never natural ecosystems, sensitive planting and design can create gardens that attract wildlife (including beneficial animals) and encourage diversity: productive gardens where plants and animals live in stable equilibrium.

Working with the system

Organic gardeners seek to work with nature to limit damage from pests and plant disease, rather than to control nature using artificial inputs. The dream of the organic gardener is sustainable gardening. It is a different dream to the utopia of a pest- and disease-free garden promoted by the garden industry. It is a more realistic approach to gardening, accepting that plants occasionally show spots and blemishes just as our bodies from time to time show imperfections.

PLANT PROTECTION THE ORGANIC WAY

• Manage the soil organically.
• Choose plants that are suited to the site and soil.
• Start with healthy seed and plants.
• Grow resistant cultivars.
• Grow flowers and provide habitats to encourage natural predators.
• Introduce biological control agents.
• Keep out pests with barriers, traps and crop covers.
• Avoid the use of pesticide sprays.

Striking sight (facing page)
Wildlife brings a beauty of its own into the garden, and gardeners should think twice before automatically seeking to banish creatures like this striking mullein moth caterpillar. Diversity is crucial to achieving a natural balance between pests and predators.

Contemporary bird scarer (right)
There is nothing new about protecting crops from birds, but organic gardeners are always ready to explore the potential usefulness of new materials – especially when they provide an opportunity to recycle, as with these discarded CDs.

This is not to say that organic vegetables are inevitably maggot-infested or that organic flowers are moth-eaten – far from it – but that rather than the intolerance promoted by the gardening industry, tolerance is required. Instead of quick fixes with their environmental side-effects, organic gardeners aim for prevention and sustainable management of pests and disease.

Strategies old and new

There is a wide range of organic techniques and strategies to keep plants healthy. Going organic is not, as newcomers often assume, simply a question of replacing artificial or chemical inputs with more natural alternatives. There is a lot more to it than just changing your brand of pesticide. Traditional methods of good husbandry – such as appropriate soil care, crop rotation, encouraging natural predators, picking off pests and diseased growth by hand, good hygiene and timing of sowing and planting – are combined with more modern techniques, including biological controls, resistant cultivars, pheromone traps and lightweight crop covers. A few so-called "organic" pesticide sprays are available, to be used as a last, not a first, resort.

The ideal is to use good gardening techniques to promote and maintain plant health, combining this when necessary with more direct methods of prevention and control. This strategy generally results in a flourishing garden. There will inevitably be times when there is nothing that can be done to save a plant, in extreme weather conditions, for example, or if it is in an inappropriate location. The organic solution is then to give in gracefully!

CAUSES OF PLANT PROBLEMS

To combat problems and, where possible, bring plants back to health it is important to understand the cause of the complaint, and whether it is an environmental or growing problem (see p.88), a nutrient deficiency (p.89), a disease (p.90) or pest attack (p.92).
1 The plant's environment includes the soil conditions; these peas are showing heat and drought stress.
2 The element magnesium is a plant nutrient required for the production of the green substance chlorophyll; here deficiency causes a characteristic yellowing of the leaves between the veins.
3 Potato blight, a fungal disease, starts with brown patches on the leaves but soon completely destroys the haulm, or top-growth, before the spores are washed down to infect the tubers.
4 Pests are animals that eat our plants. Here the common gooseberry sawfly has defoliated a redcurrant. The fruits remain intact but the bush will be badly weakened.

What can go wrong?

Most plants in a well-kept garden, or in any natural ecosystem, are healthy for most of the time. Like animals they have well-ordered defence mechanisms against invaders and only occasionally submit to ill health. When plant health problems arise, they can be caused by:

• environmental factors, such as water shortage;
• mineral deficiencies, such as magnesium deficiency;
• disease, such as potato blight;
• pests, which are animals that eat green plants.

Resisting attack

Healthy plants have a great tolerance of pests and diseases and, rather like fit young people, can readily shake off minor infections. If environmental conditions are not as good as they might be and as a result the plant is stressed, or if it is very young or old, the same infections could be life-threatening. As a general principle, the bigger the plant, the more disease or pest damage it can tolerate. A large oak tree, for example, supports many thousands of insects and mites on its leaves, not to mention fungi feeding on the leaves, stems and roots, without showing any ill effects. At the other extreme, a small lettuce seedling is totally vulnerable to the damping-off fungus *Pythium* and the very weak biting mouths of woodlice. But as the seedling grows, the epidermis thickens and woodlice cannot bite through to the soft tissue inside; the thickened epidermis also offers protection from fungal invasion.

Getting the diagnosis right

Accurate identification of plant health problems followed by knowledge of when intervention is necessary are the keys to successful organic pest and disease control. Identification requires close inspection; the most obvious symptoms may not be the real problem. Sooty mould on camellias, for example, is caused by the presence of soft scale (a sap-sucking insect). These pests secrete a sticky waste substance called honeydew on which sooty moulds thrive. Control can only be achieved by taking action against the scale insects, not the more obvious sooty moulds.

Refer to reference books or contact one of the many pest control advisory services (your local garden centre may be able to help) before deciding on a course of action, and remember that most maladies that plants suffer are not life-threatening. Divining the most appropriate action (when to act and when not to act) and formulating control strategies comes with experience. Gaining this experience is part of the fun and intellectual challenge of organic gardening.

Knowledge of plant taxonomy – how plants are grouped into families – is helpful (see also Crop rotation, pp.301–313). Plants within the same family tend to suffer from similar maladies. These family groups are not always obvious: for example, wallflowers and nasturtiums are in the same family as cabbages and other brassica crops, and cabbage white butterflies are just as happy on nasturtiums as they are on cabbage and sprout plants.

Inspect damaged or diseased plants closely. A magnifying glass or eye piece (of no more than x10) is useful. Be sure to have a look during the night as well, because many animals that eat plants are nocturnal and will be hiding out of view during the day. Monitoring traps are useful for early warning of the presence of certain pests; the yellow sticky cards widely available from garden retailers, for example, will reveal the presence of whitefly in the greenhouse long before the average gardener notices any significant problem with plant health. Early knowledge of a problem means that measures to nip it in the bud can be implemented before the plants suffer. Prevention, rather than cure, is the key to resisting attack.

GETTING THE DIAGNOSIS RIGHT

Even if the symptoms seem obvious, it is possible to make the wrong diagnosis.
1 Wilting can be caused not just by drought but by fungal diseases called "wilts", or by pest damage to the liquid transport system further down the plant.
2 This leaf looks diseased, but the malformations are caused by the feeding of tiny blister mites.
3 Sooty mould is a secondary problem; the fungal growth is feeding on waste from soft scale insects, the cause of the problem.

A closer look
A photographer's magnifying eye glass or "lupe" can be a useful tool in identifying plant problems.

Tightly bound
A severely pot-bound plant may never thrive when planted out. New roots are unable to grow out from the tightly coiled rootball.

Growing problems

The environment plants experience includes the conditions in the soil as well as the "weather", or climate above ground. So mineral deficiencies or excesses can be classified as environmental problems, just as an inappropriate level of moisture or exposure to too much wind are environmental problems. Environmental problems can have both direct effects, and also indirect effects, because they leave plants more vulnerable to attack from pathogens or pests.

Water

Shortage of water causes plants to wilt, which even for short periods weakens plants, leaving them more vulnerable to attack from pests or invasion by pathogens. Prolonged water shortages can result in stunted growth and tissue death in all or parts of the leaves. Other factors can cause plants to wilt: pest damage to the roots that prevents them from taking up water, for example, or some fungal infections called "wilts". Water shortages can have delayed effects on plants; flower drop in camellias in spring is caused by dry conditions in the previous autumn.

Plants can also wilt as a result of too much water in the soil, caused either by poor drainage or over-watering. Waterlogged soil prevents the roots from breathing. The initial response is wilting, as the roots

cease to function. This is followed by tissue death, allowing fungal and bacterial pathogens and rots to enter. Always ensure the soil is dry before watering, especially with indoor and container plants. (See *Water and Watering*, pp.63–71, for more information.)

Frost

Even frost-hardy plants occasionally have parts that are subject to frost damage, notably spring buds, young shoots, and blossom on fruit. As water in the plant cells freezes so it expands causing the cells to burst; the cells die off leaving black/brown areas of dead tissue, usually on the growing tips. Avoid frost damage by choosing later flowering or frost-hardy cultivars of some plants, delaying sowing dates, or by the use of protective covers such as cloches or fleece.

Mechanical damage

Mechanical damage can be caused by hail or heavy rain and wind, and over- or under-exposure to sun. Scorch, caused by excessive sun, is aggravated by the presence of a thin film of water on the surface of the leaf which acts like a tiny magnifying glass. The leaf surface goes brown and dries up. In tomatoes, scorch on the ripening fruits causes a condition known as greenback, where the tops of the fruit fail to redden,

A REGULAR WATER SUPPLY

Blossom end rot (right) is a disorder of tomatoes and peppers resulting from calcium deficiency, but usually caused by lack of water. The calcium may be present in the soil but unavailable to the plant due to dry conditions around the roots; this is common in pots where water supply fluctuates.

Runner beans, grown well, are prolific croppers (far right); poor cropping may well be caused by insufficient water at the flowering stage, which is critical to pod set.

remaining a yellow/green colour. Scorch can be minimised by watering early in the morning or in the evening, or by shading. Mechanical damage can also be caused to plants by trampling or misuse of equipment, especially nylon line trimmers.

Other disorders

Splitting in vegetables, bolting (flowering too early), blindness (failing to produce flower heads and fruit) and oedema (swellings) can occur in plants which, usually for environmental reasons, have suffered disturbed growth patterns. The difficulty with these conditions is isolating the cause and avoiding it.

Mineral deficiencies

Mineral deficiencies can cause plants to fail and show symptoms of "disease" (technically disorders), but in a well-ordered organic garden, with continual emphasis on the health of the soil, these are seldom a problem. When managed organically, most garden soils will provide all the nutrients plants require.

Occasionally, especially on limy soils, trace elements, although present, may not be soluble due to the high pH, and are therefore unavailable to the plant. On these occasions additional sources might need to be added (see p.61). Mineral deficiencies can also be caused by an excessive application of particular elements; overdo potassium-rich fertilisers, for example, and you may alter the soil chemistry, "locking up" magnesium so that plants develop symptoms of magnesium deficiency.

Mineral deficiencies are often difficult to confirm from symptoms alone and can easily be confused with diseases, especially viruses. If a problem persists, it may be necessary to have the soil, or the plant, analysed professionally (see *Soil and Soil Care*, pp.34–37).

MINERAL DEFICIENCIES

Mottling, marking and even crisping of leaves can all be the result not of disease, but of mineral deficiencies. Fruits may also spoil and wither.

1 Iron deficiency is one of the most common plant disorders and almost always presents as a yellowing of leaves, especially between the veins. It is especially common on alkaline soils, when it is known as lime-induced chlorosis.

2 Manganese deficiency (on potato leaves), common on peat or poorly drained soils.

3 Phosphorus deficiency (on tomato leaves) – often seen in acid soils.

4 Potassium deficiency (on French beans), often seen on light or sandy soils.

5 Bitter pit in apples, caused by calcium deficiency - again common on light, sandy soils.

6 Boron deficiency on sweetcorn; overliming can disrupt the uptake by plants of this trace element.

Plant diseases

Plant diseases result from the invasion of plant tissue by microscopic organisms. These can be fungi, bacteria or viruses. Living on the plant tissue as parasites, they cause cell damage and death, and sometimes distortions of growth rather like tumours or cancers. Organisms that cause disease are known as pathogens and the study of plant disease is the study of plant pathology. It is important to note that some organisms that are closely related to plant pathogens have beneficial relationships with our plants. Examples include the mycorrhizal fungi that act as extensions to the root hair system, and the *Rhizobium* bacteria that form the nitrogen-fixing nodules on the roots of legumes (see also p.35).

Fungal diseases

Fungi are plants without chlorophyll, and are incapable of producing their own energy by photosynthesis. Most are saprophytic (feeding on dead and decaying tissue) but some have developed the ability to overcome plant defences and feed on living plant tissue.

Common destructive fungal diseases include potato blight, clubroot in brassicas, damping off in seedlings, mildews and rusts. Some of these, like the organism that causes clubroot, have protected dormant spores that can remain viable in the soil for 40 years or more. The organism that causes potato blight is carried over from year to year on infected seed tubers, but is spread from plant to plant in the form of spores, as is the case with most fungi. The fungus that causes apple scab overwinters on infected plant remains such as leaves on the orchard floor.

The majority of fungi that cause disease usually go unnoticed, apart from their symptoms. Honey fungus, with its distinctive honey-coloured toadstools, is one obvious exception.

Most fungal diseases are more prevalent in warm, damp conditions, which allow the fungal spores to move freely in moist air and on a film of water on the surface of leaves. Fungal spores, which either pass through the soil or are carried in the wind, arrive on the plant's surface. From here they invade the plant cells. Fungal diseases are very diverse, but are grouped according to the type of disease (or symptoms) that they cause. Within these groups pathogens can be specific to their particular hosts. For example, the organism that causes powdery mildew on apples (*Podosphaera leucotricha*) is different from the organisms that cause the seemingly identical powdery mildews on plums (*P. tridactyola*) or roses (*Sphaerotheca pannosa*). On the other hand, the grey mould fungus *Botrytis cinerea* can affect a wide range of plants and plant parts.

Control of fungal pathogens is limited to trying to avoid or prevent the conditions in which they thrive. Good garden hygiene, ensuring adequate ventilation around plants, avoidance of over-watering, the use of resistant cultivars, and the judicious use of permitted fungicides (see p.103) all help avoid or limit damage.

Bacterial infections

Bacteria are single-celled organisms; they reproduce rapidly simply by dividing into two. Plant-pathogenic bacteria cause numerous soft rots, wilts, cankers,

Plant diseases
Symptoms, from left to right, of: canker on apple branch; rust on fuchsia leaf; fungal leaf spot; pear scab; apple powdery mildew; blossom wilt; rose black spot; grey mould on a pelargonium blossom; brown rot; honey fungus – fruiting bodies on tree bark.

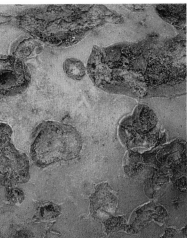

TYPES OF DISEASE

Fungal diseases (left)
The spores of fungal diseases are spread in air or, as with peach leaf curl, in water, especially rain-splash.

Bacterial infections (centre)
Potato scab is more common on dry alkaline soils, low in humus.

Viruses (right)
These (here, cucumber mosaic virus on wisteria) cannot be cured; instead, control the pests that transmit them.

blights and galls on plants. Unlike fungi, bacteria usually only enter plant tissue through wounds, caused by pruning or pests, for example. Treatment is limited to removing the affected material and prevention is usually down to simple cleanliness.

Examples of bacterial infections include common scab on potatoes, fireblight on apples and pears and other members of the Rosaceae family, and many of the cankers on fruit trees.

Viruses

Viruses are simply genetic material encased within a protein coating. They invade the cells of higher organisms, including plants, and "hijack" the cells' genetic codes for replicating themselves, diverting the cells' energy into the production of masses of viral material that spreads to adjacent cells, often severely restricting the host's growth or causing malformations and malfunctions of parts of the plant. Viruses cannot exist independently and usually rely on insects or other animals to act as "vectors" to carry them from infected to uninfected plants. Bugs such as aphids, whiteflies and leafhoppers, with their sap-sucking habits, are particularly important as plant virus vectors. Viral infections can also be passed on by vegetative reproduction from infected plants. Certification schemes exist in many countries that ensure that only virus-free plant stock is sold, most particularly of very susceptible fruits such as raspberries. "Certified Seed Potatoes" are free of viral material; they are produced in cooler climates (traditionally Scotland in the United Kingdom) where the aphid vectors of potato viruses cannot survive in sufficient numbers to spread the viral material between plants.

Viruses are too small to be seen with conventional microscopy, so they are usually named after the plant in which they were first discovered and the symptoms they cause. Control of plant viruses is restricted to planting virus-free material, the use of resistant varieties, and controlling the insect vectors of the virus.

Plant pests

Pests are those animals, large, small and microscopic, that cause unacceptable damage to plants in the garden, or reduce our enjoyment of the space that is the garden. Most creatures in the garden, however, are not pests. Many are beneficial, acting either as pollinators or helping to recycle nutrients for plants. Others feed on pest species and act as nature's own pest controllers, and there are those that have no effect on the activities of the gardener, but are part of the rich biodiversity of the garden ecosystem. The beauty of many of these animals and their interesting behaviour enhances the enjoyment of any garden, and as such they should be encouraged by organic gardeners.

Some animals do not fit comfortably into either the pest or beneficial group, as their habits change with the seasons or their life cycle, or as the vulnerability of certain plants to pest attack changes. Earwigs are notorious for destroying dahlia blooms, but in other circumstances and at other times of year they are significant predators of pests such as aphids and moth and vine weevil eggs. Even the most notorious garden pests such as slugs and snails have their part to play in breaking down rotting vegetation. It is only when plants are young and tender, or when particularly vulnerable plants such as hostas and delphiniums are left unguarded, that these animals cause so much damage.

Also, many animals feed on plants without causing significant damage and therefore in an organic garden do not deserve pest status. A good example would be the froghopper or spittle bug, often found on roses in the late spring and summer. These sap-suckers are usually present only in ones and twos on each plant (one bug per mass of spittle), whereas aphids can often appear in colonies of several thousands. Other animals are only pests when the plant is young and tender, moving on to feed on other material as it ages.

Most pests achieve pest status by feeding directly on plants, but some creatures might be considered pests because they incidentally damage plants, or because they foul the soil with their droppings. The domestic cat is one such example; it also demonstrates that pest status is often something in the eye of the beholder. Some gardeners tolerate cats, but others despise them.

Pests are frequently classified according to where they feed on the plant and their feeding habits. Although this is convenient for the smaller pests, it is in some ways an artificial distinction. Many leaf feeders also feed on stems; some sap-sucking aphids also feed on roots and flowers.

Sap-suckers

Animals such as aphids, whitefly and red spider mite, for example, have needle-like mouthparts and are known as sap-suckers. They pierce the outer epidermis of the plant and suck up the sap. Loss of sap results in reduced vigour and growth distortions. Sap-suckers can transmit plant viruses, and their waste (honeydew) soils plants, providing a sugar-rich

TYPES OF PEST

From left to right:
Sap suckers (aphids); root feeders (here, wireworms in a potato tuber); leaf feeders (capsid bug damage and a sawfly larva – some leaf feeders also eat stems); flower feeders (pollen beetles); fruit feeders (wasps on an apple); gall formers (here, a gall on an oak branch caused by a gall wasp)

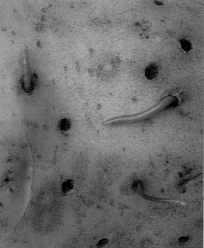

food source on which fungal moulds will thrive. Bacterial infections can also enter the plant via the wounds made by their tiny mouthparts.

Root feeders

Many insect larvae, including the caterpillars of some moths (cutworms), beetle grubs such as wireworms, vine weevil and chafer beetles, cabbage root fly and carrot flies, and many species of microscopic nematodes (often better known as eelworms), graze on plant roots. Some move between plants and others invade the root, feeding on the tap root and stem. Damage restricts nutrient and water uptake, restricting growth and causing wilting.

Leaf feeders

Many butterfly, moth and sawfly caterpillars, adult beetles and their grubs, and of course slugs and snails, graze on leaves. Other moth and fly larvae mine the leaves, leaving characteristic patterns with the transparent epidermis intact on either side of the leaf. Birds and mammals also occasionally graze on foliage. Leaf damage reduces the area where photosynthesis operates, restricting growth and fruit set, and spoiling the appearance of ornamental plants.

Stem feeders

Some moth caterpillars mine heartwood and mammals will strip bark, causing dieback in trees. Many leaf-feeding pests also consume stems. Since the stems support the leaves, damage resulting from stem-feeding is similar to that resulting from leaf-feeding.

Flower feeders

Earwigs, apple and pear suckers, thrips, blossom weevils and pollen beetles all feed directly on flowerheads and buds, which damages ornamental displays and reduces fruit set. Many bird species, including the beautiful bullfinch of northern Europe, will strip fruit trees and currant bushes of their buds in late winter and early spring, when food is scarce and the birds are at their hungriest; they can reduce the subsequent crop to nothing.

Fruit feeders

Caterpillars of some moths and sawflies, as well as some beetle grubs and fly larvae, feed directly on developing fruit. Birds and wasps also feed on ripe and ripening fruit. Direct damage is usually limited, but the soiling of fruit renders it unpalatable, and indirect damage caused by the opening up of fruiting bodies to bacterial and fungal rotting agents is often serious.

Gall-formers

Many fly and wasp larvae, as well as mites, cause galls to develop on plants. Usually plants can function perfectly well in the presence of these galls, because the pest feeds within on the gall tissue. Occasionally, however, gall-forming pests can transmit viruses. For example, the big bud mite causes gall-like swellings on currant buds, especially those of blackcurrant, but the mites also spread blackcurrant reversion virus, more damaging by far to the bushes and their subsequent yields. Galls on plants can also be caused by fungal, bacterial or viral infections.

Earwig (female with eggs)
Earwig populations should be tolerated in gardens, as they do a great deal of good. Although they are often found in holes in fruits, they are almost invariably only taking advantage of damage initially caused by other creatures.

Reducing problems by "good gardening"

A number of techniques can be used by organic gardeners to ensure that pests and diseases stay below an acceptable threshold. Most are not new, and could be described simply as "good husbandry", an aspect often overlooked by conventional (chemical) gardening in the drive to achieve other aims. Good husbandry techniques are essentially preventative. Many are common sense and have other advantages as well as reducing losses to pests and diseases.

Start with the soil

Soil can have a dramatic effect on plant health. Get to know your garden soil (see pp.34–37) and try to choose plants that will suit it. Where necessary, improve soil structure and fertility to encourage strong, balanced growth. Composted organic materials can help to reduce pest and disease levels in the soil, and to grow plants less prone to attack.

Garden cleanliness

The carry-over of pests and diseases between seasons can be prevented with good housekeeping practices. Compost garden waste, and ensure that anything that might be infected with fungal or bacterial pathogens or insect pests is well mixed into the middle of the heap, where heat generated by the breakdown of the organic material will kill them. Any plant material infested with persistent pathogens, such as clubroot-infected brassica roots, and material resistant to composting, such as the woody prunings from canker-infected trees, should be burned.

Plants carrying a viral infection should be removed and composted as soon as symptoms are identified. Viruses are incapable of existence without a living host, and will die with their hosts on compost heaps. Remove self-set (volunteer) potato and tomato plants, which often spring up on compost heaps; such plants could be infected with blight. Lift and remove any pest-infested crop rather than leaving it *in situ* for the pests to complete their development. Ensure also that pest colonies in overwintering plants, particularly brassicas, are removed where possible, and any plant remains from these crops are composted immediately, or buried in a trench, to prevent them acting as a reservoir for overwintering pests and fungal spores.

Winter digging can expose many of the overwintering stages of pests for predation by birds and surface predators like ground beetles. When tidying up the garden, spare a thought for the beetles and centipedes that play a vital role in pest control. They need safe, undisturbed locations to thrive.

Plant choice

Choose plants that are suited to the climatic conditions and soil types in your garden. These will grow well and will be less susceptible to pests and diseases. When buying in plants ensure that they are healthy – not carrying infections or pot-bound; only use certified seed from a reputable source, and be wary of gifts of plants. The primary means of dispersal for many pests and pathogens is on plants transported between gardens.

Resistance

Certain cultivars, or varieties of plants, show resistance to some pests and diseases. Resistance does not imply immunity, and on its own is seldom

Seed potatoes
Virus-free certification schemes exist for seed potatoes and some fruits; always look out for these, and for disease-resistant varieties.

Compost heap hygiene
The heat generated by the process of decay will kill many pathogens, but material infected with certain very persistent diseases, such as clubroot, should be binned or burned.

sufficient to protect crops completely. Nonetheless, resistant varieties can be an important part of an integrated control strategy, especially against virus diseases. They can be invaluable where the threat from particular pests and diseases is high.

Companion planting

Companion planting is a term used to describe the growing of different species of plant together to the benefit of one or both. The technique is often, perhaps misguidedly, thought of as a mainstay of organic pest and disease control. While there is certainly evidence to show that some plants can help to keep others healthy, it would be unwise to rely solely on companion planting to keep pests and diseases at bay. Much is written on the subject, and definitive lists of "good" and "bad" companions provided, but there is little hard evidence to show that these companionships work, or advice on what proportion of each plant is required to be effective.

Monoculture creates a pest and disease paradise, so it is worth growing a diversity of plants where possible – in all parts of the garden, not just the vegetable patch. Mixed planting can be effective and attractive, and if particular combinations work in

your garden, stick with them. What works in one situation may not be effective in another.

There is some evidence to show that the strong scent of French marigolds (*Tagetes patula*) may keep whitefly out of a greenhouse, but only when the marigolds are in flower. On a field scale, it has been shown that carrots grown with onions are less damaged by carrot fly as long as there are four times as many onions as carrots, but that the effect only lasts while the onions are actively growing, and stops once they start to produce bulbs. This may not be as effective on a garden scale.

Research is beginning to show that mixed planting can cut down on pest damage simply by reducing the chance of a pest landing on a suitable host. Cabbages interplanted with an unrelated crop such as French beans, or undersown with clover, show much lower infestations of cabbage aphid and cabbage root fly. When a cabbage root fly lands on a plant, it "tastes" it with its feet. If it lands on several suitable plants in a row, it stops to lay eggs. If the next plant is not suitable, it may fly off elsewhere.

Intercropping a disease-susceptible cultivar with a resistant one is a technique which is also looking promising, on a field scale at least. Research trials

COMPANION PLANTING

Pests that find their host plant by responding to its characteristic odour are often confused by strong-smelling companion plants. Traditional gardening tips like interplanting carrots with onions (top) and growing French marigolds in the greenhouse (below) may have a basis in science.

Mixed planting
Planting flowers around vegetables encourages pollinating and predatory insects, as well as enhancing the beauty of some vegetable crops.

have shown that lettuces can be protected from downy mildew by planting alternate resistant and susceptible plants.

Plants that attract beneficial predators and parasites (see below, and also pages 98–99) are of course "good companions" in the vegetable patch, and around fruit trees and bushes, to encourage natural pest control.

Timing

With vegetable crops and some annual flowering plants, careful timing of sowing or planting can avoid pest attack. In areas where potato blight is prevalent, for example, planting and cropping early potatoes usually misses the period when the threat from blight peaks. Sowing peas early or late ensures that flowering and pod development is completed before, or starts after, the threat from pea moth is present, avoiding damage to the peas. In general, early

sowing, provided that conditions are warm enough, allows plants to be well established before the threats from pests and diseases arrive, giving them more chance of resisting pest attack. Raising plants indoors or on heated benches allows an early start when the conditions outside are not favourable. Sturdy transplants are more able to resist attack than seedlings slowly emerging from a cold and wet soil.

Crop rotation

Keeping to a strict rotation for vegetable crops not only allows better use of nutrients, but prevents the buildup of pests and pathogens in the soil (see also p.301). With perennial crops, such as roses, strawberries, apples and pears, do not replant with the same species in the same place. New plants may fail to thrive due to high levels of host-specific pests or pathogens in the soil. The old established plants may have built up tolerance to these.

PLANTS TO ATTRACT PREDATORS

Many adult insects visit flowers for nectar or pollen even though their juvenile stages or larvae are predators. Insects are attracted to flowers by their colour (including light of wavelengths – or colours – that we cannot see) and sometimes by their scent. Big, bold, open flowers and the tiny florets of umbelliferous flowers, such as cow parsley, are particularly effective.

Typical examples of flowers that will attract beneficial insects are:
1 Gaillardias;
2 Phacelia;
3 Carrot (an umbellifer), flowering in its second year;
4 Poached egg flower, *Limnanthes douglasii*.

See also *Gardening for Wildlife*, pp.186–201

Predators & parasites for natural control

A major component of working with nature for organic pest management is allowing the natural balance of predators and parasites of pests to thrive and keep pest populations in check. The use of pesticides upsets this balance. Often pesticides are more harmful to predator populations than they are to the target pest species. In the past, pesticides have actually given new species pest status as the pesticide wiped out the predator populations. The fruit tree red spider mite is a perfect example, emerging as a pest of fruit trees only after the introduction of tar-oil winter sprays in the 1930s.

Natural predators

Many animals in the garden feed on pests. Some are more obvious than others, and get most of the thanks, like ladybirds. Some we like for aesthetic or sentimental reasons and readily inflate their importance in the pest control stakes, such as hedgehogs. But many insignificant creatures work unnoticed, keeping pest populations below threshold levels. The chart overleaf shows animals that are effective pest control agents in the garden. It is important to recognise these, so they can be encouraged and left alone to perform their business.

To build up the numbers of natural predators and parasites in your garden, aim to avoid the use of pesticides (even those mentioned at the end of this chapter). Pesticides not only have a direct effect on predators and parasites (killing them) but also an indirect effect, removing their food supply. Mixing flowering plants with vegetables and fruit encourages many general predators, such as parasitic wasps, hoverflies and lacewings, the adults of which feed on the nectar from flowers (see also facing page).

Habitats and shelters

Maintain a pond for predators that have an aquatic phase in their life cycle. Provide artificial nesting sites, such as piles of wood for solitary wasps, or overwintering boxes for lacewings (see Gardening for Wildlife, p.192). A good mulch and minimal cultivation creates ideal conditions for ground beetles (the number one slug predator), and dense, matted grass at the base of hedges provides overwintering sites for these and ladybird beetles.

Ladybird on the march
Adult ladybirds will prey on greenfly and blackfly, but the growing larvae (see overleaf) inflict the most damage on aphid populations.

Blue tit feeding young
An average pair of blue tits will collect up to 15,000 caterpillars to raise a brood.

ANIMALS THAT FEED ON GARDEN PESTS

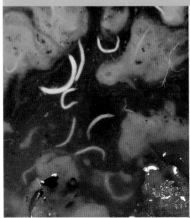

◁ Nematodes
Parasitic, microscopic roundworms; available as biological control agents (see overleaf) for the control of slugs and vine weevil. These parasites are host-specific and are completely harmless to non-target organisms. Here *Heterorhabditis megidis* is multiplying within the parasitised body cavity of a vine weevil.

◁ Centipedes
General ground-based predators, distinguished from millipedes, which are vegetarian, by having only one pair of legs per segment. They also move much faster than millipedes. Centipedes feed on slugs, slug eggs and soil-dwelling insects.

Predatory bugs ▷
Many bugs from several families (notably capsids and anthrocorids) are predators of other plant-feeding bugs; they are especially important in orchards. Right: an anthrocorid bug nymph attacks a small aphid.

Lacewings ▷
The larvae are ferocious predators of aphids and similar insects, consuming upwards of 300 during development; encourage overwintering of populations by erecting lacewing boxes (see p.192). They can also be purchased as biological control agents (see overleaf), in the form of eggs. Right: a green lacewing larva feeding on a Western flower thrip.

◁ Hoverflies
Larvae of many common species are predatory mainly on aphids. Their colour varies but is usually bright, and they resemble flattened fishing maggots. Adults can be encouraged by planting open-flowered plants. Here a number of bright green larvae are feeding on aphids on a rose shoot.

◁ Predatory midges
A number of species of tiny midges have wandering, predatory larvae that feed exclusively on aphids. Some can be purchased as biological control agents (see overleaf).
Left: *Aphidoletes* midge larvae preying on an aphid colony.

Tachinid flies ▷
Adult females of these flies, which resemble very bristly house flies, lay eggs on or near other insect hosts, especially butterfly and moth larvae, and the larvae, or maggots, develop as parasites within the host. Adults are encouraged by open-flowered plants.

Wasps ▷
The adult females of solitary species like this mason wasp (right) collect insect pests to provide food for grubs; encourage them by keeping a pile of rotting logs as a nesting site. Social wasps are also useful predators in spring/early summer, when adult females collect insect pests to feed the grubs; however, they become pests of ripening fruit in late summer and autumn.

◁ Parasitic wasps

Adult females lay eggs in other insects and the larvae develop as parasites, killing the host. Most insect species have specific wasps parasitising their larvae. A number of them can be purchased as biological control agents (see overleaf). Left: *Apantales glomeratus*, an important predator of cabbage white butterfly larvae.

◁ Beetles

Many species of ground beetle (see violet ground beetle, p.35) are predatory both as adults and larvae, feeding on juvenile and egg stages of slugs and snails, as well as ground-based insects. Rove beetles (see left) are similar to ground beetles; many species are good fliers feeding on a range of plant-feeding pests. Encourage beetles by minimising soil disturbance and with use of mulches.

Ladybirds ▷

Both the adults and larvae are predatory on aphids and other bugs. Ladybirds can be purchased as biological control agents (see overleaf). Right: ladybird larva feeding on a colony of black bean aphids.

Mites ▷

Many predatory mites feed mainly on plant-feeding mites. A number can be purchased as biological control agents (see overleaf). *Phytoseiulus persimilis* (right) is a biological control agent against red spider mite; here it is feeding on red spider mite eggs.

◁ Harvestmen

These are roving, spindly-legged ground-based predators related to spiders, but unlike spiders these have only one body part.

◁ Spiders

All spiders are predatory on insects and other arthropods, although catching systems vary and not all spiders use webs as traps. Spiders can be differentiated from harvestmen (far left) by their two clearly defined body parts.

Frogs, toads and newts ▷

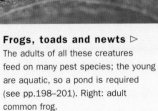

The adults of all these creatures feed on many pest species; the young are aquatic, so a pond is required (see pp.198–201). Right: adult common frog.

Lizards ▷

Many species feed exclusively on insects and other invertebrate pests, including slugs and snails. Right: an adult slow worm (a legless lizard), a major predator of slugs.

Yellow sticky traps
These traps are used to monitor the presence of pests – they cannot give effective control of infestations.

A CASE HISTORY

The glasshouse red spider mite (RSM) is a major pest of most glasshouse plants. The predatory mite *Phytoseiulus persimilis*, if introduced early enough, will completely control populations of RSM. *Phytoseiulus* are introduced, usually in an inert carrier such as vermiculite, by sprinkling into the crop. (Make sure the container is left on its side for an hour or so before this, otherwise all the mites congregate in the top layers of the vermiculite.) For *Phytoseiulus* to work, the temperature needs to be 20°C (68°F) for at least part of day, and the humidity should be kept high (at around 60%). High humidity suits the predator, but not the prey, switching the balance further in the predator's favour. As with most biological control agents the aim is not pest eradication but control: hopefully some RSM will remain in the crop to maintain a population of *Phytoseiulus* ready to kick in if the pest population starts to expand again.

Biological controls

Many predators and parasites of pests can be purchased, usually by mail order, for introduction into the greenhouse or garden. These are known as biological control agents. Some, such as lacewings and ladybirds, boost the natural populations; more often they are exotic species that are introduced to control a specific pest, like the parasitic wasp *Encarsia formosa*, a parasite of the glasshouse whitefly. Many biological control introductions work best indoors (in glasshouses, conservatories and tunnels), where movement is restricted and climatic conditions can be controlled to suit the predators' biology, but some predatory insects and mites can be used outside provided that conditions are favourable and the night-time temperature stays above the minumum required. The range of biological control agents available to the amateur is increasing all the time.

Using the controls

Details of how to use biological control agents vary, depending on the organism, but these are live cultures and the instructions must be followed to the letter (see A Case History, far left, for one illustration). Since biological control agents usually arrive by mail order and sometimes more than one release is required, check the despatch dates and likely date of arrivals. Plan ahead so that you are there to receive the live material and are in a position to use it immediately.

Take careful note of the conditions, especially temperature and humidity, that are needed, and avoid using all pesticides before as well as during application. Finally, ensure early introductions by closely monitoring plants for pests. Predator populations usually grow at a much slower rate than pest populations. In order to prevent the pest population growing away from the predators, therefore, early introduction is essential. Yellow sticky traps will pick up the first pioneers of an infestation of glasshouse whitefly, for example, indicating the time to introduce *Encarsia*.

SOME BIOLOGICAL CONTROL AGENTS

Whitefly control

Pest	Agent	Special requir
Glasshouse whitefly	*Encarsia formosa* (parasitic wasp)	Optimum temperature 18–25°C (64–77°F)
Red spider mite	*Phytoseiulus persimilis* (predatory mite)	Optimum temperature 18–25°C (64–77°F). Humidity 60%
Mealybug	*Cryptolaemus montrouzieri* (predatory beetle)	Optimum temperature 20–25°C. (68–77°F). Humidity 70%
Aphids	*Aphidoletes aphidimyza* (predatory midge larva)	Optimum temperature 21°C (70°F). Humidity high: 80%
Vine weevil	*Heterorhabditis megidis* (parasitic nematode)	Minimum soil temperature 14°C (57°F). Moist soil essential
Soft scale	*Metaphycus helvolus* (parasitic wasp)	Optimum temp. 20–30°C (68–86°F). Good light levels needed
Slugs	*Phasmarhabditis hermaphrodita* (parasitic nematode)	Minimum soil temperature 5°C (40°F). Moist soil essential
Thrips	*Amblyseus cucumeris* (predatory mite)	Optimum temperature 25°C (77°F)
Leatherjackets	*Steinernema feltiae* (parasitic nematode)	Minimum soil temperature 10°C (50°F). Moist soil essential
Chafer grubs	*Heterorhabditis megidis* (parasitic nematode)	Minimum soil temperature 12°C (54°F). Moist soil essential. Apply from mid- to late summer

Traps, barriers and deterrents

Barriers such as walls or fences around gardens to keep rabbits out have been used since medieval times; fruit cages, too, are a traditional way of protecting soft fruit crops from birds. By contrast, barriers against insect pests are a relatively recent advance. They usually consist of a net with a mesh size through which insects cannot pass – usually less than 1.5mm. This lets maximum light, water and air through, while keeping insect pests out. Insect mesh is not to be confused with fleece, an unwoven fabric. Fleece protects young plants from climatic damage and also some pests (see p.233), but its continued use prevents ventilation and provides ideal conditions for slugs and fungal pathogens to proliferate.

Know the pest's habits

Sometimes, as with carrot fly, a simple fence 45–50cm (18–20in) high will act as a barrier. The host-seeking female carrot flies keep low to the ground, as they are weak fliers and subject to being blown off-course by wind. The fence firstly prevents the low-flying carrot flies from getting into the carrot patch, but it also acts like a chimney, taking the carrot odour upwards and away from the host-seeking females.

Stronger fliers, like cabbage white butterflies, need complete crop cover to keep them out. This also protects crops from insect pests like cabbage root flies, which lay their eggs adjacent to cabbage stems after a response is triggered by alighting on appropriate leaves (see p.95). Collars (see p.304) or upturned yoghurt pots with the base removed prevent access to the base of brassica plants by egg-laying female

cabbage root flies. Insect barrier glue is a sticky non-set glue that prevents walking insects from passing. It is especially effective at controlling winter moths in orchards. The female winter moth has no wings, but climbs the tree in autumn or winter. On trees less than four years old, the glue, or fruit tree grease, should be applied on a paper band, not directly to the trunk itself. If the tree is staked, remember to put a sticky band around the stake too.

Keeping slugs and snails away

A small isolated bed protected with a water-filled moat, known as a Butcombe box (see right), can be an effective way of keeping slugs and snails away from vulnerable plants such as tender salad crops. A plethora of materials are marketed as slug barriers. Most consist of a porous material, such as a mined rock, that is dry and unpleasant for slugs to pass over. However, these barriers tend to be less effective in wet weather and seldom stay in place for long; also, slugs move under them through the soil. Recently, an electrical barrier has been developed which slugs will not pass. This incorporates a small battery, powering a conductive band around a plant pot. Copper bands (see p.205) can also be effective, setting up a static charge around pots.

Trapping and hand-picking

In small gardens the value of hand-picking pests should not be underestimated. Removing or squashing a few invaders at the start of an infestation can prevent colonies becoming established, and

Keeping slugs at bay with the Butcombe box
The wooden frame, 15cm (6in) high, has a base made of a porous membrane. A "moat", made of plastic guttering, prevents slugs from entering the box, thereby protecting the crop growing inside. The box can be filled with purchased potting compost or garden soil. If garden soil is used, treat it with the biological control nematode Phasmarhabditis hermaphrodita (see facing page) once it is in the box, to make sure that no slugs are trapped within the moat.

Ringing the changes
*Birds soon learn that scaring devices represent no real danger, so it is worth improvising a variety of devices and replacing or moving them around from time to time. Effective scarers create deterrent sounds, such as humming tape, or sights, like the reflective mirror ball (**1**). This windmill (**2**) made Blue Peter-style from a detergent bottle, does both. The hovering "bird of prey" (**3**) made from feathers and a potato is a very old idea. All of the devices on the left, together with many others, are in use at the HDRA's gardens at Yalding, Kent.*

continued action can control numbers of persistent pests such as slugs. Removing badly affected plants, pruning out damaged sections, or sometimes removing the sensitive part of an uninfested plant (as when pinching out the tender shoot tips of broad beans, which attract blackfly damage) can prevent pests spreading or becoming established.

Traps for garden pests can be used in conjunction with hand-picking. This is especially effective for slugs. As most slug activity is after dark, night-time forays into the garden with a torch are usually the best time for slug collection. Traps baited with beer or chocolate, or simply items that provide daytime refuge (such as plastic plant trays or old bits of wood or carpet) where slugs will congregate, allow slugs to be picked during the day. A simple slug trap can be made from a plastic carton filled with beer. Keep the rim just above soil level to prevent beetles falling in. Slugs will happily climb over the lip.

Introducing ducks or chickens into a garden can also control slug numbers. Ducks and bantams are particularly useful in this respect, as they tend not to cause significant damage to plants. In tunnels and on vegetable plots, chickens can be introduced for a short period between crops as part of a rotation.

The primary use of insect traps is to monitor populations, but in sufficient numbers in small areas they can help prevent pests becoming established. Pheromone traps are available for many moth pests, usually consisting of a protected sticky board and a sachet of the female sex pheromone. Male moths find the females by homing in on this pheromone's scent and are easily fooled into entering a trap and alighting on the sticky board. The removal of males has little effect on the population's viability, since surviving males will readily cover for their deceased colleagues, but in small gardens a few such traps can often either take out enough males to have an effect, or disrupt the mate-seeking process sufficiently to reduce the viability of the next generation.

Feeding pests!

When young vegetable and bedding plants are transplanted into a newly prepared bed, they become an attractive source of food for hungry slugs. Distract them with young lettuce plants, or old lettuce leaves tucked under bricks and tiles, put out several days in advance. Replace the leaves, taking the slugs away with the old ones, every few days. Some gardeners report success using French marigolds as similar "trap" crops amongst other bedding plants.

A heap of cut comfrey leaves can help to clear a bed of slugs before it is planted. The leaves, and the the slugs feeding on them, are left in place fro a few days and removed at night. Surrounding new plants with a protective ring of cut comfrey leaves can distract slugs until the plants become more established.

BARRIERS

• Individual cloches made from old plastic drinks bottles (right) offer protection from slugs to young vulnerable plants.
• Older brassica plants can be protected from birds with "cages" made from twiggy prunings (far right). A net or fleece tunnel, supported by canes to keep it off the plants, can protect rows.

Pesticides in the organic garden

As a final resort organic gardeners may use a small range of insecticides and fungicides. Although often less harmful or persistent than many synthetic pesticides, these "organic" pesticides are still poisons, and like synthetic pesticides can adversely affect non-target organisms. Their use is constantly under review by the bodies that set organic standards, and the use of copper products and derris in organic systems is likely to be banned in the next few years.

Legal considerations

The use of all pesticides is strictly controlled by law, and it is illegal to use any that have not been officially approved. The list of approved products varies from country to country. In the UK, organic gardeners may use *Bacillus thuringiensis* (Bt), insecticidal soap, pyrethrum, rape oil and derris as insecticides, and Bordeaux mixture (copper-based) and sulphur as fungicides. Quassia, neem, garlic oil and granulosis virus would be acceptable organically, but they are not registered for use in the UK, although they can be used elsewhere in Europe.

It is often thought that any pesticide of natural origin – and this usually means plant extracts – is acceptable in an organic garden. Although some such products might be effective, and relatively harmless environmentally, their use cannot be recommended unless they have been tested for efficacy and safety and officially approved for use. As the cost of testing and approval is very high, this is unlikely to happen. Some homemade products, such as nettle tea or boiled rhubarb leaves, may be relatively innocuous, but other home-made plant concoctions can be extremely poisonous, and none can be recommended.

Only spray as a last choice. And while you are spraying, think about the possible options for preventing the problem arising in future!

Sulphur dust on grapes
A traditional remedy, sulphur dust is used on demonstration crops of grapes at HDRA's restored glasshouses at Audley End.

IF YOU MUST SPRAY, SPRAY SAFELY

- Don't use a spray as a preventative measure.
- Read the label and follow instructions precisely.
- Use a good-quality sprayer.
- Spray only where necessary. Spray contact insecticides directly on the pests, or spray the whole plant if it is to be eaten by the pests.
- Only make up as much spray as you need; never store made-up spray.
- Spray only in still weather to avoid drift.
- Never spray when bees are working – the evening is often safest.
- Wear protection when spraying – rubber gloves, mask and goggles.
- Always wash your hands after spraying.

PERMITTED PESTICIDES

Spray	Source/derivation	Use against	Notes
Derris	From roots of derris and *Longocarpus* plants	Greenfly, blackfly and other aphids; caterpillars; flea beetle; raspberry beetle; sawfly larvae	Can harm ladybirds, lacewings and parasitic wasps. Safe for bees
Pyrethrum	Extracted from flowerheads of *Chrysanthemum cinerariaefolium*	Greenfly, blackfly and other aphids	Can harm beneficial insects but does not persist for long
Insecticidal soap	Fatty acids extracted from plant material	Greenfly, blackfly and other aphids; whitefly; red spider mite; soft scale; rose slugworm	Makes the pests slip off rather than harming them. Can damage some sensitive plants
Rapeseed oil	Agricultural crop	Greenfly, blackfly and other aphids; whitefly; thrips; scale; red spider mite	Do not use on fuchsias, begonias and seedlings as it can damage leaves
Bordeaux mixture	Compound containing copper and sulphur	Apple scab; peach leaf curl; potato blight	Harmful to fish, livestock and worms (due to the buildup of copper in the soil)
Sulphur	Naturally occurring mineral	Powdery mildew; rose black spot	Can harm predatory mites. Do not use on young apples and gooseberries, or "sulphur-shy" fruit cultivars
Bacillus thuringiensis	Bacterial spores that produce an insect-toxic protein	Cabbage caterpillars	Protein causes paralysis of mouthparts and gut in host. Degrades in sunlight; usually needs repeat applications

Raising plants

SOWING SEEDS AND TAKING CUTTINGS COMES AS NATURALLY
TO THE ORGANIC GARDENER AS COMPOSTING AND MULCHING

**Tools and techniques
(facing page)**
*Taking cuttings needs a little skill, but
is not difficult to master. A clean, sharp
knife that feels comfortable to use is
your greatest ally. An ordinary
penknife can be perfectly adequate.*

Seeds of success
*Those bitten by the propagation bug
soon find every corner of the garden
and greenhouse filled with
"experiments" at various stages of
growth. Taking good care of them all
can be a full-time job.*

RAISING PLANTS can be a fascinating occupation,
with many benefits, especially for the organic
gardener. Propagation, as it is known, can be carried
out on many different scales and in all sorts of
situations. Most of the equipment required is
relatively cheap and easy to obtain. You can even
take the enterprise one step further, and produce the
seed itself in your own garden.

There are two main methods of propagation.
Vegetative propagation – taking cuttings, for
example – produces plants that are genetically
identical to the parent; in effect, clones. Sowing seed
produces more varied results, especially if you save
your own seed from the garden, but the diversity in
the plants produced is all part of the fun.

The secret to successful propagation is to
understand the basics. Give your seeds and cuttings
the best conditions you can and they will repay you
by growing well. Correct temperature, light levels,
moisture and ventilation are all crucial. A greenhouse
and heated bench (see p.220) will open up all sorts
of possibilities, but excellent results can be had using
airing cupboards and windowsills – and many seeds
and cuttings can be grown outdoors.

WHY PROPAGATE YOUR OWN PLANTS?

• **It's fascinating** Propagating plants can
enhance your understanding and enjoyment of
gardening. There is something endlessly
fascinating about sowing seeds, taking cuttings
and dividing plants. You could even discover or
develop your own new plant varieties.

• **Avoid pests and pesticides** Bought-in
plants may harbour pests, such as vine weevil, in
the growing medium or on the plant. Many
commercially produced plants are regularly
sprayed with chemicals that you do not want in
your garden or home, and the growing medium
may also contain pesticides. By raising your
own stock, you can be certain that you are not
introducing unwanted pollutants into your
organic garden.

• **Save yourself money** Cut costs by investing
a little time and effort in producing your own
seeds and plants. You can produce just the right
quantity for your own needs, or grow a few
extra if you have the space. The seed saved from
one tomato will give dozens of plants; one
squash will provide more than enough seed for
the average gardener. Many cuttings can be
produced from a single plant. A surplus of
plants need never go to waste. Grow plants for
your friends, for schools, for community
gardens or to raise funds for local good causes.

• **Extend the range** Organically grown seeds
and plants are available, but, although the range
is expanding, it is still limited. By raising your
own, you can extend this range. Many rare and
unusual varieties of fruit, vegetables and
ornamentals are impossible to obtain through
seed companies and nurseries. Under these
circumstances, you will need to rely on your
own, or other people's, skills in propagation to
get hold of the plants you want.

• **Think local** Reduce transport costs by
growing what you need where you need it,
instead of relying on expensive and
environmentally damaging deliveries from
far away.

Vegetative propagation

This term basically translates as growing a whole plant from a part of a plant. It can be used for all plants except annuals and biennials, which are always grown from seed. Don't forget, though, that many of the bedding plants we grow as annuals, discarding every year, are in fact tender perennials that can be propagated by cuttings over winter, provided that you can give them warmth and shelter.

Stems, roots and even single leaves can be used, depending on the species. The advantage of raising plants in this way is that the offspring will be identical to the parent, without the genetic variation that can result when you save seed from a plant. And it is the only way to propagate plants that do not produce viable seed – for example, the lawn chamomile 'Treneague', bred not to flower.

Division

Division – cutting or pulling clump-forming plants into sections, each with roots and shoots – is the quickest and easiest way to propagate herbaceous perennials (see p.173) and gives large, flowering plants in a short time. It also reinvigorates them. Most can be divided in spring or autumn. Division also works well for plants that form clumps of fleshy storage organs – bulbs, corms or tubers – below ground, such as Jerusalem artichokes and daffodils. These can be harvested at the end of the season, separated, stored, and planted out the next spring.

Divisions of fist-sized dimensions, or fully formed bulbs, can be planted out as they are, with no need of extra warmth or protection. Smaller parts of plants, including the little bulblets, resembling garlic cloves, that form around clumps of bulbs, benefit from being potted up and grown on under cover.

Stem cuttings

Both tips and sections of stem can be put in pots of compost or into the soil to develop their own roots. While all cuttings root faster with bottom heat,

TAKING SOFTWOOD STEM TIP CUTTINGS

Choose strong non-flowering shoots 8–10cm (3–4in) long, severing them just above a leaf joint (**1**).

Trim the cutting to just below a leaf joint (**2**), and remove the leaves from the bottom half of each cutting (**3**).

Insert into a pot containing a 1:1 mix of coarse sand and coir so the first leaf is just above the level of the rooting medium (**4**). Keep this moist, but not sodden.

Cover with a plastic bag to maintain high humidity. Use two pieces of bent wire to construct a frame to support the bag so that cuttings do not touch it and rot. Keep it out of direct sunlight.

Once rooted, harden off (see pp.113 and 232) gradually before potting up, to acclimatise cuttings to the reduced humidity and more intense light levels.

provided by a propagator or heated bench, most do not need it. Shelter under glass, or on a window sill, is only necessary for cuttings taken from soft growth that would quickly dry up and fail if exposed outside. While these cuttings need a humid atmosphere it is important that they do not become waterlogged, or the soft tissue will rot, so the compost you use must be free-draining, opened up with grit or sand (see Growing media, p.114).

Hormone rooting powders are not regarded as a suitable organic input. Most plant species root effectively without any special treatment.

Types of stem cutting

While there is no harm in experimenting if the opportunity presents itself, in general take the right sort of cuttings at the appropriate time, and take more than you need, for the best chance of success.
• **Softwood cuttings** are non-woody shoots taken primarily from herbaceous plants and tender bedding plants in spring and early summer while they are producing strong, soft, fleshy growth. Stem tips are the easiest to take and root (see facing page). Some of the most successful for beginners are fuchsias, pelargoniums and nepeta (catmint). Because the shoots are actively growing, you need to provide adequate levels of moisture, light and warmth to encourage rooting, so the cuttings must be potted up and kept under cover.
• **Semi-ripe cuttings** are taken just as the current season's growth starts to harden at the base. They are useful for all types of woody plant, including small

---

ROOTING CUTTINGS IN PLASTIC BAGS

This is an alternative to rooting softwood cuttings in pots or open ground that works particularly well for carnations and fuchsias. Cut an opaque polythene bag to make a long strip about 25cm (10in) wide, and fold in half lengthways to form a crease. Spread a gritty cuttings mix along the crease. Lay the cuttings on this so that the top third sticks out at the top, then roll up the plastic like a Swiss roll and secure it with a rubber band. Water carefully, since there are no drainage holes, and stand in a warm place out of direct sunlight. When the cuttings root, remove the rubber band, unroll the plastic and pot them up.

---

shrubs such as lavenders and dwarf box, so are ideal for making quantities of edging plants. Conifers and many climbers also root well from semi-ripe cutttings. They are usually taken from deciduous species in early to late summer; cuttings from evergreens often root better if taken in early autumn. In some cases, getting the timing right is critical for success. Treat as for softwood cuttings.

Recent research has shown that longer cuttings than traditionally used can be very successful, giving bigger plants in a shorter time. Semi-ripe shoots of 30cm (1ft) or more of most shrubs can be rooted. In the case of climbers, shoots of up to a metre (3ft) can be used. Both ends are inserted into the pot and will often root. The arched stem will then produce multiple shoots, giving much denser growth than a normal cutting.
• **Hardwood cuttings** (see right) are taken from trees and shrubs while dormant. When taken from ready-rooting, hardy plants – for example blackcurrant, gooseberry, willow and dogwood – they need very little attention. Prepare a "nursery bed" (see p.314) for them outdoors in a cool, shaded area. These cuttings are most usually taken in late winter.

Layering

Many woody plants and climbers have a tendency to develop roots on stems where they touch the ground (some climbers, such as ivy, even develop aerial roots) and you can take advantage of this habit, or stimulate it in some other woody plants, to make new plants, cutting the rooted stem from the parent and either potting it up or planting it out, if well-developed enough. Layering is especially useful to increase clematis, rhododendron, camellia and magnolia, none of which roots easily from cuttings.

Layer shrubs in spring and climbers in early summer. Rooting usually takes at least a year, sometimes several. Dig a hole next to the parent plant and bend a stem into it, leaving about 15cm (6in) of the growing tip above ground. Peg the shoot down with a piece of bent wire, replace the soil and put a rock on top to hold the shoot down and conserve moisture. Wounding the buried stem can speed up rooting. Cut a slice out or twist it so the bark is damaged. When the stem beyond the stone begins to show more vigorous growth, it has rooted and can be severed from the parent plant.

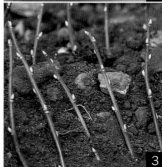

TAKING HARDWOOD CUTTINGS

Cut vigorous shoots, formed during the summer, into 25cm (9in) lengths. Remove leaves if necessary (**1**). Trim the lower end of each to just below a bud with a sharp knife. Cut off any soft growth at the top to just above a bud (**2**).

In a sheltered location, make a narrow slit or slits in the soil with a spade and fill the bottom with coarse sand. Place cuttings in this nursery bed, so that at least 7.5cm (3in) remains above ground (**3**). Refill with soil. Leave for one year, watering and weeding during the growing season as necessary. The rooted cuttings should be ready for transplanting by the following autumn.

Starting from seed

A seed is the product of a fertilised flower. It contains an embryo plant enclosed in a protective seed coat. The seed also contains food reserves that nourish the germinating embryo until it is able to feed itself.

Large-scale organic seed production is a relatively recent development. A limited but increasing range, mainly of vegetable seed, is now available through standard seed catalogues. There are also companies supplying only organically grown seed. If you cannot find an organic supply of the seed you are looking for, the next best thing is to buy seed without any chemical seed dressing, or consider growing your own seed.

What seeds need

For successful germination, seeds require moisture, air and an appropriate temperature. Most prefer to germinate in darkness, although some, especially fine seeds, need exposure to light. Success also depends on the vigour of the seed. Fresh seed, or seed that has been stored in good conditions (see p.123) will germinate more rapidly and produce more vigorous seedlings than old or poorly stored seed.

Seed can be sown directly into the soil, or into a purpose-made growing medium, such as a seed or multipurpose compost, in a pot or tray. This will supply the necessary mixture of moisture and air that the seed needs. An appropriate temperature in the soil or growing medium is essential for germination. Seeds have particular requirements which govern where, and when, particular species should be sown.

Depending on the species of plant, both low and high temperatures can inhibit germination. The most temperature-sensitive stage in the process is when the seed is first absorbing water. The growth of some tender crops, such as sweetcorn and French beans, can be permanently impaired by temperatures that are too low at this stage. The germination of onions, lettuces and celery, on the other hand, can be inhibited when the temperature is too high.

Special treatments

Over the years, vegetables and many ornamentals have been bred for fast, regular germination. Wild flowers, shrubs and trees often germinate much more erratically and may refuse to germinate unless given special treatment:

• A tough seed coat may require "scarification" – wounding so that water and air can enter (see Tough seed coats, below left).

• Many trees, shrubs and wild flowers, such as hawthorn, holly and cowslip, that are native to colder climates, need a period of low temperature before they will germinate. After sowing, stand the seed trays or pots outdoors over winter. Alternatively, mix larger seed with moist sand and store in a refrigerator for a few months. This is known as stratification.

When seedlings fail to emerge, there can of course be causes other than poor germination – such as pest and disease attack, or poor growing conditions (see pp.112–113).

TOUGH SEED COATS

Many members of the pea family, such as sweet pea, broom (*Cytisus*, top) and wisteria have tough seed coats, which gives their seeds long-term viability whilst waiting for the right germination conditions. Aid germination by scarifying the seed – nicking the seed coat with a knife, or rubbing gently between a folded sheet of sandpaper (above).

GERMINATION TEMPERATURES

Seed	Temperature range
Cabbage	5–32°C (41–90°F)
Leeks and onions	7–21°C (45–70°F)
Celery	10–19°C (50–66°F)
Sweetcorn	Over 10°C (50°F)
French bean	Over 12°C (54°F)
Lettuce (butterhead)	Below 25°C (77°F)
Tomato	Over 15°C (59°F)
Poppy	15–21°C (59–70°F)
French marigold (*Tagetes*)	18–25°C (64–77°F)
Begonia	18–25°C (64–77°F)
Busy Lizzie (*Impatiens*)	20–25°C (68–77°F)
Morning glory	18–24°C (64–75°F)
Nasturtium	15–21°C (59–70°F)
Broad bean	5°C (41°)

Sowing seeds outdoors

The simplest and most direct way of raising many plants is to sow seed outdoors. The key to success is to ensure that you sow when the soil conditions – temperature and moisture content – are just right. This skill will develop with experience.

Preparing the soil

A few weeks before the anticipated sowing date, prepare the soil to suit the plants that are to be sown. Where practical, apply a leafmould mulch to sowing areas the previous autumn. This will improve the structure at the soil surface, where germinating seedlings need it. Even freshly fallen autumn leaves will be of benefit; these can be raked off before sowing.

Do not work the soil if it is too wet – this will destroy the soil structure and give poor germination and growth rates. If mud sticks to your boots, you should abandon the work until the soil is drier.

The soil condition known as "capping", also weather-related, will prevent the emergence of seeds, but you can take measures to help germination when you sow (see panel, right).

Making a seed bed

Rake the surface to create a fine "tilth". Treading or rolling a seed bed is sometimes recommended, but it is better to allow the soil to settle for a few weeks rather than risk damaging the soil structure. This has the added advantage of creating what is known as a "stale seed bed". Disturbing the soil stimulates weed seeds near the surface to germinate. As they germinate fast and grow vigorously they can easily swamp young seedlings. To pre-empt this, leave a prepared seed bed empty for a few weeks, then hoe off the weeds that germinate, and sow immediately. This will give your seedlings a head start on the next batch of weeds to appear.

Soil temperatures

Avoid the temptation to sow seeds too early in the spring. If soil temperatures are below 7°C (45°F), the majority of seeds will germinate very slowly or not at all, and seedling growth will be slow. The longer seeds remain in cold wet soil, the more likely they are to rot or be attacked by pests. Seeds sown in a warm soil will often overtake those sown weeks earlier in cooler soil. A soil thermometer is a useful tool, giving you a good idea of how quickly your soil is warming up. Speed this process by covering the soil with a cloche or sheet of black or clear polythene for a month before sowing.

How to sow

Most seeds do not need to be buried deeply: a few millimetres is quite sufficient. Larger seeds can go in at a depth of twice their diameter. Peas can take a depth of 2.5–4cm (1–1½in) and beans 4–5cm (1½–2in). Seed can be sown in rows, in individual positions or "stations", or broadcast over a larger area.

• **Sowing in drills** Seed is sown in a shallow trench or "drill", created with the corner of a hoe, or a stick. It may be sprinkled along the row, for later thinning, or placed at the final spacing required. Water the bottom of the drill before sowing; rake back the soil to cover the seeds.

• **Station sowing** Seed is sown in individual "stations" at the final spacing required. Two or three seeds can be sown at each station if necessary, then thinned to one seedling. Station-sow along a drill, or

Soil thermometer
Different soils warm up at different rates: a soil thermometer provides accurate information as to when the soil is warm enough for sowing.

COPING WITH CAPPING

"Capping" is a condition prevalent in soils with a poor structure. Rain causes soil particles to coalesce; a hard crust then forms on top of the soil during dry weather. If your soil is prone to capping, cover seeds with a mixture of soil and leafmould, or even a seed or potting compost, instead of soil. Water the seed drill before sowing, then do not water again until the seedlings have come up. Mulch the soil with a low-fertility soil improver, particularly over winter, to improve the surface structure. Reduce the frequency of digging – or give it up entirely (see The No-dig Approach, p.326).

FLUID SOWING

Start seeds off indoors on some moist paper towel in a plastic box (**1**). Put the lid on, and keep the box at about 21°C (70°F) in a propagator or airing cupboard until roots begin to appear.

When the roots are about 5mm (¼in) long (**2**), carefully wash them off the towel and into a fine gauge plastic strainer.

Make up some fungicide-free wallpaper paste at half the normal strength, and when it has thickened, add the seeds to it (**3**), stirring gently. Try not to touch the delicate seeds.

Pour the paste and seed mix into a plastic bag and seal the top with a knot. Make a shallow drill in the soil using a draw hoe and moisten it. Cut the corner off the plastic bag and squeeze the seeds and paste out into the drill (**4**). You could also use a cake-icing bag if you have one. Cover the seeds over and firm gently with the back of a rake. Keep the drill moist in dry weather.

take out individual small holes. Station sowing can cut down on the amount of seed you use, especially for widely spaced plants.

• **Broadcast sowing** Seed is scattered over the soil and gently raked in. Useful for sowing grass, green manures and other small to medium-sized seed that has to be evenly distributed over an area. As it is difficult to cover every seed, some protection against birds may be needed. Fleece is particularly effective as it also speeds germination by warming the soil. Water after sowing if rain is not forecast.

Fluid sowing

Fluid sowing (see above) is a useful way of speeding germination indoors and sowing the germinating seeds outside without damaging their delicate roots.

Seedling emergence is often 2–3 weeks earlier than with dry sown seeds. Fluid sowing has been shown to give higher yields of slow-germinating crops such as early carrots, parsnips and onions. Outdoor tomatoes can be sown direct in climates where the season is usually considered to be too short.

Thinning

Once seedlings have emerged, they will usually need thinning. Competition for light, water and nutrients is intense, and if you do not remove the surplus you will end up with a mass of stunted plants. First remove weak, spindly and slow-germinating seedlings, simply pinching them out of the ground, then continue if necessary until no seedling touches another. You may need to thin once or even twice again as the seedlings grow and encroach on each other once more. Most seed packets give an ideal "final spacing" for the plant being grown. In the vegetable garden, this can be varied according to the way you are growing your crops (for example, in narrow beds as opposed to traditional rows) and the size you wish to harvest roots, bulbs or leafy heads.

Pest problems

Even though a seed germinates, a seedling may not emerge. Slugs, bean seed fly, mice and millipedes may all destroy it before it sees the light of day. Covers, traps and barriers (see p.101) keep some pests at bay.

Sowing under cover

Raising seedlings in pots and trays in a greenhouse, polytunnel or on a windowsill allows plants to be started earlier than might be possible outdoors, and helps to keep them safe from pests. This method is particularly appropriate for the more tender plants, but can be useful for hardy plants too. Seedlings can be growing in trays while the ground where they are finally to be planted is still occupied by other plants.

Where to sow

A greenhouse or cold frame is an excellent place in which to raise plants, providing good all-round light. "Bottom heat" is the most economic way of providing warmth – either with a thermostatically controlled heated propagator, or on a heated bench (see p.220). Flat, roll-out heating mats can be used as a flexible heat source, or soil-warming cables can be bedded in sand, in a deep bench or box Temperatures in the range of 18–21°C (65–70°F) will be sufficient for most plants.

Seedlings can be raised in the house, though it can be difficult to provide enough light to prevent them becoming spindly. A propagator is useful if extra warmth is needed for germination, though a warm airing cupboard or radiator shelf can be used instead. Check the temperature there over a few days before you sow to be sure it stays within acceptable limits. As soon as the seedlings emerge, transfer them to a light windowsill. They need to be turned every day so that the plants do not become lopsided as they grow towards the light. An open-topped foil-lined box, with the side facing the window cut away, will reflect light onto seedlings from all angles and produces more regular growth.

What to sow in

You can sow in a wide range of containers, purchased or recycled from household items. The basic requirement is that whatever you use allows adequate drainage, is robust enough for the job and is free from disease organisms and chemicals poisonous to plants.

• **Pots** Clay pots are porous, allowing air to reach the roots and moisture to evaporate through the clay,

Perfect for propagating
A sturdy work bench situated in dappled shade with an easily swept floor makes an ideal spot for sowing and potting on.

COVERING SEEDS

Covering pots and seed trays with plastic will help maintain moisture levels during the critical germination phase.

Once germination starts, you must remove the covering so that the seedlings are able to emerge properly.

Shading

Young plants on windowsills can be given temporary protection from scorching sunlight simply by taping a sheet of paper onto the glass. Open windows in hot weather too, to make sure that plants do not stifle in hot, still air.

reducing problems caused by overwatering. They are, however, more expensive than plastic, and cleaning them is much more difficult. Plastic pots need less watering, which is advantageous when using soilless growing media, which dry out faster than loam-based ones. Biodegradable pots, made of paper, coir or similar materials are transplanted along with the plant to minimise root disturbance.

• **Seed trays** Trays 5–7cm (2–3in) deep and of variable size. Wooden trays are rare these days. Plastic ones are cheaper and easier to clean.

• **Modules** Multi-celled seed trays – also known as module trays, are available in plastic and polystyrene. The plastic ones are easier to remove plants from and thus use again. Seedlings grow in individual "mini pots", so their root system is not disturbed on transplanting. "Root trainers", deeper than module trays, encourage a healthy root system, and are ideal for sweet peas, beans and sweetcorn, for example.

• **Homemade pots and seed trays** Aluminium foil take-away cartons, ice cream and margarine tubs, polystyrene coffee cups and yoghurt pots can all be used. Clean them thoroughly and make drainage holes in the bottom. Egg boxes can be used as module trays. Toilet roll centres, and homemade paper tubes, are useful for plants that resent root disturbance. Just plant them straight into the ground when the plants are ready.

Sowing the seeds

Use a proprietary seed mix or a multipurpose organic compost (see Growing media, p.114). The finer the seeds, the finer the growing medium needs to be. After filling pots or trays, lightly firm the compost before sowing. Firmed compost is less likely to slump when watered. For seed trays, a wooden block is ideal for firming evenly and gently. Fine seeds can be sown on the surface of the compost and covered by gently sifting a little more over the top. Large seeds can be pushed in individually with a finger, or dropped into holes made with a pencil or dibber.

Keeping seedlings healthy

Manage the growing environment carefully to keep seedlings and young plants healthy. Good growth is the best defence against pest or disease attack. Make sure that you start with healthy, viable seeds, a good-quality sowing medium and clean, disease-free pots. Washing used pots in soapy water will normally remove most potential hazards. Scrub off all old compost before rinsing and allowing them to dry.

• **Temperature** Keep seedlings at the correct temperature. This varies according to species and is influenced by the light levels reaching the seedlings. As a general rule, the higher the temperature, the more intense the light required. Rapid fluctuations can stunt, and even kill, plants. Do not sow warmth-loving species early unless you have the facilities to keep the seedlings adequately warm and light once they have germinated.

• **Light** Too little light leads to spindly, weak plants. Be careful about exposing delicate seedlings to direct sunlight, however. They burn very easily, especially if they have been growing in diffuse light for a while.

• **Watering** Make sure the growing medium stays moist, but do not overwater. Waterlogged conditions deprive the seedling roots of oxygen, while disease organisms thrive. Use clean, uncontaminated water. For seedlings, tap water is best. An occasional spraying with seaweed extract helps to encourage sturdy growth. An effective way to water seedlings without wetting the foliage is to stand pots or trays in water. Remove them when the surface of the growing medium is just moist, and allow to drain.

• **Stroking** Gently brushing or stroking seedlings raised indoors helps to produce stocky, firmly rooted plants (see right).

Problems

A rot problem known as damping off is common in seedlings and can spread rapidly through whole batches. It is caused by fungi that thrive in cool, wet, still conditions. Otherwise-healthy seedlings will collapse at ground level, as the stem and roots become blackened and thin. To avoid damping off:

• Practise good hygiene (see also p.228–229);
• Don't overwater;
• Ensure that ventilation is good without exposing seedlings to cold draughts;
• Don't let seedlings become overcrowded.

Ants and woodlice, not normally plant pests, can play havoc with seedlings. You can keep them off greenhouse staging with grease smeared around the legs, or by standing the legs in saucers of water, provided that no part of the staging touches the walls to give them an alternative way up.

Space

Give seedlings space to grow. Densely sown seedlings compete for limited light, water and space and diseases thrive in these conditions. Plants that suffer a check at this stage may never catch up. Using modules is one of the best ways to avoid the problems caused by overcrowding. Alternatively, you must ruthlessly thin the seedlings, or prick them out, as early as possible. Select the healthiest and most vigorous ones and remove the rest.

Seedlings in trays need transplanting (also known as pricking out) when the first pair of true leaves, rather than the initial seed leaves, appears (see below). Growing in modules avoids the need for this.

Hardening off

Young plants must be acclimatised gradually to cooler and less humid conditions. conditions. This is known as "hardening off" (see also p.232). The best place to do this is in a cold frame – or cover plants with a cloche or fleece and remove it gradually over a number of days.

Stroking seedlings
Seedlings raised under cover tend to be taller and weaker than those growing outside. Gently stroking or brushing seedlings makes them grow shorter and sturdier without harming them in any way. The plants do not need to be stroked individually. A piece of card brushed gently backwards and forwards 10–20 times over a tray of seedlings is all that is required on a daily basis. Plants seem to respond best when stroked early in the day.

PRICKING OUT

A chopstick or swizzle stick makes an excellent tool for transplanting seedlings. Before transplanting, water the compost well. Lever the seedlings gently out of the growing medium and very carefully hold them by one of the seed leaves as you lower them into a hole dibbled into the compost in the new container. Make sure the seed leaves are well above the compost's surface; if not, they are likely to rot.

Growing media

To produce healthy seedlings and grow plants in pots and containers, use a specific growing medium – a seed, potting or multipurpose compost mix. Garden soil on its own gives poor results; the complex balance of micro-organisms, air spaces and nutrient levels is easily lost in the restricted, artificial conditions of a container. You can buy organic growing media, or make your own mixture.

The ideal growing medium
• Is both moisture retentive and well aerated;
• Contains an appropriate quantity of nutrients;
• Allows a vigorous root system to develop;
• Is uniform in consistency and predictable in behaviour;
• Is free from pathogens.

Soil-based and soilless composts
Growing media, whether commercial or home-made, usually contain a carbon-rich bulk material with some other ingredient, such as sand, to improve drainage. The majority of proprietary composts now available are soilless; they do not contain any loam (which in this context means a sterilised, or pasteurised, fine-textured topsoil). This makes them lighter to handle, if not necessarily easier to manage. They are, for example, very difficult to re-wet once they have dried out.

Some plants, for example chrysanthemums and fuchsias, prefer a soil- or loam-based mix. These composts are also useful for patio and container growing, where their added weight, higher nutrient content and moisture-retaining abilities are helpful.

Proprietary composts are usually clearly labelled with their intended uses; however the development of multipurpose composts, which can be used for both sowing and growing on, has tended to blur these distinctions. In general:
• **Seed composts** Soilless; consist of equal parts of fine-textured bulking material, such as coir, and fine sand, which ensures effective drainage and aeration for germinating seeds. They contain little in the way of additional fertilisers; high nutrient levels are not necessary, and can inhibit germination and growth.
• **Cuttings composts** Very similar to the above. Often horticultural grit or perlite are used instead of sand to open up the mix still more, reducing the risk of cuttings rotting off instead of rooting.
• **Potting composts** Used to pot up cuttings once rooted, or plants once they have grown beyond the seedling stage. Similar in texture and ingredients to seed composts, but with the addition of fertilisers to sustain plant growth for an extended period of time.
• **Multipurpose composts** Similar to potting composts but with more moderate levels of fertiliser, so that they can be used for seeds and cuttings. As a consequence, older plants will need more feeding than those in potting composts.

Making your own growing media
It is perfectly possible to produce your own seed and potting mixes using easily available ingredients. This is, after all, the way most gardeners did things a few generations ago. From an organic standpoint it makes good sense too – by minimising the use of bought-in ingredients and products it reduces the need to transport heavy materials around the country; it allows garden materials and wastes to be reused and recycled; and it gives you a more intimate understanding of your garden soil, and what plants need from a growing medium. The aim is to get the right balance of bulk material, nutrients, aeration and drainage to suit the plants you are growing. For ingredients and "recipes", see overleaf.

PASTEURISING SOIL
Method 1 (Conventional oven)
Place moist, not wet, soil in a shallow tray to a depth of about 10cm (4in). Cover with foil. Put in a preheated oven at 80°C (180°F) for 30 minutes. Remove promptly, uncover and leave to cool. This process does tend to impart a rather earthy aroma to the kitchen.

Method 2 (Microwave oven)
Put moist soil in a loosely covered bowl. It must not contain any stones, as these can explode. Set to maximum and allow 2½ minutes for 900g (2lb) of soil, 7 minutes for 4.5kg (10lb). Spread the soil out on a tray to cool quickly.

Steam sterilisers are available from horticultural suppliers for processing larger quantities.

THE PEAT ISSUE

Over the last 50 years, soilless products have almost entirely supplanted loam-based growing media. They are light, easy to handle and more versatile than their predecessors. The chief reason for their success has been the use of peat: the decayed remains of sphagnum moss or other bog plants. Peat extraction, however, is responsible for the destruction of rare habitats – the unique and fragile ecosystem of a bog – so its use is not appropriate in an organic garden.

Peat-based growing media are permitted for use in commercial organic horticulture, but gardeners do not need them. In response to the concerns of organic gardeners, wildlife organisations and environmental groups, "peat-free" products have been developed. These are based on a variety of bulk materials, including coir (coconut fibre) and various composted waste products, such as bark, crop residues and municipal green waste. Using these recycled products, rather than disposing of them, reduces environmental pollution.

It is important to recognise that growing media based on different bulk products will each have their own characteristics. They should not be assumed to perform in an identical way to each other, particularly with regard to watering. Experiment on a small scale with any new medium before undertaking any large-scale growing.

INGREDIENTS SUITABLE FOR USE IN GROWING MEDIA

Composted bark
- pH 5–6.5
- Low-nutrient bulking agent
- May suppress root diseases
- Good buffering against high nutrient levels
- Unsuitable for capillary matting systems
- Too free draining on its own, best mixed with other finer material
- Unsuitable for small modules

Coir
- pH 5.8–6.5
- Unsuitable for ericaceous plants
- Adds bulk
- High potassium content
- Good aeration and water holding capacity
- Encourages root growth
- Surface dries out quickly, whilst underneath remains moist – easy to overwater

Sawdust
- Low pH
- Good bulking agent when used in combination with loam for potting mixes
- Very free draining
- Locks up nutrients
- Needs thorough composting before use

Recycled peat
- Harvested from watercourses
- Similar to normal peat
- Low-nutrient bulking agent
- May not be weed free

Leafmould (two years old)
- Low-nutrient bulking agent
- Good moisture retention and consistency
- Contains disease-combating micro-organisms
- Makes a good seed sowing medium on its own
- May grow weed seedlings
- Excellent addition to potting mixes, helps to maintain an open structure

Grit or sand
- Washed sand, free of salt and other contaminants is best
- Use coarse sand for loam-based growing media (particle sizes 0.2–2mm)
- Use fine sand for soilless mixes

Perlite and vermiculite
- Lightweight materials to improve drainage

Garden compost
- Adds bulk and nutrients
- Best used in potting media
- May help suppress diseases
- May contain weed seeds
- Batches may vary in quality and consistency

Composted municipal green waste
- Variable pH of 6–9
- Adds bulk and some nutrients (high in potassium)
- Suppresses disease
- Good buffering capacity
- Unsuitable for ericaceous plants
- Requires addition of inert material to balance nutrient status

Mushroom compost
- High pH
- Unsuitable for ericaceous plants
- Adds bulk and nutrients

Animal manures
- Not suitable for ericaceous plants
- High nutrient content
- Best composted with straw or other bulking agents
- Useful for heavy feeders like tomatoes

Comfrey leafmould (see p.207)
- Nutrient-rich bulking agent, high in potassium

Worm compost
- Ideal for plants requiring a rich mix
- Good top dressing for pot plants
- Holds large amounts of water, making it useful for inclusion in hanging baskets

Loam
- Good quality topsoil

Limestone
- Used to raise pH

Organic fertilisers (see p.61)
- Provide plant nutrients for potting mixes

MAKING TOPSOIL FROM TURF

Never waste turf that you have lifted to increase planting areas or convert to hard surfaces. Made into a turf stack, it will rot down into a crumbly, even-textured loam, ideal for use in compost mixes. Stack the turves upside down. Cover with light-excluding black polythene or old carpet for 6–12 months. The resulting loam should be crumbly and ready for sieving. Pasteurise the loam (see p.114) for use in seed-sowing mixes to destroy harmful pathogens and weed seeds. Do not sterilise it; this kills beneficial micro-flora and affects the way nutrients behave.

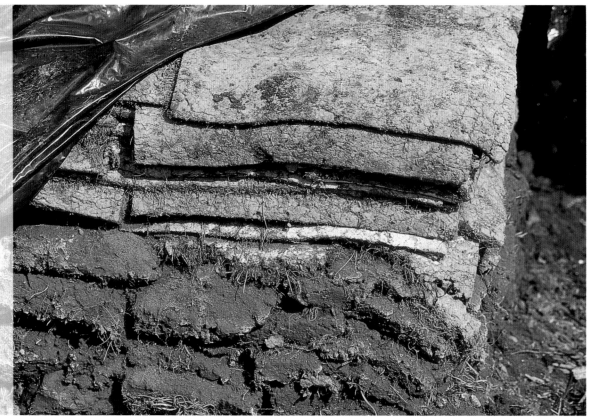

MIXING YOUR MEDIA

If garden soil will form part of your mix, first sieve it to remove stones (**1**). It is important to mix ingredients well. Make sure that the ingredients (other than any fertilizers) are damp, but not overly wet. Fertilisers are best mixed with some sand in a bucket, which will help spread them evenly through the mix. Spread the ingredients out in layers on a flat table or bench, or heap them on a hard surface (**2**), then sprinkle the sand and fertilisers evenly over the top of them. Mix the ingredients thoroughly using your hands. For larger quantities, use a spade (**3**) – or use a cement mixer. Do not store growing media for long; make up small quantities at regular intervals.

PLANT RAISING AND POTTING MIXES

Use	Ingredients	Ratio (by vol)	Comments
Seed-sowing mixtures	Leafmould alone		Often sufficient on its own if sieved
	Leafmould : loam	1 : 1	Gives good results with most seeds. Has enough nutrients until seedlings are transplanted. Too coarse for small seeds. Needs careful watering
	Comfrey leafmould : sand	4 : 1	Will provide sufficient nutrients until potting on stage.
Potting mixtures	Coir alone		Transplant seedlings promptly to avoid nutrient deficiencies
	Loam : leafmould : garden compost	1 : 1 : 1	A good basic mix, well-drained and fertile
	Peat substitute : sand : loam : garden compost	2 : 1 : 3 : 0.5	Nutrient rich
	Leafmould : worm compost	3 : 1	Nutrient rich
	Loam : manure : leafmould	3 : 1 : 1	Very rich mix for heavy feeders such as pot-grown tomatoes and peppers
	Comfrey leafmould alone	2 : 1	Good for flowering and fruiting container-grown plants
	Comfrey leafmould : grit	4 : 1	To every 35 litres (8 gals) add 144g general organic fertiliser and 28g seaweed meal
	Leafmould : loam	1 : 1	Good for permanent plantings in pots. Loam does not require pasteurisation. Use comfrey leafmould for a richer mix
	Loam : leafmould or coir	1 : 1	To every 35 litres (8 gals) add 225g (8oz) seaweed meal; 110g (4oz) bonemeal; 85g (3oz) hoof and horn; 55g (2oz) ground limestone. Nutrient rich
Cuttings mixtures	Coir : grit or perlite	1 : 1	
	Sieved leafmould : coarse sand	1 : 1	Use well-rotted leafmould

Saving seed from the garden

Seed-saving is something all gardeners can do. You might simply save a few seeds from a favourite flower or vegetable for the next season, or you might take on the more specialist task of maintaining a specific variety from a seed library or collection. The techniques you use will depend on the type of plant, and on how important it is that it is kept pure, or true to type.

When are seeds set?

A flower must be pollinated to set seed. Pollen is transferred from the male part of the flower, the anther, to the female part, the stigma. The pollen grain then grows down the style to the ovary, where it fertilises the eggs. These then develop into embryos, which will be enclosed in the seed, ready to grow into new plants.

• **Self-pollinators** Self-pollinators are plants which produce flowers that are normally fertilised by their own pollen. This can happen even before the flowers open, so there is little or no danger of one variety crossing with another.

GOOD REASONS FOR SEED SAVING

• Seed saving adds another dimension to gardening. It's a fascinating process, which extends your knowledge of how plants work.
• It is not possible to buy organically grown seed of every plant. Saving your own in an organic garden helps to ensure a supply of what you want.
• Many old and less commercial cultivars are dropped from seed catalogues, and may disappear altogether. Some of these may have excellent characteristics, particularly suited to the gardener, or may simply be your favourite flower or vegetable. By saving seed of threatened cultivars, and sharing them with others, you will be helping to conserve our genetic heritage.
• Leaving a few plants to flower and set seed will give you many more seeds than you could ever get in a seed packet, for virtually no cost. It will be fresh, too. Home-saved seed often has a high germination rate and produces vigorous seedlings.

• **Cross-pollinators** Cross-pollinators need pollen from another flower, or sometimes even another plant, to produce healthy viable seed. Pollen is transferred by insects and/or the wind. Keeping seed of cross-pollinators pure is more difficult, because they may be pollinated by other cultivars of the same plant, close relations of the same species, or by pollen from wild relatives.

Another point to consider is whether the plants are annual, biennial or perennial. Annual plants will flower and set seed in a few months, whereas biennials, such as carrots and parsnips, may require up to 18 months to do so. Many perennials may not produce seeds until several years after sowing.

Saving seed from F1 hybrids is rarely done. F1s are produced by crossing two specific parent plants; seed produced from the resulting F1 hybrid will not be true to the original, though the results might be interesting!

Selection for health and purity

It is important to keep seed free from disease (which may be transmitted in the seed) and, depending on your requirements, true to type.
• Save seed from plants that have the typical characteristics of the variety.
• Choose plants that are healthy, vigorous and yield well. Do not just choose the first plant to go to seed; you will be selecting for this characteristic, which is not usually what you want. If it is the roots of a biennial plant that are the important part, as in the case of carrots, dig them up in the autumn to choose the best. You will then need to replant them, to flower and set seed the following summer.

Cull any plants that are diseased, weak or do not appear true to type. This is known as "rogueing out".
• With self-pollinating plants, a bean with the wrong-coloured pods or a tall pea amongst a dwarf variety, for example, should be removed before seed is harvested. Off-type cross-pollinating plants need to be removed before they flower, so their pollen cannot fertilise other flowers.
• Do not grow different cultivars of the same plant

Insect pollination
Encourage beneficial insects into the garden to help plants set seed. As they move from flower to flower, pollen travels with them.

HOW THEY ARE POLLINATED

Self-pollinated
Lettuce
Zinnia
Tomato
Pansy
French bean
Sweet pea
Pea

Wind-pollinated
Beetroot
Sweetcorn (maize)
Hazelnut
Love-lies-bleeding (*Amaranthus*)
Spinach

Insect-pollinated
Aquilegia
Basil
Broad bean
Cabbage
Celery
Courgette
Foxglove
French marigold
Leek
Nasturtium
Pepper
Poppy
Primula
Radish
Runner bean
Squash and pumpkin
Sunflower

next to each other if you are saving seed. It is remarkably easy to confuse different varieties, especially if plants have died down prior to harvest.

• Save seed from several plants if possible, to maintain the genetic diversity. Although all plants of a variety may look alike, over the generations small mutations will occur, giving variations in height, maturity, colour and yield. To retain this variation, you should save seed from several plants. If you are aiming to maintain a variety long term, then larger numbers of plants are needed.

Keeping it true

If different varieties cross, then the results can be unpredictable. Generally speaking, on a garden scale, keeping true to type is more important in vegetables – where you want to be sure that you are going to get a good crop – than it is with ornamentals, where diversity can be a bonus.

If you are saving seed of a cross-pollinating plant, make sure that none of its close relatives, including weeds, are in flower in your garden at the same time. Of course pollen can be brought in from the surrounding gardens and fields too. The distance that pollen can travel varies from species to species. Hedges, fences and other barriers will cut down the risk of crossing. Where it is vital to maintain absolute purity – when growing seed for a library collection, for example – you may need to go to the lengths of growing cross-pollinating plants such as brassicas, carrots and onions in isolation cages (see p.16).

Generally, keep varieties of the same species of self-pollinating plants 2m (6ft) apart to be fairly sure that seed saved from them will stay true to type.

HAND-POLLINATING COURGETTES FOR SEED

Courgettes are pollinated by insects. Cross-breeding is common, as the pollinators move from plant to plant. For plants to breed true, you must ensure that a female flower is pollinated by a male flower of the same variety.

In the evening, choose selected flowers of both sexes before they are fully open (**1**). The females are recognisable by a swelling on the stem below the petals: this will develop into the fruit. Cover the plant with fleece overnight (or tie up or tape the flowers, as in picture **4**). The next morning, to hand-pollinate the female flower with the male, pick the male flower, tear off the petals (**2**) and insert it into the female flower (**3**), making sure pollen is rubbed from the anthers onto the style. Immediately tie the petals of the female up with raffia or twine (**4**), or seal with sticky tape, to ensure that no insects can enter bearing foreign pollen. Leave until the flower drops off.

CLEANING TOMATO SEED

Pulp the tomatoes and add a little water, then leave the mixture in a warm place to ferment. Gradually the pulp will form a mouldy cap or crust, while the seeds sink to the bottom (far left).

Drain the seeds (left) and rinse them with copious amounts of cold water, and then drain and dry them as quickly as possible.

Seed harvest and storage

Seeds come in a great variety of shapes and sizes and are produced within an equally diverse range of pods and fruits. For seed-saving purposes they can be divided into two basic categories: those that can be stored in a dried state and those which will die if they are allowed to dry out. The latter types, described as "recalcitrant", include trees with large oily seeds, such as oaks, and also many tropical plants. In this instance storage is limited to keeping the seeds in a cool, moist environment such as a sand-filled pot in the refrigerator and sowing them within a few months.

Luckily, most of the seeds produced by garden plants can be stored dry. There are two main subdivisions according to how the seeds are produced: those borne within soft fruits, such as tomatoes and squashes, and those that are dry-seeded at maturity. Dry-seeded types should be allowed to mature on the plants until the pods or seedheads have dried out. Dry pods should have a crisp feel when squeezed and should not contain any sap, moisture or green pigment when scratched with a fingernail. In climates where the seed harvest is affected by rain, harvest plants when they are as close to maturity as possible and hang them upside down in a dry, well-ventilated place to allow the seed to ripen further. Harvest soft fruits when ripe. Members of the pumpkin family require additional ripening after harvest to produce the best quality seeds, because their seeds continue to mature after the fruit is ripe.

Seed cleaning

• **Soft-fruited plants** (for example, squashes tomatoes, melons and cucumbers). Scoop out the seeds from the fruit, place in a bowl and wash off the adhering pulp. Alternatively, the seed can be mixed with water and fermented for several days (see above), allowing the action of bacteria and fungi to help clean the seed and eliminate some seed-borne diseases. The pulp and any floating seeds are drained off, leaving the viable seeds at the bottom.

To prevent the seeds from becoming mouldy, or germinating, they need to be dried quickly. Spread out washed seed on a plastic, glass or metal sheet to dry. Place the sheet in a well-ventilated spot, out of intense sunlight. Stir up the seeds every few hours to speed the drying process. Another option is to place the seeds close to a fan set to run at a cool temperature; hot air could damage the seeds. For larger seeds, drying trays can easily be constructed from fine wire mesh. These will provide excellent conditions for rapid moisture loss.

• **Dry-seeded plants** (for example, beans, brassicas, cosmos, lettuce, love-in-a-mist, peas and poppies). Seedheads and pods are harvested from the plants and threshed to clean off the dry debris when fully dry. Various threshing techniques can be used to release them.

• Put the seedheads in a sack, then tread on it, or beat it with a stick.

• Crush small pods between planks or boards.

• Open large pods individually and extract the seeds.

Dry-seeded plants
Members of the carrot family produce seeds in flattish heads called umbels. Choose the biggest umbels – these contain the best quality seed. Harvest them when the seeds are ripe and leave them to dry; they can then be winnowed.

Winnowing, the separation of seeds and chaff, can be achieved by placing the seeds in a bowl and blowing carefully – the debris is usually lighter than the seeds and is ejected from the container. A more reliable result can be obtained by using a hairdryer, on a cool setting. When you are winnowing seeds, it is a good idea to wear a facemask. Some fine chaff can irritate the lungs, throat and nasal passages.

One of the best methods involves the use of two screens or sieves, both of different gauges. The first, which is just big enough to allow the seeds to pass through, retains any chaff larger than the seeds themselves. The second, with a gauge smaller than the seeds, lets the remaining chaff drop through, leaving the seeds clean.

Pest and disease control

Having obtained your freshly winnowed seeds, look through them carefully and remove any that are diseased, mouldy or eaten by maggots. There is no point in storing seed that is already weakened by disease or pest attack.

Seeds, like any other parts of plants, can harbour unwanted organisms. These may be capable of killing the seeds, or ruining the subsequent crop. The fermentation method, used for tomatoes, has already been mentioned. Provided that seeds are very well-dried, they can also be placed in the freezer for a couple of days. This will kill some, though not all, types of weevils and their eggs.

Hot water treatment

By soaking seeds in water heated to 50°C (122°F) for 25 minutes, you can eliminate a number of seed-borne diseases. Among these diseases are black leg, black rot and black leaf spot in cabbage; target spot and bacterial canker in tomato; and downy mildew in spinach. Do this after extracting or threshing the seeds. You need to keep the temperature just right – use a thermometer and a double saucepan and make sure the temperature is constant before adding the seeds. Stir them into the water and continue to stir for the duration of the treatment. Then remove, drain and dry the seeds as usual.

Seed storage

Whether home-saved or purchased, store your seeds in the correct conditions to maintain their ability to germinate and grow for as long as possible. The drier and cooler the seeds are kept, the better. Seeds stored in breathable envelopes or packets in a cool, dry room will fare much better than in a warm damp one. Never keep seeds in a greenhouse.

There is no point in storing seed already weakened by pest or disease attack

The moisture content of seeds is usually the critical factor in determining how long they remain viable. Seeds stored in humid climates can have a depressingly short life. The answer is to dry the seeds further, to 8% moisture levels, in airtight containers. Glass jars with rubber seals are probably the best. These can be kept in a refrigerator or freezer, which will increase the lifespan of the seed even further, often up to ten times that of seed kept at room temperature and humidity. The process of seed drying is quite simple and involves the use of colour-indicating silica gel as the desiccant (drying agent). As the granules absorb moisture, they change

from blue to pink; when saturated they can be dried and used again. A very low oven (95°C/200°F) or a microwave will drive off the moisture and reverse the colour change. Repeat this whenever you need to dry the silica gel.

Drying seeds with silica gel

Put dry seeds into breathable packets or envelopes, label and weigh them. Place them in an airtight jar with an equal weight of dry silica gel. Seal the lid tightly. After a week the seeds will have reached the correct moisture content and can be stored in another airtight container, and placed in the freezer or refrigerator for long term storage. Before opening the jars and removing seeds, let them reach room temperature, which reduces the amount of moisture condensing on the inside of the jars and on the seeds they contain. It is also a good idea to let very dry seeds reach ambient humidity levels before sowing – just keep them in a room for a few days.

Getting started

The list on the right shows some of the easiest seeds to save – judged on their overall score for ease of pollination, maintenance of purity and ease of harvest and cleaning – together with more challenging projects. You can learn more about seed-saving, and even start seed-swapping, by joining your local gardening club or society – and by becoming a member of HDRA and its Heritage Seed Library programme, dedicated to preserving and giving gardeners access to old and unusual varieties.

ROUGH GUIDE TO EASE OF SEED SAVING

Easy
Basil
Broad bean
Calendula
Columbine
Coriander
French bean
Nasturtium
Phacelia
Pea
Poppy
Rocket
Tomato

Moderate
Amaranth
Cabbage
Carrot
Cucumber
French marigold
Leek
Lettuce
Onion
Parsley
Peppers
Radish
Runner bean
Squash
Sunflower

Challenging
Beetroot
Parsnip
Spinach
Sweetcorn
Turnip

SEED LIFESPANS

1–3 years	Up to 5 years	5+ years
Carrot	Basil	Artichoke
French bean	Beetroot	Borage
Leek	Broad bean	Chicory
Onion	Cabbage	Cucumber
Parsley	Cauliflower	Endive
Parsnip	Celery	Pumpkin
Pea	Lettuce	Squash
Rocket	Pepper	Watermelon
Rosemary	Radish	Calendula
Runner bean	Tomato	Cosmos
Sweetcorn	Turnip	Lupin
Begonia	Nasturtium	Mallow
Delphinium	Pansy	Morning glory
Lily	Sunflower	

Looking
good

NATURAL BEAUTY IN THE ORGANIC ORNAMENTAL GARDEN

The garden framework

THE ORGANIC APPROACH CAN BE APPLIED TO ALL ASPECTS OF HARD LANDSCAPING IN THE GARDEN

Using timber (facing page)
Sustainability of source and the avoidance of potentially toxic preservatives should govern your choice.

Long-lasting materials (below)
Building with reclaimed materials like these edging tiles preserves their use and beauty for another generation.

AS INCREASINGLY LARGE TRACTS of the earth are suffocated below tarmac or concrete, or diminished by industrial agriculture, the living landscape of our gardens becomes ever more important. The potential of our gardens as thriving ecosystems is affected by the design and composition of the garden framework.

Purchasing power

Gardens are usually multi-use environments, and they need a "framework" to meet these needs. This includes all aspects of garden construction or hard landscaping – patios, paths, driveways, fences, walls, garden buildings and special features. If the philosophy of organic gardening is to be applied to hard landscaping we need to take a detailed and critical look at materials, including the extraction of the raw materials, processing, transport, their use in the garden, how they affect garden ecology, and,

finally, recycling. Organic gardeners should be searching for sustainable ways of providing and maintaining the garden framework from the planning stage onwards, while also being mindful of how those decisions will support the green living world. We need to consider not only the design of the garden and the selection of the materials, but also maintenance requirements.

There is a greater choice of building materials for the garden today than ever before. Gardening television programmes and magazines inspire us to make full use of these materials for everything from basic paths and fences to expressing a creative talent.

Forming the guidelines

Assessing the environmental costs of garden building materials and practices is a comparatively new area, and the situation is constantly changing as companies set about improving their environmental policies. As yet there are no organic standards for hard landscaping, which is a relatively new concept. In the UK, HDRA is working to create organic standards for amenity horticulture and landscaping, in conjunction with the amenity horticulture industry. These standards will include recommendations for hard landscaping, so watch out for the HDRA logo on products, plants and even land.

In the meantime, the basic principles of organic gardening – sustainability and low environmental impact – can be applied. Some materials, such as locally sourced and well-managed timber, will always score highly in terms of being sustainable and environmentally friendly. Other materials should be avoided, due to toxicity perhaps, or the fact that extraction of the raw materials may damage natural habitats, or their manufacture may cause pollution. Sometimes compromises have to be made; some materials, such as glass, fall between these two extremes. This chapter raises the issues, and should help you to make sustainable, organic, choices whether you are building a new garden or adding structures to an existing garden.

Counting the environmental costs

Building materials and products carry environmental costs that you may not have considered. The information in the panels below, and the table opposite, will help you start to make more environmentally sound choices. Unfortunately, products rarely fulfil all the criteria that we would wish, so there will have to be compromise somewhere along the line. A balance must be struck. For example, although natural stone is a non-renewable resource, it is very durable, and should last for many generations.

Making your choices

The information needed to make informed decisions may not always be available, or easily accessible, but it is always worth asking. Where do the raw materials come from? Does the manufacturer have an environmental policy? What steps do they take to repair environmental damage?

How you can help

If your questions cannot be answered satisfactorily, let producers know that you will be making an alternative choice. Over the last decade it is public demand that has fuelled the enormous increase in the availability of organic food and "fair-trade" products (which guarantee a fair price to producers). Ecological awareness has led to huge developments in products to replace peat, in composting green waste, and the avoidance of garden furniture and related products made from tropical hardwoods. Public interest and pressure can improve things.

THE COSTS

- **Extracting the raw material** Quarrying and other extraction processes can damage habitats, water tables and wildlife. The process may cause pollution. The company may not take responsibility for repairing damaged landscape. Processes may be hazardous to human health, and products may not be fairly traded.
- **Transportation** Long-distance transport consumes energy and causes pollution.
- **Processing** Industrial processes may use fossil fuels and could cause pollution of air, land or water.
- **Sustainability** Materials may be from finite, rather than renewable, sources and may be used inefficiently. The techniques used to install them may be energy intensive.
- **Disposal** If the product cannot be composted or re-used in another form, an environmental and financial cost will be attached to its disposal.
- **Durability and maintenance** The material may not serve its purpose well, and it may require frequent maintenance.
- **Toxicity** Treated wood and masonry may leach harmful substances into the environment, and they can be hazardous to the person using them. Seek out non-toxic alternatives.

THE SOLUTIONS

- **Plan carefully** Design the garden framework to meet your needs, but also create habitats to support wildlife.
- **Consider maintenance** Hard landscaping can be designed to minimise maintenance such as strimming, and reduce weed problems. This will cut down on the use of fossil fuels, engine noise, pollution and work time.
- **Conserve soil** Use excavated soil on site. Do not mix good soil with non-organic waste.
- **Avoid damage** Be aware of products and practices that cause harm to people or the environment.
- **Use sustainable or renewable resources** Look for wood from well-managed forests, coppice products, home-grown bamboo and cob.
- **Use non-renewable resources sparingly and efficiently** For example, use metal only where its properties of strength and lightness are essential.
- **Re-use and recycle** Can existing materials in the garden be put to new uses? Are reclaimed building products available locally? Can bought-in materials be recycled or composted at the end of their life?
- **Use local resources** Locally available materials reduce pollution caused by transport.
- **Use labour rather than industrial or mechanical processing** Labour and craftsmanship are a renewable source of energy.

BUILDING MATERIALS AND THE ENVIRONMENT

Material	Sustainability	Applications	Durability	Cautions	Recycling
Wood	Sustainable if from well-managed forests	Practically all garden landscape work	Variable according to species	Ensure from sustainable forests; avoid toxic preservatives	Can be reclaimed or, ultimately, allowed to rot to "compost"
Pre-formed concrete slabs or blocks	Quarried materials, reserves limited; cement manufacture currently polluting	Paving	Very durable	Avoid large areas of unbroken, sterile paving	Use recycled slabs if available; some new slabs are made of recycled materials
Fired clay bricks or blocks	Quarried materials, energy intensive manufacture	Walling or paving	Very durable		Can be reclaimed and recycled
Natural stone and stone chippings	Quarried material, reserves limited	Walling or paving	Very durable, variable according to type	Use most local supply	Can be reclaimed and recycled
Reconstituted stone	Secondary raw materials, using reclaimed aggregates	Walling or paving	Very durable	May contain resins, or cement	Can be reclaimed and recycled
Cement mortars, concrete	Quarried materials; polluting, energy-intensive manufacture	Walling or paving	Very durable	Avoid inhaling cement powder, avoid skin contact	Can be recycled
Sand and gravel	Quarried materials	Paving, mortars or concrete	Very durable		Can be recycled
Plastics	Can be made from natural materials; most are derived from petroleum	Paving, soil reinforcing or walling	Durable, but variable according to type; some may become brittle	Avoid plastics such as PVC, which can be expensive to recycle safely; never burn plastics	Plastics can be recycled, but facilities for safe recycling are scarce
Plastics, recycled	Recycled plastic and polystyrene waste	Fencing, paving, compost bins, bed edging and in other situations in place of timber	Very durable	Will never biodegrade; do not burn; check recycled content	Can be recycled again to produce more of the same, but it rarely is
Lime	Quarried material, reserves limited	Used in cement manufacture and in lime mortars	Very durable if used correctly	Avoid skin contact, as very caustic	Old lime mortars can be reclaimed for foundation material
Wrought iron work	Quarried material; energy-intensive manufacture	Railings and decorative screens and gates	Fairly durable	Check that any metal paints used are eco-friendly	Can be reclaimed or recycled
Steel and other metals	Quarried material; energy-intensive manufacture	Sometimes used in garden barriers, also fittings, nails, etc	Fairly durable	Use only where particular properties of steel are essential	Can be reclaimed or recycled; plastic-coated metals are difficult to recycle
Wood treatments	Some products highly toxic	Used to preserve non-durable woods		Use only non-toxic products	Some wood preservatives cause burning wood to emit toxic fumes
Glass	Quarried materials, and lime, potash and metallic oxides	Greenhouse, glass bricks or mosaics	Fairly durable		All glass can be recycled
Geotextile membranes	Can be made of plastics or natural biodegradable materials	Weed-suppressing membrane; also used to separate soil from paving material	Plastics durable, biodegradability varies according to material		Not widely recycled (biodegradable plastics rot harmlessly)
Pond liners, bentonite lining membrane	Quarried material, plus polypropylene geotextile	Water retention in ponds, reed beds or wetlands	Very durable; self-sealing		Geotextile can be separated from bentonite
Pond liners, synthetic	Butyl preferable to PVC as does not contain carcinogenic plasticisers and does not pose same risk of chlorine pollution	Ponds or bog gardens	Will last up to 20 years, and can be repaired	Avoid PVC liners	Not recyclable, but can be made into granular fillers (although this requires a lot of energy)
Bamboo	Sustainable, but incurs transport costs; can be home-grown	Plant supports, screening, pergolas or guttering	Variable according to size and variety		Can be composted
Natural-fibre ropes, eg hemp, flax	Sustainable	Plant supports, and between wooden posts for boundaries	Variable according to size of rope		Can be composted

Choosing timber for the garden

Timber is potentially the most environmentally friendly of all building materials, and can provide attractive and durable paved surfaces, fences, screens and supports. In an organic garden it is important to use timber that comes from sustainably managed forests, whatever the type of wood and the country it comes from. Look out for wood with the Forest Stewardship Council (FSC) label, which guarantees that it comes from a well-managed sustainable forest. Coppice wood (see p.138) is also a sustainable resource, cut from mixed temperate woodlands. A managed coppice wood also provides an incredibly wide diversity of habitats for plants and animals.

Well-weathered wood
Naturally resistant woods such as oak and sweet chestnut can last for years without any preservative treatment.

Natural resistance

To avoid the use of wood preservatives (see also below), try to use wood that is naturally resistant to decay. The heartwood of more naturally rot-resistant species, such as oak, can be used untreated. Other woods that last well without treatment are larch (*Larix decidua*), which will last about 10 years in contact with the soil, or up to 20 years if not in contact with soil, Western red cedar (*Thuja plicata*), which will give service for about 20 years, and sweet chestnut (*Castanea sativa*), traditionally used for palings and posts. Untreated pine lasts for about five years. The table opposite gives more information.

Well-seasoned wood that has been allowed to dry out evenly is more expensive than greenwood (freshly cut undried wood), but in its favour, it tends to last longer and can be less prone to distortion as it weathers.

Once you begin to think about it, your own garden may well be able to provide a useful harvest of material for making plant supports and screens (see also pp.138–141).

Wood preservatives

Timber and posts for outdoor use and many ready-made wooden products, such as fence panels and compost bins, are usually treated with some sort of preservative before sale. Organic gardeners should, if possible, avoid treated timber and products, unless a relatively environmentally friendly product has been used. Be aware that pre-treated timber may not have any form of label to indicate that it has been treated.

Items in contact with the soil, such as posts, gravel boards and compost bins, are at most risk from decay, so they are often made of timber that has been pressure-treated with toxic chemicals such as copper arsenate and chromium arsenate (CCA), which is a very effective, long-term wood preservative. Manufacturers claim that if properly applied, the chemicals in the preservative, which are themselves highly toxic, are held very tightly within the fibres of the wood, but there are doubts concerning leaching and the release of vapours. Such chemicals have no place in the organic garden. If the use of CCA pressure-treated timber is unavoidable, always wear gloves when handling it, and wear a face mask if you are sawing. This type of timber should never be burnt as it releases highly toxic fumes.

Alternatives to conventional preservatives

Boron rods provide an alternative wood preservative, which is considered safe for people and the environment. They are made of boron compounds that have been subjected to high temperatures to form water soluble, glass-like rods. These rods are placed within drilled holes in the wood, strategically placed where decay is most likely and then plugged to secure them. When the wood becomes wet, boric acid is released, which prevents fungal decay. Boron pastes have a similar effect. At the time of writing, manufacturers of boron rods are applying for permission to make these rods available for amateur use.

Wood that is not in direct contact with the ground, and so is less prone to rot, is usually treated with less toxic preservatives. Until the use of more environmentally friendly methods of preservation are used as standard throughout the timber industry, you may prefer to ask a saw mill or fencing supplier to supply untreated wood. You can treat this yourself using eco-friendly products based on natural plant oils, resins and less toxic materials. Creosote is sometimes sold as "organic" as it is derived from material of living origin (coal tar), but it is not regarded as suitable for use in an organic garden due to its hazardous nature.

Think about the use to which the wood is to be put before making a final decision about the use of preservative-treated wood (untreated being the preferred, organic option). If it is absolutely necessary, then consider how long the timber needs to last. Tree stakes generally need only last a couple of years, after which time the tree should support itself – so using a CCA-treated stake that will survive for 25 years is totally unnecessary. Non-structural timbers, such as bed edging, and wood for a compost box, could simply be left untreated. It will of course rot eventually, but you can then simply replace it.

Railway sleepers are not generally appropriate in an organic garden because of the tar that permeates them, which may be exuded in some conditions, although some sleepers are made of hardwood that has not been treated.

"SYNTHETIC WOOD"

Waste polystyrene and plastic can be recycled and made into a material that looks remarkably like wood. Products include fencing and furniture, and sheets, planks and posts with which to make your own structures. It may not have quite the same flexible strength as real wood (check with your supplier to ensure that the material you buy is suitable for the proposed use), but has the advantage of needing no treatment to prevent decay. While it would be preferable not to use any form of plastic at all in an organic garden, this material is at least finding a use for a common waste product. But beware – some products contain only a small amount of recycled material. Check before you buy.

DURABILITY OF NATURAL WOODS IN A GARDEN SETTING

Species	Durability	Uses
Alder (*Alnus glutinosa*)	Perishable in air, but lasts many years in water	Excellent for posts and jetty supports permanently immersed in water; Venice was built on alder wood foundations
Cherry (*Prunus avium*)	Moderately durable; will last about 10 years	Not widely available, but can be used in light garden structures if local stock is found
Douglas fir (*Pseudo-tsuga menziesii*)	Moderately durable; will last 10 years	Can be used for fencing, compost bins
Larch (*Larix decidua*)	Moderately durable – 10 years in contact with the soil, up to 20 years above ground	Used extensively for fencing and pergolas; larch logs can be used for paving
Oak (*Quercus robur*)	Durable – 20 years in contact with the soil, up to 40 years above ground	Ideal for fence posts, gravel boards, compost bins, fencing, decking, boardwalks and garden buildings; can be used for paving (old beams or log rounds)
Pine (*Pinus* spp.)	Most types are not durable, lasting about five years; maritime pine moderately durable (10 years)	Can be used in all types of garden construction from fences to compost boxes and path edges, but plan to replace on a five-year cycle, or use an eco-friendly preservative to extend life
Sweet chestnut (*Castanea sativa*)	Durable – 20 years in contact with the soil, up to 40 years above ground	Ideal for fencing and pergolas
Western red cedar (*Thuja plicata*)	Durable if grown in USA; moderately durable if grown in UK	Frequently used for fence cladding, trelliswork and for light, non load-bearing structures; not as strong as oak

NOTE: Durability comparisons are made using heartwood – virtually all sap woods are considered perishable

Hard surfaces

Hard surfaces, such as patios, pathways, drives, and hard standing for utility areas, account for a large proportion of the building materials used in gardens. They often require a substantial depth of foundation material, which involves excavating topsoil.

Planning

Keep areas of continuous, unbroken paving to a minimum. They may provide a suitable setting for plants in containers, but they cannot support the same biodiversity as a border with soil.

However, paving such as broken random natural stone, with herbs or alpines planted between deliberately-left gaps, can provide a valuable habitat for garden wildlife. The stones absorb heat in summer, and give a welcome sunbathing place for lizards and other small animals, while the nearby plants provide safe cover. If laid only on a minimal foundation of sharp sand, the stones will also provide cover for invertebrates such as beetles.

Minimising weeds in paving

If you want a very neat garden, there are ways to reduce weeds. Firstly, provide an impenetrable foundation layer: a geotextile membrane under gravel, or a substantial foundation construction below slab or bricks. If the paving includes joints – filled-in gaps of about 1cm (½in) between each unit – they should be pointed with mortar, rather than filled with sand, which gives weeds an ideal rooting medium. Cement and concrete products are not the most environmentally sustainable materials (see Cement or lime?, facing page) and you may wish to consider more sustainable options. Lime mortars can be used in place of cement in many areas, including paving foundations and pointing.

ROCK FEATURES

Garden rock features raise considerable anxiety and opposition from environmentalists. This is because the rock that makes the most convincing and attractive garden features is taken from valuable habitats. Waterworn limestone, for example, is taken from a very specialised habitat, which has evolved over thousands of years, supporting plants that will not grow anywhere else. To use it in your garden is to destroy this habitat. The late Geoff Hamilton recognised this, and developed a homemade "rock", which weathers well and supports rock plants very effectively.

Natural stone is a limited resource that is best reserved for building purposes. If you do not want to make your own "rocks" you could consider using reconstituted stone made from stone dust, or reclaimed stone. A scree garden using stone chippings or crushed brick waste is another effective way to display alpine plants.

Paving setts
*Mortars for laying and pointing
paving materials can be made using
lime in place of cement.*

Excavations

Establishing an area of paving will often necessitate
the excavation of topsoil. Consider, at the planning
stage, how the soil is to be removed and what is to
be done with it. Can it be used elsewhere in the
garden – for example, for a raised bed or turf bank –
or somewhere nearby? If machines are used, ensure
they are the lightest and smallest possible. Do not
forget that energy and materials are used to create
the machine, although the environmental cost of
this will be spread over its working life. The fuel
it consumes and the noise and pollution it creates
while working are all part of the equation.

Using stone

Natural stone, such as granite, sandstone, limestone
and slate, is a very limited resource but provides a
very durable building materials. Reconstituted stone
products are made using stone dust from quarrying
operations, bonded with cement or synthetic resins.
Synthetic stone is made from minerals such as sand
and ash bonded with synthetic resins. More energy
is required to produce a reconstituted or synthetic
product than to use stone in its natural state, and the
production of the resins used can cause pollution.

Local stone may be a good choice for paving. It
forms the character of the varied regions in which
we take such a pride. All stone extraction involves
quarrying, and potentially, it is environmentally

USING LIME IN STONEWORK

Always use lime mortars consistently
throughout a construction project; do not use
cement for part of the project, or for repair
work, as it has different properties regarding
porosity, and expansion and contraction.

**General foundation mix for laying paving
slabs and other hard surfaces**
3½ parts coarse sand
1 part lime putty
25% pozzolan

Wall foundations depend on the height and
construction of the wall. The following mixes
can be used for paving or walling:

Bedding mortar for granite or flint
3 parts sand
1 part lime putty
20% pozzolan

Bedding mortar for sandstone
3½ parts sand
1 part lime putty
10% pozzolan

Coping course mortar
3 parts sand
1 part lime putty
20–30% pozzolan

CEMENT OR LIME?

The use of cement has
been heavily criticised by
environmentalists, for the
energy and emissions involved
in its manufacture and for its
inappropriate use. At the time
of writing, cement manufacture
accounts for at least 7% of the
world's emissions of carbon
dioxide (CO_2), and this figure
is steadily rising.

Lime can be used in place of
cement in mortars, renders, and
foundations in garden building
work. While both cement and
builder's lime are produced by
burning chalk or limestone in a
kiln to produce calcium oxide
(quicklime), the cement process
requires higher temperatures
and more energy. Another
important difference is that
when water is added to
calcium oxide, it turns into
calcium hydroxide, known as
"slaked lime" or "lime putty",
which can then re-absorb
CO_2 from the atmosphere,
to become calcium carbonate
once again. This cycle can be
repeated indefinitely, whereas
the lime component in cement
cannot behave in the same way.

Lime mortars can be bought,
or made using lime putty mixed
with sand, or quicklime mixed
with wet sand. The latter is the
more traditional method and is
known as "sand-slaked" or "hot-
mix" mortar. A "pozzolan" –
a substance that aids the
carbonation process – is added
to lime mortar to increase its
strength and frost resistance. A
typical pozzolan is a burnt clay
product from Cornwall.

Like cement, builder's lime
is caustic when wet, and thick
protective gloves are required.
It does not, as cement does,
pose the additional risk to the
user of inhaling silicon dioxide.

dense bricks, such as reclaimed engineering bricks, generally last longer as paving than facing brick, although some types of fired clay facing bricks can be extremely hard-wearing. Ask a reputable dealer if you are uncertain. Pleasing designs can be achieved by combining a number of different materials such as quarry tiles, bricks and bottle ends. If the area is to appear in harmony with its surroundings, some aspect of it, such as a colour or matching brick, should relate to the nearby buildings. If a combination of materials is being used, a repeated sequence of materials will make the area look well-planned. This can also be achieved by containing random materials within a uniform edging material. Selecting materials of similar depth and preparing foundations carefully will make a uniform finished level easier to achieve.

Different materials may require different laying techniques. An area that consists only of reclaimed granite cobbles would require a bedding layer of sharp sand, rather than mortar. Well-compacted rubble can be used for the base layer. For normal garden use, on an average soil, the base layer for stones, bricks or slabs will need to be 7–10cm (3–4in) deep. This should be increased to 15cm (6in) for clay soils. A bedding layer of at least 1.5cm (½in) of mortar can then be used to fix and point the surface materials. Cement mortar is normally used for bedding and pointing paving materials, and concrete is often used as the base material. Lime mortar is generally recognised as an environmentally friendly alternative (see previous page).

Gravel and stone chippings

Gravel and crushed rock – stone chippings – are obtained by quarrying. Some gravels are collected by sea-dredging, which destroys marine environments. However, secondary aggregates, such as crushed rubble from demolition works, offer an alternative to newly quarried materials, and make an attractive durable surface, in a variety of colours and textures.

For general garden use, a 2.5–5cm (1–2in) layer of chippings over a weedproof geotextile membrane will suffice. For areas of heavy pedestrian or vehicular use, lay a foundation of compacted rubble, 10cm (4in) deep for paths, and double that for driveways. Regular traffic can help to prevent seedling weeds establishing.

Collecting materials
Small quantities of reclaimed materials can be snapped up when seen, and stored until matching or complementary items are found. Here, a stack of tiles in a corner makes a mini-wildlife habitat in the meantime; many creatures will appreciate the warmth that the tiles retain after the sun has left this spot.

destructive, depending on how the company manages and restores the site. This cost is offset to some extent because natural stone should last for many generations. If it is used in its natural form, the requirement for energy-intensive processing is minimal and local craft skills are kept alive.

Reclaimed materials

Reclaimed building materials, such as brick, stone, concrete slabs, wood and quarry tiles can all be used to create new paving. Ensure that secondhand bricks for outdoor use are weather-resistant. Heavier, more

To keep the gravel in place, use an edging of wooden planks, or reclaimed bricks or tiles. Driveways need a heavier edging material; thicker timber, for example, or mortared bricks laid on a suitable foundation.

Hoggin

Hoggin is a naturally occurring mixture of clay, sand and gravel, which can be rolled to give a durable surface to patios, pathways and drives. The clay content acts as a binder. The surface is hardest in dry conditions and requires excellent drainage facilities if waterlogging and surface erosion are to be avoided. When hoggin is well laid and compacted, weeds are slow to colonise.

Certain types of subsoil with a high percentage of gravel or grit can be re-employed as a hardwearing surface material. A proportion of new aggregate may be necessary to give a stable surface, but this will be a much smaller quantity than if the whole area was paved.

Wood as a paving material

Wood is potentially the most environmentally friendly of all building materials, and it makes attractive and durable garden surfaces. However, it can be treacherous when wet, and surfaces should be grooved to create a non-slip surface.

Timber paving may take the form of decking, log rounds, heavy-duty timbers (reclaimed or new timber beams), pavers or bark and woodchip mulches. (For general advice on choosing wood and wood preservatives, see pages 130–131).

Timber decking may be constructed from new or reclaimed wood, preferably a durable hardwood like oak, which not does require a preservative. Where the deck has a structural purpose, always consult a structural engineer to check both the design and suitability of the wood.

Pre-cut heavy timber paving can be used for patios, pathways and drives. It combines well with other materials such as decorative aggregates or reclaimed slate to create attractive patterns. Log rounds (see below) make good stepping stones, or an informal paving material, held in place with a retaining edge. A base layer may be needed on damp, clay soils. Use the spaces between as planting pockets, or fill with grit or with fine silver sand, soft enough to be walked on barefoot.

For the ultimate soft surface, choose bark or woodchip mulch, in a thick layer over a weedproof membrane, both economical and easy to lay.

TIMBER FOR GARDEN PATHS AND SURFACES

Decking	Mulches	Wood rounds and pavers
Timber decking can be constructed in a great variety of different patterns. It may be set above, or level with, adjacent surfaces. A 5mm (¼in) gap should be allowed between each decking board for drainage. Decking may also be available as preformed squares (see below), but check for preservative use when purchasing these.	Bark- and wood-chip mulches come in many grades, styles and colours, which you can select to suit the location. A "play grade" bark mulch can provide a soft landing area underneath play equipment. The recommended depth for a domestic play area with no high equipment is 30cm (12in). For paths, use a 10cm (4in) layer. A retaining edge of planking, for example, may be needed. Top up mulches annually.	Log rounds are short lengths of round branches or tree trunks, which may or may not have had their bark removed. They can be used as stepping stones in a mulch or turf path, or butted up together as an informal surfacing material. Use shallow rounds, 10–15cm (4–6in) deep, for pedestrian areas. Chunkier rounds, up to 20cm (8in) deep, are more suitable for heavy use.

Walls, fences and screens

Boundary and screening walls perform the same function as fences, but a wall is normally of a more solid and bulky construction requiring substantial foundations, and if well built will afford greater strength and durability. Walls absorb more heat than fences; this is slowly released during the night, giving a slightly warmer micro-climate for adjacent plants. Solid walls standing alone do not make good windbreaks; they can create more turbulence than permeable barriers which filter the wind.

Garden walls

Walls in gardens account for the use of many tonnes of quarried materials, a finite resource, so recycled materials should be used wherever possible. Stone walls should ideally only be built where their strength and durability are actually needed. Substantial walls can also be built from reclaimed heavy-duty timbers, and they do not require large quantities of quarried foundation materials.

Walls can be a wildlife habitat in the garden. The dense evergreen growth and protection of an ivy-covered wall will shelter nesting or roosting birds and many insects. Drystone walls are an ideal habitat for small mammals and reptiles and scree plants.

Garden wall
Low walls need only simple building skills and can increase the planting opportunities in your garden. This small retaining wall creates a raised bed with good drainage for sun-loving plants. Leave gaps in the mortar, or poke holes in it with a pencil when it is wet, to about 15cm (6in) deep; you may encourage the nesting of masonry bees, a beneficial insect.

Alternatives to brick and stone

In areas where timber and natural stone were scarce or too expensive, walls were traditionally made of cob – local mud mixed with straw or heather. A well-built cob wall can last for years. They are usually less weather-proof than stone, and to last need damp-proof foundations and a coping – like a tiny roof overhanging the sides, traditionally of thatch or slate. A render of lime mortar will protect the sides. Mud can also be made into unfired bricks for "lump-wall" construction, but unless you have a suitable clay-containing soil, lime or cement must be added to make the bricks durable.

Rammed earth or "pisé" walls consist of clay-containing earth built up in layers between removeable shuttering. "Wattle and daub", a hazel lattice covered in mud and straw, or a mixture of mud, straw and cow manure, is another variation on the theme. If you have space, straw bales make cheap building units, but need a good coat of render.

An effective and environmentally friendly acoustic barrier consists of a framework of woven, freshly cut willow, filled with soil, into which the willow stems root. Variations include a soil-filled framework of dried willow, in which ground-cover plants are established. Dense, compressed reed walls designed to reduce noise are also available.

A hedge (see pp.148–149) is without doubt the most environmentally beneficial garden barrier. But hedges take time to mature, require trimming, and occupy space. Fences provide a practical alternative where space is limited and a secure definition of boundaries is an immediate priority.

Fences

Wood is the most commonly used fencing material, and is, potentially, the most environmentally friendly. Unfortunately, most fencing is made from non-durable softwoods, and strong chemicals may have been used to preserve it (see also p.130). In fact, as fence panels are rarely in contact with the ground, which is where wood is most at risk from decay, a simple water-repellent stain should protect them. Fence posts are most at risk from decay at ground level, where wood, air and soil meet. Posts made of oak or sweet chestnut are recommended for their

natural durability. Concrete post bases extend the life of a wooden posts and make them easier to replace.

Conventional wooden fencing includes the familiar larchlap, close-board and palisade. However, fencing panels can also be made from compressed woody prunings, and other natural materials such as reed and heather. Such panels can be homemade or bought. They are particularly suitable for lightweight screening within the garden, as are trellises and screens made from bamboo.

Bamboo canes may have travelled half a world to the UK. Growing your own, for plant supports, light structures and screens, is an environmentally friendly alternative. The canes must be dried slowly, for three to six months. Lash them together with cord. They can also be drilled, but do not nail as they will split.

Other materials

Fences, barriers and posts made from "synthetic wood" (see p.131) can be useful; they have a long lifespan and never rot. There is, however, the question of how they are to be ultimately disposed of. Other fencing products made of plastics or a combination of plastic and wire can be difficult to separate and recycle and at present only add to the problems caused by landfill and incineration.

Metals, also non-renewable and using energy-intensive production processes, are best reserved for special applications; for example, around balconies and roof gardens where their strength and lightness is essential. Decorative iron work may also be required to preserve the architectural style of a building, and it can often be found in salvage yards

Preferred fencing choices
• *Homemade or locally made panels from coppice products or garden prunings.*
• *Untreated woods from sustainable forests.*
• *Panels made of natural vegetative materials such as heather, reed or bamboo.*
• *Sustainable woods treated only with eco-friendly products.*
• *Recycled or scrap wood.*

Avoid
• *CCA pressure-treated timbers.*
• *Creosote-treated timber.*
• *Tropical woods and any wood from poorly managed forests.*
• *Plastics and recycled PVC.*

BAMBOOS FOR CANES

Many hardy species can be grown for canes in the UK. Canes 2–3m (6–10ft) long take around three years to grow. Cut them above a joint, where they are solid, to stop rain getting into the base of the cane, leading to rot. Look for:
Phyllostachys aureosulcata var.
   aureocaulis (far left), *P. nigra*
   (centre), *P. violascens,*
   P. viridiglauscens and *P. vivax*
Pleioblastus simonii
Pseudosasa japonica (near left)
Semiarundinaria fastuosa
Yushiana anceps, Y. maculata and
   Y. maling

Coppice products

Renewable and sustainable, natural and versatile coppice products and garden prunings can provide the organic gardener with a number of indispensable building materials.

Coppice wood is the term given to poles and branches produced by a "stool" – a tree stump or root plate that is cut at ground level every few years. The stool continues to live, and grows new wood after each harvest. A pollarded tree is managed in a similar way, except that the branches are cut at a greater height, usually just out of reach of grazing animals, from a permanent trunk called a "bolling".

Most deciduous trees are suitable for coppicing, and they can be harvested on a cycle, ranging from annually for willow, to every 20 years for larger ash or chestnut poles. Hazel for fencing spars is generally harvested on a six- to eight-year cycle. Chestnut is used for traditional hop poles and ash for hurdles. They are harvested on a 15-year cycle.

An ancient craft

Coppicing and pollarding usually extend the natural life of a tree. An ash tree lives for about 200 years, whereas if it is coppiced regularly it will continue to grow from the same root plate for 1000 years or more. Coppiced ash trees growing on waterlogged

soil in Bradfield Woods, near Bury St. Edmunds, have been dated at 1000 years old.

The most commonly coppiced trees in Europe include hazel, ash, sweet chestnut, oak, alder, sycamore, willow, hornbeam, maple and lime. When carefully managed, an area of coppice can support a great diversity of flora and fauna and is one of the richest habitats of a temperate climate.

Using stems from the garden

Woody material from garden pruning can be used in the same way as coppice wood. Garden trees and shrubs can provide small-diameter wood with a huge range of durability, flexibility, strength and colour. It is well worth experimenting with the species in your own garden.

Ornamental dogwoods (*Cornus alba* cultivars), willows (*Salix* spp.), and ash trees (*Fraxinus* spp.) provide some of the richest bark colours for decorative panels in woven screens. For a paler, cleaner look, branches can be stripped of their bark. Other useful material includes the pruned lower limbs of larger trees, such as cedar and cypress. These, and other conifer species, often have naturally curved lower branches and branchlets, which lend themselves to bentwood trellis work if they have to

THE SUSTAINABLE BARBECUE

Rather than buying charcoal sourced from unsustainable, poorly managed woodlands and tropical forests, look for local charcoal from managed woods. Where there are initiatives to bring ancient coppice woods back into production, charcoal is a valuable by-product. Selling it locally reduces transport costs.

Coppiced poles
Below: using a bill hook to harvest hazel poles from a regularly coppiced stool. Centre: cut poles stacked for drying. Far right: one of the simplest screens to construct, from trimmed poles lashed together with twine. This one will support runner beans.

be removed. Conifers do not in general lend themselves to coppicing. Many will die if cut back into bare wood. However, both yew and the shrubby juniper (*Juniperus communis*) re-grow well from hard pruning, provided that it is not done very often. If you need to cut an overgrown specimen of either down to size it will generate useful material.

Many species that are normally brittle can be used if they are cut in spring when the rising sap makes the branches more flexible for bending and weaving, especially if very young shoots are used. Otherwise, the normal time to cut coppice wood is during winter, when the trees are dormant.

Hedge clippings from species such as privet (*Ligustrum ovalifolium*) are flexible enough to be used for small trellises. Older, thicker hedge wood from renovation work is useful for making frameworks for larger panels.

All types of prunings, especially those with twigs too small for other applications, can be made into compressed brushwood panels.

Making plant supports

Supports for climbing plants can be made from coppiced wood, or even shrub and hedge prunings that are of a suitable length. They will last for a year or two if in contact with soil, longer if not. Twiggy materials are best for plants such as sweet peas that cling on with tendrils; straight rods work well for twining climbers.

When using willow, strip the bark from the lower part of the rod (or whole stem if you like) to stop it rooting. This is easily done when newly cut.

Create wigwams with flexible rods. For greater stability for heavier climbers such as roses, weave fine willow rods in spiral fashion around the wigwam frame to create a continuous woven band around the base. You can also use lengths of strong-stemmed climbers such as wisteria and honeysuckle for weaving.

To make an arch-shaped bentwood trellis, use a large bench or area of firm ground and lay out the framework pieces: two uprights and main cross pieces. Wire together the tops of the two uprights to form an arch. Either nail or bind the cross pieces between the uprights to strengthen the arch. Then use finer stems to criss-cross the framework in the pattern of your choice.

A use for Leylandii timber

A little-known fact about the notorious Leyland and Lawson cypresses (x *Cupressocyparis leylandii* and *Chamaecyparis lawsoniana*) is that they can provide durable woods for external use. Their timber is not often available in the UK, so you may look upon an inherited overgrown screen of Lawson or Leyland cypress with renewed interest, and begin to think of them as a more valuable resource than fodder for the chipper or shredder. If you can, dry the poles in a shed or garage for a year or more; they will give longer service than if used freshly cut.

Depending on the size of the trees, their trunks may be used to make fence posts, pergolas and arches; side branches with a natural curve are useful for the tops of arches and pergolas, while others can be woven into trellises. Sadly, neither tree will regrow from the cut stump.

MAKING A HAZEL OR WILLOW SCREEN

Drive main uprights into the ground. For a screen up to 1.2m (4ft) high, their diameter should be around 4–5cm (1½–2in). Set them about 60cm (2ft) apart, with 30cm (12in) of their length below ground.

Position vertical spacers between the main uprights. These are usually of a smaller diameter than the main uprights (about 2.5cm/1in) and are just pushed into the soil until stable enough to weave around.

Cut greenwood for the weavers, about 1.5cm (⅝in) in diameter. Weave these rods in and out of the posts. Make sure that each new weaving rod you add in overlaps the last weaver securely, and is neatly tucked into the weave. The ends of the weavers should overlap the end uprights by about 5cm (2in) for stability. Use a single weave as shown, or if fine willow or hazel is available, three rods or more can be used for each row.

For taller screens, more substantial posts, 7.5–10cm (3–4in) in diameter, are required every 1.2–2m (4–6ft), with uprights and spacers set in between, as above.

Living willow screens and structures

Freshly cut green willow rods can be made into an elegant lattice fence, which subsequently takes root and grows to produce a green, living screen. Vigorous species of willow such as *Salix daphnoides*, *Salix purpurea* and *Salix alba* hybrids are most commonly used, although any species with flexible branches of sufficient length and strength will suffice. The flexibility of willow rods allows them to be made into all kinds of structures including arbours, tunnels, domes and sculptures. Screens made from living willow are very strong, and they make effective windbreaks where other materials fail. The rods are cut and used fresh during winter to ensure that they will root. As the willows become established, vigorous new growth is made each season. This must be pruned back in the winter to maintain the structure. When siting a willow screen, which is sometimes known as a "fedge" because it is a cross between a fence and a hedge, remember that the summer growth can be wide-spreading – up to 1m (3ft) on either side.

Making a simple willow wall

You need a selection of willow rods, sorted into bundles of similar length, and a length of weed-suppressing membrane approx 1m (3ft) wide to run the length of the screen, plus a metal rod and lump hammer to make holes, and secateurs and twine.
• Firstly, roll out the membrane and secure it either by digging in the edges, or with large wire staples.
• Using the metal rod, make planting holes in a straight line down the centre of the membrane, 15–20cm (6–8in) apart and 30cm (1ft) deep. Select fairly thick, straight rods and push these into the holes to form the uprights.
• Now use lighter rods to establish diagonals. Make an angled planting hole at 45° beside each upright. Push rods in and weave them diagonally across four uprights. Mirror this on the other side with planting holes angled in the opposite direction on the other side of each upright.
• Using fine long rods, create a band of firm weaving across the top. Finally, tie down the loose ends in decorative arcs across the top.

Living willow structure
Living willow can be used to create an amazing range of screens, tunnels, domes and other structures. If neglected, the willows will grow into full-sized trees. Sadly, you may not be around to take care of your structure for ever, so on clay soils prone to shrinkage, a willow structure should not be planted closer to a building than the final mature height of the willow species being used.

SPECIES SUITABLE FOR COPPICE CRAFTS

Species	Bendability	Durability	Applications/Notes
Hazel (*Corylus avellana*)	Good	Good 3–8 years	All types of bent and straight wood trellis work, and woven panels
Ash (*Fraxinus excelsior*)	Good when young	Moderate 2–3 years	All types, traditionally used for hurdles; can be riven (split) into fine wands or spars for binding
Chestnut, sweet (*Castanea sativa*)	Good	3–8 years	Often reserved for frameworks and posts
Common oak (*Quercus robur*)	Only young branches	Good 3–8 years	Round wood used for frameworks and posts – riven rod and saplings flexible
Sycamore (*Acer pseudoplatanus*)	Moderate	Poor 1–3 years	Can become weak when dry; can be used for small panels
Willow (*Salix* spp.)	Excellent	Moderate 3–5 years	Suitable for tight weaving and also living screens or "fedges" where it will survive much longer
Elm (*Ulmus* spp.)	Good	Low–moderate 1–4 years	Easy to work when young and green; young rods used as bonds (ties)
Poplars (*Populus* spp.)	Good	Moderate 1–3 years	Traditionally used for making brooms
Birch (*Betula* spp.)	Good when young, only becomes brittle on drying	Poor	Besom brooms; small panels in larger works
Privet (*Ligustrum ovalifolium*)	Good	Moderate–good 3–5 years	Bentwood trellis
Juniper (*Juniperus* spp.)	Good	Good	All types of trellis and light structures
Bamboos (see p.137)	Flexible when fresh	4–8 years, depending on diameter	Cannot be nailed – pre-drill or bind together with cord
Dogwoods (*Cornus* spp.)	Good, very flexible	Moderate 3–5 years	Retains colour when dry
Apple (*Malus* spp.)	Good	Poor 1–3 years	Suitable for small trellis
Peach, cherry, plum (*Prunus* spp.)	Poor–fair	Poor 1–3 years	Suitable for plant supports
Sumach (*Rhus* spp.)	Very good	Moderate–good 3–5 years	Highly flexible for more complex weaving – handle with gloves since some species have highly irritant sap
Lime (*Tilia* spp.)	Fair	Poor	Woven panels in larger works
Holly (*Ilex* spp.)	Fair	Poor	Suitable for weaving
Eucalyptus	Good	Moderate	Suitable for all types of bentwood or woven panel
Bay laurel (*Laurus nobilis*)	Good	Moderate	Good for weaving
Cotoneaster	Good, esp. fine shoots	Moderate	Good for weaving
Broom (*Cytisus* spp.)	Good	Fair	Good for weaving and making besom brooms
Honeysuckle (*Lonicera* spp.)	Good	2–3 years	Useful for weaving around a framework of other wood
Wisteria	Good	2–3 years	Useful for weaving
Clematis	Good	2–3 years	Fine stems useful for decorative weaving around framework of other wood; larger older stems more suitable for trellis frameworks

GARDEN USES FOR POLES AND PRUNINGS

- **Twiggy supports** for peas and tall-growing perennials.
- **Poles, screens and wigwams** for climbing beans.
- **Decorative wigwam supports** for ornamental climbers.
- **Woven baskets and screens** – look out for local short courses in weaving to learn how to make simple projects.
- **Edging for beds** – nail stout poles between pegs, as shown left, or weave more flexible rods between more closely spaced pegs to create "mini-hurdles".
- **Making besom brooms** – bind bunches of brushwood from birch or broom tightly with twine, then drive a sharpened hazel pole into the top of the bunch. Useful for lawns – or Halloween!

Woody plants and climbers

LIKE THE SET ON A STAGE, TREES, SHRUBS AND CLIMBERS
PROVIDE THE BACKDROP FOR THE FLOWERS' PERFORMANCE

TREES AND SHRUBS supply the permanent setting for a garden. Trees provide structure and height, create shade, and add depth to a garden scene and also add much character. Hedges are planted to enclose the garden, or to create subdivisions and rooms within it. Shrubs offer structure and seasonal interest and create a permanent background for flowers. They demand relatively little attention, cover large areas of soil efficiently, suppress weed growth and, with some careful selection, can provide year round variety and interest.

Woody plants provide excellent cover for birds, mammals and insects, and are an important source of food and nesting material. In exchange for board and lodging, these creatures will play a vital part in maintaining a garden organically. Woody plants are the slowest to develop, but in return live longest. During the first few years little progress is noticeable, but then you suddenly become aware that the tiny sapling planted years ago has matured into a wonderful tree.

The importance of trees

The old saying "Weed as if you die tomorrow, plant trees as if you will live forever" should be put into practice more often. Many people are reluctant to plant trees, thinking they will never see them reach maturity. If the word maturity conjures up visions of old, gnarled oaks, then you are right. If, on the other hand, you would be satisfied with a trunk sufficiently large to comfortably wrap your arms around and a canopy sufficient to provide shade for afternoon tea, then you should be out there digging a hole for it now. Planting a tree is always special, making it the perfect way of commemorating a landmark occasion such as a birth or a wedding.

Plant a tree to celebrate a special person or event

Trees play a vital role in our environment. They clean up the air we breathe, absorb dust and noise, provide food and shelter for wildlife, and play an important role as a climatic thermostat. During summer they create welcome shade that is several degrees cooler than that cast by a building. During cold winter weather their network of branches creates air pockets, trapping air and creating a sheltered microclimate.

Choosing the right tree

The main criteria to consider when planting a tree are its suitability for the soil conditions and climate and its ultimate size. There is a wide range of small

TREES FOR SMALL GARDENS

Acer griseum, A. campestre,
  A. palmatum and cultivars
Cornus kousa var. *chinensis*
Crataegus monogyna
Enkianthus campanulatus
Euonymus europaeus
Laburnum anagyroides
Liquidambar styraciflua
Malus 'Golden Hornet',
  M. 'John Downie'
Morus nigra
Prunus (many)
Sorbus (many)

Colour and shape
The red stems of Cornus alba *(facing page) add brilliant colour to the winter garden. The narrow growth habit of* Liquidambar styraciflua *(right) makes it ideal for small gardens, providing height without taking up too much space. In autumn its foliage turns stunning deep shades.*

FOR ATTRACTIVE BARK

Acer capillipes, A. griseum,
  A. pensylvanicum
Arbutus x *andrachnoides*
Betula (most)
Cornus alba cultivars,
  C. stolonifera 'Flaviramea'
Eucalyptus gunnii
Euonymus alatus
Hydrangea aspera cultivars
Luma apiculata (syn. *Myrtus*
  luma)
Prunus serrula
Rosa glauca
Rubus cockburnianus
  R. thibetanus 'Silver Fern' (right)
Salix acutifolia 'Blue Streak'
S. alba 'Britzensis'
S. x *sepulcralis* var. *chrysocoma*

FOR AUTUMN COLOUR

Acer (many; right, the field
  maple, *Acer campestre*)
Amelanchier lamarckii
Aronia melanocarpa
Berberis thunbergii
Cercidiphyllum japonicum
Cercis canadensis
Cornus alba, C. controversa,
  C. 'Eddie's White Wonder',
  C. kousa var. *chinensis*
Cotinus coggygria
Crataegus monogyna
Ginkgo biloba
Hamamelis mollis
Hydrangea quercifolia
Laburnum anagyroides
Liquidambar styraciflua
Malus 'Golden Hornet', *M.* 'John
  Downie', *M. tschonoskii*
Morus nigra
Nyssa sylvatica
Parrotia persica
Prunus sargentii, P. x *verecunda*
  'Autumn Glory'
Quercus coccinea 'Splendens',
  Q. palustris, Q. rubra
Rhus typhina
Sorbus alnifolia, S. 'Joseph Rock'
Viburnum opulus, V. plicatum
  'Mariesii'

trees suitable for small gardens such as those in the genera *Sorbus* and *Cornus*, many maples, crab apples and *Amelanchier lamarckii*. In a small garden, in particular, it is also important that the tree rewards you with the maximum interest all year round. Attractive bark, leaf colour, autumn colour and fruits, ornamental and edible as well, are all options. The proposed location of the tree will also have a bearing on your choice.

Make sure the tree is suited to your garden. You may have wonderful childhood memories of the weeping willows at the lake's edge in the park, but these trees really need the moisture to be found by a lakeside, and the amount of space provided by a park with a lake, rather than the average back garden with a pond.

Siting trees

Horror stories often blame trees for damage to houses – foundations ruined by tree roots, drains completely blocked and so on. Tree roots themselves, however, rarely cause damage to buildings. Most problems only occur on clay soils where the clay either shrinks, following severe dry weather, or heaves (expands), usually after a tree has been removed. A healthy tree takes up large quantities of water from the soil and during exceptionally dry spells clay soils can dry out and shrink. When a tree is removed, it is no longer drawing water out of the soil; this can cause clay soils to heave.

Tree roots sometimes do find their way into broken drains, where over time they expand, causing the drains to crack. On heavy soils in particular, birch, cherry, apple, pear and plum should be planted at no less than 4m (12ft) from the house. Ash, false acacia, chestnut, lime, plane, sycamore and willow should be planted no less than 7m (22ft) away, whilst oak and poplar are safest kept at a minimum distance of 12m (40ft) from the house or substantial outbuildings.

Use common sense when planting trees. Look at the sun's position during the day, and imagine where the shadows will be. Make sure your favourite breakfast corner will not be cast in deep shade. Remember tree roots will spread beyond the crown, affecting moisture and nutrient levels in the soil in the surrounding area.

Pleaching, pollarding and coppicing

With regular pruning and training, it is possible to grow potentially large trees in confined spaces. Beech, lime, plane and hornbeam are often used for a hedge or stilted hedge, which is like a hedge grown on tall trunks, creating a clearing underneath. They can also be pleached, in which case the branches are trained horizontally along a framework and sideshoots are pruned back to the main branches. All these styles provide height and screening, without taking up much room, but will only be successful if pruned annually, to give them the trim, crisp outline required.

In established gardens people often struggle with large trees that cast too much shade and overpower the whole scene. Many tall trees, such as chestnuts, limes and willows, can be pollarded, meaning that they are cut back to the main stem at about head height. This needs to be done every seven to ten years. Traditionally trees were pollarded to provide wood for domestic use while keeping the young shoots out of reach of grazing animals. Coppicing, a similar practice, involves cutting the wood down to a stool at ground level. Coppiced hazel is popular as it provides pliable stakes, useful in the garden.

Eucalyptus trees are often grown as coppiced or pollarded shrubs in shrub or mixed borders since their bluish-white foliage is very attractive as a backdrop to other plants, and is particularly popular with flower arrangers.

Choosing the right shrub

Interesting foliage shapes and colours, attractive stems, flowers and fruits, and also bird life, are some of the features brought into the garden by shrubs. They can act as backdrop, ground cover or feature plant, depending on how and where they are used. They may be evergreen, have special coloured foliage, be variegated or have good autumn colour. There are tiny shrubs such as rock roses suited to the front of a border or rock gardens whilst some rhododendrons can attain the size of a house.

We have a huge selection of shrubs to choose from, suiting most conditions and tastes. A little homework will help you to find the right plants for your garden. These few hours spent will save you many hours tending shrubs in the years to come. The acid-loving, stately rhododendrons, in all colours and sizes, flower between late winter and early summer; hydrangeas announce the coming of

MATCHING TREES AND SHRUBS TO SOIL TYPES

Clay soil	Dry soil	Chalky soil
Acer platanoides △	Acer negundo, A. tataricum subsp. ginnala	Acer campestre, A. platanoides
Aesculus △	Betula (below)	Arbutus unedo *
Betula pendula	Calluna vulgaris	Cornus mas
Chaenomeles △	Enkianthus campanulatus	Cotoneaster * (some)
Cornus △	Erica	Euonymus
Corylus avellana	Eucryphia *	Forsythia
Cotinus coggygria	Fothergilla monticola	Fuchsia magellanica
Cotoneaster * (some) △	Gaultheria *	Hebe
Euonymus europaeus	Genista	Hypericum *
Hedera helix *	Gleditsia	Lonicera * (some)
Hypericum calycinum * △	Ilex aquifolium *	Mahonia aquifolium * (below)
Ilex aquifolium cultivars * △ (below)	Juniperus *	Morus nigra
Laburnum x watereri 'Vossii' △	Pieris	Olearia *
Philadelphus (some) △	Pinus *	Paeonia delavayi, P. lutea
Phyllostachys *	Rhododendron *	Philadelphus
Prunus	Robinia	Pittosporum *
Ribes sanguineum △	Rosa pimpinellifolia	Prunus (Japanese cherries)
Roses	Rosmarinus officinalis *	Pseudosasa japonica
Salix (many)	Santolina *	Roses (most)
Viburnum lantana △ , V. opulus △	Vaccinium *	Sorbus aria, S. intermedia
Weigela		Syringa
	* evergreen	Vinca *
* evergreen		Weigela
△ particularly suited for alkaline soils		
		* evergreen

autumn with their dainty lacecaps or spherical snowballs; viburnums with gorgeous scents flower at virtually every time of year, and ground-covering euonymus is tough and reliable. *Viburnum tinus* can be planted as an evergreen hedge or back-of-the-border shrub, whilst *V. plicatum* 'Mariesii', with its elegantly layered habit and lacecap-like white flowers, is a feature in its own right, deserving a prominent position.

The dogwoods such as *Cornus alba* 'Sibirica' and *C. stolonifera* 'Flaviramea' offer little in the way of flower, but start performing in autumn when their leaves turn pink and red, followed by stems that glow deep red and shine lime green respectively. This effect can be enjoyed till late winter, when they should be cut back again. They can be planted on their own, but the effect becomes much more intense when planted in groups of five or more, where space allows.

Establishing a shrub border

Once established, shrubs, especially those that are evergreen, are effective weed suppressants, but until they have reached that stage there are several ways of dealing with the bare soil. Shrubs can be planted more densely than needed, thinning them out as they mature. If carefully dug up during the dormant season, the thinned-out shrubs can be transplanted to a new area. Alternatively, the space surrounding the shrubs can be filled with ground-covering herbaceous perennials, such as pulmonaria and the ornamental deadnettles (*Lamium*), which will gradually disappear as competition from the growing shrubs increases. Another option is to plant through a permeable weedproof membrane, which is then covered in a gravel or bark mulch to hide it (see *Weeds and Weed Control*, p.76–7. See also pp.154–7 for planting, maintaining and pruning shrubs.)

Ground-cover shrubs

Plants for ground cover have become very popular since the mid-20th century, as they can reduce labour requirements considerably. A successful scheme should require little or no looking after once it is well established, making it the most labour-saving type of planting available. Starting with a weed-free area, even young plants require little

maintenance during the establishment years. The best plants to use as ground cover are evergreen or densely twigged ones with a low, spreading habit, such as *Stephanandra incisa* 'Crispa' and cotoneasters. This prevents light from penetrating through to the earth, discouraging weed growth. Several conifers such as *Juniperus communis* 'Repanda', *J. horizontalis* cultivars and *Tsuga canadensis* 'Branklyn' (often also called 'Prostrata') are effective, but are sometimes criticised for not offering any seasonal changes. Hebes on the other hand produce flowers over prolonged periods, but can be short-lived, particularly in colder areas. Certain ground-cover roses, such as 'Max Graf', grow into a colourful animal- and intruder-repellent cover, though as they lose their leaves in winter they are not the most effective weed-suppressing plants, and their thorns can make weeding unpleasant!

GROUND-COVER SHRUBS

Calluna vulgaris ★
Cotoneaster horizontalis ★ (left),
  C. microphyllus ★
Erica ★
Euonymus fortunei and cultivars ★ △ ⊌
Gaultheria ★ ⊌
Hebe albicans ★, *H. pinguifolia* ★
  H. 'Youngii' ★
Hedera ★ ⊌
Hypericum calycinum ★ ⊌
Leucothoe walteri and cultivars ★ ⊌
Mahonia aquifolium ★ ⊌,
  M. repens ★ ⊌
Pachysandra terminalis ★ ⊌
Rosmarinus officinalis Prostratus
  Group ★ △
Rubus pentalobus ★, *Rubus tricolor*
Sarcococca hookeriana var. *humilis* ★ ⊌
Stephanandra incisa 'Crispa'
Viburnum davidii ★
Vinca ★ ⊌

★   Evergreen
⊌   Shade-tolerant
△   Rabbit-proof

TIPS FOR PLANTING GROUND COVER

• Young plants give the quickest effect.
• Space plants at a little less than their maximum spread.
• Prepare soil well to encourage quick growth.
• Mulch for initial weed control and to aid establishment.
• Avoid invasive plants where this could be a problem.
• Match vigour if mixing plants.
• Control weeds by hand or hoe until plants have covered the ground.

Hedges and windbreaks

When low-level screening or a windbreak is required in a garden, a hedge is ideal. It will create an attractive background, whilst also offering food and shelter to wildlife. In a very exposed location, if space is available, it is worth planting a proper shelter belt, consisting of several rows of mixed trees and shrubs that will catch the wind and disperse it, to protect the garden from severe winds. A mixture of deciduous and evergreen trees and shrubs is best, planting the lowest ones on the windward side. This way the force of the wind is broken as it filters through and is pushed upwards.

Which plants to use

Both trees and shrubs can be used for hedging. Your choice of plant, or plants, will depend not only on appearance, and how you want to maintain the hedge – neatly clipped, for example, or billowing with blossom – but also whether the plants are suited to your soil and climate, and whether the hedge is in a very windswept site or not. Amongst the best choices for cold exposed sites are beech, privet and *Cornus mas*. Plants chosen for coastal sites must in addition tolerate salt-laden winds. And if the hedge is intended to keep out browsing animals such as deer, you must obviously choose species that do not appeal to the marauders, but are not toxic, as for example yew is.

Formal hedges

Evergreens are the classic choice for clipped hedges, giving a solid backdrop of colour and structure year-round. Yew (*Taxus baccata*) and box (*Buxus* spp.) are traditional garden hedges with a smooth finish; box is ideal for lower hedges as it grows more slowly than yew. An interesting alternative to box is *Ilex crenata*, an evergreen holly with small rounded leaves which also lends itself to crisp clipping. Privet (*Ligustrum* spp.) is commonly planted. It is tough but only partially evergreen, and can look somewhat dull in winter. Beech (*Fagus sylvatica*) and hornbeam (*Carpinus betulus*) are deciduous, but will retain their dried leaves, rustling in the wind as they glow coppery orange in winter sunlight (see below right). A fast effect is often obtained with leylandii (X *Cupressocyparis leylandii*) but, being a tall forest tree, it will carry on growing rapidly to a huge height unless you are very strict with the pruning from an early age. Let it grow to within 30cm (12in) of the desired height and then start pruning the top. The hedge will require pruning at least twice a year to keep it under control.

Semi-formal hedges

Not all hedges need to be crisply trimmed, and flowering and fruiting hedges are among the richest food sources for wildlife (see also pp.193–7). For a more relaxed effect, try *Viburnum tinus*, which can be loosely clipped into cloud-like shapes. In warmer climates *Griselinia* makes an attractive hedge, as do fuchsias. Several flowering shrubs lend themselves to being grown as a hedge, either crisply or loosely cut. For a late winter show the soft yellow flowers of *Cornus mas*, followed in late summer by shiny red edible berries, are unusual. The spring-flowering forsythias can also make a good hedge. Berberis, with its prickles, will discourage intruders; it makes a good flowering boundary.

Another way of creating an informal screen is to plant a willow "fedge", or living willow screen. Fresh willow branches are inserted into the ground during the winter months and are woven into a screen. By spring they will root, and start growing. The new shoots can then be woven into the existing structure. (see also *The Garden Framework*, p.140.)

HEDGE-PLANTING TIPS

• Bare-root plants are the cheapest. You can buy mixed bundles of native species. Or, grow your own plants from hardwood cuttings (see p.107).
• Plant evergreens in autumn and deciduous species from autumn to early spring.
• Don't just dig individual holes: prepare a strip 60–90cm (2–3ft) wide.
• Don't forget tree guards to protect from grazing animals.
• Provide shelter initially in windy areas.
• Mulch for weed control and water retention. Water in dry weather during the first year.

CLIPPING HEDGES

With the exception of fast-growing hedges such as
leylandii and *Lonicera nitida* that need to be pruned
twice or even three times a year to keep them tidy,
most established hedges, like the beech hedge, right,
can be pruned once. If you prune twice, give the first
cut after the frosts are over, as sensitive shoots of box, for
example, can be damaged. Otherwise it is best to prune
in late summer after the main growth season is over.
This way you can enjoy a crisp, neat hedge till the
following spring. Prune hard, getting as close to the last
cut as possible, or your hedge will soon get too fat or
too tall. Only the looser-growing flowering hedges like
Viburnum tinus should be pruned with a light hand,
following the natural contours formed by the shrubs.

HEDGING PLANTS

Aucuba ★ ⋙
Berberis gagnepainii △ ,
  B. thunbergii △ , *B. thunbergii* f.
  atropurpurea △
Buxus (box) ★ ⋙ △
Carpinus betulus (hornbeam)
Chamaecyparis cultivars ★
Cornus mas ⋙ △
Crataegus monogyna (hawthorn) ★
x *Cupressocyparis* cultivars ★
Elaeagnus x *ebbingei* ★ •
Escallonia ★ •
Euonymus fortunei cultivars ★ △ •
Fagus sylvatica (beech, left)
Forsythia △
Fuchsia magellanica △ ○
Griselinia littoralis ★ • ○
Hippophae rhamnoides ★ △ •
Ilex aquifolium cultivars (holly) ★ ⋙
Laurus nobilis (bay) ★
Ligustrum (privet) ★ ⋙ •
Lonicera nitida and cultivars ★ ⋙
Olearia x *haastii* ★ •
Potentilla fruticosa cultivars ★
Prunus laurocerasus cultivars ★ ⋙ ,
  P. lusitanica ★ ⋙
Quercus ilex ★
Rhododendron (some) ★ ⋙ △
Rosa rugosa and cultivars
Rosmarinus officinalis ★ •
Taxus baccata (yew) ★ ⋙ △
Thuja ★
Viburnum tinus ★

★ Evergreen ⋙ Shade-tolerant
△ Rabbit and/or deer proof
• Tolerates maritime conditions
○ Moderately hardy

Climbing plants

Climbers are a versatile way of increasing height and variety in planting, whilst taking up little space. Traditionally climbers are guided along walls, fences and trelliswork, or up pergolas and freestanding supports. They can also, however, be grown through other plants. You might, for example, let a rambling rose such as 'Bobbie James' clamber through a tree or shrub.

Climbers in host plants

When climbers are planted in association with trees or shrubs, it is best to choose ones that will not strangle their host and that will flower at a time when the host plant is not in flower, fruit or autumn colour. This way one will not detract from the other, and a long-lived partnership can be established.

To avoid a shrub being smothered and strangled opt for climbers that are not too vigorous and can be cut back regularly. Suitable plants include the summer-flowering clematis hybrids, such as the *C. viticella* and *C. texensis* cultivars, which can be cut back to 30cm (12in) in winter, or the truly herbaceous climbers such as the golden hop, *Humulus lupulus* 'Aureus'. Alternatively, annual climbers can be used, like the stunning blue morning glory or evocatively scented sweet peas. More tender perennials like *Eccremocarpus scaber* can also be grown as annuals. Care must be taken when planting annuals at the base of woody plants to give them sufficient water since there will no doubt be strong root competition.

Plant the climber as far away from the root of the tree or shrub as is practical – and remember that it will tend to grow towards the light.

Vigorous climbers such as wisterias can be grown on a freestanding support as long as they are pruned rigorously. If you shy away from rigorous pruning, grow them at the very least on a sturdy, chunky pergola, or on a house wall, somewhere where you can enjoy their scent. The most powerfully fragrant climbers for arches and arbours include wisteria, honeysuckles, many roses and *Jasminum officinale*.

Climbing techniques

Climbing plants have different adhesion techniques. The easiest to deal with, perfect for surfaces where you cannot fix climbing supports, are the self-clinging ones such as ivy and *Parthenocissus henryana* which have tiny roots or suction pads that adhere to the surface. Care must be taken that they do not cause damage to old brick, mortar or plasterwork. If you live in a listed house, it is safer to fix vine eyes into the mortar, attach galvanised guiding wires, and grow the following types of climber which all need support. Some, such as wisteria, are twiners, that wind up ropes, poles or branches. Others, like sweet peas, cling on with the help of little tendrils, whilst the leafstalks of clematis twine themselves around twigs, string or wire. Spined plants, such as roses,

Cascade of scent
Site a wisteria, one of the most elegant of climbers, where you can enjoy its delicious scent when laden with flowers in early summer.

claw their way up by hooking themselves onto their support. This is effective when they are scrambling up vegetation masses, as would happen in the wild, but they need to be tied in if you want to guide them along walls or posts.

Wall shrubs are usually categorised together with climbers, but they tend to be shrubs that are slightly frost sensitive and need the shelter of a wall, or have a lax growing habit and benefit from some kind of support (*Ceanothus* 'Gloire de Versailles', for example), rather than true climbers. They are usually pruned and tied back to the wall, so they can benefit fully from the sheltered, sunny position in which they grow.

Training climbers

It pays to spend some time during spring and early summer, when climbers are growing rapidly, to guide them along their support. For many plants, particularly roses, terminal buds are the ones producing flower buds, while the sideshoots produce only foliage. When branches are trained in a near horizontal position, all those sideshoots will start growing vertically, and, like the terminal bud, will produce flowers. So, by tying the branches down to an existing framework and training them across, rather than upwards, you will ensure a much better crop of flowers, which can be enjoyed at eye-level.

Tying in
Ties made of natural fibres rot with time and are unlikely to cause constriction. But check ties regularly on a plant whose stems are expanding rapidly, and loosen them if necessary.

Never use plastic or metal ties, as these will cut into the wood as the branches grow and fatten, cutting off the sap stream, and creating a weak point. Natural fibres will rot eventually, and will snap and release the branch as it expands. By then the plant has usually been fixed again at a higher point and will stay in place. It is still advisable though to check climbers regularly, loosening tight ties and tying in new shoots. The younger the growth, the more pliable it is.

If you are allowing your climber to scramble up into a difficult-to-reach spot, make sure you choose one that does not need regular pruning to do well.

CLASSIC CHOICES

Requiring no pruning

Clematis montana is one of the more vigorous spring-flowering clematis. Its dark green foliage complements well the blush-pink flowers that appear in late spring. Although it dislikes being pruned, its vigorous habit occasionally necessitates severe cutting back. This should take place after flowering.

Hydrangea petiolaris will happily work itself up a north-facing wall, making it ideal to hide unsightly garage walls or sheds. Although it will take a few years to establish, its flaky, rust-brown stems will soon charm you, as it produces its fresh green foliage in spring, soon to be followed by the delicately scented white lacecap flowers.

Parthenocissus henryana is a deciduous, self-clinging climber which has attractive foliage and stunning autumn colour. Its vigour makes it ideal to cover a façade, or let it clamber through a tall pine, where its autumn foliage can contrast beautifully.

Requiring pruning

Clematis viticella is a summer-flowering clematis with many cultivars and hybrids that lend themselves well to annual cutting back to 30cm (12in). This promotes vigorous new growth that can then be carefully trained to produce flowers at eye-level.

Climbing roses should be pruned annually, removing the old flowering stems, and thinning out some of the older stems to encourage new growth at the base. The flower stems should be cut back to the main stem, leaving approximately two eyes, before they are tied in again in as horizontal a position as possible.

Wisteria sinensis needs to be pruned in two stages. In summer, when the main growing season is over, the new shoots are pruned back by about half. In winter these shoots are then further shortened to two buds. This may seem elaborate, but will give so much joy when the heavily scented trusses of delicate lilac flowers appear the following spring.

RESISTANT ROSES

Old and English roses
'Charles de Mills'
Gertrude Jekyll ★
Redouté ★
Winchester Cathedral ★

Rugosa roses ★
'Blanche Double de Coubert'
'F. J. Grootendorst'
'Roseraie de l'Haÿ'

Hybrid musks ★
'Buff Beauty'
'Penelope'

**Modern shrub and
ground-cover roses**
Bonica ★
'Cerise Bouquet'
'Fritz Nobis'

Wild roses and their hybrids
R. filipes 'Kiftsgate'
R. pimpinellifolia hybrids
R. sericea f. pteracantha

Hybrid teas & floribundas ★
Just Joey
Remembrance

Patio roses
'Cécile Brünner'

Climbers (cl) & ramblers
Albéric Barbier'
'Climbing Cécile Brünner'
'Félicité Perpétue'
'Maigold' ★ (cl)
'Paul's Himalayan Musk'
R. banksiae 'Lutea'
'Sander's White Rambler'

★ *repeat-flowering*

Roses

Loved by many gardeners, roses are often considered as one of the most noble of garden flowers. They can be difficult to grow, and account for a high proportion of pesticides used in non-organic gardens. With careful selection, and good growing conditions, however, roses can be grown successfully organically. Few are truly disease resistant, but some species and cultivars are known to be less susceptible than others (see panel, left). Providing good growing conditions will help to keep them healthy.

Choosing which roses to grow

Certain roses are less suited to organic gardening than others. Bush roses, such as the hybrid tea and floribunda (cluster-flowered) types, dislike competition at root level and so are often grown as a monocrop in a rose bed. They require ample spacing, dislike underplanting, and due to the fact they are grown *en masse*, tend to be more susceptible to pest and disease outbreaks.

Species and shrub roses are better suited to the organic garden. They are less sensitive to competition from other plants and are often less susceptible to diseases and pests. Most are of greater value to wildlife and are much less labour demanding, as they require less pruning and deadheading. Look out for roses with rose hips. These are popular with pollinating insects, provide an excellent food source for birds and mammals, and create a colourful seasonal display. The more informal habit of species and shrub roses means that they look more at home in a mixed border. Species roses, such as *R. glauca* or *R. moyesii*, can be mixed into a shrub or herbaceous border. Most rugosa roses make a good, thorny hedge, with glossy hips.

How and where to plant roses

Roses will perform at their best in an open, sunny site. Good air circulation, and a moisture retentive, but well drained, soil will help to prevent disease build up. Avoid planting in sites susceptible to waterlogging, in very acid or alkaline conditions or on very chalky soils.

Where possible, grow roses in a mixed border. Low-growing plants can be grown around the outer edge of a bed of bush roses – which dislike competition – to add diversity and encourage natural predators. If replanting roses in the same place is unavoidable, exchange the soil with that from another part of the garden, to a minimum depth of 45cm (18in).

Prepare a deep planting hole, and incorporate well-rotted manure or garden compost with a sprinkling of bone meal for a kick-start. Plant during the dormant season. If container-grown, it is also possible to plant when in leaf. Trim the roots of bare-rooted plants, removing damaged ends, and soak them in water whilst preparing the hole (see also p.153). All bush roses should be pruned hard on planting, cutting stems back down to the second or third bud, depending on where you find an outward-pointing one.

Aftercare

Mulch the soil each spring. Depending on its richness, use a medium- to high-fertility soil improver (see p.40). Where necessary, water roses growing against a wall, or up a tree, where the soil will tend to be rather dry in spring and early summer. Deadhead bush roses, such as floribundas or hybrid teas, regularly, to encourage continuous flowering. Cut the flowering stem back to a complete, outward-pointing leaf. Do not deadhead roses which will later bear attractive fruit. Watch out for aphid attack, particularly early in the season. Other pests to look out for include frog hoppers and winter moth, as well as diseases black spot, powdery and downy mildew and rose rust (see *Plant Health*, pp.84–103, and the *A–Z of Plant Problems*). Remove fallen leaves, and renew the mulch in early spring before the buds start to grow.

Pruning roses

Prune roses when they are dormant. As part of general hygiene, remove dead or diseased wood. Cut this out and make sure you destroy all twigs and debris after pruning. Always cut above an outward pointing bud (see p.156). Even if no actual bud is visible at a leaf scar, one will be formed if cut at that point. Roses can be kept young and vigorous by cutting out the oldest stems entirely on a three- to four-year cycle. Each year, remove one or two of the oldest stems at the base of the plant. This is the only pruning required by species roses. All shrub roses should be left unpruned for the first few years. Repeat-flowering shrub roses should be pruned

Fruit for the birds
Roses that flower once only in summer, such as Rosa glauca, R. moyesii *and* R. rubiginosa, *will produce colourful, bird-attracting rose hips in the autumn.*

leaving approximately half to two-thirds of their height. The less they are pruned, the more natural the shape of the shrub; the harder they are pruned, the better the flowers will be. If at all, once-flowering roses should be lightly pruned, reducing them by one-third. Bush roses, including floribundas, hybrid teas, polyanthas and miniatures tend to be kept as compact roses, taking them down to half or even a quarter of their original height.

Resistant roses
Breeders are still searching for the fully disease-resistant rose, but these roses (below, from left to right) all show some resistance: 'Charles de Mills', 'Blanche Double de Coubert', 'Buff Beauty', Bonica, R. filipes 'Kiftsgate', 'Frühlingsmorgen', 'Gertrude Jekyll' *and* 'Just Joey'.

Looking after woody plants

All plants benefit from being planted in a well-prepared site. The better the soil, the quicker establishment will be. Remove all weeds, particularly perennial ones (see *Weeds and Weed Control*, p.78–81). Starting with a clean slate eliminates unnecessary competition for water and nutrients.

If you are planting up a new border, prepare the whole area – digging and adding soil improvers as necessary, depending on the state of the soil and the type of plants. Acid-loving (ericaceous) plants such as azaleas are happy with leafmould or, at most, garden compost. Rapidly growing shrubs and repeat-flowering plants such as lavatera rely on a lot of energy to perform their task. They prefer a high-nutrient soil improver such as well-rotted manure.

Native species, such as birch and hawthorn, should not need any additional feeding.

When planting a mixture of species with different requirements, prepare the whole area with a low-fertility material such as leafmould, then add compost or well-rotted manure to individual planting holes, as appropriate.

When planting a single specimen tree or shrub, particularly on poor soils, prepare a generous hole 1–1.5m (5ft) in diameter, and around 45cm (18in) deep, or twice as deep as the rootball. If planting in a lawn, chop up the turf and put it in the bottom of the hole. On heavy soils, gently fork over the base and sides of the hole to allow roots to penetrate.

Selecting and obtaining stock

As there are, as yet, no recognised organic growing standards for ornamentals in the UK, the supply of organically grown trees and shrubs is very limited. The options are to make do with "conventionally grown" plants, or raise your own organically.

Woody plants are either container- or field-grown. The latter are usually larger and stronger than container-grown plants, giving you more plant for your money. Unless they have been rootballed – lifted with a ball of earth around the roots, which is subsequently wrapped in a hessian-type cloth – the roots must not dry out, and need to be covered in soil quickly, either by heeling the plant in temporarily or planting it straight away.

It can be tempting to plant a large tree, hoping it will mature quickly. In fact a young tree will establish more quickly, with less aftercare, and will soon catch up with or even overtake a larger specimen. However if there is a need to screen some eyesore, it may justify the extra cost of starting big.

When to plant

Although container-grown stock can be planted at any time of the year, the ideal planting season for all woody plants, bare-rooted or not, is between autumn and spring. Trees planted in early autumn will benefit from the still-warm soil, making new roots before winter sets in. Spring-planted stock may not get the chance to establish their roots before the start of the drier seasons, making them more

Bare-rooted plants
Never let bare-rooted stock sit around drying out. Unwrap the bundles, separate out the young trees (here including field maple, hazel, blackthorn and hawthorn) and plant them as soon as possible.

susceptible to drying out. In mild climates, it is possible to plant throughout winter, as long as the ground is not frozen or waterlogged.

Planting woody plants

Soak the rootball well before planting. As you position the plant in the hole, stand back to check it is upright, and showing its best side. Spread out its roots, if bare-rooted, or tease the roots gently from the edge of the rootball if container-grown. If staking is required (see below), put in the stake now to avoid damaging the roots. Backfill the hole with the removed soil, mixed with an appropriate soil improver if necessary. Tread down the soil firmly, then water well.

Do not be shy about pruning trees and shrubs when planting. Bare-rooted plants will have suffered root damage, however carefully they have been handled. Trimming damaged and dried roots will encourage new feeder roots to form. To compensate for the reduced root capacity it is equally important to prune the top growth. The more damaged the roots, the harder you should prune the branches. It is also important to remove any diseased or damaged shoots and if necessary, shape the plant.

To promote rapid establishment keep young plants moist and free from weeds or grass. Mulch an area of at least 1m (3ft) around each plant with a loose mulch or a mulch mat (see below and also pp.76–7). For really low maintenance, plant through a permeable membrane, covered in mulch or gravel.

Stakes and shelters

Trees shorter than 1.5m (5ft) do not need a stake, unless planted on a very windy site. Larger trees and shrubs usually need to be staked (see right) or even

anchored when planted. This is to stop the wind rocking the plants in the soil, which impedes good root establishment, and to prevent them from being blown over. A large, semi-mature tree, with a good, solid rootball, can be anchored by constructing a square or triangular wooden frame over the rootball, fixed to posts rammed into the soil. This underground structure firmly anchors the rootball.

A tree planted as a large specimen may need to be staked for 3–5 years, until it is securely anchored by its own roots, but in most cases the stake can be removed after a year or two. Use a stake to suit the situation; there is no point in using a preservative-treated stake that will last for 25 years or more when the tree is only to be staked for a couple of years. Attach the tree to the stake with a rubber or natural tree tie. To prevent it rubbing, attach the tie at the top of the stake, and use a spacer, or tie the tie in a figure of eight.

Check tree ties at least once a year, and loosen, or remove them as necessary. If they are allowed to tighten around the stem, they will reduce the sap flow, impeding growth.

Where necessary, young plants can be given extra protection with tree or shrub shelters. These are tubes manufactured from twin-walled polypropylene that acts as a mini-greenhouse, and protects the plants from rabbit, deer and strimmer damage.

Aftercare

Water new plantings during dry periods. When planting larger trees, it is advisable to coil a special perforated plastic irrigation and aeration pipe around the rootball, leaving one end exposed at ground level, blocked off with a stop tap collar. When

Single and double stakes
Use a short stake, supporting the trunk or stem at around a quarter of its height, rather than supporting the entire stem to the crown. A low-level stake allows the upper part of the tree to move in the wind, which encourages it to make strong new anchoring roots, and strengthens the whole trunk. Double stakes are useful where a large or containerised rootball prevents staking hard up against the stem.

PLANTING IN TURF

If planting a tree or shrub in a lawn, clear the turf from an area at least 1m (3ft) in diameter around it to limit competition from the grass plants. Keep the area weed-free with a loose mulch or by planting through a geotextile membrane or mulch (tree) mat (see also pp.76-7).

Where to cut
Prune at an angle (top) just above an outward-pointing bud. Shrubs with opposite buds (above) should be pruned level, as close to the buds as possible.

watering, the water can be poured straight into the pipe, so that it reaches the roots directly, as it seeps out through the holes, avoiding waste.

Mulching with an organic soil improver (see pp.40–41) during establishment years will help to retain moisture and suppress weeds, which will promote rapid growth. If a tree or shrub has been planted into grass, keep an area of 1sq m (1sq yd) around it mulched and weed-free. Vigorous grass growth can outmatch a newly planted tree.

Rhododendrons should be deadheaded after flowering when young or if under stress, so the plant can concentrate all its efforts on producing new growth. Once established this is no longer necessary.

Pruning trees, shrubs and roses

As part of general hygiene measures, check plants regularly for any dead or diseased wood. Cutting this out will help to control disease outbreaks.

Formative pruning is usually applied to young plants, correcting the shape where necessary. It may also be applicable where a mature plant has outgrown its space, or when a neighbouring plant has been removed, leaving the remaining plants lopsided.

A rejuvenating, or renewing, prune will encourage a shrub or tree to produce strong new shoots.

Think before you prune, making sure that the cut will enhance the shape of the bush. Generally this means cutting just above an outward pointing bud. If the cut is made above an inward pointing bud, the new shoot will grow through the centre of the bush,

spoiling its natural shape, as well as making it dense and airless, increasing the risk of disease. Furthermore, inward-growing shoots tend to receive little direct light, making them weak and straggly.

When to prune

If you are unsure when is the best time to prune a shrub, be guided by its flowering time. Spring-flowering shrubs, such as forsythia, produce flower buds along the stems during the preceding autumn. These buds open to flower in the spring. When flowering is over the shrub will come into growth; this is the time to prune it. Shrubs flowering in late spring and summer, such as mock orange (*Philadelphus*), will come into growth in early spring, producing new shoots, which in turn will have flower buds by early summer. These can be pruned at any stage between leaf-fall in autumn through to late winter. If you are concerned about the hardiness of the plant, is it better to prune at the end of winter, as the network of branches will trap air, creating a protective microclimate in cold weather.

How to prune

Generally speaking, it is safe to prune hard those trees and shrubs which put on more than 30cm (12in) of growth in a season. The harder these plants are pruned, the more vigorously they regenerate. Plants that grow slowly, putting on less than 30cm (12in) per year, do not take kindly to severe pruning, so avoid it unless absolutely necessary. Any cuts you do make should be gentle, formative trimming.

PRUNING SHRUBS

Shrubs that perform well with annual hard pruning	Shrubs that need only light pruning
Buddleja davidii, B. alternifolia	Aucuba japonica and cultivars
Caryopteris	Berberis
Cornus alba and C. stolonifera cultivars	Buxus sempervirens
Cotinus coggygria cultivars (right)	Cotoneasters
Deutzias	Daphnes (right)
Eucalyptus	Magnolias
Forsythia	Potentilla fruticosa cultivars
Fuchsias (hardy)	Prunus
Hydrangeas	Rhododendrons
Hypericums	Taxus baccata
Philadelphus	Viburnums
Roses	
Rubus	
Salix (some)	

These shrubs could be pruned hard to rejuvenate, but would take several years to recover completely.

Regenerative pruning of old shrubs

In established gardens, it is sometimes necessary to prune old, mature shrubs that have outgrown their allocated space. If you want your plants to perform well recompense them for the efforts they will have to make to recover their vigour. After pruning, feed the plants and keep the soil moist particularly during dry periods, by applying a generous mulch of medium- to high-fertility organic matter, such as garden compost or well-rotted manure, depending on the species.

Some take well to hard treatment, whilst others have to be tackled gently. Plants that have been pruned regularly cope better with a hard prune than those that have never been touched. If in doubt, the pruning can be undertaken over a two- to three-year period, selecting each year half or one third of the oldest wood. Not all old shrubs will cope with such treatment, and you must be prepared for some losses.

Pests and diseases

In organic gardening, pest and disease management is all about prevention rather than cure. By choosing the right plant and planting it in the optimum position to ensure strong, balanced growth, the likelihood of it suffering a disease attack is small. Prepare the soil well and provide good aftercare, observing sensible hygiene rules, such as removing and destroying dead and diseased material and promoting good air circulation (see also *Plant Health*, pp.94–6).

A little tolerance is also to be advised. Plants are part of the natural world, and are inevitably going to be less than perfect; a few leaf spots here or a nibbled leaf there is not going to be life-threatening.

Propagation

Although a slow process, there is something enormously satisfying about growing a tree from seed. A species of any woody plant (that is, without a cultivar name) can be grown from seed, but will take years to reach any size. Plants grown by means of vegetative propagation reach flowering stage much sooner, but still take several years to become sizeable. Remember that if you want to reproduce special characteristics in a named cultivar, such as flower or foliage colour, vigour and habit, it is important to propagate the plant by vegetative means.

• **Seeds** Many woody plants do not shed their seeds till late summer or autumn, a rather inhospitable season for small seedlings to germinate and survive. Nature has therefore incorporated a protective mechanism, hardening off the seeds so they need to undergo prolonged exposure to cold weather before they can germinate. You may need to imitate this and chill, or stratify, the seeds (see p.108). If unsure of the conditions required, it is safest to sow the seeds as soon after harvest as possible, keeping them outdoors in a cool, shady place. If they have not germinated after the first winter, do not despair; some need two cold spells before coming to life. Keep the soil moist at all times. For these slow germinators, use a general purpose potting compost. As a general rule of thumb, cover the seeds with a layer of compost as thick as the seed itself.

• **Cuttings** Most woody plants are either propagated from semi-ripe or hardwood cuttings (see p.106–7). Collect semi-ripe cutting material in late summer, particularly from evergreen shrubs such as *Prunus laurocerasus* 'Otto Luyken' and conifers. With conifers it is often possible to take heeled cuttings, pulling off new sideshoots from the main stem with a little heel of hardened wood. Otherwise take stem-tip cuttings. Shrubs such as dogwoods and willows root easily from hardwood cuttings taken at the end of winter.

• **Layering** If only one or two young plants are needed, many woody plants can be layered (see p.107).

RABBIT- AND DEER-PROOF PLANTS

Azaleas (★)
Bamboos ★
Buddleja
Box (*Buxus*) ★
Choisya ★
Clematis
Cornus sanguinea
Pampas grass (*Cortaderia*) ★
Daphnes ★
Euphorbias (★)
Gaultherias ★
Hydrangeas
Hypericums (★)
Lonicera spp., including honeysuckle (★)
Peonies
Philadelphus
Rhododendrons ★
Yew (*Taxus*) ★
Vinca ★

★ evergreen
(★) some species evergreen

NB Even these plants may be vulnerable to attack in exceptional winter conditions

SOME PESTS AND DISEASES OF WOODY PLANTS AND CLIMBERS

Aphids
Bacterial canker
Caterpillars (various)
Clematis wilt
Coral spot (left)
Fireblight
Honey fungus
Peach leaf curl
Phytophthora root rot
Powdery mildews
Rhododendron bud blast
Rose black spot
Scale insects
Silver leaf
Vine weevil

For more information, see the *A–Z of Plant Problems*, p.368–95.

Herbaceous plants

WHILST A PERMANENT BACKGROUND IS CREATED BY TREES
AND SHRUBS, HERBACEOUS PLANTS ADD SEASONAL VARIETY

Show time (facing page)
*Little beats flowering plants for
creating impact in the garden: the
scene-stealing flamboyance of oriental
poppies may be fleeting,
but these perennials will flower
year after year.*

Nature's way (below)
*A continental-style, naturalistic
planting where the soil is covered by a
matrix of ground-covering plants, out
of which arise seasonal highlights.
Vegetation is planted in clumps or
drifts or scattered through as solitaires,
mimicking natural vegetation cover.*

THE TERM "HERBACEOUS" APPLIES, botanically, to
plants that do not form a persistent woody stem.
"Herbaceous" is, however, commonly used as
shorthand for "herbaceous perennial", to mean
plants such as hostas, delphiniums and the like, that
die down in the winter, and return every spring.
These plants may also be referred to simply as
"perennials". This chapter covers the whole
spectrum of herbaceous plants – annuals, biennials,
bulbs and half-hardy perennials grown as annuals, as
well as herbaceous perennials, including grasses.

Hardy annuals and bedding plants create long-
lasting colour, whilst perennials come and go like
performers on a stage, each contributing its part to
create a spectacular show.

There is a huge range of plants to choose from in
this group, from tiny to gigantic, and flowering from
winter through to autumn. Plants may be grown for
their foliage alone, for their flowers, or for both.
The colour spectrum is unrivalled, covering all
shades imaginable. It is possible to find suitable
plants for all garden environments, from dry to wet,
sunny to shaded.

Herbaceous perennials

Although a few early perennials such as *Doronicum
orientale* kick off the spring season, the main
performance starts in early summer and lasts into
autumn, with delights like *Aster pringlei* 'Monte
Cassino' carrying on till the start of winter. Many
border perennials, such as helianthus, originate from
prairie environments and stand up to hot, dry
summer conditions. Others come from woodland
habitats, preferring cool shade. Many of these finish
flowering before summer, as by then trees leave little
moisture for comparatively shallow-rooted perennials.
Cranesbills (hardy geraniums), decorative deadnettles
(*Lamium*) and tiarellas are reliable shade-loving
plants. Other perennials originate from wetland
areas, growing along streams and lakes, and require a

moist soil. Many have large leaves from which high levels of moisture evaporate. Gunneras, ornamental rhubarb (*Rheum*) and rodgersias are very bold in character, adding drama to a garden scene.

Annuals and biennials

Plants, both hardy and half-hardy, that germinate, flower, set seed and die within one year, such as marigolds, are known as annuals. Biennials, such as foxgloves, take two years to complete this process. Both can be more labour demanding than bulbs, perennials and woody plants as you have to sow them each year, though if content, some may self-seed and return year after year.

Tender perennials

Perennials that do not normally survive a cold winter are usually classified, with annuals, as bedding plants, as they too need to be replanted annually.

Plants such as pelargoniums or felicia can be over-wintered in a frost-free greenhouse, cutting them back and re-potting them at the start of spring.

Bulbs

Most bulbs are late winter and spring flowering, but there are those that flower in summer and autumn. Shade-loving woodland bulbs like cyclamen and snowdrops (*Galanthus*) come to life once trees have shed their leaves, allowing water and light to penetrate to the woodland floor. They then come into leaf, flower and set seed before spring draws to a close. Others, such as tulips, originate from areas where summer creates near desert-like conditions. They too come to life between autumn and late spring. Avoid large, highly hybridised tulips and daffodils, as they can have difficulty building up enough energy to keep on producing those huge flowers. Instead opt for the species, or closely related selections.

HOW THEY GROW

Annuals
Completing the cycle of seed to seed in one year, annuals (**1**, the annual poppy 'Danish Flag') can create an intense patch of colour over many months.

Biennials
These plants need one year to build up a large, strong, basal plant which will flower, set seed and die the following year. A few short-lived perennials are often treated as biennials to avoid disease (for instance hollyhocks, **2**, which are prone to rust).

Perennials
Faithfully returning year after year, perennials (such as aquilegias, **3**) provide reliable colour, with attractive foliage and seedheads if the right ones are chosen.

Bulbs
Late winter and early spring flowering bulbs (such as tulips, **4**) are ideal to interplant amongst perennials and spring bedding and under deciduous trees and shrubs. Planting among other low plants will help disguise the leaves as they die down

GRASSES

Strictly speaking, grasses are either herbaceous perennials or annuals, but deserve to be in a category of their own. Their care and planting method is very similar to that of perennials. Some, such as the infamous gardener's garters (*Phalaris arundinacea* var. *picta*) are invasive and should be used with caution, but many, such as most species and cultivars of *Stipa*, *Miscanthus* and *Calamagrostis*, are well-behaved and deserve a warm welcome. *Stipa arundinacea* and *S. tenuissima* may self-seed, but unwanted seedlings can be hoed off.

Grasses can play an important role in our gardens. The flowering spikes of the taller ones, such as *Molinia caerulea* subsp. *arundinacea* 'Transparent' and *Stipa gigantea* (left), provide great height whilst remaining translucent, creating a net-curtain effect. Grasses' slender, elegant foliage and feathery flowers add softness to a planting scheme. Grasses bring movement into the garden, creating ripples when planted in larger masses and rustling in the breeze. Many dry gracefully to warm tones of yellow and rust, adding a statuesque note to winter scenery, particularly on frosty mornings when *Miscanthus* cultivars such as *M. sinensis* 'Malepartus' can be seen standing to attention.

With their simple elegance and boldness, grasses look stunning *en masse*. In smaller gardens, use them individually as feature plants, either repeating through a planting or singled out. Most grasses have sufficient personality to stand completely on their own. A single specimen of *Molinia* 'Windspiel' creates a sparkling fountain of very fine flower spikes, effortlessly reaching 2m (6ft). They arch gracefully when weighed down with dew drops, only to spring upright again when dry, and in autumn turn a coppery orange which fires up in late afternoon sunlight.

Planting styles

Herbaceous perennials can be planted in beds or borders by themselves, or mixed with bedding plants, shrubs or roses. They can be placed in bold groups, lingering drifts or in small clumps, all depending on the plant, its character and the effect you are trying to achieve. You can opt for a special colour scheme, using one, two, three or more colours, suiting your taste and the garden situation.

Traditional borders

Britain is renowned for its sumptuous herbaceous borders. They display carefully coordinated colour schemes, where plants blend with each other in seasonal succession. Popular at the start of the 20th century, herbaceous borders were usually part of larger gardens maintained by small armies of gardeners, and had to be stunning for six or eight weeks of the year only. Today, many garden owners expect the same of their gardens but have a great deal less space. The mixed border provides an answer,

offering a home for shrubs, roses and all kinds of herbaceous flowers, so that height, structure and interest can be provided the whole year round. There are herbaceous and annual climbers, which look particularly effective scrambling over and through shrubs and trees (see *Woody Plants and Climbers*, p.150). Annuals and bedding plants can be used to extend the season, filling gaps where early bulbs and perennials have finished.

Traditional mixed, and even more so herbaceous, borders can be hard work to maintain to the immaculate standards needed for them to look stunning. The secret is careful planning (see pp.164–169) and regular attention to keep everything looking at its best (see *Planting and Aftercare*, pp.170-173).

The Continental approach

To cut down on the labour and other requirements of a traditional herbaceous border, a new naturalistic, environmentally sound approach to herbaceous

Consider the environment
To a large extent, site and soil dictate planting style. Moisture-loving plants, such as the mimulus, irises and ferns below, must have damp conditions if they are to thrive and look "at home". Facing page: brown and sere, many plants, especially grasses, can give the winter garden a haunting beauty.

perennial planting was initiated in Germany during the 20th century. Having been further developed in the Netherlands and other European countries, it is broadly referred to as the Continental style.

This style is usually applied to large-scale planting, and is particularly suited to public spaces, but there is no reason why the basic principles cannot be used in small gardens.

Creating the look

The principles of the Continental style of planting, based on common sense, are easy to understand. Plants are chosen to suit the habitat. Unlike our traditional borders where plants are grouped simply for their aesthetic value, the aim is to create plant communities that will require management rather than maintenance. These communities are allowed to evolve and develop. Plant species can migrate, increase or decrease as circumstances change, just as they would in a natural setting.

> # Seek out the right plants for the provided habitat and plant them the way nature intended

Out of a permanent ground cover rise perennials, bulbs and grasses, planted in drifts, clumps or as solitaires. Plants, categorised by habitat, are used accordingly, regardless of geographic origins. Depending on whether they originate from woodland, woodland margin, meadow, steppe, rock, water margin or water they will be used in the corresponding environment in the garden.

Furthermore, by observing a plant's natural growth habit, it is possible to mimic its normal growing patterns. Certain plants, such as mulleins, scatter themselves about by shedding their seeds away from the plant. Others, such as Michaelmas daisies (*Aster*) have spreading rootstocks and are best planted in drifts or clumps. By imitating these reproduction processes a much more natural effect will be obtained than when perennials are planted in the traditional clumped manner. Finally, to discourage weeds, the ground is covered (as would be the case in nature) with a permanent mulch such

as gravel or crushed stone, or with ground-covering vegetation. For a naturalistic effect it is preferable to work with generous drifts of one or more intermingling species, repeating key plants.

Reducing the workload

This naturalistic style of planting does not depend on regular maintenance. Initial ground preparation should ensure freedom from perennial weeds. If plants have been chosen correctly to suit the site, there is no need to add soil improvers or fertilisers. Ground cover means weeding is reduced to a minimum once plants are established. The plants receive no fertilisers or nutrient-rich mulches, nor any additional watering, so they tend to be squat and sturdy, cutting out the need for staking. Apart from some selective deadheading, the plants are only cut down once a year, in the late winter. Many plants have attractive seedheads that provide homes during winter for predatory insects. Frosts enhance their architectural outlines, whilst their bonnets of snow give a cosy look to the winter garden.

It is important to monitor the progress of more vigorous plants or those that self-seed in great quantity. Remove as necessary to prevent them taking over completely.

ATTRACTIVE AUTUMN AND WINTER SILHOUETTES

Allium cristophii,
  A. sphaerocephalon
Achilleas
Asters
Calamagrostis x *acutiflora* 'Karl
  Foerster' ★, *C. brachytricha* ★
Eremurus robustus (foxtail lily)
Foeniculum vulgare 'Purpureum'
  (purple-leaved fennel)
Heleniums
Iris sibirica cultivars
Miscanthus sinensis cultivars ★
Molinia caerulea cultivars ★
Oenothera cultivars
Phlomis russeliana
Rudbeckia fulgida var. *sullivantii*
  'Goldsturm'
Sedum 'Herbstfreude',
  S. spectabile cultivars,
  S. telephium 'Matrona'
Solidago (goldenrod)
Stipa arundinacea ★,
  S. calamagrostis ★, *S. gigantea* ★,
  S. tenuissima ★

★ grass

Planning a flower bed or border

Whichever style of planting you opt for, it is important to adapt the planting to suit the space. Long or deep beds and borders framed by wide spaces and seen from a great distance need to be planted boldly, in generous groups so that the plants retain their identity, even from far away. Failing to do this will make the scheme look chaotic with little flecks of colour blurring into one another. Small planting areas in confined spaces are viewed intimately and should be planted accordingly. Use a wide range of plants in small numbers to create optimum variety.

Siting a border

The most versatile sites are free of shade from trees or tall buildings, to ensure the maximum amount of sunlight during the day, in summer and winter. Hedges provide a dark green backdrop for the flowers, whilst walls or fences offer support for climbers. They will also create a warmer, sheltered microclimate, where more delicate plants which normally would be classified as half-hardy (for instance *Melianthus major* or some of the more exotic euphorbias) should be able to survive the winter with little or no extra protection. A sheltered area also helps to reduce the need for staking taller perennials like delphiniums.

Character or solitaire plants

To avoid the whole bed looking fussy or "busy", repeat one or two instantly recognisable "character plants" at regular intervals. Particularly suited are those with striking large or vertical leaf shapes, or a bold, long-lasting flower. Sedums, grasses and daylilies (*Hemerocallis*) are useful aides. These plants will create a rhythm, and their repetition will enable you to draw all parts together into a coherent unity. A well-chosen character plant – for example, a grass

FLOWERS FOR CUTTING

Perennials

Acanthus mollis and *A. spinosus*, *Anaphalis triplinervis* ○, anthemis, aquilegias, astilbes, asters, *Bergenia cordifolia*, *Centaurea dealbata* ○, coreopsis, *Dianthus* (pinks), dictamnus, *Doronicum orientale*, echinops ○, eryngiums ○, *Gypsophila paniculata* ○, foxgloves, heleniums, *Helianthus* (sunflowers), heuchera, hostas, *Lathyrus latifolius*, *Liatris spicata*, *Limonium platyphyllum* ○, linaria, honesty (*Lunaria annua*) ○, lychnis, monardas, peonies, poppies: *Papaver nudicaule* and *P. somniferum* seedheads ○, phlox, physostegia, rudbeckia, salvias, scabious, *Trollius europaeus*, zantedeschia

Bulbs and tubers

Agapanthus, alliums ○, alstroemerias, crocosmias, dahlias, *Dierama pulcherrimum*, *Galtonia candicans*, lilies, narcissus, *Schizostylis coccinea*

Grasses

Cortaderia ○, molinias ○, stipas ○

○ suitable for drying

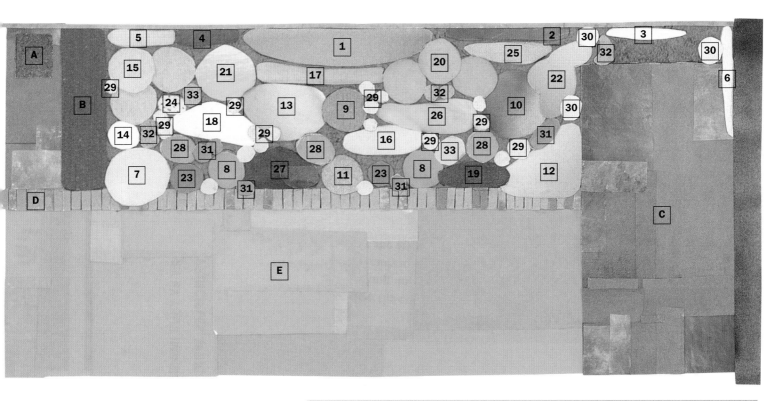

or hosta – can also stand as a solitaire, creating a focus in a planting scheme in a small bed, or in a well-chosen container.

Flowers for picking

Even in the smallest garden, it is possible to grow flowers that can be harvested (see panel, facing page). Some, such as lilies, are useful as scent providers in the house. Nasturtiums, calendulas, daylilies (*Hemerocallis*) and violets are edible and make wonderful decorations in salads (see also p.331 for more edible flowers). Many cut flowers on sale are produced using high inputs of pesticides. There is a wide choice of plants that you can grow organically to produce your own flowers for cutting, to be used fresh or dried.

Planting annuals and bedding plants

Some gardeners like to dedicate beds especially to bedding but, from an ecological point of view, they are best mixed in with other plants, even in the vegetable garden. Besides adding a colourful note, their flowers attract predatory insects such as hoverflies and lacewings, which control pests. Short-lived plants like forget-me-nots, cornflowers (*Centaurea cyanus*) and California poppies (*Eschscholzia*) are perfect gap-fillers around newly planted perennials, trees and shrubs.

A TRADITIONAL MIXED BORDER

This plan shows a traditional border, facing south-west and backed by a timber fence. Climbers clad the fence, while a few woody plants provide a permanent outline. The perennials are planted in drifts. The bulbs should be planted in the background, as they flower when the perennials are still low, so their dying foliage will be hidden by the emerging perennials as spring progresses.

KEY TO PLANTS USED

Climbers/wall shrubs
1 *Ceanothus* x *delileanus* 'Gloire de Versailles'
2 *Chaenomeles speciosa* 'Nivalis'
3 *Clematis armandii* 'Apple Blossom'
4 *Clematis* 'Perle d'Azur'
5 *Rosa* 'Maigold'
6 *Schizophragma integrifolium*

Shrubs
7 *Artemisia* 'Powis Castle'
8 *Caryopteris* x *clandonensis* 'Heavenly Blue' x 2
9 *Perovskia atriplicifolia* 'Blue Spire'
10 *Rosmarinus officinalis*
11 *Salvia officinalis* 'Purpurascens'

Perennials
12 *Alchemilla mollis* x 4
13 *Agapanthus campanulatus* x 3
14 *Aster pringlei* 'Monte Cassino'
15 *Campanula lactiflora* 'Prichard's Variety' x 3
16 *Coreopsis verticillata* x 5
17 *Doronicum orientale* x 3
18 *Echinacea purpurea* 'White Swan' x 4
19 *Geranium* x *magnificum* x 2
20 *Helenium* 'Butterpat' x 3
21 *Helianthus* 'Lemon Queen'

22 *Hemerocallis citrina* x 5
23 *Nepeta racemosa* 'Walker's Low' x 2
24 *Papaver orientale* 'Black and White'
25 *Pulmonaria saccharata* 'Mrs Moon' x 3
26 *Rudbeckia fulgida* 'Goldsturm' x 7
27 *Salvia* x *sylvestris* 'Mainacht' x 4
28 *Sedum* 'Herbstfreude' x 3

Bulbs
29 *Allium cristophii* x 20
30 *Cyclamen hederifolium* x 6
31 *Muscari azureum* x 50
32 *Narcissus* 'Tête-à-Tête' x 50
33 *Scilla siberica* x 100

Design elements
A Compost heap
B Beech hedge
C Terrace
D Brick mowing edge
E Lawn

Preparing a planting plan

Prepare a scaled drawing of the planting area. Using the same scale as for the plan, cut out circles of paper to represent the expected spread of each plant, so you will know how many plants fit into the area. Position the key plants and any shrubs or roses first, then place the larger perennials, which are often the late summer ones, gradually working down to the smaller ones near the front.

Avoiding gaps

Place shade-loving, spring-flowering woodland perennials and bulbs such as scented violets (*Viola odorata*) and lungwort (*Pulmonaria*) near the base of deciduous shrubs at the rear of the border. Many early spring flowerers, such as *Doronicum orientale* and bulbs, die back long before summer starts. Although their small size and early flowering period may tempt you to put them near the front, they will leave you with a gap for the rest of the year. If you place them further back in the border, taller plants can grow up in front of them, not only hiding the empty gaps but also masking the dying foliage. Likewise with an oriental poppy. Once it has finished flowering in early summer, it dies back

totally. Put a spreading, high-summer flowering plant like gypsophila next to it, allowing it to spread over the space left by the poppy. Remember that your aim is to have an even spread of colour and interest throughout the year. Use foliage plants to supplement, and complement, the flowers.

Doing your homework

When faced with the choice of many cultivars, there are several criteria to assist in making your choice. Hardiness and suitability to soil type and aspect are the starting point. Colour also plays an important role. Considering period and length of flowering enables you to provide colour during the months when little happens. Flowering height depends on whether you require a plant to attain a particular size to fit in with its neighbours. If height is not important, consider a smaller plant, as it is less likely to require staking.

Disease resistance is another important factor in any garden, let alone an organic one. Certain plants are more susceptible to diseases like mildew or rust. Nurserymen have been working hard to produce cultivars that are more resistant. If in doubt, opt for an old, well-established cultivar that has proved its

PLAN FOR A DRY SUNNY SITE

This plan is inspired by the naturalistic Continental movement and would suit a dry, sunny front garden, low in labour input but looking interesting the whole year round. Low woody plants such as lavenders, hyssop and cotton lavender (santolina) provide a permanent structure. Key plants, such as the fennel, grass and eryngiums, add seasonally changing interest. The whole area could be covered in a permeable polyester fleece before planting and afterwards the area mulched with gravel.

KEY TO PLANTS USED

1 *Aurinia saxatilis* x 3
2 *Crocosmia* x *crocosmiiflora* 'Solfatare' x 39
3 *Eryngium alpinum* x 11
4 *Eryngium variifolium* x 14
5 *Euphorbia characias* subsp. *wulfenii* x 4
6 *Foeniculum vulgare* 'Purpureum' x 2
7 *Hyssopus officinalis* x 7
8 *Lavandula angustifolia* 'Hidcote' x 12
9 *Lavandula* x *intermedia* Dutch Group x 14
10 *Molinia caerulea* subsp. *arundinacea* 'Windspiel' x 4
11 *Santolina pinnata* subsp. *neapolitana* 'Sulphurea' x 33
12 *Sisyrinchium striatum* 'Aunt May' x 17
13 *Thymus serpyllum* x 18

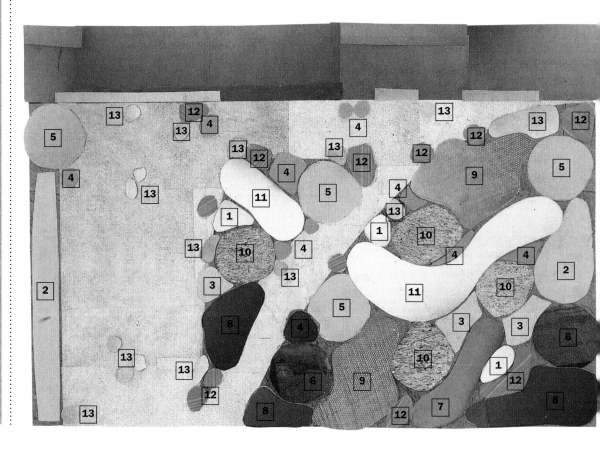

Winter's grace
Certain perennials, such as sedums, dry beautifully, creating attractive silhouettes that stand well into winter.

EVERGREEN PERENNIALS AND GRASSES

Acanthus mollis, A. spinosus
Achillea 'Coronation Gold',
　A. 'Moonshine', *A.* 'Taygetea'
Agaves
Ajuga reptans
Anthemis punctata subsp.
　cupaniana
Anthemis tinctoria
Armeria maritima
Artemisias (many)
Asarum europaeum
Bergenias
Campanula latiloba,
　C. persicifolia
Carex pendula
Cerastium tomentosum
Dianthus (pinks)
Dierama pulcherrimum
Doronicum orientale
Epimediums (many)
Eryngiums (some)
Euphorbia amygdaloides var.
　robbiae, E. characias, E. x *martinii*
Geranium x *cantabrigiense*
　G. macrorrhizum
Helictotrichon sempervirens
Hellebores
Heuchera
x Heucherella
Iris foetidissima
Kniphofia (red hot pokers –
　larger cultivars)
Lamium galeobdolon,
　L. maculatum
Limonium platyphyllum
Liriope muscari
Luzula sylvatica
Sisyrinchium striatum
Stachys byzantina
Stipa arundincea, S. gigantea
Tellima grandiflora
Verbascum olympicum,
　V. phoeniceum
Veronica gentianoides 'Variegata'
Viola riviniana Purpurea Group
　(syn. *V. labradorica*)

worthiness. Wildlife value is also important in organic gardens; choose plants providing edible seeds or berries, nesting material or shelter (see pp.186–197).

Improving an existing border

Many borders are a collection of interesting plants accumulated over years. Memories from gardens visited, presents from friends and family, have been popped into convenient spaces, with little regard for their neighbours. The best intentions of moving them into a more deserving position at a later date are soon forgotten. The result can be an uncoordinated collection without colour or texture associations, and an erratic spread of flowering through the seasons. It is worthwhile reworking such collections completely.

During the season, make a list of the plants, noting flowering height, colour and period of interest. Assess it to see which seasons are thinly represented and look for plants that will cover those periods. Many borders look stunning from early to high summer, after which they gradually fade into autumn. There are many wonderful perennials, particularly from the daisy family (Compositae, or Asteraceae), that are excellent colour providers during late summer and autumn. Heleniums, helianthus, rudbeckias and echinaceas are just a few.

To avoid staring at a neatly cut stubble field for the whole of late autumn, winter and early spring, plant early spring perennials and bulbs (see also Avoiding gaps, p.166) and some perennials that are evergreen (see right) or whose flowers are followed by attractive seedheads. Birds love the seeds and insects occupy the hibernation hotels provided by the empty stems and seedpods. The slightest frost will transform the garden into a magic winter landscape (see also Attractive autumn and winter silhouettes, p.163).

Having drawn up your planting plan, you can get to work. During autumn, winter or early spring, deal with existing plants. When the ground is not too wet, and there is no frost, lift plants that are to be moved or need dividing. Heel them in elsewhere, or cover with a damp sack or tarpaulin if they are to be replanted shortly. Be ruthless, discarding any that do not perform well or that you simply dislike. Take this opportunity to dig out any perennial weeds, too. Divide the crowns of plants you are keeping (see p.173) before replanting as this will rejuvenate them, and give you several more specimens.

Colour schemes

The perception and use of colour is very personal. What one person perceives as dark blue, another sees as dark green. A person may love pinks, whilst another hates them, preferring oranges. You are the person who spends most time with your garden, so choose the colour combinations that excite you. Although it is an exciting challenge to plant a border according to a very specific colour combination, simply following the colours dictated by the seasons can be equally rewarding.

Colour theories and their applications

As white light shines through a prism, it breaks up into the colours of the rainbow – red, orange, yellow, green, blue, indigo and violet. With the exception of indigo, the same colour arrangement is obtained when mixing various combinations of the primary colours of yellow, red and blue. Yellow and red make orange, red and blue produce purple and violet tones, whilst blue and yellow create green.

These colours, when brought together, form the "colour wheel". All the colour theories below draw on this concept.

Opposing or contrasting colours

Using the colours that lie opposite each other in the colour wheel, the following combinations can be found: red and green, blue and orange or yellow and purple. In gardening terms, these are usually restricted to yellow and purple, and blue and orange. The effect of using these combinations can be bold and lively if intense shades are used, whilst the opposite is achieved if pastel tones are selected.

Using the right proportions in these mixtures is vital. Although a wonderful flower colour, blue reflects little light, and needs to be used in association with a higher proportion of the lighter orange tones to provide a good contrast. Likewise, dark purple is a rich colour, but will only show to best effect when surrounded with twice as much refreshing yellow.

HOW COLOURS CHANGE WITH THE SEASONS

Spring starts off with masses of fresh colour. By early summer everything still looks fresh and crisp, with pure whites, clear pinks, true blues and reds dominating the scene. As summer progresses and the heat shimmers on the horizon, it is time for warm yellows, velvety reds and rusty oranges. By the time autumn arrives, the faded colours of asters and chrysanthemums announce that the year is coming to its close.

Throughout the year, the importance of green as a colour should not be underestimated. Evergreens give the garden much needed structure in winter, and throughout the growing season, the changing backdrop of greens forms a perfect foil for colourful flowers. Tapestries of colour both subtle and striking can be created using the many varying shades of foliage alone.

Adjoining colours

A more subtle arrangement can be achieved by using adjoining colours from the wheel. Yellow, orange and red are the so-called hot colours, whilst pinks, purples, blues and mauves are known as the cool ones.

Many gardeners tend to shy away from hot colours, preferring the soft pastel tones in the cool range. Warm colours have the ability to brighten up a dull day, bringing sunshine into the garden when the weather does not oblige. When using these hot reds and yellows, it is important to include the shades that lie between these two main colours, ie the range from pale to deep yellow, orange to dark red, mirroring this colour spectrum in flower and foliage where possible. Failing to do this can create harsh contrasts, as the linking colours are missing. The result would be like decorating a room in just black and white. The grey tones are the ones that would bring harmony into the space, removing the harshness.

Monochrome planting

Monochrome planting schemes are thrilling when good, but a bland anti-climax when not carefully orchestrated. The secret to successfully using one flower colour only is to introduce as many different shades as possible both in foliage and flower, to create the variety and contrast needed. When planting a white garden for example, make full use of silver, grey and blue foliage as well as pale, mid- and dark greens. Besides pure white, include cream and green-tinged flowers, and those that are white with an undertone of blue, pink, mauve or yellow. These colour variations, mixed with interesting foliage shapes, create variety and add a degree of apparent spontaneity that makes the garden more exciting and interesting.

All bar one

Although it is possible to have different colour schemes for each season, in reality it is hard to orchestrate such a display, particularly at the change-over stage between seasons. Depending on weather conditions, some plants may come into flower earlier or later than usual, upsetting the carefully planned succession. In small gardens it can be particularly difficult for a plant lover to adhere strictly to a

specific colour scheme. You may love cool colours, using only blues, pinks and purples, but at the same time have a soft spot for oriental poppies, with their huge, pillar-box red flowers. Try omitting one colour out of the spectrum, creating a display with the remainder. The awkward colours to blend are oranges and pinks – the notorious clashers. Remove shades of pink and reddish-pink and you are left with blues, purples, yellows, oranges and reds. Eliminating oranges and orange-reds, leaves blues, purples, yellows and pinks.

Complementary blues
The metallic blue of eryngiums can add a harmonious touch to a border of cool, blending colours, or a vibrant contrasting note when placed in amongst oranges and reds.

Planting and caring for herbaceous plants

When planting a new perennial flower bed or border, it is vital to start with a clean base, free from perennial weeds. If the area was previously lawn, chop up the turf and dig it into the soil. If time allows, grow a green manure (see pp.56–57) in the season prior to planting to improve the soil.

For a traditional herbaceous border, add a medium- to high-fertility organic soil improver such as compost or well-rotted manure at the digging stage – or spread it over the surface before planting. On poor soils you may also add a general slow-release fertiliser such as blood, fish and bone to help plant establishment and promote growth. Grasses and bulbs cope better with less fertile soil, requiring a low- to medium-fertility soil improver, if anything at all. Where a naturalistic herbaceous perennial scheme is planned, with plants selected to suit the existing soil conditions, no soil improvers should be required.

For annuals, the requirement is for a moisture-retentive soil rather than nitrogen-rich feeding that will encourage leafy growth instead of flowers.

Beautiful bulbs

Bulbs such as Allium giganteum *(here among the oat-like* Stipa gigantea) *can provide many years of colour, requiring little attention.*

Buying plants

Most herbaceous plants are transplanted into their final growing spot; hardy, and some half-hardy, annuals can also be sown direct.

Whether home-grown or purchased, plant out vigorous, healthy plants to give them the best start. You may be able to find organically grown plants and bulbs, but these are not widely available as yet.

Few nurseries sell bare-rooted perennials these days, although this is preferable from both an environmental and economic standpoint. When buying container-grown plants, those in smaller pots are usually the better buy. A full pot of herbaceous perennials can often be divided before planting, giving you more for your money.

Some tender perennials, such as F1 hybrid pelargoniums and busy Lizzies, can be grown from seed, but most are vegetatively propagated (see pp.106–107). If you have a light, frost-free spot, purchase small plantlets in early spring, and grow them on indoors until they can be planted out. When buying annual bedding such as lobelia, choose young plants that are not pot- or tray-bound. Once the roots have been restricted in this way, the plants tend to flower before they are fully grown.

Starting from seed

Starting from seed is a cost effective way of obtaining large quantities of plants, particularly annual bedding, and you can be sure that the plants are raised organically. Most hardy annuals, and many half-hardy annuals, particularly the large-seeded ones such as French marigolds (*Tagetes*) and nasturtiums, are easy and cheap to grow from seed. Raising your own plants also gives you the chance to try some of the more unusual annuals, such as the blue lace flower (*Trachymene coerulea*) or the green-flowered tobacco plant *Nicotiana langsdorffii*.

Herbaceous perennials from seed will take a year or two to reach flowering size. Raising perennials from seed is mostly restricted to true species; seed sown from those with a cultivar name is unlikely to produce a plant identical to the parent. Some perennials, such as aquilegias, will self-seed freely. The flower colour may bear no relation to the parent plant, but that is not necessarily a bad thing.

Most seed packets recommend a suitable sowing period for annuals, but it is worth experimenting with later sowings to fill gaps left by early-flowering perennials or bulbs. A display for late spring or early summer can be achieved from autumn sowings of hardy annuals such as love-in-a-mist (*Nigella*), which can be sown direct, or raised in modules and planted out after the ground has been cleared.

Many hardy annuals, such as calendula (pot marigold), *Phacelia tanacetifolia* and the poached egg plant (*Limnanthes douglasii*), will self-seed. Self-sown plants tend to be much sturdier, and flower earlier, than those you sow yourself. Unwanted seedlings can simply be hoed off, or transplanted to a more appropriate site.

Harden off young transplants well before planting out. If necessary, protect against slugs and late frosts.

Planting perennials and grasses

Bare-rooted plants are available only at certain times of year, but container-grown plants can be planted at any time. Soak the plants well, in a bucket of water, before planting, so that the compost is thoroughly wetted. Dig a hole large enough to take the rootball comfortably, loosening the soil at the base to help the roots penetrate to lower levels of soil moisture. Firm plants in after planting, and water in, even if the soil is moist. This will eliminate air pockets, ensuring the roots make good contact with the soil.

Planting bulbs

Bulbs prefer a well-drained, humus-rich soil. If you fear the position may be too wet, or the soil too heavy, incorporate plenty of sharp grit into the soil, or put some grit or coarse sand in the bottom of the planting hole. As a rule of thumb, plant bulbs at a depth twice that of the size of the bulb.

Avoid planting bulbs at the front of a bed or border. The dying foliage will be unsightly and it is vital that you allow the leaves to die back naturally for around six weeks after flowering, rather than cutting them off or tying them up in knots.

Bulbs are normally planted when dormant. Only the very small bulbs such as snowdrops and winter aconites are best transplanted while in leaf, just after flowering, as they can easily dry out. If you have to plant them as dry bulbs, soak them for 24 hours in lukewarm water prior to planting. For spring

displays, bulbs must be put into the ground in autumn; summer- and autumn-flowering bulbs are planted in spring.

Watering herbaceous plants

Where possible, select plants to suit the soil type, to cut down on the need for additional watering. Prepare the ground well before planting, breaking up any compaction to encourage extensive rooting. If appropriate, improve the soil's water-holding capacity by adding bulky organic soil improvers (see p.40-41) before planting, and keep the ground well mulched once planted up (see overleaf). If watering is needed, soak the soil thoroughly rather than giving it a light sprinkling. To reduce evaporation losses, water in the early morning. Alternatively, water in the evening, though this increases the risk of slug damage.

HARDY ANNUALS THAT SEED READILY

Many hardy annuals readily self-seed and perpetuate themselves year after year. They include poppies, pot marigolds (*Calendula*), eschscholzias, nasturtiums, antirrhinums and nigella, whose feathery leaves (above) decorate a late summer show of *Salvia patens* 'Cambridge Blue' and ageratums. These young self-seedlings, produced by summer-flowering plants, will survive winter and flower early the following year. You may need to thin them and, if you like, transplant some to other parts of the garden.

Reasons for mulching
After planting, apply a mulch. A deep layer helps both to conserve moisture in the soil and control weeds. Choose a mulching material that is in keeping with the style of planting.

RABBIT-PROOF PERENNIALS

Aconitum (monkshoods)
Astilbes
Campanula lactiflorae,
   C. latifolia
Cortaderia (pampas grass) ★
Crinum
Crocosmias
Foxgloves (*Digitalis*)
Epimediums
Euphorbias (★)
Hardy geraniums (★)
Helianthus (sunflowers)
Hostas
Hypericum (★)
Irises
Red hot pokers (*Kniphofia*)
Leucojum
Melissa
Nepeta (Cat mint)
Peonies
Poppies (★)
Veratrum
Vinca (periwinkle) ★

★ evergreen
(★) some species evergreen

Staking perennials

The flowers of the taller herbaceous perennials, such as delphiniums, may need support of some sort to prevent wind damage, or simply to stop them flopping over their neighbours. The need for support can be reduced by selecting shorter, stockier varieties or cultivars, or in the case of peonies, those with lighter, single flowers. Excess food and water will also encourage taller and less sturdy growth.

Traditionally, perennials were staked with bushy hazel twigs, put in place as the plants came into growth. They provide a sturdy and unobtrusive support that can be removed at the end of the season and composted. The twigs are placed around the base of the plant, and folded over the centre, at two-thirds of the final height, creating a dense network of fine branches that supports the flowering stems as they grow up through the twigs. Hazel twigs may be available from a local coppice wood, or from an organisation selling coppice products. Another option is to circle the plant with bamboo canes and then create a network of garden twine between them.

There are all sorts of proprietary supports available. Quick and easy to use are the galvanised metal or plastic circles with a grid, or L-shaped plastic-coated wires, which hook into each other. Suitable candidates for this type of staking are clump-forming perennials such as heleniums, phloxes and chrysanthemums. Large clumps that threaten to fall in one direction can quickly be propped up with hefty supports made from a metal stake, bent to form a semicircular hoop.

Some very tall plants, such as delphiniums, may require staking on an individual basis. Each stalk may have its own cane, supporting the bloom for most of its height.

Always use natural fibres for tying up plants. They are less likely to strangle a plant, and can safely be composted. To avoid eye injuries, top canes with purchased, or homemade, cane toppers.

Mulching and feeding

There should be no need to feed annuals and biennials. A suitable short-term mulch, such as leafmould or fine bark, will help to keep the soil moist. Cocoa shells are also suitable for annual plantings, but may be too rich for a fertile soil.

A much wider range of mulches can be used on perennial plantings to retain moisture, control weeds and feed the soil (see also pp.76-77). Choose one that is appropriate to the planting. Gravel, for example, would suit a dry, prairie-style bed, whereas bark or leafmould is more appropriate in a woodland setting. Always apply a mulch to moist, weed-free soil.

Fertile soils should be mulched with bark, leafmould or green-waste compost, whereas poorer ones may need a medium- or high-fertility material like garden compost, mushroom compost or well-rotted manure until fertility builds up. Alternatively, apply a dressing of a general organic fertiliser.

Avoid using the same mulch every year if it is likely to alter the soil pH. Mushroom compost, for example, tends to be alkaline, whereas pine needles would tend to acidify the soil.

Deadheading and cutting back

Regular removal of flowers as they die will help to keep annuals and biennials looking good, and may extend the flowering period. Avoid doing this with plants such as honesty and love-in-a-mist (*Nigella*) if you want to retain their attractive seedheads.

Removing flowers from some perennials, such as phlox, will encourage sideshoots to flower, and delphiniums, lupins and many achilleas may develop a second flush of flowers if cut back. Otherwise, resist the temptation to remove flowerheads as they fade. Be patient, and wait a few weeks to see if the plant produces seedheads that will add a decorative element during winter months, provide food for birds and small mammals and hiding places for insects. Dead flower stalks and leaves also protect plants against severe cold weather. Some, such as sedums, remain attractive right through winter. Others start rotting at the base, and will succumb to wet and windy weather. Have an occasional tidy up, removing unsightly material. What is left at the end of winter can be raked off.

Dividing perennials

While annuals and biennials must be grown from seed, perennials can also be propagated by vegetative means – division and cuttings. Splitting perennials reinvigorates the plant as well as producing more, identical plants, so it should be done regularly once plants are mature whether you need to increase your stock or not. Divide herbaceous perennials when plants begin to die back in the centre, look congested or show a reduction in vigour. This can be after two to three years in the case of vigorous plants, whilst those that are slow to establish may stay undisturbed for 15 years or more.

During autumn, winter or early spring, when the ground is not too wet to work and there is no risk of frost, lift plants and divide them up. Grasses prefer to be divided in the spring. With the exception of woody-based perennials, such as *Achillea* 'Moonshine', other perennials can easily be divided. Dig up a clump and insert two forks, back to back, into the middle. By pushing the two handles towards and away from each other, the roots are gradually teased apart. Repeat this until you have the number of plants you require. Really tough or fleshy rootstocks, such as hostas, may have to be chopped up with a spade or knife.

Once bulbs become overcrowded they do not flower so freely. Lift bulbs as they are dying back or when they are dormant. The clump can usually be teased apart by hand, and individual healthy bulbs can then be replanted.

Other ways of making more plants

Soft, stem-tip cuttings (see p.106) can be taken from early spring through to early summer from many perennials, including penstemons and veronicas.

With some perennials, including delphiniums and dahlias, you can take basal stem cuttings; in spring, pull new shoots carefully from the base, or crown, of the plant when they have four or five leaves, trim the base neatly and root them in small pots of free-draining cuttings compost.

Spring tidy
Dead or dried growth left on plants over winter can provide wildlife with food, shelter and nesting materials. In spring, clear away old stems and foliage and divide and plant new plants as necessary, then remove any weeds before mulching.

Lawns and lawn care

FROM PERFECT TURF TO MEADOW MIXTURES, ALL TYPES OF
LAWN CAN BE MANAGED ORGANICALLY

Clean sweep (facing page)
Autumn leaves need to be swept from the lawn to keep it healthy, but should never be burnt: pile or bag them up to make leafmould (see p.50). You can fashion a besom, or lawn broom, yourself by binding a bundle of twiggy prunings to a wooden shaft. An alternative if leaf fall is not too heavy is to mow over the leaves and leave them, shredded, in situ as a light mulch. They will soon disappear, being taken down into the soil by worms and other creatures.

DESPITE NEW TRENDS for decking and patios, for many gardeners the lawn remains an essential part of the garden, typically British, and something gardeners the world over try to replicate.

Lawns provide different things for different people, forming an important part of a garden's design, a foil for more colourful planting, access through the garden, or simply an area for play and relaxation. A lawn creates a sense of space, to be used or viewed as an open area that lets in light and provides views to the garden beyond. Managed organically, this green carpet can also contribute richly to the biological diversity of the garden.

For the organic gardener the lawn is as much an ecosystem as the pond or hedgerow. Nature abhors a monoculture, and "weeds" will soon try to move in to a new lawn. You may want a formal, striped, relatively weed-free lawn, or you may prefer a more relaxed green sward made up of a diversity of plant species. Both types of lawn can be created organically, though the former will require a lot more care and attention than the latter.

Organic lawns are exciting habitats in their own right, full of variety, and with great value to insects, birds and other wildlife. By accepting that a wide variety of different plants can exist together in a lawn in addition to grass, organic gardeners can create rich habitats that support a range of insects and other creatures. Adjusting mowing and cultural regimes can create meadows or wild areas, allowing flowers to self-seed, insects to feed and breed, and birds to forage for food and collect nesting materials.

PRINCIPLES OF ORGANIC LAWN CARE
- Choose grass seed to create the type of lawn you require, and to suit the location.
- Maintain good soil structure to promote grass growth.
- Increase frequency of mowing as growth increases, but never mow too short.
- Leave mowings on the lawn surface during summer to feed the grass.
- Rake out moss before it accumulates and smothers grass.

Grass roots level
An organic lawn containing a variety of grasses and flowers can become a useful habitat for insects and a feeding ground for birds.

Cutting the grass

The frequency and height of cut of an organic lawn should be adjusted to suit the use to which the lawn will be put. By varying them you can create a formal appearance, or a more natural look. With such a vast range of mowers available it is important to choose one that suits you and your lawn. The table below describes the main types, which use one of two cutting systems, either cylinder blades or rotary blades. For a small, level lawn a hand-powered mower is ideal, but for larger areas of grass, powered mulching mowers bring several benefits.

Cutting the lawn

Grass can grow year-round provided conditions are warm and moist enough, but you will only need to mow regularly between spring and autumn. Frequency of mowing depends on the speed of grass growth. During spring a weekly trim may be sufficient, but for neater lawns and play areas this can be increased to twice a week from late spring onwards. Grass growth decreases again in autumn, requiring less frequent mowing. In winter grass may still grow slowly, but conditions are usually too wet to mow, so it is best to avoid mowing except during prolonged warm and dry periods. The length of cut depends very much on the quality of grass in your lawn and how the lawn is being used. Long grass withstands drought better than shorter grass and also provides stronger competition for weeds. Most lawn areas can be cut to about 3cm (1¼in).

Family lawns used for play can be cut shorter, to perhaps 2.5cm (1in) in spring and autumn, but slightly shorter in summer. For a fine lawn finish grass can be cut very short, down to as low as 1.5cm (½in) in summer on level, quality lawns. Take care not to scalp the surface if the area is slightly bumpy, and always leave grass longer if weather is dry to help it withstand drought.

What to do with lawn clippings

Grass mowings are a good source of nitrogen, which is released as they decompose. Where possible, leave them on the lawn to feed the grass; otherwise recycle them in other ways. During the main mowing season, late spring and summer, mow regularly so that short clippings can be left on the lawn to rot down naturally. Consider investing in a mulching mower which cuts and then recycles finely chopped grass back down to the soil surface.

In early spring and autumn, and when the grass is long, clippings are best collected in the grass box on your mower. Left on the lawn, they can smother growth, cause discolouring, or encourage disease. They are a useful material for recycling elsewhere in the garden and should never be burned or discarded.

• Use them as a compost activator.

• Add to the compost heap (see p.44).

• Mix with autumn leaves in a leafmould heap.

• Use as a mulch round trees, shrubs, fruit bushes and vegetables.

CHOOSING A MOWER

Hand-powered	Powered cylinder	Rotary	Mulching mowers
Only use cylinder cutting blades (see right). Cylinder hand-powered mowers are cheap, efficient and economical to use on small formal lawns, providing extra exercise too. They are a good choice for organic gardeners who do not wish to use electricity or petrol. Hand mowers cannot cope with long grass, so mow frequently. Keep blades sharp and well adjusted.	All cylinder mowers use a cylindrical blade cutting against a solid base plate. This, combined with a roller, gives lawns that much sought after stripe. Powered cylinder mowers are usually larger and more expensive than rotary models (see right), and are the best choice for those on flat, even sites wanting to produce a quality lawn. Power supply: petrol, mains electric. (NB: All new petrol mowers run on unleaded fuel.)	Rotary mowers have a single blade rotating at great speed, and while most have wheels, hover versions are also popular. The latter can often cope with longer, rougher grass as well as slightly sloping sites. Rear rollers give a striped effect. Cheaper models do not collect clippings; it is usually worth buying one that does. Power supply: petrol, mains electric and battery models available.	This development of the rotary mower is an excellent choice for organic gardeners with large lawns. Grass cuttings are chopped finely, then blown down into the turf. Deposited close to the soil surface they quickly decompose, or are taken down by worms, to feed the soil. Mulching mowers have been shown to improve grass growth, recycling nutrients back into the lawn, and so decreasing the need for additional feeding.

Clear contrast
These grass paths may not be immaculately maintained, but look well-groomed in this context, forming neat strips of green carpet between "beds" of rough grasses and wild flowers.

Mowing patterns

Elaborate patterns can be created on large areas of grass by cutting to different heights to add interest and enhance design. Leaving some areas uncut can create wildlife habitats. Summer mowing is a regular task, and for some a time-consuming chore, so simply mowing paths or formal areas keeps these looking good while leaving some areas undisturbed for wildlife. Regular stripes running up and down a lawn are an effect created by using a cylinder mower or one fitted with a rear roller. Cutting alternately up and down the lawn, then again across it in both directions can produce an interesting checkerboard effect, too. With a little imagination quite elaborate patterns can be developed.

Edging the lawn

Neatly cut edges really set off a lawn, with regular trimming keeping them in good condition. Start by cutting a clean edge, using a spade or half-moon edge cutter. Long-handled shears allow you to clip edges without bending. Power tools, including adapted nylon line trimmers with wheeled heads that allow both horizontal and vertical edges to be cut, make light work of edging large lawns. They are fast and efficient, but larger models can be heavy for extended use. Most are electrically powered, but some use rechargeable batteries. Follow safety advice carefully, and wear goggles as debris can be thrown

up into your face. Where a section of lawn edge has become worn or damaged it can be easily repaired.

Repairing damaged edges

Use a spade to cut out the damaged section of lawn, removing a patch with a clean straight edge along the inside. Lift and rotate this through 180°, replacing the outer edge with the cleanly cut inner edge. Fill the damaged area, now within the lawn, with seed compost mixed with grass seed (see pp.182–3), and cover with clear plastic until the seed germinates.

Trimmed to shape
Shears will be needed to keep this play furniture made from turf-covered mounds in trim.

Improving the lawn

A lawn is made up of millions of plants and, as elsewhere in the organic garden, a good soil structure and adequate fertility are essential for vigorous growth. Strongly growing grass prevents weeds getting established, shrugs off pests and diseases, and withstands drought. Lawns are one of the few areas of the garden permanently covered with growth, preventing bulky organic soil improvers from being dug in. However, they can be applied as a "top-dressing", to build and maintain soil structure and health. Supplementary feeds may also be necessary.

Feeding the lawn

Feeding is not an annual necessity. If grass growth and colour is good then do not feed; you will only encourage more grass growth, which means more mowing! If growth is poor then apply a general organic fertiliser (see p.61) or a complete organic lawn feed over the whole lawn in early spring. Garden compost, spread thinly, can also be used if you have enough to spare. An application of seaweed meal or extract in spring and summer improves grass growth and colour. If growth continues to be slow, feed again in summer, and consider top-dressing in autumn to improve soil structure.

Liming lawns

Acid soil conditions encourage a buildup of thatch (see below) and cause poor grass growth. Acid soil also favours moss and certain other weeds, like sheep's sorrel. If the pH is below 5.5–6.0, lime the area to bring it up to around 7. Ground limestone or dolomitic lime (see p.61), evenly sprinkled over the lawn and gently raked in, is the appropriate organic treatment. Repeat annually until the required pH level is reached.

Scarifying

Thatch is the name given to the layer of fibrous material and organic debris which can accumulate on the soil surface in the depths of a lawn. It can prevent water reaching the soil, encourage diseases, and stop grass thickening up. Where necessary, remove thatch by vigorous raking, using considerable downward pressure. This process is known as

LAWN CARE TOOLS

Lawn rake (right)
Useful for scarifying – raking out accumulated debris and moss, which can build up over time. A lawn rake is also useful for collecting fallen autumn leaves.

Besom or yard broom
Used to scatter worm casts, spread a top-dressing and brush off morning dew before mowing.

Garden vacuums and wheeled leaf collectors
These make life easier when collecting autumn leaves from large areas. A lawn mower can also be used for this task, chopping the leaves as they are collected in the grass box before adding to the compost heap.

scarification. Powered scarifiers are also available to buy or hire. Scarifying is is best done in early autumn, when it will encourage the grass to thicken up by producing sideshoots. If large bare patches appear after scarifying, sow with grass seed.

Aerating

This process creates holes in the soil to allow air and water to penetrate. It can be very beneficial on compacted areas of lawn. It can also be very hard work, so only attempt it where compaction is a real problem. The best time to aerate a lawn is early autumn, when the soil is moist. If you use a hollow-tined aerator, which takes out a core of soil about 10cm (4in) deep, then once every three years should be enough. The alternative is to simply spike the grass, using a fork on small areas, or a powered machine on larger lawns. However, spiking does compress the surrounding soil, so a hollow-tined aerator is to be preferred, particularly on heavy soils.

Top-dressing

The sprinkling of various soil-improving materials onto the lawn surface is a process known as top-dressing. These materials are applied in layers thin enough for the grass to grow up through. For a greater effect, particularly on compacted areas of the lawn, use a hollow-tined aerator before applying the top-dressing, which can then be brushed down into the channels. Good soil structure encourages worm activity which in turn improves drainage. Worms also help take surface debris down into the soil.

Applying a top-dressing

Autumn and spring are both good times to apply a top-dressing. Start by mowing the grass to a length of about 2.5cm (1in). Do not cut lower or the dressing may smother the grass. If the lawn contains thatch, moss or large weeds then scarify before mowing. If you are going to aerate the soil with a hollow-tined aerator, do it at this point.

Sprinkle the top-dressing mix evenly over the whole area to a depth of up to 1cm (½in). Hollows can be filled slightly more, and by adding a top-dressing regularly through the year these can be firmed and filled to gradually level the lawn surface.

Brush or rake the top-dressing through the grass onto the soil surface below using a besom brush or stiff broom. Heavy rain will help do this if you time the treatments to coincide with wet weather.

MATERIALS FOR TOP-DRESSING

A top-dressing mix is made by mixing together a bulky organic material with loam and/or sharp sand or fine grit. Fine leafmould and municipal green waste compost are ideal bulky organic materials for autumn use. Richer materials like garden compost, if you have it to spare, can be used in the spring. The following general recipes can be adapted to suit your particular soil type. All quantities are parts by volume.

For heavy soils where the soil sits wet, or moss is a problem
3 parts sharp sand
1 part loam
1 part bulky organic material

For light, free-draining sandy soil
2 parts loam
3 parts bulky organic material

AT-A-GLANCE GUIDE TO SEASONAL LAWN CARE

Spring	Summer	Autumn	Winter
• Rake and scarify to remove moss and thatch.	• Continue to mow regularly, lowering the height of cut if growth is strong. Take care not to scalp lawns, leaving bare patches where moss and weeds can establish.	• Collect fallen leaves from lawns.	• Continue collecting fallen leaves which can smother grass.
• Aerate poorly drained lawns; brush sand into the holes to create drainage channels.		• Aerate compacted areas.	• If soil is acid, apply ground limestone to reduce acidity.
• At the start of the season set the mower blades high to leave grass longer. Adjust frequency of mowing according to grass growth.	• Leave grass slightly longer during hot, dry periods, and when drought is forecast.	• Scarify if necessary to rake out moss and accumulated thatch.	• Avoid walking on frosted lawns.
• Use a broom to scatter worm casts before mowing.	• Trim edges after mowing.	• Reduce frequency of mowing, and raise height of cut.	• Mow during very mild spells if grass is looking untidy.
• Cut new lawn edges, and repair damaged ones.	• Continue raking out moss.	• Apply a top-dressing mix to improve soil structure.	• Get mowers cleaned and serviced before storing away for winter in a dry place.
• Repair bare patches.	• Dig out weeds by hand, filling holes with potting compost.	• Fill in hollows in lawns by spreading potting compost or a top-dressing.	
• Feed lawns with an organic fertiliser or compost.	• If growth is poor, feed with an organic fertiliser to improve vigour and colour, and to increase resistance to weed infestations.	• Plant crocus and dwarf bulbs under turf for spring displays.	

Lawn problems

A single-species lawn is a virtual monoculture – a very unnatural state of affairs. Left to its own devices a lawn soon becomes a more varied community of plants, including coarser grasses and wild flowers, and much more attractive to a wider range of wildlife. Some gardeners spend a great deal of time preventing anything other than grass from growing in their lawns. Others take a more balanced approach, and are happy to tolerate "weeds" such as clover and daisies.

Some weeds can be positively beneficial. The roots of clover (see also left) fix nitrogen from the air in the soil, providing the plant with a ready source of this essential nutrient and so cutting down the need to add fertiliser. Grasses growing in close association with clover can take up small amounts of nitrogen released into the soil. Small-leaf clover resists drought well, remaining green in dry conditions. And how do you make a daisy chain without daisies?

Weed control

By following the advice on lawn care in this chapter, your lawn should reward you by growing strongly and resisting weed infestations. If weeds do become a problem various methods can be used.

• Remove individual weeds like daisies, plantains and dandelions by hand, using an old kitchen knife or special tool, such as a daisy grubber.

• Fill in holes left after removing weeds with soil or a potting compost, and sow grass seed into this.

• Avoid mowing too low; short grass offers less competition for weeds, and cutting too short can weaken grass, which will make it easier for weeds to invade.

• Scarify to remove debris and improve conditions for grass growth.

• Improve drainage with a hollow-tined aerator to prevent waterlogged conditions which harm grass and encourage moisture-loving weeds and moss.

Common lawn weeds

Different soils and situations encourage their own types of weeds. Identifying problem weeds can tell you something about these and help point you in the right direction to control them. Mind-your-own-business quickly spreads in moist, shaded areas. Daisies are a good indication of high soil alkalinity. They are more numerous on compacted soil, and on lawns mown very short. Clover grows well on poor soils. Feeding the lawn will tend to deter it (but see also The Value of Clover, left). Sheep's sorrel can become a problem where acid soil conditions prevail. Liming soil to bring soil pH back to neutral can help. Plantain and thistles grow where grass is thin or patchy.

Lawn pests include ants, leatherjackets and moles (see the A-Z of Plant Problems for advice).

How to control moss

Moss can develop for a variety of reasons. It relishes moist areas where drainage is poor, and will also thrive on drier soils where soil fertility is poor and acidity high. Moss colonises areas in shade, and spreads over soil where grass is mown too short. Rake out moss regularly with a lawn rake, each spring and autumn if the problem is bad. Bare patches should be re-seeded. Feed a poor lawn to strengthen grass growth, and set mower blades to about 2.5cm (1in) to avoid mowing too short. Improving drainage and making an acid soil more alkaline by applying ground limestone or dolomitic lime (see p.178) will also discourage moss.

Remember that moss is valued by birds for nest building, so consider leaving a mossy patch for them to obtain nesting materials, or leave piles of raked-out moss in an open position for them to collect.

Renovating a neglected lawn

If you need to renovate a neglected or overgrown lawn, a series of steps can be taken (see facing page) that should bring it back into fine form. Although this can be done at almost any time during the growing season it is best to tackle the job during spring, when grass is in active growth. Do not expect instant results, but in time you will bring the lawn area back under control. This approach should certainly be easier and cheaper than digging up the old lawn and sowing or laying a new one. One exception is where the old lawn is very uneven, with bumps and hollows over the whole area. In these circumstances a fresh start would be best.

LAWN RENOVATION

1 Cut long grass down. For this you will probably need a powerful rotary mower, setting the blades at their highest cutting height. Mow the area, collecting all the clippings. Lower the blade a little and mow the area again. Continue this routine until the long grass has been brought down to about 5cm (2in) in height.

2 Rake over the lawn to remove debris and congested growth. As this leaves a very untidy surface, mow the area again.

3 Dig out large weeds by hand. Check the soil pH with a kit. If it is below pH 5.5–6.0, lime the area to bring the pH back to around 7.

4 Fill any holes with potting compost, then sprinkle a pinch of grass seed over the top. This will grow over and spread to fill the hole.

5 Apply a suitable lawn fertiliser evenly to the whole area.

6 If areas appear waterlogged, use a hollow-tined aerator to make vertical holes up to 15–20cm (6–8in) deep over the area and brush sharp sand down into the holes to create drainage channels.

7 Repair any bare patches by raking over the surface with a lawn rake, removing stones, dead grass, weeds and debris, and loosening the soil surface. Add potting compost to level the surface if necessary. Sow a suitable grass seed mixture, and keep watered until germinated.

8 Over the coming weeks mow more often, at least once a week, and twice if possible.

9 Follow the annual care regime outlined on pp.178–9 to maintain the lawn in top condition, encouraging strong grass growth and discouraging weeds. Gradually fill hollows and remove bumps, and top-dress the whole lawn area each autumn.

LAWN PROBLEMS

Many lawn problems can be solved using cultural methods.

1 Worms benefit grass growth, but their casts can cause problems if trodden on and compacted. Disperse worm casts by brushing with a besom broom when dry.

2 Sitting water after heavy rain can be a sign of surface compaction or poor drainage. Try to alleviate it by hollow-tined aeration.

3 Prevent thick layers of moss building up by raking it out or by scarifying. Identify and remedy the cause to prevent it recurring.

4 Rosette-growing weeds like plantains cleverly avoid being damaged by mowing by hugging the ground. Hand-digging them out individually is the best solution. An old kitchen knife makes an ideal weeding tool.

Making a new lawn

Good preparation lays the foundations of a healthy lawn. Check out soil structure and fertility (see *Soil and Soil Care*, p.33-37) and make any necessary improvements a month or two in advance of laying the turf. Soil improvement is much easier to do at this stage than when the lawn is established.

The site should be firm, level and free from bumps and hollows, and free from perennial weeds. If it has been dug over, consolidate the soil by walking up and down the area on your heels. Rake the area to remove stones and lumps, levelling the surface by eye. A top-dressing of general organic fertiliser can be raked in at the same time.

Turf or seed?

Seed is cheaper than turf, involves less work and gives a greater choice of grass mixes, but:
• Weeds may overwhelm grass seedlings;
• It may be a year before the lawn can take hard use;
• Seed is more dependent on good weather.
Turf gives an immediate effect and the lawn can be used after a few weeks; there is also no need to protect turfed areas from birds or cats, as there is with seeded ground. However:
• Turf must be laid within 48 hours of arrival;
• The choice of grass mixes is limited;
• Quality turf may be hard to find, and expensive.

A new lawn from turf

The quickest way to create a lawn is by laying turf. You may not be able to find organically grown turf, but it is always worth checking with suppliers as the range of organically grown products is increasing all the time. It pays to invest in good quality seed-raised turf unless you are growing a natural meadow and do not mind coarser grasses and wild flowers. These days it comes delivered in narrow rolls rather than in squares. It must be laid as soon as possible, certainly within a day; it will soon deteriorate if left rolled up.

How to lay turf

Turf can be laid almost all year round, but is best laid during the moister spring and autumn months, when warm temperatures encourage growth and

Designing in practicalities
Areas of lawn used for access can soon show signs of wear (near right), so stepping stones or a path may need to be installed. Edges of lawns can be protected from damage by sinking an edging strip along them. These usually come as flexible rolls of plastic or metal, and must be pushed well down so that they will not damage the mower. Where border plants spill over onto the lawn (far right), consider laying an edging of bricks or paving slabs flush with the lawn surface. This will act as a path for wet weather as well as allowing the mower to be run over the edge of the grass and onto the paving when cutting the grass.

rainfall reduces the need to water. Start by rolling out one roll along a straight-edged board. Tamp down the turf with the back of a rake to settle it onto the soil. Once a single row is in place, put the board on the laid turf to distribute your weight evenly. Working from it, unroll more turf alongside. Butt up adjoining strips tightly, as turf can shrink slightly to leave gaps. Continue, staggering any joins so that you do not get a seam running across the lawn.

When creating a curve, do not stretch and bend lengths of turf, as this can result in a very uneven surface. Cut curves once turf is laid, with a sharp, long-bladed knife. Use a length of hosepipe to mark out a smooth curve; for a straight edge use a board as a guide, cutting with a knife or half-moon edger. Keep the final level of the turf slightly above any paths, paving or patio alongside it so that you will be able to run the mower right over the edge. Finally, draw a little soil up along edges to stop them drying out until the grass has rooted down and established. Once it has, the edge can be re-cut.

Aftercare

Turf takes a few weeks to root down into the soil. Until then it will need regular watering using a lawn sprinkler to prevent it drying out or shrinking, if daily showers do not do this for you. If shrinking does occur, fill gaps between adjoining strips with a seed compost and sow with grass seed.

Once it has settled, your new lawn will start to grow and require mowing. Wait until the turf has rooted down before walking over it with a mower. You can gauge this by tugging at an area to see if roots hold it down. Set mower blades quite high for the first few cuts, just topping the grass to keep it tidy. Lower the height once it has established.

A new lawn from seed

Sowing grass seed is the cheapest way to produce a lawn. You can choose a seed mix that suits growing conditions and the use to which the lawn will be put. You can also sow wild flowers and clover at the same time to create a richer environment that will be more attractive to wildlife. Sow in the damper months of spring or autumn, although lawns can be sown in summer in wetter areas. When preparing the site, make sure the finished surface is firm and level.

Complete soil preparations well before you intend sowing, to allow time to create a "stale seedbed". Leave the area bare for a few weeks, and weed seeds close to the soil surface will germinate. If the weather is dry during this period, water the soil to encourage weed germination. Hoe the weeds off just before sowing the new lawn, leaving a fine tilth on the surface. This removes many weed seedlings that would otherwise have competed with the grass.

How to sow

To sow seed evenly it helps to divide up the area into square metre (sq yard) plots with string or long canes. Measure out sufficient seed for a single plot, then divide it into two lots. Sprinkle the first half evenly over the soil in one direction, then sow the second batch at right-angles to this. Mixing the seed with sand can help you to sow more evenly, as you can see where you have sown. Gently rake the seed into the soil surface to cover it slightly and hide it from birds. On small areas consider spreading netting over the area to keep off birds until the seed has germinated. Always sow at the recommended rate given on the seed box. Sowing too thickly results in weak, congested grass growth; sowing too thinly leaves gaps where weeds can get a hold.

Aftercare

If the weather is dry, irrigate with a lawn sprinkler to keep the soil surface just moist. During warm weather grass seed should germinate within 14–21 days. Bird protection netting can then be removed, but continue irrigating gently if conditions turn dry. Try to avoid walking over newly emerged grass until it is a few centimetres tall. Check over the area regularly and pick out any emerging weeds by hand. Once the new grass has grown to about 6–7.5cm (2½–3in) it can be given a light trim. If you have a mower with a rear roller, run this up and down to gently firm the new grasses and settle the soil surface. About three days later the grass will have grown up straight again and can be mown. Only mow lightly, setting the blades high to trim off the very tips of the grasses. Over the coming weeks cutting frequency can increase and the blades be lowered for a shorter cut. Regular mowing encourages grasses to develop new growth from the base, eventually producing a thicker and more robust lawn.

GRASS SEED MIXTURES

Beautiful lawns are made up of many different grasses, each offering different growth characteristics which together make a dense green sward. Choosing the right lawn seed mix of grasses is important in the organic garden. If you are sowing a new lawn from scratch then you can select a blend of different grass types that will suit the conditions of the area, the use the lawn will be put to, and the finish required. Hard-wearing mixes can be chosen for lawns used for football and play, while different mixes would be better for a shaded site, or for growing into a fine quality lawn. Grasses grown in meadows or left longer to flower and seed will attract a variety of insects and butterflies.

Rye grass
Hard-wearing perennial grass that provides a good utility lawn, withstands a certain amount of drought and looks superb.

Red fescue
Both slender and creeping varieties of red fescue grow strongly to provide thick growth which is hard-wearing and reasonably tolerant of drought.

Meadow grasses
Smooth-stalked varieties are used in blends for fine lawns.

Other grasses
Chewings fescue, browntop bent and crested dog's tail are just some of the other grasses used in lawn seed mixtures. By choosing blends which combine grasses with a variety of characteristics you will produce a lawn that looks good and performs well in your chosen situation.

Country casual

The tranquillity of a traditional flowering meadow can be recreated in all but the smallest gardens.

CUTTING CONSIDERATIONS

Always aim to cut meadows on a sunny day after a period of dry weather. The process of cutting and raking away the debris is designed to release as much seed back onto the soil surface as possible. In addition to ensuring that the seedheads of the majority of flowering plants are ripe and splitting, a period of dry weather will make the whole process easier.

Small areas can be cut by hand using shears. On larger sites the growth can be scythed. There is a knack to using a traditional scythe, with its long, curved blade, that can soon be learned. Today the gardener is more likely to use a nylon line trimmer for the job. Petrol models are available for hire, and are especially useful for cutting growth on banks and uneven sites, although the noise is a drawback.

Meadows and wild flowers

For the organic gardener keen to encourage wildlife into the garden, an area of rough grass and flowers is a rich habitat enjoyed by butterflies, bees, spiders, and other insects, invertebrates and small mammals. Compare a meadow to a clean-cut lawn and you will see how one is teeming with life while the other is bereft of visible activity.

You can simply leave an area of grass uncut and see what grows. Grasses and flowers (plants otherwise regarded as weeds in this situation) will develop, flower and set seed. The grass must be cut at some point, or else shrubby plants will start to move in. Cutting at the correct time ensures that seeds are released and scattered to grow another year. To encourage spring-flowering species, cut from midsummer; to encourage summer-flowering species, delay mowing until early autumn.

Leave the mown grass on the surface for two or three days to release any ripe seeds, then rake away all the debris, which can be composted. Removing the cut grass helps to keep the fertility down, allowing wild flowers to flourish.

The floral content of these rough weedy lawns can be enriched by clearing small areas and sowing or planting specific wild flowers. From field scabious to primrose, yarrow to clover, a wide range of flowers are available to suit different soils and situations, and to flower at different seasons.

Sowing a wild flower meadow

Numerous seed mixes are available that contain different selections of wild flowers and grasses, suited to different soil types and situations. Ideally choose species that are native to your locality. Do not collect seed from the wild. You could perhaps collect seed from a friend's meadow planting. Sowing this fresh seed straight away often results in far better levels of germination than packet seed.

Wild flowers grow best on poorer soils, not on cultivated and enriched garden soil. The poorer the soil the better, as this will help prevent invasion by vigorous weeds such as nettles and docks, and also reduce the vigour of the grass, which can be very competitive. If a new wild flower lawn is being sown, start by digging over the area, turning over the richer topsoil and burying it beneath poorer subsoil. If your topsoil is deep, remove it and replace it with poorer soil.

Firm the soil down and rake level as you would when preparing a new lawn, but without adding any compost or fertiliser. Leave the area for a few weeks after preparation, then hoe off any germinating weeds to produce a stale seedbed (see also p.183) to sow into. Wild flower seeds and grasses can be broadcast over the area and raked into the surface, or plugs of wild flowers planted out between areas of sown grass. New meadows are best established in spring, sowing seed at the specified rate, and keeping areas watered until seeds have germinated and seedlings established.

Alternatives to a traditional meadow

If your soil is very fertile, a wild flower meadow is unlikely to do well. For a similar visual effect, consider instead sowing a "Farmer's nightmare" mixture of annual cornfield weeds such as cornflowers, field poppies and corn marigolds, combined with barley seed (see also p.194). This gives a magnificent spring

and summer annual display, but the ground will be bare over winter. As long as the plants are allowed to seed, and the ground is gently dug over each year in early spring, one sowing should last for many years.

Another way to give flowering interest to an existing lawn is by adding small bulbs (see right).

Raising wild flowers as plug plants

Flower seed can be expensive to buy, especially if you have a large meadow to develop. While a basic seed mix may provide a good general meadow it is worth choosing a few other, more choice wild flowers to raise separately in "plug" or module trays. These should be grown on until they have reached a larger size before planting out, rather as you would summer bedding. Planting out in clumps or wide drifts will add character to the meadow, although the greater the diversity of plant species included in the meadow, the wider its appeal and value to wildlife. It helps to raise and keep a few plants in reserve to fill gaps where the germination of seed sown directly was poor.

Never dig up plants from the wild, however successful they appear to be in their natural habitat.

BULBS IN GRASS

Autumn is the ideal time to plant bulbs under turf to create spring flower displays. These will enrich the lawn environment with blooms that are attractive to many insects. Crocus, snowdrops, snake's head fritillaries (above) and dwarf narcissus grow up well through turf to produce a colourful seasonal display. Some can be planted using a bulb planter, taking out a core of soil and turf, dropping in the bulb, then replacing and firming down the plug. Smaller bulbs can be spread out over an area after peeling back the turf just 2.5cm (1in) or so deep. Loosen the soil slightly, space out the bulbs, then fold back and water down the turf.

After flowering in spring, allow six weeks before cutting down the leaves of bulbs. This foliage is needed to produce food for the bulb to ensure a repeat flowering performance the following year.

Aim to give the lawn a trim in late autumn, or even during winter if conditions allow, so that bulbs grow up through a neat, low green carpet.

Meadow mowings
Leave mowings on the surface to dry out, then shake them well to release their seed as you collect them up.

Gardening for wildlife

ORGANIC GARDENS ARE AT AN ADVANTAGE WHEN IT COMES TO ATTRACTING AND VALUING WILDLIFE

Inviting in the guests (facing page)
You can attract a variety of beautiful visitors such as birds and butterflies into your garden by creating the right habitats and conditions for them.

A GARDEN TEEMING WITH WILDLIFE is a pleasing and relaxing place to be – good for your well-being and for the feelings it brings of continuity and inter-action with the wider world. Butterflies and birds are as much of a delight as flowers and fruits, but lesser creatures can be equally stunning and are a vital part of the natural food chain.

Safe havens

With the continuing increase in urban sprawl and the intensification of modern farming, which places great reliance on the use of pesticides, the private garden has become vitally important as a safe habitat for wildlife. It is estimated that the collective area of domestic gardens in the UK now covers twice the area of existing nature reserves. More and more wild creatures are finding in gardens not just a refuge but their only chance of long-term survival.

Organic gardens have a head start when it comes to attracting wildlife as pesticide use is minimal. Natural predators and parasites, which keep pests and diseases under control, in turn provide food for larger creatures. The use of bulky organic manures encourages a thriving microflora and fauna in the soil – and these in turn are the first vital link in the food chain. There is no need to be concerned that more wildlife will result in more pests: studies have shown that organic farms support a greater abundance and diversity of wildlife species than conventionally managed farms, and there is, if anything, a decrease rather than an increase in the number of pests.

Creating the right conditions

With a little extra planning you can easily increase the range of creatures visiting, and living in, your own garden. If you are really keen to promote the right conditions for wildlife you can create a mini-nature reserve, with every plant carefully selected for its wildlife value. You can also incorporate plenty of wildlife-friendly ideas into an existing garden without having to make it look untidy or wild. A wildlife-friendly garden can look just as good as, or even better than, any other garden plot.

The basic requirements of all the creatures that visit your garden are the same: food, somewhere to live and breed in safety, and water for drinking and bathing. This chapter describes how you can provide these necessities of life in your garden to support a diverse range of creatures.

Don't expect too much too soon; you can only create the most suitable conditions for visits by wild birds, beasts and insects – not drag them into your garden by force. Despite your best efforts, you may find totally different species are drawn to your garden than those you originally intended to attract.

CREATURES GREAT AND SMALL

Birds and small mammals are obvious delights for the wildlife gardener, but smaller creatures can be just as beautiful and fascinating to observe. These are just some of the invertebrates that might visit a summer garden:
Dragonflies (top) **and damselflies** will fly some distance from water. Watch some of the males defend their territory against any other insect – even butterflies.
Shield bugs (centre) feed on grasses, wild legumes and shrubs. They are often devoted parents.
Velvet mites, tiny red creatures, are garden friends. They swarm on hot, dry pavements and eat pests such as red spider mites.
Violet ground beetles (see p.35) are one of the most spectacular ground beetles, with iridescent purple edges to their smart black wing cases.
Crab spiders (bottom) have as many distinctly different colours as birds. Females are often paler but both sexes can change colour according to their background.

Making wildlife feel at home

Wildlife refuge
*Though we do not understand all the
intricacies of the natural world, keeping
your garden free of harmful chemicals
and providing the right habitats ensures
that as many creatures as possible, such
as this female stag beetle, can continue
to share your garden.*

Every creature needs somewhere safe to rest, sleep and breed, so it makes sense to provide some shelter for the wildlife in your garden. This may be in the form of a purpose-built home, such as a nest box (see pp.191–2), but creatures will also live very happily in compost heaps, under mulches and in log piles, as well as being quite content to make their home in or under a hedge.

Before you rush to dig a pond or put up a bat box, first take a look around your garden and identify the areas that are already attractive to wildlife. Then earmark any other areas that, with a little change in management, could be improved upon.

Hedges and edges

A hedge is an excellent place for creatures to take shelter from predators or the weather, court, mate and feed, as well as build a nest. In windy winter conditions a hedge is warmer and stays dry at the

base. A hedge base full of leaf litter is also a rich food source for insect eaters – not only birds but also hedgehogs, voles and shrews.

To avoid disturbing any nesting birds, hedge cutting should be delayed until mid- to late summer. Fruiting hedges can be left uncut until the birds have eaten the berries. The base of the hedge should remain undisturbed; there is no need to rake out fallen leaves.

If your garden is small, try creating a "fedge" along your boundary by growing ivy, honeysuckle, and clematis through a chain-link fence, or clothe your walls and fences with climbing plants. Train the plants so that the base of the support is well covered, and do not trim growth back too closely. Dense evergreen climbers make the most effective wildlife refuges. Many small birds, such as wrens and tits, will hide in thick ivy on cold winter nights. Tawny and little owls appreciate tall, ivy-clad trees, and if some of the branches are decaying, woodpeckers will welcome both the source of food and possible nest-sites. Leave dead branches in place if they are not in immediate danger of falling so that they, too, can provide food for insects and shelter for birds.

Wildlife corridors

Creating wildlife corridors through your garden will enable smaller creatures to come and go while remaining hidden from their predators. Thick shrubs and hedge bases provide excellent protection, but ground-cover plants linked to areas of longer grass and herbaceous beds will also provide good cover for creatures on the move. If you erect a fence, try to raise it off the ground a little so that small animals such as hedgehogs can squeeze underneath.

Lawns

To create the best variety of habitat, alternate areas of mown grass with patches of longer grass. Birds such as song thrushes and starlings need open areas of short turf to feed on, while amphibians require longer grass. Try to leave uncut grass wherever you can without making things look too untidy – along the base of an informal hedge, for example, or under trees. A neat path of short-mown turf through slightly taller grass that grows next to uncut areas of

NEAT vs. NATURAL

One of the harder aspects of
wildlife gardening is to strike a
balance between super-tidy and
messy designs. A happy medium is
one of beneficial neglect with a
careless abandon in the planting –
think of a trailing wild rose bush
sprawling its stems across long grass,
a group of sunflowers left to self-
seed, or a drift of cowslips romping
unchecked through a lawn.

But the nostalgic country or
cottage style of gardening is
not the only option with wildlife
appeal; there's no need for your
garden to look neglected or old-
fashioned. More modern styles
of "meadow" planting, with
drifts of herbaceous perennials
threading through grasses (see also
pp.162–163), are not only visually
spectacular but benefit wildlife as
well. Flowers and seedheads provide
food for butterflies, goldfinches and
other seed-eating birds, and leaving
the seedheads over winter will
give birds a long-lasting "store
cupboard", as well as being easy
on busy gardeners.

Nooks and crannies

If you want to encourage creatures into your garden, make a leafmould heap or leave a log pile in a sheltered spot (above) for them to nest in. Frogs, hedgehogs, newts, beetles and timber hoverflies may all make use of a cool, dark, probably damp site. By contrast, weasels, shrews, wood mice, toads, slow worms, spiders and even pupating butterflies and moths will be attracted to the crevices and gaps in sunny drystone walls (above right) and stony banks.

vegetation can add structure to an area that might otherwise look unkempt and neglected. Do not cut or mow all areas of long grass on the same day. If you have to cut a large area of rough grass, start at one end and work inwards from one side to allow creatures an escape route. Never cut grass in a circle – mice and frogs become trapped like rabbits in a cornfield.

Sheds and compost heaps

Garden sheds can provide useful hiding places for different species. Butterflies may creep inside to hibernate, so leave the shed door open on sunny autumn afternoons and shut it late in the evening. Remember that garden birds will sometimes nest in the most unlikely places; they might appreciate your shed as much as you do!

If you regularly make a leafmould heap, you may well have a hedgehog sleeping in it for at least part of the year. Leave a gap in the chicken wire, or whatever supports your leaf heap, so that a hedgehog can get in and out easily.

Grass snakes occasionally lay their eggs, and hibernate, in compost heaps. If you are privileged enough to have snakes visiting your garden, and want them to stay, make a large compost heap in a sunny position. Snakes, like swallows, often return to the same nest site year after year but they need the heat of decaying vegetation to hatch their eggs, so

you will need to rebuild the heap every year. The safest times to disturb the heap are during early October, or from mid-April to mid-May when the snakes have emerged.

Under cover

Small creatures love to lurk under mulches. A wood-chip or bark mulch will shelter beetles, centipedes and the like, while thicker mulches of hay and straw may be frequented by frogs, toads, shrews, spiders and newts. In winter try to leave some mulch undisturbed for creatures to hibernate in.

Make mounds or banks in a sunny part of the garden by piling up rubble and packing it loosely with topsoil, leaving small gaps between stones. Not only is this a good site for attractive plants that need good drainage, such as thymes, sea campion (*Silene maritima*) and rock roses (*Helianthemum*), but it is also the best habitat for hibernating amphibians or, in summer, basking lizards. Weasels also love to hide inbetween stones, though they may also like short lengths of drainpipe in dry, undisturbed garden areas.

Hedgehogs prefer a more substantial log-pile, with the base logs stacked at least 10cm (4in) apart. Position the logs in a sheltered spot, under trees or thick shrubs where they will not be disturbed. The hedgehog will gather dry leaves to make its nest, so make sure there are some inviting leaves close by.

Buying and building shelters

You can buy a variety of purpose-built boxes for a whole range of creatures to shelter and raise a family in. The design can be simple or intricate, as long as it fulfils the needs of whatever it is you aim to attract. The residents are unlikely to be fussy.

Hedgehog and frog boxes

Hedgehog boxes can be particularly important in urban areas where shelter is scarce. Finding a suitable shelter for winter is hard in neat gardens, so keep hedgehogs happy by siting a box (below) under a hedge or thick shrub where they will be undisturbed. Frog boxes can also be of benefit in a garden: place these in a north-facing, shady spot out of the wind.

Bird boxes

Even if there are already many suitable nest sites, a bird box may encourage a normally shy species of bird to stay on your plot. Bird boxes can be made of untreated wood or "woodcrete" (a proprietary concrete/sawdust composition). The latter version is useful if your garden has predatory squirrels or even woodpeckers with a taste for young birds. All bird boxes should be positioned with an easy means of access for you to be able to clean the box out periodically. Site your bird box on a warm, sheltered wall, tree trunk or shed, well away from predators, rain and direct sunlight. Cats can climb up and reach into boxes from all sorts of unlikely angles, as can grey squirrels, so position the box carefully. If there are a lot of cats about it may be worth having several different designs of nest box in your garden. Predators often learn that a particular box pattern may contain food – chicks or eggs.

> ## A bird box may encourage a normally shy species of bird to stay on your plot

Ideally, bird boxes should be cleaned out every autumn. Remove any nest material and rinse the box out with hot soapy water to keep it fresh for the next visitors. Bird fleas do not attack humans, but it is probably a good idea to wear gloves. Allow the box to dry thoroughly before closing it up again.

WHAT BOX FOR WHICH BIRD?

The size of the entrance hole determines which species can, and cannot, use a bird box.
• Boxes with entrances 2.5cm (1in) in diameter are suitable for blue, marsh, willow and coal tits; wrens and goldcrests may occasionally use it for shelter rather than nesting in.
• Entrances 2.8cm (just over 1in) in diameter will attract the same birds listed above, plus the pied flycatcher.
• Entrances 3cm (1¼in) in diameter are appropriate for all the birds mentioned above, plus the great tit and tree sparrow.
• Robins, wagtails and fly-catchers prefer an open-fronted box sited low down in a hedge bottom or at the base of a thorny shrub.

Prefab house
Ready-made hedgehog boxes can be bought in a variety of designs. Site one under a hedge or shrubbery. Put bacon rinds in the box in late summer to encourage a hedgehog to investigate.

FIVE-STAR ROOMS

These sophisticated ready-made boxes are designed to house (from left to right) lacewings, mason bees and bats. Though blue tits may use a bee box as a "feeder", don't panic – they will be unable to reach the deeper layers of eggs in their self-contained cells. The tiny bat boxes (about 5cm/2in square) should be positioned high above the ground. If you live close to an old-fashioned yellow sodium street light, you may be able to watch the bats feeding on any insects attracted to the light.

Insect hotels

Insects also appreciate having somewhere to live in winter. Ladybirds, earwigs and other insects hibernate naturally in tufts of rough grass, dead leaves and hollow plant stems, so delay cutting down flower stems and clearing your borders until the spring.

You can buy neat wooden boxes for lacewings to hibernate in, or make a simple insect "hotel" from a plastic bottle and some corrugated cardboard (below).

Making your own lacewing hotel

• *Saw the bottom off an empty 2-litre soft drink bottle (it does not need to be washed out).*
• *Cut a piece of corrugated cardboard about 80–100cm (32–36in) long, roll it up and slide it inside the bottle.*
• *Push some thin wire through both sides of the bottle base to stop the cardboard falling out.*
• *Tie a string around the bottle neck, leaving the top on, and hang the "hotel" up in a sheltered position. (In the UK, hang the bottle in place by the end of August).*

Plastic food containers can also be pressed into service for housing ladybirds and other predators. Make a series of small holes in the lid of a square tub with a knitting needle and stuff the inside with straw, then place the tub on its side under a bush or large herbaceous plant to keep it dry over winter.

Bees, especially orchard mason bees (*Osmia*), which are useful early season pollinators, can be given extra help with supplementary shelter. They will happily colonise holes drilled in blocks of wood or paper drinking straws stacked in a waterproof box, or you can buy special bee-boxes. Mason bees emerge early, so the boxes need to be erected in early spring before the apple buds burst. An open, sunny, preferably south-west-facing site is essential.

Bat roosts

Bats are quite common in built-up areas, even in large cities. They need temporary and permanent roosts. A pipistrelle can eat up to 2,000 small insects, such as midges, per hour, so they are good to have about!

A bat box should be made of untreated timber and have rough wood inside so the bats can happily hang upside down. It should be sited as high as possible – at least 3m (10ft) above ground level, away from bright lights and prevailing winds. There should also be plenty of air space in front of it. Planting night-flowering annuals nearby will encourage moths and other insects to feed, which will in turn attract the bats. Try night-scented stock (*Matthiola bicornis*) or tobacco plants (*Nicotiana*). As with bird boxes, the bats may take a while to settle in.

Food for all

Wild birds in gardens are often very reliant on food put out for them because supplementary feeding encourages a larger population than the habitat can naturally support. Once you have started to feed birds you must continue, as they will always come to the bird table for food rather than searching for their own during the short winter days.

Feed the birds with black sunflower seeds, fat balls and mixed seeds rather than peanuts, which can contain harmful aflatoxins. Keep bird feeders as clean as possible – food poisoning is not confined to humans! If possible, move the feeder's position every few months to avoid a build-up of harmful bacteria.

It is better, wherever possible, to grow plants that will supply birds with their own food source rather than develop their over-dependence on humans. Berried shrubs attract a number of species, as do seed-heads and grasses; leave some herbaceous plants to run to seed. Sunflowers, rudbeckias and echinaceas make excellent garden plants as well as good food for many garden birds – hang up an old seedhead for blue tits. Once birds find a regular food supply they return regularly, which is greatly to the gardener's advantage. It has been estimated that a song thrush will eat over 10,000 caterpillars, flies, snails and other pests during a single breeding season. Note, however, that many cultivated fruits are as attractive to birds as they are to humans.

Birds are not the only creatures that come to a garden to feed. An organic garden is likely to provide rich pickings for both vegetarian and carnivorous wildlife visitors of all shapes and sizes. With a little extra thought you can provide them with even better fare. Natural foods that can easily be included on your menu for wildlife include nectar, pollen, greenfly, caterpillars, slugs, berries and seeds.

Flower food

Flowers are not only pleasing to our eyes; they are attractive to many insects, which flock to feed on the energy-rich pollen and nectar they supply. In turn, these insects will feed birds, bats and other predators. Flowers grown to feed wildlife do not have to be native wild flowers – cultivated blooms can be even more nectar-rich and will extend the season. Many of the best-suited flowers for insects

SHRUBS WITH FRUITS OR SEEDS FOR BIRDS

Alder (*Alnus*): tits, especially long-tailed tits; finches; tree sparrows.
Barberry (*Berberis*): thrushes; flycatchers; finches; tits; nuthatches.
Bilberry (*Vaccinium*): whitethroats; greenfinches; chaffinches; starlings; sparrows.
Daphne: blackbirds; flycatchers; finches; whitethroats.
Elder (*Sambucus*): robins; thrushes; blackbirds; dunnocks; wrens; tits; starlings; pigeons.
Juneberry (*Amelanchier*): starlings; whitethroats; finches; robins.
Privet (*Ligustrum*): tits; hawfinches; greenfinches; sparrows; song thrushes; robins.
Spindle (*Euonymus*): thrushes; blackcaps; tits, including long-tailed tits; finches.

WILD FLOWERS FOR WILDLIFE

A meadow (see also pp.184–5) is one of the richest habitats of all for wildlife, containing not only flowers but also the grass species that are essential to the life cycle of many butterflies (see facing page, below right).

The rich insect population will in turn attract small mammal predators such as voles and shrews, which can forage in safety amongst the long growth. Never isolate a patch of meadow in the midst of a mown lawn or completely surrounded by paths or hard surfaces. Allow the meadow to lead and blend into denser growth so that creatures have a secure route in and out.

Farmer's nightmare

A meadow does require time to develop, and a careful mowing regime. For a quick and easy-to-grow colourful display that will positively crackle, buzz and hum with wildlife in the garden, try sowing a patch with a mixture of annual cornfield weeds, commonly referred to as "Farmer's nightmare". For a really authentic effect, mix in some barley or wheat seed. Sow the seed in autumn or spring into weed-free ground. Once the plants have set seed in late summer or autumn, remove the remains to the compost heap. Dig the ground over in late winter, and see what comes up the following spring. Some species may need to be resown if they have not seeded well, or if the seeds have been eaten by birds.

If you want to tailor your own mix, look out for white campion, corn chamomile, corn cockle, cornflower, corn marigold, wild pansy, scarlet pimpernel and the red poppy, *Papaver rhoeas*.

Unlike many meadow species, cornfield weeds thrive in ground that is disturbed every year, so you can move your wildlife attraction around if necessary – ideal if you are gradually reclaiming a large garden.

are smaller, old-fashioned cottage garden varieties; avoid over-bred, blowsy double blooms. Different flowers suit different feeding methods, so grow a range of flowers to suit all tastes. Bumble bees, for example, have much shorter tongues than Red Admiral butterflies, but longer ones than hive bees. Grow deep-throated flowers such as sage, marjoram, foxgloves and nasturtiums for bumble bees; nemesia, lemon balm, mahonia and viburnums for hive bees, and sedum and buddleja for butterflies to feed on. Simple, flat-opening flowers such as fennel are best for hoverflies, parasitic wasps and other small insects.

Most insects prefer different food plants at various stages of their life cycle, or even at different times of day. The peak nectar flow of flowers varies from species to species throughout the daylight hours, and you may find it interesting to plot a butterfly's progression from one food source to the next as the nectar comes on-stream.

Plants as nurseries

Butterflies also need somewhere to lay their eggs. Caterpillars feed on foliage rather than nectar and pollen, and they can be quite specific about which plants they will eat; some species are quite limited in their range of food sources. It is best to identify which butterflies are visiting your garden before you plant specific caterpillar food-plants. A great many

butterfly and moth species feed on grass, so leaving an area where the grass can grow tall is important. Some caterpillars hibernate, and many pupate, on grass stems over winter, so wait until late spring before cutting back long grass.

Grubs and caterpillars are in turn food for birds, predatory beetles, parasitic wasps, voles and amphibians. Many creatures regarded as garden pests are actually a valuable food source for other creatures. A pair of blue tits, for example, may eat around 7–8,000 insects per brood – mostly grubs of the apple sawfly and apple blossom weevil. They are also partial to aphids and codling moth pupae over winter. So give nature a chance before you take action against a pest attack; you may find that the job has been done for you. Clusters of aphids left on strong, established plants that can tolerate them, for example, will make a "nursery" for parasitic wasps and predators to feed and breed on.

Frogs and toads will live all year round in a garden if they can find a food supply, and their taste for small invertebrates – especially slugs – makes them the gardener's friends. Mealworms and angler's maggots make good extra amphibian fodder – buy them from specialist pet stores or fishing shops. Toads in particular can be taught to take food from your finger and will quickly learn to reappear at the same place at their regular feeding time.

NATIVE SPECIES

Most, though not all creatures in this country are adapted to feeding on native plant species. If you would like to grow native species, try to find out what would naturally grow in your area before you plant – these plants will stand the best chance of attracting most creatures and of thriving, not just surviving, in your individual site and soil.

Talk to your local Wildlife Trust, or contact Flora for Fauna, who also have an excellent website: http://www.nhm.ac.uk/science /projects/fff. Type in your postcode to receive a list of plants that grow (or have grown) in your particular neighbourhood.

FOOD PLANTS FOR CATERPILLARS

Many butterfly and moth caterpillars are specific to just a few species of plant. Here are just a few:

Grasses Gatekeeper, Grayling, Meadow Brown, Small Heath, Large Heath, Ringlet, Speckled Wood, Marbled White, Orange-tip, Small White, Essex Skipper, Large Skipper, Small Skipper

Lady's smock Orange-tip

Sorrel, common and sheep's Small Copper, Beech-green Carpet Moth, Blood Vein Moth, Forester, Yellow Shell

Sweet marjoram Plume Moths

Blackthorn Brown Hairstreak, Chinese Character; Lappet Moth, Phoenix Moth

Groundsel Cinnabar Moth

Blackberry Green Hairstreak, Grizzled Skipper, Common Emerald Moth

Garlic mustard Green-Veined White, Orange-tip

Mullein Mullein moth (caterpillar shown on p.85)

Nettle Comma, Painted Lady, Peacock, Small Tortoiseshell, Red Admiral, Beautiful Golden Y Moth, Green Carpet Moth

FLOWERS FOR HONEY BEES

Arabis
Broad and field beans (*Vicia faba*)
Borage (*Borago officinalis*)
Blackberry, raspberry and
  hybrid berries
Carrots
Candytuft (*Iberis*)
Dog rose (*Rosa canina*, right)
Heather (*Erica*)
Mignonette (*Reseda odorata*)
Parsnips (*Pastinaca sativa*)
Russian sage (*Perovskia atriplicifolia*)
Rosemary (*Rosmarinus officinalis*)
Rosebay willowherb (*Epilobium
  angustifolium*)
Verbascums
Vervain (*Verbena officinalis*)
Virginia creeper (*Parthenocissus
  quinquefolia*)
Wallflowers (*Erysimum*)
Woad (*Isatis tinctoria*)

FLOWERS FOR BUMBLE BEES

Anise hyssop (*Agastache anisata*)
Bergamot (*Monarda*)
Bird's foot trefoil (*Lotus corniculatus*)
Clover, red and white
  (*Trifolium*)
Globe artichoke (*Cynara scolymus*)
Goldenrod (*Solidago*)
Horehound, (*Marrubium vulgare*)
Honeysuckle (*Lonicera*, especially
  L. periclymenum, right)
Knapweed (*Centaurea scabiosa*
  and *C. nigra*)
Lobelia cardinalis
Lungwort (*Pulmonaria saccharata*)
Perennial cornflower (*Centaurea
  montana*)
Phacelia (*Phacelia tanacetifolia*)
Red valerian (*Centranthus ruber*)
Shasta daisy (*Leucanthemum* x
  superbum)
Viper's bugloss (*Echium vulgare*)
Yarrow (*Achillea vulgaris*)

FLOWERS FOR HOVERFLIES AND OTHER BENEFICIAL INSECTS

Blackthorn (*Prunus spinosa*)
Brambles (*Rubus fruticosus*)
Buckwheat (*Fagopyrum esculentum*)
California poppy (*Eschscholzia californica*)
Convolvulus, annual (*Convolvulus tricolor*)
Corn marigold (*Chrysanthemum segetum*)
Cornflower (*Centaurea cyanus*)
Coriander (*Coriandrum sativum*, left)
Cow parsley (*Anthriscus sylvestris*)
Dog rose (*Rosa canina*)
Fennel (*Foeniculum vulgare*)
Figwort (*Scrophularia*)
Hawthorn (*Crataegus monogyna*)
Ivy (*Hedera helix*)
Phacelia (*Phacelia tanacetifolia*)
Sweet alyssum (*Lobularia maritima*)
Yarrow (*Achillea millefolium*)

FLOWERS FOR ADULT BUTTERFLIES

Aubrieta
Buddleja (especially *B.* x *weyeriana* and *B.* x *weyeriana* 'Sungold')
Candytuft (*Iberis umbellata*)
Hebe (particularly 'Great Orme' and 'Midsummer Beauty')
Field scabious (*Knautia arvensis*)
Honesty (*Lunaria annua*)
Hyssop (*Hyssopus officinalis*)
Hemp agrimony (*Eupatorium cannabinum*)
Ice plant (*Sedum spectabile*)
Irish heath (*Erica erigena*)
Ivy (*Hedera helix*)
Lady's smock (*Cardamine pratensis*)
Lavender ('Munstead' is one of the best)
Marjoram (*Origanum*; wild forms are best)
Mint (*Mentha* spp., especially apple mint)
Michelmas daisy, left (especially *Aster* x *frikartii* 'Mönch')
Small scabious (*Scabiosa columbaria*)
Sweet rocket (*Hesperis matronalis*)
Sweet William (*Dianthus barbatus*)

Ponds for wildlife

A pond, even a tiny one, can be the heart of your wildlife oasis. Your pond will be used by a wide range of creatures for many and various purposes. Some will drink from it, or hunt for food over it. Others will use it for cover, to feed and breed in. Some will spend their whole lives in the pond, and others will use it for only part of their life cycle.

A pond is not the only worthwhile water supply in a garden. Even the smallest water container will act as an "outside aquarium", and be excellent for birds and amphibians. Birds need water for daily bathing, as well as drinking. They will come to fresh clean water in any shallow type of container; even an upturned dustbin lid or washing-up bowl can be pressed into service. Sink the container into the ground, or build a ramp of bricks up to one edge to make it accessible for thirsty hedgehogs as well.

If you have young children and an open pool is inappropriate, consider a bubble-fountain or a wall-mounted basin, or cover your pond with a safety grating of rigid mesh until they are older.

Ponds for wildlife

A pond is best sited in a sunny position, away from overhanging trees, with an area of rough grass or plants along at least one edge to act as a refuge and feeding ground for amphibians. A pond in shade will support some life, but there will be a greater diversity of species in full sun. If your pond is visible from the house, create an area of short grass on the side of the pond nearest the window so you can watch what is going on.

Creating a wildlife pond

The size of a pond depends obviously on the site available – but it should be at the very least a metre square. At least one side should gently slope, to allow small creatures safe access. Most wildlife will inhabit areas of shallow water around the margins. There should also be a deeper area, at least 60cm (24in), in the centre, which will remain frost-free during winter, and cool in summer. There are various materials available to line a pond – you can choose from concrete, bentonite clay, ready-made plastic moulds or a butyl sheet liner (see *The Garden Framework*, p.129). A butyl liner is the most flexible, and probably the easiest to deal with when creating an irregularly shaped pond. Natural clay, available in a mat form, will last the longest. You need to allow plenty of overlap to anchor the liner securely around the edges – your supplier will be able to help with the size required if given the intended dimensions of the pond. The pond can be filled with rain or tap water. If using tap water, wait at least 48 hours for

NEW FRIENDS

Creatures that may visit or live in garden ponds:

Frogs (right)
Newts
Bats
Whirligig beetles
Pond skaters (centre)
Water measurers
Water boatmen
Water snails
Diving beetles
Damselflies and dragonflies – some of them are inquisitive and will investigate people!
Swallows (far right)

the chlorine to dissipate before introducing floating or oxygenating plants. Wildlife will move in rapidly of its own accord, and within a year your pond should have a full complement of creatures.

New ponds often suddenly turn an alarming vivid green, caused by a sudden surge in the number of small algae. The water clears eventually, but to hurry things along put some barley straw or lavender clippings in a fine mesh plastic net bag and weight it so it just floats. Beneficial micro-organisms rapidly colonise the straw or lavender and destroy the algae.

Planting the pond

A good assortment of plants will provide food and shelter for an extensive range of creatures. Plant a mixture of floating, oxygenating and shallow water species. Algal growth is encouraged by sunlight, so, to keep the water clear, aim to keep half to two-

DIGGING AND LINING A POND

Early spring is the best time to create a new pond. This gives plants and wildlife time to settle in before the following winter.

• Dig the hole slightly larger than you want the pond to be to allow for any protective under layer. At least one side should slope gently (15–30°), and there should be an area about 60cm (24in) deep, depending on the severity of your winters, which will remain frost free. A shelf for marginal plants in pots can be useful.

• Remove all sharp stones, roots and anything else that might puncture the lining. Firm the sides and edges and make sure that the edges are all level. For additional protection gently smooth a 10cm (4in) layer of builder's sand all around the inside of the hole. Lay a protective underlay, such as old carpet, cardboard or custom-made pond underlay.

• With assistance (a butyl liner is heavy) lay the liner over the hole, with a 30cm (12in) overlap around the edges. Let it dip halfway into the hole, and weigh down the edges with heavy stones. Put some soil in the middle if you are going to plant directly in the soil.

• Fill the pond. The weight of water will mould the liner to the shape of the pond. Bury the edges of the liner under turf or stones to protect it from the light.

UK PLANT SPECIES FOR PONDS

Oxygenating/submerged	Floating plants	For shallow water
Hornwort (*Ceratophyllum demersum* and *C. submersum*) Water milfoil (*Myriophyllum spicatum* and *M. verticillatum*) Water starworts (*Callitriche*, such as the UK native *C. stagnalis* – especially valuable for newts, which prefer to lay their eggs wrapped in a single leaf)	Duckweed (*Lemna*) Waterlilies for a small pond need to be carefully selected, as the native species are too vigorous. Try the fragrant *Nymphea odorata* cultivars, such as 'W.B. Shaw', or *N. pygmaea* and *N. tetragona*	Arrowhead (*Sagittaria sagittifolia*) Bogbean (*Menyanthes trifoliata*) Burr-reed (*Sparganium ramosum*) Brooklime (*Veronica beccabunga*) Flowering rush (*Butomus umbellatus*) Greater spearwort (*Ranunculus lingua* and the larger flowered cultivar 'Grandiflorus') Sweet flag (*Acorus calamus*) Water plantain (*Alisma*)

thirds of the surface covered with plant growth. Use species as native to your area as possible. Avoid planting some of the more invasive alien species – often on offer in garden centres – especially if there is any chance that they may be inadvertently released into the wild. Particular pond thugs to resist include Australian swamp stonecrop or New Zealand pigmyweed (*Crassula helmsii*), water fern (*Azolla filiculoides*) and parrot's feather (*Myriophyllum aquaticum*). When planting in baskets, use a special, low-nutrient aquatic compost or garden subsoil.

Pond maintenance

Once a pond is established, it may not need much maintenance from the wildlife's point of view. Some insects prefer overgrown, muddy ponds, and frogs certainly don't mind weedy water. You may prefer a slightly more "managed" pond, but try not to disturb it unless really necessary.

During the summer, remove excess blanket weed; twist it round a stick or rake it out. Free-floating plants such as duckweed can be lifted out with a sieve. Leave any debris or plant matter on the pond side overnight, to allow creatures to escape back into the pond, then add it to your compost heap.

Vigorous and invasive pond plants can be cut back or removed gradually; reduce the volume of submerged plant foliage, such as pond weed, by about a third. Late summer is the best time, before creatures hibernate. Avoid disturbing a pond early in the year, or in very cold weather. Other pond plants can be divided every two or three years if necessary.

Cover the pond with netting for a few weeks in autumn if it collects large quantities of falling leaves, or remove the leaves by hand. Also remove dead and decaying foliage, or this will add nutrients to the water, encouraging algal growth. Always leave some debris at the bottom of the pond, however.

POND ALLIES

1 Tadpoles
Migrating frogs will tend to colonise a suitable pond within a year or two. If none appear, the pond is either unsuitable or cut off from their migration. If the latter, introduce some frogspawn taken from a healthy garden pond within, if possible, half a mile of yours. Do not take it from the wild.

2 Floating leaves
Floating leaf cover helps to prevent a pond from clogging up with algal growth. Aim for a 50–60% cover of the surface of the pond.

3 Plants with submerged and semi-submerged stems and leaves
These plants (here, for instance, golden club, *Orontium aquaticum*) provide food and shelter for water-dwelling creatures, and make egg-laying sites for newts.

4 Ramshorn snails
These snails are scavengers, helping to keep pond water clean by feeding on algae and plant debris.

The rest of the garden

Amphibians spend more time on land than in the water, so if you want these creatures to visit be sure to provide some safe cover for them. Undisturbed areas, such as long grass, thick mulches and heaps of stones or logs, provide safe havens and hibernating sites for frogs, toads and newts. At least part of the pond edge should consist of plants to provide good cover. You may also like some mown grass to allow a good view of the pond. To avoid harming emerging frogs, mow this grass regularly, starting in mid-spring before young creatures start to leave the pond. Always check for froglets after heavy rain.

Algal blooms

One of the most common pond problems is an algal "bloom" – the water turning the colour of pea soup, or silting up with swathes of blanket weed. This is usually a symptom of warm, nutrient-rich water. The "pea soup" is generally a short-lived phenomenon, appearing in spring as the weather warms up, then vanishing once the oxygenating plants start into growth. Blanket weed can be more persistent; it can be physically removed by winding it round a stick, or raking it out. Barley straw or lavender clippings can also be used (see p.99), and the following measures will help to avoid it:

• Have submerged oxygenating plants occupying around 25–33% of the volume of water.

• Let floating plant foliage cover at least half and no more than two-thirds of the surface to shade the water.

• If it is necessary to top up the water level, use rainwater rather than mineral-rich tap water.

• Use aquatic compost rather than the usual garden growing media when planting aquatics in pots, or a very low-nutrient homemade potting mix.

• Clear the pond annually, if necessary.

THE UNWANTED LIST

1 Great pond snail
While this snail (*Lymnaea stagnalis*) will eat algae and organic debris, it can also damage plants. If there are too many in your pond, float fresh lettuce leaves on the surface in the early evening. Remove, with attached feeding snails, in the morning.

2 Invasive plants
Avoid planting invasive and alien plant species (such as this parrot's feather). Sadly, you may find that some pond and garden centres sell inappropriate species, so check before you buy.

3 Algae
Blanket weed (shown) and other algae thrive in light conditions in nutrient-rich water. An algal "bloom" can turn a pond to green soup overnight.

4 Fish
Don't introduce fish to a wildlife pond – they will upset the natural ecosystem. Some, such as this stickleback, may arrive as eggs on birds' feet. They should only survive in numbers that the pond can sustain.

Container gardening

CONTAINER-GROWN PLANTS CAN GIVE THE GARDEN A
WELCOME INJECTION OF COLOUR, FRAGRANCE AND FOCUS

GROWING PLANTS IN CONTAINERS allows you to create a garden within a garden, or even where there is no soil at all. If you simply want to maximise your growing space, then the plainest plastic tubs will do. But with a wider choice of pots, windowboxes, urns, troughs and other improvised containers, moods and styles can be created – perhaps a lush tropical theme, an exotic eastern look, or even the glory of an old-fashioned cottage garden. By using containers you can let your imagination run riot, following fashion or your latest enthusiasm, safe in the knowledge that you can change it all next year with little effort.

Deciding what to grow

Use containers to grow almost any type of plant, ornamental or edible, annual or perennial, dwarf or climbing. A shrub or climber in a large pot (see p.207) can act as an attractive focal point, while a colourful assortment of pots and planters will revitalize a backyard or liven up a dull corner where nothing much will grow. You could also grow a pot full of mixed salad on your patio (see p.210), or provide a tumbling riot of fragrance and colour throughout the summer from a hanging basket or a wall-mounted pot (see p.215). You can even create your own miniature wildlife garden in a windowbox. The compost mix can of course be tailored to grow plants that would not enjoy your garden's soil. The main rule of container gardening is to select the most appropriate plants for the conditions where the container will stand.

Containers and the organic approach

One of the prime tenets of organic gardening is to create a healthy, fertile soil that provides plants with all they need – so growing plants in the restricted environment of a container cannot be considered truly organic. Container-grown tomatoes could not, for example, be legally marketed as an organic crop. But containers do have a valuable role in our gardens – especially in towns and cities – and they can be certainly be managed along organic lines, with the appropriate choice of compost mix and without the use of synthetic feeds and pesticides.

Creative use of space (facing page)
Evergreens with strong shapes are good value in small spaces, and sticking to one choice of material for the pots prevents a cluttered look. A sheltered corner or patio may allow you to grow more tender plants such as the oleander and citrus here; they will appreciate the extra heat stored and reflected by the stonework.

Urban oases
Keen container gardeners are liable to let their enthusiasm spread to cover the tops of walls, posts, windowsills and even garden seating with a growing collection of plants. Introducing such variety into urban environments, especially with flowering plants, softens the hard landscape and turns the smallest paved courtyard, balcony or even rooftop into a welcome refuge for wildlife.

Container considerations

Plants will grow in anything from terracotta pots to an old bucket. A container can be new, reclaimed or recycled, as long as it has drainage holes and is sturdy enough to be filled with potting compost. Where frosts are likely, containers should also be frost-proof.

Choose the container to suit the site or design style you have in mind. A Versailles box or "aged" stone urn will give a very different feel from florists' buckets or a brightly painted wooden box. You don't have to spend a lot to be smart. Simple containers like the tubs below can be used to formal effect if planted up identically and arranged with care.

Drainage

All containers must have drainage holes in the base. To allow good drainage, fill the bottom of the container with coarse material before adding the growing mixture. To add weight, use large (3cm/1¼in) gravel. Broken-up polystyrene packaging is a lightweight alternative and also a good way of recycling material. Aim for a layer 4cm (1½in) deep for most containers. If the pot is made of stone or terracotta, and freezing is likely, a drainage layer one-fifth of the total depth of the pot will give it some protection. Standing the pot on bricks or purpose-made "feet" also improves drainage if necessary.

Container sizes

Appropriate size depends on what plants you intend to grow. For ease of management – both feeding and watering – the larger the container the better; do not, however, put a small slow-growing plant straight into an overlarge pot. A large pot containing several plants is easier to look after than many individual

MATERIALS AND FINISHES

Wood and wicker
Rough-sawn wood gives a rustic look, and may deter slugs. Oak, cedar and sweet chestnut do not need a preservative. Planed wood can be neatly painted, for window boxes for example. Wickerwork baskets can be lined with plastic.

Stone and terracotta
Sales and salvage yards are good sources for old stone troughs, sinks and clay pots. "Age" new terracotta by painting with yoghurt and keeping the pot in a damp, shady spot. Paint machine-made pots with tile or blackboard paint. Glazed pots need less watering (see p.66) and look good with bamboos and Japanese maples for an "eastern" theme.

Plastic
Good-quality plastic pots can be long-lasting, and are light enough to move around easily. They can be reused and painted.

Metal
Galvanised buckets give a modern look – or recycle large tin cans for a cheery display.

pots. Any container should be at least 15–20cm (6–8in) deep, with most plants appreciating a greater depth. Remember that containers that taper towards the top can make potting-on difficult. If the container needs to be moved from time to time, for example under cover in winter, remember that you may have to lift it. For large pots, improvise a trolley with a strong board fitted with four castors.

Growing media

Use an organic, peat–free, multipurpose or potting compost – homemade or purchased – to fill pots and containers. Do not stint on quality; your plants will be growing in a restricted environment and need the best. The growing medium should of course suit the plants you are growing. Plants that thrive in dry situations will need a freer-draining, poorer mix than a pot full of leafy vegetables. A tub of annuals can get by with a general multipurpose mix, while a fruit tree, which is to be in the container for many years, will need a richer mix, preferably one based on loam or soil. These have the advantage of being heavier, and the additional weight can stop pots of tall plants blowing over. A soilless mix, being lighter, is useful for hanging baskets and on balconies, and where containers need to be moved around. Recipes for a range of homemade potting mixes can be found on pp.116–117.

Feeding and watering

Plants in tubs, pots and other containers are fed with the same range of composted organic materials and organic fertilisers that are used on open ground (see *Soil and Soil Care*, pp.32–61). These are applied as a top-dressing to the container. In addition, liquid feeds (see overleaf), which supply nutrients in a more readily available form, can be watered on or applied as a foliar spray. How much and how often container plants need to be fed will depend on the richness of the growing medium used, the volume of the container and the plants being grown. Some guidelines are given throughout this chapter.

How often a container plant needs watering also depends upon the plant type, its size in relation to the container, the type of container (terracotta dries out more quickly than plastic), the site (a windy site increases the demand for water), the weather and the season. Never let containers dry out – plants are

much more prone to problems if they are short of water, and dry compost is difficult to re-wet. A regular water supply is particularly important for cropping plants. In practice, most container plants need daily watering during summer, even after rain, and very little in winter. Always direct water under the foliage. (See also *Water and Watering*, p.66).

Pests and diseases

As with all organic growing, keeping plants growing well is the best defence against pests and diseases. Potbound plants in overcrowded pots with an erratic supply of water will be more prone to pests such as red spider mite and aphids. Pots and tubs are often in hot and dry locations, where plants may suffer from pests that would not be found in the open ground.

By using clean compost, you can avoid many soil-borne pests and diseases, but root-eating creatures may still move into a pot, where their effects can be devastating. Vine weevil grubs can soon kill plants in containers and baskets; a biological control agent (see p.100) is available. Grow flowers to attract predators to keep other pests in check (see p.96), and deal with any problem as it arises; check plants regularly and pick off pests, diseased shoots or leaves as you notice them. Remove sickly and badly infested plants.

Winter protection

Move tender plants indoors over winter if necessary, or protect plants with fleece. Wrap up pots so that neither the pot nor the plant roots freeze.

Pest control

Slugs and snails may be less of a problem in containers than in the open ground; however, if one does make the climb, there will be nothing to distract it from the prized plant within. Try deterring them with a barrier around the pot: a strip of either grease or non-drying glue or, as here, of copper – or stand the pot in a saucer with an integral, battery-powered electric fence (see p.101)!

HOMEMADE MOCK STONE PLANTER

1 Select two strong cardboard boxes, one smaller than the other by 5cm (2in) on all sides.
2 Mix 3 parts of concreting sand with 1 part each of coarse coir and cement. Mix in water to form a stiff mortar.
3 Cover the bottom of the larger box with 5cm (2in) of the mortar, tamp it down to remove air bubbles, and insert 5 corks to form drainage holes.
4 Centre the smaller box within the larger one.
5 Fill the space between the boxes with mortar to a depth of about 15cm (6in). Tamp the mortar down with care.
6 Leave for a week to set hard.
7 Remove the boxes, push out the corks and brush with a wire brush for a rustic appearance.
8 Brush with yoghurt or liquid manure. Green algae will grow.

Organic liquid feeds

Liquid feeds provide plants with nutrients in a readily available form. Although this goes against the organic principle of feeding the soil, not the plant, there are times when a liquid feed can be necessary in an organic garden. Suitable liquid feeds are made from manures, plant and animal wastes, and rock minerals. These are basically the same materials that are used for feeding the soil, but in a different form, and they are subject to the same constraints as to source of supply.

Suitable organic liquid feeds can now be bought from most good garden centres as well as from specialist suppliers, or can be homemade. The latter are almost as easy to make as their principal ingredients, comfrey and nettles, are to grow.

GROWING COMFREY IN THE GARDEN

Comfrey is a fast-growing hardy perennial, growing up to 1m (3ft) tall. The cultivar 'Bocking 14' was selected by Lawrence D. Hills, the founder of HDRA and one of the pioneers of organic gardening. 'Bocking 14' is high-yielding and has a particularly high potash content★. It does not set seed, nor does it have a creeping root – features of other species of comfrey that enable them to spread rapidly.

Plant 'Bocking 14' in spring and summer as root cuttings or pot-grown cuttings. Once established, the leaves can be cut three or four times a year. The last cut should be in early autumn at the latest. Feed the plants every year or two with a high-fertility soil improver or high-nitrogen fertiliser. Grass mowings applied in spring, with shredded prunings added in the autumn, can be an effective feeding regime.

★A sample analysis of comfrey concentrate made from 'Bocking 14' contains, per litre, 79mg of nitrogen (N); 26.4mg phosphorus (P); and 205mg potassium (K).

When to use liquid feed

Container plants, where the volume of compost is limited, are the main candidates for liquid feeding. Young plants being raised in modules may also need feeding if planting out is delayed. Liquid feeds in the garden should only be used as a short-term solution where soil is poor, or soil conditions or root damage prevent a plant taking up sufficient nutrients. In the latter case, the feed is best applied as a foliar spray to the leaves. Organic liquid feeds should never be used as an alternative to good soil care and management.

Feeding plants in pots

How much, and how often you need to apply a liquid feed will depend of the type of plant, its size in relation to the volume of the container, how vigorously it is growing or how big you want it to grow, and the quality of the growing medium. Observation, with experience, is the key. A young tomato plant newly transplanted into its own pot, for example, should not be fed, whereas a tomato plant covered in fruit may need feeding three times a week. A slow-growing shrub will not require a liquid feed, while a tub full of annuals may benefit from a weekly dose.

Remember that you can overdo it. It is counter-productive to encourage excess leafy growth in a tomato plant or a pot of annual flowers, for example, as you will only delay the production of fruit or flowers. And slow growth does not necessarily mean a shortage of food; cold weather, root damage or overwatering can also slow growth, especially of young plants. In these cases, liquid feeding could simply make things worse.

Purchased liquid feeds

When buying a liquid feed, check the ingredients carefully to ensure that additional, non-organic ingredients have not been added. Choose one with an organic symbol of approval if available. Purchased liquid feeds may contain a mixture of ingredients to give a balanced product – either for general use, or with a high potash content for feeding tomatoes and other fruiting plants. Ingredients used to produce commercial organic liquid feeds are:

• **Liquid manures** Usually cow, poultry or sheep

manure (not from intensive systems).

• **Fish emulsion** A by-product of the fishing industry, not from fish caught specifically for this purpose.

• **Rock phosphate** Micronised so that it stays in suspension.

• **Plant extracts** For example, vinasse, sugar beet derivatives and seaweed (see also below).

Seaweed extract

Seaweed extract is a plant growth stimulant rather than a liquid feed; it contains little in the way of major plant foods. What it does contain is a wide range of trace elements, plus ingredients such as plant hormones and specific carbohydrates that can stimulate plant growth.

Seaweed extract can be used in various ways, at various stages of plant growth, to produce a range of effects. It seems to work best if applied to the soil or roots early on in the life of the plant, and as a foliar spray later on. To use seaweed extract, soak seeds in seaweed extract for a few hours prior to sowing to increase the rate of seedling emergence, or apply extract to the soil around young plants to increase their root growth (two applications at four-week intervals); or apply to the soil or foliage of young plants to "green-up" leaves, which increases the chlorophyll content. Seaweed extract can also be applied to the soil to reduce the possibility of some root diseases, and as a foliar spray to discourage sap-feeding insects and possibly increase resistance to frost.

Homemade liquid feeds

Liquid feeds can be made using comfrey or nettle leaves. Be aware that both can have a strong smell.

Comfrey leaves are rich in plant foods. The leaves decay rapidly, releasing the goodness they contain. They can also be used as a mulch or compost activator. Comfrey leaves tend to be slightly alkaline, so the liquid feed should not be used on acid-loving plants. Comfrey liquid is high in potash and has reasonable levels of nitrogen and phosphate; it is good for fruiting plants, although its nitrogen levels may not be sufficient for a fully grown hanging basket.

Nettles make a general liquid feed, which is a little low on phosphate, but also supplies magnesium, sulphur and iron. Young nettles cut in spring contain the highest levels of major nutrients.

RECIPES FOR LIQUID FEEDS

Comfrey
• Steep 3kg (6lb 12oz) comfrey leaves in 45 litres (12 gal) of water.
• Cover with a lid.
• Use undiluted after four weeks.

Nettle
• Steep 1kg (2lb 4oz) leaves in 10 litres (2¼ gal) of water.
• Cover with a lid.
• Use after two weeks, diluted one part nettle liquid in 10 parts water.

Comfrey concentrate

Comfrey leaves can also be made into a concentrate. Pack cut leaves into a plastic container with a hole in the bottom (a water butt, bucket, or a drainpipe with an end cap are all good options) and cover with a lid. Place a collection vessel under the hole, and after two to three weeks a dark liquid will drip out. To use, dilute the concentrate in 10–20 parts water. For example, tomatoes in pots can be fed with concentrate diluted 1:15 with water three times a week once the fruits start to form. The concentrate can be stored for a few months in a cool, dry place.

Concentrate collecter
Stuff a pipe with comfrey leaves and collect the concentrate as it drips out. For smaller quantities, use a plastic bottle inverted over a container.

COMFREY LEAFMOULD

Comfrey leafmould can be used neat as a potting compost, or as an ingredient of a potting mix. Fill a plastic bucket or dustbin with alternate 10cm (4in) layers of damp, two- to three-year-old leafmould (see p.50) and chopped comfrey leaves. As the comfrey leaves decompose, the goodness they contain is soaked up by the leafmould. When the comfrey leaves have disintegrated (usually after two to five months), the leafmould is ready to use.

Ornamentals in containers

As well as the usual annual bedding plants, shrubs and perennials, grasses and even small trees can be grown in pots and troughs, provided that you choose them carefully. Take a good look at the site where you propose to position your containers; plants will grow well as long as they are in the right place. Gloomy shade is not the right place for sun-loving pelargoniums, and ferns will turn brown and sad if they are scorched and dry. Most rock-garden plants, succulents such as houseleeks and drought-tolerant shrubs such as lavender and rosemary will thrive in the hot, dry conditions of a sunny patio. Shade-loving shrubs that grow well in pots include *Fatsia japonica*, mophead hydrangeas, *Mahonia* 'Charity', skimmias and *Viburnum davidii*. Dwarf trees and shrubs are ideal, but others can do well even if they would naturally grow quite large. As the pot restricts the roots, the top growth will also be limited. There are a great many small conifers to choose from, in greens, greys and golds and attractive year-round. Many are sold as rock-garden plants, but larger specimens also look good: try *Abies balsamea* 'Nana' or *Chamaecyparis pisifera* 'Boulevard'.

The best herbaceous perennials for containers are those with a long season of interest – bold foliage plants such as ferns and hostas, for example, or long-flowerers such as the hardy geraniums. In a shady corner, elegant dicentras and astilbes are striking.

Container size

Large plants like climbers and small trees need plenty of space for their roots to develop; they will not flourish if you skimp on the pot size. The bigger the container, the more plants you can plant. A trough measuring 1m x 30cm x 30cm (3ft x 12in x 12in), for example, will support three small shrubs (for example, small species of hebe, euonymus or spiraea) and a couple of ivies. Underplant with bulbs for winter and spring interest; in summer, bedding plants can be tucked around the edges. By contrast, alpines, rockery plants, sedums and houseleeks will all thrive with a smaller, shallower root run.

Composts

Choose the compost to suit the needs of the plant. Many shrubs will do well in a nutrient-rich, soil-based compost. Add up to 20% extra grit for plants that need good drainage. Add sulphur chips to reduce the pH to below 6 for acid-loving plants. A soil-based or soilless multipurpose compost will suit most annuals, grasses and bulbs. Use a mulch such as coarse bark or stone chips for a decorative finish that also helps to retain moisture.

Feeding and watering

Long-term shrubs or other perennials that you want to grow on to make large specimens should be repotted in spring. Use a pot 5–7.5cm (2–3in) wider than the previous one, and fill the gap with fresh

Clematis 'Arctic Queen'
Containers need not be used purely for low-level patio groupings. Climbers such as this clematis can add a dramatic flourish of colour and height to a corner or grouping.

compost. Otherwise top-dress the existing pot annually in spring, adding a 2.5cm (1in) layer of a nutrient-rich organic material such as garden or worm compost. If you have used a decorative mulch, just push this to one side, add the organic material, then redistribute the mulch. If plants need extra nutrients during the growing season, a scattering of a general organic fertiliser will help, or feed regularly with a liquid feed. Never let the plants dry out.

Climbers in pots

Climbers in containers can be tied to an existing wall, fence or trellis, or can be given their own independent supports in the pot: twiggy garden pruning such a hazel, replaced annually, for example, or a more permanent wire, cane or trellis framework. A compact cultivar of clematis that can be cut down to the ground each winter will grow happily in a 35cm (14in) diameter pot; try *Clematis florida* 'Flore Pleno' or 'Sieboldii', or *C.* 'Comtesse de Bouchaud'. Plant in a free-draining, soil-based potting compost with the crown 7.5cm (3in) below the surface. Provide tall, twiggy prunings for support. Pinch out new shoots to two leaves until flower buds appear, to give a bushy plant covered in flowers. Other good choices for pots are scented climbers such as jasmine and honeysuckle, or annual climbers such as sweet peas and nasturtiums.

Grasses in pots

Some perennial grasses like hot, dry conditions and grow well in containers. Grow blue-grey *Festuca glauca* and *Koeleria glauca* or bronze *Carex comans* in pots of their own, or as a foil for flowering plants. The mosquito grass *Bouteloua gracilis*, with distinctive purple-brown flowers, makes a more unusual container specimen. Grasses are less demanding of nutrients than many other container plants.

Hardy annuals and biennials

Many hardy annuals will give only a short display; grown in pots, they can easily be replaced. They are among the best plants for attracting bees and beneficial insects into the garden. Try alyssum, *Convolvulus tricolor*, dwarf rudbeckias or calendulas, or even some of the modern dwarf sunflower cultivars. Biennials such as wallflowers, daisies and forget-me-nots give valuable early flowers the following spring.

A pot full of bulbs

A selection of bulbs planted in a pot in early autumn can provide a succession of flowers from midwinter through to late spring. Choose bulbs that flower at different times and that are planted at different depths. Plant at least two or three of each cultivar. A small and colourful, summer-flowering shrub in the middle of the pot will continue the show.

Stunning displays
Exploit the flexibility and adaptability containers can provide. Grow a tree or shrub in a large container (above, far left) as a central feature in a garden without soil, plant a combination of annuals and bulbs (centre) for an instantly eye-catching temporary display, or tailor your compost mix to include a greater range of plants, such as houseleeks (right), in containers.

Vegetables and herbs in containers

Almost any vegetable can be grown in a container. Courgettes, tomatoes, potatoes and aubergines do well in large individual containers in an appropriate location. Salads, spring onions, chard, leaf beet, French beans, beetroot, carrots, radishes and oriental brassicas can be grown in a mixed pot (see facing page for some planting suggestions), or in greater quantities on their own. Avoid vegetables with deep roots such as parsnips, and those with a long, slow growing season such as cauliflower and Brussels sprouts, or with high demands for food and water, such as pumpkins.

Both useful and beautiful

Remember that vegetables can look good too, and an "edible" container can look as striking as one filled with ornamentals. You might also like to add some herbs and edible flowers. Container growing is particularly useful where herbs do not like your soil conditions. If you garden on heavy clay, for example, a free-draining compost mix can allow you to grow herbs such as rosemary, sage and thyme. In cool climates, pots of basil can be started off in the greenhouse and moved outside to a warm, sunny spot when the weather improves.

Grow annual flowering plants such as calendula (also edible) or *Convolvulus tricolor* to attract predators to improve pest control, too.

Container size and compost mix

Vegetables each have different growing requirements. A seedling salad crop (see p.332) can be grown in compost that has already been used once, while heavy feeders need a stronger mix (see Growing media, pp.114–117). Generally, the larger the container the better, as vegetables need a good supply of food and a consistent supply of water to do well. Growing several plants in one large container may give better results than using individual pots, and the plants will be much easier to look after.

As containers come in all shapes and sizes, it can be easier to talk volume than rather than dimensions (see panel, below left, for some examples). Measure the approximate volume of a container by filling it with compost from a bucket of known volume. In general, use a container that is at least 20cm (8in) deep. Seedling salads can go in shallower pots or trays, as long as you keep them watered. Heavy feeders like tomatoes and courgettes need a container at least 25–30cm (10–12in) deep. Carrots grow well in containers, and are easily protected from carrot fly by draping fleece over the pot. Grow early, short- or round-rooted varieties such as 'Amsterdam Forcing' and 'Early Scarlet Horn', in a container at least 15cm (6in) deep. Pull the bigger carrots first, leaving the others to grow.

SOME COMPOST REQUIREMENTS

Aubergine 10 litres (2½ gal) per plant.
French beans 2.5 litres (4 pints) per plant.
Beetroot, kohl rabi Minimum depth of compost 20cm (8in); plants 7.5–10cm (3–4in) apart.
Leaf beet and chard 4 litres (7 pints) per plant.
Courgettes 30–40 litres (6–9 gal) per plant.
Leek Minimum depth of compost 20cm (8in), plants 4cm (1½in) apart.
Sweet peppers 5 litres (1 gal) per plant.
Tomato 15 litres (3¼ gal) per plant.

GROWING TIPS

• For a quick impact, raise plants in modules, rather than sowing direct.

• Never let pots dry out. Many vegetables are likely to bolt or split if the water supply is erratic.

• Line clay pots with plastic to cut down on water loss.

• Choose dwarf or miniature cultivars.

• Feed with a general or potash-rich liquid feed (see p.206) as appropriate. Seaweed extract will give a plants a boost.

• The *A–Z of Vegetables and Salad Crops*, pp.338–366, gives the feeding requirements of individual crops. You can adapt this to container-growing.

EDIBLE MIXTURES FOR POTS

The recipes listed here are each designed to be crowded into a deep, 40cm (16in) pot. Even the flowers are edible!

Fitting everything in relies on regular attention, thinning out (and eating) excess plants as they grow, tying up and staking as required, and eating everything as young as possible.

Use a good quality, rich potting compost, keep the pot well watered and liquid-feed those pots that include tomatoes once the first fruits have set.

Simply salads

1 x tomato 'Shirley' or other reliable tall (not bush) cultivar
12 x 'Markana', semi-leafless peas
4 x lettuce 'Red Fire' or similar loose leaf lettuce
4 x lettuce 'Frisby' or other compact loose leaf lettuce
4 x salad rocket
6 x compact, variegated nasturtium 'Alaska'

Pretty in purples

5 x purple-podded French bean 'Royalty'
5 x Chinese leaf celery
8 x baby beetroot 'Tardel'
4 x chervil
1 x creeping golden thyme
3 x viola 'Johnny Jump Up'

Aztec delight

5 x mini sweetcorn 'Minipop'
6 x purple kohl rabi 'Azur Star'
3 x coriander (for leaf)
3 x parsley
3 x trailing tomato 'Tumbler'
4 x summer savory

Edible delights

Tall, sun-seeking sweetcorn allows plenty of room for smaller plants to be tucked in beneath it, to grow and tumble over the rim of the pot.

Fruit in pots

Dessert apples
Choose a compact apple cultivar like 'Jester' for successful container-growing. With most apples and pears you will need to grow two or more varieties to ensure successful pollination.

While most fruits can be grown in containers, they need regular attention if they are to flourish, and will not appreciate being neglected for a few weeks' summer holiday. The crops from these plants will be less heavy than from plants in the ground, and their productive lifespan considerably shorter.

Which fruits to grow

Figs, which only crop successfully when their roots are restricted, do well in containers. Apples, plums, pears and cherries can make attractive, productive pot plants. The more tender fruits, such as apricots, nectarines and citrus, benefit from the mobility of a pot, which can be moved into the protection of a glasshouse in winter, and put outside in suitable summer conditions. Check on the pollination requirements of each fruit; if it is not self-fertile, you may need to grow more than one plant to ensure successful cropping. There is no need to grow trees on dwarfing rootstocks; the restriction of the pot will limit size. In fact, a more vigorous stock can be the better choice, as it will grow a more resilient tree. Dwarf peaches and nectarines, which make ideal patio fruits, are now available.

GROWING TIPS

• Never let the compost dry out.
• Give fruit in pots a sunny, sheltered spot.
• Turn the pot around every week or two if positioned next to a wall.
• Thin the fruit if necessary, as the plant will only be able to support a relatively small crop.

Of the soft fruit, strawberries are most suited to containers. Blueberries also do well, and in pots can be given the acid soil they need wherever you are. Gooseberries and red- and whitecurrants trained as standards look attractive in pots and are convenient to pick. A grape vine will also make a standard (see p.263) for a small crop of dessert fruit. Choose autumn-fruiting raspberries if you want to grow them, as they crop on fresh new growth, but they may have to be replaced every year. Blackberries and other hybrid berries are just too vigorous for containers.

Pots and composts

Plant fruit as you would any other potted plant, into a container only 5–8cm (2–3in) larger than the

FRUIT TREES AND BUSHES FOR POTS

Fruit	Container growing requirements
Apple	Choose compact cultivars on rootstocks M26 or MM106; prune as a pyramid or bush
Pear	Compact cultivars on Quince A or C rootstock; prune as a pyramid or bush
Cherry	Self-fertile sweet cherry cultivars on Colt or hexaploid Colt rootstocks; train as a pyramid
Plum	Self-fertile dessert cultivars on Pixy or St. Julien A rootstocks; train as a pyramid
Peach and nectarine	Naturally dwarf "patio" cultivars or traditional cultivars on St Julien A rootstock; train as a pyramid or bush
Fig	Needs a 38cm (15in) pot; prune to a multistemmed, shrubby habit, removing older wood to encourage young growth
Blueberry	Needs a well-drained compost with a low pH of 4–5.5
Red- and whitecurrant, gooseberry	Look good trained as standards
Grape vine	Train as a standard; replace every three years
Strawberries	Use a 15cm (6in) pot for each plant, or several plants in a larger pot; plant in late summer; keep outside over winter; crop for one year only. Plants can then be planted out into open ground if available

existing rootball. The size of the container can be increased, if necessary, at the next repotting. A container measuring 45cm (18in) in diameter, 38–45cm (15–18in) deep, is a reasonable ultimate pot size for most fruits. Strawberries can thrive in much smaller pots. Grow several plants in a larger pot, a "strawberry tower" with planting pockets on the sides, or even in a window box.

Use a nutrient-rich, soil-based compost. Feed with high-potash liquid feed when the fruits start to swell. Give the plants a nitrogen-rich fertiliser in late summer. Top-dress every spring, removing the top 2–5cm (1–2in) of compost and replacing it with worm or garden compost. Repot every alternate winter: remove the plant from its pot, and gently tease away as much old compost as you can; cut away thick woody roots, taking care not to damage the fibrous roots, and repot into fresh compost.

This general regime, combined with regular watering (which may mean twice a day at times) and prompt attention to problems, should ensure that fruits grow well. However, because organic methods concentrate on growing in open ground, there is relatively little experience to draw on of managing container fruit organically; you may find that with experimentation, you can get better results.

CITRUS FRUITS IN CONTAINERS

With their glossy foliage and bright fruits, citrus can make attractive patio plants. Growing them in containers means that they can be given the right conditions in both summer and winter.

• Use a nutrient-rich, soil-based compost, and add 20% horticultural grit to improve drainage.

• In summer, stand the pots outside in a warm, sheltered place. Water them freely, but make sure the pots drain well. Liquid-feed the plants regularly, using a high-nitrogen organic feed from spring to midsummer, and then a general feed until autumn (see also p.206).

• In winter, bring the pots into a greenhouse or conservatory – the minimum temperature needed varies with the type of citrus you have, but is likely to be at least 7°C (45°F) at night, and slightly higher during the day. Water less frequently, allowing the compost to partially dry out between waterings.

• Top-dress established plants with fresh compost in spring.

PLANTS FOR HANGING BASKETS

Trailing foliage plants

Helichrysum petiolare
Plectranthus australis
Plectranthus amboinicus
Various ivies (*Hedera*)
All the above are easy to grow
from cuttings (see p.106).

Flowering plants

Convolvulus major T
Convolvulus minor U
Black-eyed Susie (*Thunbergia
    alata*) T
Fuchsias T/U
Dianthus chinensis U
Begonias T/U
Pelargoniums T/U
Petunias T/U
Campanula fragilis T
Erigeron 'Profusion' T
Trailing lobelias T
Sanvitalia procumbens T
Scaevola aemula T

T trailing
U upright

Plants for winter baskets

A winter-flowering hanging
basket can be planted up in
early autumn once the summer-
flowering plants have passed
their prime. A dwarf conifer
surrounded by dwarf spring
bulbs and tulips looks good.
The conifer could be planted
out in spring to make way for
summer plants. Other good
winter choices are:

Variegated periwinkle (*Vinca
    major* 'Variegata')
Ivies (*Hedera*)
Small shrubby plants such
as *Euonymus fortunei* and
x *Chamaeycyparis pisifera*
Winter-flowering heathers

Variegated varieties, where
available, will give a brighter
show in dull winter weather.

Hanging baskets

Hanging baskets are an excellent way of decorating a wall or post, adding colour and interest. They can also increase the growing space in a greenhouse. Ornamentals, herbs and even tumbling tomatoes can all be grown successfully in baskets.

Go for the largest basket you can manage; buy a bracket that will take its weight, and attach it securely. A 40cm (16in) basket can be rather heavy to handle, but is easy to look after. A 35cm (14in) basket will do for general use, but a 30cm (12in) basket is really too small. An open wire framework increases the planting area, which ultimately makes a better show. It needs to be lined, however, and will dry out more quickly than a solid basket.

Liners and compost

Avoid sphagnum moss, the traditional liner, as its harvesting can cause environmental damage. Liners made from alternative, often recycled, materials are available, or you can make your own. An old woollen jumper can be cut to fit a basket, or you can use hay twisted into ropes. Hay does tend to grow some interesting surprises during the summer; unwanted additions can be snipped off with scissors.

"Mock moss", made from wool or coir and often dyed green, is the closest alternative to real moss. It is available loose, or in pre-formed sheets. Winter baskets can also be lined with conifer cuttings 15–20cm (6–8in) long, together with a little wool inside to seal any gaps.

A soilless compost is best as it reduces the weight of the basket. Improve water retention by adding an organic moisture retainer, based on coarse seaweed meal. Use worm compost in the mix (up to 25% volume) to increase the level of plant foods and improve the water-holding capacity.

Basket plants

Baskets look their best with a combination of trailing and upright plants, and plants with a long flowering season are most suitable. Choose a selection of plants to suit the season and location of the hanging basket. Half-hardy plants, both foliage and flowering, are usually used in summer baskets. Trailing plants should be planted around the rim, and through the mesh of wire baskets. Do not stint on numbers if you want a really good display. With ornamentals, aim for a plant every 5–10cm (2–4in), in all directions.

Caring for baskets

Water baskets daily – even in wet weather. Twice a day may be necessary in hot or dry, windy weather. Once a basket has dried out, it is very difficult to re-wet. Take the opportunity when watering to look out for pests and diseases, and snip off any infested foliage. If a whole plant is unhealthy, remove it and replace it with another plant. Regular deadheading helps to prolong the life of a basket display.

A weekly feed of a high-potash organic liquid feed (see p.206) is necessary for tomatoes and flowering plants. For baskets of herbs use a general-purpose liquid feed at fortnightly intervals. Seaweed extract added to the feed can be beneficial.

BASKET TIPS

• Raise basket plants in root trainers (see p.112), as the resulting root ball is an ideal size to pass through the liner into the compost.
• In cool climates, hang a newly planted basket in a greenhouse or a sheltered spot for a few weeks first to give it a good start.
• Wrap wool moss around the rim of a wire basket to prevent it cutting through stems.
• Avoid windy sites, such as the corner of a building; the basket will dry out more quickly.
• To prevent a basket swinging in the wind, tie the back of it to the bracket behind.

Improvised linings
Conifer clippings make one of the cheapest linings for hanging baskets, as do discarded woollen jerseys.

Gardening under cover

GREENHOUSES, SPACIOUS POLYTUNNELS, FRAMES AND CLOCHES
– ALL SHELTERS EXPAND YOUR GROWING HORIZONS

Full house (facing page)
A modest greenhouse can provide the inspiration you need to raise your own plants – organically, of course.

Collectable cloches (below)
These beautiful hand-blown glass cloches now have antique value, but in the organic garden are put to good use rather than gathering dust on a shelf. Our gardening forefathers expected tools and equipment to last a lifetime, and took care of them accordingly.

WALK INTO A GREENHOUSE or polytunnel (polythene tunnel) and feel the atmosphere change – savour the different smells, and marvel at the luxuriant growth. In here you can enjoy your organic garden whatever the weather. There may be new and interesting crops to care for, tender plants safe from frost, and seedlings destined for both the flower and food garden germinating weeks early.

Greenhouses and polytunnels trap the sun's energy, raising the temperature and creating an atmosphere where plants thrive. This chapter covers the selection and use of unheated structures that, with the addition of a heated bench and some winter insulation where necessary, can be used all year round, with minimal energy consumption.

Protection from the elements can also be provided, on a smaller scale, with cold frames, cloches and crop covers. A cold frame is a useful adjunct to a greenhouse, as a halfway house for hardening off tender plants and seedlings. It can also stand alone as a place to grow tender crops such as melons in summer, and salads in winter. A frame can also be used to provide unheated winter protection against the rain for alpine plants, and for cuttings and autumn-sown seeds.

Cloches are movable structures, again valuable for use in hardening off and for growing tender crops that benefit from extra warmth early and late in the season. Cloches can also be used to warm up the soil to give direct-sown crops a good start, or to bring on an early strawberry crop. Although cloches are primarily employed in fruit and vegetable growing, they can also be a useful form of protection for ornamentals.

Crop covers are the simplest form of protection of all – simply sheets of lightweight materials that are laid directly over plants to protect against adverse weather conditions and pests.

This chapter describes the range of structures and materials, from greenhouses to fleece, that are available, and how to get the best from them.

ADVANTAGES OF A COVERED SPACE

- Raise plants to flower or crop elsewhere.
- Save money on plants, especially bedding.
- Keep salads cropping all year and produce other out-of-season crops.
- Grow fruit and vegetables that need a good, long season to succeed outdoors.
- Grow exotic and tender fruit, vegetables and flowers which would not survive outside.
- Protect plants through adverse weather.
- Provide high-quality, organically grown pot-plants for the house.

Greenhouses and polytunnels

Lean-to greenhouse
*Plants in a lean-to structure can
benefit from the heat absorbed by a
wall during the day, then released at
night when temperatures fall.*

The biggest difference between a greenhouse and a
polytunnel is cost. Where limited space means only a
small structure is possible a greenhouse is the best
choice. It will be more pleasing to look at, needs less
maintenance, gives the best light transmission, and at
this size the cost differential is less. With larger
structures, over 20sq m (200sq ft), a polytunnel is the
best choice for cost-effective food production.

Glass is transparent, admits more light than
polythene, warms the house more quickly, and
retains heat for longer. Plants, particularly those with
a high light requirement, such as tomatoes, grow
better under glass than under polythene. Glass lasts
indefinitely whereas polythene becomes brittle and
breaks down with age.

What size of greenhouse?

Whatever the size of greenhouse, there will be times
when it is not large enough. A popular size is 1.8m
(6ft) wide and 2.4m (8ft) long. A path 60cm (2ft)
wide down the middle allows 60cm (2ft) each side
for the plants. A better arrangement is a greenhouse
that is 2.4m (8ft) wide and 1.8m (6ft) long. This
arrangement allows 90cm (3ft) either side of a
shorter path, giving some additional plant space.

Where space is limited, a lean-to greenhouse may be
an option. The problem of lack of light from one
side can be partially alleviated by painting the wall
inside the greenhouse white. A sunny wall is best for
a general-purpose greenhouse. A lean-to greenhouse
on a wall that does not get any direct sun is good
for cuttings, and for growing ferns and plants whose
natural habitat is the forest floor.

Materials for greenhouse frames

The most commonly used materials are aluminium
and wood. Aluminium is light and strong and needs
little maintenance. Aluminium greenhouses vary a
good deal in quality. Glazing bars consist of
T-sections in the poorer quality ones; H-sections
make for a sturdier, better-quality structure. On a
windy site, the latter is advisable.

Wooden greenhouses may be manufactured from
various types of wood. Cedar is very durable and
does not require toxic wood preservatives. It is a
good choice if you can be sure that it comes from a
sustainable, managed source. Wood is a better
insulator than aluminium, but the thicker glazing
bars required exclude more light.

Greenhouse glazing

Glass is the most usual glazing material, toughened
for safety if necessary. An alternative is polycarbonate
plastic – a twin-walled, lightweight, tough material
that provides good insulation. On the down side,
however, it is not "see-through" and allows only 85%
light transmission, as opposed to 97% for glass.
Adequate vents for good air circulation and
temperature control are vital (see facing page). If you
spend the day away from home, an automatic vent
opening system could be a good investment. Even in
spring, unexpected sun can cause a rapid temperature
rise if vents are closed and plants can suffer.

Choosing a polytunnel

A polytunnel consists of a framework of galvanised
steel hoops. One that is short and wide is preferable
to a long, narrow tunnel covering the same area, as
ventilation is better with this configuration.
Polytunnels have a much moister atmosphere than
greenhouses, so good ventilation is vital. Fit large

Side issue
Polytunnels may have vertical or sloping sides. If a polytunnel is less than 7m (22ft) wide, choose a model with vertical sides, so that every bit of space can be used.

doors (or double doors) at each end for maximum through-draught. Sides that roll up to reveal several feet of mesh netting are another possibility for providing extra ventilation.

What type of cover?

A polytunnel is covered with a single plastic sheet, stretched over the hoops. Covers can vary in thickness, lifespan, light transmission and cost. Some sheets are treated on one side to prevent drips – this treatment also aids insulation. The lifespan of a cover varies from three to seven years according to quality. It can be increased by a year or so by sticking anti-hotspot tape to the hoops before fitting.

Other plastic-covered structures

A solar tunnel has a PVC cover, reinforced with a fabric, fitted in sections. It is easier to clad, and the green colour gives a more pleasant appearance. A Keder house consists of a steel frame with a moulding bolted on the outside at 2m (6ft) intervals. This moulding supports the cover, which consists of two extremely tough, long-lasting, plastic sheets kept apart with 25mm (1in) bubbles. Excellent ventilation is afforded by sides which lower, or by roof sections that lift.

GREENHOUSE VENTILATION

Ventilation is essential for both temperature and disease control. Unlike ventilation, which can be controlled, draughts are bad for plants and should be eliminated, especially at the base and eaves. Ideally, the area of the roof vents should equal one-fifth of the floor area, but few greenhouses have this amount. Additional vents are sometimes available as an optional extra, and are well worth the extra investment. A louvre vent (left), fitted opposite the door and near to the floor, is more effective than additional roof vents because it acts as an air intake, replacing the warmed air that leaves through the roof vents.

Lime wash can be painted on glass to provide shading in high summer.

A sliding door is preferable to a hinged one as it does not catch the wind and can be used as a variable vent.

Equipping greenhouses and tunnels

The range of uses, and seasons of use, of a greenhouse or polytunnel can be greatly extended by adding a few extras. Good staging or benching, a waterproof power supply (fitted by a qualified electrician), a heated bench or propagator, and guttering that will direct water from the roof into a water butt will all prove invaluable.

This chapter assumes that no heating is provided under cover other than that supplied by a heated bench or propagator, with added insulation for winter. This is the most energy-efficient way of running most greenhouses and tunnels. Additional heating can of course be added if required.

Staging

If full use is to be made of a greenhouse or polytunnel, some form of staging will be needed. Slatted staging allows good air flow, which helps to control fungus disease, but it is cold in winter. A good compromise is to have slatted staging for summer use, covering it in winter with polystyrene slabs, protected by a plastic sheet. Cavity wall insulating slabs from a builders' merchant are ideal for this purpose.

Plants can be protected from several degrees of frost by standing them on polystyrene and covering them with one or two layers of fleece.

Narrow shelves above staging give an additional area for pots and trays. They are particularly useful for young plants, such as tomatoes, which require a lot of light. Wide shelves should not be fitted, as they block light from the plants below. Stand plants on higher shelves on trays, so water does not drip on plants below.

Heated bench

A heated bench is an economical and energy-efficient way of providing heat. The gentle "bottom heat" it provides will speed the germination of seeds early in the season, give a boost in cold weather to plants in containers, and can provide protection against light frost. To make a heated bench, soil-warming cables are buried in a 10cm (4in) deep bed of moist sand. A strong bench is needed to support the weight. A lighter alternative is an aluminium tray or bench, or roll-up mat, with a flat heating element incorporated into it. A thermostat can be fitted to regulate the temperature.

A box made from transparent polycarbonate with a hinged lid that fits over a heated bench provides extra protection, for raising tender plants, or keeping plants frost-free over winter. Fleece can be used as a cover instead of polycarbonate, but it is second-best.

On a smaller scale, you can simply purchase a heated propagator, which just needs to be plugged in to provide the same bottom heat.

Insulation

Insulation in winter and early spring helps to reduce the risk of frost damage and to maintain the highest possible temperature. In a greenhouse, the best insulation for the lower half is polystyrene slabs. The upper part of the greenhouse can be lined with bubble plastic. Twin-wall plastic with large bubbles (5cm/2in diameter) is best. The glazing bars of most

Plants on show
Although rarely possible on this sort of scale, staging makes good use of space and displays plants to best advantage.

SOIL BEDS UNDER COVER

Plants grown in a soil bed (far left) within a greenhouse or polytunnel are much easier to manage and require much less attention than those grown in the restricted environment of pots and growing bags. Appropriate soil improvement, following organic principles, avoids the need for liquid-feeding. Raised edges (left) allow bulky soil improvers to be added as a mulch.

A soil rather than concrete floor also helps to keep the atmosphere cooler in hot weather.

aluminium greenhouses have a channel on the inside. Clips are available that lock into this channel and hold the bubble plastic in place. If the glazing bars have no channel, curtain wires can be stretched along the ridge and eaves to support sheets of bubble plastic. In wooden greenhouses, insulating curtains can easily be put up with drawing pins. When insulation is removed, label each piece ready for refitting in the autumn. In a polytunnel, wires can be erected to support sheets of bubble plastic.

Shading

In summer, a greenhouse may become too hot. Plants will overheat and wilt; sunlight may scorch leaves and cause tomato fruits to develop a condition known as greenback. Shading cuts out some sunlight and prevents overheating – but, unless it can be easily removed, it will also cut out light on dull days. A well-ventilated greenhouse will require the minimum of shading and possibly none at all.

The simplest method of shading is to paint the outside of the glass with lime wash. Shading on the roof is more effective than on the sides. The side facing the midday sun should be shaded first and the effectiveness checked before applying any more. Blinds, which can be raised or lowered depending on the weather, are more efficient. They are fitted to the inside of the house, and may get in the way of tall plants that reach the roof. Green plastic sheeting,

fleece or netting fixed inside on supports can be used to protect individual, vulnerable plants and seedlings. Shading is not needed in a polytunnel.

Soil beds

Growing in the greenhouse soil, rather than in pots, is to be recommended for plants that are to spend their whole lives in the greenhouse. Plants, are much less trouble to look after when grown in the soil than in a pot or growing bag, particularly those which have high food and water requirements, such as tomatoes. The soil should be managed in the same way as the soil outside – using organic manures, compost, green manures and fertilisers to build fertility as required. Liquid feeding should not be required.

Soil beds, as opposed to concrete flooring, help to keep the air in a greenhouse moist. Organise the area into beds, preferably of a size that means that you do not have to tread on the soil.

A crop rotation (see also pp.301–303) must be used to prevent pest and disease build-up in the soil. As space is limited, and many greenhouse crops are related, a good rotation can be difficult to achieve. It may be necessary simply to avoid a crop for a year or two, or grow it in containers placed on a plastic sheet over the soil. If problems do build up, then it may eventually be necessary to change the soil to a depth of at least 30cm (12in).

Fruit in the greenhouse
Sweet melons (right) and grapes are traditionally grown to fruition under glass in cool climates, but you can also give winter shelter to tender fruits in pots, such as peaches and nectarines, not to mention herbs like bay. A greenhouse or polytunnel can also be used to force delicious crops of early strawberries (see p.226).

What to grow under cover

A greenhouse or polytunnel can be the engine-room of the kitchen garden, providing a host of young transplants for plots outside (see Propagation, pp.111–113). Some crops are, however, traditionally grown to harvest under glass – most especially the more tender, fruiting vegetables, such as tomatoes, cucumbers, peppers and aubergines (see pp.224–225). However, hardy crops can also be grown to crop out of season – either earlier or much later than they would outside. The "hungry gap", between late winter and summer, when outdoor crops are scarce, can be filled with midwinter sowings of spinach, spring cabbage, calabrese, peas, cauliflower, potatoes and other traditional outdoor crops. Choose cultivars suited to indoor growing (see left). Crops may either be sown direct in soil beds, or raised in a heated propagator or on a heated bench, then transplanted into the soil or potted up. Protect against frost where needed.

At the other end of the season, valuable greens for autumn and winter salads and stir fries can be sown, from late summer onwards, up to four weeks later than the recommended outdoor sowing times. Suitable crops include chervil, salad rocket, French sorrel, giant red mustard, corn salad, endive, American land cress and baby beetroot. You don't need a lot of room to produce a few meals' worth of fresh vegetables out of season. All of the projects on pp.226–227 work on a small scale.

Flowers

A greenhouse or polytunnel can supply almost continuous colour for the home and garden. Bedding plants, basket plants, container plants, half-hardy border perennials, hardy perennials, biennials, pot plants and cut flowers are all easy and rewarding to grow. As well as raising plants to flower elsewhere, grow some to add colour to the greenhouse or polytunnel itself. Sweet peas, sown in mid-autumn, will flower abundantly in spring. Half-hardy climbers such as morning glory and black-eyed Susan thrive in the protected conditions. Hardy annuals, such as pot marigolds, can be sown in autumn in pots or soil beds; they will then provide early spring colour and food for beneficial insects for pest control. French marigolds are worth growing among tomatoes and other crops as they may be effective in repelling whitefly.

CROPPING CALENDAR*

Season		Crop
Spring	Crops to harvest 4–8 weeks earlier than those outdoors	Cabbage, cauliflower, calabrese, lettuce (1) Peas (2) Potatoes, spinach, cress (3) Radish, watercress (4) Carrots (3 or 4) Strawberries (in pots or growing bags)
	Flowers for cutting	Sweet Williams, Brompton stocks, spring bulbs (6); sweet peas (2)
	Plant raising for growing inside	Tomatoes, peppers, aubergines (1) Sweetcorn (2) Cucumbers, courgettes, melons (5)
	Plant raising for growing outside	Bedding plants, patio and conservatory plants, basket plants* (1) Brassicas (1) Peas and beans (2) Courgettes, pumpkins and squashes (6)
	Plants being grown from cuttings	Hanging basket plants• Plants for pots and tubs
Summer	Fruit for harvesting	As sown in spring: aubergines, courgettes, cucumbers, melons, peppers, sweetcorn, tomatoes
	Plants being propagated	Hardy biennials from seed Half-hardy perennials from seeds and cuttings Hardy perennials from seeds and cuttings
Autumn	Fruit for harvesting	As in summer: aubergines, courgettes, cucumbers, melons, peppers, sweetcorn, tomatoes
	Flowers for cutting	Chrysanthemums, antirrhinums, stocks
	Seed-sowing and planting for winter crops under cover	Carrots (4, sow early autumn) Lettuce, endive, chicory, kohl rabi, Oriental greens and other winter salads and stir-fry leaves; raise in modules or sow direct depending on available cropping space Plant parsley in the corner of a soil bed
Winter	Food ready for harvest	Parsley planted in autumn Crops sown in autumn: carrots, kohl rabi, winter salads and stir-fry leaves
	Flowers for cutting	Chrysanthemums, narcissus, anemones Sweet peas••
	Plant raising	Broad beans and peas•• Onions, early cauliflowers and cabbages: sow in pots or modules on a hot bench; move to staging, prick out if appropriate. Keep frost-free
	Plants being protected from winter cold	Half-hardy container plants, such as cannas, standard fuchsias and bougainvillea Tender perennials, such as argyranthemum

* These plans could be fully realised in a 72sq m (84sq yd) greenhouse or polytunnel. They can be adapted for smaller structures

Key
1 Sown in modules, and finally transplanted into soil beds; could be sown in pots early in the season then pricked out into the modules
2 Sown in root trainers then transplanted into soil beds
3 Sown directly into soil beds
4 Grown from seed to maturity in containers
5 Sown individually in pots
6 Transplanted into beds the previous autumn, after summer crops have finished

• In late spring, hang up planted-up hanging baskets inside to give them a good start. Move outside when conditions are favourable
•• Sow in root trainers, germinate on hot bench and move to staging as soon as germination is observed

Fruiting crops under cover

Fine fruits (facing page)
An unheated greenhouse or polytunnel is a perfect environment for growing warmth-loving fruiting crops such as tomatoes (1), aubergines (2), cucumbers (3) and peppers (4).

Tomatoes are a popular crop for a cool greenhouse or polytunnel. Aubergines and peppers can also give excellent results, though they need slightly higher temperatures and do not give such high yields. All three belong to the same botanical family (see pp.304–313), making crop rotation difficult. To ring the changes, alternate them with crops from another family – cucumbers or melons, for example (see facing page) – or use pots and growing bags.

Starting off

Young plants may be bought from late spring onwards – but for the best choice of cultivars, and organic plants, raise your own on a heated bench or in a propagator. You can start tomatoes as early as midwinter if you can keep them frost-free. If not, sow in spring, 8–10 weeks before the last frost.

Tomato cultivars are available specifically for growing under cover, but most outdoor cultivars grow well in an unheated greenhouse or tunnel. "Indeterminate" types make best use of limited space, making tall plants with a single vertical stem, known as cordons. Bush and trailing types do well in pots and baskets. Aubergines and peppers make more compact, bushy plants, to 75cm (30in) tall at most.

Germinate seeds in a warm spot, pricking out the seedlings into 7.5–10cm (3–4in) pots. Keep these growing in a warm place (12–16°C/54–61°F depending on the plant). Once the first flowers show they can be planted in a soil bed or into pots or growing bags.

Soil beds, pots or growing bags?

To grow in soil beds in a greenhouse or polytunnel, apply a medium-fertility soil improver such as garden or worm compost to the soil, and check that the soil temperature 10cm (4in) below the surface is at least 14°C (56°F). If not, move the plants into a pot one size larger and wait. If plants have got rather leggy, they can be planted in the soil a few centimetres deeper than they were in the pot. Spacing will depend on the cultivar. Follow the advice on the seed packet. Never crowd plants; it encourages disease.

To grow in pots, use 21–25cm (8–10in) pots filled with a rich organic potting compost. Arrange them at a spacing appropriate to the crop and cultivar.

Organic growing bags are available to buy. Two plants per bag are easier to manage and give larger yields than the three usually recommended.

Watering and feeding

Watering and feeding should be adjusted to the growth rate of the plants. Early in the season, take care not to overwater or overfeed. Both can be disastrous. Once plants are growing well, however, do not let them go short of water. Cropping will be reduced, and tomatoes and sweet peppers may develop a condition known as blossom end rot (see p.88). Plants in pots and bags may need watering twice a day in hot weather. Start feeding with an organic liquid feed (see pp.206–207) once the first fruit has set. Plants grown in soil beds will not need so much watering, or feeding if the soil is in good heart.

Support and training

To support cordon tomatoes, attach a length of twine to the greenhouse frame above each plant, and tie the other end loosely around the stem at the base of the plant. As the plant grows, twist the tip around the string. Alternatively, tie the stem in to a tall cane. Taller aubergines and peppers may also need support.

Sideshoots growing from the main stem of cordon tomatoes must be pinched out when small, leaving the single main stem to grow tall. Sideshoots are not removed from bush tomatoes, peppers or aubergines.

Stopping

An indeterminate tomato will keep growing while conditions are suitable, but in cooler climates in an unheated greenhouse, plants are usually "stopped" after 4 or 5 flower trusses form. Simply cut off the growing tip of the plant. This encourages the development and ripening of the existing fruit, rather than new growth that will flower too late to crop. Aubergines and peppers need not be stopped, but limiting the number of fruits produces larger ones.

Harvesting

Harvest tomatoes when they are ripe. Peppers may be picked green, before they mature, or left to ripen, which will give a smaller crop. Aubergines are picked when the skin is still shiny and taut.

Supporting stems
In addition to the support given by twine, canes or frames, bottomless pots filled with compost around the base of tomato plants will encourage rooting from the stem and hence a more stable plant. It also makes directing water to the roots more efficient.

GREENHOUSE CUCUMBERS

Modern greenhouse cucumber cultivars prefer warmer, more humid conditions than tomatoes, so grow them away from the door or side vents. They are vulnerable to soil-borne stem and root rots, so rotate them with other crops or grow in growing bags or 30cm (12in) pots. Where greenhouse temperatures are regularly below 20°C (68°F) at night during the growing season, grow a ridge variety instead.

• Sow seed of greenhouse cultivars edgeways, one seed per 7.5cm (3in) pot.

• Germinate with bottom heat of at least 20°C (68°F).

• Keep the seedlings at around 20°C (68°F); move them to 12cm (5in) pots as necessary.

• Keep the compost moist but not waterlogged.

• Plant out when minimum night temperatures reach 20°C (68°F).

• All-female F1 cucumbers produce fruit on the main stem, so they can be grown up a single cane or string with plants 45cm (18in) apart, just like cordon tomatoes. They are very productive grown in this way and take up little space. Remove all flower buds and sideshoots from the first 30cm (12in) of the main stem; after this, remove sideshoots but leave the flower buds – you should get one cucumber at each leaf joint.

If you have sufficient space, train sideshoots out horizontally on netting or wires, pinching them out after two leaves and removing secondary shoots.

• Water regularly. Once fruits start to swell, liquid-feed pots and growing bags weekly.

• In hot weather, spray the greenhouse floor with water once or twice a day to maintain a humid atmosphere.

• Cut fruit regularly to maintain cropping.

Other under-cover crops

Even if space is limited, there are still ways to enjoy a taste of home-grown fresh fruits, vegetables and salads, and even cut flowers, often well before or after local garden produce is available.

Watercress

Watercress is quick and easy to grow. Germinate the seeds on a hot bench or in a propagator in a pot of multipurpose compost that is standing half-submerged in a tray of water. Prick out seedlings into modules or root trainers, and stand them, half submerged, in a tray of water.

Seal the small holes in a growing bag with electrician's tape. Remove most of the plastic from the top of the growing bag by cutting three large square holes. Soak the compost. Plant five plants in each hole, equally spaced. Begin harvesting as soon as the shoots are large enough and harvest regularly.

Strawberries

Strawberry plants forced under cover will only crop once, but produce a mouthwatering treat a month earlier than outdoor plants. In late summer, peg runners (see p.248) from garden plants into individual 15cm (6in) pots of multipurpose compost, or peg them down onto the surface of the compost using twine threaded through two drainage holes. When rooted, cut them from the parent plant and "plunge" the pots outdoors, sinking them into a bed of gravel of leafmould to keep the roots frost-free. Strawberries need a period of cold to initiate flower

bud formation. In midwinter, move the plants into to the greenhouse or polytunnel. When growth begins, feed once with an organic liquid feed (see pp.206–207). Cover flowering plants with fleece at night if frost is likely. Remove covers during the day to allow pollinating insects to reach the flowers. Flowers can be dusted with a little cotton wool to assist pollination. After harvest, discard the plants.

Stir-fry leaves and salad mix

Make use of any spare bench space with a crop that matures quickly. Stir-fry leaves and salad mixes (see pp.332–333) can be grown on a bench in a container 15cm (6in) deep, filled with an organic multipurpose compost. Sow seeds very thinly in rows every eight weeks from early spring until mid-autumn. Water the compost without wetting the leaves. Pick individual leaves as required.

Sweetcorn

Sweetcorn is very successful when grown under cover. Pollination of almost 100 per cent is achieved if at least nine plants are grown. The crop matures quickly and can use the same space occupied by early potatoes or another early crop. Some cultivars grow to 2m (6ft) tall, so choose a short cultivar unless you have a lot of headroom. Sow seeds individually in deep pots or root trainers in late spring. Plant out into a soil bed, in a block pattern, with plants 30cm (12in) apart. If red spider mite is a problem, there is a biological control (see p.100) that can be used.

Crops under cover (1)
This page, from left to right: sweetcorn needs the whole height of the house to grow; watercress grown in a wet growing bag can be harvested on a cut-and-come-again basis; you may find it hard to resist picking off the short but sweet crop of forced strawberries one by one.

New potatoes for Christmas

Save a few tubers from a crop of early potatoes, such as 'Swift', 'Maris Bard' or 'Rocket'. Leave them in the sun to turn green, then store until late summer. Then, plant in a 15 litre (3 gal) tub with drainage holes. Put a 15cm (6in) layer of multipurpose or potting compost into the bottom of the container and place three tubers, buds upwards, on top. Cover with 7.5cm (3in) of the compost, then water in. As the shoots grow, continue to fill the container with compost, always leaving the top of the shoots in the light. You can use the contents of used growing bags, or other once-used growing media to save costs.

Water regularly, taking care not to allow the compost to dry out – feeling the weight is a good test for moisture content. The foliage can be supported with four canes (fitted with cane caps to protect your eyes) pushed inside the rim of the pot, supporting two horizontal circles of string; or the stems can be allowed to trail from the pot. Protect from frost. Stop watering when the leaves and stems die off. Empty the contents on Christmas morning and harvest the new tubers.

Chrysanthemums

Pot-grown chrysanthemums fit in well with summer greenhouse crops and will produce colourful, long-lasting blooms for cutting in mid- to late autumn, when garden flowers are scarce. Started off under cover in spring, they can stand outside in summer, just when the covered space is needed for tomatoes and other fruiting crops; when these come to an end, the chrysanthemums can come in to flower.

Initially you will have to buy small plants or rooted cuttings. Specialist nurseries offer the widest choice. From then on you can propagate your own plants each year from the overwintering "stool" of the previous year's plants, if healthy. Take cuttings in spring (see p.106) and root on a heated bench or in a propagator at 13–18°C (55–65°F). When they are well-rooted, pot each one up into a 9cm (3½in) pot, and grow them on the greenhouse staging.

When the plants have made 15–20cm (6–8in) of growth, pinch out the growing tips, leaving 4–5 leaves below. This will make the plants grow bushy. When they have filled the small pots, pot them on into 23cm (9in) pots using a nutrient-rich growing medium, based on garden or worm compost (see pp.42–49 and 52–55). Harden them off gradually before standing outside for the summer.

As the plants grow, tie the stems to canes for support. Fix the tops of the canes to a horizontal wire to prevent the plants blowing over. Water as needed and feed weekly with an organic liquid feed. As autumn draws in, watch out for early frosts; protect flower buds with fleece if necessary. In mid-autumn, bring the plants under cover for flowering.

Cut flowers when the outside petals are expanded and the centre petals still tightly packed. Crush the end of the stem before placing in water. After flowering, cut off any growth above 15cm (6in) and put the pots under the staging. During winter, give only enough water to prevent dehydration. In spring, bring the pots into better light and increase watering. Then, to start again, take cuttings from the new shoots, and discard the parent plant.

Crops under cover (2)
This page, from left to right: compact and fast-growing salad crops and young stir-fry leaves are perfect gap-fillers, and many can be grown into winter (see also p.332); new potatoes can be grown in a tub or used growing bag in a corner until ready to harvest for a midwinter treat; other late offerings from the greenhouse or polytunnel can include your own chrysanthemums – either large showy blooms like these, or those with cheerful sprays of open flowers.

Management tips under cover

Plants under cover may be sheltered from some of the harsher aspects of life outdoors, but they are also completely reliant on you, the gardener, for water, food, and protection against harmful organisms that will also thrive indoors, with a ready supply of tender plant material and cosy hiding places. They may also suffer from the down-side of being under glass or polythene – a build-up of excess heat and humidity – without your intervention. With "good housekeeping" you can provide the conditions that plants, rather than pests and diseases, need to thrive.

Climate control

• Control temperature by insulation and ventilation – shade only as a last resort.
• Keep lengths of fleece cut to size. During heavy frosts, cover tender plants with one or more layers.
• Invest in a maximum/minimum thermometer to monitor temperature and help you to manage appropriate ventilation and insulation.
• On mild winter days fully open doors and vents but remember to close them in mid-afternoon. If you are not at home, leave the doors closed.
• When warm days are followed by cold nights, close a polytunnel well before sundown to obtain a layer of condensation on the sheet. This provides some insulation against the cold.

A healthy environment

• Keep the house very tidy – store pots and other equipment elsewhere.
• Keep the glass or plastic clean – it may need to be washed down several times a year.
• Clear out and scrub down the structure at least once a year. Use hot, soapy water and finish off with a powerful jet-rinse with a hose.
• Do not smoke in the greenhouse or tunnel.
• Prune out dead and diseased parts of plants – clean the secateurs before moving to another plant.
• Dispose of dead plants, or those badly infected with pest or disease, immediately.

Pests and diseases

• Raise your own plants where possible to avoid the risk of bringing in pests and diseases.
• Check bought plants and their compost. Quarantine them in another area for a week or two before introducing them to the greenhouse or polytunnel.
• Use crop rotation to prevent the build-up of soil-borne pests and diseases.

NATURAL PEST CONTROL

The enclosed, sheltered environment of a greenhouse or polytunnel provides ideal conditions for the microscopic pests predators known as biological controls. These are available to combat glasshouse whitefly (top picture), red spider mite, aphids, thrips, vine weevil, scale and slugs. For more details see *Plant Health*, p.100.

Film of moisture
Closing polytunnel doors early will result in a layer of condensation building up on the inner side of the polythene as the outdoor air cools down in the evening, buffering sharp falls in temperature inside.

USING STRAW BALES

Straw bales can provide an extra root run and moisture reservoir for tomato plants. Use organically-sourced straw – tomato plants are very susceptible to chemical residues. Soak the bales in water and apply a high-nitrogen organic fertiliser over 2 to 3 weeks, so that they start to decompose. Wrapping the bales in polythene can help to retain moisture and warmth, but take care in hot summers that conditions do not become too warm for plant roots. Then plant each tomato in a mound of potting mix on the surface of the bales. Feed them throughout the season exactly as you would plants in pots and growbags.

• Inspect plants daily for signs of pest or disease. Problems build up rapidly in a closed environment.

• In summer, mist plants that are susceptible to red spider mite with a fine spray of water.

• Use yellow sticky traps to monitor pests.

• Use biological control agents (see p.100) to deal with regular pest problems. Remove sticky traps before introducing flying biological control agents.

Soil, composts and feeding

• Wherever possible grow plants in soil beds rather than pots or growing bags.

• Use organic techniques to keep the soil fertile and healthy.

• Pot up plants promptly as necessary, to prevent them exhausting their compost and getting pot-bound. This also helps to keep pests at bay.

Watering

• The appearance of the surface of a soil bed is not always a good indication of the moisture level; check below as well. Check pots by feeling the weight.

• Make an inspection hole towards one end of a growing bag that allows compost to be tested with the finger tips.

• Whenever possible water in the morning; avoid watering in the evening.

• Wet the soil rather than the plants.

• Use a good quality watering can with a long spout and a removable, fine rose. A can with an on/off trigger can make watering more precise.

• Use rainwater whenever possible, but water seeds and young seedlings with tap water; they are more vulnerable to disease and hence need cleaner water.

• Water seeds and seedlings from below, standing pots and trays in a container of water. Remove when the surface of the compost is wet.

• Before use, leave tap water to stand in the greenhouse for a few hours to warm up and to allow excess chlorine to escape.

• Periodically check the effectiveness of watering – feel the weight of pots at the front, middle and back of benches. Check the edges of beds – they may be getting less water than the middle.

• In warm weather, "damp down" in the morning – wetting paths and other surfaces to increase humidity.

• In autumn keep foliage as dry as possible.

• In winter use a smaller watering can, to make it easier to apply a smaller quantity of water.

Cold frames, cloches and crop covers

Cold frames, cloches and crop covers can provide valuable temporary or longer-term protection for food crops and ornamentals. They are cheaper, require less space, and are more flexible in their use than a greenhouse or polytunnel.

Cold frames

A traditional cold frame is a low, wooden- or brick-framed structure with a sloping roof made from glazed wooden frames, known as lights. These lights may be hinged to form a lid that can be propped up, or they may slide across or be removed entirely, allowing the degree of ventilation to be varied according to what is in the frame. This type of frame is not widely sold these days, but it is relatively cheap to make one at home, especially if recycled timber or bricks are used. Rigid plastic may be used for glazing where weight or safety must be considered. Making your own also means that the frame can be custom-built to fit the available space. Sit wooden frames on bricks to prevent the timber rotting.

The modern cold frame is a lightweight, aluminium structure with glass all round – very like a large cloche. These are more flexible in many ways as they are more easily moved, but they do not provide the same degree of insulation, and are not as sturdy as their old-fashioned counterparts.

Site a cold frame where it will get good light in winter and spring. Shading can be added in summer, and insulation in winter, if needed. If you are going to grow crops in the frame, then prepare the soil covered by the frame to suit the crop in mind. If using the frame to stand out pots and trays, a layer of gravel makes a good base. This can be laid over a weedproof membrane. If this is firmly fixed around the base of the frame, it will help to keep out slugs.

Cloches

Cloches are designed to be moved around the garden as required. They come in many different shapes and sizes, and vary widely in price. Tunnel cloches, supported by wire or plastic hoops, are designed to protect a row of plants; wider versions can be used to cover the whole width of a 1.2m (4ft) vegetable bed. Where pest protection is the main requirement, tunnel cloches may be covered with netting, mesh or fleece instead of plastic. Other types of cloche may be used individually, or put together to cover a row. Designs such as the traditional bell cloche (now available in clear plastic) are intended to cover individual plants.

Shape, height, width, ventilation, degree of frost protection, and ease of watering and repositioning are all points to consider when choosing a cloche. Those shaped like the letter "A" give plants near the edges little headroom; wider cloches with vertical or near-vertical sides are more versatile.

Filling the frame

The great advantage of a frame is that it provides both protection and excellent ventilation. This is particularly useful when hardening off plants. Cold frames can also be used to protect hardwood cuttings and trays of slow-germinating seeds of trees and other hardy plants during winter, and to give shelter from winter rains to alpine plants and dwarf bulbs.

GETTING THE BEST FROM A FRAME

Use your cold frame to:
• Harden off seedlings and transplants.
• House trays and pots of slow-germinating seeds, such as trees and wild flowers.
• Grow tender crops such as melons and cucumbers.
• Grow early and late salad crops.
• Create nursery beds for brassica transplants.
• Protect hardwood cuttings over winter.
• Protect alpines in pots from winter rains.

CLOCHES

Cloches come in all shapes and sizes (**1**); even open-weave baskets can protect against birds and rabbits, and frost at night. Simple "mini-cloches" made from sawn-off plastic bottles (**2**) will protect individual young plants. Be sure not to trap a slug inside. A Victorian glass cloche (**3**) makes an attractive addition to any garden. Polycarbonate sheeting has now largely replaced the glass panes traditionally used to make functional A-shaped cloches (**4**), good for low, bushy plants.

HARDENING OFF

Plants protected by frames and cloches must be gradually acclimatised to the cooler, drier outside environment, although this may not take as long as for plants grown within a greenhouse or polytunnel, especially as the season progresses. First, prop up or slide off frame lights for part of the day (right), then for the whole day, then at night as well for a couple of days before removing the plants.

Plant growth under a cloche can be especially soft and tender, as the space is so enclosed. A spell of dull weather is ideal for hardening them off, as they will be less likely to be scorched by strong sunlight. Remove the cloche (far right) for a short time in the evening, replacing it before nightfall for several days.

THE MANY USES OF CLOCHES

• Warm up soil in spring prior to planting or sowing.
• Help to establish newly set out transplants.
• Protect plants from birds, rabbits and other mammals.
• Protect plants from insect pests.
• Protect half-hardy crops from light frost and cold winds.
• Harden off plants grown in a greenhouse or polytunnel.
• Cover parts of rows of salads to stagger maturity times.
• Protect food crops such as parsley and broad beans over winter.
• Protect autumn-sown flowers (for example, larkspur and cornflower) over winter.
• Force cut flowers such as anemones in early spring.
• Extend the season into early winter for herbs and salads.
• Protect cuttings of hardy perennials in winter.
• Protect strawberry flowers from frost – remove in daytime for insect pollination.
• Cover herbs in late winter for an early crop.
• Keep hardy salads cropping over winter.

Choosing cloches

Traditional glass cloches are undoubtedly attractive, and give better light transmission and frost protection than plastic ones. It is also easier to see what is going on inside without removing the cloche. Plastic-covered cloches, however, are relatively cheap, lightweight and less likely to break. The disadvantages of plastic cloches are that they give less frost protection (unless twin-walled) and are more likely to blow away in the wind. Plastic also has a shorter lifespan. Exposure to sunlight decays it, causing it to become opaque and brittle. Better-quality cloches will use plastic that is more resistant to damage by sunlight.

Cloche practicalities

Most cloches have to be removed to water the plants beneath. A few models incorporate features that allow watering without removal, but it is always important to check plants regularly. Adequate ventilation is also essential in cloches – simply to prevent plants overheating, to facilitate hardening off, or perhaps to give pollinators access to flowers – for example, of strawberries. Some cloches have holes in the ends, covered by "hit-or-miss" discs. For these to be effective, the holes have to be large in

LIMITATIONS OF CLOCHES
• Frost damage is possible when temperatures fall below -2°C (28°F).
• They may encourage soft growth that collapses when the cloche is removed.
• Weed germination and growth is speeded up.
• The enclosed atmosphere under a cloche encourage diseases, which can go unnoticed.
• Watering can be difficult.

relation to the area of the ends. It is, however, equally important that a cloche can be closed at both ends, or it can become a wind tunnel.

Horticultural fleece

Fleece is a lightweight, synthetic fabric, bonded rather than woven, that can be laid directly over plants. It lets in air, light and water. Fleece is easily damaged, and may only last a couple of seasons. Thicker grades can last longer. Outdoors, fleece can be used as a temporary cover to protect vulnerable plants against the elements, and pests, until the plants are sturdy enough to survive alone. To keep pests out, it is advisable to cover the seeds or plants right from the start. When the plants are to be uncovered, remember to remove the fleece gradually, replacing it at night at first, to harden plants off.

For short-term protection, for example when frost is forecast and could harm new bedding plants, strawberries in flower, or tender crops in a greenhouse or polytunnel, the fleece can be put on overnight and then removed during the day. Fleece can also be used to form windbreaks for young or vulnerable plants.

Cropping under fleece

Fleece can be used as a long-term cover to protect a crop throughout its life – for example, it makes an excellent barrier to carrot fly – but this does have disadvantages. Weeds will thrive under fleece, as will diseases that are encouraged by the more humid atmosphere. And, since the material is opaque, it has to be removed in order to check what is going on underneath. Frequent removal and replacement will be necessary to weed and inspect for pests and disease problems. Some of these disadvantages can be avoided by using fine plastic mesh instead of fleece to cover crops.

Mesh fabrics

Lightweight, fine mesh plastic net fabrics are also available for garden use to protect plants. Much tougher than fleece, this type of material can last for 10 years or so. It can be laid directly over plants, or stretched over tunnel cloche hoops. These fabrics do not give as much protection against frost as fleece does, but they do give plants some protection against the elements and from the same range of pests. Most pests will be excluded by the standard mesh size, but to form a barrier against tiny creatures such as flea beetle, ultra-fine mesh (0.8mm) should be used.

A covering of fine mesh has the advantage of being "see-through", so that you can check the progress of plants (and weeds) without continually removing the covering. Conditions are less humid too, so diseases are less likely to develop. Mesh can be left in place throughout the life of a crop, or until it outgrows the height of supported covers and tunnels – but only do this if absolutely necessary. In general, it is best to remove coverings as soon as plants can survive without them.

Pests excluded by crop covers

Fleece and mesh, securely fixed, will protect crops from flying pests such as carrot fly, flea beetle, cabbage root fly, cabbage white butterflies, aphids and onion fly. Rabbits will also be deterred, but not slugs and other soil-dwelling pests, which attack crops from below.

FIXING FLEECE

Weigh fleece down with small bags of soil or wooden planks, or use the proprietary plastic pegs sold for this purpose. Alternatively, staple the edges of the fleece to two wooden battens. Unwind the fabric to release extra material. With wooden-edged raised beds, you can pin or staple the fleece directly to the edging (top picture) on one side.

To make a windbreak, tuck the fleece under a horizontal length of twine looped between canes (bottom picture). Catch the fleece under the twine when you wind it around the canes to help prevent slipping.

Covered crop
Fleece provides good protection against many pests, including cabbage root fly, carrot fly, whitefly and flea beetle. Lay it loosely over the plants and hold it down all around. Tuck some slack in at the edges and release this as the plants grow.

Grow your own

ENJOY THE FRESHEST, MOST DELICIOUS ORGANIC PRODUCE

Growing fruit

BLOSSOM IN SPRING, SHADE IN SUMMER AND ABUNDANCE AT
HARVEST – FRUIT IS THE TREASURE TROVE OF THE GARDEN

FRUIT HAS BEEN part of our diet since we gathered
our harvest from the wild forests. Now tamed,
improved and cultivated, fruits offer instant
gratification as the original nutritious fast food,
straight from the plant. Associations with time and
place, accretions of history, myth and folklore all add
to the spice – for example, apples, once associated
with the fall of Adam and Eve, were held in low
esteem from the 13th century until their
rehabilitation as the just fruits of honest toil in the
16th century. In our times too, fruit surely earns its
place in a garden.

All fruits are attractive in blossom, some also
deliciously scented to give promise of the juicy
bounty to come. Fruit is sufficiently versatile to be
restricted and managed to fit even a small garden –
trained against a wall or fence, for example. Where
there is space, however, the crown of an apple or
pear tree provides dappled shade and much sought-
after medium height to the plant architecture of the
garden. Finally, the harvest is both luscious and
beautiful. There may be no fruit in some years,
but generally there is surplus to spare for friends –
and for wildlife.

All-round attraction
*Every garden should have an apple
tree – not only productive but
beautiful in flower, leaf and fruit, with
silvery bark on branches that become
ever more gnarled and characterful with
age. Even at the end of its life it yields
fragrant logs for burning.*

**Currants and berries
(below)**
*Soft fruits from the supermarket chiller
cabinet cannot compare with those
warmed and ripened by the sun in
your own garden.*

WHY GROW FRUIT ORGANICALLY?

- **Fast food** Fruit is the ultimate fast
food, which can be eaten straight from the
plant.
- **Produced without pesticides** Organically
grown, there is no need to peel or scrub the
fruit before eating.
- **Connect with the seasons** Summer
strawberries, autumn apples – harvesting your
own fruit connects with the living seasons.
- **Endless choices** With hundreds of apples to
choose from as a starter, the range of fruits and
cultivars is amazing.
- **Fresh and tasty** Home-grown fruit can be
harvested and eaten at the appropriate time –
not to suit the shops.
- **Less work for more** Growing most fruit
takes little time in comparison with the
returns.
- **Local production** Saves on food miles;
allows you to taste fruits and cultivars which
would never make it to the shops.
- **Enhance the garden** Fruit trees and bushes
can be attractive garden plants in their own
right.
- **Anyone can do it** Fruit can be fitted into
even the smallest of plots.
- **It can be fascinating** Growing fruit can be
a rewarding hobby.

Deciding what to grow

This chapter deals with a range of fruits suitable for temperate climates. This covers both sweet and sharp fruits, from strawberries, cane fruits and small-berried bush fruits through to top fruits such as apples, pears, plums, figs, cherries and peaches. Also included are hazelnuts.

You will have your personal preferences for the fruits you like. It is important also to know what will succeed in your conditions and what you have space for. The paragraphs that follow explain the needs of different fruits and will help you make successful choices. Once you have considered all the potentials and pitfalls of your site, together with the local weather, you will be in a good position to decide what to grow and where. You may have walls or fences in your garden. These may be open to the sun most of the day, sunny for part of the day or cold and facing away from the midday sun. You may have a garden with limited space. There are possibilities for all these situations.

Some fruits may benefit from growing against a wall, especially in less favourable conditions, but most fruit also grows well in the open garden. The free flow of air in this situation helps to reduce disease infections.

Many fruits are very attractive to birds, squirrels and foxes and will need to be grown inside a netted cage or netted individually. These include cherries and all the soft fruits – currants and berries.

Coping with the elements

Although most of the fruits described in this book are hardy, few, if any, will cope with frost when in blossom or in early fruit. It is vital to avoid planting into frost pockets and to avoid creating new frost pockets by erecting fences or establishing plantings that trap and hold frost rather than letting it drain away. Frost, being cold, drains downwards to the lowest point. Fruit trees and bushes can, therefore, be planted above the danger level and thus escape damage. It is worth remembering also that some fruit, such as some cultivars of strawberry, need a period of frost in winter to initiate flowering for the next year's crop.

Wind has the obvious effect of damaging branches. Less obvious is the fact that pollinating insects cannot settle in blustery weather and this will affect the size of the harvest. Some gardens are naturally sheltered. If not, thought needs to be given to creating shelters against the wind.

Without doubt the greatest contribution to a successful harvest comes from the sun. Sunshine provides energy for plants to grow, ripens wood and improves the flavour and colour of fruits. If your garden receives little sun, you will be greatly limited in what you can successfully grow.

Latitude also affects choice of fruits. The further away from the equator you are, the shorter your summer will be and it simply may not be long enough to ripen some fruits. If you live in a cool region with a short season you are unlikely to ripen good dessert grapes without a greenhouse, for example. Other fruits often grown under cover in cooler areas (see also pp.216–229) include figs, peaches and apricots. In warm regions these fruits bear bountiful crops without protection; on the other hand, in these areas apple varieties, from cooler climates, will struggle with the heat.

Altitude above sea level is another important consideration. At higher altitudes the season is shorter and there is simply insufficient warm daylight time to ripen some crops. Above 120m (400ft) the possibilities are more limited: damsons, early ripening and cooking varieties of apples, currants, strawberries and most cane fruits will be the main choices.

Arctic raspberry
An unusual fruit that you will be very unlikely to see in the shops, but like alpine strawberries is easy to grow, and ornamental too. The flavour of the berries produced by these mat-forming herbaceous perennials is subtly different to that of the conventional raspberry. Plants reach a mere 15–20cm (6–8in) tall, and die back in winter. To ensure good pollination, more than one cultivar must be grown.

How much space?

If your garden is small, you may have to adapt your plans for fruit to fit the available space. Many types of soft fruits are popular with birds and will need netting. This is easier to do when they are grown in a plot together. You may decide that even just two raspberry plants, grown up each side of a freestanding post, are better than none. Even in the smallest garden, however, you can grow plentiful supplies of strawberries along the edge of a border or path, or in containers. Many tree fruits will also, with careful maintenance, be productive in a pot (see also *Container Gardening*, pp.212–213).

A single fruit tree can, when mature, produce a generous crop, but some cultivars of top fruit need other trees nearby that are compatible pollinators in order to set a crop. A single pear tree of the variety 'Louise Bonne de Jersey' in your garden, for example, is unlikely to set a crop – unless your neighbour has a compatible cultivar.

But remember that thanks to the development of dwarfing rootstocks for many fruit trees, and their amenability to training (see pp.244–245), two or more trees need not dominate a garden. If you are very partial to apples and keen to plant several cultivars, but have limited space, you could use a wall or fence to grow cordons which need only 75cm (30in) between trees.

Will it grow in my soil?

Fortunately most soils are perfectly suitable for growing fruit. Shallow chalky soils, however, do pose problems that are hard to rectify, partly because the soil is too shallow for good rooting and partly because it is very alkaline. Some fruit can still be grown in these conditions but raspberries, in particular, will struggle.

Blueberries and cranberries need very acid conditions (pH 5.5 or less) and most fruit thrives in slightly acid soil. However the majority of fruits will tolerate alkaline conditions. Raspberries are an exception and become iron-deficient in soils with a pH higher than 6.5. This will show as a yellowing of young leaves on new growth and will ultimately shorten the potential life of the planting from 12–14 years to, perhaps, eight. You will still be able to harvest an adequate crop in this time, however, so all is not lost. It is very difficult to make alkaline soils more acid but very acid soils can be made less acid by applying ground limestone or dolomitic lime.

The acidity of the soil is not the only factor. The structure of soil is also important. In good, friable soil, plant roots are able to ramify freely and deeply and make good use of the nutrients already present.

It comes as no surprise, perhaps, that fruit prefers a deep rich loam that is free-draining but moisture-retentive. You may not have these conditions to offer but much can be done to improve soil structure, open up heavy soils and increase the water-holding

Space-saving forms
Cordons and espaliers can not only be grown against walls and fences, but also freestanding, with the support of a strong post and wire system, to form attractive screens.

FRUITS FOR
SUN AND SHADE

Must have sun
Apples
Apricots
Figs
Grapes
Hybrid berries
Peaches
Pears
Plums
Nectarines
Strawberries
Sweet cherries

**Will tolerate light or
part-day shade**
Acid cherries
Blackberries
Blackcurrants
Damsons and gages
Gooseberries
Raspberries
Red- and whitecurrants
Worcester- and jostaberries

Mulching
Fruit trees benefit from a thick strawy mulch in late spring, but draw it away slightly from the actual trunk. Rake off and compost the straw in winter to remove any pests and disease spores lurking within.

capacity of light soils (see *Soil and Soil Care*, pp.33–61). If starting with a very poor soil, start to improve it a year in advance of planting.

Drainage

Fruits are composed largely of water and so adequate supplies are essential (see overleaf). In very wet localities, on the other hand, the main preoccupation will be with drainage (see also p.64). Roots will rot and fungal pathogens attack where drainage is poor. Perhaps the most dramatic effect can be seen in raspberry plantings, where root rot (*Phytophthora fragariae-rubi*) can rapidly run along waterlogged rows, killing canes as it spreads.

Preparing the site

Fruit is a long-term investment. In the case of fruit trees you may expect 50 years of cropping or more, depending on the rootstock used (see p.242). You might imagine that maintaining such a crop will need regular inputs of organic fertilisers, manure and compost. This is not necessarily the case. Giving fruit a good start is, on the other hand, of fundamental importance. It is difficult to improve conditions after planting, whereas prior to planting

there is ample opportunity to create the soil structure and fertility to give trees, bushes and canes a running start. A well-established plant has an extensive root system that can forage for nutrients more efficiently than a weak plant. Details of soil improvement using well-rotted manure and garden compost are given under individual fruits. For alternatives and further information, see Bulky organic soil improvers, p.40.

Supplementary feeds

Spraying with dilute seaweed extract (see p.207) is extremely beneficial for fruit, especially in spring and early summer. Both trees and bushes will take up nutrients more effectively, receive a full range of trace elements and have enhanced hardiness to frost damage if given regular seaweed sprays.

Watering needs

If you only have a small number of fruit trees and bushes you may be able to supply adequate water by watering can or hand-held hose. Where this is impractical, the best solution is to install permanent irrigation lines of seep- or soaker hose (see p.68). A mulch (see below) of straw or other organic matter applied in late spring will help conserve water. Large, established trees should not need watering.

Mulches

Specific recommendations for planting and feeding are given for each fruit type on the following pages. As a general rule, however, with the exception of strawberries and some others, you will not need to add compost or fertilisers more than once every two or three years. An important addition to this is the use of organic mulches.

The most common materials used for mulching fruit are straw and hay, although weathered and part-composted shredded prunings and woodchips are excellent if enough is available. You can use your own shreddings or buy in a bagged product.

Mulches need to be applied thickly to damp soil in late spring when it has had a chance to warm up. Apply hay and straw up to 10cm (4in) deep and shreddings 5cm (2in) deep, keeping a clear area of about 15cm (6in) diameter round tree trunks and the base of plants to deter voles and mice from chewing at the bark. Mulches not only suppress weeds and retain moisture but can also contain significant levels of nutrients. Hay and straw, for example, will release considerable amounts of potassium during the course of a season. Shreddings contain fewer nutrients but add to organic matter levels and improve soil structure. Pale-coloured mulches should be removed in winter to allow dark soil to absorb heat on early spring days and radiate it up into branches at night, protecting fragile emerging blossoms. Removing the mulch will also clear away some disease spores and overwintering pests.

Plant health

The best approach to maintaining healthy fruit crops is to be watchful, keeping a regular check on how plants are growing. In this way signs of any problems are seen early on and can be dealt with before they become serious. Incipient disease infections can often be pinched or pruned out and pest colonies despatched with a wipe of the thumb. See right for general guidelines to keep your fruit healthy. Potential pests and diseases are given for individual fruits, with more detailed advice in the *A–Z of Plant Problems* (see pp.367–395).

Weeds – tolerance or zero tolerance

Control of weeds in fruit is just as important as for vegetables, except where fruit trees are growing on vigorous rootstocks. If we recognise that many weeds are, in fact, wild flowers, we instantly change their status. Many of them are valuable in attracting beneficial insects and have an important place in orchards. In close proximity to bush and cane fruits and low-growing fruits such as strawberry and alpine raspberry, however, they are less beneficial, competing with the crop plants for light, water and nutrients; if very rank, they can reduce air flow and increase the likelihood of fungal attack.

Hoeing and hand-weeding are still the most effective ways of removing weeds growing in open soil. There is often a flush of weed growth before mulches are applied in spring. Once mulches are in place, they should severely curtail weed growth. Some perennial weeds may penetrate the mulch and these will have to be removed by hand.

Since perennial weeds are so awkward to remove from growing fruit, it pays to do your utmost to clear ground well before planting (see pp.78–79).

Gooseberry sawfly larva
This pest can rapidly strip the foliage from both gooseberry and redcurrant bushes. When young, the larvae are very small and prefer to feed in the centre of the plant. You need to look carefully and regularly right into the heart of bushes in order to find and pick off the pests before they can do too much damage.

FRONT LINE DEFENCE
Prevention is the key to healthy fruit.
- Plant pest- and disease-resistant cultivars.
- Choose the right site.
- Never plant fruit where similar fruit has been growing.
- Prune plants to create an open growth habit, to allow good airflow between branches.
- Do not overfeed with nitrogen.
- Remove damaged and diseased fruit, shoots and foliage.
- Remove mulches over winter.
- Use a liquid seaweed foliar spray.
- Protect from birds with netting or a fruit cage.
- Provide shelter and the right kind of plants and flowers for creatures that eat pests. Fruit pest predators to encourage:
Anthrocorid bugs (see p.98)
Earwigs (see pp.93 and 192)
Blue tits (see p.191)
Lacewings (see pp.98 and 192)
Ladybirds and their larvae (see pp.99 and 192)
Typhlodromid mites
Hoverfly larvae (see pp.98 and 197)
Most need no more welcome than an unsprayed garden, but in many cases providing appropriate habitats and food plants too will make all the difference (see *Gardening for Wildlife*, pp.186–202).

Choosing cultivars

There is more to choosing a cultivar than liking the name. There are fruit cultivars for different seasons, different climates, different flavours; there are also cultivars with known resistance to some pests and diseases. When making your selections you should bear the following points in mind:

• **Season of harvest and use** If you have room you may wish to extend your season of harvest with cultivars that succeed each other in maturing or fruits that are suitable for storing. There are late-cropping cultivars of apples and pears that do not actually ripen until stored for a while.

• **Disease and/or pest resistance** If you have a particular local problem, such as apple canker, you should look for resistant or less susceptible varieties.

• **Suitability for your local climate** Cultivars that do well in a warm climate may perform poorly when planted in a garden with a shorter, cooler season and vice versa. Some older cultivars have strong local associations and these are worth seeking out for general robustness and reliability.

• **Flavour** Not all cultivars have good flavour and personal tastes vary. If you can, try before you buy.

• **Pollination requirements** See below and under individual fruits for further information.

Pollination

Fruit will not form unless flowers are pollinated. Many fruits, including the majority of soft fruits, are self-fertile: they do not need pollen from another plant or tree to set flowers. Many cultivars of plum and a few cherries are self-fertile; many apples are to some extent self-fertile but benefit greatly from cross-pollination with another apple cultivar. Some cultivars are not able to set a crop on their own and need to be planted within bee-flying distance of another cultivar that is both compatible and in flower at the same time. If you are short of space, the next door garden is usually close enough.

The Royal Horticultural Society classification system for fruit into flowering groups is generally accepted as standard and most fruit suppliers now use this system in their listings to help customers choose cultivars that are compatible and will pollinate each other. Some apples are referred to as "triploids". This refers to their genetic structure and means that the flowers are "male sterile", producing little or no pollen. These generally need two pollinators, of different cultivars, to set a good crop.

Cherries are particularly complex as, apart from the few self-fertile cultivars such as 'Stella', they all need pollinators and are extremely fussy, in general, as to who supplies the pollen. There are several instances of total incompatibility and no crop can result from these matches.

Rootstocks

Most fruit trees are not grown on their own roots. Instead they are grafted in the nursery onto the roots of compatible trees, usually of the same type. Apricots, however, are grafted onto plums, and pears

Cordon companions
A row of apple or pear cordons, here trained against post and wire supports, can be made up of different cultivars to fulfil pollination needs.

onto quinces. Rootstocks enable propagation of cultivars that do not root from cuttings, and help to control the size of the tree. Depending, for example, on the rootstock selected, the same cultivar of apple might grow 2.4m (8ft) tall, or 9m (30ft). Further information on rootstocks is given under each fruit.

Own-root trees

Figs are always grown on their own roots, and all other tree fruits can be. They need careful managing as they can be enormously vigorous, resulting in trees up to 10.5m (35ft) tall that take five to eight years to crop. In collaboration with fruit breeder Hugh Ermen, HDRA has been working for some years on establishing systems for growing trees on their own roots. Providing that vigour can be controlled, there are benefits for the organic gardener in better health and longevity (for the tree!) and less need for scrupulous weed control, as the trees will grow strongly despite competition, once established. In due course apple trees on their own roots will become available to gardeners.

There is scope for experimentation and innovation with these own-root trees. Orchards of such trees allow for imaginative floral underplantings, as the resulting competition for water and nutrients helps to control the natural vigour of the fruits.

Family trees
Two or more cultivars can be grafted onto the same rootstock to produce a single tree that bears different fruits on different branches; not only a novel talking point, but also a practical way of growing cultivars needed to pollinate each other in a small space.

Newly grafted fruit trees
Specialist fruit nurseries graft many hundreds of young trees each year, binding shoots from chosen cultivars onto the roots of other trees that will control height and vigour. The plant tissue fuses naturally at the graft point or "union".

Pruning and training

All fruit needs to be pruned for best results. Pruning aims to achieve a number of objectives:

• **Removal** of dead, diseased and damaged material.
• **Creating a balance** between light penetration and light interception. With too many leaves, sunlight cannot enter the crown to ripen fruit; too little foliage and not enough photosynthesis takes place.
• **Opening up** the branch framework to allow better air circulation and lessen risk of fungal infection.
• **Pruning** out colonies of pests.
• **Shaping** of trees.
• **Control** of vigour.

Before starting to prune it is important to understand how trees and bushes grow. There are essentially two phases of growth. In spring there is a surge of new growth as each tree tries to ensure that it can compete for light with its neighbours. In midsummer this growth slows down and energy is then devoted to ripening the fruit already on the trees and producing new fruit buds for next season. Late in the summer there may be a short, second phase of leafy growth. You can take advantage of this pattern by pruning in winter if you want a plant to make more growth, and in summer if you need to

FREESTANDING TREE FORMS

Dwarf bush
A rounded or goblet shape with an open centre: no central trunk beyond the point where the canopy branches. The restricted height makes for ease of picking. Good for apples, pears, plums and damsons, and cherries in warm areas or sites.

Dwarf pyramid
A tree with a central trunk and branches arranged in increasing length from top to bottom to give a flame or cone shape. Suited to apples, pears, plums and damsons.

Container fruit
Small bushes and standards can be created to grow in pots, useful where tender fruit needs moving under cover in winter. Most types of fruit can be used including redcurrants and gooseberries.

Standard tree
The traditional form for orchards of, in particular, apples and pears, allowing livestock to graze safely beneath trees. The crown can be above head height on a full standard, making ladders a necessity for picking and pruning. Not suitable for small gardens.

control vigour. Formally trained fruit trees – fans, espaliers, pyramids, cordons and palmettes – are thus pruned principally in summer to keep tight control of the shape. Formative pruning of young trees is, on the other hand, usually done in the winter, with the exception of plums and cherries, which are highly susceptible to silverleaf disease infection in winter.

It is important with tree fruit to recognize a flower/fruit bud from a leaf or shoot bud. The latter are generally fairly flat and pointed and lie close to the stem. Fruit buds are usually rounder and fatter and point slightly away from the branch. Some fruit types produce flowers on one-year-old wood, others on older wood – see the individual pages for details.

Trained forms

The craft of training fruit into architectural forms has its origins in France and Belgium. In Britain, the Victorians embraced the idea of formal shapes with enthusiasm, creating boats, goblets, winged pyramids and candelabra in ever more elaboration. The most common and useful forms for modern gardens are oblique or upright cordons (single stem), fans and espaliers. These shapes suit many soft fruit types too. Apart from the attractiveness of the shapes achieved, training trees in this way allows fruit to be grown on a wall or on wires, thereby taking up less space. It suits small gardens admirably and makes productive and attractive use of walls and fences.

FLAT-TRAINED TREES

A system of parallel horizontal wires will be needed to support all these forms.

Cordon
A single trunk with clusters of short fruiting shoots, or spur systems, along its length. They can be vertical but are ususallly set at an angle. Cordons trained with two or more parallel main stems are known as double or multiple cordons. Good for apples, pears and plums.

Espalier
A central trunk with opposing pairs of horizontal arms. Most usually 3-, 4- or 5-tiered. A low, single-tiered espalier is also called a "stepover". Suited to apples and pears.

Palmette
Similar to an espalier, but the arms radiate upwards at a 45° angle. A very formal shape, popular in Victorian Britain. Suited to apples and pears.

Fan
Branches divide and radiate outwards from a point 60–75cm (2–2½ft) above the ground. The branches are not parallel, but spread like fingers to cover the wall space allocated. Best suited to plums, cherries, figs, peaches and apricots, but can also be used for apples and pears.

Restoring overgrown fruit trees

An old, tangled fruit tree is not an uncommon sight in gardens. Planted by an enthusiastic gardener or a relic of an older orchard, the tree has been neglected and left unpruned for many years. Some such neglected trees are tall and wide on their vigorous rootstocks; others are weak, stunted and sickly. The latter type rarely become productive and are usually riddled with disease.

Decisions to make

Since renovating a tree is laborious, it is worth deciding in advance whether the effort is justified or not. The following questions should be considered:

• **How diseased is the tree?** High levels of canker, mildew and scab are not good signs.

• **Are there signs of vitality and vigour?** If extension growth annually is negligible, pruning hard may stimulate new growth but this is not always the case.

• **Does it fruit, and are the fruits of good flavour?** Not all old trees are of rare or sought-after cultivars. Flavour is a matter of personal preference, and each gardener will need to decide for themselves.

• **Does the tree contribute to the overall design of the garden?** Gardens have become smaller and occasionally large trees are left that are not in scale with the plot and create excessive shade. It may be better to start again with a new tree on a dwarfing rootstock or several trees trained as cordons.

Apples and pears

With few exceptions large old trees were originally formed as open-centred, goblet-shaped bushes. The aim is to restore them to this with a basic framework of six to eight main permanent branches spaced evenly round the tree. This work should be done in winter.

• Start by removing all growth below the point at which the main branches start. Cut or pull out all suckers growing round the base.

• Examine the tree from below and choose the main branches that you will retain.

• Saw off all strong upright branches, any growing across the centre and any damaged or diseased.

• The centre of the tree should be open to air and light. Remove any growth in the centre to leave the main branches free of laterals for the first 60cm (2ft) from the trunk.

• Now remove all other large branches that are not wanted for the framework that arise from the trunk or near the centre of the tree.

• Work along each retained branch with pruning saw and secateurs, shortening sideshoots and thinning spur systems (the knobbly clusters of short stems) to leave up to three or four well-spaced fat fruit buds on each spur system and no rubbing, crossing or congested branches.

• With time branches can get very long. If a long branch droops, growth at the tip will slow down or stop. Restoring vigour to old trees is part of the health package. If this has happened, prune back the leader to a single strong outward-pointing shoot. As you prune, cut out any diseased tissue.

In the following summer there may be considerable growth round the pruning cuts. This must be managed, or the tree will, in a few years, revert to its former state.

• In midsummer rip off any new young shoots in the centre of the tree or below the point where the main branches start.

• In winter thin out new sideshoots at major pruning cuts to leave single young laterals that will form new fruiting spurs in two years' time.

Thereafter prune the tree as an open centre bush (see p.268).

Plums and gages

Restoring overgrown plums requires less dramatic pruning. Trees do not need to be as open and airy as apples and pears. The work must be carried out between late spring and early autumn to avoid silverleaf disease. The ideal time is just after cropping.

• Reduce the height and width of the tree to a manageable size by sawing off large branches to a point where an outward-facing shoot or branch arises.

• Remove all damaged, diseased, crossing and rubbing branches.

• Thin out the remainder of the canopy if necessary so that light can penetrate and no shoots are touching.

USEFUL EQUIPMENT

Once you have decided to restore a tree, you will need to be properly equipped. Minimum requirements are:
• Bow saw – for large branches over 4cm (1½in) diameter.
• Pruning saw – for branches up to 4cm (1½in) diameter.
• Secateurs – for thinning out laterals. Since you may be climbing in the tree or up a ladder, a secateur holster is very useful.
• Ladder – steps are dangerous in this work; an extending ladder is required with rope to lash it to branches and prevent slipping. If you have several fruit trees, a specialised fruit tree ladder, tapering at the top and with a supporting leg (see left), is a very useful investment.
 It is always advisable to work with someone else in case of accident, and to help pull out tangled branches.

As with fruits pruned routinely, wounds on properly pruned fruit trees will heal perfectly adequately without the use of wound paints.

CULTIVAR CHOICE

Early
'Elvira', 'Honeoye', 'Rosie'

Mid-season
'Cambridge Favourite',
'Cambridge Late Pine',
'Darselect', 'Eros', 'Hapil',
'Pegasus'

Late
'Auchincruive Climax', 'Florence'
'Symphony', 'Rhapsody'

Perpetual
'Aromel', 'Bolero', 'Challenger',
'Mara des Bois' (large fruit but
wild flavour), 'Marastil'
(Note: perpetual or
"remontant" types are grown
for a late harvest. To achieve
this, you must remove all
flowers that form until late
spring. Otherwise they will
produce nearly all their fruit in
summer.)

Under glass or polythene
'Elvira', 'Rosie'

Resistant to powdery mildew
'Bolero', 'Cambridge
Favourite', 'Challenger', 'Mara
des Bois', 'Marastil', 'Rhapsody'

**Resistant to verticillium
wilt and crown rot**
'Bolero', 'Darselect', 'Rhapsody'

Resistant to red core
'Auchincruive Climax',
'Rhapsody', 'Symphony'

**Less susceptible to grey
mould (botrytis)**
'Eros', 'Pegasus', 'Symphony'

**Less susceptible to vine
weevil**
'Florence', 'Symphony'

Tucking straw under fruits
*Keeping the fruits clean and dry
(right) will reduce the risk of spoilage
by rots and mildew.*

Pegging down runners
*You can peg a few runners into pots
(far right) to root to increase your
stocks of plants, provided that the
parent plant shows no sign of disease.
Otherwise, all runners should be
removed regularly.*

Strawberries

The taste of the first strawberry of the year is
undoubtedly more exciting than the sound of the
first cuckoo. You could be harvesting your first crop
within 12 months of planting.

The earliest cultivars start cropping in late spring
– even earlier, if grown under cover. The main
season then extends through the summer with late
season "perpetual" types continuing the harvest into
autumn. By choosing appropriate cultivars (see left)
it is possible to harvest outdoor strawberries from
early summer until the first frosts of autumn. In a
small garden, however, you should limit yourself to
one or two varieties, as less than 12 plants of each
provides a frustratingly small harvest. The healthy,
productive life of a strawberry plant is about three
years.

Strawberries do not freeze well except as a purée
and cannot be stored as whole fruit. Eat them
immediately or refrigerate for a day or two.

Site and soil

Strawberries need winter cold to initiate flowering
and summer sun to grow and ripen fruit. An open
site in full sun is best. Relatively unfussy about soil,
strawberries will grow in an acid soil with a pH as
low as 5.5. Free-draining, slightly acidic, sandy loams
with good levels of organic matter suit them best.
High fertility is not a good idea as it will tend to
encourage big leafy plants at the expense of fruit.
Good drainage, however, is extremely important, as
is adequate water at most stages of growth. If your
soil is not a sandy loam, you can still grow good
strawberries by attending to soil structure and
drainage (see pp.38–41). Strawberries can also be
grown in containers (see pp.212–213).

Buying plants

Strawberries are bought in various forms: bare-
rooted runners, pot-grown plants and cold-stored
runners. This allows for flexibility in planting times.

Strawberries reproduce by throwing out long
stems (stolons) at the end of which young plantlets
(runners) form. These root while still attached to the
parent. The traditional bare-rooted runners are best
planted as soon as they become available in summer.
They can be planted as late as autumn but should
then be deflowered in their first year as they will be
weakened by growing a crop while still so young.

Pot-grown plants can be planted in autumn or
early winter and can even be held back for planting
until late spring if weather conditions are not
suitable. If bought in winter, keep them out in the
cold to ensure flowering. They can be allowed to
fruit in their first year.

Cold-stored runners are held back in growth by
keeping them artificially cool. They are sold in early
summer for immediate planting, whereupon they
rush into growth and produce a crop late in the
season. They will then crop normally in the
following years.

Preparation and planting

Before planting, dress the bed with 2–3cm (1in) of leafmould and lightly work it in. If your soil is particularly poor, add either well-rotted manure at one wheelbarrow to 8–10sq m, garden compost at twice that rate or pelleted chicken manure (see p.60).

• **Space plants** 30–45cm apart (12–18in) in the row with 75cm (30in) between rows.

• **Scoop out** holes large enough to spread out bare roots or to fit a potted rootball.

• **Set the plants** with the crown above the soil level (do not bury the centre of the plants) and firm soil with the fingers or knuckles.

• **Water** the plants in well.

Caring for the crop

Be alert for problems, and take precautions to prevent damage to the fruits (see panel, right). In dry weather keep plants well watered, especially while fruit is swelling. If soil has been well prepared, strawberries will not need additional feeding during the season. Remove all runners that form; up to three runners on a healthy plant can be retained, however, to make new plants.

Harvest fruits when they are fully coloured all over and eat them straight away – not that you will need prompting! After all the crop has been picked, trim off all foliage to leave a few centimetres of stalk to protect the newly emerging leaves. Remove all this, with the straw, to the compost heap. This will take away any lingering pests or diseases and reduce the risk of re-infection.

A light dressing of garden compost or similar soon after tidying away foliage at the rate of one 10-litre (2-gallon) bucket per sq m (sq yd) will stimulate healthy new growth.

Looking ahead

You will need to plan to move your strawberry bed somewhere new every three years. Ideally you should allow six years before returning strawberries to a strawberry bed, or planting raspberries there as they share many soil-borne diseases. In small gardens you may have to settle for three years. In the interim the bed could be used to grow annual flowers or salad crops or other short-lived plants. This means you will need to identify at least two plots for strawberries over the long-term.

CULTIVAR CHOICE

Early
'Glen Moy', 'Malling Jewel'
(virus-tolerant), 'Redsetter'

Mid-season
'Glen Ample', 'Glen Prosen',
'Malling Joy'

Late
'Glen Magna', 'Leo', 'Malling
Admiral'

Autumn-fruiting
'Allgold' (yellow), 'Autumn Bliss',
'Terri-Louise', 'Zeva'

With the exception of 'Malling
Jewel', 'Allgold' and 'Zeva', the
above have resistance to raspberry
aphid. 'Redsetter' and 'Autumn
Bliss' are resistant to root rot.

Raspberries

The soft, rich and juicy berries of raspberries follow on with perfect timing from the strawberry season. Raspberries are normally grown in rows, but even a small garden can find room for two or three plants grouped round a single 1.5m (5ft) stake. As well as cultivars spanning the summer season you will also find "autumn-fruiting" types. These produce fruiting canes in a single year, providing a harvest from late summer until the first frosts of autumn. Summer raspberries crop on canes grown the previous year, so their first crop will be harvested in the second season after planting. Autumn-fruiting types will produce a small crop in the first year.

Raspberries freeze well but otherwise will keep for only one or two days in a refrigerator.

Site and soil
Raspberries grow in relatively cool areas with shorter summers as well as in warmer climates. They prefer fertile, free-draining soil with a pH of 6.5 or below. Raspberries are not happy in alkaline soil and grow very poorly in chalk. They will suffer permanently from iron deficiency (see p.89), which cannot be corrected easily. They need sunshine for at least half the day but can tolerate breezy locations provided they are well staked and tied.

Good drainage is vital as raspberries are prone to an aggressive root rot that thrives in waterlogged soils. Equally important is adequate water in summer as raspberries root close to the surface and can quickly suffer from water shortage.

Buying plants
Raspberries are usually sold as bare-rooted plants called "stools", for winter planting. It is essential to buy certified virus-free stock from a reputable supplier, as raspberries are very prone to viruses. Good quality stock will crop for up to 14 years if well managed, perhaps eight if your soil is alkaline.

Soil preparation and planting
Raspberries, blackberries and strawberries share some unpleasant soil-borne diseases. For this reason these fruit types should not replace each other when a planting becomes exhausted. If planting into previously cultivated soil, you will need to do little more than add garden compost or well-rotted manure at the recommended rate (see p.40).

Remove all perennial weeds before planting, then erect a post and wire support. A double support system (see below) allows more canes but takes up more space. Set the stools 35–45cm (15–18in) apart (or for more vigorous cultivars, such as 'Autumn Bliss', around 50cm/20in apart) in a line under the wires up to the soil mark on the cane stub.

In spring buds will break first on the cane stub before new growth emerges from below ground. As soon as this happens, cut off the stub to soil level.

Caring for the crop

Attend to weeding and watering and any pests and disease problems (see panel, right) as soon as seen. Feeding during the season should not be necessary. An annual dressing of compost after harvest and fertiliser in spring (see below) should be sufficient. If growth is weak, plants may be showing infection by virus rather than lack of nutrition, and they need to be removed and burnt.

By early summer the new canes will be growing well and a small forest of new growth, known as spawn, will be emerging. Keep hoeing or cutting off any spawn forming outside of the row until the soil is warm enough to mulch heavily. Use straw or hay. Newspaper six or seven pages thick under the mulch will smother out unwanted spawn and weeds, but it does hinder rain penetration.

Thin out the new canes to about 10 or 12 per 1m (3ft) of row when they are about 75cm (30in) tall, removing weak or diseased canes first. Canes of autumn-fruiting types do not need thinning. Restrict them to a band about 30cm (12in) wide. Tie in the canes loosely to the wire supports as they grow.

After the harvest

As soon as possible after fruiting, cut down all fruited canes of summer crops to ground level. Try not to leave an untidy stub, which can be an entry site for pests and diseases. Spread garden compost along the row to help decompose the dead stubs.

Thin the new canes if necessary to leave about eight to ten for every 1m (3ft) of row and tie in firmly to the wires. Leave autumn-fruiting types loosely tied, even after harvest. In autumn loop over the top of each cane and tie it to the top wire. This makes canes more stable in windy weather. In late winter untie the cane tips and prune back to a bud just above the top wire. At the same time, cut back all canes of autumn-fruiting crops to ground level and mulch with garden compost to cover the stubs and help them rot. Remove the old straw mulch and compost it before adding compost. In alternate springs, spread seaweed meal at 125g per sq m (4oz per sq yd) and chicken manure pellets according to manufacturer's instructions to give plants a boost.

Summer raspberries
The fruiting canes are tied in to support wires, while new canes grow up in the spaces between, to be tied in when the fruited canes are pruned out.

Blackberries and hybrid berries

Blackberries grow wild, but if you want to have your own personal supply of this usually heavy-cropping, juicy, late summer fruit, then grow your own. Not all wild blackberries are sweet but most cultivated ones are.

In the last century many crosses, principally between raspberries and blackberries, were carried out to produce a range of interesting hybrid berries. These include loganberries, tayberries, tummel-berries, boysenberries and many others. These fruits are mostly earlier-cropping than blackberries, and sweet, but with a similar growing habit.

You will harvest your first crop in the second summer after planting and can anticipate full cropping in the year after that.

Site and soil

Most blackberries and hybrid berries are vigorous, if not rampant, growers and need plenty of space. The ideal situation is against a wall, fence or post and wire arrangement similar to that used for raspberries (see p.251). It is important to give plants sufficient space for the long canes to be tied in. Beds prepared at the base of walls or fences should be at least 1m (3ft) wide.

Blackberries are easy to grow and are not fussy about soil. Hybrid berries generally need more

> ## Blackberries are vigorous and easy to grow, and are not fussy about soil

warmth and similar conditions to raspberries – a free-draining, slightly acid soil.

It is possible to grow blackberries in partial shade or a site facing away from the sun, but hybrid berries grow best in full sun.

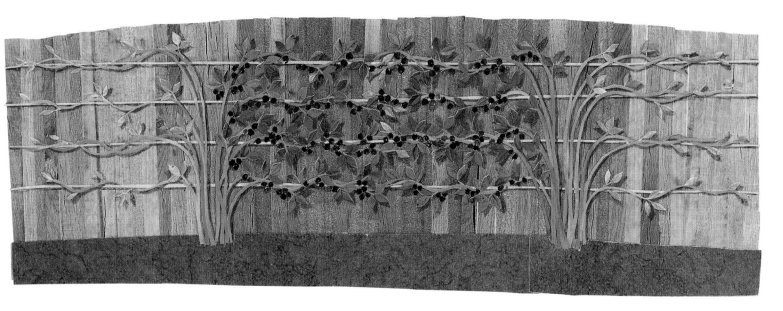

Buying plants

Plants are sold as bare-root stools in the same way as raspberries. If you have a small garden, look for some of the less vigorous cultivars, such as 'Marion' or 'Merton Thornless'. Most cultivars are thorny but a few are thornless. These are, in some cases, also less vigorous but seem to have less flavour than the thorned cultivars. The season for these berries extends from midsummer through to late autumn.

Preparation and planting

Prepare the soil as for raspberries (see p.251). Each plant may need as much as 7.2m (24ft) of space to tie in the canes depending on the cultivar. Erect posts as for raspberries and set wires 25cm (9in) apart from 60cm (24in) above soil level up to about 1.5m (5ft). If you are planting against a fence or wall, a similar wiring arrangement will be needed.

Plant a single stool at the centre of the support or space plants according to vigour (see Cultivar Choice, facing page) if you are growing several. Bury each stool up to the soil mark on the stub and firm it in.

In spring buds will break on the stub and later new growth will emerge from below soil level. As soon as this happens, cut off the old stub at soil level.

Pruning and training

In the first year a few canes only will grow. Tie all these in to one side as they grow. By midsummer you will need to attend to this weekly as growth is rapid. There are three methods of tying in: roping, where the canes are divided into equal numbers and tied as they develop in loose "ropes" along each wire; weaving, where canes are trained individually in informal loops up and down the wires; and fans, which are used for stiff-stemmed types like 'Oregon Thornless', where the canes are tied in a rough fan-shape across the framework. If cane tips touch the soil they may root and produce a new plant.

In the second year, this growth will flower and fruit, and new canes will grow. Tie the new canes in, following one of the methods above, to the opposite side. This is known as the "alternate bay" system (see above). Allow up to 30 new canes per plant, although some cultivars produce many fewer.

After fruiting, cut out all fruited canes to the ground and spread garden compost over the cut stubs to help them decompose quickly.

Caring for the crop

After a few years the plants will throw up suckers away from the main stool. These can be hand-pulled as they appear.

Blackberries need little feeding. If vigour declines, apply garden compost, well-rotted manure or pelleted chicken manure. Hybrid berries will benefit from a dressing of garden compost every two to three years.

Keep the crop well watered. In early summer, mulch the soil with straw or hay as for raspberries (see p.251). Root spread is extensive so all exposed soil round the plant should be covered to at least 1m (3ft) from the stool.

"Alternate bay" training
The simplest way to train blackberries is with the fruiting canes tied in on one side, and the new growth on the other. With several plants, alternate the sides so that fruiting canes meet fruiting canes, and new growth grows toward new growth.

PROTECT THE CROP

Plant healthy, virus-free stock in an appropriate spot. Netting against birds may be needed. Train new canes away from old ones (see above) so that diseases such as rust and purple blotch are not transferred from old to new foliage. Cover stubs of cut-down canes with compost to help them decompose.

Raspberry beetle maggots may be found in fruits. Remove mulches in autumn to allow birds access to the soil to help clear up capsid bugs and raspberry beetles.

Pests and diseases are less likely to be a problem where plants are growing in appropriately managed soil, and where the garden environment encourages natural predation.

See the *A–Z of Plant Problems* for more details.

Blackcurrants

Blackcurrants, nutritious and rich in flavour, are hardy and reliable, although late frost can damage blossoms and reduce the crop. The berries can be eaten raw, cooked or pressed for their juice. Blackcurrants have a particularly high vitamin C content and, in common with all soft fruits, are best consumed soon after picking to gain maximum nutritional benefit. However, they are suitable for freezing and make excellent preserves.

Blackcurrants are always grown as bushes. You will harvest a moderate crop after two years, reaching full cropping after three or four years.

Site and soil

As blackcurrants are pruned hard, they generally need quite fertile conditions but are otherwise unfussy about soil types. They do grow into quite broad bushes even with pruning and are not suited to trained shapes such as fans in the way that redcurrants are. A single bush can be quite productive, so you need not be put off growing blackcurrants if you have a small garden. Choose a sunny spot receiving sunshine most of the day for best results. Bushes become drawn and spindly if too shaded, and sunshine also improves the flavour of the berries.

Buying plants

Blackcurrants are generally sold as one-year-old plants. A good plant will have a few branches and a strong fibrous root system. Some nurseries may sell container-grown young plants which can be planted at any time of year provided enough water is given to help establishment. It is always preferable,

however, to plant in early winter or, if that is not possible, very early in spring when the soil is workable and not too wet.

There are cultivars that are resistant to some of the pests and diseases of blackcurrants, particularly to mildew, leaf spot and leaf midge (see Cultivar Choice, left, and Protect the Crop, facing page). Others are particularly valued for their flavour and extra high vitamin C content.

Preparation and planting

It is important to prepare the ground well.
• Mark out a site large enough to accommodate the number of bushes you plan. Allow a spacing of 1.5–1.8m (5–6ft) apart – unless you are using the "hedge" system (see facing page) – or 1.5m (5ft) each way for a single bush.
• Clear the site of all perennial weeds and, if drainage is poor, double-dig the plot (see p.322). If cutting a bed from lawn, dig the turf under, carefully removing dandelion or other perennial weed roots.
• Just before planting, work in well-rotted manure at the rate of one 10-litre (2-gal) bucket to every 2sq m (20sq ft) or garden compost at twice that rate. If organic matter levels are low and you are not digging in turf, apply about 2–3cm (1in) of leafmould as well and lightly dig it in.
• Set the plants 1.5–1.8m (5–6ft) apart (or use the alternative closely spaced "hedge" method, see opposite) and plant them about 5cm (2in) deeper than the soil mark to encourage further roots to form on the buried stems. Cut back the branches, leaving one or two buds on each above soil level.

"Destructive" method of pruning blackcurrant bushes (right)

This method only works well if you have three plants or multiples of three. Divide the bushes into three groups of equal number. Starting in the autumn after the first crop has been taken, prune off all growth on all plants in one of these groups. Leave the others unpruned.

Rotate your way round all three groups in successive years so that eventually, in any year, you will have one set of plants growing new branches and two sets cropping.

This system is reasonably effective at reducing disease infections.

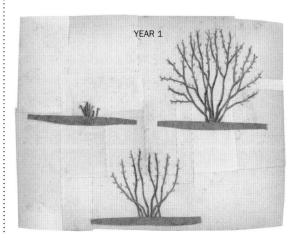

YEAR 1

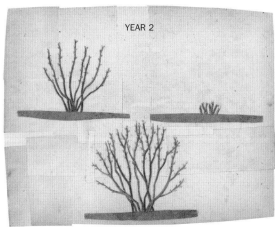

YEAR 2

Currant events
Apart from the harvest of luscious, juicy fruits (left), the key time in the blackcurrant year is late autumn to winter, when they should be pruned – traditionally, as above, by sawing out thick old branches at the base to leave younger wood that will crop well in coming years.

Feeding

Feed bushes with garden compost, well-rotted manure or organic fertilisers at least every three years at the rate recommended or every other year on poorer soils. A well-managed planting should last over 20 years. Mulch bushes in late spring with straw or hay.

Pruning

Blackcurrants fruit mainly on the previous season's wood. The aim of any management is, therefore, to encourage as much healthy new growth as possible to fruit the following year. It is not necessary to create an open centre to the bush. In the first year the new plants will produce branches from above and below ground and there will be no crop. No pruning is necessary. In the second year the existing branches will fruit and grow. New branches also grow from below ground. They are pruned in autumn, traditionally by removing, each year, up to one-third of the oldest branches as close as possible to soil level (see above). This process does not start until the autumn of the third year. Start with those lying closest to the ground. In some cases a good new shoot can be found near the base of an old branch. Prune back to this if it is well placed.

Alternatives to traditional pruning

These include the "destructive" method (see left), which prunes bushes in groups of three on a three-year cycle, and the "hedge" method. With this method it is possible to gain a bigger harvest early in the life of a new planting by close planting at 90cm (36in) apart. Once the bushes start to become crowded you can then either remove every other bush in winter and thereafter use the "traditional" method, or sustain the system by removing all fruited wood every autumn.

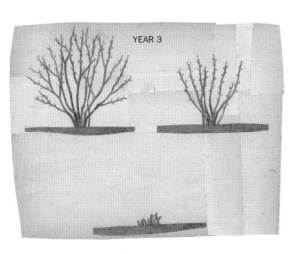

YEAR 3

PROTECT THE CROP

Plant healthy, virus-free bushes in an appropriate location. Cultivars resistant to big bud mite, mildew and leaf midge are available.

In winter and early spring, pick off any swollen buds which will be infested with the big bud mite. If infestation is severe, prune back hard to remove infested branches. Look out for aphids on young shoots and leaves from spring onwards. Squash these by hand, wash off with jet of water, or spray with an appropriate insecticide. Cut out any mildewed shoots. Sow flowers to attract natural predators (see pp.96–99).

Plants infected with the reversion virus, which can be transmitted by the big bud mite, will begin to crop poorly. Where reversion is identified, the only answer is to remove the bushes and start afresh.

See the *A–Z of Plant Problems* for more details.

Red- and whitecurrants

CULTIVAR CHOICE

Early-cropping
'Jonkheer van Tets';
'Laxton's Number One'

Mid-season
'Red Lake'; 'Stanza'

Late
'Rondom'; 'Rovada'

Whitecurrants
'White Versailles'; 'White
Grape'; 'White Dutch';
'White Pearl' (all cultivars here
crop mid-season)

A redcurrant bearing a full crop of ripe berries is truly stunning. These berries may not be as sweet as strawberries but they are an essential ingredient of summer pudding, make an excellent jelly and wine and, with their high pectin content, are very useful for mixing with fruits that set poorly when making jam. They also freeze well.

There are cultivars available to span a season of harvest during the main summer months. The redcurrant is, perhaps, more dramatic in fruit with its brilliant red berries but some connoisseurs prefer the white for its slightly sweeter flavour. All the

advice given here for redcurrants also applies equally to whitecurrants.

Unlike blackcurrants, which fruit almost exclusively on wood grown the previous year, redcurrants crop on short shoots that grow from a permanent framework of branches. They can thus not only be grown as bushes, but also as cordons and fans, and even as standards (see grapes, p.260).

Redcurrants will start cropping as soon as there are branches which are two years old. The crop will increase annually to reach a peak after five years or so. A well-managed bush might last up to 30 years, although 15 to 20 is more usual.

Site and soil

Although closely related to blackcurrants, redcurrants have a different habit of growth and rather different requirements, needing less fertile conditions. They are fully hardy, tough, reliable and rather unfussy about soil. They are well suited to growing as cordons or fans and will even crop in cool situations where they receive only short amounts of direct sunlight.

If you plan to grow these currants as cordons or fans you will need a fence or wall equipped with horizontal wires, or a post and wire structure to support them (see also blackberries, see p.252). Birds enjoy these fruits, so you will need to net them.

Buying plants

Plants are usually sold bare-root or container-grown as one-, two- or three-year-old plants. To grow as bushes, look for plants with a good fibrous root system, a short single stem and three or more young branches of about pencil-thickness at the base. For trained shapes start with one-year-old plants.

Preparation and planting

For bushes, mark out a site large enough to accommodate the number of bushes you plan. Allow for a spacing of 1.2–1.5m (4–5ft) apart. Space cordons 40–45cm (15–18in) apart. A fan will grow to about 2m (6ft) wide.

To prepare the soil, follow the advice given for blackcurrants. Just before planting, work in garden compost or any other medium-fertility soil improver except farmyard manure, at the rate of one 10-litre (2-gal) bucket to every square metre (10sq ft). Heavy dressings of manure are not recommended for redcurrants, as plants grow too vigorously and branches can tear away in high winds.

Plant bare-root bushes in winter; pot-grown plants can be planted at any time but will establish better if planted in winter. Dig out a hole large enough to accommodate the roots comfortably and spread the roots out evenly in the hole. Replace the soil, ensuring that the plant is planted at the level of the original soil mark. If a one-year-old plant has more than one stem arising from the base remove all but the best; a branched two- or three-year-old bush should have a single "leg", or length of clear trunk, below the point where the branches form.

Pruning and training

Unlike blackcurrants, redcurrants fruit on wood that is at least two years old. Whether grown as trained forms or bushes, redcurrants are pruned to encourage short, stubby fruiting shoots known as spurs. Winter pruning (see below) forms and maintains the basic shape and size of the plants, while additional summer pruning restricts the amount of growth on them, by shortening all shoots on the main framework branches. Summer pruning also helps to remove disease and any aphids present.

Summer pruning

To summer-prune, first identify the leading shoot of each branch (the one at the tip that extends the length of the branch) and do not prune it. (If the leading shoot is exceptionally long, choose a shorter shoot below it and leave this unpruned.) Prune all other sideshoots to five leaves. This pruning is important:

• It removes pest colonies at shoot tips;
• It removes soft sappy growth, which is most susceptible to American gooseberry mildew and other fungal infections;
• It improves air circulation, reducing the risk of infection by mildew and other diseases, which thrive in still air between congested growth;
• It controls vigour, restricting stem and leaf production in favour of promoting fruit and fruit bud development.

Caring for the crop

Mulch all plants in late spring with hay or straw. This will conserve moisture and suppress weeds. Do not overfeed redcurrants. A dressing of garden compost every three years should be adequate for their needs. Clear away suckers (shoots growing around the base of the plant) to leave a single clear stem by pulling, cutting or chopping them away, ideally when they are still small.

PROTECT THE CROP

The currant blister aphid can colonise undersides of leaves from bud burst. Encourage natural aphid predators. Pick off badly infested leaves, or spray with a suitable insecticide if widespread. Check from mid-spring for gooseberry sawfly larvae, which can defoliate a plant. Pick off, or spray with derris. Clear up fallen leaves in autumn, especially if currant leaf spot has caused early leaf fall.

PRUNING AND TRAINING REDCURRANTS IN WINTER

Bush	Cordon	Fan
At planting Cut back all branches by half to an outward facing bud. Shorten any sideshoots to two or three buds.	**1** Only one upright stem should be retained. In the winter after planting cut this back by up to half of the new growth and reduce sideshoots to two or three buds.	**1** After planting reduce to a single stem and prune this back to leave a short "leg" of about 25cm (10in).
Year one and two Repeat this process in subsequent years until a bush is formed with eight to ten main branches, each with a strong leading shoot and spur system forming lower down. Keep the centre of the bush open by pruning out shoots growing towards the centre. Start summer pruning (see above).	**2** Repeat this process each winter until the plant has reached the desired height. Start summer pruning from the third year (see above).	**2** After the first growing season a number of branches will have grown out. Remove any growing towards or away from the wall or supports. Tie in the best placed four branches, using canes to keep them straight, in a fan shape. Leave the centre open. Cut all four branches back by half. Remove all others.
Subsequent years Once the bush is formed, each winter prune back the leading shoot by up to half and continue to reduce all side growth to two or three buds. Remove any old, congested and weak spur systems.	**3** Thereafter in winter cut back the leader to one or two buds of new growth or prune back to a new leader slightly lower down the stem. Remove old, congested and weak spur systems. To create a double or triple cordon allow two or three stems to grow upright, training them parallel to each other.	**3** In the next year allow two good branches to grow from the buds near the tip of each of the existing branches and tie them in. Spur back all growth lower down to two or three buds in winter. **4** Continue this process until the space is filled leaving at least 15cm (6in) between the tips of branches at the outside of the fan. Do not allow any strong upright branches to grow as these will tend to dominate and reduce vigour on lower-angled branches. Start summer pruning (see above) once the fan is formed. **5** Thereafter each winter, prune the new spurs as above, occasionally reducing or removing spur systems. After several years the lowest two branches may become weak. These can be removed and the next tier brought down to replace them.

Gooseberries

If you claim to have no interest in gooseberries,
there is a fair chance it is because you have never
tasted a fine dessert fruit, taut with flavour.

Gooseberries can be grown as bushes, cordons,
fans and standards. A well-managed bush will last 15
to 20 years and will crop in the second summer
after planting. Gooseberries freeze well but
otherwise do not store for long.

Site and soil

Gooseberries and redcurrants are closely related and
advice on site and soil for redcurrants (see p.256) is
equally applicable for gooseberries. Gooseberries can
also be grown with little direct sunlight, except that
choice dessert cultivars are better grown where they
will receive sunlight for at least half the day.

Buying and planting

Buy, plant and prepare the soil following the general
advice given for redcurrants (see p.256).
Gooseberries can be rather droopy in habit and it is
important to keep fruit away from contamination by

soil, which can in turn lead to fungal infections or
attack by slugs and snails. Site gooseberries where
there is a good airflow, keep the bushes pruned to an
open centre, and push in four canes around each
bush, about 30cm (12in) away from the stem and
angled slightly outwards. Join them with string or
light wire at a height of about 40–45cm (15–18in)
so that new branches are forced to be more upright.
In subsequent years these canes can be moved
outwards and the wire raised or removed. The other
option is to train plants as cordons.

Caring for the crop

Feeding and watering Follow the mulching and
feeding information for redcurrants (see p.257).
Pests and diseases Gooseberries share the same
pests and diseases as redcurrants (see p.257).
American gooseberry mildew and the gooseberry
sawfly are the two main problems. Mildew-resistant
cultivars are an effective method of avoiding this
disease. In spring, look out for mildewed shoots and
leaves, then developing fruit. Cut it out. Check from
mid-spring, for gooseberry sawfly larvae, which can
defoliate a plant. Pick off where practical, or spray
with derris. Finally, look out for aphids on young
shoots in spring; squash these by hand, wash off with
jet of water, or spray with an appropriate insecticide.

Pruning

Gooseberries are pruned and trained as for
redcurrants (see p.257) except that spurs are left
longer in winter, pruned to three or four buds rather
than two, to allow more fruits to grow.

CULTIVAR CHOICE

Early-cropping
'Bluecrop'
'Earliblue'

Mid-season
'Berkeley'
'Herbert'
'Ivanhoe'

Late-season
'Coville'

Blueberries

The lowly, prostrate bilberry of woodlands and mountain slopes has a tall cousin – the highbush blueberry. The rich blue, cooked berries of this plant make wonderful sweet pies. It also displays fine autumn colouring. Unfortunately blueberries only thrive in very acid soils, meaning major soil modifications or growing in pots for most of us.

Fruiting will start in the second summer after planting, reaching full cropping after five or six years. The season lasts from mid- to late summer.

Site and soil

Blueberries need damp but not waterlogged soil with high organic matter levels and a soil pH between 4 and 5.5. Choose a sunny site, although some shade will not be a problem. Protection from late frost is important. Bushes are informal in shape and not trained; no supports are needed.

Buying plants

A single plant will crop reasonably but better results will be achieved with two or more bushes to cross-pollinate. Buy two- or three-year-old plants, usually pot-grown, checking that they are not root-bound.

Preparation and planting

Never forget that blueberries need very acid conditions. You will need to test the pH of any compost or manure that you use. Garden compost is frequently alkaline and manure cannot be guaranteed to be acid. Only use rainwater when watering in plants. If you do not have suitable soil conditions, grow blueberries in a large pot or tub.

Plant bushes in late autumn or early winter spacing them 1.5m (5ft) apart. Mulch with composted bark or pine needles.

Caring for the crop

Feeding and watering Keep the mulch topped up annually. Remember not to use tap water on plants.
Pests and diseases Problems are rare.
Harvesting Fruits ripen over a period of weeks and should be picked when they are soft, fully blue and come away easily. Fruits can be frozen successfully or are suited to preserving.

Pruning

Blueberries fruit on two- and three-year-old branches. The aim of pruning is to keep a good supply of new branches, removing a number of branches that are four years old or more each year. In the first two or three years prune out any very weak growth or branches growing in a more horizontal plane close to the soil.

In subsequent years continue to remove weak growth; cut out crossing branches and wood that has stopped fruiting. Prune out branches growing close to soil level or pointing downwards.

Grapes

Grapes are expensive to buy. You can grow your own vines in a relatively small space provided that you restrict their ample growth with regular pruning and trimming. A vine will even crop well in a pot. The first crop will be harvested three years after planting. Cultivars are broadly defined as "wine" and "dessert" with the latter further subdivided into "vinous", "muscat" and "sweetwater" according to sweetness. Sweetwater grapes are the sweetest.

Grapes can tolerate a wide range of climates, but for the best results with fine dessert grapes in cooler regions you will need to grow under glass. Outdoors in such situations grape-growing is restricted to a few dessert types and wine varieties, white being much more successful than red.

Grapevines are always grown on supports in a variety of shapes. Two of the simplest and most popular are the cordon and the double Guyot (see facing page). The cordon is ideal in a glasshouse where the vine is to be trained vertically, with a central stem growing up one wall or upright then across the roof, and also for vines grown outside on pergolas, trained up one pillar and then across the canopy. It consists of a single, upward-growing main stem or rod from which each year shoots grow, are trained out sideways, bear fruit and are then pruned back hard in winter. The main stem will gradually become more gnarled as it ages, but new shoots will always resprout from the stump of the previous year's fruiting stems. Vines are renowned for their long lifespan and capacity to reshoot from old wood.

Where space is plentiful, for example in a large glasshouse or vinery, multiple cordons can be grown, with two or more vertical main stems trained out and upwards from the base in a candelabra shape. They must be widely spaced to allow fruiting sideshoots to grow out sideways from each. You can also train a single main stem up a pergola pillar, then allow it to fork into two or more to achieve greater coverage across the canopy.

The double Guyot makes good use of horizontal space, reaching only 1.2m (4ft) or so in height. It is the traditional way of growing wine grapes outdoors on a post-and-wire system, either freestanding or along walls and fences. It makes good use of the fact that, as with most woody climbers, the best flowering and fruiting shoots are produced on stems that are trained out horizontally. Each year, two strong stems that grew the previous year are trained out sideways along the bottom wire (grape-growers call these the "rods"), and shoots from these are trained up vertically to bear fruit. In winter the rods, with their fruited sideshoots, are cut back to the central stump and new rods trained in.

Site and soil

Grapevines are generally vigorous and need plenty of room for their roots as well as their branches. They also benefit from maximum sunlight, warmth

Double Guyot

Train the vine so that the vertical fruiting shoots are well spaced, to allow plenty of sun to fall on the fruits. Ensure that you have a group of three strong shoots in the centre. When the fruiting arms or rods are pruned out, two of these can be tied down along the bottom wire to form next year's structure. The third is a reserve in case one shoot fails. If by any mischance two or all of the central shoots are lost, you can retain last year's rods, cutting back the vertical fruited shoots to two or three buds.

and an airy site, especially when they are grown against walls and fences. They need good ventilation under glass. Vines are very hardy, and generally flower late enough to avoid damage to blossom from spring frosts.

With the exception of just a few cultivars, grapes prefer a free-draining, slightly alkaline soil with good levels of organic matter to maintain adequate moisture. Rich soil high in nutrients is not ideal; it is likely to produce lush growth at the expense of fruit. If your soil drains poorly you will need to incorporate plenty of coarse grit into your soil; on very heavy clay soils a land drainage system (buried terracotta pipes leading to a soakaway, for example) may be need to be installed.

Buying plants

Grapevines are bought either as bare-rooted or container-grown plants, usually about a year old. In wine-making regions where the serious vine pest phylloxera is present, vines are grafted onto resistant rootstocks, but in countries such as the UK where phylloxera is not prevalent, grapevines are raised from cuttings to grow on their own roots. The ideal time to plant is in winter, but container-grown grapes can be bought at any time and planted when convenient. All grapes are self-fertile – their flowers will pollinate each other – making it possible to grow just one vine.

Planting under glass

In a free-standing greenhouse aim to plant one vine at the base of the wall opposite the door. According to the size of the greenhouse you will then be able to train in either one or two parallel rods along the roof.

In a lean-to glasshouse grapes are planted at the base of the front wall and trained up the inside of the glass, towards the top of the back wall in order to get the longest possible rods. For a single rod (cordon) plant 1.2m (4ft) apart or twice that for a double.

If your greenhouse has a concrete or paved floor you will need to plant outside and train the vine in through a hole.

Fix wires 30cm (12in) apart along the length of the roof glass, preferably 15cm (6in) away from the glass. For a single cordon in a free-standing greenhouse, run one wire along the apex of the roof to support the main rod.

TRAINING GRAPES UNDER GLASS

	Cordon	Double Guyot
After planting	Cut back the young vine by at least two-thirds to a strong bud. This will encourage good rooting before the plant has to support a crop.	Prune back the young stem to leave about 15cm (6in) above soil level at a bud.
In the first year	Allow only the top bud to grow for a single cordon, two for a double, three or more for a multiple cordon. Rub out all other buds. During the summer tie in the rod(s) to a cane(s) vertically up the back wall or start to train it/them up the roof of the lean-to. Pinch back any sideshoots to five or six leaves and any shoots from these to one leaf. **Early winter** As soon as the leaves have fallen, prune back the new leader by half to two-thirds of the year's growth. Remove entirely any sideshoots that have formed below the top of the front wall of a lean-to or below about 1m (3ft) otherwise. Any shoots forming above that should be pruned back to a single good, fat bud.	**In summer** Tie in the leader that forms vertically. Remove any competing shoot that arises low on the stem and pinch back all other sideshoots to five or six leaves. In winter cut back all growth to a bud just below the bottom wire about 40cm (15in) above soil level.
In the second year	**During the growing season** Tie in the leader as it grows and treat sideshoots as in year one. Remove any flower trusses that form. The vine will be allowed to fruit in the third year. If you are growing a multiple cordon you can allow further laterals to become permanent rods at this stage. **In winter** Repeat the pruning as for year one, aiming to leave one spur about every 30cm (12in) of rod. Remove all other growth and any forming below the desired height as in the first year.	Allow three buds to grow out and tie them loosely upright to a supporting cane. Remove all shoots arising below these and pinch back any sideshoots as in year one. **In winter** pull down the two outer rods and tie them to the bottom wire. Shorten them to a bud to leave about 60cm (24in) of growth. Reduce the remaining central shoot to leave three or four good buds.
Third year onwards	Continue the process of pruning and tying in as in previous years but when the leader has reached the planned limit of growth cut the new growth back hard each winter to leave one or two buds or to a shoot further back. From the third year fruits can be allowed to form. Fruits grow on new wood and routine pruning aims at an annual programme of replacement. After buds have broken in spring, select the best shoot and train it in. Rub out all but one other (as a spare) and keep this pinched back after two leaves. Aim to allow one bunch per 30cm (12in) of rod, ie one bunch per lateral. On each lateral select the strongest looking flower cluster, pinch out all others and stop the shoot two leaves beyond the flower cluster. Any laterals not carrying flowers can be left to grow to about 60cm (24in) and then stopped. **During the season** it is essential to attend weekly to pruning until late summer. Pinch back all sub-laterals that form to one leaf. Pay special attention to ensure that vents and windows are not covered by growth. Keep the house very well ventilated to reduce fungal infections as soon as frost is no longer a threat. **Each winter** cut back the laterals to a strong bud near the base. If these spurs become excessively long, train in a new better placed shoot in summer, retain this and saw off the old stub. Untie the tip of the rod and allow it to droop towards the floor to ensure even bud burst. After growth starts, tie it back up to its wire.	Shoots arising from the horizontal laterals are trained in vertically and pinched out two leaves beyond the top wire. These will now carry fruit. Remove entirely any sideshoots that form on these and, once bushes are growing well, pick off any leaves directly shading the bunches. Tie in three replacement leaders as in year two, pinching out any sideshoots to one leaf. In winter cut out entirely both lateral arms and pull down two new leaders to replace them. Trim these and the central leader as in the previous year. **In subsequent years** This process now continues annually. Eventually to retain the shape it may be necessary to allow the three replacement shoots to grow from lower on the main stem and then cut back to these.

Planting outdoors

There are various training systems used for grapes grown in the open either on a wall, or on a post-and-wire system for wine grapes. For wall-trained grapes set wires at 30cm (12in) apart horizontally starting at a height of 40cm (15in). For wine grapes the top wire should be set at about 1.2m (4ft).

In all situations soil must be well prepared. Attend to any drainage problems and then cultivate an area of soil at least 2 x 2m (6 x 6ft) beyond the planting site. Incorporate well-rotted manure or, preferably, garden compost and seaweed meal at 125g per sq m (4oz per sq ft) and include leafmould if your soil is either very heavy or very light. Add a small handful of bone meal to each planting hole.

Plant up to the original soil mark, ensuring that you plant at least 30cm (12in) away from the base of any wall. This area is often very dry and receives little rain. Firm the plant in well and water it in thoroughly.

If the soil pH is below 6 add dolomite lime (see p.61) in spring to raise it closer to neutral and work it in lightly.

Training and pruning

The pruning needed to form and maintain the vine will depend on the desired shape (see table above). The main pruning to shape is always carried out in winter. It is essential that woody stems of vines are only pruned while the plants are dormant; the plants are so vigorous that if cut while in growth, they will "bleed" sap profusely, weakening the plant. Pruning during the growing season, although no less essential for good cropping, consists in the main only of pinching or trimming back young shoots to restrict growth.

Thinning the fruit

Thinning is not essential for grapes grown for wine. Dessert grapes, whether grown indoors or outdoors, should be thinned for best results when the grapes are no bigger than a small pea. Use a small pointed stick and pointed scissors. Avoid touching the fruits with your fingers as it removes the bloom, spoiling the finish and increasing the possibility of infection with grey mould (botrytis). Cut off about half the berries to leave plenty of space between each grape in a broad-shouldered bunch. Further thinning may be necessary in midsummer if the berries are still too tightly packed.

Feeding and weeding

Keep vines well irrigated in summer but stop watering once the grapes begin to ripen in late summer. A mulch of straw applied in late spring and removed in autumn will keep down weeds and help to conserve moisture, as well as providing some potash.

Each year in late winter alternate between a dressing of garden compost to cover as much of the root area as possible and dolomitic limestone if it is needed. If deficiencies show, use seaweed meal or the appropriate material (see p.61).

Harvesting the bunches

To harvest wine grapes, cut through the stalk a few centimetres above the bunch. With dessert grapes, avoid touching the fruit; it will spoil its attractive "bloom" and can cause bruising. The shoot can be severed on each side of the bunch's stalk to form a handle (see right).

The fruit is best eaten soon after harvesting but can be kept for short periods; leave one side of the stem longer if the grapes are not to be eaten immediately: placing the long end in water will preserve the freshness of the fruit. If some bunches are slow to ripen, remove shading leaves to let in more sunlight.

A STANDARD GRAPEVINE

Grapevines grow extremely well in containers, trained in many shapes – but a simple standard works well. The main stem will need the support of a sturdy stake about 1.2m (4ft) tall that extends down to the base of the pot. Fix a wire-framed hanging basket upside-down on top of the stake (a small, spoked wooden wheel could also be used); this will give extra support to the fruiting shoots, and allow them to cascade down in an attractive fountain shape.

A generous-sized pot is essential, filled with a soil-based compost with added grit (see p.205, and also pp.114–117) to give weight and stability. Feeding will be required (see also *Container Gardening*, p.206) and regular, plentiful watering during summer.

To form the standard, in the first year train a single stem vertically as for the double Guyot. In winter, if the stem is strong and extends well above the stake, prune it to a healthy bud at the height of the top of the stake. (If growth is weak, cut back the leading shoot by half and complete the above process the following winter.) Leave only the top 3–4 buds and rub off all the others on the stem, removing any sideshoots completely at the same time. The next and each subsequent year, as shoots grow, train them over the support (up to 12 as the vine becomes established), and let each bear one or two bunches of fruit, then in winter, cut them back to 2–3 buds.

PROTECT THE CROP

Fungal diseases – downy and powdery mildew, and botrytis (grey mould) are the major problem on vines, indoors and under cover. They can affect all stages from buds and flowers, to leaves and fruits. Grow cultivars with some disease resistance if possible. Careful management of the growing environment is the only effective way to prevent them getting out of hand. They thrive where soil is dry and the atmosphere humid. Water, copiously, plants growing under cover or against a wall, through the season until fruit is ripening. Prune out excess growth through the season to reduce humidity around leaves and fruit. Provide maximum ventilation in greenhouses. Cut out diseased fruit bunches. At the season's end clear up all plant debris; scrub down the greenhouse; scrape old bark from dormant stems with a blunt knife. Most pests – vine weevil and under cover, glasshouse red spider mite, whitefly and mealy bug, can be dealt with by using biological controls (see p.100).

Harvesting dessert grapes
Create a handle for each bunch by cutting the stem on either side of it, so that you do not need to touch and spoil the fruit.

Apples

Providing a harvest from a succession of cultivars from midsummer through to the late-keeping fruit from store in spring, apples must offer one of the longest periods of fresh supply of any fruit. Such is the interest in apples that the range of cultivars runs into the thousands with many historic cultivars still stocked by specialist nurseries.

Over many centuries apples have evolved, been selected and bred to suit a very wide range of situations. There are now cultivars to suit warm and cool climates with rootstocks to match. The rootstocks (see below) determine the ultimate size of the tree, its precocity in cropping and its useful life expectancy.

Site and soil

In general this fruit grows best on rich, free-draining soil with a pH of 6.5. If your soil is less fertile you can compensate, not only by your soil treatment, but also by using a more vigorous rootstock or even growing the tree on its own roots. Plant on an open site in full sun but protected from the wind. Avoid frost pockets. Apples do not perform well at altitudes above about 120m (400ft) in cool regions.

Apples are suited to growing as formal trained shapes against walls and fences or, for improved air flow, on free-standing post and wire supports. Walls that face the setting sun are ideal; cooking apples can be grown on a cool wall. Avoid very hot conditions.

Buying plants

The ideal time to buy trees is in late autumn or early winter for immediate planting. At this time they are usually sold with bare roots but container-grown trees can be found at most times of year, though cultivar choice is likely to be much reduced.

To ensure healthy, good quality trees, buy plants with a certificate showing that they are free of virus. Buy one-year-old trees, known as "maidens" (single, unbranched vertical stems) or "feathered maidens" (with a few small sideshoots). Plants of this age are relatively cheap and can be pruned to your preferred shape from the outset. It is also possible to buy pre-formed young bush or espalier trees two or three years old at greater cost.

The shape of the trees

Freestanding trees may be grown as bush trees (the most popular shape, easy to form and maintain) or pyramids, a narrower variation (see also p.244). Standard trees, with a tall clear trunk, are only seen today on large estates and in traditional orchards, as their height makes them difficult to prune and pick.

The aim of pruning and training with the bush is to form an open-centred crown with a main framework of four to six flat-angled permanent branches above a short clear trunk. The pyramid has a central trunk from bottom to top, with branches that are pruned to be shorter at the top than the

CULTIVAR CHOICE

Dessert, early
'Discovery' (RS, RM), 'Epicure' 3 (RS, RM), 'Irish Peach' 2

Dessert, mid-season
'Blenheim Orange' 3 T (dual purpose), 'Egremont Russet' 2, 'Ellison's Orange' 4 (RS, RM), 'Fortune' 3 (RS), 'King of the Pippins' 5 (RS, RM), 'Lord Lambourne' 2, 'Orleans Reinette' 4, 'Queen Cox' 3, 'Red Devil' 3 (RS, RM), 'Ribston Pippin' 2 (RS) T, 'Saint Edmund's Pippin' 2, 'Sunset' 3 (RS), 'Winston' 4, 'Worcester Pearmain' 3 (RS)

Dessert, late
'Ashmead's Kernel' 4, 'Brownless Russet' 3, 'Court Pendu Plat' 6 (RS, RM), 'D'Arcy Spice' 4, 'Pixie' 4, 'Tydeman's Late Orange' 4

Culinary
'Annie Elizabeth' 4, 'Arthur Turner' 3, 'Bountiful' 3 (RM), 'Bramley's Seedling' 3, 'Crawley Beauty' 7 (RS, RM), 'Edward VII' 6 (RS, RM), 'Emneth Early' 3 (RS, RM), 'Grenadier' 3 (RS), 'Reverend W. Wilks' 2, 'Woolbrook Russet' 4

Numbers refer to pollination groups. Cultivars will cross-pollinate with others in the same or neighbouring groups.
RS Resistant to scab
RM Resists powdery mildew
T Triploid; needs two non-triploid pollinators

APPLE ROOTSTOCKS

Rootstocks	Effect	Height	Planting	Notes
M27	Very dwarfing	1.5–1.8m (5–6ft)	1.2–1.8m (4–6ft)	Needs permanent staking; crops very early in life
M9	Dwarfing	1.8–3m (6–10ft)	2.5–3m (8–10ft)	Needs a fertile, rich soil and permanent staking; crops very early in life
M26	Dwarfing	2.4–4m (8–12ft)	3–5m (10–15ft)	Good on lighter soils; strong root system; crops after two or three years
MM106	Semi-dwarfing	4–5.5m (12–18ft)	4–5.5m (12–18ft)	Suitable for poor soils or traditional orchards; strong root system; crops after two or three years
MM111	Vigorous. Semi-vigorous on poor soils	6–9m (20–28ft)	5.5–7.5m (18–24ft)	Strong root system; crops after two to three years; suitable for traditional orchard
Own-root trees	Vigorous	Over 9m (28ft) unless grown at close spacing	Best grown as cordon 75cm (30in) apart or pyramid at 2.5m (8ft) apart	Very strong root system; needs summer pruning to control vigour; crops after three or four years

CRAB APPLES

These small-fruited apple trees can be grown as cordons but are usually grown as informal trees, valued for the ornamental features of their blossom, attractive foliage and fruits. Crab apples make good pollinators; *Malus* x *zumi* 'Golden Hornet' is popular for orchards. *Malus* 'John Downie' makes particularly good crab apple jelly.

bottom of the tree, giving a cone shape. It is preferable to start with a feathered maiden or an older tree correctly trained for the shape. Ideally branches should not lie directly above each other or arise immediately opposite each other. To form and maintain bushes and pyramids, see overleaf.

Apples trees can also be trained flat. The cordon and espalier shapes (see p.245) suit their growth habit and pruning needs best, although fans and palmettes are also possible. Trees to be trained flat need a strong framework to support them and hold the branches in place. Purpose-made metal supports can be bought, or you can erect a post and wire system. Wires can also be strained across walls or fences. Set the top wire or rail at a height of about 2m (6ft), although on a wall this could be higher. Wires are set 30cm (12in) apart, starting at 75cm (30in) from the ground.

Cordons are usually planted obliquely at an angle of 45–60°, pointing up the slope on sloping ground, as this has some effect in controlling vigour. Space trees 75cm (30in) apart and use M26 or MM106 rootstocks. Use M27 for vigorous cultivars such as 'Jupiter' and 'Bramley'.

With espaliers, it is possible to have tiers of branches ascending as high as space and inclination permits but it is most usual to have three tiers at 45cm (18in) intervals. It is also possible to have a single tier ("step-over") at 75–90cm (30–36in) above the ground. For a three-tier espalier erect a post and wire support structure with wires at 60cm, 1.1m and 1.5m (2ft, 3½ft and 5ft).

Planting distances for espaliers will depend on the rootstock (see p.265). All rootstocks except M9 are suitable; only use M27 where you plan a single tier espalier or "step-over".

To form and maintain bushes, cordons, espaliers and pyramids, see overleaf.

Good neighbours (facing page)
Cordons (main picture) not only look beautiful, but are a useful way of growing several apple cultivars in close proximity, where space for several freestanding trees cannot be found. Coordinating the flowering time of cultivars in crucial in achieving good cross-pollination and thus heavy crops. (Pictured, from left to right: 'King of the Pippins', 'Kidd's Orange Red', and 'Red Devil' in flower.)

PLANTING AN APPLE TREE
• Prepare a hole at least 1m (3ft) in diameter on light soils, twice that size on poor-draining heavy clay or silt soils. You will need a stake 1m (3ft) long and a lump hammer or mallet, a tree tie, some well-rotted manure, leafmould if the soil is particularly heavy or light, bone meal, seaweed meal and any organic fertilisers required to amend inherent deficiencies (see p.61).
• Mark out a circle to the required size.
• If planting in a grassed area, slice off the turf and stack it to one side.
• Dig out topsoil to a spade's depth and stack it separately.
• Loosen the subsoil in the bottom of the hole with a garden fork. Also, on heavy soils, lightly loosen soil round the sides of the hole.
• Knock in the stake off centre on the side from which the prevailing wind blows.

• Either drop turf upside down in the hole and chop it with a spade, or, if you do not have turf, add leafmould (see below).
• Half-fill a 10-litre (2-gal) bucket with well-rotted manure, mix in 135g each of seaweed meal and bone meal and any other fertilisers required, and then mix this into the set-aside topsoil. If no turf is being turned in, add a bucket of leafmould.
• Attach the tree loosely to the stake so that it will be planted no deeper than the original soil mark. A cane or batten placed across the hole will help you gauge the depth.
• Return half the soil to the hole, untie the tree and shake it gently to settle soil round the roots. Add a little more and tread the soil gently to firm the tree in.
• Return the remainder of the soil, firm it in and attach the tree to its stake.

PRUNING AND TRAINING APPLES AND PEARS

When	Bush	Cordon	Espalier	Pyramid
On planting (maiden or feathered maiden) and in the first year	**On planting** Prune back the main stem to a bud about 75cm (30in) from the ground for all dwarfing rootstocks, 1.2m (4ft) for MM106 and 1.5–1.8m (5–6ft) for MM111. Look for a point just above at least four good buds pointing in different directions. For feathered maidens prune to leave four good sideshoots. If the angle of these is above 30° to the horizontal, train them downwards with a clothes peg or peg weight.	**On planting** Attach a cane to the wires for each tree at an angle of 45–60° (see also p.245). Prune the stem by about half to a strong bud facing along the line of the cane. **In late summer** Tie in the tree to the cane.	**On planting** Prune back to a point just above the lowest wire with three well-placed buds below it and tie it to the wire. Tie in a cane on each side at 45° to the wires facing opposite directions to support the growing branches. Allow the three buds to grow. **Late summer** Tie in one shoot to each cane, leaving the central one to grow vertically. Tie this to the second wire.	**On planting** If feathers (sideshoots) are suitably placed, reduce each by half and prune back the leader to a bud 20–25cm (8–10in) above the highest feather or branch. Remove all badly placed feathers.
After one year (year one)	**Winter** The four buds or feathers will have grown into young branches. Cut these back by half, to a downward-facing bud. Remove any laterals (sideshoots) growing directly upwards or downwards from these branches. Any lower shoots from the main stem below the main branches can be left but shorten them by half. They will help to thicken the trunk and can be removed after they have fruited. Cut out any shoots growing up in the very centre of the tree.	**Winter** Prune back the previous year's growth on the main stem by between one-third and a half. Reduce all laterals arising directly from the trunk to three buds. **During late summer** Tie in the extension growth of the leader to the cane.	**Winter** Pull down the new branches to the horizontal, but leave the tips pointing slightly upwards. Move the canes out to these tips, retaining the 45° angle. Prune to a bud just above the second wire as at planting, and fix angled canes to make the second tier.	**Winter** Prune back the central leader (the main stem) to 20–25cm (8–10in) of its new growth, cutting to a bud pointing in the opposite direction to the previous year. Cut back all side branches to 20cm (8in) of new growth, cutting to a downward-facing bud. Remove all sideshoots on the lowest branches within 30cm (12in) of the central trunk. Prune back all other sideshoots on all branches to a bud at 15cm (6in).
After two years (year two)	**Winter** Cut back the branch leaders (the main shoots extending their spread) by half of the previous season's growth, to a downward-facing bud. Prune back any shoots near the branch tip that are competing with this leader. Remove any strong upright growth, any sideshoots growing directly under the branches and any growing across the centre of the bush. Remove the lowest sideshoots on the branches to leave them clear of growth for the first 45–60cm (18–24in) from their point of origin. This creates an open, airy, light centre.	**Midsummer** When growth of new wood slows and begins to turn brown at the base, cut back all shoots arising directly from the main stem to three leaves above the cluster of leaves right at the base. Prune growth arising from last year's laterals that is longer than 25cm (10in) to one or two leaves. **In mid-autumn** Cut back shoots over 25cm (10in) to one or two leaves. Any new growth since the summer pruning should be removed at the base. **In winter** Cut back the leader by about one-third.	**During summer** Tie in the new growth on both tiers as in year one. Repeat the winter training and pruning for the third tier. Start pruning laterals as for cordons (see left).	**Winter** Maintain a pyramidal shape by pruning the leader and side branches as for year one every winter. Once the desired height and girth are reached, pruning should consist of cutting back to a better placed lateral further into the canopy or reducing the leader to a 2–3cm (¾–1¼in) stub at a bud. **Summer** Keep the centre of the tree close to the trunk free of growth – light levels are low here and growth poor.
In subsequent years	**Summer** Pull off or rub out any new growth from below ground, in the centre of the tree or arising from the main trunk. **Winter** Treat leaders as in year two. These branches will, after eight years or so, become quite long; if necessary, shorten to a well-placed, flat-growing branch further down. Leave all laterals to form natural branching side-growth. These will carry the fruit. When 4–5 years old, remove them entirely. Remove all strong upright growth, branches growing towards the centre, damaged or diseased wood. (If a mature tree is not fruiting well, some strong upright shoots can be made to crop by tucking them under other branches or tying them down in an arch.)	**Winter** Continue winter-pruning the leader until it has reached the desired height. Thereafter it can be pruned in summer at a leaf to 3–5cm (1¼–2in) of growth. When spur systems become very complex or excessively long, reduce them or remove them. **Summer** Prune all laterals and sub-laterals every summer as for year two (see above).	**Summer** Once branches have reached the end of their wires, the canes can be dispensed with and summer pruning can be carried out from then on as for cordons. After 10 years or more the lowest tier may be considerably less vigorous than the top tier. This can be remedied by completely removing the top tier and training in two new branches in the following years. Old and congested systems can be renovated as for cordons.	**Winter** Continue to maintain a pyramidal shape as for year two (see above). **Summer** Keep the centre of the tree free of growth as for year two (see above).

Looking after the fruit

It is important to keep weeds under control around trees, especially during their early years of establishment. They compete for food and, more importantly, nutrients. For weaker rootstocks, M27 and M9, good weed control under the canopy is essential throughout the life of the tree. Thick straw mulches 8–10cm (3–4in) deep will help to smother weeds and conserve moisture. Lay this in late spring, removing it in winter to the compost heap (see also p.240). Grass can be allowed to grow up to the trunk of well-established standard trees on MM111.

Feed trees if they show signs of decline with well-rotted manure or garden compost applied in early spring. This is likely to be about every three years for M26, more frequently for M9 and M27 trees. Trees on MM106 and MM111 will not need feeding after the first 10 years, unless they are growing in particularly poor soil.

Pruning

Once established, all tree forms benefit from winter pruning, which aims to keep a balance between older fruiting wood and new, vigorous growth. Trained forms – cordons, espaliers and fans – need extra pruning in summer to keep their shape. See facing page for details. To renovate neglected trees, see pp.245–246.

Thinning the fruits

It is normal in summer for many fruitlets to drop naturally but these may not be the ones you would have selected. For the best quality and size of fruit it is important to thin fruitlets early. Start thinning about six weeks after most petals have dropped.
• Remove the "king fruit" at the centre of the cluster. This is usually slightly larger and distorted.
• Thin the remaining fruitlets to leave one per cluster and 10–15cm (4–6in) between each fruitlet. Select the best fruitlet, discarding any that are affected by sawfly, or damaged or distorted.
• If fruit set is poor and the crop is light, leave two fruitlets in some or all the clusters.

Harvesting

First indication of ripeness will be the development of colour to the skin and a few windfalls on the ground. Test by gently lifting and twisting individual

fruits in the palm of your hand. If they come away easily they are ready for picking. Fruit of early cultivars can be eaten from the tree; later cultivars need time to develop their flavour after picking.

Storing fruit

Late cultivars will not ripen until they have been in store for a while. A domestic fridge is ideal for storing apples but a frost-free shed, cellar or loft will be adequate. Aim for cool, dark, slightly damp conditions. Only store perfect fruits.
• **Slatted boxes or shelves** Traditionally apples were stored in purpose-made slatted boxes or drawers. A good substitute is a vegetable crate. Lay apples in a single layer, not touching each other.
• **Individual wrapping** Wrap each apple in a square of tissue paper or newspaper, ensuring each fruit is completely covered. Fruit can be laid in boxes or vegetable crates in layers.
• **Polythene bags** Use large polythene bags, making four small holes in the lower part of the bag with a biro or pencil. Fill each bag with about 2kg (4lb) of fruit, and fold the neck of the bag loosely; do not tie it. Do not store different cultivars in the same bag or box; ethylene given off by the earlier cultivars as they ripen will affect the later ones. Check fruit in store regularly and discard or use any that show signs of deterioration.

CULTIVAR CHOICE

Dessert, early
'Beth' 4, 'Fondante d'Automne' 3, 'Glow Red Williams' 3 (RS), 'Gorham' 4 (RS), 'Jargonelle' 3 (RS), 'Merton Pride' 3 T, 'Onward' 4, 'Précoce de Trevoux' 1

Dessert, mid-season
'Beurré Hardy' 3 (RS), 'Beurré Superfin' 3, 'Conference' 3, 'Concorde' 4, 'Doyenné du Comice' 4, 'Louise Bonne of Jersey' 2, 'Thompson's' 3

Dessert, late
'Beurré d'Anjou' 2, 'Glou Morceau' 4, 'Joséphine de Malines' 3, 'Olivier de Serre' 3 (needs warmth)

Culinary, late
'Bellissime d'Hiver' 2, 'Black Worcester' 3, 'Catillac' 4 T, 'Uvedale's St Germain' 2 T, 'Vicar of Winkfield' 2 T

Numbers refer to pollination groups. Cultivars will cross-pollinate within the same group or in the group immediately before and after. However, the following will not pollinate each other: 'Glow Red Williams' – 'Louise Bonne of Jersey'; 'Seckel' – 'Fondante d'Automne'; 'Onward' – 'Doyenné du Comice'.

T Triploid: these cultivars need two pollinators that are not triploids themselves
RS Resistant to scab

Pears

The soft, melting, buttery flavour of European pears has invited the naming of many cultivars as "beurré". The fact that so many old cultivars bear French names shows how valued the pear was in France. The long season and warm conditions of the Continent suit them well.

Pears are quite long-lived trees, but the quality and size of fruit starts to decline after 30 or 40 years. The earliest cultivars are ready in midsummer and can be eaten straight from the tree. The majority are picked from early to mid-autumn and need at least two or three weeks after picking to ripen. Late-storing cultivars will keep well into winter. Other than early cultivars, pears should not be left to ripen on the tree, as flavour will be poor.

Site and soil

Pears enjoy warmth and an early start to the season. Blossoming is several weeks earlier than apples which means that the cooler the climate or the higher the altitude the less likely they are to succeed. There are a very few pear cultivars suited to cooler zones, none of them particularly choice. In these situations growing under glass (for example, fan-trained against the wall of a lean-to glasshouse) may be your best option. Advice given for soil conditions for apples also applies to pears.

Buying plants

Pears need to be pollinated by another compatible cultivar (see Cultivar Choice, left) so grow at least two cultivars and choose carefully. Pears are more difficult to store than apples but cultivars are available to span a season from midsummer through to winter without special storage conditions.

Follow the general buying advice given for apples. Bear in mind, however, that pears are slower to come into cropping than apples. Unless you are training a cordon or espalier, it is worth buying a tree grown for three years in the nursery to shorten the time before you harvest a crop. For a pyramid shape (see below) buy a tree with the centre leader still intact. Part-trained trees are available. Prepare the soil and plant as for apples (see p.266).

Pruning and training

Pears can be grown as open-centred bushes or, as apples, trained as formal shapes. Walls that face the midday or setting sun are ideal, with the warmest walls used for the more delicate or best-flavoured varieties. Pears grow well as a dwarf pyramid as this takes advantage of their natural habit of growing a strong central leader. The pyramid shape makes good use of sunshine as higher branches do not shade lower ones.

Train and prune cordons, espaliers and pyramids as for apples (see p.268). For an open-centred bush tree, initial formative pruning follows the pattern given for apples, unless you have bought a tree already three years old. At this stage routine pruning each winter can begin as follows:
• Reduce the leading shoots of each branch by one-third to a half, and remove any shoots competing with the leader near the tip (see p.268).

PEAR ROOTSTOCKS

Rootstock	Effect/Notes	Eventual max. height	Planting distance
Quince C	Dwarfing; suitable for all forms of tree	2.4–3m (8–10ft)	3–4.5m (10–13ft)
Quince A	Semi-dwarfing; suitable for bush, trained forms on poor soils, traditional orchards	3.6–4.5m (12–13ft)	3.6–4.5m (12–13ft)
Pear	Vigorous; suitable for traditional orchards, perry pears	9–12m (28–40ft)	10–12m (30–40ft)

Always prune out any diseased wood, cutting back well into healthy wood.

• Leave all one-year-old laterals unpruned unless they are strong growing and upright or badly placed (see p.268).

• In the following year new one-year-old laterals will appear and fruit buds will form on the unpruned laterals, now in their second year, and sub-laterals will grow out from them. Cut back into the two-year-old wood to leave shoots with four to six fruit buds on them.

• For the next two years prune back any extension growth on these spurs to the growth ring. New one-year-old laterals will arise from the main branches during the following years to give spurs of varying ages. Treat all side-growth as detailed above.

• Once a spur has completed four years it should be removed with a sloping cut to encourage a new lateral to restart the process.

Caring for the crop

As for apples (see p.269). Trees on pear rootstocks will not need feeding and grass can be allowed to grow up to their trunks, once the trees are established. Thin fruits as for apples.

Harvesting and storing

Not all pears have strong skin colouring, making the judging of ripeness difficult. When the approximate anticipated picking time for a cultivar arrives, start testing individual fruits. Hold the bulbous end of the fruit in the heel of your hand with your index finger on or near the stalk. Tilt the fruit gently upwards. It will come away easily when ready for picking. With

The more delicate-flavoured varieties are best grown against a warm wall

the exception of very early cultivars, pears need to ripen off the tree.

Pears are more difficult than apples to store well. General advice given for apples is relevant but it is better not to wrap pears. It is important to know when a cultivar is likely to ripen but outward signs are not dramatic; there will be a slight yellowing of the skin colour. Bring batches in to room temperature to complete ripening – it may take a further two to three weeks. When ripe, pears are soft at the stalk end and will give when pressed gently.

PROTECT THE CROP

In spring, pear leaf blister mite attacks expanding young foliage, causing pink blisters, which later turn black. Pick off infested leaves. Pick up and destroy fruitlets that fall in early summer. They may contain pear midge larvae (see picture below). Where this pest is a problem, mulch the soil, in spring, with black plastic or other impermeable sheeting to prevent the midge larvae returning to the soil.

Look out for aphids on young shoots; squash these by hand, wash off with a jet of water, or spray with an appropriate insecticide. Sow flowers to attract natural predators (see p.96). A grease-band can reduce an aphid infestation on a free-standing tree by keeping ants, which farm aphids, out of the tree. Mulch trees to keep soil moist, and water in periods of prolonged dry weather.

In autumn, remove mulches and rake up all fallen leaves, or mow them so they are taken into the soil quickly to remove scab spores. Apply greasebands to trees and stakes (see p.101). Keep these in place until early spring to protect against winter moth. Remove any fruit still hanging in tree, and hang up fat for the birds. In winter prune out any diseased wood.

See the *A–Z of Plant Problems*, p.367, for more information.

Plums, gages, damsons and bullaces

Plums and gages are fruits of high summer continuing through into autumn, when damsons also become ripe. Plums and damsons are often found in relatively cool regions with shorter seasons such as the north of England. Damsons are certainly very hardy and are even used as perimeter windbreak trees in some windy regions. Bullace is very similar to damson but has a round fruit. Nevertheless plums, gages and damsons all flower earlier than pears and in regions where late spring frosts are common rarely fruit well. It is not worth expending effort on growing gages in cool regions with unpredictable temperatures in spring.

Large-crowned mature plum and damson trees are a common sight and damsons particularly are nearly always grown as informal, bushy trees, as are bullaces. Plums and gages, however, are well suited to growing as fans or cordons on a wall or free-standing support.

Site and soil

Good drainage is essential but otherwise plums and their close relatives are not unduly fussy about soil.

All three crops grow best in sunny conditions, sheltered from frost and high winds. Gages and dessert plums will benefit from being grown against a warm wall, particularly if this protects them from late spring frosts.

Buying plants

For general advice, see apples. There are many self-fertile cultivars (see Cultivar Choice, left); those that

CULTIVAR CHOICE

Dessert plums and gages, early
'Early Laxton' 3, 'Opal' (sf) 3

Dessert plums and gages, mid-season
'Blue Tit' (sf), 'Cambridge Gage' 5, 'Jefferson' 1, 'Kirke's Blue' 4, 'Victoria' (sf) 3

Dessert plums and gages, late
'Coe's Golden Drop' 2, 'Golden Transparent' (sf) 3, 'Laxton's Delight' 3

Culinary plums and gages, early
'Czar' (sf) 3, 'Early Prolific' 3 (syn. 'Early Rivers'), 'Pershore' (sf) 3

Culinary plums and gages, mid-season
'Belle de Louvain' (sf) 5, 'Purple Pershore' (sf) 3

Culinary plums and gages, late
'Marjorie's Seedling' (sf) 5, 'Warwickshire Drooper' (sf) 2

Damson (all self-fertile)
'Merryweather', 'Bradley's King', 'Farleigh', 'Prune' (syn. 'Shropshire')

sf Self-fertile, need no pollinator. Numbers refer to pollination groups. Cultivars cross-pollinate others in the same group or the one immediately before or after.

PRUNING AND TRAINING

	Plum bush (from a maiden)	Plum cordon (from a maiden)	Plum fan (from a maiden)
After planting	If maiden trees have laterals, prune off all except four good, well-placed ones at a height of 90cm (36in). Remove all other feathers. If there are no feathers cut to a suitable bud at the same height.	Cut back the main stem by about one-third, cutting to a bud, and reduce all sideshoots to three buds.	As the tree starts to grow in spring, reduce the young stem to either two sideshoots or two buds about 75cm (30in) from the ground. Tie them in to canes on supporting wires at an angle of 45° on each side. If there are four well-placed sideshoots, tie two further in at an angle of 60° on each side.
In the first year			**Late summer** Cut back branches by half the new growth to a leaf and tie in to canes. Set a cane below each branch and two above to begin forming a fan. Remove shoots crossing the centre.
After a year's growth	**Late spring** Reduce the new branches by half to an outward-facing bud.	**Early summer** Pinch out all new growth on sideshoots to leave six leaves once they are long enough. **Late summer** Reduce sideshoots further so that only three leaves are left. **Late autumn** Tie in the new leader to a cane at an angle of 45° or train it upright; upright growth will be more vigorous.	**Summer** Allow three laterals to grow out from these branches on each side and tie them in, one to each cane. Remove all others. At the end of the summer reduce these new branches by half the growth they have made.
In subsequent years	**Late spring or late summer** Prune lightly, only to remove growth that is damaged, diseased, too long or badly placed. Fruits will form on two- and three-year-old wood and at the very base of year-old growth. If damsons and plums on 'Pixy' rootstocks become congested growth can be thinned.	**Every summer** Prune as above. Once the leader has reached the desired height, cut it back annually to a single leaf of new growth or a weaker shoot slightly lower down. Tie this shoot to the cane. If spur systems become long, crowded or complex, thin, reduce or remove them.	From now, on laterals can be allowed to form and are pruned annually as for cordons (see left). Pruning back of leaders will be necessary once they have reached the required length. New branches can be allowed to fill any vacant space and tied in to canes but the centre should always be left open. Any upright growth in the centre will tend to dominate, weakening growth on the other fingers of the fan.

are not, or only partly so, will need a pollinator. Part-formed fans can be bought but you may prefer to start with a feathered maiden and form your own tree to the planned shape. Rootstocks – see below.

Preparation and planting

Follow general advice given for apples. For fans and cordons, prepare supporting wires as for apples.

PLUM ROOTSTOCKS

Pixy
Dwarfing; suitable for all gardens. Allow to crop after three years.
Eventual height: 2.1–2.5m (6½–8ft).
Spacing: 2.5–3m (8–10ft) for a pyramid or bush; 5m (15ft) for a fan.

St Julien A
Semi-dwarfing; suitable for larger trees and orchards. Allow to crop after three or four years.
Eventual height: 3–4m (10–12ft).
Spacing: 4–5m (12–15ft) for a bush or pyramid; 5.5m (17½ft) for a fan.

Caring for the crop

• **General care** As for apples (see p.269).
• **Pruning** To form tree shapes, see above. Plums, gages, damsons and bullaces are all fruit types that are prone to silver leaf disease. They are particularly susceptible to infection when trees are dormant. Apart from the initial cutting back, all pruning must be done between late spring and early autumn to reduce possibility of infection. Cut out affected growth, cutting well back into healthy wood. Disinfect tools afterwards. Also prune out dead or diseased wood.
• **Thinning** In a good year, some cultivars will set a great deal of fruit. After the natural fruit drop in early summer, thin the remaining fruitlets with scissors to about 5–10cm (2–5in) apart. Failure to do this may lead to branches breaking under the weight of the crop.
• **Harvesting** There is no doubt when a plum, gage or damson is ripe. It will be fully coloured (but note that they come in many colours, including green) and soft. Fruits will pull away easily.
• **Storing** Fruits do not store for long but can be frozen or used in preserves. Once picked, keep them cool until you are ready to use them.

PROTECT THE CROP

From midwinter, check for plum leaf curling aphid on buds and twigs. Squash, hose off, or use an appropriate pesticide. Prune out heavily "curled" shoot tips. Encourage natural aphid predators. In spring, remove any withered blossom or shoot tips – caused by the brown rot fungus. Plum moth caterpillars may be found in prematurely ripened fruit. A pheromone trap, in late spring, may protect single trees. Remove fallen fruit in autumn. See also Pruning, left, for silverleaf, below.

CULTIVAR CHOICE

Sweet cherries
The following cultivars are self-fertile:
'Stella' 4, 'Sunburst' 4, 'Lapins' (Cherokee) 4, 'Starkrimson' 3

The following cultivars are not self-fertile and are listed in "incompatibility" groups. Only those in different groups will pollinate each other, provided the flowering periods overlap. The self-fertile cultivars listed above will provide pollen for any of those in the groups below.

Incompatibility groups (flowering periods in brackets)
1. 'Early Rivers' (1), 'Roundel' (3)
2. 'Merton Favourite' (2), 'Waterloo' (2), 'Merton Bigarreau' (3), 'Merton Bounty' (3), 'Van' (3)

Cultivars 'Noir de Guben' (1), 'Merchant' (3), and 'Bigarreau Napoléon' (4) are all self-infertile but are compatible with any of the above cultivars in overlapping flowering groups.

Acid cherries
'Morello' (self-fertile) (5) – will pollinate sweet cherries in flowering groups 4 or 5.

Cherries

Cherries are normally referred to as sweet or acid. Sweet cherries are eaten straight from the tree and have either white ("white heart") or dark ("black heart") flesh. Skin colour also varies from "white", which are actually flushed with scarlet, to very dark. Sweet cherries ripen in midsummer; acid cherries ripen slightly later. These cherries are grown for culinary use and are very sour eaten raw.

Initial pruning to shape trees is similar for each type. Thereafter it is very different, as acid cherries fruit on branches produced the previous year, whereas sweet cherries fruit on older branches and are pruned as for plums.

Most acid cherries are self-fertile, as are a few sweet cherries. In general, however, sweet cherries are not and have very complicated compatibilities for pollination (see Cultivar Choice, left). Cherries will start to crop in their third year.

Sweet cherries

• **Site and soil** Sweet cherries flower even earlier than plums. The blossom is not frost-tolerant, so it is advisable to give cherries the warmest spot in the garden. Sweet cherries are most commonly grown as a fan against a wall that receives sunshine for most of the day. Wires will be needed, spaced 30cm (12in) apart. In regions where late spring frosts are not a problem it is possible to grow cherries as informal "bush" trees. Cherries have similar soil requirements to plums (see p.272).

• **Rootstocks** Good dwarfing rootstocks for cherries are gradually now becoming more widely available (see below). This is an important

development because tall trees are difficult or impossible to net – and birds love cherries. Wall-trained cherries are easily netted and ideal for the garden.

• **Buying plants** For general advice, see plums and apples (pp.265 and 272). Take care to choose cultivars that will pollinate each other or are self-fertile (see Cultivar Choice, left). Acid cherries will pollinate sweet cherries in appropriate flowering groups.

• **Preparation and planting** As for apples (see p.266).

• **Pruning and training** Informal bushes and fans are formed and pruned as for plums (see p.273).

• **General care** Follow advice for apples (see p.269). Keep at least 1m (3ft) square or diameter circle free of weeds round each tree.

• **Thinning** Cherries do not need thinning.

• **Harvesting** Cherries should be picked as soon as they are ripe. Pull by the stalk not the fruit. Either eat immediately or place in a fridge. Cherries do not store but can be frozen.

Acid cherries

• **Site and soil** The requirements of acid cherries are not very different from sweet types. They do, however, flower later and can therefore be grown on cool walls, although a warmer aspect is preferable. In warmer regions they grow successfully as bushes out in the open but netting will be necessary as for sweet cherries. Late frosts will damage blossom. Fan-trained trees will need wires 15cm (6in) apart.

• **Buying plants** As for sweet cherries. The most common cultivar is 'Morello'. This, like most other acid cultivars, is self-fertile, and needs no pollinator.

ROOTSTOCKS

Rootstocks	Effect	Eventual height	Planting distance
Gisela 5	Dwarfing: modern successful rootstock, allowing for the first time really dwarf cherry trees	2–2.5m (6–8ft)	2.5–3m (8–10ft)
Hexaploid Colt	Dwarfing: 25% smaller than standard Colt (see below)	2.25–2.7m (7½–9ft)	2.5–3m (8–10ft)
Colt	Semi-dwarfing: a well-proven rootstock but still quite large trees for netting	Average 3–3.5m (10–12ft)	3.6–4.5m (12–13ft)

Cherry fan
Fan-trained cherries are a great deal easier to net against birds than freestanding trees.

PROTECT THE CROP

Cherries are susceptible to most of the problems that can affect plums (see p.273), with the exception of plum fruit moth. Cherry blackfly (below) can appear on young shoots in late winter. Squash, hose them off, or use an appropriate pesticide (see p.103). Encourage natural aphid predators (see pp.96–97). Prune in the growing season, not when dormant, to reduce the risk of silver leaf infection. Protect the crop from birds before it ripens. It may also be necessary to protect buds from bullfinch and blue tit damage in winter. Where practical, allow birds access at other times, to help control pests. Pests and diseases are less likely to be a problem where plants are growing in appropriately managed soil, and where the garden environment encourages natural predation.

- **Rootocks** Acid cherries are grown on the same rootstocks as sweet cherries.
- **Preparation and planting** As for apples (see p.266).
- **Pruning and training** Although extremely similar to the sweet cherry, the acid cherry has a very different habit of growth. Unlike sweet cherries, acid cherries fruit on wood produced the previous year. Initial training is similar to plums but thereafter differs markedly.

Form a bush as for a plum (see p.273). Once established, pruning of cherry bushes consists of removing a proportion of older three- and four-year-old wood to a younger side-branch.

For a fan, initial pruning and training is similar to plums. The aim is to have, after two or three years, a basic framework of short permanent branches, filling half the space available with the centre half empty. In the following year, allow new shoots to grow from this framework and fill the available space, tying them in to a fan shape with branch tips about 12–15cm (5–6in) apart.

In subsequent years, fruit will form on these one-year-old shoots. At the same time new shoots will grow as laterals. Choose two of these for each branch close to the base and about 15cm (6in) apart. Remove all others. After harvest in mid- to late summer, cut the fruited wood back to the best of the two shoots retained, with a preference for the lower one. If there is space both new branches can be kept. Tie in the new growth.

After some years the framework branches will have become extended as replacement wood never forms exactly at the base. Some branches may need pruning back harder to a dormant bud. Do this on a few branches successively over a period of years.
- **General care** As for sweet cherries.
- **Harvesting** Acid cherries do not pull away easily from the tree. Use scissors or secateurs to cut the stalks close to the branch. Fruit is ready when it is very dark in colour and soft to the touch. Fruits can be used to make jam or wine, preserved in a jar of brandy, or cooked for immediate use. Cooked cherries can be frozen.

Peaches and nectarines

CULTIVAR CHOICE

Peaches
'Duke of York', 'Garden Lady' (dwarf), 'Peregrine', 'Rochester', 'Terrace Amber' (dwarf), 'Terrace Diamond' (dwarf), 'Waterloo'

Nectarines
'Early Rivers', 'Garden Beauty' (dwarf), 'Lord Napier', 'Terrace Ruby' (dwarf)

PROTECT THE CROP

Peach leaf curl disease infects leaves as they unfold in spring, causing red blistering and distortion. A temporary shelter to keep rain off until all leaves have appeared reduces infection. Watch out for scale, glasshouse red spider mite and aphids in the greenhouse and very hot, dry locations. Sooty moulds may be the first symptoms. Water plants well in dry weather and introduce appropriate biological control agents. See also Apricots (facing page).

Peaches and nectarines are sun-lovers and their warm, luscious and juicy flesh arouse images of the Mediterranean and Middle East. The flesh is yellow, white or pink and, in the case of "cling" peaches, does not separate readily from the stone. Nectarines really only differ in the skin, which is smooth rather than hairy, although they need even more warmth than peaches and crop little more than half as well.

The main cropping period is mid- to late summer, but under glass the season can be advanced quite considerably given sufficient warmth and light.

Peaches and nectarines can be grown in pots. The dwarf cultivars are specially suitable for this.

Site and soil

Peaches flower very early in spring and the blossoms are not hardy. For this reason peaches and nectarines are normally grown against a warm, sunny wall. It is not uncommon to see peaches grown against the back wall of a lean-to greenhouse, where they will flourish in the frost-free, warm environment. They can be grown as free-standing trees in warm regions but growing them against a wall gives the added advantage of being able to protect them easily from the winter rain that spreads peach leaf curl (see *A–Z of Plant Problems*). Peaches and nectarines prefer a slightly acid soil which is deep and fertile. Alkaline soils tend to induce yellowing of the leaves (chlorosis).

Buying plants

For general advice see apples (see p.265). Only one rootstock is used, the plum rootstock St Julien A (see p.273). In general it is best to choose a maiden and train it yourself. You may be able to find a well-grown pre-trained three-year-old fan, which will then save you the initial years spent in creating the basic framework. It is also possible now to buy very dwarf cultivars suitable for growing in pots or the open ground but not suitable for fan-training.

Preparation and planting

Aim to plant your trees in the first half of winter as they break into growth quite early. Follow the general advice given for apples (see p.266). Trees need staking for the first two or three years.

Forming the tree

Peaches and nectarines are very similar to acid cherries in that they fruit on young wood. Follow advice on forming trees for acid cherries (see p.275). Carry out all pruning between late spring and early autumn to avoid silverleaf (see pp.273 and 390).

Pollination

Peaches are nearly all self-fertile but benefit from hand-pollination, moving from flower to flower, dusting lightly with a soft paintbrush on a warm, dry day when flowers are fully open. Do this several times over a fortnight, as flowers open in sequence.

Looking after the fruit

• **General care** As for apples (see p.269). Peaches must be kept weed-free throughout their life.
• **Thinning** For the best size and quality of fruit, thinning is essential. Thin in two phases: when fruitlets are the size of grapes, thin to one fruit per cluster, and then later, when they are walnut-sized, to leave one fruit every 15cm (6in) approximately.
• **Harvesting** Fruits will be soft to the touch and fully coloured when they are ripe. They bruise easily and should not be dropped. Fruits do not store.

Apricots

Apricots, delicious as they are, are not as commonly grown as peaches. This is quite probably because they need both adequate water and a long, warm, dry growing season, making them difficult subjects. If you can meet the conditions, it is well worth trying. Apricots are all self-fertile, so you can happily grow just one tree. The season lasts from mid- to late summer with earlier crops possible under glass.

Unlike most fruits covered so far, apricots prefer a slightly alkaline soil. Good drainage is essential, especially for heavier soils. Dieback, a common disease in apricots, is exacerbated by cold, wet winters and waterlogged soils.

Apricots flower in late winter. Except in warm areas, it is therefore usual to grow them as a fan against a sunny wall or under glass, where the blossom can be protected from frost damage. Where frosts at flowering time are rare they can be grown as free-standing trees.

Buying plants

Follow the general advice given for apples and plums (see pp.265 and 272). Apricot cultivars are all self-fertile. A number of rootstocks will be offered (see below).

Preparation and planting

As for peaches (see facing page).

Forming trees

For establishing bushes and fans, follow the advice given for plums (see p.273) to create the basic framework and for general management. Fruit forms at the base of one-year-old shoots as well as older wood.

Fans Once a fan is established, follow the advice for plums to prune and train new shoots and sideshoots that grow from the basic framework. Remove entirely any shoots growing towards the fence or wall. In cool regions there is very likely to be varying amounts of dieback. This should be pruned out to healthy wood as soon as it is seen and a new shoot trained in during summer.

After some years, long and congested spur systems should be shortened, thinned or removed with a sloping cut that faces upwards.

Pollination

In cooler areas and if trees are grown under glass, hand-pollination will improve fruit set (see Peaches, facing page).

Looking after the fruit

General care Follow the advice on watering, feeding and weeding for other tree fruits.

Thinning In warmer regions there may be excessive blossom. This will lead to a tendency to biennial cropping, bearing only every other year, if not thinned. After the main natural spring drop of fruitlets, take out any remaining damaged fruitlets and thin the trusses to leave one fruit per cluster about 7–10cm (3–4in) apart only if the set is heavy.

Harvesting Fruits part easily from the stalk and are soft to the touch when ripe. They will not store.

CULTIVAR CHOICE

'Alfred'
'Farmingdale'
'Hemskirke'
'Moorpark'

PROTECT THE CROP

Apricots have a similar range of pests and diseases to peaches but are generally healthier and do not suffer from leaf curl. Silverleaf can be a problem (see Plums, p.273).

The most common problem is dieback, a fungal problem that is prevalent in cool climates and soil is often very wet. Whole branches die back and sap oozes out of wounds near the branch base. Avoid winter pruning and keep trees growing strongly to reduce infection. Prune out all affected branches to healthy wood.

Brown rot and grey mould (botrytis) can cause fruits to rot. Remove infected fruit, and prune to allow good ventilation. Brown rot fungus can also cause blossom wilt and dieback.

Pests and diseases are less likely to be a problem where plants are growing in well-managed soil and the garden environment encourages natural predation.

ROOTSTOCKS

Rootstocks	Effect	Eventual height	Planting distance
St Julien A	Semi-vigorous; suitable for bushes and fans	4.2–4.5m (12–13ft)	4.5–5.5m (13–17½ft) – for fans or bushes
Seedling peach	Vigorous; tolerates wetter conditions than seedling apricot; free-standing trees	6–8m (20–25ft)	5–6m (15–20ft)
Seedling apricot	Vigorous; free-standing trees	7.5–9m (23–28ft)	5.5–7m (17½–22ft)

Figs

It is not difficult to grow figs, exotic though they may seem. The main problems in cooler temperature climates are to restrain their vigour and to bring them into fruitful cropping. In a Mediterranean climate figs may crop twice in a year but in cooler situations once a year is more usual. Figs will not crop successfully in cool, short summers. No pollination is necessary as the flowers form inside the embryo fruits and are self-fertile. Figs are grown on their own roots and not grafted onto rootstocks.

Site and soil

Figs do best in warm, dry and sunny locations with a long growing season. In cooler climates figs are best grown against a wall receiving maximum sunshine. The wall needs to be at least 3m (10ft) high as figs are vigorous and each fan tree will take up to 3–4m (10–12ft) in width. Horizontal wire supports will be needed at 30cm (12in) intervals. Alkaline soils suit figs better but it is not necessary to add lime unless the pH is less than 6.

It is common practice to restrict fig tree roots, and therefore the vigour of the tree, by growing the tree in an excavated pit 60–90cm (24–36in) square, lined with concrete blocks or bricks. The pit should be dug 60cm (24in) deep and the bottom 30cm (12in) filled with stones, rubble or old mortar. Trees restricted in this way fruit much more readily.

Ripening figs
New embryo pea-sized fruitlets form as the current season's figs ripen. These fruitlets will overwinter and then start to swell during summer.

PRUNING AND TRAINING

	Fig bush	Fig fan
On planting	The basic framework is formed as for a plum (see p.273).	Advice for fans outside or under cover is almost identical but glasshouse-grown figs need a more open branch structure with more widely spaced arms. Initial pruning to create the basic framework is as for peaches and acid cherries (see p.275) but allowing about 30cm (12in) between the skeleton branches.
In subsequent years	**Spring** Remove all branches growing into the centre to keep it open. Cut out any frost-damaged wood and thin out branches to prevent congestion. The most productive branches are young, short and thick. All spindly growth should be removed. The aim is to produce an open framework of flattish branches to allow maximum light penetration. In warmer climates, where hot sun is more of a problem than frost damage, aim for a more upright shape to help shade the centre. After a while some long bare branches will form in the tree. Cut these back in spring to one bud to generate a new branch.	**Spring** After all danger of severe frost is past, start by removing all frost-damaged wood, crossing or badly placed branches and weak spindly growth. Clear away all suckers arising at or below ground level. Cut out all old branches that have produced fruit to one bud and prune back a number of one-year-old shoots nearer the centre of the fan similarly to encourage new branches. Tie in the remaining unpruned sideshoots to an open fan shape, filling the wall but leaving the centre slightly open. Do not allow any strong upright growth in the centre. **By midsummer** New shoots will have arisen along the length of the branches. Except where replacement branches will be needed, pinch these back to five leaves. Embryo figs will then form on these to grow and ripen the following year. **Autumn** Remove all part-formed or unripened figs to leave only pea-sized embryo figs on the tree.

Fan under glass
The branches are trained wide apart to reduce the risk of crowded growth encouraging disease in the still air of a closed environment, and also to minimise shading of the fruits by leaves.

In hot, dry climates this practice will not be necessary. Trees can be grown as a free-standing bush with unrestricted roots. They may reach 8m (25ft) in height eventually. Figs are well suited to container growing (see pp.212–213).

Buying plants

Look for two-year-old container-grown specimens with two good branches for a fan, three or four for a bush, arising 60cm (24in) above soil level. Unless you live in a warm region or have the opportunity to grow figs under glass, choose an early or mid-season variety.

Preparation and planting

For open-centred bushes follow advice for apples. For wall-trained fruit grown in a pit, it is important to provide adequate nutrition to give the tree a good start. Once the pit is prepared, add to the soil to be returned:
• One 10-litre (2-gal) bucket of garden compost
• One small spadeful of chopped well-rotted manure (or use chicken manure pellets applied in spring)
• 75g (2oz) bone meal
• 75g (2oz) seaweed meal
• Ground limestone, if the soil is below pH 6.

Tease the roots out from the potting compost. Set the tree in the hole and work the above mixture well round the roots, firming the tree level with the original soil mark. To train and prune as a bush or fan, see above.

Feeding and weeding

Keep wall-trained trees free of weeds at all times. Bush trees can be vigorous and may be grassed down once established. Unrestricted trees will not need feeding. Pit-grown trees will, however, need feeding annually as their roots are restricted. Every other spring apply one 10-litre (2-gal) bucket of garden compost or half a bucket of well-rotted manure to the surface. In intervening years apply a measure of chicken manure pellets and 75g (2oz) seaweed meal.

Regular watering will be necessary for crops grown under glass or pit-grown against a wall outside in dry weather.

Picking the fruit

In a temperate climate fruits outdoors will ripen in late summer. Fruits hang down when ripe and are very soft to the touch. They may have split skins. Figs are best eaten fresh or can be dried.

PROTECT THE CROP

Outdoor-grown figs are relatively problem-free. Fruit may need protection from birds. In autumn, protect the embryo figs from frost damage if this is likely to occur. Pick off any diseased fruits and leaves; cut out any branches that have died back, cutting well back into healthy wood.

Figs under cover, or in a very hot dry situation – against a wall for example – may suffer from glasshouse red spider mite, soft scale and other greenhouse pests. Check plants regularly, and introduce the relevant biological control agent. Prune and train to give an open shape to reduce the risk of grey mould developing.

Clear up fallen leaves and debris at the end of the season, and remove any figs that have not ripened (but not the tiny embryo fruits that will produce the next season's crop).

See the *A–Z of Plant Problems*, p.367, for more details.

CULTIVAR CHOICE

'Kentish Cob' Also called 'Longue d'Espagne', the most commonly grown cultivar; excellent flavour, fairly hardy. Pollinators: 'Gosford', 'Gunslebert'

'Gunslebert'
Hardy, vigorous and heavy-cropping; some resistance to canker and big bud. Late cropping. Pollinators: 'Cosford', 'Kentish Cob'

'Butler'
Large nut, heavy cropping, vigorous and hardy; good flavour; some resistance to canker but susceptible to big bud. Mid to late cropping. Pollinator: 'Ennis'

'Ennis'
Irregular cropper, sometimes biennial, but excellent flavour; tends to produce empty nuts. Pollinator: 'Butler'

'Cosford'
Moderate crop but very fine flavour. Pollinators: 'Gunslebert', 'Kentish Cob'

Snapped stems
Snapping or "brutting" hazel stems reduces vigour and helps nuts to ripen. It also makes the plant more likely to bear female flowers.

Hazelnuts

In Britain, cultivated hazelnuts are generally referred to as cobnuts, although in America the name "filbert" is more common.

Site and soil
Hazels grow best in a full sun and a free-draining soil with a pH of 6–7. While adequate fertility is important, too much will lead to large, unproductive trees. The trees are fully hardy, but flower extremely early. It is important therefore to choose a frost-free site. Commercial nut "plats" (plantations) are frequently sited on hillsides and slopes to ensure that frost "drains away". Although nuts are wind-pollinated they need protection from strong winds and will benefit from windbreak hedges.

Buying plants
Spacing for nut trees is wide; each tree will eventually take up an area of 3.5m (11ft). Buy two-or three-year-old well-rooted trees.

> ## For good quality, easy-to-pick hazelnuts, grow a single-stemmed tree

Hazelnuts are not self-fertile and need to be pollinated by another cultivar; not all cultivars are mutually compatible for this purpose. If, however, you have wild hedgerow or woodland hazels nearby, you should have no problem with pollination. Cultivar Choice (see left) includes advice on compatibility.

Preparation and planting
Follow the general guidelines for apples (see p.266), allowing a cultivated weed-free area at least 1m (3ft) in diameter around each tree.
• Prepare the site in autumn ready for planting soon after leaf fall.
• Just before planting, add bone meal at the rate of 125g per sq m (4oz per sq yd).
• If rabbits are a problem you will need to fit a spiral tree guard to the trunk.
• Plant the tree to the same depth as it was in the nursery (look for the soil mark) and firm it in well.

Forming the tree
Hazels can be allowed to grow as a multiple stemmed, bush-like tree, as wild nut trees do. However a single-stemmed tree, or standard, with an open goblet-shaped crown produces better quality nuts that are easier to pick. It is also easier to weed and mulch a single stem. To train a standard:
After planting
• Remove all shoots growing from below ground to leave a single main stem. Prune off any growth to a height of about 45cm (18in) above soil level. The crown can then form naturally above this point.
In subsequent years
• In late summer each year, snap in half long laterals of 30cm (12in) or more of current season's growth (see picture, below left). The snapped portion is left hanging down to aid location in winter. This process, called "brutting", reduces vigour, helps nuts ripen and encourages weaker growth, more likely to bear female flowers.
• Regularly prune out any shoots growing around the base of the tree.
• In winter, prune out any strong upright growth or damaged branches and "brutted" laterals to three or four buds in winter.
• Keep the tree to a height convenient for picking by pruning back tall branches to a suitable outward-facing lateral.

Looking after the plants
Keep trees free of weeds and mulch with straw early in autumn. Remove this mulch in winter. Apply well-rotted manure every three years in spring at the rate of one wheelbarrow to 10sq m (9sq yd), increasing the frequency only if growth is poor. Nuts do not need thinning.

Harvesting the crop
The harvesting period is from late summer, when the husks are still green and the nuts juicy, through to mid-autumn, by which time the shells and husks are brown and the kernels firm and fuller flavoured. The last crop to be harvested can be stored until midwinter. Hazelnuts cannot normally be stored for long as they dry out more quickly than other nuts. For short-term storage, keep nuts refrigerated.

PROTECT THE CROP

Fungal leafspots and powdery mildew may appear on the leaves in summer. Mulch plants well, and water in very dry weather. Pick off, or cut out, badly infected leaves and shoots; clear up all plant debris in the autumn.

The major problem of hazelnuts in many areas is the squirrel which harvests ripe nuts. Little can be done against this creature. Nut weevils may attack young nuts, creating a round exit hole in the ripe nut. The percentage of the crop attacked is usually too small to warrant attention.

Pests and diseases are less likely to be a problem where plants are growing in appropriately managed soil, and where the garden environment encourages natural predation.

Growing herbs

KNOWN FOR THEIR FRAGRANCE, FLAVOUR AND HEALING PROPERTIES, HERBS ARE EASY TO CULTIVATE ORGANICALLY

Choosing herbs (facing page)
Plant a selection of herbs that reflects your own taste. Choose plants for their fragrance, foliage, culinary use, or simply for their beauty alongside garden ornamentals.

Strong medicine (below)
The mandrake, a powerful plant in many folk mythologies, grows here within a symbolic woven "cage". Some medicinal herbs should be sited with care in a family garden.

WALK INTO ANY HERB GARDEN for a sensory experience – the plants it contains will have been selected for their scent as well as their appearance, and have rich associations with human history. Here are plants that have, over many centuries, helped people to sleep, soothed pain, repelled insects, calmed fractious babies and flavoured intoxicating drinks. Herbs are still worth growing today for their useful qualities, as well as for the fact that they are beautiful to look at. This chapter will tell you about growing herbs organically, along with information about how to harvest, store and use various herbs. It also includes details about which herbs are suitable for different soil types and situations, as well as how to stop invasive herbs from taking over the garden.

What is a herb?

The broadest definition of a herb is of a plant that people use or have used for a specific purpose. Nowadays herbs are most commonly known for their culinary, medicinal, aromatic and decorative qualities. In earlier times, people relied on herbs for an even greater number of uses: some were utilized in dyeing and cleaning fabrics; others had a role in ritual and ceremony; and many were used in everyday life as flavourings for food and drink, to promote good health, and to cure illness.

Annuals, biennials, perennials, bulbs, shrubs, climbers and trees can all have herbal value. In many cases, it is the leafy part of the plant that is used as a herb, but different parts, such as roots, fruits, seeds and flowers, even the bark of some trees, are utilized according to the species.

Herbs are plants that people have found useful throughout history

The majority of herbs are safe to handle and consume, but not all of them. Some herbs can be toxic to humans and animals even in small doses, so they need to be treated with respect. Never use anything that you are not sure is completely safe, and consult a medical herbalist first if you want to use herbs for their medicinal properties.

Growing herbs organically

Herbs are easy plants to grow, beautiful to look at, and, in many cases, free from pest and disease problems. Growing them yourself means that you can have fresh supplies to hand when you need them, and using organic methods means you can be sure they have not been treated with pesticides.

Growing herbs of any kind will increase the diversity of a garden, one of the key principles behind a successful organic system. With such a huge range of herbs to choose from, there is almost certainly one for every situation. Herbs can be selected to climb, creep, tumble, form dense carpets, or be trained up walls. Some will be happy in boggy soil, others on top of walls, in between paving stones,

HERBS TO ATTRACT WILDLIFE

For bees
Borage, chives, lungwort, sage, thyme, teasel, mint

For beneficial insects
English marigold, fennel, yarrow, dandelion, angelica, coriander, feverfew, tansy

For butterflies and moths
Evening primrose, catmint, hemp agrimony, valerian, lavender, coltsfoot, purple loosestrife

For birds
Poppy, rose, teasel, elder, hawthorn

See p.289 for an index of common and botanical names

Out of the blue
Borage flowers are characteristically blue, but more unusual white flowers can sometimes be found.

under trees and in meadows – success depends on matching the right plant to the available conditions. They also vary in size, from the tiny, ground-hugging Corsican mint *(Mentha requienii)*, to stately giants such as angelica or lovage reaching 2m (6ft) high. Herbs can be grown for their appearance alone. Some plants have spectacular flowers, some are valued for their foliage, and they all have something to contribute to a garden.

Many herbs attract wildlife: birds eat the seeds and berries, butterflies and bees enjoy the nectar and pollen, while beneficial insects will lay their eggs near sources of aphids and other pests. Some examples are given above. Dense plantings of ground-covering herbs such as thymes provide habitats for many beneficial creatures, including beetles, spiders and even frogs and toads.

Growing herbs for flavour

Herbs impart an enormous range of flavours to both sweet and savoury dishes. They can be added to soups, sauces, stews, salads, casseroles, pies, flans and anything else you can eat! Although it is possible to buy dried herbs, their flavour is far better when used fresh. Recipes that list dried herbs can be adapted for

fresh herbs just by doubling the quantities given. With practice you should be able to judge quantities according to taste. A good suggestion is to start with just one or two herbs in a recipe until you become familiar with the flavours and learn how to combine them for the best effects.

Preparations and decorations

Another tradition is the use of aromatic herbs to repel moths or insects and to keep stored clothes or linen smelling sweet. These mixtures are effective and still popular today, either sewn into bags or stored loose in containers as pot-pourri.

Herbs are also an important part of the cosmetics industry, finding their way into bath oils, shampoos, creams and lotions. Many old-fashioned preparations are simple to make yourself and much cheaper than buying products off the shelf.

The role of herbs in rituals and ceremonies was more evident in ancient times, but vestiges still remain, such as the way we decorate our homes with mistletoe, ivy and holly in midwinter. Other herbs are today appreciated simply for their decorative role, either in the garden, or in fresh or dried flower arrangements.

Where to grow herbs

Herbs grow well in all sorts of situations, from a few culinary herbs planted in a window box to a rambling wild garden full of teasels, nettles and brambles. Plant according to your personal taste, and how you intend to use the herbs: a few herbs can be scattered throughout a garden, but if you plan to go into large-scale production of herbs for cooking or drying it will be easier to dedicate a separate area to them. For best results, group herbs by their growing requirements rather than by their use.

Creating a herb garden

Formal herb gardens are based on a system of paths and beds, often edged with low-growing hedges. To remain neat this type of garden requires quite a lot of maintenance, with hedges trimmed two to three times a year and careful attention paid to weed control. Thorough preparation of beds and paths at the outset is essential to prevent weed problems later on.

Group herbs by their growing requirements rather than by their use

An informal herb patch is equally attractive, or herbs can be mixed in amongst other flowers, shrubs and even vegetables. Put them in beds and borders, against walls and fences, in fact, anywhere that you have space!

Shade-tolerant herbs

Herbs that enjoy dappled shade thrive on the edges of shrubberies or by patches of small trees. Add a low-fertility soil improver on an annual basis in order to mimic the leaf litter layer that occurs naturally in woodland areas. Vigorous ground-cover herbs can become rampant in favourable conditions, so cut them back regularly and remove runners to control their spread, or plant them in containers.

Drought-tolerant herbs

Drought-tolerant herbs look stunning growing together in a location where they will have full sun in well-drained soil. A naturally dry part of the garden will be ideal. Use a gravel mulch around the plants to help control weeds and keep the area immediately around the base of the plants dry. These herbs will also grow well in containers, where you can provide ideal soil conditions for them, and which you can move around the garden to make best use of the sunniest spots.

Herbs for damp soil

Herbs that like damp soil will grow well in a naturally boggy area, or you can create one by the edge of a pond (see *Gardening for Wildlife*, pp.198–201). In dry summers you will need to keep the water levels in the pond or bog garden topped up. Again, some of these species can become invasive once they are established in the garden.

Herbs for paved areas

Choose low-growing herbs that thrive in dry conditions for planting amongst paving slabs. Fill the cracks with compost and sow the seed directly into position in spring. Keep watered and avoid walking on the herbs until they become established.

Herbs for a vegetable patch

Leafy herbs such as chervil, coriander, summer savory and dill all enjoy the slightly richer soil normally found in a vegetable garden. These types of herb are best sown direct in the spring once the soil is warm enough.

Herbs in containers

Many herbs grow well in containers, which is a good way of providing suitable conditions if your soil is not ideal (see also *Container Gardening*, p.210). Use any container with drainage holes and a minimum depth of about 30cm (12in).

Put a layer of large stones or broken crocks at the bottom of the container, then fill it with general-purpose organic potting compost (see pp.114–115). For herbs such as rosemary, which prefer a light soil, mix compost with gravel or grit to ensure adequate drainage. Use no more than one part grit to five parts compost, depending on the herb's requirements. Check moisture levels at least once a day in sunny weather, and water if necessary.

Caring for herb plants

Most herbs are relatively easy to grow organically. Follow these guidelines to ensure successful cultivation of your chosen herbs.

Soil preparation and planting

Check the preferred soil conditions of your chosen herbs (see p.280) before planting. Many herbs thrive in a free-draining, low-nutrient soil. If your soil is heavy, incorporate a low-fertility soil improver to improve drainage. Constructing raised beds will also help. For a short-term solution, add a couple of handfuls of grit or gravel to the bottom of the planting hole. Other herbs that prefer a more fertile soil may benefit from the addition of a medium-fertility soil improver. Remove any weeds, especially perennial weeds such as couch grass.

Maintenance

Remove flowering stems from shrubby herbs such as lavender and sage after flowering. Prune these herbs in the spring to control the size of the plant and to prevent them becoming bare and woody at the base.

Always remove flowers if you want to harvest the maximum quantity and quality of leaves. Pinch out growing tips to encourage bushy growth, and cut out any plain shoots on variegated herbs. Established clumps of perennials are best divided every two to three years, in spring or autumn (see *Herbaceous Plants*, p.173). It can be worth taking cuttings each year from tender shrubby herbs such as some lavenders and variegated sage, which may not survive the winter.

Propagation

Many herbs are easy to raise in the garden. Annuals and biennials such as parsley and basil are grown from seed. Some perennials, such as fennel and chives, are also easy to raise from seed, and may self-sow. Remember that cultivated varieties do not always come true from seed, or seed is not produced. In this case, vegetative propagation is the only option – by cuttings, layering, or division depending on species.

Invasive herbs

Vigorous herbs will take over if left to their own devices. These species are excellent for growing in wild areas, where they will be controlled by equally vigorous neighbours. In other situations they need to be restricted: bury a large plant pot, a bucket with the bottom removed, or a permeable sack with extra drainage holes, and plant invasive herbs inside. Cut back any vigorous growth and rooted creeping stems, and divide every two to three years. Other invasive herbs are prolific self-seeders: remove flower heads before seeds form, or hoe off the seedlings in spring.

Tough and tender
Known for their versatility, hardy pot or English marigolds (Calendula, below right) grow vigorously in most soils, although they prefer fine loam. They self-seed readily, so remove any dead flower heads if you want to prevent too much seed dispersal. By contrast, the tender herb basil needs warmth and sun, and protection from wind, frost and scorching. Grow seedlings (below) under cover and plant out only when the weather is warm enough. In cooler climates basil may be best grown in a greenhouse or polytunnel.

VIGOROUS HERBS

Invasive herbs
Chinese lantern
Comfrey
Creeping Jenny
Mint
Soapwort
Madder
Horseradish
Tansy

Vigorous self-seeders
Chives
Evening primrose
Lady's mantle
Lemon balm
Sweet cicely
Teasel
Coltsfoot
Jacob's ladder
Feverfew
Pot marigold
Borage

See p.289 for an index of common and botanical names

Border invader
With its large, robust rosette of leaves, borage is an opportunistic self-seeder: although it is a beautiful plant, it will crowd smaller neighbours.

POPULAR HERBS

◁ BASIL

Tender perennial grown as an annual. H 30–45cm (12–18in). Cultivars vary in leaf size, colour and flavour.

Ideal location Greenhouse, polytunnel or sunny, sheltered spot outdoors. Light, free-draining, fertile soil. Grows well in containers.

Cultivation Sow under cover in late spring and early summer at 13°C (55°F). Apply a medium-fertility soil improver before planting out. Pinch out tips for bushy growth; remove flowers to promote leaf production.

◁ BAY

Evergreen shrub or small tree. Frost-tender, especially when young. Golden-leaved 'Aurea' is particularly tender. H 3–6m (10–20ft). Can be pruned to limit size. Good for topiary.

Ideal location Sheltered, sunny spot in light, free-draining soil. Good in pots.

Cultivation Add a medium-fertility soil improver on planting and mulch every spring. Prune in summer if necessary. In exposed areas protect from wind scorch and frost. Prone to attack by bay sucker and scale insect.

CHIVES ▷

Hardy perennial. H 30cm (12in). Both leaves and flowers can be used. The purple flowers are attractive to bees.

Ideal location Sunny, in moist fertile soil, but tolerates shade and most soils.

Cultivation Add a medium-fertility soil improver before planting. Cut back to 5cm (2in) after flowering to promote fresh growth. Sow seed in late spring. Divide established clumps in spring or autumn.

FENNEL ▷

Hardy perennial. H 2m (6ft). Leaves, stems and seeds are all used. The flowers attract many beneficial insects. The cultivar 'Purpureum' has bronze foliage.

Ideal location Sunny position, in free-draining, fertile soil.

Cultivation Add a medium-fertility soil improver on planting. Cut back dead flowering stems in spring. Sow seed in spring; may self-seed. Established plants may be divided in spring or autumn.

◁ LAVENDER

Hardy, evergreen shrub. H 60–100cm (24–39in). Flowers are very popular with bees and butterflies. Many forms, including more tender prostrate, dwarf, pink- and white-flowered varieties.

Ideal location Sunny, sheltered spot with light, free-draining soil. Will not tolerate waterlogged ground.

Cultivation Trim in spring. Remove flower spikes after flowering. Plants may need replacing every 3–5 years. Take cuttings in spring or summer, or layer in spring.

◁ MINT

Hardy perennial. H 3–100cm (1–39in). Many types available, including ginger mint, spearmint, peppermint and pennyroyal. Invasive habit, spreading by runners and seed. Plant in containers to limit spread.

Ideal location Light shade; moist but not waterlogged soil.

Cultivation Add a medium-fertility soil improver on planting and when dividing. Cut to ground level in autumn. Divide every 2–3 years. To propagate, take root cuttings or divide established plants.

PARSLEY ▷

Biennial. Quite hardy, but needs winter protection in cold regions. H 30cm (12in). Curly and flat-leaved varieties.

Ideal location Partial shade and moist, fertile soil. Good in containers.

Cultivation Sow in modules in gentle heat (18°C/65°F is ideal) or direct into the ground when soil is warm. Sow in spring and summer for summer harvest, and in late summer for a winter crop grown under cover. Vulnerable to carrot fly and virus.

ROSEMARY ▷

Evergreen shrub. H 1–1.5m (4–5ft). Many types, not all hardy, including dwarf, prostrate and variegated cultivars. Dwarf types can be clipped for hedging.

Ideal location Sheltered, sunny spot. Free-draining, low-fertility soil. Cannot tolerate waterlogged soils.

Cultivation Prune in spring. Tender cultivars need winter protection. Take softwood cuttings in spring, semi-hardwood in summer. Layer established branches in spring.

◁ CORIANDER
Annual. H to 70cm (28in). Grown for leaves and seed. Special selections for leaf production available.
Ideal location Sunny, in light but fertile soil. Benefits from cloche or polytunnel protection in cool climates.
Cultivation Sow direct from spring to autumn for continuous supply of leaves. Runs to seed quickly in hot weather. Add a medium-fertility soil improver before sowing. Pick leaves regularly for use or leave to flower for seed production.

THYME ▷

Evergreen shrub. H 30cm (12in). Many types, including lemon-scented, golden and variegated. Creeping thymes make good ground cover.
Ideal location A dry, sunny spot with poor, free-draining soil. Dislikes wet winter conditions. Grows well in gravel, paving and rock gardens.
Cultivation Trim after flowering. Layer in spring, or take cuttings in early summer. Creeping thymes may be divided.

◁ SAGE
Evergreen shrub. H 60–90cm (24–36in). Many types, including purple and variegated cultivars. The flowers attract bees.
Ideal location: Sunny. Poor, light, free-draining soil.
Cultivation Prune in spring. May not always survive the winter, so take cuttings in case. Prone to powdery mildew. Take cuttings from new growth in spring and early summer.

FRENCH TARRAGON ▷

Perennial. H 60cm (24in). Popular for flavouring vinegar. Has a much finer flavour than Russian tarragon, which can be invasive.
Ideal location: Sunny, in light, free-draining, low fertility soil. Cannot tolerate waterlogged soil.
Cultivation Remove flower spikes to encourage leaf growth. Protect roots from damp over winter. Cannot be grown from seed. Divide, or take root cuttings, in spring.

COMMON AND BOTANICAL NAMES

Specialist herb nurseries usually sell herbs under their botanical names. In most garden centres you may also find that apart from a small selection of culinary herbs, the plants are scattered about under their botanical names. Many plants that are used as herbs are beautiful garden plants in their own right. Look at the list below, and you may well find that you are already growing a number of these herbs, or their close relatives. Always check that a herb is edible before use.

Alpine strawberry *Fragaria vesca*
Angelica *Angelica archangelica*
Artemisia *Artemisia*
Basil *Ocimum basilicum*
Bay *Laurus nobilis*
Borage *Borago officinalis*
Box *Buxus*
Bugle *Ajuga reptans*
Catmint/catnip *Nepeta cataria*
Chamomile *Chamaemelum nobile*
Chervil *Anthriscus cerefolium*
Chinese chives *Allium tuberosum*
Chinese lantern *Physalis alkekengi*
Chives *Allium schoenoprasum*
Coltsfoot *Tussilago farfara*
Comfrey *Symphytum officinale*
Comfrey, dwarf *Symphytum grandiflorum*
Coriander *Coriandrum sativum*
Corsican mint *Mentha requienii*
Creeping Jenny *Lysimachia nummularia*
Creeping savory *Satureja spicigera*
Curry plant *Helichrysum italicum*
Dandelion *Taraxacum officinale*
Dill *Anethum graveolens*
Elder *Sambucus nigra*
Marigold (English) *Calendula officinalis*
Evening primrose *Oenothera biennis*
Fennel *Foeniculum vulgare*
Feverfew *Tanacetum parthenium*
Foxglove *Digitalis*
Garlic *Allium sativum*
Garlic chives *Allium tuberosum*
Ginger mint *Mentha x gracilis*
Gipsywort *Lycopus europaeus*
Guelder rose *Viburnum opulus*
Hawthorn *Crataegus monogyna*
Hedge germander *Teucrium x lucidrys*
Hemp agrimony *Eupatorium cannabinum*
Honesty *Lunaria annua*
Horseradish *Armoracia rusticana*
Hyssop *Hyssopus officinalis*
Jacob's ladder *Polemonium caeruleum*
Lady's mantle *Alchemilla mollis*
Lavender *Lavandula*
Lemon balm *Melissa officinalis*
Lily-of-the-valley *Convallaria majalis*
Lovage *Levisticum officinale*
Lungwort *Pulmonaria officinalis*
Madder *Rubia tinctorum*
Marshmallow *Althaea officinalis*
Marsh woundwort *Stachys palustris*

Meadowsweet *Filipendula ulmaria*
Mint *Mentha*
Orris *Iris germanica* subsp. *florentina*
Parsley *Petroselinum crispum*
Pennyroyal *Mentha pulegium*
Peppermint *Mentha x piperita*
Periwinkle *Vinca major, V. minor*
Pineapple mint *Mentha suaveolens*
Poppy *Papaver*
Pot/English marigold *Calendula officinalis*
Purple loosestrife *Lythrum salicaria*
Rose *Rosa*
Rosemary *Rosmarinus officinalis*
Sage *Salvia officinalis*
Santolina *Santolina chamaecyparissus*
Sea holly *Eryngium*
Soapwort *Saponaria officinalis*
Spearmint *Mentha spicata*
Summer savory *Satureja hortensis*
Sweet Cicely *Myrrhis odorata*
Sweet violet *Viola odorata*
Tansy *Tanacetum vulgare*
Tarragon, French *Artemisia dracunculus*
Tarragon, Russian *Artemisia dracunculus* subsp. *dracunculoides*
Teasel *Dipsacus fullonum*
Thyme, common *Thymus vulgaris*
Thyme, creeping *Thymus serpyllum, T. praecox*
Valerian *Valeriana officinalis*
Wall germander *Teucrium chamaedrys*
Water figwort *Scrophularia auriculata*
Water mint *Mentha aquatica*
Winter savory *Satureja montana*
Woodruff *Galium odoratum*
Yarrow *Achillea millefolium*

Harvesting and preserving herbs

Small amounts of herbs can be picked throughout the growing season and used immediately. Harvesting large amounts of herbs for drying, or using them in some other way, requires a different approach. Whichever you do, always harvest thoughtfully, without stripping a plant bare. As a general rule, never harvest more than about a third of a plant at any one time. Vigorous plants, such as mint and comfrey, can be cut back to ground level two or three times a season without doing them any harm.

Saving seeds (below right)
Tie a bunch of harvested herbs, wrap them gently in newspaper or a paper bag, and then dry them upside down to collect the seeds.

HERBS TO PRESERVE

Culinary herbs that dry well
Bay
Mint
Rosemary
Sage
Tarragon
Thyme

Herbs to dry for decoration
Chinese lantern
Honesty
Poppy
Sea holly
Teasel
Yarrow

Herbs for freezing
Basil
Borage flowers
Chervil
Chives
Fennel leaf
Parsley
Summer savory

Herbs to flavour vinegar
Elderflowers
Chive flowers
French tarragon
Garlic
Lavender flowers

See p.289 for an index of common and botanical names

Knowing when to harvest

Allow perennial herbs to become established before harvesting them. This will usually be in or after the second year of growth. Never harvest from plants that look weak or are struggling to grow.

The majority of leafy herbs reach their maximum flavour just before the flowers open. After that point, the texture and flavour of leaves change as the plants put energy into flower and seed production. Remove all flowers to extend the production of tender leaves, unless you are growing the herbs for flowers or seed.

Herbs harvested for drying need to be collected with as little moisture on them as possible. The ideal conditions for this will be a dry, warm, but not too sunny day. The ideal time is after overnight moisture has dissipated but before strong sunlight has caused the volatile oils to evaporate. In most cases this is around mid-morning, depending on the climate and weather conditions.

Always use sharp secateurs or scissors to harvest the herb in order to avoid damaging the plant unduly. Collect your plant material quickly, and then bring it indoors immediately to minimise any deterioration in flavour and quality.

Preparing herbs for storage

Drying is an excellent way of preserving herbs for use out of season. Many leaves and seeds keep their flavour well, and, stored correctly, should last up to a year. Providing the ideal range of temperatures and ventilation for drying individual herbs is not easy in a domestic situation, and if you dry herbs at home you may find that the drying process results in some loss of flavour and colour. Some herbs do not retain their flavour well when dried, and are best used fresh or preserved in some other way (see facing page). Check all the plant material carefully before you dry it and discard any parts that are diseased or damaged.

There are two main methods of drying herbs: either suspended in bunches, or lying flat on racks or trays. Electric dryers are available to buy. Whichever method you use, it is best to dry each type separately as they tend to dry at different rates. Choose a dark, clean, dry, well-ventilated location, free from dust and insects. Always dry herbs out of direct sunlight, which causes loss of colour and flavour.

Poppy seedheads
Dried poppy seedheads can look very decorative. When the "pepperpot" tops of the seedheads open, the seeds can be shaken out.

DRIED HERB RECIPES

A simple pot-pourri
Rose petals
Lavender flowers and leaves
Lemon balm leaves
Marigold petals
Use equal amounts of these dried herbs. Mix together and put in a bowl or closed container. As the aromas fade, you can add a few drops of an essential oil of your choice to restore the fragrance.

Soothing bath bag
1 tablespoon chamomile flowers
1 tablespoon lavender flowers
2 tablespoons oatmeal or cornmeal
Mix the ingredients well, then place in the centre of a square of muslin, or a fine, large handkerchief. Gather the edges together, and tie securely with ribbon or string.

Hang the bag in the flow of the hot tap as the bath is running. You can also use the bag as a gentle body scrubber, which releases a soothing, milky juice from the oatmeal or cornmeal.

Sweet bag for linen or clothes
Make a small sachet of fine lawn or muslin. Fill with equal amounts of dried herbs selected from the following, according to preference (both flowers and leaves can be used):
Lavender
Artemisia
Rosemary
Cotton lavender (santolina)
Sage
Pennyroyal mint
Lemon balm

Drying in bunches

Keep the bunches of herbs small; a good guideline is to gather up no more than enough stalks to fit comfortably in your hand. Hang the herbs upside down; this helps to preserve their appearance if you are planning to use them for decorative purposes. Use rubber bands to tie up the bunches as these will shrink with the herbs. Be aware that these rubber bands will eventually perish and need to be replaced. Finally, tie a large paper bag or sheet of newspaper loosely over the flower heads (see facing page) if you are aiming to collect the seeds.

Drying on racks or trays

To dry herbs flat, strip the leaves from each stem and arrange them in a single layer on a rack or tray. Try to inspect the herbs regularly to ensure they are drying properly, and turn any of the larger leaves frequently to ensure that they dry evenly. Look also for anything that shows signs of mould or decay and remove it. The herbs are ready when they are crisp to the touch but not brittle. They should crumble but not shatter when you crush them.

Once dried, store the herbs in airtight containers to prevent them reabsorbing moisture from the atmosphere. Glass jars, tins or screw-top containers are all suitable. Keep them in the dark in a cool, dry place. Most dried herbs will retain their flavour for up to a year, but are best renewed after that time.

Freezing

Freezing retains the flavour, but not the appearance, of herbs. It is an excellent way of preserving leafy herbs that do not dry well, such as basil, parsley, fennel leaf and chives. To freeze these herbs, wash, chop and place them in ice-cube trays. Cover with water, and freeze. Remove the cubes from the trays and store in plastic bags or boxes in the freezer until needed. To use, add to dishes at the end of the cooking time. They are particularly good for soups, stews and sauces.

Herb-flavoured vinegar

Some herbs have traditionally been used to flavour vinegars. These vinegars make excellent ingredients in mayonnaise and salad dressings, and any other recipe that requires vinegar. Use a mild-flavoured vinegar such as cider or white wine vinegar; malt vinegar is not suitable as its flavour is already too strong.

Place the chopped or crushed herbs in a bowl and pour the vinegar over them. Cover and leave for about two weeks for the flavour to develop, making sure the herbs stay immersed. Strain the mixture through muslin or filter paper, and check for flavour. If it is not strong enough, repeat the process with a new lot of herbs. If it is too strong, dilute with plain vinegar. Store in clean bottles or jars, but make sure the vinegar does not come into contact with metal lids as this will cause corrosion.

Growing vegetables

VEGETABLES ARE THE LOGICAL STARTING POINT FOR ANYONE WHO WISHES TO TAKE CONTROL OVER THE FOOD THEY EAT

THERE EXISTS NO STRONGER connection with the living soil, the earth and the changing seasons than through eating the food you yourself have sown, nurtured and harvested. Vegetables can be grown virtually anywhere – a garden in the traditional sense is not essential to produce safe, healthy food. The results with some types of vegetable growing are quick – sprouted seeds, for example – and will be ready to eat in a matter of days. Most can be harvested within a few weeks or months, although some can take longer to begin bearing. The desire to grow fruit follows on logically as knowledge and experience with vegetables grows. If you are new to both, it pays to start small and gradually expand your edible horizons.

Growing vegetables organically is a positive, empowering, rewarding and for some a deeply spiritual experience. Above all it is deeply satisfying, enjoyable and fundamental to our very existence, with many health benefits. The shared enthusiasm for growing food cuts through barriers of class, race and culture like no other. Plants of all types can bring people and communities together, but none succeed quite like those that we eat. However much food you decide to grow, or whatever constraints you have to work with, growing at least some of your own vegetables organically satisfies more than the fundamental human desire to eat healthy, fresh, uncontaminated produce – it is also a way of minimising our impact on the wider environment.

The bigger picture

Many common fruits and vegetables travel for thousands of miles around the planet before they reach their final destination. Transport is often by air, followed by road, both of which consume vast amounts of fossil fuels which contribute to atmospheric pollution leading to global warming.

The number of so-called "food miles" travelled by supposedly "fresh" produce can be enormous, resulting in much food being eaten a long way from where it was grown. Cultivars created for the rigours of travel and longevity, rather than nutritional value and flavour, are the direct fallout of worldwide monocultures and the move toward increased globalisation. These growing systems depend almost exclusively on high, unsustainable inputs of energy, artificial fertilisers and synthetic chemical pesticides. Concerns over food safety are increasingly frequent, ranging from worries over pesticide residues to the many uncertainties surrounding the widespread use of genetically modified food crops.

Environmental benefits

Growing your own vegetables, and growing them organically, provides not only safe, uncontaminated food but also has significant environmental benefits. Food miles are virtually eliminated, organic waste can be recycled through techniques like composting, and threats to our health are reduced. Increasing attention is being focused on the "localisation" of food, where produce grown locally, using environmentally friendly and sustainable, organic techniques, is sold directly to the people of that region. Such initiatives reconnect people with where their food actually comes from, but growing your own is still the ultimate in "locally-grown" food.

Food for the soul (facing page)
Whether you grow vegetables in an allotment setting with the companionship of other gardeners, or in the seclusion of your own garden, nurturing your own crops to harvest can provide a peaceful, satisfying and healthy respite from the stresses and strains of everyday life.

WHY GROW YOUR OWN ORGANIC CROPS?
• Produce is fresher
• Grow crops you cannot buy
• Better flavour and higher nutritional value
• A positive, empowering and healthy activity
• Helps to educate future generations about where food comes from
• Helps build communities
• Many environmental benefits
• Control over what you eat
• You can do it anywhere
• Kinder on nature

GENETICALLY MODIFIED ORGANISMS (GMOs)

All organisms contain genes, which pass the blueprint for that particular organism on from one generation to the next. In nature unrelated species cannot interbreed, so the genes of a fish could never end up in a plant – but this bizarre notion is now a reality. Genetic engineering (GE) has made cross-species transfer of genes possible: the characteristics carried by the introduced gene become part of the new organism. Vitamin A-enhanced rice, for example, contains genes from a daffodil.

There are both ethical and safety concerns about GMOs. Although the developers, and others, are happy that the technology is safe for human health and the environment, others disagree. This is why GM plants and animals are not organically acceptable.

GM crops have been introduced rapidly, without extensive testing, on the grounds that they are similar to un-engineered crops. But the process involves creating gene combinations which could not have occurred naturally. Once released into the environment, genes that "escape" from the GM parent plant, via soil bacteria or cross-pollination, will be impossible to retrieve. Once incorporated into wild plants, we can only surmise what the outcome might be.

At the point of writing, no GM crops are yet available to gardeners, but developments on the horizon include peculiar colours, such as blue carnations and roses; grass which does not need mowing; and novel perfumes. This novelty may prove to be more costly than we can possibly imagine.

International flavour
Here, Chinese leaves grow next to English lavender; experimenting with crops from different cultures is part of the fun.

Past, present and future

Organic gardening is not about simply looking back or nostalgia for what went before, especially where vegetables are concerned. Successful organic growing techniques have been developed over many generations through observation, trial and error. Working in harmony with nature allows us to observe natural systems closely and learn from them all the time, as we discover new approaches to growing food and develop fresh, often innovative techniques. Growing organically is about putting into practice the findings of the latest scientific research, choosing cultivars that are naturally resistant to pests or diseases, using proven cultural practices alongside new, experimental ones and encouraging and fostering nature's own checks and balances.

A rich heritage

Preserving and maintaining the best of the past for future generations is inextricably linked to organic gardening. Many "heirloom" or "heritage" vegetable cultivars are the result of selective breeding over many generations and are specifically suited to the unique growing conditions found in a particular locality. Preserving this genetic diversity ensures that a rich and varied gene pool remains available for future breeding, as well as giving us a fascinating insight into our global vegetable heritage.

Making space for food

It is possible to grow organic vegetables successfully in virtually any space that receives sunlight. In the developed world, most of us live and work in towns and cities where space is usually at a premium, but this need not be a barrier to growing your own food. Growing vegetables in a limited space does at times require a degree of ingenuity and innovation,

> Becoming partially self-sufficient in certain kinds of food, especially vegetables, is a realistic option available to us all

but coupled with patience, experience and a willingness to learn you will succeed.

The image of self-sufficiency still held by many remains a distant dream. Total self-sufficiency, tarnished as its image often is by crankiness and eccentricity, is impractical for most of us. Whether you simply grow a supply of fresh summer salads in a pot on a windowsill, or plant an entire garden with a cornucopia of edible plants, you will have taken an important step that is good for both you and the world around you.

Getting started with vegetables

You can read books, talk to other gardeners and think about it forever, but the best way to start growing vegetables is simply to have a go. Your first few successes will give you confidence, and you will soon start to get a feel for what works well in your conditions.

Deciding what to grow

There are so many possibilities when first starting to grow vegetables that it is helpful to ask yourself a few questions, to set priorities, and then plan accordingly. Would you like to produce staple vegetables, or unusual types not easily available in shops? Do you have facilities to store vegetables over winter? If so, consider growing suitable ones for storage or freezing. How much time do you have to spare? Some vegetables need more attention than others. Take a look at the section on vegetable families (pp.304–313) to find out more about the range that can be grown. The *A-Z of Vegetable and Salad Crops* contains more detail for individual crops.

Where to grow vegetables

The ideal place to grow vegetables is often described as a fertile, well-drained and moisture-retentive soil, in a flat, sunny but sheltered position. Most gardeners do not have these "perfect" conditions, but still grow excellent vegetables by making the best of what they have. When selecting a site for your vegetables, consider the following points:

• **Sun and shade** Deep shade will severely limit the growth of vegetables, but some can tolerate light shade, including lettuce, chard, beetroot and kohl rabi. In cool climates, position tall vegetables so that they will not cast a shadow on lower-growing ones, but in hotter climates use them to provide welcome shade.

• **Drainage** Vegetables will not thrive in a waterlogged site, which is better used for something else, such as a pond or bog garden. Improve heavy soil gradually by adding low-fertility organic material and consider growing on raised beds (see p.322).

• **Shelter** Protect exposed sites with permanent or

Choice crops
Below, clockwise from top left: radishes, easy to grow; sweetcorn, a family favourite; 'Lollo Rosso' lettuce; the black kale 'Nero di Toscana'.

CROPS AND CLIMATE

On the following pages, reference made to warm and cool climates is intended as a general guide to help you to decide which vegetables to grow, in what part of the garden, and whether or not they need some form of protection. The information is tailored to suit temperate climates, which have a relatively narrow range of temperatures. "Cool climate" refers to mild-to-cool summers and cool-to-cold winters, where rainfall occurs all year round and summer and winter are linked by intermediate spring and autumn conditions – as in the United Kingdom. "Warm climate" refers to warm-to-hot, often longer summers and cool winters. The terms "under cover" or "unheated protection" indicate where vegetables can be grown successfully under some form of unheated cover – cloches, frames or a greenhouse or polytunnel (see *Growing Under Cover*, pp.216–233).

TOOLS AND EQUIPMENT

Handle tools before buying to assess which model feels most comfortable. The following basic items will make lighter work of jobs around the vegetable garden:

• Compost bin and leafmould container – for recycling green waste to make soil improvers.
• Fork – for general cultivation, lifting root crops, aerating soil, and moving and incorporating bulky organic material.
• Hoe – for surface weed control, creating seed drills, earthing up and surface cultivation depending on type.
• Labels – for naming plants and cultivars, recording dates.
• Rake – for breaking up and levelling soil, seedbed preparation, covering seed drills.
• Spade – for digging, general cultivation, deep weed control. Use a "border" spade, with a smaller head, if you have back problems.
• Sticks, string – for marking rows.
• Trowel or hand fork – for hand-weeding and making planting holes.
• Watering can – for irrigation.
• Wheelbarrow – for collection and transportation of bulky materials.

temporary windbreaks such as hedges, fences or netting. Protect individual crops with barriers, cloches or other covers, especially when young.
• **Slopes** Use terracing to prevent soil erosion. Position rows or beds across the contours of a site, rather than up and down. Be aware that the bottom of a slope can be a frost pocket.
• **Space** Select vegetables to suit the space available. Even quite small areas can be very productive, using vertical as well as horizontal growing space. Remember to allow space for making leafmould and compost when planning the layout.
• **Dogs and footballs** Depending on what else you use your garden for, you may conclude that growing vegetables is just not compatible with the other demands on it. In this case, consider having a vegetable plot in an allotment or community garden.

Growing methods

There are many ways of growing vegetables: in rows, beds or containers; on their own, or mixed with flowers and shrubs. Both this chapter and others will help you choose the method that suits you.

Preparing the ground

You may already have a clear piece of land suitable for growing vegetables, but if not there are various

organic methods of preparing it. You could dig up part of the lawn, remove existing plants from flower beds, or use a light-excluding mulch to clear a weedy patch. (See *Weeds and Weed Control*, p.79, and The no-dig approach, p.328, for more details.)

Before you start growing, find out more about your soil and start to look after it organically. Use organic soil improvers and fertilisers as necessary to build the fertility. (See *Soil and Soil Care*, pp.32–61, for all the information you need.)

Plans and records

Even if you are only growing a few vegetables to start with, it makes sense to draw up a simple plan for a crop rotation (see pp.301–303). Keep a close eye on what happens through the season, so you can deal with any problems and adjust growing conditions accordingly.

Keep records. This is helpful for all gardeners, not just beginners. At its simplest, this could simply mean writing the cultivar name and sowing date on a plastic label used to mark a row. Soon you will be able to record information on yields, pests and diseases, weather conditions and what grew well where. Don't worry if not everything goes according to plan! Even experienced gardeners will tell you that they still get surprises.

Starting small
A small plot is easy to manage and can still produce a good range of vegetables. Being overambitious may result in more crops than you are able to care for successfully, which can lead to disappointment.

Planning the produce year

Forward planning can help you to get the best results from growing vegetables, put your fantasies into practice and harvest fresh produce all year round. Thinking about the whole year ahead also helps to spread the workload. It enables you to put time aside for important jobs such as making compost, collecting autumn leaves, incorporating green manures and applying soil improvers, as well as the more obvious tasks of sowing, planting and harvesting.

Spread the harvest

The majority of vegetables from a spring start are ready to harvest between early summer and late autumn. Crop and cultivar choice, combined with a

Some vegetables have a range of cultivars that crop at different times of the year

range of sowing and planting times, makes it possible to avoid summer gluts, and to spread the harvest over a longer period. In cool climates, grow crops under cover and use protective barriers to further extend the cropping season at both ends. (See *Growing Under Cover*, pp.216–233.)

The hungry gap

In cool climates, the period between late winter and late spring is known traditionally as the "hungry gap", because there is not much to harvest from the garden at this time. To fill this gap, grow vegetables that are hardy enough to stand through the winter, such as leeks or kale, or that mature very quickly from an early spring sowing, such as radish or seedling salads.

One of the difficulties in filling the hungry gap with hardy vegetables is that they need to be in their final growing position by midsummer, when the ground may still be occupied by summer crops. In this case, allocate less space to summer vegetables, or try intercropping smaller summer crops with winter ones (see p.318 for more about intercropping).

Cultivar choice

Some vegetables, such as cabbage (see below, right), carrot, cauliflower, leeks, lettuce, onions and peas, have a range of cultivars for different seasons; some can even be available to harvest all year round. Cultivars described as "quick" or "early" are especially useful at both the beginning and the end of the growing season, as they produce a crop more quickly than main crops. Others have been bred to tolerate cold conditions in winter.

Successional sowing is another way of spreading the harvest, particularly suitable for fast-maturing crops. This means that you sow a small amount of the same crop at intervals of two to three weeks. A good rule of thumb is to sow the next batch of seeds when the previous ones are just starting to show as seedlings. Suitable vegetables include corn salad, kohl rabi, lettuce, radish, rocket, spinach, spring onions and turnips.

Storage

Crops such as potatoes, pumpkins and onions can be stored in good condition for many months over winter (see pp.334–5). Freezing can also help to extend the "eating" season of some vegetables.

VEGETABLES FOR THE HUNGRY GAP

Brussels sprouts
Chard
Kale
Leaf beet
Leeks
Parsley
Radish and radish pods
Seedling salads
Sprouting broccoli
Winter cabbage
Winter cauliflower
Winter spinach

CABBAGE THROUGH THE YEAR

• **Spring cabbage** Sow in late summer; plant out in early autumn; harvest in late spring and early summer. Suitable cultivars: 'Durham Early', 'Pixie', 'Spring Hero'.

• **Summer cabbage** Sow in mid- to late spring; plant out in early summer; harvest in late summer and early autumn. Suitable cultivars: 'Golden Acre', 'Greyhound', 'Hispi'.

• **Winter cabbage** Sow in mid- to late spring; plant out in midsummer; harvest from late autumn until late winter. Suitable cultivars: 'Celtic', 'January King', 'Red Drumhead'.

Vegetable & salad crop planning chart

Organic vegetables and salads can be picked fresh – from the garden, from under a cloche or from an unheated greenhouse or polytunnel – at most times of year except in very harsh climates. Add to this crops from store (excluding the freezer) and the out-of-season selection expands further.

The key to all-year-round fresh vegetables and salads is good planning, and this chart will help you to do just that. It shows when crops can be sown, when they will be growing, and when they vacate the space for another crop to move in. It is also a useful overview of the sheer range of crops that you can grow in the garden.

Inevitably the chart gives an overview, rather than specific dates and times for specific areas. Exact timing will depend on growing conditions in your location (and in that year), the cultivars you grow, and the stage at which you harvest your crops.

CROP			Jan	Feb	Mar	Apr	May	Jun	Jul	Aug	Sep	Oct	Nov	Dec	See page
Artichoke, Chinese		PE				P——P									338
Artichoke, globe	*	PE				P——P									338
Artichoke, Jerusalem		PE		P———P											338
Asparagus – from seed	+	M PE		SH S——————S					T						339
Asparagus – one-year-old crowns	+	PE				P——P									339
Asparagus pea	*	M					S——S								339
Aubergine				SH———SH		PI–PI	P–P								340
Bean, broad – spring-sown				Ss———————Ss											340
Bean, broad – autumn-sown													S———S		340
Bean, French	*					SP Ss——————Ss									340
Bean, lablab/hyacinth		M						SH P–P							309
Bean, runner	*						S——————S							341
Beetroot	*	M		Ss——————————Ss											341
Beet, leaf/perpetual spinach	*	M			S———S			S———S SU						SC 342
Broccoli – calabrese	*	M			Ss———————Ss				S–S TuP					342
Broccoli, nine-star (perennial)		M PE			S———S T———T										343
Broccoli – sprouting	*	M			S——S T———T										342
Brussels sprouts		M		SH—SH S——S			T—T							343
Cabbage, Chinese	*	M							Ss———————Ss TuP					344
Cabbage – spring		M								S	T———T				343
Cabbage – early summer	*	M		SH———————SH P———————P										343
Cabbage – summer (including red)	*	M			S——S T——————T									343
Cabbage – autumn (including red)	*	M					S——S T———T							343
Cabbage – winter		M					S——S T———T							344
Cardoon						S——S									344
Carrot – early cultivars	*	M		Ss———————Ss											345
Carrot – maincrop					Ss———————————Ss									345
Cauliflower – spring		M						S	T						345
Cauliflower – early summer		M		SH T–T							SP			345
Cauliflower – late summer		M			S——S			T						345
Cauliflower – early autumn		M				S			T					345
Cauliflower – autumn		M					S		T					345
Cauliflower – winter		M					S			T				345

Key to symbols and colours used

S	Sow *in situ* outdoors	PP	Plant outdoors under protection e.g. cloche, frame, low polytunnel	——— Duration of sowing/planting period
Ss	Successional sowing/cropping *in situ* outdoors	TuP	Transplant to unheated greenhouse/polytunnel	Actual period of growth in the cropping situation
SsU	Successional sowing/cropping in unheated greenhouse/polytunnel	T	Transplant to cropping position	Cropping area *not* occupied
SH	Sow in heated protection	+	Full cropping commences second season after sowing/planting	Fresh harvest period
SU	Sow in unheated protection i.e. unheated greenhouse/polytunnel	*	Optional earlier sowing in heated protection	Forcing period
SP	Sow under outdoor protection e.g. cloche, frame, low polytunnel	M	Crop can also be raised in modules and transplanted	Available from store
P	Plant outdoors	PE	Perennial crop	
PI	Plant indoors i.e. greenhouse or polytunnel	SC	Suitable as a seedling cutting crop	

CROP			Jan	Feb	Mar	Apr	May	Jun	Jul	Aug	Sep	Oct	Nov	Dec		See page
Cauliflower – mini	*	M					Ss———————Ss									345
Celeriac				SH————SH SU————SU P–P												346
Celery – self-blanching					SH———SH		P–P									346
Chicory – red						Ss————————Ss TuP										348
Chicory – sugarloaf, for mature heads		M					S————————S								348
Chicory – sugarloaf, seedling crop				SsU————SsU Ss——————————Ss SsU										SC	348
Chicory – Witloof/forcing			|||||||||||||||||||||		S—S				|||||||		348
Corn salad					S————————S		S———S SU————SU								349
Courgette, marrow	*						S									349
Cress, American land					Ss———————————————Ss										350
Cucumber (outdoor), gherkin	*						SH P–P									350
Cucumber – indoor						SH SU PI										350
Dandelion		PE	||||||||||||||||| S———S ||||||||||||||||||||||||||||||								332
Endive	*	M				SH———SH PP Ss———Ss SP								SC	350
Florence fennel	*	M				S————————S TuP								SC	351
Garlic				P———P								P———P		351
Good King Henry	+	PE				S————————S									352
Green-in-the-snow						Ss————————Ss TuP							SC	332
Hamburg parsley					S————————S		S—S							352
Kale/borecole – winter and spring crop	*	M				S———S T——————————T							SC	352
Kohl rabi	*	M			Ss———————————————Ss SU									352
Komatsuna	*	M					Ss————————Ss SU						SC	353
Leek	*	M			S————————S T——————————T								353
Lettuce – summer and autumn	*	M			Ss———————————————Ss								SC	353
Lettuce – outdoor winter crop		M							S————————S					353
Lettuce – protected winter crop		M							S————————S					353
Melon, sweet						SH———SH PP									354
Mibuna greens		M		—————SsU Ss————————————————Ss SsU—————							SC	355
Mizuna greens		M		—————SsU Ss————————————————Ss SsU—————							SC	355
Mustard, cress (incl. Greek), salad rape				Ss————————————————Ss SP———SP								SC	332
Mustards, Oriental		M					Ss————————Ss TuP						SC	355
New Zealand spinach	*	M					S									355
Okra						SH———SH PP–PP								–

CROP			Jan	Feb	Mar	Apr	May	Jun	Jul	Aug	Sep	Oct	Nov	Dec		See page
Onion – bulb, sown early in heat		M		SH——SH		P										356
Onion – bulb, sown outdoors				S——S												356
Onion – bulb, from spring sets					P——P											356
Onion – bulb, sown in autumn										S—S						356
Onion – bulb, from autumn sets											P——P					356
Onion – mini/pickling					S——S											356
Onion, spring/bunching				Ss				Ss	S—S							356
Oriental saladini				SU Ss			Ss		S—S SU					SC	333
Pak choi		M						Ss——Ss SP							SC	357
Parsley – leaf		M			SH—SH S—S P	S——S									288
Parsnip			S——S													357
Pea – early, spring-sown	*	M			S——S											357
Pea – early, autumn-sown											S—S				357
Pea – maincrop					Ss——Ss										357
Pepper, sweet/chilli					SH——SH P–P									358
Potato – early, in unheated protection				P											358
Potato – early					P——P										358
Potato – maincrop					P——P										358
Potato – autumn/winter crop							P——P							358
Pumpkins, squash	*					S								359
Purslane – summer				SU—SU S——S								SC	360
Purslane – winter (claytonia)				S——S		S——S SU				SC	349
Radish – leaf				Ss——Ss		S–S SP				SC	332
Radish – summer				SP Ss			Ss SP——SP				360
Radish – winter						S——S					360
Radish – mooli						S——S					360
Red orache				Ss		Ss	S—S				SC	361
Rhubarb – from crowns	+	PE	P——P					P——P			361
Salad rocket				SU Ss		Ss	Ss——Ss SU			SC	361
Salsify				S——S							362
Seakale, forced in situ	+	PE	S P								363
Scorzonera				S——S							362
Seakale beet/Swiss chard	*	M		S——S		S—S SU				SC	347
Shallot				P						P—		363
Sorrel		PE		S——S		S——S				363
Spinach – summer crop				SU Ss——Ss					SC	363
Spinach – winter crop						Ss——Ss SU			363
Swede				SP—SP S——S						364
Sweetcorn				SH—SH P–P SP					364
Tomato – outdoor/unheated protection				SH—SH PP P–P				365
Tomato – indoor with heat			SH—SH PI–PI						365
Turnip				SP Ss——Ss				366
Watercress		M		Ss——Ss				226

Crop rotation

Crop rotation is the practice of growing related vegetables in different areas in consecutive years. Vegetables from the same botanical family (described in detail in the pages that follow) are susceptible to the same pests and diseases. Parsnips, for example, belong to the same family – the Apiaceae – as carrots, and are also a favourite of the carrot fly.

Some vegetable relationships are easy to grasp: the peas and beans all belong to one family, as do the onion, shallot and garlic tribe. But the parts of the plant eaten – their shape and flavour – are not always a good basis for guesswork. Brussels sprouts, for example, would obviously seem to belong with cabbages in the Brassicaceae family, which they do – but so do swedes, radishes and turnips. Beetroot, on the other hand, is related to spinach and chard. Sometimes it is only when vegetables flower that clear family resemblances can be seen; the flowers of the Solanaceae – tomatoes, potatoes, peppers and aubergines – are remarkably similar (see p.312).

If members of the same family are grown in the same place year after year, there is a tendency for soil-borne pests and diseases to become established. In small plots, moving vegetables just a few metres may not have much effect on pest and disease control, but it is still worth doing for other benefits.

• **Nutrient availability** Vegetables differ in their nutrient requirements, so moving them around the growing area helps to prevent the soil becoming depleted locally and makes best use of the soil.

• **Soil treatments** Some crops need soil amendments to do well, others make good use of residual fertility left by a previous crop. Grow crops with similar requirements together, so you can apply the appropriate soil treatments for them. This means that all parts of the vegetable area will receive the same treatment over the period of the rotation.

• **Weed control** Some vegetables, such as marrows and potatoes, produce weed-suppressing foliage and are easy to weed. Others, like onions and carrots, are more difficult to weed and do not have a growth habit that competes well. Alternating vegetables with these characteristics helps keep weeds under control.

• **Soil structure** Plant roots occupy different levels of the soil. Alternating deep- with shallow-rooting vegetables has a positive effect on soil structure.

How long is a crop rotation?

Three or four years is the usual recommended minimum for a crop rotation, but it can certainly be longer. If you know that your soil has a serious, persistent problem, such as potato eelworm, onion white rot or clubroot, you may need a much longer rotation to grow susceptible crops with any success.

Planning a crop rotation

Plan your own rotation according to the crops you want to grow, or use the examples overleaf to get started. Remember that you do not have to grow the same vegetables every year, although there will probably be some favourites you want to repeat.

• **Make a list** of the vegetables you want to grow over a whole season, and in roughly what quantities.

• **Group vegetables together** according to botanical family (see pp.304–313 for details).

• **Draw a plan** of the growing area. Divide it into equal-sized sections according to how many years the rotation is to last. If using several different areas of the garden for growing vegetables, treat each one separately, changing the crop each year for the period of the rotation. Distribute the vegetables around the sections, keeping families together. If one family does not fill a whole section, try to combine it with another that requires similar soil treatments. Fast-maturing crops, and those from miscellaneous families (see above right), can be fitted into gaps.

Vegetable families
Keep crops in the same family together (here, potatoes and tomatoes, both Solanaceae), moving them from plot to plot each year.

BASIC COOL-CLIMATE ROTATION

Move the crop groups around the plots clockwise each year

Plot 1: Solanaceae, Cucurbitaceae

Manure in spring, then grow potatoes, tomatoes and courgettes. After harvest, sow/plant overwintering autumn onions, garlic and leeks, and/or a green manure for soil improvement.

Plot 2: Apiaceae, Chenopodiaceae

Carrots, parsnips and celery, and beetroot, spinach and chard (below), with lettuces inbetween. Use grazing rye or phacelia as a green manure over winter.

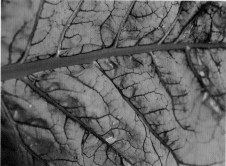

Plot 4: Alliaceae, Papilionaceae

After harvesting the onions, garlic and leeks planted the previous year (see Plot 1), grow peas and beans. Plant the green manure winter tares to overwinter, liming beforehand if necessary as brassicas will follow.

Plot 3: Brassicaceae

Grow summer brassicas, then plant winter brassicas with lettuce and other intercrops inbetween. Add compost in spring and summer. Mulch winter brassicas with leafmould over winter.

ROTATION FOR A WARMER CLIMATE

Plot 1 Add compost in spring. Grow tomatoes, aubergines and peppers, then to overwinter, garlic, onions and broad beans.

Plot 2 Sweetcorn, intercropped with salads in the early season. Follow with a green manure.

Plot 3 Add manure in spring, then grow pumpkins, squashes and courgettes.

Plot 4 Onions, garlic and broad beans planted the year before (see Plot 1). Grow salads over winter. Add leafmould in spring.

- **Be flexible** and prepared to adapt your plans, while sticking to the rotation principles. Unexpected weather and other crop disasters can affect everyone.
- **Keep records** of what you planned, and what actually happened! This will be useful information if you want to adjust the rotation in following years.

Soil treatments in a rotation

- **Compost, manure, and other medium- to high-fertility soil improvers** Use for heavy feeders such as potatoes, leeks, cabbage family and marrows. Apply in spring before planting.
- **Lime** Add to cabbage family section to control clubroot, in the autumn before planting, but only if necessary to raise pH, not routinely. Do not lime when growing potatoes, as it can encourage scab.
- **Leafmould and other low-fertility soil improvers** Beneficial preceding root crops; apply anywhere as a mulch to improve structure, especially over winter.
- **Green manures** Take account of the family that green manures belong to and use them to follow a crop from the same one. In this way, any problem affecting that family is more likely to appear in the green manure rather than the crop. Use them over winter, sowing in late summer or autumn, or as catch crops (see p.318) in spring and summer. Do not use grazing rye before sowing seeds direct as it inhibits germination when it decomposes.

Growing perennial vegetables

Perennial vegetables, which can stay in the same spot for many years, obviously do not fit into the usual crop rotation. Asparagus and rhubarb are best given their own, separate beds. Others, such as globe artichokes and seakale, make beautiful border plants, given sufficient space. Good King Henry and sorrel, much smaller plants, can also be fitted into a border.

As with all perennial plants, appropriate soil preparation, including removal of all perennial weeds, is essential before planting (see *Herbaceous Plants* p.170, and also the *A-Z of Vegetable and Salad Crops*). When replacing them, do not replant on the same site. Check for pests and diseases on perennial crops, especially those such as nine-star broccoli that are related to other vegetables. Pests and diseases that become established on perennial crops can be a source of infection for other plants.

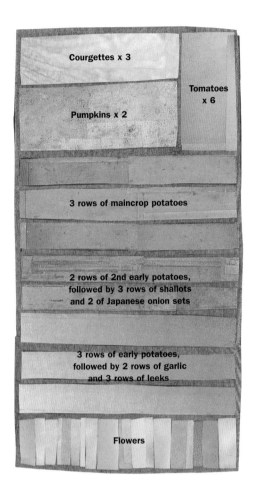

Courgettes x 3

Tomatoes x 6

Pumpkins x 2

3 rows of maincrop potatoes

2 rows of 2nd early potatoes, followed by 3 rows of shallots and 2 of Japanese onion sets

3 rows of early potatoes, followed by 2 rows of garlic and 3 rows of leeks

Flowers

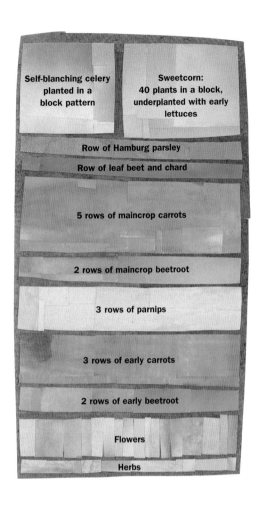

Self-blanching celery planted in a block pattern

Sweetcorn: 40 plants in a block, underplanted with early lettuces

Row of Hamburg parsley

Row of leaf beet and chard

5 rows of maincrop carrots

2 rows of maincrop beetroot

3 rows of parnips

3 rows of early carrots

2 rows of early beetroot

Flowers

Herbs

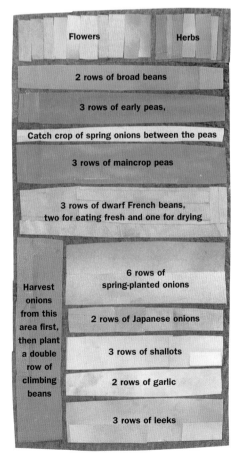

Flowers

Herbs

2 rows of broad beans

3 rows of early peas,

Catch crop of spring onions between the peas

3 rows of maincrop peas

3 rows of dwarf French beans, two for eating fresh and one for drying

Harvest onions from this area first, then plant a double row of climbing beans

6 rows of spring-planted onions

2 rows of Japanese onions

3 rows of shallots

2 rows of garlic

3 rows of leeks

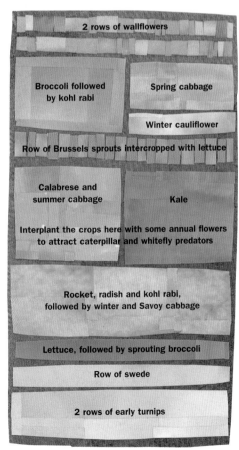

2 rows of wallflowers

Broccoli followed by kohl rabi

Spring cabbage

Winter cauliflower

Row of Brussels sprouts intercropped with lettuce

Calabrese and summer cabbage

Kale

Interplant the crops here with some annual flowers to attract caterpillar and whitefly predators

Rocket, radish and kohl rabi, followed by winter and Savoy cabbage

Lettuce, followed by sprouting broccoli

Row of swede

2 rows of early turnips

4-YEAR COOL-CLIMATE ROTATION FOR A LARGE PLOT *(Scale: 1:50)*

This plan will supply a good range of seasonal vegetables, fresh and from store. Flowers are for cutting and herbs for the kitchen; both will attract beneficial insects. Crops stay in their groups and move plot clockwise each year:

Year One

1 4
2 3

Year Two

2 1
3 4

Year Three

3 2
4 1

Year Four

4 3
1 2

The Group 1 crops (top left)
Big feeders from the Solanaceae and Cucurbitaceae: in spring, dig in the grazing rye (see Group 4), then apply manure (or equivalent) for them. After harvesting the early potatoes, plant Alliaceae to grow over winter; they need no feeding.

The Group 2 crops (below left)
Peas and beans, as legumes, fix their own food, but benefit from a leafmould mulch. Harvest some overwintered onions early to make way for climbing beans. Spring-planted onions join their overwintered relatives. Follow on with winter tares to fix nitrogen for next year's brassicas, and lime in the autumn if the soil needs it.

The Group 3 crops (below right)
Brassicas and salads. Dig in the winter tares, or add garden compost or equivalent in spring. Mulch with leafmould in the autumn to make a good seedbed for next year's root crops.

The Group 4 crops (top right)
Mostly root crops, which need no extra feeding, using up last year's leftovers. Apply compost in spring where celery, leaf beet and sweetcorn are to grow. Follow with grazing rye for winter cover.

PROTECT THE CROP

Brassicas may make up a high proportion of the crops you grow, so it is important to use a good crop rotation to try to avoid clubroot (**1**), the most serious disease of brassicas. Spores can survive in the soil for 20 years in the absence of a host crop. Avoid bringing in the disease on plants and soil.

Cabbage root fly larvae also attack the roots of this family, causing plants to wilt and die (**2**). Young plants can be protected with a root fly collar (**5**) or a crop cover. Fleece can also be used to protect young plants from flea beetle, and netting may be needed against pigeons, which enjoy young plants at any time, but when hungry in winter they will strip standing mature crops.

From late spring onwards, various moths and butterflies, such as the large cabbage white, may lay their eggs (**3**) on brassica plants. The resulting caterpillars (**4**) can be picked off by hand, if wasps have not removed them first.

Because some form of brassica crop can be growing at any time of year, cabbage whitefly and mealy aphids can build up in numbers. It pays to remove all members of this crop family once a year – in early spring for example – to break the cycle.

For more information and advice see the *A-Z of Plant Problems*.

Brassicaceae – the cabbage family

Family members

Agricultural mustard★ (*Sinapis alba*)
American land cress (*Barbarea verna*)
Brussels sprout (*Brassica oleracea* Gemmifera Group)
Cabbage (*Brassica oleracea* Capitata Group)
Calabrese (*Brassica oleracea* Italica Group)
Cauliflower (*Brassica oleracea* Botrytis Group)
Chinese cabbage (*Brassica rapa* Pekinensis Group)
Cress• (*Lepidium sativum*)
Fodder radish★ (*Raphanus* spp.)
Kale or borecole (*Brassica oleracea* Acephala Group)
Kohl rabi (*Brassica oleracea* Gongylodes Group)
Mizuna greens• (*Brassica rapa* var. *nipposinica*)
Mustard• (*Brassica hirta*)
Oriental mustards• (*Brassica juncea*)
Pak choi• (*Brassica rapa* Chinensis Group)
Radish• (*Raphanus sativus*)
Rocket• (*Eruca vesicaria*)
Salad rape• (*Brassica napus*)
Seakale (*Crambe maritima*)
Sprouting broccoli (*Brassica oleracea* Italica Group)
Swede (*Brassica napus* Napobrassica Group)
Turnip (*Brassica rapa* Rapifera Group)
★ *Green manures*   • *Suitable as a seedling cutting crop*

Members of the large and diverse brassica family are grown for their leaves, buds, roots, stems or shoots. They thrive in cool, moist climates and are very nutritious, being rich in minerals and vitamins. Many familiar "western" vegetables, such as cauliflower and cabbage, belong to the brassica tribe; it also includes oriental vegetables like Chinese cabbage and mizuna greens. Some, such as kales, sprouting broccoli and Savoy cabbage, need a long growing season, but they are very hardy and provide useful winter food. Empty ground between larger winter brassicas is useful for catch and intercropping. However, careful choice of cultivar and close spacing can produce smaller, meal-sized heads of vegetables such as cabbage and cauliflower. Some brassicas make good seedling cutting crops (see p.332).

Soil treatment and crop rotation

Brassicas need a firm, moisture-retentive soil, not thriving where moisture is limited. In a crop rotation, this family follows on from the nitrogen-fixing pea and bean tribe (see p.308). A green manure crop of winter tares or clover provides leafy brassicas with all the nitrogen they need. In the absence of a green manure, a medium-fertility soil improver, such as compost, can be applied to the brassica bed. Acid soils should be limed in autumn prior to growing brassicas.

Brassicas are easily raised from seed or by planting ready-grown "starter" plants. Western brassicas tend to be sown in spring and summer; many Oriental types, which tend to bolt in hot, dry conditions and when the day length is increasing, are best sown in the shortening days after midsummer – providing useful autumn crops. Fast-growing crops like rocket and radish, directly sown, will be ready quickly; kohl rabi and calabrese can crop in as little as eight weeks. A succession of sowings will maintain a supply. Many brassicas, however, are slow-growing and take months to reach maturity. Avoid tying up the growing space for this long by sowing in a nursery bed or modules, and transplant when the ground becomes available.

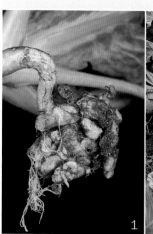

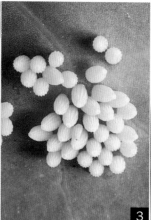

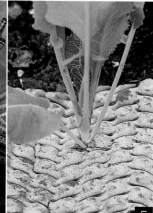

MEET THE FAMILY

The members of this diverse group, which includes annuals, biennials and perennials, would all, ultimately, produce the same, characteristic flower, with the four petals arranged in a cross.

Some forms of brassica can be picked at almost any time of year. Leafy crops include kales (**1**) and cabbages for winter (**2**), spring (**3**) and summer use (see p.297). The immature flowerheads of calabrese, cauliflowers (**4**) and sprouting broccoli are eaten; Brussels sprouts develop small, cabbage-like heads along a tall stem.

Cress, mustard, radish and salad rape are used as sprouted seeds, and many can be eaten as seedling crops. The perennial vegetable seakale is grown for its forced shoots, harvested in mid- to late winter. Kohl rabi produces crisp and juicy swollen stems. Radishes can even be grown for their peppery seed pods.

Root crops include swedes, turnips and radishes. Spring and summer radishes tend to have small roots, apart from the long white "mooli" types. Winter radishes are much larger.

Oriental brassicas, such as pak choi and oriental mustards are fast-growing, producing tasty, nutritious leaves and shoots that are good in salads and stir-fries.

Some brassicas have a typical strong, mustardy flavour, but others, such as kohl rabi and calabrese, are more delicate. Many can be eaten raw, as well as cooked or pickled.

Brassicas may not be an obvious choice for an ornamental garden, but some are very attractive. Red, curly and "ragged-leaved" kales can look stunning over winter. Kohl rabi, in purple or green, makes an interesting addition, and the glaucous green of many cabbages and cauliflowers makes a perfect foil for brightly coloured annuals. Oriental mustard greens and some "mini" cabbages could be grown as bed edging.

Alliaceae – the onion family

Family members

Garlic (*Allium sativum*)

Leek (*Allium porrum*)

Onion (*Allium cepa*)

Shallot (*Allium cepa* Aggregatum Group)

Welsh onion (*Allium fistulosum*)

Tree onion (*Allium cepa* Proliferum Group)

Plants in the onion family have a pungent flavour and many produce typical "drumstick" flowerheads, if left to flower. Crops include tiny pickling onions, multi-coloured shallots, slim young spring onions, pungent garlic, and red, white and yellow globe onions. All are hardy, cool-climate crops.

Spring onions, a quick filler crop, are eaten as slim young plants, leaves and all. Onion, shallots and garlic are usually harvested once they are mature; when dry, they can store well for many months (see p.335). Leeks, which do not produce a bulb, are grown for their long white, cylindrical "shank". They can be left in the ground to harvest in the winter months.

The herbs chives and garlic chives (see p.289) also belong to this family; their leaves and flowers can be eaten. The perennial Egyptian or tree onion produces aerial bulbs in place of flowers, and these may sprout and grow *in situ*. Flowers of leeks and garlic may also produce tiny bulbs in place of seed.

Growing the crop

Members of this family are simple to grow. By choosing a range of types and cultivars, they can be available all year round, either fresh or from store. Spring onions and leeks are grown from seed, the latter raised in a seedbed for transplanting in early summer (see p.315). Onions and shallots are grown from seed or sets (immature bulbs), and garlic is planted as cloves only. Garlic must undergo a period of cold to crop well, which is why it is traditionally planted in autumn. Shallots may also be planted in autumn, and late summer is the time to sow or plant the Japanese onion cultivars for an early crop.

Soil and spacing

Members of this family prefer a well-drained, relatively fertile soil. Avoid rich feeding, which encourages disease and cuts down on storage life. Soil that has been fed for a previous crop, such as potatoes or brassicas, should suffice. Leeks can benefit from a medium- to high-fertility soil improver on poorer soils.

Bulb onions and leeks respond well to variations in plant spacing (see p.316), which can be used to supply the size of plant you prefer. A crop of slender gourmet leeks, for example, can be grown as close as 5cm (2in) apart.

PROTECT THE CROP

Onion white rot (centre) attacks bulbs and can survive in the soil for 20 years or more. Try to avoid introducing it on plants and soil, and use a crop rotation.

Where onion fly is a problem, the maggots tunnelling into bulbs, protect the crop with a lightweight crop cover.

Various fungi may attack onion foliage. Downy mildew (top) is common in wet seasons, its dark spores turning leaves black. Clear up infected debris and use a crop rotation. The orange pustules of leek rust (bottom) appear in summer. It may look alarming, but plants will often grow away from the disease in autumn.

Cucurbitaceae – the cucumber family

Family members

Courgette, marrow, summer squash (*Cucurbita pepo*)

Cucumber, gherkin (*Cucumis sativus*)

Luffa (*Luffa cylindrica*)

Melon (*Cucumis melo*)

Pumpkin, gourd, winter squash (*Cucurbita maxima*, *C. moschata* or *C. pepo*)

Watermelon (*Citrullus lanatus*)

Members of the cucumber family, also known as cucurbits, are typically vigorous plants with big, bold leaves and yellow, trumpet-shaped flowers. They require a lot of space. Trailing cultivars can be trained to scramble over arches or up netting. Bush cultivars are more compact.

This family is grown mainly for its fruits, which may be eaten young or mature. They come in a wonderful array of shapes, colours and sizes. Flowers and seeds can also be eaten. All are tender annuals that need warm conditions to do well. In cool climates, courgettes (also known as zucchini), marrows, pumpkins, squashes and outdoor cucumbers can crop outdoors if raised in warmth and transplanted into warm soil, after the last frost. In warmer regions they can be sown direct outside. Melons need warm conditions and are usually best grown in a cool greenhouse or cold frame.

Greenhouse cucumbers also need the warm, humid conditions provided in a greenhouse or polytunnel.

Cucumbers, courgettes and summer squashes are eaten young and picked regularly to maintain the supply. They tend to have a mild flavour. Melons are picked when ripe, and pumpkins and winter squashes are left to mature on the plant, to develop a tough skin for storage. Some are bland and watery while others develop a sweet, rich, densely textured flesh – excellent for soups and stews.

Growing the crop

All members of this family benefit from a dressing of medium-fertility soil improver, such as compost, on planting. Unless you are growing for competition or in a container, no further feeding is required. In an outdoor crop rotation, they can be included in the potato or brassica beds, or given their own section.

Once planted, most outdoor cucurbits need little attention and make good weed-suppressing plants. Melons and indoor cucumbers will require more training, watering and feeding.

In most cases, the flowers – which are either male or female – must be pollinated to set fruit. Greenhouse cucumbers will, however, be bitter if pollinated. "All-female" hybrid cultivars avoid the task of removing male flowers to prevent pollination.

PROTECT THE CROP

Some cultivars show some resistance to cucumber mosaic virus (above). Protect young plants from slugs. Powdery mildew may be a sign of a dry soil; late in the year it will not affect the crop. Under cover, biological controls can be used to control pests like red spider mite. Crop rotation, good ventilation and hygiene are the best defence against diseases such as mildew and sclerotinia.

Fascinating fruits

All of the cucurbits, even the common-or-garden marrow (far left), are striking in appearance. Squashes show some of the widest variety of form, from the glowing lantern-like spheres of 'Atlantic Giant' (centre) to the curious, infolded 'Turk's Cap' (below).

PROTECT THE CROP

Use crop rotation to avoid a buildup of foot and root rots.

Autumn- and early spring-sown seed of peas and beans may be taken by mice. Traps can be set under wire netting; later sowings may be safer.

The pea and bean weevil eats notches out of leaves from early spring. Plants growing well can usually withstand the damage; if necessary, young plants can be protected with a crop cover, put on at sowing time.

The black bean aphid first appears on the tips of broad beans. Nip out infested shoots. Early sowings are less prone. Early and late sowings of peas can be made to miss the pea moth, whose larvae eat peas.

Broad bean chocolate spot is an early season disease, common in wet soil. Powdery mildew on peas tends to occur on dry soils, later in the season.

Young French and runner beans are attractive to slugs and snails. In cooler areas, the first crop is best transplanted, rather than directly sown, with individual bottle cloches added for extra protection.

For more advice see the *A-Z of Plant Problems*.

Pea and bean flowers
The Papilionaceae take their name from the Latin for butterfly, based on the appearance of their flowers (right, pea; far right, broad bean). Sweet peas, lupins, clovers, gorse and broom are also members of this family.

Papilionaceae – the pea and bean family

Family members

Alfalfa ★ (*Medicago sativa*)
Asparagus pea (*Lotus tetragonolobus*)
Broad or fava bean (*Vicia faba*)
Clover ★ (*Trifolium* spp.)
Fenugreek ★ (*Trigonella foenum-graecum*)
Field bean ★ (*Vicia faba*)
French bean (*Phaseolus vulgaris*)
Lablab or hyacinth bean (*Dolichos lablab*)
Lupin ★ (*Lupinus angustifolius*)
Pea (*Pisum sativum*)
Runner bean (*Phaseolus coccineus*)
Trefoil ★ (*Medicago lupulina*)
Winter tares or vetch ★ (*Vicia sativa*)
★ *Green manures*

The vegetables in this family, once part of the Leguminosae, are still widely referred to as legumes. They are grown primarily for their fleshy pods and/or seeds. Legumes characteristically develop root nodules containing bacteria that fix gaseous nitrogen from the air. When the nodules decay, nitrogen is released into the soil, which is why the green manures in this family are so valuable.

Peas and broad beans are hardy, cool-season crops, growing best below 15°C (59°F). French and runner beans are frost-tender and need warmer conditions to thrive.

Young broad bean pods and shoot tips can be eaten, but the green, white or red seeds are the main crop. Traditionally, peas are shelled from their pods, but mangetout and sugarsnap pea pods are eaten whole.

Peas can vary in height from 60cm to 3m (2–10ft), and most are supported with twiggy branches or wide-mesh pea netting. "Leafless" cultivars, with more tendril than leaf, are self-supporting when grown in a block.

Dwarf French beans are ideal for small spaces and containers. Climbing cultivars (known as pole beans) will twine up canes or sticks in a wigwam or double row. They do best in warm-to-hot weather and are much more tolerant of dry conditions than runner beans.

Runner beans are generally climbers, although dwarf cultivars are available. The edible flowers can be red, white, salmon-pink or bicoloured red and white, making an attractive feature trained up a trellis or wigwam. The pods are long and green.

Soil and crop rotation

Legumes thrive in a well-drained but moisture-retentive soil which has been fed for a previous crop such as potatoes. In a rotation they can be followed with brassica family crops, which will make use of the nitrogen provided by the pea and bean nodules, provided that roots have been left in the ground.

RING THE CHANGES

There is more to French beans than green pods. Pods also come in purple, yellow, green with red flecks and other combinations. If left to fatten up, plump fresh beans may be podded like peas, or they can produce dry beans – a high-protein crop for winter use. The range of colours and patterns of dried seed reveal their true diversity. Saving seed is easy – which is probably why so many heirloom cultivars still exist, making a strong presence in HDRA's Heritage Seed Library.

Climbing beans were originally grown as ornamentals, and still can be today. 'Viola Cornetti', for example, has purple stems and edible deep purple pods (left), stunning grown with annual climbers such as morning glory, or the firebrand flower clusters of *Ipomoea lobata* (*Mina lobata*). Tall peas also make an attractive feature, particularly the wide red pods of 'Carouby de Mausanne'. The crimson-flowered broad bean, a jewel in the Heritage Seed Library crown, can provide a blast of early season colour.

The lablab or hyacinth bean is one of the most attractive, with its purple-pink flowers set against green-bronze leaves. Maroon pods follow (below), edible when cooked. It is a tender plant, however, needing a minimum temperature of 18°C (64°F).

Chenopodiaceae – the beet family

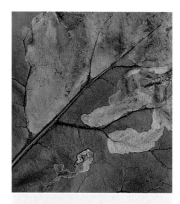

PROTECT THE CROP

The crops in this family are relatively trouble-free, although some tend to bolt in adverse conditions. Beet leaf miner (above) has little effect on beetroot, but can spoil leaf beet crop. Remove affected leaves, and squash the maggots within the "mines". Downy mildew can be a problem on young spinach when the air is moist.

Concentrated colour
Rich, dark colours of both roots and leaves (below, of ruby chard and spinach) are a hallmark of this family.

Family members

Beetroot (*Beta vulgaris* subsp. *vulgaris*)

Chard, Swiss chard or seakale beet (*Beta vulgaris* Cicla Group)

Good King Henry (*Chenopodium bonus-henricus*)

Leaf beet, perpetual spinach or spinach beet (*Beta vulgaris* Cicla Group)

Red orache, or mountain spinach (*Atriplex hortensis* 'Rubra')

Spinach (*Spinacea oleracea*)

This family includes both leaf and root crops suitable for warm and cool climates. Spinach and red orache are fast-growing, leafy "catch" crops. Spinach is best sown in the cool temperatures of spring and autumn as it rapidly goes to seed in hot, dry weather. Sow little and often for a good supply.

Beetroots

Beetroot is grown for its substantial, juicy roots, commonly dark red, but gold, white and bicoloured types are available. Its deep green and magenta leaves are decorative and can also be eaten when young, either raw or lightly cooked. Fast-growing baby beet are eaten when only 2.5–5cm (1–2in) across. Larger roots of maincrop cultivars can be stored for winter use. "Bolt-resistant" cutivars are used for early sowings.

The leafy beets

Leaf beet and chard are known by a confusing range of names. The former has large, mid-green leaves; the latter tends to have a dark green glossy leaf with a wide, prominent midrib, which can be eaten as a separate vegetable. The midrib colour ranges from white through yellow, orange and luminous pink to glowing red. Leaf beet and chard are easy to grow, much less prone to bolting than spinach, can be picked over a period of many months, and withstand low winter temperatures. Two sowings, one in spring and one in autumn, should give a year-round supply.

The little-known perennial Good King Henry is an old-fashioned salad plant. Its leaves can be picked early in the year; the flowering shoots are also eaten. It prefers a good rich soil and tolerates some shade.

Growing the crops

Crops in this family all prefer a fertile soil that does not dry out easily. They are often included in the "roots" section of a rotation, on soil that has been improved for a previous crop. They may appreciate a mulch of a medium-fertility soil improver on poorer soils. Spinach beet and chard can be raised in modules for transplanting, and beetroot is suitable for "multi-sowing" (see p.317). All can be grown in a cool greenhouse for out-of-season cropping.

Asteraceae – the lettuce family

Family members

Cardoon (*Cynara cardunculus*)

Chicory (*Cichorium intybus*)

Endive (*Cichorium endivia*)

Globe artichoke (*Cynara scolymus*)

Jerusalem artichoke (*Helianthus tuberosus*)

Lettuce (*Lactuca sativa*)

Salsify (*Tragopogon porrifolius*)

Scorzonera (*Scorzonera hispanica*)

Vegetables in the Asteraceae family range from the compact annual lettuce to the magnificent perennial globe artichoke, which can grow to 2.5m (8ft) tall. Depending on the crop, the leaves, shoots, flower buds, roots or stem tubers may be eaten.

Lettuce is perhaps the most widely grown member of this family, eaten, along with chicory and endive, as a salad. All three can be very decorative, with leaves in diverse shapes and colours. Some lettuce cultivars produce a hearted lettuce; individual leaves can be picked from the "loose leaf" types over several weeks. Chicory and endive are often blanched to reduce their bitterness, and chicory roots can be forced, to produce pale young shoots known as chicons. Using a selection of cultivars and cloche protection, these crops can provide leafy salads all year round. They also do well in an unheated greenhouse, and are useful as seedling crops, for intercropping and for growing in containers.

Jerusalem artichokes are simple to grow, producing starchy, edible stem tubers and stems up to 3m (8ft) tall. Some cultivars produce a rather unexpected "sunflower", with the characteristic flower form of this family – masses of small ray petals surrounding a central boss of florets.

Perennial globe artichokes and cardoons, very similar in appearance, produce large, thistle-like blooms if allowed to flower. The stems of cardoons are blanched in autumn; the large, immature flower buds of the globe artichoke are eaten in early summer.

Salsify and scorzonera are little-grown root crops, the former white-skinned, the latter black. They are harvested in autumn, or lifted as required in winter. The following spring, the shoots can be blanched for eating, or left to produce edible flower buds.

Soils and situations

The plants in this family prefer well-drained soils. The leafy crops can be fitted into a vegetable plot rotation or put among ornamentals. Cardoons and globe artichokes need a lot of space and would not look out of place in an ornamental border. The roots can join other root crops in a crop rotation, while Jerusalem artichokes make a good windbreak.

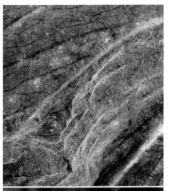

PROTECT THE CROP

Lettuce is the most pest- and disease-prone member of the Asteraceae. Common pests include slugs, cutworm, leaf aphids and root aphids. Young plants can be protected against slugs by barriers and traps. Crushed eggshells may have a short-term effect used as a barrier (see above).

Under cover, downy mildew (top) and grey mould (botrytis) can be a real problem, especially in cool, damp conditions. Crop rotation, good hygiene and ventilation can reduce the problem.

Cultivars with resistance to aphids, downy mildew and various physiological disorders are available.

Lettuce alone
The Asteraceae family includes not only crops but many ornamentals, including asters (as the name would suggest) and chrysanthemums, and also weeds such as dandelions and lawn daisies. Far left: lettuces growing with related ornamental daisies; left: salsify flowerhead going to seed.

Solanaceae – the potato family

PROTECT THE CROP

Using resistant cultivars is a good way to protect potatoes and greenhouse tomatoes in particular against a range of probems. Potato blight, a fungal disease also attacking tomatoes (see below), can be a major problem in a wet season. Little can be done to prevent it. Early potato crops may avoid it, and clearing up all potential sources of infection can delay its start. Biological controls can combat whitefly, red spider mite and aphids under cover. See also the *A-Z of Plant Problems*.

Family flowers
Below, from left to right: flowers of aubergine, potato and tomato. Potatoes were first grown as ornamental plants when introduced to the UK.

Family members

Potato (*Solanum tuberosum*)

Tomato (*Lycopersicon esculentum*)

Pepper, sweet (*Capsicum annuum* Grossum Group)

Pepper, chilli (*Capsicum annuum* Longum Group)

Pepper, hot (*Capsicum frutescens*)

Aubergine (*Solanum melongena*)

Potatoes, despite being frost-tender, crop well in cool climates. Other members of this family – tomatoes, aubergines and peppers – need warmer conditions and good light levels for reliable cropping. They are popular crops for a cool greenhouse or polytunnel (see pp.224–5), but may also be sown under cover then transplanted outside when conditions are right.

Potatoes aplenty

Potatoes need quite a lot of space but are easy to grow, and the amateur grower has a far wider choice of cultivars, over 100 in the UK, than is ever seen in food shops. They store well for winter eating.

Potatoes are planted as tubers. Always use certified "seed" tubers. Spring planting is the norm; a late summer planting can, with protection, give a winter crop (see p.227). Some potatoes will produce true seed, in small green tomato-like fruits, but these are rarely used for growing (and are poisonous if eaten).

Tender fruit crops

Homegrown tomatoes, left to ripen on the plant, surpass anything shop-bought for flavour. Again, the diversity on offer to the gardener is staggering – from compact, manageable, bushy plants to "indeterminate" cultivars that would grow metres tall if not stopped; from tiny, cherry-sized fruit to those that make a meal in themselves, in red, yellow, orange and green. Tomatoes can be grown in pots, baskets and growing bags. More vigorous cultivars are easier to manage grown directly in the soil.

The taste of peppers can be sweet or hot-to-blistering, the latter known as hot or chilli peppers. Sweet peppers can be cropped when green, or left to ripen to red, yellow, orange or purple. Hot peppers usually produce smaller, longer more pointed fruit.

Aubergine fruits are now typically a dark, shiny purple, but the originals were a very egg-like white. Modern cultivars bearing no more than four or five fruits per plant make cropping more reliable. Both aubergines and peppers grow well in containers or in the soil, doing best under cover in cool climates.

Soil and rotation

All do best in a fertile soil, rich in organic matter, where manure or rich compost has been applied. They follow on well from a grazing rye green manure.

Apiaceae – the carrot family

Family members

Carrot (*Daucus carota*)

Celeriac (*Apium graveolens* var. *rapaceum*)

Celery (*Apium graveolens*)

Florence fennel (*Foeniculum vulgare* var. *dulce*)

Hamburg parsley (*Petroselinum crispum* var. *tuberosum*)

Parsley (*Petroselinum crispum*)

Parsnip (*Pastinaca sativa*)

Skirret (*Sium sisarum*)

Turnip-rooted chervil (*Chaerophyllum bulbosum*)

This is a diverse group of crops with a range of flavours. The family likeness appears when they flower – tiny individual flowers are produced in creamy white, umbrella-shaped flowerheads, known as umbels (see the carrot flowers below). They are very attractive to beneficial insects.

Carrots and parsnips are traditional root crops; Hamburg (turnip-rooted) parsley, turnip-rooted chervil and skirret are less well known. Celery and celeriac leaves and stems have the same distinctive flavour, as does the knobbly swollen stem base of celeriac, which is eaten more like a root crop. Florence fennel "bulbs" (in fact stem bases) have a crisp texture when raw, and a mild aniseed flavour.

Its attractive feathery foliage can be used in place of the herb fennel. Best sown after midsummer, Florence fennel is the fastest of these crops to grow. Most others need a long growing season. Parsley, a herb, is often grown along with these vegetables.

Growing the crop

Carrots and parsnips are direct-sown hardy crops that may be left in the ground for use over winter, or harvested for storage. Early carrots, quicker to crop, are eaten fresh. Both crops prefer a light soil which has been fed for a previous crop, such as brassicas. On stony or heavy soil, consider growing early carrots in a container (see p.210).

Celery and celeriac will bolt if growth is checked. They are best sown in modules and transplanted when the soil has warmed up. The soil should be rich in organic matter, so it never dries out, dressed with a medium- to high-fertility soil improver.

Although the members of this family have differing soil requirements, they are kept together in a traditional rotation as they are prone to the same problems. On a bed system, where the ground may be divided up into more than four distinct areas, they can be given separate beds.

PROTECT THE CROP

Carrot roots may fork in stony soils (**1**). The major pest of this family is carrot fly; the larvae feed on the roots of all members. Discoloured foliage, here on parsley (**2**), may be noticed before root damage – here on a carrot (**3**). Barriers and crop covers are the most effective way to prevent damage.

Parsnip canker, a disease of parsnips only, is exacerbated by carrot fly damage. Good drainage and close spacing can prevent it.

Violet root rot affects this and several other crop families, especially on wetter soils. Avoid growing susceptible plants on an infected site for at least four years.

F1 HYBRIDS

You will see some cultivars in seed catalogues marked "F1". This means that they are F1 hybrids – obtained by crossing two specifically selected parents. F1 hybrid plants are usually very vigorous and uniform in appearance, and can perform very well. They often show good resistance to certain pests and diseases, and some are available as organically produced seed. One of the main drawbacks with "F1s" is that plants from a single sowing tend to all crop at once. Sowing little and often avoids this.

Alternatives to seed
Just as potato tubers left in the light will sprout both roots and shoots (right), so other crops multiply by vegetative means. Jerusalem artichokes are grown from tubers, like potatoes, and seakale from sections of fleshy root known as "thongs". Onions and shallots can be grown not only from seed, but also from small bulbs known as "sets". Garlic is always grown this way. Asparagus, globe artichokes and rhubarb crop much more quickly if grown from divisions or "offsets" taken from a mature plant (see also Herbaceous Plants, p.167) rather than seed.

Sowing and planting vegetables

This section looks at growing vegetables outdoors. Plants can also be raised in a greenhouse, or other protected situation, to avoid adverse outdoor conditions, or simply for convenience. For more details, see *Raising Plants* and *Growing Under Cover*, and the *A-Z of Vegetable and Salad Plants*.

Choosing seeds

Organic seed is produced to recognised organic standards, without the use of artificial fertilisers or pesticides. "Conventional" seed is produced using artificial fertilisers and pesticides, and its use is acceptable when organic alternatives are unavailable.

Where possible, use good-quality organically grown seeds from a reliable source, or save your own. If organic seed is not available, check on the seed packet to make sure that the seed you use has not been treated with pesticide dressings after harvest.

Heritage or heirloom varieties (see p.16) are available from seed libraries. Cultivars developed using genetic modification (GM) techniques (see p.294) are not appropriate in an organic garden.

Seed formats

Most vegetable seeds are sold dry and loose inside a foil or paper packet. Various treatments and formats can make sowing easier and enhance performance.

• **Coated/pelleted seed** Each seed is coated in clay to make handling and station-sowing easier. Check that no pesticide is present in the coating.
• **Chitted or pre-germinated seed** Pre-germinated seeds (usually cucumbers) are sent by post with their seedling root already growing.
• **Primed seed** Seeds are germinated under ideal conditions then "dried back" before being dispatched for immediate sowing or storing at 5°C (41°F). Emergence is rapid, even and unaffected by fluctuating soil temperatures. Primed seeds include carrot, celery, leek, parsley and parsnip.
• **Seed tapes** Seeds are embedded in a biodegradable paper tape which is laid in a drill. Thinning is unnecessary.

Always keep seed in a cool, dry place. For details on seed storing, and lifespan of seeds, see p.120.

Alternatives to seed

Some vegetables are raised vegetatively – from tubers or offsets, for example. This may be because they rarely set seed, because seed-raised plants are very variable, or because vegetative propagation is faster. Even where seed raising is possible, you may prefer to buy plants. This may be to save waiting time – asparagus, for example, is not cropped until its third year, so one-year-old plants, known as crowns, are usually planted. Crops such as tomatoes and cucumbers need to be raised in warm conditions which you may not be able to provide. Buying in plants avoids the problem, and may not be any more expensive if you only need a few plants. Even the very basic crops such as cabbage and Brussels sprouts can be purchased – as module-grown "starter" or "plug" plants. These are useful where space, time and conditions for plant raising are limited. They may be available locally, or by mail order. When buying mail order, open plants on receipt, water and stand in a well-lit spot. Always buy organically grown plants, sets and tubers wherever possible.

Sowing vegetables

When sowing outdoors, seed may be sown *in situ*, where the crop will grow and mature, or in a nursery bed, or seedbed, for transplanting later. A seedbed is used primarily for brassicas that take up a lot of space for a relatively long time. Plants can also be raised in a greenhouse, or on a sunny windowsill or other protected situation, to avoid adverse outdoor conditions or simply for convenience.

Warming the soil

Cool-climate vegetables like beetroot will germinate in spring as soon as soil temperatures reach 5°C (41°F) or above. Warm-climate crops like French beans need at least 13°C (55°F), and must not be sown or planted out until all risk of night frosts has safely passed. Soil can be warmed prior to sowing using cloches, garden fleece or black polythene. A dark mulch also warms up quickly in spring. Non-permeable materials like polythene also help to keep the soil dry – seeds will rot in cold, wet conditions.

On a bed system (see p.322), an entire bed can be warmed for early spring sowings using fleece (see also Fixing fleece, p.233). It can be pulled back, seeds sown into the warmed soil (or young plants planted), and then replaced.

Thinning

Unless seeds are sown very thinly or multi-sown (see p.318), some seedlings need to be removed to allow others space to develop. Thin in stages, leaving each seedling just clear of the next until the recommended spacing is reached. Water before and after thinning, disturbing the soil as little as possible. Plants in nursery beds may also need thinning prior to transplanting.

Transplanting from nursery beds

Water young plants thoroughly before transplanting, to minimise root damage. Always handle plants by their leaves. Loosen the soil with a fork and keep as much soil on the roots as possible. Lift plants in cool conditions and transplant immediately, into holes just large enough to take the roots, with the lower leaves just above the soil. Firm the soil, then water in and keep moist. Wilting is common but plants soon recover. In very hot weather, cover new transplants with lightweight material, such as fleece, that will provide some shade. Remove it after a few days when the plants have perked up.

Thinning carrots
Most vegetables need thinning if seed germination has been successful. Carrots are sown as thinly as possible, to avoid the need to for thinning and thus reduce the risk of attack by carrot fly. Thinnings of some crops (though not carrots) can be replanted to fill any gaps, or used in salads.

Transplanting leeks
Slow-growing vegetables can be sown in pots or modules until the harvest of early crops makes space available in beds. Leeks can be raised in pots or seed trays, or closely spaced in a seedbed on a spare piece of ground. Water them well before transplanting to individual blocks of planting holes, 15cm (6in) deep and 15–23cm (6–9in) apart. Drop a single plant into each hole, but do not fill the hole with soil. Instead, water in thoroughly to settle soil gently around the roots.

Using space effectively

Using spacing techniques, combined with suitable cultivars and, where possible, a bed system of growing (see p.322) will help make the best use of any growing space. Where there is no need to walk between rows, vegetables can be grown using closer-than-traditional spacings. The practice of growing vegetables in long rows, with the soil between them hoed regularly, grew out of changes to agricultural practice during the 18th century. This system still has its merits used on an allotment-sized plot, but in a garden context, better results can often be achieved by block planting, spread out evenly across the bed or growing area, using equidistant or square spacing.

Good use of space
On narrow beds, no space need be wasted on paths between rows of crops, and vegetables can be grown in rows spaced more closely, or at equidistant spacing in either a square or staggered formation.

- **Equidistant spacing** Plants are grown in staggered rows and each plant is an equal distance apart from all the others. The between-plant spacing is an average of the recommended in-row and between-row spacings. For example, plants normally grown 15cm (6in) apart in rows 30cm (12in) apart, can be grown equidistantly at 23cm (9in) apart each way. Plants receive equal amounts of light, moisture and nutrients and soon form a canopy over the soil, which helps to reduce weeds.
- **Square** Plants are grown at the same spacing in the row as between the rows, resulting in a square pattern. This is useful where only two or three plants can be fitted across a bed. A planting "grid" can easily be made by pressing a straight edge into the soil to mark out evenly spaced lines at right angles to each other. Sow or plant where the lines cross.

Achieving the pattern

To achieve the desired plant layout using transplants, simply plant out at the required spacings. For vegetables sown *in situ*, either station-sow, planting 2-3 seeds at each position where a plant is required, and thin later to leave just a single plant, or sow in drills and carefully thin seedlings in each row. Crops such as beetroot can also be multi-sown *in situ* to a desired pattern.

The effect of plant density

The spacing of vegetables such as onions and cabbages affects their final size; up to a certain limit allowing them more space means they grow larger. By reversing this and growing them more densely, with less growing space, the result is vegetables of a smaller, often more convenient size. In most cases overall yield is also increased. There is a lower limit below which closer spacing becomes counter-productive, because plants are simply too close together to be able to develop to a harvestable size. Using equidistant spacing is generally the most effective way to influence plant size and can be varied to suit different vegetables.

Bulb onions illustrate the influence of spacing on size. For large bulbs, an equidistant spacing of 20 x 20cm (8 x 8in) is ideal. By reducing this to 15cm (6in) between plants each way, smaller, medium-sized onions are produced. At an equidistant spacing of 60cm (2ft), summer cabbage will produce the largest heads possible, but if the spacing is reduced to 30cm (1ft) there will be a higher total yield of smaller heads, which are generally more convenient for use in the kitchen. Recommended in-row and block spacings for individual vegetables can be found in the *A–Z of Vegetables and Salad Crops*.

"Mini-veg"

An extreme example of how very close spacing can succeed is the use of "mini", "baby" or "high density" vegetables. These are cultivars selected because they respond well to very close spacing. They are useful for very small beds, such as the square-foot garden (see below) and containers (see p.210). The between-plant spacing for a crop such as leeks can be as little as 13mm (½in). Mini vegetables produce small, meal-size harvests over a long period if sown little and often.

"Square-foot" gardening

Using this technique, modest harvests of a wide range of vegetables are possible over a long period. The idea of square-foot gardening was developed in the USA. It requires little space or time and can also be a good "start-up" technique for a child or adult who has not grown vegetables before. A useful harvest can be achieved from an area no more than 1.2 x 1.2m (4 x 4ft). The area is divided up into 16 squares of 30 x 30cm (12 x 12in) using string. Different vegetables are grown in each square, at close, equidistant spacings. Various cultivars, including the "mini" types, are suitable. Taller and climbing crops are grown on the side of the bed furthest from the sun to avoid shading others. Crop rotation principles are followed (see also p.301).

Multi-sowing

Multi-sowing simply means sowing several seeds in the same place, either *in situ* or in 5cm (2in) modules, and allowing all to grow to fruition. The seedlings are left unthinned and, if module-grown, are planted out as a complete cell "unit", spacing them at around twice the normal spacing. The result is several smaller roots or bulbs, instead of one large one. Crops suitable for multi-sowing include beetroot, leeks and bulb onions (4–5 seeds sown per

Top plot:

Garlic x 9	Potato x 1	Cabbage x 6	Parsley, chives and sweet marjoram
Leaf beet x 5*	2 rows curled cress + 2 dwarf calendulas	Leek x 16	Broad bean x 3
Radish x 16	Celeriac x 5	Lettuce x 4	Turnip x 16
Sugarsnap peas x 16 (2 rows)	Sugarsnap peas x 16 (2 rows)	Potato x 1	Oakleaf lettuce x 4

Centre plot:

Celeriac x 5	Basil x 2	Dwarf French beans x 4	Parsley, chives and sweet marjoram
Leaf beet x 1	Parsley x 2 + 2 dwarf calendulas	Leek x 16	Chinese cabbage x 4
Cutting crop of mizuna greens *	Kohl rabi x 9	Mini sweet-corn x 4	Mini sweet-corn x 4
Tomato x 1 + 2 dwarf nasturtiums	Tomato x 1	Climbing beans x 3 + 2 French marigolds	Climbing beans x 3 + 2 French marigolds

Bottom plot:

Celeriac x 5	Garlic x 6	Claytonia x 4	Chives
Leaf beet x 1	Parsley x 2	Green-in-the-snow x 6	Chinese cabbage x 4
Mizuna x 4	Winter lettuce x 4	Chinese leaf celery x 3	Chicory frisee x 4
Corn salad x 6	Radicchio x 3	Winter lettuce x 4	Onions x 8

A YEAR IN A SQUARE-FOOT PLOT

These plans show one way to take a 1.2m (4ft) square plot through the year. At the height of the season it should provide at least three or four servings a week of various crops, and at the least productive times will supply salad leaves, herbs and garnishes. The plot even includes edible flowers.
• Grow taller and climbing plants on the side furthest from the sun to avoid shading others.
• Thin out plants as they fill the square, and eat the thinnings.
• Harvest plants at the earliest possible moment.
• Whenever a new crop is planted, add compost or leaf-mould, according to its needs. Mulch potatoes with compost.
• Have module-grown plants ready to fill empty squares for continuity of cropping.

Top
Planting of the crops shown here begins in midwinter and continues through the spring, to crop in spring and summer.
★ Thin leaf beet to one plant only to crop later.

Centre
The plot in summer and early autumn, with new crops growing in almost every square.
★ Leave 4 plants of mizuna to grow larger for late crops.

Bottom
Late autumn/winter, with hardy leaf and salad crops, and the garlic cloves and onion sets planted to overwinter.

Recommended cultivars:
Broad bean 'Bunyard's Exhibition'
Cabbage 'Greyhound'
Celeriac 'President'
Leek 'King Richard'
Sugar pea 'Dwarf Sweet Green'
Potato 'Swift'
Radish 'Scarlet Globe' and 'Sparkler'
Sweetcorn F1 'Minipop'
Turnip 'Snowball' and F1 'Market Express'

Multi-sowing
These red-skinned bulb onions have been multisown, five seeds to each 5cm (2in) module cell, then transplanted to a bed. As the cluster of plants develops, each bulb finds its own growing space and reaches only a modest size.

station or module cell), round cultivars of carrot (4 seeds per cluster) and salad or spring onions and chives (10 seeds per cluster).

Intercropping and undercropping

Intercropping is the sowing (or planting) of fast-growing or small vegetables, in rows or patches, on unused ground between slower-growing main crops. Many combinations of crop and intercrop can be used, but the guiding rule must always be that the "intercrop" should not be allowed to thrive at the expense of the main crop and must be harvested before the slower crop needs the space. Spring

onions, small lettuces and many other summer and winter salad crops are particularly good intercrops. The space between winter brassicas can be usefully filled with a wide range of intercrops. Tall plants like sweetcorn, which cast little shade, can be undercropped with lower-growing plants like dwarf French beans, lettuce or mizuna, or spreading vegetables such as courgettes and pumpkins, to make maximum use of space. Shade-tolerant vegetables like lettuce and spinach can be sown between rows of climbing beans.

Catch and double cropping

Catch crops are fast-maturing vegetables sown on spare ground between the clearance of one main crop and the planting of another. Leaf lettuce, radish, rocket, seedling cutting crops and fast-growing green manures are good examples. With double cropping, seeds of fast-maturing crops are sown between slower-growing station-sown crops such as parsnips, and harvested before the latter need the space.

Successional sowing

Sowing fast-maturing vegetables like lettuce and radishes little and often, at 2–3 week intervals, avoids gluts and gives a continuous supply over many months. Suitable crops also include calabrese, corn salad, kohl rabi, rocket, seedling salads (see p.332), spinach, spring onions and turnips.

GOOD CROPS FOR INTER- AND UNDERCROPPING

Chicory
Corn salad
Endive
Lettuce (right, among leeks)
Mizuna
Pak choi
Radish
Salad rocket
Seedling cutting crops
Spinach
Spring onion

Courgettes, squashes and pumpkins also make good, weed-suppressing undercrops for tall plants such as sweetcorn (far right) and runner beans.

Vegetable care

Once established, many crops need little maintenance. Check them over regularly though, and provide any extra care they need to ensure high yields.

Watering

Stress caused by lack of water can cause bolting, make plants more susceptible to pest and disease attack, and reduce yields. Seedlings and transplants should never dry out. Once established, watering thoroughly but infrequently is more effective than little and often. Water that soaks down into the soil encourages deep rooting and helps plants draw on reserves during dry spells. Some crops benefit from water at particular stages of growth (see below). Do not overwater; excessive, unnecessary watering can reduce the flavour of crops such as tomatoes.

Apply water at the base of plants in the evening, when evaporation is less (or if slugs are a problem, early in the morning). Use a can with a fine rose for small seedlings, or a watering lance fitted to a hosepipe. Crops needing lots of water, such as runner beans, can have bucketfuls poured around their roots. Seep- or soaker hose can also be used (see *Water and Watering*, p.66).

Feeding

If the soil has been prepared appropriately in advance, most crops should need no extra feeding. Long-term crops may benefit from mulching with a medium- or high-fertility soil improver (see overleaf).

Hoeing (above)
A hoe with a sharp blade is used to skim over the surface of the soil, cutting through seedling weeds, which then shrivel and die in the sun. As crops mature and cover the soil with a leafy canopy, the need for hoeing is reduced.

Close planting (left)
In this dense planting of lettuces in a block, the close canopy of leafy rosettes shades the ground well, reducing the loss of soil moisture and hence the need to water. Weeds are also suppressed.

KEY STAGES FOR WATERING

If the weather is dry during the critical periods below, plants must have water to crop well.
- French beans, broad beans: at start of flowering; when pods are forming.
- Lettuce: 7–10 days before harvest.
- Summer cabbage, summer and autumn cauliflower: 2–3 weeks before harvest.
- Courgettes: once fruits begin to form.
- Peas: when flowering and as pods form.
- Potatoes: when tubers are marble-sized.
- Sweetcorn: when flowering starts and when cobs are swelling.
- Runner beans, tomatoes: flowering onwards.
- Calabrese, celery, spinach: whenever dry.

Attracting predators
Grow flowers in the vegetable patch to attract beneficial insects that will aid pollination and keep down pests.

Plant supports (1)
This page, left to right: Broad beans are easily kept from flopping by enclosing them in twine tied to stakes. Climbing French beans will soon cover an open obelisk of woven willow and twine. Short, twiggy sticks pushed in the soil are the ideal support for peas.

Mulching and weed control

Mulching bare soil reduces water loss through evaporation and prevents germination of weed seeds. If a high- to medium-fertility soil improver is used, this also adds plant nutrients. Apply mulches to warm, moist soil in spring and summer.

Weeds compete for food, light and moisture – so keep vegetables as weed-free as possible. Sow your seeds in drills or stations so you can distinguish them from annual weeds; only broadcast-sow vegetables which you can readily identify at the seedling stage, such as carrots. Vigorous crops may need only a single weeding before they outgrow competition. See *Weeds and Weed Control* (pp.73–83) for mulches and techniques suitable for a vegetable plot.

Plant problems

Healthy, well-grown plants are more resistant to pest and disease attack. Pest- and disease-resistant cultivars should be used where problems are known to exist. Pests attack vegetables above and below soil. They range from large animal pests such as rabbits, which cause general damage, to microscopic eelworms that attack specific crops such as potatoes. Knowledge of pest life cycles aids control, as can timing of sowings to avoid pest-prone periods of the season. Pest control can range from hand-picking slugs and snails to using natural biological controls. Physical barriers can prevent some pests laying their eggs near crops. Do everything you can to prevent disease, as it can spread rapidly. Virus diseases are difficult to control and plants should be destroyed. The risk of infection with some fungal diseases can be reduced by raising soil pH (see pp.61, 302). Crop rotation (see p.301) plays an important role in reducing the severity of other soil-borne diseases and some pests.

Certain problems with vegetables are caused by bad cultural practice or mineral deficiencies in the soil. Bolting happens when plants "run to seed" prematurely and is caused by drying out, sudden fluctuations in temperature, sowing at the wrong time or module-grown plants becoming root-bound. Poor fruit or pod set can be caused by lack of pollination, drought or erratic watering.

Plant protection

Half-hardy vegetables planted in spring are vulnerable to cold and frost. They can be protected with cloches or fleece. Protection can also be given to vegetables such as outdoor tomatoes in early autumn to help ripen late fruits.

Training and support

Vegetables such as climbing beans will spiral up canes, although they may need to be guided to their supports and tied in until they start to climb. Peas

have tendrils which will cling to twiggy sticks or wide-mesh pea netting. Trailing pumpkins, cucumbers and squashes use tendrils to climb up trellis, over fences and into trees.

Tall non-climbing vegetables such as taller varieties of Brussels sprouts, broad beans and cordon tomatoes, will need the support of sturdy stakes.

Blanching and forcing

Some vegetables such as endive and scorzonera can be made more palatable by blanching – excluding light from all or part of a growing plant for a certain period, which turns the leaves pale and yellow. Curly endive is sweeter-tasting if blanched for around 10 days. Rhubarb, seakale and Witloof chicory are forced in complete darkness from a "dormant" state to produce tender leaves and shoots. Where perennial crops such as rhubarb are forced regularly, grow several plants so that the forced plant can be rested for a season or two before being forced again. Seakale can be harvested annually. Chicory is discarded once the "chicons" are harvested.

Harvesting

Harvesting requirements vary widely. Leeks and potatoes, and some cultivars of other vegetables will stay in good condition for weeks. Others, such as early cabbage and calabrese, need picking almost as

soon as they are ready. Peas and runner and French beans will stop producing more pods if not picked regularly. Get to know your crops so you can get the very best from them. Whatever you are harvesting, try to eat it as soon as possible. Fresh produce has the best flavour and the highest nutritional value. Sweetcorn must be the most extreme example of this, tasting best if cooked within 15 minutes of picking. On the other hand, vegetables such as winter squashes and onions can be kept in good condition for months. See Storing Vegetables, p.332.

Traditional rhubarb forcers
These pots have been left on long after the forcing period is over, simply because of their ornamental value.

Plant supports (2)
This page, left to right: Squashes scramble over a support of canes bound together with twine. Cordon tomatoes need tying to a sturdy support such as a bamboo cane. Runner beans will spiral up a frame of bamboo canes.

EDGING MATERIALS SUITABLE FOR RAISED BEDS

Bamboo rolls
Upended bottles
Bricks
Concrete blocks/slabs
Kerbstones
Logs★
Railway sleepers
Roofing tiles
Slates
Timber★
Synthetic "wood" (see p.131)
Woven willow or hazel (see p.141) ★★

★ Should be untreated, or treated with environmentally-friendly preservative (see p.130).
★★ Soil along bed edges may dry out rather quickly

Beds on show (facing page)
The bed system at Yalding, in Kent, one of the HDRA's demonstration gardens. Entire beds can easily be covered with sheets of garden fleece or fine mesh, low polythene tunnels or cloches in order to warm soil, raise earlier and more tender crops, extend the growing season, provide winter protection and protect crops from certain pests.

Growing in beds

Growing vegetables in narrow beds, divided by access paths, has many advantages over traditional row cropping. On a traditional vegetable plot, soil improvers and fertilisers are applied across the whole area, and then dug in. The soil between the rows is compacted as crops are watered, fed, weeded and harvested. A "bed system" breaks with this constant cycle of compaction followed by cultivation.

The most important factor when setting up beds for vegetable growing is that you should be able to reach the centre of the bed easily without over-stretching, or having to walk on the soil. Although rectangular beds are easy to set out and manage, beds can be of any shape as long the centre is reachable from the path.

Beds can be flat or raised, edged or with no edging, dug, double-dug or not dug at all. Choose the combination that suits you.

Flat or soil-level beds

A flat bed, without any edging, is the simplest and least labour-intensive to set up. Each corner of the bed is marked with a post, and string is tied between them to define the edge. The height of the bed relative to the paths will increase, however, if the soil is medium to heavy, and it is well dug (see below). Soil improvers will also tend to raise it, while the paths become lower due to compaction. Flat beds are best suited to light soils, which would tend to dry out rapidly if raised up.

Raised and edged beds

Edging provides a neat, sharply defined boundary between bed and path. It contains the soil on the bed, and any mulching material on the path. Edging is to be recommended on medium to heavy soils where the level of the bed tends to rise above the path. Where topsoil is thin, edging allows the bed to be built up with soil that can be dug out from the paths, or imported from elsewhere. Raised beds are especially useful on heavier soils where drainage is poor.

An edge 10–30cm (4–12in) high is adequate in most situations. Beds raised to 60cm (2ft) are useful where there is difficulty in bending, if cultivation is done from a wheelchair or where there are serious

ADVANTAGES OF A BED SYSTEM

• Beds help maximise even the smallest growing space.
• Beds can look very attractive, giving a tidy, organised appearance to a vegetable-growing area.
• All work is done from the paths, avoiding compaction and damage to soil structure.
• Soil improvers, fertilisers and water are concentrated on the growing areas, not wasted on paths.
• Drainage is improved and the soil warms up faster in spring.
• Rounded beds with a convex profile have an increased surface area.
• Lack of compaction reduces the need for digging – and only the growing area, not the paths, need be dug.
• Vegetables can be grown at close, equidistant spacings, increasing yields from the area.
• Spacing can be manipulated to vary the size of individual vegetables such as onions.
• Close, even spacing creates a dense canopy of leaves, smothering out weeds.
• Crop rotation (see p.301) is much easier to plan and manage.
• Crops can be harvested whatever the weather without damaging the soil.

drainage problems. The main drawbacks with raised beds are the initial cost of materials, the labour required and drying out at the bed edges. Choose the edging material to create the look you require (see panel, far left).

"No-dig" or double-dug?

The soil in a bed is treated in the same way as the soil on an open plot. If the soil is dug regularly, this is done working from wide wooden boards to avoid compaction. Beds are particularly appropriate where a no-dig system is used (see p.326). At the opposite extreme is the intensive deep bed – prepared by double digging and incorporating soil improvers to a depth of around 60cm (2ft). A low-fertility soil improver such as leafmould can be incorporated as the bed is dug initially. This deep cultivation is useful where the soil is compacted. It results in a deep,

fertile zone with an open, free-draining structure into which roots can easily penetrate. Medium- to high-fertility materials, if required, should only be mixed into the top 15–20cm (6–8in). Increases in yield are noticeable and plants are more tolerant of drought. Loosening of the soil and the addition of soil improvers can produce a noticeable increase in bed height, so edging may be required.

Planning a bed system

For most purposes, square or rectangular, narrow beds, 90-120cm (3-4ft) wide, allow easy access to the centre of the bed, although the exact width will depend on your height and reach. An average bed length of 3m (10ft) avoids having to walk too far to reach the other side. Beds can be grouped formally where food production is the main objective, or in patterns for a decorative "potager" effect.

Paths

Paths should be a minimum of 30cm (1ft) wide, with some up to 60cm (2ft) for wheelbarrow access. Bare paths will require hoeing to control weeds. Light-excluding natural-fibre carpet covered with woodchips or sawdust is effective and clean to walk on. A porous membrane covered with gravel, pine needles, bark or similar can also be used. More formal paths of slabs or bricks can look more elegant

Small beds with brick paths
Brick paths roughly 45cm (18in) wide allow access to crops in all weathers and are convenient for wheelbarrows. They look good, too.

but are more expensive. Grass paths can be effective between vegetable beds, provide an all-weather surface and look attractive. If grass is used, the paths should be set up to the width of your lawn mower, and brick or other permanent edging should be used to act both as a "mowing edge" and to prevent grasses invading the beds. The clippings can be used as a mulch.

> The addition of soil improvers tends to raise the beds, while paths sink as they become compacted

Siting and orientation

Beds should be in an open, sunny position. Wherever possible, rectangular beds should run north–south to minimise shade from taller crops. In other situations, grow tall-growing crops on the side of the bed furthest from the sun.

Sowing and planting

Always work from the paths or from a wide wooden plank across the bed. A length of wood that fits inside the edge of raised beds is ideal for marking out seed drills and planting positions. For more information on spacing techniques suitable for beds see Using space effectively, p.316.

If several different crops are to be grown in the same bed, keep each together in a block, at equidistant spacings, or with the rows running across the bed. Tall crops that need support, such as climbing beans, can be grown in rows down the middle of beds running north–south, with smaller crops either side. In beds running east–west, tall crops are better grown in separate beds, or in blocks with rows running across the bed, to minimise shading. Wide-spaced vegetables such as Brussels sprouts are planted in staggered rows along, rather than across, beds, with other vegetables intercropped between.

Watering

Water by hand or use a semi-automatic system of seep- or soaker hose (p.66) if all the vegetables in the bed have the same watering requirements. Soil near the sides of raised beds may need extra water.

Growing mushrooms

Mushrooms of various types, from the familiar white button mushroom to the more exotic oyster mushroom and the shiitake can be grown relatively easily by the gardener. Several are available year-round. They are eaten raw or cooked and some can be dried. Different types can be grown successfully in shaded and cool parts of a garden as well as in sheds or cellars. There is no need for soil or light, but cropping can be sporadic and unreliable if the required conditions are not met.

What is a mushroom?

Mushrooms are fungi – plants which, lacking chlorophyll, are unable to manufacture their own food. They rely on other organisms – living or dead plants or even animals – for their needs. Suitable materials, or "substrates", on which to grow mushrooms include logs, untreated sawdust, wood chips, coffee grounds, strawy manures or even newspaper and cardboard. The fungi break the substrate down to compost in the process of digesting it for food.

For most of its life a fungus exists as a network of fine filaments – the mycelium – growing through a substrate. The edible part, the mushroom, is a "fruiting body", which produces spores. This only appears when conditions of nutrition, humidity, temperature and light are correct.

Growing mushrooms

To grow your own mushrooms, you will be supplied with live "spawn" – the mycelium – growing in a suitable substrate. In some cases this simply has to be put in the correct location to grow; alternatively you may use the spawn to inoculate a substrate, such as hardwood logs, a pile or bed of compost or even a roll of kitchen paper.

Organic kits for growing the familiar cultivated mushroom, consisting of a container filled with an inoculated compost, are quite widely available. Starter kits for other, less usual species are available from specialist suppliers.

Growing on logs and sawdust

Hardwood logs, 5–15cm (2–6in) in diameter and cut in the dormant season, are inoculated in spring. Birch, beech and oak give the most reliable results.

Small wooden dowels, which are supplied already colonised with mushroom mycelium, are inserted into pre-drilled holes.

The logs are kept in warm and moist conditions while the mycelium colonises the wood. It can take from 6-12 months from inoculation to fruiting, which can then continue for several years. Bags of moist sawdust from untreated timber can be mixed with spawn, then kept in a warm spot while the mycelium grows. These are then moved to a bright, cool location for fruiting.

Growing on bulky organic material

Growing methods vary with each type of mushroom but in general spawn is mixed with moist, well-rotted manure, compost, straw or other organic material (which should be free of other fungi) and placed in bags. Mycelium growth is then encouraged in moist conditions at a temperature of around 20°C (68°F). Fruiting begins several weeks later.

GROWN ON ORGANIC MATERIAL

Field mushroom (*Agaricus campestris*) White cap, pink to brown gills on underside.
Morel (*Morchella esculenta*) Grey-brown, spherical cap; strong, aromatic flavour.
Parasol (*Macrolepiota procera*) Large cap has brown scales on a pale background.
Shaggy ink cap (*Coprinus cornatus*) Elongated egg-shaped shaggy cap; disintegrates to black and ink-like. Delicious eaten young.
Shiitake (*Lentinus edodes*) Widely cultivated; strong, smoky flavour. Dries well.
Spring agaric (*Agaricus bisporus*) The common cultivated mushroom.
Wood blewit (*Lepista nuda*) Dense flesh; young caps blue-violet, violet underneath.

GROWN ON LOGS OR SAWDUST

Chicken of the woods (*Laetiporus sulphureus*) Yellow brackets; texture and taste of chicken.
Grey oyster (*Pleurotus ostreatus*) Large, oyster-shaped fruiting bodies. Widely cultivated.
Lion's mane (*Hericium erinaceum*) Waterfalls of icicle-like spines; mild, sweet flavour.
Nameko (*Pholiota nameko*) Cap orange-brown; delicious Japanese mushroom.

MUSHROOMS IN THE GARDEN

Integrated into the garden, mushrooms look good as well as producing a tasty crop. The traditional field mushroom (*Agaricus campestris*), for example, can be sown in a lawn. It fruits in the autumn and may crop for several years if the conditions are right. The sides or corners of timber-edged raised beds can be replaced with hardwood logs which are then inoculated with mushroom spawn. A slow compost heap can be used to produce shaggy inkcaps. This species will also grow, along with the king stropharia (*Stropharia rugoso-annulata*) in a border mulched with woodchip or straw.

A note of caution
Mushrooms often appear at a considerable distance from where they were first introduced. The identity of any unfamiliar-looking mushroom must always be checked before eating. Many species are poisonous.

The "no-dig" approach

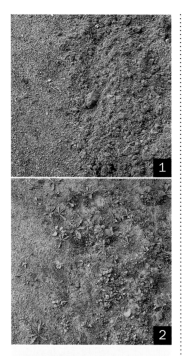

THE EFFECT OF DIGGING

This demonstration shows how digging the soil can increase weed numbers, by bringing dormant seeds from lower levels to the surface, where they will germinate. On a bare piece of ground (**1**), the soil on the right is cultivated, while that on the left is left untouched. Three weeks later (**2**), many more weed seedlings have germinated on the dug soil than on the undisturbed side. Fewer weeds, and therefore less time spent weeding, is one of the great benefits of the no-dig approach.

"No-dig" is an organic technique which can be used for growing all types of vegetable. In no-dig, apart from any initial cultivation required, the soil is never turned over. Soil improvers, which in a no-dig system often have a dual role as a mulch, and fertilisers are spread over the soil surface but are not incorporated – this job is left to earthworms and other organisms. Earthworms improve drainage through their burrowing activities, while their crumbly, aerated casts enhance soil structure. Soil organisms further decompose what the worms drag down, releasing food for the growing plants, and forming humus. Some soil disturbance is inevitable when sowing, planting and harvesting, but this is minimal compared with that caused by digging. In the long term, digging is detrimental to soil structure, resulting in increased losses of soil moisture and organic matter.

The main drawbacks of no-dig are that it can take longer to improve a poor soil and that soil-inhabiting pests are not exposed to predators. Combining the best elements of digging with no-dig techniques is generally the most pragmatic approach. The soil may need initial cultivation before going no-dig – for example, if it is badly compacted – and it can still be turned over occasionally, such as when incorporating green manures. No-dig is particularly successful when combined with a bed system, where the soil is not walked on (see p.322).

Contrary to popular opinion, a no-dig plot does not require huge quantities of mulch materials. Compost and manure is added in the same quantities as on a dug plot. Potatoes (see facing page) are the only crop that must have an extra thick mulch; it is essential to prevent green tubers.

Getting started

To get the best results from no-dig, the soil should be in a reasonable condition, structurally, at the outset. This may involve digging to improve drainage and relieve any compaction. If you are unsure about the condition of your soil, the information in *Soil and Soil Care* (pp.32-61) will help you determine whether or not digging is necessary, and what soil treatments may be required.

THE BENEFITS OF A NO-DIG SYSTEM
• The repeated effort of labour-intensive digging is no longer required.
• Soil structure is preserved and, in time, enhanced.
• Soil organisms flourish in the stable conditions of undisturbed soil.
• Losses of organic matter and moisture are greatly reduced.
• Fewer weed seeds are brought to the surface.

On soil that does not have any major problems, the no-dig approach can be adopted straight away. If the plot is weedy, or you are converting a patch of lawn, it can be cleared without digging, using a sheet mulch (see overleaf). Ahead of sowing or planting, appropriate soil improvers are spread evenly over the soil, or are concentrated on planting positions for widely spaced crops like courgettes. Organic fertilisers and lime, if required, can be lightly raked in before spreading any bulky soil improver.

Sowing and planting

Most crops are grown in the same way as they would be on a dug bed. In an established no-dig system, the surface soil will be fine, crumbly and ideal for seed sowing. Seed is sown in drills or stations. Transplants are set into holes made with a trowel. Any layer of soil improver or mulch should be scraped back prior to sowing or planting, then spread back as the plants begin to grow.

Weeds and weeding

On a no-dig plot, weeds are drastically reduced as dormant seeds are not brought to the surface. An organic mulch further reduces weed numbers and retains soil moisture, but is not essential.

Light hoeing is effective on bare soil and gradually depletes the reserve of weed seeds. Any perennial weeds should be loosened with a fork and lifted out, disturbing the soil as little as possible.

Harvesting

You may be able to simply pull root crops out of the ground. If not, use a fork to loosen them gently, causing minimal disruption to the soil.

GROWING NO-DIG POTATOES

In climates where potato foliage is at risk from frost damage, it is usually advisable to plant a no–dig crop slightly later than normal. The mulch tends to reduce soil temperature, and the plants may be more susceptible to frost damage.

Planting

1 Hoe off, or cut or mow down any vegetation on the growing area.

2 Soak the ground well if dry. Spread manure, compost or a nitrogen-rich organic fertiliser over the ground at the appropriate rate (see p.40).

3 Lay out seed tubers on the ground at the required spacing. Where there is a risk of frost, plant them into a trowel hole.

4 Cover each row with a 7.5cm (3in) layer of hay or old straw. Mark the position of each row to avoid standing on the tubers.

As they grow

1 Check regularly for shoots emerging through the mulch, and ease any through that are pushing up the mulch rather than growing through it.

2 Top up the mulch as the plants grow, covering the area between the rows too.

3 When the plants are close to meeting across the row, cover the mulch with a thick layer of grass mowings to exclude light and keep the tubers from going green.

4 Add more grass as necessary. Birds love to pull the mulch apart but will play a useful role in controlling pests at the same time.

Harvesting

To harvest a few potatoes, simply pull back the mulch and pick as many tubers as you require. They will be sitting on the soil surface. Replace the mulch and leave the rest to keep growing. To harvest the whole crop, lift or rake off the mulch. Lift all tubers, checking for any which may have developed below ground level. Replace the mulch.

Green manures and no-dig

Green manure crops (see p.56), which are usually dug into the soil, can still be grown on a no-dig plot. Annual green manures, such as mustard, are cut down or hoed off and left as a mulch. Perennial green manures such as clover and grazing rye (which will tend to regrow if cut down even though it is an annual) are cut down and killed off with a light-excluding mulch, or by growing a no-dig crop of potatoes.

Sheet mulching

Sheet mulching with various materials (see below) is an easy, highly effective way of clearing ground – such as a weedy plot or a lawn. It is particularly useful when establishing a no-dig system. You can get a crop from the land in the first year, without any digging. Where resources are limited, concentrate on clearing a small, manageable area first.

MATERIALS FOR SHEET MULCHING

A sheet mulch is made up of two or three layers.

Base layer
(Biodegradable; excludes light)
Large sheets of cardboard
Cardboard boxes, flattened
Newspapers, full thickness

Middle layer
(Soil improver; anchors base layer)
Garden compost
Grass clippings
Leafmould or fallen leaves
Well-rotted manure
Mushroom compost (NB: high lime content)
Shredded soft prunings
Spent straw or hay

Top layer – optional
(Retains moisture; looks good)
Straw
Hay

Mulch when soil is warm and after heavy rain. Mulching cold soil delays warming up, slowing plant growth and increasing the risk of slug damage. These chard plants (right) have been raised in modules and planted through a sheet mulch.

Laying a sheet mulch

Cut down any vegetation first, and dig out any woody weeds. Lay the base layer, overlapping the "joins" between sheets of cardboard or paper by 30cm (12in) to exclude light. This is best done on a still day; the soil must be warm and moist.

To hold this layer down so it smothers weeds, add a covering layer no more than 10cm (4in) deep, especially along overlapping edges. The choice of material for this depends on what is available and the fertility of the soil. Ground that has been uncultivated for some time, or which was a lawn, is often very fertile and crops will grow surprisingly well with no additional feeding. If the ground is poor, use a medium- or high-fertility soil improver, such as well-rotted manure or garden compost, for the covering layer. Fresh or spoiled straw can be spread as a 5cm (2in) layer over the top, to keep it looking neat and tidy, and to help conserve moisture. Watering the entire area will settle the layers and stop materials blowing away.

As the base layer decomposes, the covering layer sinks onto the soil surface, where it is incorporated into the soil by worms, increasing soil fertility.

Growing through a sheet mulch

In the first year potato tubers, and transplants such as brassicas, courgettes and pumpkins, can be planted through the mulch into the soil, in pockets loosened with a trowel; mix in some compost if available. Initially plants may need more frost protection than usual, as the mulch cuts off the warming solar radiation that usually comes from the soil at night. Use fleece, or alternatively, plant a little later.

Small seeds and root crops are unsuitable for sheet mulches in the first year, but in the following season the surface of the ground should be crumbly and very suitable for sowing all types of seed. It is useful to continue to keep the soil mulched to prevent the germination of weed seeds, protect the soil from capping after heavy rain, and conserve moisture.

Perennial weeds such as docks and thistles may push up through a sheet mulch. To remove them, simply loosen the soil around their roots and ease them out. A second year of sheet mulching may be needed to control them completely.

Once a sheet mulch has cleared the ground, the area can be maintained using no-dig techniques.

Edible landscaping

Many vegetables are not just delicious to eat, they are also gorgeous to look at. Edible landscaping takes account of the ornamental aspects of edible plants alongside their practical value. It also means you can grow edible plants in a garden without the need for a separate vegetable area.

An edible landscape can be large or small, formal or relaxed, and include fruit, vegetables, herbs and flowers. A famous example is at Villandry in France, designed to complement the Château on a grand scale, where vegetables provide blocks of colour within a formal layout of paths and beds edged with clipped hedges. At the other extreme is a mixed border, where both edible and ornamental plants all tumble about in merry confusion.

Potager gardens

A potager is an edible garden planted specifically for its ornamental as much as its edible qualities. Maintaining a balance between appearance and yield can be difficult, and careful planning is needed to keep it looking good all year round. Planning for either summer or winter is easier, with the garden "at rest" during one of these seasons.

Creative planting

Edible landscaping offers the creative gardener the opportunity to try out all sorts of unusual planting combinations. Vegetables are appreciated for their colour, leaf shape and texture, overall form and as visual statements. They can be trained up screens, trellis or other plants to provide height, or used to create colourful shapes and patterns at ground level. Allowing some vegetables to go to seed often results in unexpected delights; lettuces, for example, turn into elegant tapering towers up to 1.2m (4ft) high. They are no good for eating at that stage, but look delightful! Onions and leeks left to run to flower produce ball-shaped flowerheads at the top of tall stems: striking, colourful and attractive to bees.

Tower power
Red and green lettuce make attractive spires when left to go to seed. The display may be short-lived, but this is a cheap and cheerful way to improvise a formal effect.

Beautiful plants are healthy plants

Plants in an edible landscape need to be healthy and flourishing to look their best. Pay careful attention to maintaining the soil in good condition and, just as you would in a traditional vegetable plot, remember the principles of rotation (see p.301) when planning from one year to the next to produce best results. Replacement or substitute plants kept in reserve at varying stages of growth will be useful to take the place of any damaged or unhealthy plants, keeping the display looking good.

Eating the landscape

Harvesting inevitably leaves gaps in an edible landscape. Solve this problem by using varieties that can be picked over a long period, such as kale or loose-leaf lettuces. In addition, select crops that still look good after the edible part has been harvested, such as French and runner beans or courgettes. It helps to grow "temporary" plants beside others that will expand to fill the gaps. Raise extra plants in pots or modules as replacements for those you eat.

Potager style

Colourful crops planted in patterns can rival the brightest bedding displays, and are edible too.

VEGETABLES AND HERBS FOR EDGING

For summer and autumn

Compact lettuce, especially 'Lollo Rosso' and 'Lollo Verde'
Curly endive
Curly parsley
Red-leaved plantain
Strips of seedling crops
Dwarf Savoy cabbage

For winter

Lamb's lettuce
Mizuna
Ornamental cabbage and kale
Rosette pak choi

Perennials

Chinese (garlic) chives
Chives
Marjoram
Salad burnet
Sage, purple and green varieties
Thyme
Winter savory

BEAUTIFUL VEGETABLES

Vibrant colours

Asparagus pea (red flowers)

Aubergine (purple flowers and rich purple fruits; or try 'Easter Egg', with white fruits)

Beetroot 'Bull's Blood'(dark red foliage)

Broccoli 'Romanesco' (lime-green curds)

Crimson-flowered broad bean

Giant red mustard (red/green leaves)

Kale 'Cavolo Nero' (greenish-black leaves)

Kale 'Ragged Jack' (pinkish-grey leaves)

Leek 'St.Victor' (purple/blue)

Pumpkin (orange fruits)

Purple- and yellow-podded French beans

Radicchio (red/white leaves)

Rainbow chard (yellow, white, red, pink and orange stems)

Ruby chard (above left)

Red cabbage (purple/blue leaves)

Height and drama

Globe artichokes (above right)

Cardoons

Cucumber, trained

French beans, climbing

Green and bronze fennel

Pumpkins and squashes, trained

Radishes grown for seed pods

Runner beans

Seakale

Good leaf shape or texture

Buckshorn plantain

Courgette

Endive, curled

Kale, frilly

Lettuce, oakleaved or frilly

Mizuna

Parsley, curled

Pumpkin (below left)

Edible flowers

Borage (blue or, rarely, white)

Calendula (orange)

Chives (pink or purple)

Cowslip (yellow)

Daisy (pinky-white)

Lavender (mauve, white or pink)

Nasturtium (below right; yellow/orange/red)

Rose (pink/red flowers taste best)

Sage (purple/pink)

Viola (purple, rarely white)

LEAFY SALAD CROPS

All these plants can be grown as seedling crops. Those marked ** are best grown only as seedlings when used for salads; all others can be grown as seedlings, semi-mature or mature plants.

Mild
Chard **
Chervil
Chinese cabbage
Coriander
Corn salad *
Dill
Leaf beet **
Lettuce
Pak choi
Spinach **
Summer purslane
Winter purslane *

Bitter
Chicory *
Dandelion
Endive

Hot
Garden cress **
Garden mustard **
Greek cress **
Green in the snow *
Land cress *
Mibuna
Mizuna *
Oriental mustard *
Radish leaf **
Rocket *
Texel greens **
Watercress

* Good for a winter crop in a cool climate
** Best grown as seedling crops for salads

More detail on growing these crops can be found in the *A-Z of Vegetable and Salad Crops*.

Cutting salads
Harvest seedling salads when about 10–15cm (4–6in) high, leaving a short stem to regrow.

Growing salads

A great number of vegetables can be used to make delicious salads, but for gardeners the term "salad plants" normally refers to leafy crops that are suitable for eating raw. These vary widely in their origins, flavours, colours and textures. Some flowers are also edible (see p.331) and make colourful additions to salad mixtures.

Salads all year round

It is possible to harvest something fresh and leafy almost all year round, with a bit of planning. Salads are perhaps especially welcome in winter when fewer fresh vegetables are available.

Spring and autumn Choose quick-maturing varieties that will produce a crop within a few weeks of sowing. Protect with cloches or fleece, or grow in a greenhouse or polytunnel, to extend cropping time.

Summer The widest range of salads can be grown in summer, both seedlings and mature plants. Make sure they never go short of water at this time of year, to discourage premature bolting. Some salads are mild, many more are stronger, so grow a mixture for a blend of flavours. Chicory, endive and

dandelion are all quite bitter, but blanching mature plants will produce milder, more tender leaves. Cover flat varieties with a plate, and upright ones with a pot or bucket – or tie the leaves together. It takes one to three weeks, depending on the season.

Winter Salads sown in late summer will be ready to harvest in early winter, and with protection, or in mild winters, some can be harvested right through the winter. In harsh climates, grow seedling crops indoors on windowsills in shallow trays or pots.

Techniques

Salad plants can be grown to maturity, harvested at the seedling stage or when semi-mature. Seedling or semi-mature crops can be harvested much earlier, within a few weeks, and the harvest can go on over a longer period.

Seedling salads

Seedling salads are harvested when immature. Seeds can be mixed before sowing, providing an instant mixed salad. Seedling crops are shallow-rooting, so will grow well in containers with a minimum depth of about 10cm (4in) as well as in the soil. They do not need particularly fertile conditions, but do benefit from a soil or growing medium that retains water well. These crops have a high water requirement, so make sure you can water them easily in dry conditions. Weed-free conditions are important. If weeds are a problem, use the stale seedbed technique (see p.75).

Sowing seedling salads

Sow seedling salads direct into a fine seedbed or container, either broadcast over the whole area, or in shallow drills approximately 10cm (4in) wide. Aim for a spacing of about 2 cm (¾in) between seeds. Water well to encourage germination. In hot, dry or windy conditions, it is helpful to cover the seeds with horticultural fleece or windbreak netting until they germinate.

• **Intercropping and catch cropping** Quick-growing seedling crops make good use of space amongst slower growing, widely spaced vegetables such as cabbages, potatoes or courgettes. They will be ready to harvest long before the larger crop needs

the space. Another option is to sow seedlings when the ground is empty for short periods.

• **Successional sowing** Sow a new batch of seeds every 2-3 weeks to ensure continuity of harvesting.

Harvesting

Seedling salads are ready to harvest as soon as they are about 10–15cm (4–6in) high, usually within a few weeks. Use a sharp knife or scissors to cut the leaves, or pick by hand, leaving a stem of about 2cm (¾in). The plants can regrow, and you will be able to cut them two or three times over the following weeks. The life of a seedling patch varies depending on weather conditions and season. Seedling crops do not stay fresh for long once harvested, so pick them just before you want to eat them.

Semi-mature salads

Sow seeds at a wider spacing than for seedling crops, leaving about 15–20cm (6–8in) between plants. Alternatively, sow in modules and plant out, or simply transplant some seedlings to a similar spacing. To harvest, pick individual leaves from the outside as the plants develop, leaving the growing tip intact.

Storing vegetables

Certain vegetables can be stored through the winter, to eat fresh when produce from the garden is scarce. Some very hardy crops, such as parsnips and Jerusalem artichokes, can be left in the ground over winter, but there are disadvantages to this. It increases the likelihood of pest damage, and any disease present will have the opportunity to spread. In addition, the soil may become frozen solid in cold weather, making harvesting difficult.

Many vegetables can be stored successfully without any special equipment as long as you are able to provide the right conditions. Once your vegetables are in store, they need to be inspected regularly. Adjust conditions if necessary, and remove anything that shows signs of decay to stop it spreading.

Harvesting for storage

Best results will be obtained from maincrop cultivars that mature towards the end of the season and are harvested in cool conditions.

- **Harvest vegetables just as they reach maturity.** Picking too early means they will not have developed their full flavour; leave it too late and they become fibrous and woody.

- **Only store best-quality produce.** Anything that is blemished or has pest and disease damage will only deteriorate, and may also spread rots to other, sound fruits and vegetables.
- **Handle with care.** Even quite sturdy crops, such as potatoes, are easily bruised. The damage may not be apparent at first, but it may allow rots to set in once in store.

Where to store vegetables

The ideal storage conditions for individual vegetables vary according to type. In general, the best place is somewhere cool and dry, with an even temperature, and free from mice and other pests. A basement or cellar is ideal, but an unheated shed or garage, or an unheated room in the house is also suitable. Lift storage containers off the floor on boxes or pallets, and keep a supply of old blankets, sacks or rugs for extra insulation if required.

Storage requirements

Details of storage conditions for crops that last well through the winter are given opposite. Some other crops can also be stored for shorter periods:

- **Tomatoes** Harvest green tomatoes at the end of the growing season, before the first frost. Whole vines can be uprooted, then hung in a cool, dry place to continue to ripen slowly. Alternatively, harvest fruit individually, wrap in paper and store on trays or in boxes. To encourage ripening, place tomatoes in a closed paper bag or box with a ripe apple or banana.
- **Cabbages** Firm red and white winter cabbage will store for several months if harvested before the first frost. It is crucial to leave the roots intact, or cut with a 15cm (6in) stem. Place on pallets or slatted shelves and keep at 0–4°C (32–39°F). Cover with straw, sacks or thick layers of newspaper if temperatures drop.
- **Leeks and Brussels sprouts** Both can normally be left in the ground all winter, but if very harsh weather is forecast you can bring a temporary supply into the house for convenience. Dig up entire plants, with roots intact, and place in a bucket with just enough water to cover the roots. In a cool place, they should stay fresh for up to a week.

Drying and storing beans
Choose varieties recommended for storage, such as these borlotti beans. Leave the pods on the vine until dry and crisp. Shell the beans and store in an airtight container.

CROPS TO STORE

1 Potatoes

Lift and leave exposed to dry for a few hours. Store in thick paper sacks, tied or folded loosely at the neck. Potatoes must be stored in the dark to prevent them turning green and developing high levels of solanine, a toxic alkaloid. Frost protection is essential. Ideal temperature 5–10°C (41–50°F).

2 Onions, shallots and garlic

Harvest garlic when the first 4–6 leaves turn yellow. Leave onions and shallots until all the leaves have fallen over naturally. Lift carefully, and leave in a warm, dry place for a couple of weeks. In fine weather, do this outdoors, lifted off the ground on racks or pallets. Otherwise, bring them under cover to finish drying. Bulbs are ready to store when the skins are papery and rustle when handled. Plait into ropes or hang in net sacks in a place where air circulates freely. Ideal temperature 2–4°C (36–39°F).

3 Carrots, parsnips, beetroot, celeriac, swede

Remove excess soil gently; do not wash or scrub as this may damage the skin. Remove leafy tops by twisting close to the crown. Place in shallow trays or boxes, separating layers with moist sand, coir, untreated sawdust, fine leafmould or sieved soil. Ideal temperature 0–4°C (32–39°F).

4 Pumpkins and winter squash

These need a few weeks of sunny weather at the end of the season to develop a tough skin for optimum storage. Harvest before the first frost. Cut with a long stalk, leaving part of the vine attached. As this dries, it hardens and protects the stem, which is otherwise vulnerable to rotting. Store in a dry, airy place, if possible on slatted shelves or in nets for good air circulation. Can last 6–9 months if well-ripened at harvest. Ideal temperature 10–15°C (50–59°F); storage at higher temperatures causes the flesh to become fibrous.

A-Z of Vegetable & Salad Crops

Notes on the entries

- **Botanical name and family** These tell you more about plant relationships – how the crop fits in, if at all, to a rotation plan and whether it may share preferences and weaknesses with other crops (see also pp.301–313). This is followed by a general description of the crop.

- **Seed to harvest** The usual time taken to achieve a crop. Sometimes Planting to Harvest, for crops that are vegetatively propagated.

- **Crop diversity** In some cases none at all, especially for crops that do not lend themselves to commercial cultivation and those, like some of the salad leaves, that are only one step away from the wild. Other crops are bewilderingly – or perhaps excitingly – diverse, with a huge array of cultivars to choose from; in some cases recommendations are given.

- **Site** All crops will perform better for you if given the site and soil conditions they prefer.

- **Soil treatment** The recommendations given are suggestions for an "average" soil, if such a thing exists. What is actually needed will depend on many factors. If your soil has good organic matter levels and you grow green manures, you can cut down on the use of soil improvers and fertilisers – unless you are looking to grow bumper-sized crops. A dry, poor soil might need more improvement than is suggested, especially to increase water-holding capacity. See also *Soil and Soil Care*, pp.33–61, and *Growing Vegetables*, pp.295–296; also individual vegetable families (pp.303–313).

- **Ideal pH range** See pp.37 and 61 for more information.

- **Sowing** Covers timing and options for both outdoors and under cover. Methods are described in more detail in *Growing Vegetables*, pp.314–318 (including techniques such as multi-sowing and intercropping), and in *Raising Plants*, pp.104–123. Minimum germination temperature figures give an idea of when, and where, a particular crop can be sown – direct in the soil, or raised in the warmth of a propagator or airing cupboard, for example. Knowing when the soil outside is warm enough for sowing does come with experience, but if you are new to vegetable growing, or have moved to a new area, a soil thermometer can be useful.

- **Spacing** For rows, the recommended distance between plants in the row is given first, and then the distance between rows. Block planting refers to equidistant planting, and indicates the space each way that each plant will need. For a further explanation of growing in beds and rows, see p.322.

- **Plant care** See also pp.319–323. Problems referred to here are covered in detail in the *A–Z of Plant Problems*, following on from this section.

- **Harvesting** Personal preference sometimes plays a part in deciding when to harvest, but general recommendations are given here, together with an indication of whether the crop is best eaten fresh, or can be stored short- or long-term.

Further information

The HDRA's three open gardens, at Ryton, Yalding and Audley End (see p.403 for details), are tremendous sources of advice and inspiration for anyone interested in growing food. What you see will depend on when you visit, but all have plenty on show (at Ryton, year-round) to suit gardens both large and small. The wide variety of crops and growing methods displayed change yearly as new cultivars and techniques are tried. At Ryton you will also see cultivars being grown for seed to continue the crucial work of the Heritage Seed Library; Yalding makes a speciality out of growing crops in innovative and ornamental ways; while at the historic Walled Kitchen Garden at Audley End, the very best of gardening tradition is preserved.

At all three sites, organically raised seed, both of vegetables and green manures, can be purchased, and at the appropriate season young plants may also be available. Through its shops and its dedicated mail-order service, the Organic Gardening Catalogue (see p.402 for details), HDRA offers one of the most comprehensive ranges of vegetable cultivars, including not only unusual crops and varieties but all the "tried-and-tested" organic favourites with good pest and disease resistance. Members of the Heritage Seed Library also gain access to "heirloom" and other commercially unavailable varieties through its Seed Swap and Seed Guardianship schemes.

Artichoke, Chinese

Stachys affinis LAMIACEAE

An Oriental root vegetable, easy to grow but little known because the small spiral tubers are fiddly to clean. It requires a relatively long growing season in a large area, and can become invasive, but it is suitable for containers. Grows 45–55cm (18–22in) tall.

PLANTING TO HARVEST 20–28 weeks.
SITE Will tolerate some shade.
SOIL TREATMENT Low-fertility soil improver.
IDEAL pH RANGE 6.5–7

Planting

To get an early start, tubers can be sprouted in trays of compost in a warm spot, or individually in pots, until the shoots are 6cm (2½in) tall. Plant direct in April, 10–15cm (4–6in) deep.

Spacing

ROWS 23 x 45cm (9 x 18in)
BLOCK PLANTING 34cm (13½in)

Plant care

Drawing up a little soil around the base of the plants will help support their stems. Weed until established; the vigorous growth will then crowd out any weeds. Water well in dry spells to encourage good tuber formation. If grown in containers, feed weekly with diluted comfrey liquid (1 part to 15 parts of water) from midsummer onwards.
PROBLEMS Few. Occasionally attacked by lettuce root aphid, which can cause wilting.

Harvesting

Harvest when the leaves have died down. Tubers shrivel after a week in the fridge so only lift when needed. They withstand most winters outdoors, but in cold areas mulch with straw against frost. Chinese artichokes sprout again from very tiny tubers, so after harvesting dig the ground thoroughly and remove all fragments if you do not want them to return.

Artichoke, globe

Cynara scolymus ASTERACEAE

This perennial plant – 1.2–1.5m (4–5ft) tall with a 90cm (36in) spread – is easy to grow but produces a relatively small crop for the space, making it more suitable for a larger plot. It makes a fine addition to an ornamental planting. The large spiky heads (flower buds) are eaten. Allowed to open, they become inedible, but bees love the magnificent peacock-blue thistle flowerheads.

PLANTING TO HARVEST Around 28 weeks in the first season. Thereafter, crop in May or June.
CROP DIVERSITY Heads usually green, but there is a purple form.
SITE Sunny, sheltered. Avoid heavy or wet soils, where it is less likely to survive the winter.
SOIL TREATMENT Apply a high-fertility soil improver, plus a low-fertility soil improver on dry soils.
IDEAL pH RANGE 6.5–7

Planting

Can be raised from seed, but with variable results; only some will produce good heads. They are usually grown from offsets (or divisions) taken from plants in April. Select only the best for division and discard the rest.

Spacing

At least 1 x 1.5m (3 x 5ft).

Plant care

Water until established. Mulch with hay or compost. Protect from frost by covering the crown with straw or bracken. Remove in the spring before growth starts. The productive life of artichokes is 3–4 years, so take offsets from a third of your plants every year to keep supplies going.
PROBLEMS Usually trouble-free. Aphids may be a nuisance but can be washed off using a hose.

Harvesting

Globe artichokes produce several large heads from July to September. Harvest them when plump but still tender, with scales still tight, and eat fresh. Removing side buds will increase the size of the main head. Cook heads whole and eat the fleshy pads at the base of the scales. Before eating the heart at the top of the stem, remove all of the fibrous "choke".

Artichoke, Jerusalem

Helianthus tuberosus ASTERACEAE

Not for small gardens, this perennial crop provides good cover for birds and amphibians, crowds out many weeds, and makes a useful summer windbreak. It sometimes produces pretty sunflower-like blooms. The edible parts are the knobbly tubers that grow in the soil.

PLANTING TO HARVEST 16–20 weeks.
CROP DIVERSITY Tubers are smooth or knobbly, creamy-yellow or red.
SITE Sun or partial shade. Avoid poorly drained soils.
SOIL TREATMENT Apply a medium-fertility soil improver before planting. High-fertility materials produce larger tubers.
IDEAL pH RANGE 6–7.5

Planting

Plant tubers 15cm (6in) deep in February or March.

Spacing

ROWS 30cm x 1m (12in x 3ft)
BLOCK PLANTING 45cm (18in)

Plant care

Support with stout stakes and wires or individual canes in windy areas. Earth up 4–10cm (1½–4in) of soil around the roots in early summer for additional support. Watering in dry weather and removing flower buds will increase the yield. When leaves turn yellow in late summer, cut stems to 15cm (6in).
PROBLEMS Usually trouble-free. Occasionally attacked by slugs and wireworms.

Harvesting

Tubers do not store well once harvested so they are best dug when required for the kitchen, after the leaves have turned yellow. Replant some for the next season if required. Remove all tubers if you want to clear the area.

Cultivar choice
Globe artichoke
'Green Globe'; 'Purple Globe'; 'Romanesco'.
Jerusalem artichoke
'Fuseau' – smooth tubers; 'Sunray' – shorter variety, often has a sunflower-like flower.
Arugula *See Rocket*

Chinese artichoke

Globe artichoke

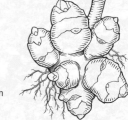
Jerusalem artichoke

Asparagus

Asparagus officinalis ASPARAGACEAE

A perennial crop, easy to grow once established. It provides a gourmet harvest of delicious spears from April to June. Yields are relatively small for the growing area needed, but a bed can crop for 20 years. It is vital that all perennial weeds are cleared before planting.

SEED TO HARVEST 2–3 years.
CROP DIVERSITY Plants are either male or female. Traditional cultivars produce a mixture of both. All-male F1 cultivars give slimmer spears in larger numbers over a longer season. Female spears are said to be more succulent. Most spears are green, but a purple cultivar is available.
SITE Will grow in a wide range of not too fertile soils. Good drainage is essential, as is a deep root run. Lime if pH is below 6. Foliage can grow to over 90cm (36in) tall, so avoid windy sites.
SOIL TREATMENT Dig over well, removing all weeds. Add a medium-fertility soil improver in the winter before planting.
IDEAL pH RANGE 6.5–7.5

Sowing

Can be raised from seed. To shorten time to cropping, buy one-year-old plants, known as crowns. Module-raised plants are also available.
UNDER COVER F1 hybrid seed is costly, so it is advisable to sow it under cover. Sow in large modules or 9cm (3½in) pots in February. Maintain a temperature of 13–16°C (55–61°F) until plants are 10–15cm (4–6in) tall.

Harden off and plant out in June.
OUTSIDE Sow open-pollinated asparagus seed March–April on a prepared seedbed 2.5cm (1in) deep in rows 46cm (18in) apart. Thin to 15cm (6in). Select the best seedlings to plant out in spring as one-year-old crowns.
MINIMUM GERMINATION TEMPERATURE 10°C (50°F).

Planting

MODULE-GROWN TRANSPLANTS Plant up to early summer, at a depth of 10cm (4in).
ONE-YEAR-OLD CROWNS Plant without delay in March and early April. Dig a trench 25cm (10in) deep, 30cm (12in) wide, forming a mounded ridge of soil along the bottom. When sitting on this mound the crowns should be 10cm (4in) deep. Spread out the fragile roots carefully, then gently fill in the trench to the level of the crowns. Keep filling as they grow, always leaving 8–10cm (3–4in) of stem showing.

Spacing

ROWS Asparagus grown in single rows will crop for longer as it takes more time for the bed to become congested. Space plants 30–40cm x 2m (12–16in x 6ft).
BEDS Asparagus is traditionally grown in 3-row beds, with 30cm (12in) between plants and rows, and 1.3m (4½ft) between beds.

Plant care

Keep watered in the first year to establish. Protect young shoots with horticultural fleece in cold springs. Well-grown plants may need support in summer. Weeding is a crucial job – once perennial weeds are established they are almost impossible to eradicate. Mulch once the spears have emerged with a medium- or low-fertility soil improver (the latter on fertile soil) to control weeds and feed the foliage, or fern. Hand-weed as necessary; do not hoe as asparagus is shallow-rooted. Cut the fern close to the ground once it turns yellow in

the autumn. Asparagus beetle can overwinter in old stems, so prompt removal is important.
PROBLEMS Asparagus beetle, slugs, violet root rot.

Harvesting

Cut spears sparingly at first until crowns are established. Hybrid cultivars can be cut lightly in the second year after planting as crowns or module-grown plants. In the third year harvest for 6 weeks, and from then on for 8 weeks if plants are growing well. Asparagus is ready to cut when spears are 15cm (6in) tall. Cut the spears 2.5–5cm (1–2in) below soil level. Cut all spears during the harvest period to maintain a supply. Asparagus is best eaten fresh. Store in a fridge for no more than 3–4 days.

Asparagus pea

Lotus tetragonolobus
PAPILIONACEAE

An attractive half-hardy annual with small, winged, edible pods. Its bright green leaves and crimson flowers make it worth growing for its appearance alone. It enjoys light but fertile, open soils and a sunny site, and will succeed in hot, dry soils where true peas fail. It can also be grown in containers. No soil treatment is needed before sowing if soil was improved for a previous crop. Otherwise, apply a low- or medium-fertility soil improver depending on soil conditions. Sow under cover in April and May in trays or modules, barely covering the seed. Harden off and plant

---

Asparagus: The Four-year Sacrificial Crop

Useful if you have sufficient land, especially on an allotment with a known weed problem or where you do not want to tie up an area for 10 years or so. Once this system is established, the asparagus can be fitted into a normal vegetable crop rotation pattern, with a much shorter wait for the crop to come into harvest.

YEAR 1 Prepare a bed and on it station-sow open-pollinated seed, 10cm x 25cm (4in x10in) apart. Keep the plants weed-free as they grow and develop, and cut the fern back in autumn.
YEAR 2 Prepare and sow another bed. Cut a few of the fattest spears (not more than one per 45cm (18in) of row) from the first bed.
YEAR 3 Sow another bed. Cut about a third of the fattest spears from the first plot, and a few from the second.
YEAR 4 Sow another seedbed. Cut all spears from the first plot, which can then be dug over and used for a different crop; harvest the one- and two-year-old beds as above.

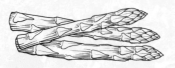

Asparagus

Asparagus pea

outside six weeks after sowing. Sow outside from mid-April to the end of May, 2cm (¾in) deep. Space in rows 10–15cm x 30cm (4–6in x 12in) or in blocks 20cm (8in) each way. Watering once flowers have set makes pods more tender. Cropping starts 8–10 weeks after sowing. Pick pods regularly when 2–3cm (1in) long; they quickly become stringy and tough. Picking is easiest in the evening, as the leaves fold down.

Aubergine

Solanum melongena SOLANACEAE

A tender, tropical plant best grown under cover. Can be grown outside in a good season in a very warm, sunny location, though it must be sown indoors. Aubergine (or eggplant) plants are relatively compact and bushy.

SEED TO HARVEST 16–24 weeks.
CROP DIVERSITY Most cultivars have purple fruits, and may be round, long or oval. Some have egg-like white fruits.
SITE Well-drained, fertile soil. Grow in a very warm, sheltered site in the south, or in a cool polytunnel or greenhouse. Aubergines need temperatures of 25–30°C (75–86°F) for good production. Growth is stalled below 20°C (68°F). Aubergines also do well in pots and other containers, which can stand outside in good weather.
SOIL TREATMENT Apply a medium-fertility soil improver before planting into soil. In pots, use a rich multipurpose compost.
IDEAL pH RANGE 6.5

Sowing

MINIMUM GERMINATION TEMPERATURE 21°C (70°F). Sow under cover in gentle heat from mid-February to March. Prick out into 10cm (4in) pots, and keep at 16–18°C (60–64°F). When first flowers appear plant in a soil bed under cover, or into 20cm (8in) pots or growing bags. Put plants outside only when danger of frost has passed.

Spacing

40–45cm (16–18in) each way.

Plant care

Tall plants may need a cane for support. For good-sized fruits, allow only 4 to 6 to grow on a plant. Keep well watered. Feed container plants with a high-potash organic liquid feed once fruits have started to set.
PROBLEMS Glasshouse red spider mite and whitefly; aphids.

Harvesting

Harvest once required size is reached, when skin is still shiny.

Beans, broad

Vicia faba PAPILIONACEAE

The broad or fava bean is a hardy, reliable crop that thrives in cool conditions. It can be sown in autumn or spring for midsummer harvest. Dwarf and shorter varieties can be grown in large containers. Broad beans will fix nitrogen in the soil. The sweet-scented flowers attract bees.

SEED TO HARVEST Spring-sown crops: 12–16 weeks. Autumn-sown crops: 28–35 weeks.

CROP DIVERSITY Dwarf and tall cultivars with green, white (pale green) or red seeds. Green-seeded plants are said to be tastier than white. Longpod varieties tend to be hardier than shorter-podded "Windsors". Most are white-flowered; there is also a crimson-flowered heritage variety.
SITE Open, sunny site; winter crops may need shelter. Will not do well on dry or waterlogged soils. Lime-tolerant.
SOIL TREATMENT Apply a low-fertility soil improver to light soils before sowing.
IDEAL pH RANGE 6–7

Sowing

MINIMUM GERMINATION TEMPERATURE 5°C (41°F).
UNDER COVER For early crops, sow in boxes or biodegradable tubes; transplant with 3–4 true leaves. Rapid growth of young plants limits root diseases; also useful if mice tend to eat seeds.
OUTSIDE In late autumn, sow extra-hardy cultivars in well-drained, sheltered sites. In spring, sow from February to April. Plants stop growing well at temperatures above 15°C (59°F).

Spacing

ROWS Usually grown in double rows, 15–20cm (6–9in) between plants, 60cm (24in) between rows.
BLOCK 20–30cm (8–12in).

Plant care

Pinch out the growing tips once the bottom flower clusters have opened, to deter black bean aphid. Earlier sowings are usually less prone to attack. Tall varieties may need a support of canes and string when pods swell, especially on windy sites.

PROBLEMS Mice; pea and bean weevil; black bean aphid; broad bean chocolate spot; broad bean rust; foot and root rot.

Harvesting

Harvest pods when beans can just be felt through them, before they get large and tough. Young pods may be eaten whole. Broad beans freeze well.

Beans, French

Phaseolus vulgaris PAPILIONACEAE

These produce good crops (often more reliably than runner beans) in a relatively small space but need warm conditions for a successful start. Usually eaten as young fresh pods, in drier regions these can be used to produce a crop of dry beans. Also called string, haricot or kidney beans.

SEED TO HARVEST 7–13 weeks. Dwarf cultivars start earliest. 16–18 weeks for dry beans.
CROP DIVERSITY Available in climbing or dwarf cultivars, with round (pencil) or flat pods. The lilac, purple and white flowers are decorative; the pods can be striped, violet or yellow as well as green. Yellow pods have a more waxy texture and a good flavour. For growing under cover, pick a compact dwarf variety, or if space allows grow a climbing variety, which may be less prone to disease as there is a better flow of air around the plants.
SITE Warm site and soil, sunny and sheltered. Can be grown in an unheated greenhouse or polytunnel, or in containers.

Cultivar choice
Aubergine 'Long Purple' – first introduced in 1905; 'Black Beauty' F1; 'White Egg'; 'Italian Pink Bicolour'.
Broad beans 'Aquadulce Claudia'; 'Super Aquadulce' – hardiest for autumn sowing; 'Green Windsor'; 'White Windsor' – spring sowing only; 'Witkiem Manita' – early-maturing, white-seeded; 'Red Epicure' – reddish beans that retain their colour if steamed; 'Crimson-flowered' – HDRA's broad bean, only available in the UK to members of the Heritage Seed Library; 'Futura' – tolerant of chocolate spot; 'The Sutton' – dwarf cultivar.

Aubergine

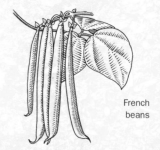

French beans

SOIL TREATMENT None needed on a reasonable soil, or one improved for a previous crop. If not, add a medium-fertility soil improver before sowing.
IDEAL pH RANGE 6.5–7.5

Sowing

MINIMUM GERMINATION TEMPERATURE 13°C (55°F)
UNDER COVER To get an early start for plants for dry bean production, and for early crops, sow in April under cover in deep wooden boxes lined with newspaper, or in biodegradable tubes, root trainers, or 9cm (3½in) pots. Harden off before planting outside only after the last frost.
OUTSIDE Sow from early summer, when the soil is warm enough, until late June. Warm the soil with cloches or black plastic to benefit early sowings. The last sowings, which should be dwarf varieties, may need cloche protection. Sow 5cm (2in) deep. Expect about 75% germination – always put a few extra beans in at the end of a row for transplanting into gaps.

Spacing

ROWS Dwarf beans: 5–7cm x 45–60cm (2–3in x 18–24in), depending on cultivar. Climbing beans: Grow up wigwams or in double rows 60cm (24in) apart, with 1.5m (5ft) between double rows. Sow 2 seeds per support, with 10–12cm (4–5in) between supports. Closer spacing is possible in containers but does increase risk of disease.
BLOCK PLANTING Dwarf beans: 15–20cm (6–8in). Close planting delays harvesting by a week or so.
UNDER COVER Use wider spacing to lessen the risk of disease.

Plant care

Use bottle cloches to prevent pests taking the seeds and eating seedlings. Use tall cane or pole supports for climbing beans. Taller dwarf cultivars may benefit from the support of twiggy sticks. Watering as the pods develop increases yield.
PROBLEMS Mice; bean seed fly; slugs; red spider mite; black bean aphid; halo blight; viruses.

Harvesting

Pick fresh beans as soon as they are large enough. Check plants at least every other day, as beans develop very quickly and plants can stop producing as soon as a single pod is allowed to mature. Purple and yellow pods are easier to spot than the green ones. The beans freeze well, and can also be turned into chutney. Do not pick fresh beans from a drying crop as this will delay maturity. Leave the pods to dry on the plants until they rattle. Drying can be completed indoors in bad weather. Hang whole plants upside down in a warm airy place until dry.

Beans, runner

Phaseolus coccineus PAPILIONACEAE

A frost-tender perennial, usually grown as an annual. A prolific cropper, with attractive flowers and long, rough pods that are eaten young before the seeds develop. Easy to grow. Most climb to 3m (10ft) or so, making a useful and attractive screen, if grown in a row, or wigwam. Runner beans produce a tuber, which can be stored over winter (or may survive in light soil) to produce plants the next season. These may be less vigorous than those grown from seed.

SEED TO HARVEST 12–16 weeks.
CROP DIVERSITY Flowers can be scarlet, white, bicoloured or salmon. Pods are always green, but seeds may be white, black or purple-speckled. Dwarf cultivars, growing to around 38cm (15in) tall, are available.
SITE Sheltered, sunny, with moisture-retentive soil to allow deep rooting. Dwarf cultivars can be grown in containers.
SOIL TREATMENT Grow on soil improved for a previous crop. Where necessary, apply a low-fertility soil improver to ensure a good water supply, or grow on a "compost trench" (see p.48).
IDEAL pH RANGE 6.5

Sowing

MINIMUM GERMINATION TEMPERATURE 12°C (54°F)
UNDER COVER Sow in May in deep trays, biodegradable tube pots or root trainers. Transplant after the last frost in warm soil.
OUTSIDE Station-sow, 2 seeds per station, from late May to early July once the soil has warmed up; a second sowing for a later crop is worthwhile.

Spacing

ROWS In double rows – 15cm x 60cm (6in x 2ft), or up a circular cane wigwam. Bush varieties – 15 x 60cm (6in x 2ft).
BLOCK PLANTING Dwarf cultivars only, 30cm (12in).

Plant care

The plants need a strong framework of 2.5m (8ft) bamboo canes to support the fully grown plants and their crop. Mulch well once plants are established. Water regularly in dry weather once the first flower buds appear to encourage more flowers. The flowers must be pollinated to produce pods.
PROBLEMS Birds; slugs; root aphids; bean seed fly; foot and root rots; halo blight. Poor pod set (see also *Poor/no fruit set*, p.385) can be due to frosts at flowering time; water shortage; poor weather reducing the activity of pollinating insects; a site too exposed for the insects; or sparrows pecking at flowers.

Harvesting

Pick young pods 17cm (7in) or so in length. Regular picking encourages more pods to form.

Beetroot

Beta vulgaris subsp. *vulgaris*
CHENOPODIACEAE

Easy and quick to grow, beetroot can be sown outdoors over a long period, from March to June.

SEED TO HARVEST 7–13 weeks.
CROP DIVERSITY Roots can be red, yellow or white, and round, cylindrical or long. Bolt-hardy cultivars (resistant to bolting caused by cold weather when young) are good for early sowings. The green and red foliage is attractive, but the old cultivar 'Bulls Blood', with its deep red foliage, is most colourful. Suitable for mini-veg.
SITE Open, sunny. Beetroot is salt-tolerant – useful in coastal gardens – but does not tolerate

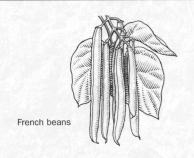
French beans

Cultivar choice

French beans Dwarf: 'The Prince'; 'Tendergreen'; 'Mont D'Or' – yellow pods; 'Purple Queen' – purple pods; 'Aroza' RZ – resistant to the common mosaic virus. Climbing: 'Blue Lake'; 'Viola Cornetti'. For drying: 'Brown Dutch' – golden brown seeds; 'Horsehead' – dark red seeds.
Runner beans 'Scarlet Emperor' – traditional variety from 1906; 'Czar' – white-seeded (can be left to produce a dry bean crop); 'Enorma Elite' – slim, stringless pods; 'Painted Lady' – less vigorous plants, bicoloured flower; 'Hestia' – dwarf, bicoloured flower.
Beetroot 'Boltardy'; 'Pronto'; 'Moneta' (monogerm) – resistant to bolting; 'Forono' – for storage, cylindrical; 'Monaco' – mini-beet; 'Golden' – yellow flesh; 'Chioggia' – red and white flesh.

an acid soil. The round "ball" cultivars grow well in containers.
SOIL TREATMENT Nothing required on a fertile soil or one improved for a previous crop. Apply a low-fertility soil improver to light or heavy soils.
IDEAL pH RANGE 6.5–7.5

Sowing

Seeds are usually multi-germ: each produces several seedlings. Monogerm types are specially bred to produce a single seedling from each seed.
MINIMUM GERMINATION TEMPERATURE 7°C (45°F)
UNDER COVER Start sowing in late February or early March. Sow in modules, 2 seeds (or 2–3 monogerm seeds) per cell. Thin to strongest seedling. For multi-sowing, allow 4–5 seedlings per module. Use a small-rooted cultivar. Harden off when plants have 3–4 true leaves before transplanting outside.
OUTSIDE Sow from March or April until late June, or a fort-night later in mild areas. To grow beet for storage, sow globe or long cultivars in May and June.

Spacing

Spacing can be adjusted to some extent depending on the cultivar and size of root required.
ROWS Early and quick crops: 10 x 23cm (4 x 9in).
Maincrops: 7.5 x 30cm (3 x 12in).
Mini-beet: 2.5 x 15cm (1 x 6in).
Multisown: 22 x 22 cm (9 x 9in).
BLOCK PLANTING 12.5–15cm (5–6in) apart.

Plant care

Water often in hot, dry weather or the roots will become woody.
PROBLEMS Usually trouble-free.

Harvesting

Harvest roots as soon as they are the right size. For storage, harvest in autumn. Roots can be left in the soil over winter but may become tough and slug-eaten. Twist, rather than cut, the tops off. Store beets in a cool, dark and humid place, such as a box of moist sand.

Beet, leaf

Beta vulgaris Cicla Group
CHENOPODIACEAE

Also called perpetual spinach or spinach beet, with edible stems and leaves. It can crop year-round. Similar in flavour to spinach, but more reliable.

SEED TO HARVEST 8–12 weeks.
CROP DIVERSITY None.
SITE Tolerates salt-laden winds and some shade. A good winter crop under cover.
SOIL TREATMENT Apply a low-fertility soil improver if soil was manured or composted for a previous crop. Otherwise use a medium-fertility improver, or a low-fertility material with a nitrogen-rich organic fertiliser.
IDEAL pH RANGE 6.5–7.5

Sowing

MINIMUM GERMINATION TEMPERATURE 8°C (46°F)
UNDER COVER Sow the "multi-germed" seeds in modules in March and April. Thin to the strongest seedling, or plant in clumps for a seedling crop. Harden off before planting outside. For a winter crop under cover, sow in August.
OUTSIDE Station-sow, half a

thumb deep, in March and April to crop over the summer and autumn. Sow in July and August to crop over winter and spring.
SEEDLING CUTTING CROP Broadcast thinly in early autumn for cutting in winter under cover.

Spacing

ROWS 23 x 38cm (9 x 15in)
BLOCK PLANTING 23cm (9in)

Plant care

Water in dry weather. Mulch to retain moisture; use a medium-fertility soil improver to boost growth.
PROBLEMS Beet leaf miner; beet leaf spot.

Harvesting

Pick leaves from the outside first as soon as they are big enough to eat. Cutting crops are ready very quickly; take the first cut at about 5cm (2in) tall. Allow to regrow slightly taller before the next cut. To rejuvenate older plants cut all the leaves off just above the soil to encourage new growth.

Broccoli, sprouting and calabrese

Brassica oleracea Italica Group
BRASSICACEAE

Sprouting broccoli is hardy and easy to grow. It is in the ground from midsummer until the next spring. Each plant can take up to 1sq m (10sq ft) of ground, but repays this by cropping when vegetables are scarce. Calabrese is a tasty, fast-maturing, green-headed broccoli, cropping from early summer to autumn. It is

smaller and less hardy, but produces larger, denser heads.

SEED TO HARVEST Sprouting broccoli: 8–12 months; calabrese: 11–14 weeks.
CROP DIVERSITY There used to be little choice with sprouting broccoli, but modern cultivars can be earlier to crop, with larger spears. A white sprouting cultivar is also available. Calabrese cultivars are early, mid-season and late.
SITE Open, but protected from strong winds. Calabrese will crop on less fertile soils than other brassicas and is suitable for early and late cropping under cover.
SOIL TREATMENT Apply a medium-fertility soil improver, or a low-fertility soil improver with a general organic fertiliser, in the spring before planting – or plant after a nitrogen-fixing green manure crop.
IDEAL pH RANGE Sprouting broccoli 6–7.5; calabrese 6.5–7.5.

Sowing

MINIMUM GERMINATION TEMPERATURE Sprouting broccoli 7°C (45°F); calabrese 5°C (41°F).
UNDER COVER Sow sprouting broccoli in modules or in a seed bed from April to mid-May. Harden off before planting out. Calabrese resents root disturb-ance and must be sown in modules or biodegradable pots. For an early crop, sow in March. Harden off and plant outside 4–5 weeks after sowing. Overwinter a late summer sowing of an early-maturing calabrese in an unheated polytunnel or greenhouse to crop the following spring.
OUTSIDE Sow sprouting broccoli

Cultivar choice
Broccoli Sprouting broccoli:'Rudolph' – can start cropping in December; 'Purple Sprouting Early' – a reliable, traditional cultivar; 'Claret' F1 – the first hybrid; 'Red Arrow' F1 – a shorter, bushier plant with masses of shoots; 'White Star' – white sprouts. Calabrese: 'Trixie' – tolerant of clubroot; 'Emperor' and 'Shogun'– resistant to downy mildew.

Borecole *See kale*

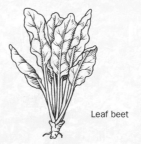
Leaf beet

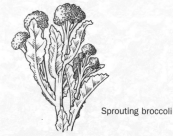
Sprouting broccoli

in a seedbed from mid-April to mid-May. Scatter seed thinly in drills 2–2.5cm (¾–1in) deep, aiming for 7.5cm (3in) between plants. Transplant in June and early July. Station-sow calabrese, 2–3 seeds per station, thinning to a single seedling. Sow April to July to crop from early summer through to autumn.

Spacing

Transplant deeply (with lowest leaf on the surface of the soil) to reduce the danger from cabbage root fly and encourage a good root system; firm around plants after planting.

ROWS Sprouting broccoli: 60cm (24in) apart, allowing 75cm (30in) between rows for easy picking. With calabrese, close spacing produces small heads maturing at once. Wider spacing gives more side shoots and larger central heads over a longer period. Close spacing: 8 x 60cm (3 x 24in). For maximum yield: staggered rows, 15 x 30cm (6 x 12in). For largest central heads: 20 x 45cm (8 x 18in).

BLOCK PLANTING Sprouting broccoli: 60cm (24in); calabrese: 20cm (8in).

Plant care

Protect young plants from cabbage root fly (see p.304); use crop covers of fleece or mesh to keep out other pests. Sprouting broccoli may need staking over winter; earthing up stems during the growing season encourages extra rooting. Water calabrese regularly in dry weather. If water is restricted, one good soak 2–3 weeks before harvest is best. Mulch with compost after cutting the central heads to en-courage sideshoot production.

PROBLEMS Cabbage root fly, mealy cabbage aphids, cabbage caterpillars, clubroot; flea beetle; birds. Calabrese may also get downy mildew.

Harvesting

Snap off sprouting broccoli shoots when buds show but before they open. Regular picking encourages more shoots. Harvesting period can last up to 2 months. Cut the central head of calabrese before flowers open. Expect 2–3 further pickings of small side-shoots.

Broccoli, 9-star

Brassica oleracea BRASSICACEAE

A short-term perennial producing small, cauliflower-like heads. Sow seed in mid-spring. Thin to 15cm (6in), then transplant into a rich, firm soil in early autumn. Leave 90cm (36in) between plants. Each plant produces 6–9 heads to harvest in the spring. Pick all heads, even if inedible, to stop them going to seed. Apply a medium-fertility soil improver each year after harvesting. Replace plants after three years. Control diseases and pests, especially mealy cabbage aphid and cabbage whitefly, as they can spread to other brassica crops.

Brussels sprouts

Brassica oleracea BRASSICACEAE

A hardy, cold weather crop for an autumn and winter harvest from a spring sowing. Needs a long growing season, but crops over a long period. Mature plants are very hardy. Their wide spacing leaves room for intercropping (see p.318) when young.

SEED TO HARVEST 20 weeks.
CROP DIVERSITY Early, mid and late season; dwarf (35cm/14in) and tall (75cm/30in) cultivars. Modern cultivars produce tighter, more compact sprouts. Green and red cultivars available.
SITE Open, full sun, in firm soil.
SOIL TREATMENT Add a medium-fertility soil improver, or a low-fertility improver plus a general organic fertiliser, in the spring before planting – or plant after a nitrogen-fixing green manure crop. Mulch with grass mowings or apply a chicken manure fertiliser mid-late July if plants are not growing vigorously.
IDEAL pH RANGE 6.5–8

Sowing

MINIMUM GERMINATION TEMPERATURE 7°C (45°F)
UNDER COVER For the earliest crop, sow in March in a seedbed or large module trays. Harden off and plant 6 weeks after sowing.
OUTSIDE Sow from mid-March to mid-April, starting with the early cultivars. Sow thinly in rows, 4cm x 20cm (1½in x 8in), in a seedbed. Plant out from late spring to early summer.

Spacing

Transplant deeply (with the lowest leaf on the surface of the soil) to reduce the danger from cabbage root fly; firm around plants well after planting.
ROWS Space short cultivars 45cm (18in) apart, tall cultivars 60cm–1m (24–36in) apart; allow 75cm (30in) between rows for ease of picking. Closer plantings give more uniform maturity of smaller sprouts.
BLOCK PLANTING 45–75cm (18–30in) depending on cultivar.

Plant care

Stake well on windy sites. Earth up stems as they grow for additional support. Remove pest- or disease-infested leaves.
PROBLEMS Flea beetle; mealy cabbage aphid; cabbage root fly (may also affect the sprouts); cabbage whitefly; birds; cabbage caterpillars; clubroot; downy mildew; brassica white blister.

Harvesting

Sprouts taste best after a frost. Harvest from the bottom of the stem, leaving those higher up to develop. To harvest a week's supply, pull a plant up and put it outside with its roots in a bucket of water to keep fresh. Can be frozen, but best eaten fresh.

Cabbage

Brassica oleracea BRASSICACEAE

A hardy crop that thrives in cool conditions and can be available all year round. Can grow large; choose varieties, or change plant spacing, for smaller heads.

SEED TO HARVEST 20 weeks.
CROP DIVERSITY Spring cabbage: sow in autumn, eat in spring as loose leaves – "spring greens" – or once hearts have developed.
Summer and autumn cabbages: sow in spring to mature in four to six months. May be ball- or pointed-headed.

Brussels sprouts

Spring cabbage

Cultivar choice
Brussels sprouts 'Oliver' F1; 'Peer Gynt' F1 – early cropping; 'Noisette' – tasty, pick over a long period; 'Braveheart' – late season, good disease resistance; 'Rubine' – red.

Calabrese *see Broccoli, sprouting and calabrese*

Winter cabbages May be white or Dutch – large, very tight, white heads, harvested during winter from a spring sowing, storing for months once cut – or Savoy: bubble-textured, with dark green leaves, very hardy and will stand all winter from a spring sowing. Crosses between these two types are also very hardy. Red cabbage, distinctive in looks and flavour, is usually grown to mature in late summer–autumn. It is often not as hardy as overwintering types but stores well.

Mini-veg: Some cultivars can also be grown as mini-veg.

SITE Open, sunny site. Tolerant of exposure. Some cabbages, such as smaller Savoys, look attractive in a flower garden.

SOIL TREATMENT Apply a medium-fertility soil improver, or a low-fertility soil improver plus a general organic fertiliser, before planting – or plant after a nitrogen-fixing green manure. Do not overfeed cabbages that are to overwinter. If growth is too lush it may not survive frost.

IDEAL pH RANGE 6–8

Sowing See table below.

MINIMUM GERMINATION TEMPERATURE 7°C (45°F)

UNDER COVER For extra-early crops sow an early summer cultivar in modules or trays in February or March. Harden off and plant out as soon as the soil is workable. An early crop can also be grown under cover. Later sowings can be made in trays or modules under cover.

OUTSIDE Sow thinly in a seed-bed. Transplant 5–6 weeks later.

Plant care

Protect seedlings and young plants from cabbage root fly (see p.304). Water transplants until established.

PROBLEMS Cabbage root fly; mealy cabbage aphid; cabbage caterpillars; flea beetle; clubroot; brassica white blister; pigeons.

Harvesting

Cut as needed. Spring cabbages on fertile soil can give two crops: after cutting the head, make a cross-cut on the remaining stalk, and several small cabbages will develop. Autumn and winter cabbages can be stored (see p.334).

SOWING AND SPACING FOR CABBAGE

Type	Sow in	Spacing in rows & blocks*
Spring	August	30cm (12in), or 10cm x 30cm (4 x 12in) thinning to 30cm (12in), eating the thinnings as spring greens.
Early summer	February, March	35–45cm (14–18in)
Summer	March	35–45cm (14–18in)
Autumn	May	50cm (20in)
Winter	May	50cm (20in)

* spacing can vary depending on variety choice and size of final head required (see also p.316)

Cabbage, Chinese

Brassica rapa var. *pekinensis*
BRASSICACEAE

Chinese cabbage has an upright head and is dark to pale yellowy-green in colour. A quick-growing and mild-flavoured late summer and autumn crop, good stir-fried and raw in salads. Prone to bolting if growth is checked by transplanting or drought.

SEED TO HARVEST 8–10 weeks.
CROP DIVERSITY Heads may be dense or loose, short and barrel-shaped or taller and cylindrical.
SITE Humus-rich, moisture-retentive soil. Tolerates some shade in summer. Good as a late season crop under cover.
SOIL TREATMENT Apply a low- to medium-fertility soil improver before planting.
IDEAL pH RANGE 6.5–7

Sowing

MINIMUM GERMINATION TEMPERATURE 10°C (50°F)
UNDER COVER Sow in modules from May to August; choose bolt-resistant cultivars to sow before midsummer. Harden off before transplanting. Late crops can be planted out under cover in September.
OUTSIDE Station-sow, or sow thinly, from mid-June to August.

Spacing

ROWS 30 x 45cm (12 x 18in)
BLOCK PLANTING 35cm (14in)

Plant care

Water regularly in dry weather. Mulch with a low-fertility soil improver to retain moisture. Grow under fleece or fine mesh netting if flea beetle is a problem.
PROBLEMS Flea beetle; caterpillars; slugs; clubroot.

Harvesting

Cut semi-mature or mature heads. Stumps may sprout new leaves.

Cardoon

Cynara cardunculus ASTERACEAE

A large perennial, closely related to globe artichokes, 1.2–1.5m (4–5ft) tall with a 90cm (3ft) spread. It is easy to grow, but produces a small crop for the space. Although a perennial, cardoon is grown as an annual for eating. The stems, when blanched, are the edible parts. It is beautiful in flower in its second year if not harvested.

SEED TO HARVEST 34 weeks.
SITE Sunny, sheltered. Avoid heavy or wet soils. Can be grown in large pots and mixed borders.
SOIL TREATMENT Apply a high-fertility soil improver, plus a low-fertility soil improver on dry soils. Can be grown on a compost trench (see p.48).
IDEAL pH RANGE 6.5–7

Sowing

MINIMUM GERMINATION TEMPERATURE 13°C (55°F)
UNDER COVER In spring, sow 2–3 seeds in a 9cm (3½in) pot in a sandy compost in gentle heat. Thin to one seedling and harden off. Transplant after the last frost when plants have 3–4 leaves.
OUTSIDE Cardoons can be sown direct. Station-sow 3–4 seeds, 2.5cm (1in) deep, in April.

Cultivar choice
Cabbage Spring cabbage: 'Flower of Spring'; 'Wintergreen' – for spring greens; 'Spring Hero' F1 – ball-headed. Early summer: 'Greyhound'. Summer cabbage: 'Minicole' F1 – compact, stands in good condition for weeks; 'Stonehead'. Autumn cabbage: 'Cuor di Bue'; 'Winningstadt'. Winter cabbage: 'January King'; 'Tundra' F1; 'Holland Late Winter'. Red cabbage: 'Red Drumhead'. Savoy: 'Vertus'; 'Wirosa' F1; 'Ormskirk Late'.
Chinese cabbage 'Green Rocket' F1 – cylindrical type for later sowing; 'Tip Top' F1 – good resistance to bolting.
Cardoon 'Gigante di Romagna'.

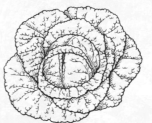
Savoy cabbage

Chinese cabbage

Spacing

50cm x 1.5m (20in x 5ft)

Plant care

Cardoons need regular watering to produce large succulent stems, and a compost or hay mulch. On a dry day in early autumn, blanch stems by pulling them into a bundle. Wear gloves. Tie with soft string. Wrap a collar of cardboard or thick newspaper round leaves to exclude light. Tie tightly. Stake the collar on exposed sites.
PROBLEMS Usually trouble-free. Aphids are an occasional nuisance but can be washed off using a jet of water from a hose.

Harvesting

Cardoons are ready after about a month of blanching, and will stand blanched until hard frosts. Lift plants with a fork, cut off the roots and outer leaves. If the weather turns cold, cut and store in a dark, frost-free place. Eat leaf midribs and hearts, raw or cooked.

Carrot

Daucus carota APIACEAE

Carrots are not suited to all soils and can be a challenge to grow. Using a selection of cultivars, you can harvest carrots almost all year round. They can be closely spaced, giving a good yield from a relatively small area.

SEED TO HARVEST Early cultivars: 9 weeks. Maincrop cultivars: 20 weeks.
CROP DIVERSITY Early cultivars are used for the quickest crops, sown in succession through the season, and for crops under cover and in containers. Maincrop cultivars have larger roots, for summer and autumn harvest; also suitable for winter storage. Root shape can be small and round, slender or broad, short or long, cylindrical or tapering. Most are orange, red or yellow; purple and white cultivars exist, mainly in seed library collections. Can be grown as mini-veg.
SITE Medium to light, stone-free soil in a sunny, open site. Shorter varieties grow well in containers. Early and late crops can be grown under cover.
SOIL TREATMENT No additional feeding is needed on reasonable soil, or on soil manured or composted for a previous crop. Mulching with a low-fertility soil improver in the previous winter can be beneficial. Do not sow immediately following a grazing rye green manure crop.
IDEAL pH RANGE 6.5–7.5

Sowing

Germination is often slow and uneven. Improve by using primed seed (p.314), or fluid-sowing pre-germinated seed (see p.110).
MINIMUM GERMINATION TEMPERATURE 7°C (45 °F)
UNDER COVER Best sown direct as roots do not develop well if disturbed. Round-rooted cultivars may be started off in modules; short-rooted cultivars may be raised in biodegradable tubes, which are transplanted whole. For growing under cover, sow from February to August; February to June for transplanting outdoors.
OUTSIDE Start sowing early cultivars as soon as soil is warm enough, in February or March. Maincrops can be sown from April to June. For winter storage, sow in late May or June so the roots are not too large when they are lifted in the autumn. Scatter seed thinly in shallow drills, 2cm (¾in) deep, or station-sow 3–4 seeds per station.

Spacing

Early (quick) cultivars are often grown at wider spacing than maincrops to aid rapid growth.
ROWS Sow thinly in rows 15cm (6in) apart. Thin early carrots to 7cm (3in). Thin medium-sized maincrop roots to 4cm (1½in), up to 7cm (3in) for larger roots.
BLOCK PLANTING Sow broadcast, then thin to 7–15cm (3–6in).
MINI-VEG 1cm (½in) x 15cm (6in).

Plant care

Keep weed-free when young. Water well in dry weather.
PROBLEMS Diseases and disorders are rarely a problem. The main pest is carrot fly: to avoid this pest, grow the crop under fleece or fine mesh netting. Carrots sown in early June miss the first generation of fly attack and are large enough to survive a second generation attack. Carrot fly may be attracted by the scent of crushed carrot foliage, so sow thinly to minimise the need for thinning. Thin in the evening, not in bright sun when carrot flies will be active and scent the damaged leaves. Feed thinnings to pets or bury deep in the compost heap. Onions may offer protection. Grow 4 rows of onions for every row of carrots.

Harvesting

Pull roots while young. Maincrop roots may be left in the ground over winter and dug as required.

In cold areas protect with a straw mulch. Storage in the ground is not advisable in heavy soils or where carrot fly is a problem. Lift October–November for storage.

Cauliflower

Brassica oleracea BRASSICACEAE

Cauliflowers can be difficult to grow well. They need moisture throughout the growing season, so autumn- and spring-heading types are easier. Most are large plants which can be in the ground for up to a year. For small gardens, early summer and mini-cauliflowers are best.

SEED TO HARVEST Summer and autumn cauliflowers – 16 weeks. Winter cauliflower – 40 weeks. Mini-veg – 15 weeks.
CROP DIVERSITY A wide range of cultivars is available, suited to different growing and cropping seasons from early summer to winter. Most are white, but can also be orange, green and purple-headed. Suitable for mini-veg.
SITE Open sunny site; avoid frost. Fertile, moisture-retentive soil.
SOIL TREATMENT Apply a medium-fertility soil improver, or a low-fertility soil improver plus a general organic fertiliser, before planting – or plant after a nitrogen-fixing green manure.
IDEAL pH RANGE 6.5–8

Sowing

Best sown in modules or pots to reduce transplanting check. For sowing times and spacings, see the table overleaf. Harden off and transplant as soon as possible – around 6 weeks after sowing.

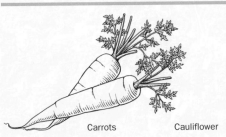

Carrots

Cauliflower

Can also be sown outdoors in a seedbed, leaving at least 5cm (2in) between seedlings.
MINIMUM GERMINATION TEMPERATURE 7°C (45°F)

Spacing
See table below.

Plant care
Cauliflowers resent any check to growth. Mulch, and water in dry weather to keep growth active. Firm around plants in frosty or windy conditions. Protect heads against frosts, rain and heavy dew in autumn by tying up leaves. This will also keep curds white. Modern varieties often have leaves that naturally protect the heads.
PROBLEMS Clubroot (see p.304). Protect against cabbage root fly, whitefly and caterpillars with a fine mesh cover. Small, premature and deformed heads are usually the result of a check to growth, often by transplanting or drought. "Whiptail" (narrow leaves, curds fail to develop) is caused by boron deficiency, usually when soil is too acid.

Harvesting
Select tight, small-curded heads. Curds starting to separate or turn yellow or brown are a sign of overmaturity and deterioration. Mini-cauliflowers will not stay in good condition for long. Cauliflowers keep for a week in the fridge, or can be hung upside down for up to 3 weeks in a cool dark shed – occasionally mist with a fine water spray to keep humid.

Celeriac

Apium graveolens var. *rapaceum* APIACEAE

Celeriac produces a large, celery-flavoured "bulb" – a swollen stem. Leaves can also be used to season dishes. A close relative of celery. Easier to grow, though it still needs a long season of unchecked growth to crop well.

SEED TO HARVEST 26 weeks.
CROP DIVERSITY There is little variation. Some cultivars are less prone to discolour when cooked.
SITE Needs a fertile, moisture-retentive soil to do well. Will grow in sun or semi-shade.
SOIL TREATMENT Apply a medium- to high-fertility soil improver, or a low-fertility soil improver with a nitrogen-rich organic fertiliser.
IDEAL pH RANGE 6.5–7.5

Sowing
MINIMUM GERMINATION TEMPERATURE Germinates best at 10–19°C (50–66°F).
UNDER COVER Sow in gentle heat (16°C/65°F) in February and March, or April and May if no heat available. Sow in trays or modules, thinning or pricking out into individual pots when large enough to handle. Harden off before planting out in May after the last frost. Take care not to bury the crown of the plant.

Spacing
30–38cm (12–15in) each way.

Plant care
Water in dry spells. Mulch to retain soil moisture. From mid-summer onwards remove lower leaves to expose the crown.
PROBLEMS May suffer from the same pests and diseases as celery, but is generally trouble-free.

Harvesting
Harvest from late summer to the following spring, starting when bulbs are large enough. Store in the ground if possible, covering with dry straw or bracken for protection against severe frosts. Can be lifted and stored indoors but quality will deteriorate.

Celery

Apium graveolens APIACEAE

Celery produces crisp, crunchy, succulent stems. Traditional trench celery is quite demanding of soil conditions and requires attention over a long growing season. Self-blanching celery is less labour-intensive and easier to grow but is not as hardy, nor so delicate in texture or flavour.

SEED TO HARVEST Self-blanching and green celery – 11–16 weeks. Trench celery – 9 months.
CROP DIVERSITY Trench celery is a traditional crop for late autumn with white, pink or red stems that are blanched before use. Self-blanching cultivars have creamy yellow stems, paler when grown in a block. American green cultivars have green stems that are not blanched.
SITE Must have fertile, moisture-retentive, well-drained soil. Prefers an open site, but tolerates some shade. Grows well in deep containers.
SOIL TREATMENT Apply a high-fertility soil improver, or one of low-to medium fertility with a nitrogen-rich organic fertiliser. For trench celery, in early spring

SOWING TIMES AND SPACINGS FOR CAULIFLOWER

Harvest	Sow indoors	Sow outdoors	Spacing in rows	Spacing in blocks
Early summer	Early October; early February		45cm (18in) x 60cm (24in)	53cm (21in)
Late summer	March	March (sheltered sites only)	45cm (18in) x 60cm (24in)	53cm (21in)
Early autumn	Late April	Late April	50cm (22in) x 60cm (24in)	55cm (22in)
Autumn	Mid-May	Late June	60cm (24in) x 66cm (26in)	64cm (25in)
Winter, frost-free areas only		Late May	70cm (28in) each way	70cm (28in)
Spring *		Late May	60cm (24in) x 66cm (26in)	64cm (25in)
Mini-cauliflowers	April to early July	April to early July	10cm (4in) x 23cm (9in)	12.5cm (5in)

* These plants should be grown "hard", that is with very little nitrogen, if they are to survive the winter.

Cultivar choice
Celeriac 'Prague Giant'; 'Prinz' – good resistance to bolting; 'President'.
Celery Trench cultivars: 'Hopkins Fenlander'; 'Solid Pink' – hardy trench cultivar, first introduced in 1894; 'Solid White'. American green: 'Tall Utah'. Self-blanching: 'Golden Self-Blanching'.

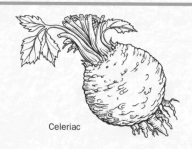

Celeriac

dig a trench 38–45cm (15–18in) wide, 30cm (12in) deep. Mix soil improvers, as above, into the soil removed, then fill in the trench to a depth of 7.5–10cm (3–4in). Use the remaining soil to blanch the celery as it grows. Trenches should be 1.2m (4ft) apart. Apply a general organic fertiliser to the trench bottom before planting if needed.
IDEAL pH RANGE 6.5–7.5

Sowing
UNDER COVER Sow in trays or modules in gentle heat in March and early April, no more than 10 weeks before the last frost. Sow on the surface of the compost, or cover only lightly. Germination can be slow and erratic. Fluid sowing *(p.000)* can improve it. Prick out into biodegradable pots. Thin modules to one seedling as early as possible. Plant out when conditions are warm enough. Plants may bolt if subjected to temperatures below 10°C (50°F) for more than 12 hours when young. Protect with cloches if necessary. If seedlings are growing fast and the weather is unfavourable for planting out, snip them down to 8cm (3in) tall with scissors to slow growth. Keep the plants under cover until outdoor conditions are suitable.
MULTI-SOWING Self-blanching celery only. Sow 6–8 seedlings per module, thinning to 2–3.
MINIMUM GERMINATION TEMPERATURE Germinates best at 10–19°C (50–66°F)

Spacing
ROWS Trench celery – 30–45cm (12–18in) between plants, 150cm (4ft) between trenches.
BLOCK PLANTING For self-blanching celery: 15–30cm (6–12in). Closer spacing gives a high yield of more slender stems.
MULTI-SOWING Self-blanching celery only: 20cm (8in).

Plant care
Water frequently and regularly in the growing season. Remove discoloured outer leaves. Blanch trench celery stems (see Cardoon) once plants are 30cm (12in) tall. Surround a block of mature self-blanching plants with straw to blanch outer rows.
PROBLEMS Celery crown rot; celery leaf miner; slugs; celery leaf spot; calcium deficiency caused by irregular water supply.

Harvesting
Harvest trench celery in the autumn, about 9–10 weeks after blanching begins. Blanched celery will stand in the ground for about a month in good condition, but is a magnet for slugs. Harvest self-blanching celery July–September. Celery is not totally hardy and will not survive prolonged frosts. When severe cold is forecast, lift plants and store in a cellar or in cool moist sand. Can be lifted and heeled in in a dark cold frame. Keeps for a week in the fridge.

Chard

Beta vulgaris Cicla Group
CHENOPODIACEAE

Easy-to-grow relative of beetroot also called seakale beet, grown for its stems and leaves. It crops for many months. Leaves have thick, often beautifully coloured midribs. The plant is attractive enough for an ornamental plot.

SEED TO HARVEST 8–12 weeks.
CROP DIVERSITY Swiss chard has white midribs. Other cultivars have midribs in ruby-red or a rainbow of colours.
SITE Will tolerate salt-laden winds (useful for seaside gardens) and some shade. The glowing stem colours are glorious in an autumn border. A good winter crop in an unheated polytunnel or greenhouse.
SOIL TREATMENT Apply a low-fertility soil improver if soil was manured or composted for a previous crop. Otherwise use a medium-fertility improver, or a low-fertility material with a nitrogen-rich organic fertiliser.
IDEAL pH RANGE 6.5–7.5

Sowing
MINIMUM GERMINATION TEMPERATURE 8°C (47°F)
UNDER COVER Sow individual seeds in modules in March and April. The seeds are "multi-germed", with several seedlings emerging from one seed. Thin to the strongest seedling, or plant as a clump for cutting as a seedling crop. Harden off before planting outside. For a winter crop under cover, sow in August; or for a seedling cutting crop, broadcast thinly in early autumn.
OUTSIDE Station-sow about half a thumb deep in March–April to crop in summer and autumn. Sow July–August to crop over winter and the following spring.

Spacing
ROWS 23 x 45cm (9 x 18in).
BLOCK PLANTING 30cm (12in).

Plant care
Water if necessary in dry weather. Mulch to retain moisture. Use a medium-fertility soil improver if growth needs a boost. Over-wintered crops can stand most winters unprotected but give a finer crop with the protection of cloches or horticultural fleece.
PROBLEMS Beet leaf miner.

Harvesting
Pick leaves from the outside as soon as they are big enough. Rejuvenate older plants if leaves have become coarse by cutting all the leaves off just above the soil. Cutting crops are soon ready; take the first cut when about 5cm (2in) tall. Allow to grow slightly taller before the next cut.

Chervil, turnip-rooted

Chaerophyllum bulbosum
APIACEAE

An unusual root vegetable that although very slow to germinate is easy to grow.

SITE Sunny, open; fertile soil.
SOIL TREATMENT Apply a medium-fertility soil improver, or grow on land manured or composted for a previous crop.
IDEAL pH RANGE 6.5–7.5

Sowing
Only suitable for sowing outside as it requires a period of cold to initiate germination. Sow in late summer–early autumn, covering seed lightly. Sow with another winter salad as seeds will not germinate until the spring.
GROWING IN ROWS 15–20cm x 30cm (6–8in x 12in).
BLOCK PLANTING 20cm (8in).

Cultivar choice
Chard Swiss Chard – white ribs; 'Bright Lights' – pink, red, yellow, orange and white ribs; 'Charlotte' – red ribs

Chilli peppers *see Peppers*

Celery

Plant care

Once germinated, plants have a relatively short growing season; do not let them suffer growth checks. Water regularly in dry conditions, and keep weed-free. **PROBLEMS** Usually trouble-free.

Harvesting

When leaves die back after mid-summer, roots are nearly mature. Start to use when leaves are quite withered, twisting off remaining leaves. Roots are said to improve in quality if left in the ground for a few weeks. Dig as required on light well-drained soils. Otherwise, lift and store in damp leaf-mould or sand. Eat roots boiled.

Chicory

Cichorium intybus ASTERACEAE

A hardy perennial, usually grown as an annual. Chicories have a distinctive, slightly bitter taste, and are a useful, colourful salad crop for the winter. Their leaves come in a wide range of shapes and colours; some produce hearts, and some can be forced or blanched to reduce bitterness Good ornamentals in containers.

SEED TO HARVEST Variable.
CROP DIVERSITY Witloof chicory is grown primarily for forcing. Roots are lifted and forced in the dark in winter to produce blanched plump shoots, knows as chicons (called endive in France). Red chicory (also known as radicchio) has red or variegated leaves. Some cultivars have a compact heart, others remain loose-leaved; some can be forced. Individual leaves can also be picked. The best colour develops with shortening days and cool nights, though new cultivars are naturally red. Not always hardy in cold winters. Cutting chicory produces small rosettes of leaves for cutting.

Sugarloaf chicories look rather like large, green cos lettuce when mature, and are harvested in autumn. Plants are drought-resistant once established, and withstand light frosts. Can be grown as a seedling cutting crop.
SITE Avoid very light or heavy soils. Tolerate some shade. Witloof chicories need deep soil to produce good roots for forcing. Grow non-forcing types in a cool polytunnel or greenhouse for early and late crops, and over winter. Chicories are decorative enough for containers or at the front of a border.
SOIL TREATMENT None needed on most soils, especially on soil improved for a previous crop.
IDEAL pH RANGE 5.5–7.5

Sowing

See table below.
MINIMUM GERMINATION TEMPERATURE 10°C (50°F). Germination rates are usually high; use thinnings for salads.

Plant care

Water until established in dry weather, then should survive dry conditions without watering. May need fleece or cloches if hard frosts are forecast. Dig roots to start blanching suitable varieties in late autumn and winter.
PROBLEMS Usually trouble-free. Slugs can be a problem on forced and blanched chicories.

Harvesting

FORCED CHICORY Cut chicons when tips show through soil (if blanched with soil) or 10–13cm (4–5in) tall under cover. Cut 2.5cm (1in) above the neck. Roots may grow another shoot.
SUGARLOAF Cut when large enough. The stump may resprout.
RED CHICORY Cut once hearts form, leaving stumps to resprout, or pick individual leaves. Quite frost hardy; cover with a cloche to harvest over winter. Harvest seedling cutting chicory when a few centimetres tall.

SOWING TIMES AND SPACING FOR CHICORY

Chicory type	Crop type	Sowing time	Location	Final spacing in rows
Witloof and other forcing types	Roots for forcing	Mid-June to early July	Outside	20 x 30cm (8 x 12in)
Sugarloaf	For mature heads in autumn	June and July	Outside	25 x 30cm (10 x 12in)
Sugarloaf	For smaller heads, or semi-mature cutting crop over winter	July and August	In modules, to transplant into soil beds or containers under cover	25 x 30cm (10 x 12in)
Sugarloaf	Seedling cutting crop	January and February, September	Under cover	Sow broadcast, or in bands 15–20cm (6–8in) wide and 20cm apart
Sugarloaf	Seedling cutting crop	March–August (mid-summer crops may be rather tough)	Outside	Sow broadcast in patches
Red chicory, early cultivars	Leaves and hearts in summer	Late April and May	Outside, or in modules under cover	20–35cm (8–14in)
Red chicory	Leaves and hearts in autumn	June and early July	Outside	20–35cm (8–14in)
Red chicory	Protected winter crop	August	In modules, to transplant under cover	20–35cm (8–14in)

Cultivar choice
Chicory 'Brussels Witloof' – for winter forcing; 'Grumolo Verde' – cutting chicory, frost-resistant broad green leaves, Lovely rosette habit in winter; 'Palla Rosa' – raddichio, grown for leaves, hearts or forced for chicons; 'Red Rib' – Italian dandelion; bright red stem and veins with dark green leaves (a salad stunner!); 'Sugar Loaf'– large conical green heads; 'Treviso' – red, non-hearting, extremely hardy, can be forced.

Chicory "chicons"

Claytonia

Montia perfoliata PORTULACACEAE

Mild-flavoured hardy annual salad plant, also known as miner's lettuce and winter purslane. Leaves, stems and flowers are all edible; valuable for spring and autumn use, and as a winter salad grown under cover. Plants have attractive bright green, fleshy, triangular leaves and a white flower; they are small, and ideal for inter-cropping and edging. They grow wild in some areas. Best on a light sandy soil, but not really fussy, and will also grow in light shade. No special soil treatment is needed. Sow March and April for summer use; July and August for autumn cropping; and September for cropping over winter, in seed trays or modules. Transplant when large enough. Broadcast thinly for a seedling cutting crop, or sow in rows. Claytonia will self-sow freely if you let it flower, so you may only need to sow it once. Thin plants to leave 10–15cm (4–6in) each way. Cover with a cloche to crop through winter – though it will survive without. Claytonia is usually trouble-free. Pick individual leaves as soon as large enough. Plants continue to grow for many weeks.

Corn salad

Valerianella locusta
VALERIANACEAE

Small, hardy annual salad plant also known as lamb's lettuce or mache, with a mild flavour.

Usually grown for autumn and winter use, it can be grown in a cool greenhouse or polytunnel over winter. The large-leaved English or Dutch type has more elongated leaves. The French type is a more compact rosette of a plant with smaller leaves. Extremely hardy, corn salad grows almost anywhere; no special soil treatment is required and it is generally trouble-free. Sow it in rows, or broadcast in wide drills; thin to 10–15cm (4–6in) each way. Sow in March and April for summer cropping; July and August for winter use; or August and September for winter cropping under cover.

Pick individual leaves when large enough, or cut whole plants. Good for intercropping. Corn salad will self-sow freely in the garden if you let it flower. Seedlings can be transplanted or hoed off if not needed.

Courgettes and marrows

Cucurbita pepo CUCURBITACEAE

Large, often very vigorous, half-hardy plants, with a diversity of shapes, colours and sizes of fruit. Undemanding and rewarding to grow. Heat-tolerant. Courgettes are also known as zucchini.

SEED TO HARVEST Courgettes: about 6 weeks after planting out. Marrows: 7–8 weeks.
CROP DIVERSITY Plants are classified according to the type of fruit; many are multipurpose. Courgettes are immature marrows, selected to crop

heavily: fruits are green or yellow with smooth, thin, hairless skins, for eating young. They usually have a bushg habit. Marrows have elongated cylindrical fruits, yellow, green or striped, with tougher, sometimes hairy skins. Trailing or bush cultivars available.
SITE Sheltered, in full sun. The foliage and fruits of bush varieties can look stunning in an ornamental garden. Courgettes can be grown under cover for an early crop.
SOIL TREATMENT Apply a low- or medium-fertility soil improver depending on soil condition. Rich feeding will produce a lot of foliage at the expense of the fruit. Can also be grown on a compost trench (see p.48).
IDEAL pH RANGE 5.5–6.8

Sowing
MINIMUM GERMINATION TEMPERATURE 15°C (59°F)
UNDER COVER Sow in late spring, 3–4 weeks before you expect the last frosts. Push 2 seeds into 9cm (3½in) pots; remove the weaker seedling. Harden off well before planting outside when all danger of frosts has passed. Transplant carefully as plants dislike root disturbance.
OUTSIDE Sow direct in early summer in mild areas. Protect with bottle cloches for extra warmth at the start.

Spacing
All the cucurbits are vigorous plants; where space is limited, choose the more compact bush cultivars. Trailing cultivars will grow beneath tall crops such as runner beans or sweetcorn.
ROWS Bush cultivars: 60–90cm x

90–120cm (24–36in x 36–48in) Trailing cultivars: 1.2–1.8m x 1.8m (4–6ft x 6ft)
BLOCK PLANTING Bush: 90cm (36in). Trailing: 1.2m–1.8m (4–6ft).

Plant care
Keep weed-free until established. Water only until established, unless you are aiming for the heavyweight prize at your local flower show. When growing well, mulch with straw, hay or a low-fertility soil improver. Trailing varieties can be trained up a strong support, or pegged out into a circle. Early in the season, or in response to stress, male flowers may be produced in the absence of female flowers. Pick and eat them. Courgettes under cover may need hand-pollination (see p.120). Push a board underneath large marrows to lift them off wet soil.
PROBLEMS Slugs, especially on young plants in cold and wet weather; cucumber mosaic virus; powdery mildew.

Harvesting
Once a courgette grows into a marrow the plant stops producing more fruits, so keep picking even if you have a surplus. For storage, leave marrows on the plant as long as possible to develop hard skins before the first frosts. When they feel hard and sound hollow if tapped, pick fruit and expose the underside to the sun for 10 days or so to complete the ripening process. Well-ripened marrows will store for 6–12 months in an airy place at 7–10°C (45–50°F). Courgettes will keep in the fridge for 2–3 weeks.

Claytonia

Corn Salad

Cultivar choice
Corn salad 'Large-leaved'; 'Vit' – French.
Courgettes and marrows Courgettes: 'Patriot' F1 and 'Defender' – cucumber mosaic virus-resistant; 'Jemmer' F1 – yellow fruits.
Marrows: 'Custard White'; 'Long Green Trailing'; 'Vegetable Spaghetti'; 'Tromboncino'.

Cress, American land

Barbarea verna BRASSICACEAE

A hardy biennial with a strong watercress flavour. Fast-growing, it can be harvested almost all year. Does best on more fertile soils. Summer crops need light shade. A useful winter salad grown under cover, and suits an ornamental bed. Will self-seed if left to flower. Apply a medium-fertility soil improver if soil has not been improved for a previous crop. Sow in modules, or direct. Sow in July and August for cropping winter to spring; in August for winter cropping under cover; March–June for summer cropping. Row spacing: 15 x 20cm (6 x 8in); block planting 15cm (6in). Water in dry spells. Flea beetle may be a problem. Start picking individual leaves when they are large enough. Will crop over a long period.

Cucumbers and gherkins

Cucumis sativus CUCURBITACEAE

Cucumbers are tender annual, trailing plants, grown outdoors or under cover for summer cropping. Gherkins are short-fruited types, harvested young and usually pickled.

SEED TO HARVEST 12 weeks.
CROP DIVERSITY Outdoor cucumbers: traditional ridge cultivars are rough, spiny fruits, 10–15cm (4–6in) long; newer cultivars (usually F1 hybrids) have smoother skins and are longer. There are trailing and bushy types of ridge cucumber, often needing to be pollinated to set fruit. Apple cucumbers are ridge types with round yellow fruits. Grow them outdoors, in a polytunnel or under cloches. European or greenhouse cucumbers have long, smooth fruits, setting without pollination. They become bitter if pollinated, in fact, so all-female cultivars have been bred to avoid pollination. They are for growing under cover.
SITE Grow outdoor crops in a warm, sheltered site, with fertile, moisture-retentive soil. Outdoor types need average temperatures around 18–30°C (64–86°F) and are damaged below 10°C (50°F), tolerating some shade in summer. Greenhouse cultivars need high humidity and night temperatures of at least 20°C (68°F). They can be grown in border soil, large containers, growing bags, or on straw bales. Cucumbers can be an unusual ornamental feature if grown up a fence or archway.
SOIL TREATMENT Apply a low- to medium-fertility soil improver before planting, or grow on a compost trench (see p.48). On heavy soils, mound up the earth before planting on top of the mound.
IDEAL pH RANGE 5.5–7

Sowing

Sow under cover in a heated propagator or similar to maintain a temperature of at least 20°C (68°F) until the seeds germinate. Seedlings must be kept where the night temperature is at least 16°C (60°F) for outdoor cultivars, and 20°C (68°F) for greenhouse cultivars. Use modules or bio-degradable pots to avoid disturbing the roots. Sow seeds on their side at a depth of 1.5cm (⅔in). Start outdoor crops May–June, no more than a month before the last frost is expected. Sow in April for a greenhouse/polytunnel crop, or in May if no additional heat can be supplied. Harden off before transplanting outside; outdoor plants may need cloches after planting to establish well. When planting, leave the rootball slightly proud of the soil surface to reduce risk of stem rot.
MINIMUM GERMINATION TEMPERATURE 20°C (68°F)

Spacing

ROWS Trained: 45 x 100cm (18 x 39in). Grown on the flat: 60–75cm (24–30in) x 1.3–1.6m (4–5ft), depending on the cultivar.
BLOCK PLANTING About 75cm (30in) depending on cultivar.

Plant care

Train trailing types up netting, wires, canes or strings; nip out the growing point when plants reach the top of the support. Ridge types will also grow on the flat; pinch out the growing point when 5–6 leaves have formed to encourage bushy growth. Water regularly throughout the growing season, and mulch plants grown on the flat with straw to keep fruit clean. Remove any male flowers appearing on greenhouse cucumbers. All-female types may produce male flowers, particularly if stressed – take these off at once. Do not remove male flowers from ridge cucumbers or gherkins. Check the seed packet to know which cucumber type you have.
PROBLEMS Slugs and aphids (mainly outdoors); glasshouse red spider mite, outside too if hot and dry; powdery mildew; cucumber mosaic virus; stem rots.

Harvesting

Cut fruits once large enough – check plants regularly for any monster fruits lurking unseen. Best kept in a cool room, wrapped in plastic film, rather than a fridge. They pickle well.

Endive

Cichorium endivia ASTERACEAE

A slightly bitter-tasting salad vegetable related to dandelions and chicory. It is easy to grow and can be harvested most of the year. It withstands a light frost, but a winter crop needs protection. Eat as a seedling crop, picked as loose leaves, or as blanched, mature heads. Fares better than lettuce in the low light levels of winter. Suitable for containers.

SEED TO HARVEST 7–13 weeks for mature heads. Quicker for seedling and loose leaf harvest.
CROP DIVERSITY There are two types. Escarole, also called Batavian or scarole, is a broad-leaved, hardy, upright plant, good for winter cropping. Frisee or curled endives are short, squat plants with frizzy leaves, more heat-tolerant and mostly used for summer and autumn crops.
SITE Not fussy, but winter crops need a well-drained, sheltered site on relatively infertile soil. Light shade tolerated in summer. The Frisee types are very attractive. A useful winter crop in a cool polytunnel or glasshouse.

Cultivar choice
Cucumbers Outdoor: 'Marketmore' – cucumber mosaic virus-resistant; 'Bush Champion' F1 – compact. Outdoor/indoor: 'Slice King' F1 – good disease resistance; 'Burpless Tasty Green' F1 – mildew resistant; 'Pepinex 69' F1 – all-female for cold greenhouse and polytunnel; 'Futura' F1 – powdery mildew resistance, all-female for cold greenhouse and polytunnel; 'Crystal Apple' and 'Crystal Lemon' – round, pale greenish yellow fruits; 'Boothby's Blond' and 'White Wonder' – cream-skinned heritage varieties.

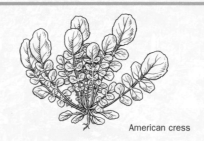

American cress

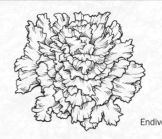

Endive

SOIL TREATMENT None needed where soil has been improved for a previous crop. Otherwise, apply a low-fertility soil improver.
IDEAL pH RANGE 5.5–7.5

Sowing

If temperatures fall below 4.5°C (40°F) for 20 days or more, then endive seedlings will bolt.
MINIMUM GERMINATION TEMPERATURE 20°C (68°F)
UNDER COVER Sow in April for growing under cover, May for transplanting outdoors. Best raised in modules for transplanting. Sow again in autumn for a protected winter crop.
OUTSIDE Sow June–early July in shallow drills for autumn harvest. Sow in August for a winter crop (protected under cloches or in frames). Sow April–September for harvest as a seedling crop, or as young leaves. Grow early and late sowings under cloches or in an unheated polytunnel or greenhouse.

Spacing

ROWS 30 x 35cm (12 x 14in)
BLOCK PLANTING 30cm (12in)

Plant care

Water in dry weather. Use cloches in cold weather. Mature plants can be blanched (p.332).
PROBLEMS Slugs; aphids. Basal rots can be a problem in winter – grow in well-drained soil, and keep leaves dry.

Harvesting

Cut seedling crop when 10–15cm (4–6in) tall. Pick leaves as needed or when of convenient size. Cut mature heads, blanched if preferred. Cut stems may regrow to provide another crop of leaves.

Florence fennel

Foeniculum vulgare var. *dulce*
APIACEAE

An unusual vegetable that can be difficult to grow well. The edible part is the aniseed-flavoured, swollen white base of the leaf stalk. The fine, feathery leaves are also delicious. Its short growing season makes fennel, or finocchio, a useful catch crop, though it tends to bolt if growth is checked by drought or cold. It can withstand light frost.

SEED TO HARVEST 10–15 weeks.
CROP DIVERSITY Modern cultivars, resistant to bolting, are available for earlier sowing.
SITE Warm and sunny, with a well-drained, moisture-retentive soil. Avoid heavy soils. Pretty enough to grow in a flower garden. Suitable for growing in a cool polytunnel or glasshouse for an early or late crop.
SOIL TREATMENT Enjoys soil manured or composted for a previous crop. Add a low-fertility soil improver before planting.
IDEAL pH RANGE 5.5–7.5

Sowing

MINIMUM GERMINATION TEMPERATURE 15°C (60°F)
UNDER COVER Resents root disturbance so modules or bio-degradable pots are preferable to trays. Sow April–July, using bolt-resistant cultivars before mid-June. Sow mid-July–early August for a late crop to grow under cover. Thin to one seedling per module; harden off before transplanting when they have 3–4 true leaves.
OUTSIDE Sow from May to July using bolt-resistant varieties

before mid-June. Station-sow in pinches 1cm (½in) deep at 2-week intervals for a succession of crops until the first frosts.

Spacing

ROWS 30 x 30cm (12 x 12in)
BLOCK PLANTING 30 x 30cm (12 x 12in)
MULTI-SOWING Fennel is sometimes eaten as a seedling crop, stir-fried with other edible greens. When growing seedling fennel, station-sow at 5cm (2in) by 30cm (12in) and do not thin.

Plant care

Early and late sowings may need frost protection. Mulch with a low fertility soil improver. Water regularly for maximum tenderness and size, and to avoid bolting. When bulbs are egg-sized, earth them up to half their height to keep them white and succulent.
PROBLEMS Slugs; bolting. Grow bolt-resistant varieties; do not transplant; water regularly.

Harvesting

Cut bulbs just above ground level when the size of a flattened tennis ball. Cut stems often grow a second crop of tasty leaves for use in salads. Fennel keeps for 2 weeks or more in the fridge, but tends to shrivel if stored too long.

Garlic

Allium sativum ALLIACEAE

An easy, surprisingly hardy crop that needs a long growing period to crop well, but takes up little space. Garlic is grown from cloves rather than seed. Buy garlic specifically for planting, rather

than that sold for eating. The latter may carry diseases, and is unlikely to be a cultivar adapted to your particular region. However, garlic will adapt to the local day length and temperature over the years, so you can develop your own strain by saving cloves to plant, from healthy plants only.

PLANTING TO HARVEST 16–36 weeks. Not raised from seed.
CROP DIVERSITY The diversity can be bewildering, including pinky-purple and white-skinned cultivars. Some are short-dormancy, storing only until Christmas. These tend to produce larger cloves and bulbs than the long-dormancy cultivars, which should keep until the following spring or later. Some crop well from a spring planting, but most must be planted in autumn. Most garlic grown in the UK is soft-necked, and does not flower. This makes it ideal for plaiting. Hard-necked garlic produces a flowerhead, but this does not detract from the cropping.
SITE Open situation. Garlic is usually grown over winter, so it needs a soil that does not become waterlogged. It can easily be fitted into an ornamental garden, and can also be grown in containers.
SOIL TREATMENT Soil improved for a previous crop is ideal. Do not plant in freshly manured soil.
IDEAL pH RANGE 6–7.5

Planting

Divide bulbs into cloves immediately before planting. To produce good-sized bulbs, most cultivars need 1–2 months when the soil is below 10°C (50°F), so it is best planted in late autumn. Some cultivars can be planted in

Florence fennel · Garlic

February. Plant cloves, pointed end-up, into position with the tip 2.5–10cm (1–4in) below the soil surface – more shallowly the heavier your soil. Where soil is likely to be very wet over winter, plant in pots filled with a free-draining loam-based compost and stand outside.

Spacing
ROWS 7.5–10cm x 25–30cm (3–4in x 10–12in)
BLOCK PLANTING 18cm (7in)

Plant care
Water in spring if dry. To improve yields of stiff-stemmed garlic, cut back the flowering stem by half 2–3 weeks before harvest.
PROBLEMS Onion white rot; leek rust.

Harvesting
Harvest in July or August once leaves begin to turn yellow. Dig up carefully before leaves have died back to keep the skin around the bulb intact. Leave to dry in the open, or in a cool dry shed. Lay out on a slatted shelf, or hang up. Once dry, plait into ropes or tie in bunches.

Good King Henry

Chenopodium bonus-henricus
CHENOPODIACEAE

An old-fashioned perennial salad plant, growing 90cm (36in) tall. It prefers a moist soil and tolerates some shade. Sow in spring with 40cm (16in) between plants. Harvest young leaves and flowering shoots in the second year. Ready early in the year. Divide plants every two to three years.

Hamburg parsley

Petroselinum crispum var. *tuberosum*
APIACEAE

Grown for its white, parsnip-like roots, harvested in late autumn and winter. The leaves can be used for parsley flavouring. Needs a long growing season.

SEED TO HARVEST 30 weeks.
SITE Moisture-retentive soil where it can root deeply. Can be grown in light shade.
SOIL TREATMENT None needed where soil was improved for a previous crop. Benefits from a low-fertility soil improver applied as a mulch over the previous winter.
IDEAL pH RANGE 6.5–7

Sowing
MINIMUM GERMINATION TEMPERATURE 7°C (45°F)
UNDER COVER Not appropriate.
OUTSIDE Sow March–April in drills 1cm (½in) deep. Germination can be slow. Cover with cloches or clear plastic to speed it up. Can also be sown in July for an early crop the next year.

Spacing
ROWS 20 x 30cm (8 x 12in)
BLOCK PLANTING 20cm (8in)

Plant care
Keep weed-free when young – sowing a few quick-germinating radishes will mark the row until the parsley shows. Mulch established plants for moisture retention and weed control. Cover crops left in ground over winter with straw or bracken.
PROBLEMS Parsnip canker.

Harvesting
Dig from early autumn through to the following early spring. Flavour is better if stored in the ground, rather than lifted for indoor storage.

Kale

Brassica oleracea Acephala Group
BRASSICACEAE

Also known as borecole, this is one of the hardiest winter vegetables, easy to grow and tolerant of a range of adverse conditions. Best eaten after frost early in the year when fresh crops are scarce, but can be available from late summer on. Useful for growing after an early crop such as broad beans or early peas. Some cultivars are very pretty.

SEED TO HARVEST 7 weeks for the quickest types. Will stand in good condition for a long time, giving a long harvest period.
CROP DIVERSITY Kales range in height from 30cm (12in) to 90cm (3ft) or more. Leaves may be curly, plain, ragged, fringed or blistered, in plain green or purple, or both.
SITE Does better on poorer soils than other brassicas. Does not need to grow into a large plant to produce a useful crop. Will tolerate exposed sites and some shade, but not poorly drained soil.
SOIL TREATMENT Apply a medium-fertility soil improver, or a low-fertility soil improver plus a general organic fertiliser – or plant after a nitrogen-fixing green manure. Do not make soil too rich; the resulting lush late growth may not be frost hardy.
IDEAL pH RANGE 6.5–7.5

Sowing
MINIMUM GERMINATION TEMPERATURE 7°C (45°F)
UNDER COVER Sow in trays or modules in February for a summer crop, May for a winter crop.
OUTSIDE Sow thinly in a seedbed in April–May, in shallow drills. Transplant 6–8 weeks later. The "rape" kales, such as 'Pentland Brig', may be sown direct as late as July or early August. Station-sow 3–4 seeds and thin to 1 seedling when large enough.

Spacing
Dwarf cultivars: 30–45cm (12–18in). Tall cultivars: 60–76cm (24–30in). Some taller cultivars can be spaced only 45cm (18in) apart if cropped when young.

Plant care
Water seedlings until established.
PROBLEMS Cabbage caterpillars; cabbage whitefly; cabbage root fly; mealy cabbage aphid; pigeons; clubroot.

Harvesting
Pick leaves as needed from mature plants, or from young plants for a quicker harvest. Often tastier after a hard frost. Sprouting shoots can be picked in early spring.

Kohl rabi

Brassica oleracea Gongylodes Group
BRASSICACEAE

A small, fast-growing member of the brassica family, with an unusual appearance. The spherical swollen stems, sitting just above ground level, are picked at tennis-ball size. Can be sown and harvested almost all year

---

Cultivar choice
Kale 'Cavalo Nero'; 'Darkibor' F1; 'Dwarf Green Curled'; 'Nero di Toscana'– long, strappy, dark green, blistered leaves; 'Pentland Brig' – leafy sprouts for spring picking; 'Red Russian'; 'Redbor' F1 – purple curly kale; 'Tall Green Curled'.
Kohl rabi 'Green Delicacy'; 'Azur Star' – purple; 'Cindy' F1 RZ – early-maturing.

Gherkins *see Cucumbers and gherkins*
Globe artichokes *see Artichokes, globe*
Haricot beans *see Beans, French*

Kohl rabi

Hamburg parsley

round. Makes a good catch crop, or an interesting addition to an ornamental garden. Can be grown in containers.

SEED TO HARVEST 5–9 weeks.
CROP DIVERSITY Green cultivars are usually grown for spring and summer crops; the hardier purple cultivars for autumn and winter use. New hybrid cultivars grow larger without becoming woody.
SITE Open. Suitable for early and late cropping under cover.
SOIL TREATMENT Apply a low-fertility soil improver or one of medium-fertility on poor soils.
IDEAL pH RANGE 6–7

Sowing

Sow every few weeks for a regular supply as kohl rabi will not stand in an edible condition for long once ready.
MINIMUM GERMINATION TEMPERATURE 10° (50°F)
UNDER COVER Sow in modules from late February through to August. Plant out when no more than 5cm (2in) high. Sow in September to grow under cover.
OUTSIDE Sow direct March–August. Use the hardier purple varieties for later sowings.

Spacing
ROWS 18 x 30cm (7 x 12in)
BLOCK PLANTING 25cm (10in)

Plant care

Water in dry weather. Kohl rabi is fast-growing and tends to be problem-free – though it is susceptible to the same pests and diseases as other brassica plants.
PROBLEMS Flea beetle, cabbage root fly; mealy cabbage aphids; clubroot.

Harvesting

Quick to mature, so check regularly. Cut older varieties when no larger than a tennis ball. Modern varieties can grow to 10cm (4in) in diameter. Late crops can be left in the ground unless heavy frost is forecast, or store for up to 2 months in boxes of moist sand. Has a fresh, crisp, juicy taste eaten raw or lightly cooked.

Komatsuna

Brassica rapa var. *perviridis* or var. *komatsuna* BRASSICACEAE

This versatile, leafy Japanese crop, also known as mustard spinach, has a milder "bite" than the Chinese mustards, but more flavour than the cabbages. It can be sown almost all year round and eaten at any stage from seedling to large plant. Mature plants can be 18cm (7in) tall by 50cm (20in) wide. It can be sown from early spring to autumn outdoors, from mid-winter to late autumn under cover. Soil conditions and pest and disease problems are the same as for Chinese cabbages.

Leeks

Allium porrum ALLIACEAE

A hardy crop for an autumn and winter harvest. Leeks do not take up much space, and are generally easy to grow. They can be harvested over a long period as they will stay in the ground in good condition for many months. Their strong root system does wonders for soil structure.

SEED TO HARVEST 16–20 weeks.
CROP DIVERSITY Early cultivars: for late summer and autumn use. Usually taller and slimmer and less hardy than later cultivars. Late cultivars: for winter and spring use. Usually shorter and fatter. A few cultivars have decorative purple foliage. Can be grown as mini-leeks, a milder alternative to the spring onion.
SITE Open site in fertile soil that retains moisture but does not become waterlogged in winter.
IDEAL pH RANGE 6.5–7.5
SOIL TREATMENT High-fertility soil improver; medium-fertility if following a broad bean/pea crop; or low-fertility improver with nitrogen-rich organic fertiliser.

Sowing

MINIMUM GERMINATION TEMPERATURE 7°C (45°F)
UNDER COVER Multi-sown leeks only. From February sow 4 seeds per module cell. Plant out, unthinned, when 20cm (8in) tall.
OUTSIDE Sow from March to early May in a seed bed. Sow seeds 2.5cm (1in) deep, 2.5cm (1in) x 15cm (6in). Transplant to final site. Sow mini-leeks direct in position; do not transplant.

Planting

Transplant at 10–15 weeks old, 20cm (8in) tall – though they can be transplanted when larger. The main planting time is in June, but it can go on into early August if waiting for other crops to finish and clear the site. Water seedbed well before digging up transplants; do not trim roots or leaves. Use a dibber to make holes 15cm (6in) deep. Drop a single leek into each hole and water in (see p.315). Do not fill in the hole.

Spacing
ROWS 7.5–15 x 30cm (3–6 x 12in).
BLOCK PLANTING 15–23cm (6–9in) each way.
MULTI-SOWN 23cm (9in)
MINI-LEEKS 1.5 x 15cm (¾ x 6in)

Plant care
Water until established if dry.
PROBLEMS Leek moth; leek rust – this shows as bright orange pustules on the leaves. It often disappears in the autumn, once the weather has turned cool and damp.

Harvesting
Lift leeks as required. Generally they will stand in the ground for many weeks in good condition, though early cultivars may not survive really hard weather.

Lettuce

Lactuca sativa ASTERACEAE

This universal salad ingredient has undergone a revolution in the last decade or so. Crisp or butter-head, hearted or loose leaf, frilly or plain, there is a lettuce to fit every taste, season and garden.

SEED TO HARVEST 4–14 weeks, depending on cultivar and season.
CROP DIVERSITY Butterheads: hearted lettuces with soft, almost greasy leaf. More tolerant of drought and heat than other types so usually grown in summer. **Crispheads:** crunchy crisp leaves forming solid hearts. Heat-tolerant for summer cropping. Some are suitable for winter growing in an unheated greenhouse. **Romaine or cos:**

Leeks

Hearting lettuce

Cultivar choice
Leeks Early to mid-season: 'King Richard' – for a very early crop, mini-leeks and multi sowing; 'Prenora'; 'The Lyon' – first introduced in 1886. Late season: 'Conora'; 'Giant Winter' – introduced in 1905; 'Musselburgh' – traditional favourite; 'St Victor' – purple leaves.

Lamb's lettuce *see Corn salad*

upright habit with more substantial, crisp, tasty leaves and a loose heart. Slower to mature than butterhead and crisphead types. Better grown in cooler weather in a humus-rich, moist soil. Hardier than most lettuces; some can be grown outside over winter. Many are suitable for seedling cutting crops.

Loose leaf, leaf lettuce, salad bowl: Non-hearting, with a diverse range of leaf colour and shape. Individual leaves can be picked over many weeks. Slow to bolt. Suitable for seedling crops.

Some lettuce cultivars can overwinter in a cool greenhouse or polytunnel. Cultivars resistant to root aphid and tolerant of downy mildew are available.

SITE Most soils, except dry or poorly drained. Appreciates light shade in the summer. Suitable for intercropping between rows of peas or brassicas or underneath tripods of runner beans. Also good for growing in containers and in an ornamental garden.

SOIL TREATMENT None needed where soil is regularly improved for vegetable growing. On poor soil apply a medium-fertility soil improver.

IDEAL pH RANGE 6–7

Sowing

Choose an appropriate cultivar to suit the sowing time.

MINIMUM GERMINATION TEMPERATURE 5°C (42°F). Germination is inhibited in hot weather, above 25°C (77°F).

UNDER COVER For summer and autumn crops, sow in modules or trays from February to early July. Once temperatures rise, outdoor sowings are likely to be more successful. For continuous supply, sow at 2-week intervals or select a range of types and cultivars. After hardening off and planting out, protect early and late sowings with cloches – or grow in an unheated greenhouse as necessary. For overwintering crops, either outdoors or in an unheated greenhouse, sow in late August or early October, depending on the cultivar.

OUTSIDE Sow a 1m (3ft) row of each cultivar at fortnightly intervals from April, when the ground is warm enough, until early September. Thin out when large enough to handle, using the thinnings as transplants if required. Bare-root transplants will not do well in summer. When temperatures are high and likely to inhibit germination, sow between 2pm and 4pm and water well. The critical period is a few hours after sowing.

Seedling cutting crops are most useful at the start and end of the season: make early sowings under cover in late February and March; sow outside when conditions are suitable. Avoid summer months, then sow again in late August outside, and under cover in September. Broadcast seed thinly in patches at 3-week intervals.

Spacing

ROWS 15–38 x 20–34cm (6–15 x 8–14in), depending on cultivar.

BLOCK PLANTING 20–34cm (8–14in), depending on cultivar.

Plant care

Water until established, and in dry periods, to prevent leaves becoming tough and bitter. Keep greenhouses and polytunnels well ventilated to reduce the risk of mildew and botrytis in overwintering crops.

PROBLEMS Slugs – if these are a real problem, raise the lettuce in modules and plant out as sturdy young plants, protected with bottle cloches; aphids; lettuce root aphids; cutworm; downy mildew; grey mould; bolting, which can be a problem in hot weather, so choose bolt-resistant cultivars for growing in high summer.

Harvesting

HEARTED LETTUCE Cut as soon as they have hearted as they will quickly bolt. Cos types will stand a little longer.

LOOSELEAF Pick leaves from the outside of the plant as needed.

SEEDLING CUTTING CROPS Harvest when 5cm (2in) tall, about 4 weeks after sowing; 2–3 subsequent cuts can be made.

Melon, sweet

Cucumis melo CUCURBITACEAE

Sweet melons grow on a trailing vine in the same fashion as their close relative, cucumber. Melons are tropical plants that need temperatures of 25–30°C (77–86°F) to grow and crop effectively, so need continuous protection in cool climates.

SEED TO HARVEST 12–20 weeks.

CROP DIVERSITY Cantaloupe melons, with grey-green or ochre skins and pale green or orange flesh, are the most suitable types for growing in the UK as they can tolerate cooler temperatures. Musk and winter melons can be grown in a heated greenhouse.

SITE Grow under cloches, in a cold frame, or in a greenhouse/polytunnel, in a warm, well-drained soil rich in organic matter, but not too fertile. Suitable for containers.

SOIL TREATMENT Apply a medium-fertility soil improver, or low-fertility soil improver plus a general organic fertiliser.

IDEAL pH RANGE 6.5–7

Sowing

MINIMUM GERMINATION TEMPERATURE 18°C (64°F)

UNDER COVER Sow in spring, usually late April or May, about 6 weeks before the last frost. Sow in 6–9cm (2½–3½in) pots, with the seed sown on its side. With expensive F1 seed, sow 1 per pot only. Thin, if necessary, to 1 seedling per pot. Once germinated, keep light and warm – 13–16°C (55–61°F). Do not sow too early, as you do not want plants to become pot-bound. Pot on into 13cm (5in) pots if necessary.

Planting

Put cloches in place a few weeks in advance to warm the soil. Plant out in June into a slight mound, about 4cm (1½in) high, to help keep the stem just above ground and therefore dry and free from rot. Water in rather than firming the soil.

Spacing

GROWN ON THE FLAT 1 x 1–1.5m (3 x 3–5ft)

TRAINED UP CANES OR NETTING 38cm (15in) for a single cordon, 60cm (24in) for a double cordon.

Cultivar choice

Lettuce Butterhead: 'All Year Round' – sow spring to autumn; 'Marvel of Four Seasons' – red curly leaves, best in spring and autumn; 'Buttercrunch' – good in hot weather; 'Troubadour' RZ – overwinter under cover; 'Winter Crop' – overwinter outside. Crisphead: 'Iceberg' – summer; 'Roxette' – resistant to downy mildew; 'Webb's Wonderful'. Cos: 'Little Gem' – quick-maturing, compact plants, resistant to root aphid; 'Bath Cos' – huge heads, first introduced in 1880; 'Winter Density' – autumn sowing outside; Loose leaf: 'Frisby' – compact, fast-growing, stands well, sow at any time of year. 'Salad Bowl' red and green oakleaf type. Winter-heading: 'Imperial Winter' – grow outdoors over winter for spring cutting.

Marrows *see Courgettes and marrows*

Sweet melon

Plant care

Protect from cold weather. Once fruiting, shade from hot sun. As flowering starts, allow pollinating insects access to plants under cover, or hand-pollinate. Water plants regularly. Feed those in containers with a high-potash feed once flowers have set.
PROBLEMS Aphids; glasshouse red spider mite; glasshouse whitefly; verticillium wilt; sclerotinia.

Training

PLANTS GROWN ON THE FLAT Plants can be left to scramble over the ground, a bench, or up netting. After 5 leaves have developed, pinch out the growing tip. Allow 4 lateral shoots to develop, spacing them out so they grow in different directions. If space is short, under cloches for example, allow only 2 laterals to grow.
TRAINED PLANTS Allow 1–2 shoots to grow per plant, training them up canes or netting. Pinch out the growing tip when 2m (6ft) long to encourage sideshoots to grow. Tie in these sideshoots, and pinch out their growing tip after 5 leaves to encourage further sideshoots to grow; these will flower. Support fruits, when tennis ball-sized, with a netting sling.
ALL PLANTS Pinch out the growing tip of each flowering shoot at 2 leaves beyond the flower. Leave 4–5 fruits of uniform size to grow on each plant, picking off the rest when gooseberry-sized.

Harvest

Melons are ready to pick in late summer and early autumn. Ripe fruits are sweet-smelling.

Mibuna greens

Closely related to Mizuna greens (see below). They grow more or less in the same way, but are less vigorous, and less tolerant of heat and cold.

Mitsuba

Cryptotaenia japonica APIACEAE

A hardy evergreen plant, also known as Japanese parsley. The delicately flavoured stems and leaves are used raw in salads. Mitsuba, a woodland plant, enjoys moist soil and light shade. Sow *in situ* in spring or autumn, leaving 15cm (6in) between plants, or grow under cover for winter cropping.

Mizuna greens

Brassica rapa var. *nipposinica* BRASSICACEAE

Attractive leafy crop, with a mild mustardy flavour, eaten raw or lightly cooked. Its green feathery leaves can be cut as a seedling crop, picked individually from larger plants, or cut as a whole head. Makes pretty edging. Will crop over winter with protection.

SEED TO HARVEST Seedling crop 3 weeks; semi-mature plants 6–8 weeks; mature plants 8–10 weeks.
CROP DIVERSITY Green and purple-leaved cultivars.
SITE Not fussy, as long as the soil does not dry out. Summer crops can take light shade. Good for intercropping when kept small by regular picking. Suitable for winter cropping under cover. Will grow in containers.
SOIL TREATMENT None needed if soil improved for a previous crop. Use a low- to medium-fertility soil improver on light soils.

Sowing

MINIMUM GERMINATION TEMPERATURE 7°C (45°F)
UNDER COVER Sow in modules from March/April for transplanting outside. Sow direct or in modules September to March for growing under cover.
OUTSIDE Sow April to August.

Spacing

Seedling cutting crop: Sow thinly in bands or patches. Semi-mature plants: 10–20cm (4–8in). Mature plants: 30cm (12in).

Plant care

Water in dry weather.
PROBLEMS Clubroot; slugs; flea beetle. Where flea beetle is a problem, grow under fleece or fine mesh netting.

Harvesting

Cut seedlings when a few centimetres high. Pick individual leaves when plants are large enough, or cut the whole head.

Mustards, oriental

Brassica juncea BRASSICACEAE

Mostly hardy, leafy greens, with a hot mustardy flavour. Pick individual leaves for salads and stir-fry in autumn and winter. Can be grown as a seedling crop for cutting. Useful for intercropping.

SEED TO HARVEST 6–13 weeks.
CROP DIVERSITY Variety of leaf shapes and colours are available.
SITE Open site. Suitable for late cropping in an unheated greenhouse/polytunnel, or containers.
SOIL TREATMENT None needed if soil improved for a previous crop. If not, apply a low- or medium-fertility soil improver.
IDEAL pH RANGE 6.5–7

Sowing

MINIMUM GERMINATION TEMPERATURE 7°C (45°F)
Best sown direct but can be transplanted from modules. Some cultivars can be sown in spring and late summer; others are for late summer sowing only.

Spacing

For harvesting young leaves: 15 x 15cm (6 x 6in). Larger plants: 35 x 35cm (14 x 14in). As a seedling cutting crop: broadcast seed thinly.

Plant care

Water as necessary in dry weather.
PROBLEMS Clubroot; flea beetle – to protect against flea beetle, grow under fleece or mesh.

New Zealand spinach

Tetragonia tetragonioides AIZOACEAE

Unusual-looking half-hardy perennial usually grown as an annual. Unlike true spinach it thrives in hot, dry conditions. Seed is slow to germinate and is best soaked in water for 24 hours before sowing. Raise in modules and plant out after the

Mizuna greens

Oriental mustard

New Zealand spinach

Cultivar choice
Melons 'Amber Nectar'; 'Ogen'; 'Sweetheart' F1.
Mizuna 'Mizuna Greens'; 'Purple Mizuna'.
Oriental mustards 'Green-in-the-Snow' – very hardy; 'Giant Red' – leaves develop deep red colour in cold weather; 'Green Wave'; 'Osaka Purple'.

Mooli *see Radish*

last frost, or sow direct once the risk of frost has passed. Plants are low and sprawling; space at least 45cm (18in) apart. The thick, fleshy leaves and shoot tips are picked as required, starting around 6–7 weeks after sowing. Usually pest- and disease-free.

Onions, globe and bulb

Allium cepa ALLIACEAE

A popular long-season, frost-tolerant crop. Simple to grow from sets, and undemanding if you want to grow kitchen-sized bulbs. In areas of low summer rainfall, autumn-planted onions may be more reliable. The huge onions at flower shows are usually grown from special giant strains, traditionally sown on Boxing Day.

SEED TO HARVEST Spring-sown seed: 20–24 weeks; autumn-sown seed: 42 weeks; spring-planted sets: 18–20 weeks; autumn-planted sets: 36–38 weeks.
CROP DIVERSITY Red, white and golden-brown skinned types; can be oval or cylindrical in shape. Specific cultivars are used for autumn planting. A wider range of cultivars is available as seed than as sets.
SITE Onions prefer an open, sunny situation but tolerate a little shade. Autumn sown/planted onions need full sun and must have good drainage. Onions can look good amongst other plants, but dislike being crowded.
SOIL TREATMENT None needed if soil was improved for a

previous crop. If not, add a low- to medium-fertility soil improver, depending on the soil condition.
IDEAL pH RANGE 6–7

Sowing
MINIMUM GERMINATION TEMPERATURE 5°C (45°F)
If sowing in spring, for a late summer harvest:
SEED, UNDER COVER Sow in trays or modules in February/March. Harden off and plant out when about 10cm (4in) tall. Multi-sowing: sow 6 seeds per module and do not thin.
SEED, OUTSIDE Station-sow several seeds per station, as soon as soil is warm enough, usually by April. Thin to 1 seedling, or leave several to grow on if multi-sowing.
SETS Plant sets March/April. They need a period of cold to initiate root formation, so plant as early as possible once soil is workable. Push sets into the soil, so the tips are just visible, with the pointed end upwards.
If sowing in late summer/autumn for early summer harvest:
SEED Timing of sowing to suit geographical location is critical, to ensure that seedlings will survive the winter, but will not bolt early in the spring. Sow in August – in the 2nd week in the north, the 4th in the south. Sow thinly in rows. Thin to 2.5cm (1in) in autumn, and in stages to the final spacing in spring.
SETS Plant from September to November, when the ground is fit to walk on. Push sets in as for the spring-planted crop.

Spacing
ROWS Bulb size is influenced by spacing. For medium-sized

bulbs: 4 x 30cm (1½ x 12in); for larger bulbs, 10 x 30cm (4 x 12in).
BLOCK PLANTING 10–15cm (4–6in)
MULTI-SOWN 25cm (10in).

Plant care
Hand-weed carefully as roots are very shallow. In spring, apply a nitrogen-rich fertiliser to over-wintered onions if required.
PROBLEMS Onion fly; onion thrips; onion downy mildew; onion neck rots; onion white rot; bolting (fluctuating weather conditions often the cause; red cultivars are especially prone).

Harvesting
Harvest to eat fresh when large enough. When onions stop growing, the leaves fall over and turn brown. Allow them to fall naturally; do not bend them over. Gently pull the onions up. In dry weather, spread them out on slatted trays or a bench in the sun for the skins to ripen. In wet conditions dry off under cover. Avoid bruising bulbs. Once skin is rustling dry, hang onions in nets or string into ropes. Store in a cool, airy location. Use thick-necked bulbs first, as they rarely store well. Autumn-sown onions should not be stored long-term.

Onions, spring and pickling

Allium cepa ALLIACEAE

Onions that are harvested after only 8 weeks or so. European spring or bunching onions form a slim plant with a white or red shank, mild-flavoured for salads.

Pickling or mini onions have small bulbs used fresh or for pickling.

SEED TO HARVEST 8 weeks.
CROP DIVERSITY Red and white cultivars. Hardy cultivars of spring onions are grown over winter.
SITE Open site preferred, but will tolerate a little shade. Can be grown under cover for an early crop. Spring onions can be grown over winter. Suitable for growing in containers.
SOIL TREATMENT No treatment needed if soil was manured or composted for a previous crop. If not, apply a low- to medium-fertility soil improver, depending on the soil. Pickling onions tolerate poorer soils than other types.
IDEAL pH RANGE 6–7

Sowing
MINIMUM GERMINATION TEMPERATURE 5°C (41°F)
UNDER COVER Sow in early spring and late summer direct into soil beds.
OUTSIDE Spring onions: sow in spring and summer every 3 weeks for a continuous supply. For an early spring crop, sow suitable cultivars in August. Pickling onions: sow in March and April.

Spacing
Sow thinly in rows 10cm (4in) apart, or in bands 7–10cm (3–4in) wide, 15cm (6in) apart. Aim for 1–2.5cm (½–1in) between seeds.

Plant care
Water in dry conditions. Protect winter crops in severe weather.
PROBLEMS Onion fly; onion white rot; onion downy mildew.

Harvesting
Pull spring onions to eat when

Cultivar choice
Onions, bulb and globe From seed: 'Hygro' F1; 'Ailsa Craig'; 'Bedfordshire Champion'; 'Red Brunswick' – for spring sowing; 'Long Red Florence' – red, torpedo-shaped; 'Senshyu Yellow'; 'Express Yellow' – autumn sowing. From sets: 'Jet Set'; 'Sturon Globe'; 'Red Baron' – spring planting; 'Radar'; Senshyu Yellow' – autumn planting.
Onions, spring and pickling Spring onions: 'White Lisbon'; 'Red Beard'; White Lisbon Winter Hardy'. Pickling onions: 'Paris Silverskin'; 'Brown Pickling'; 'Purplette'.

Onions, bunching/Welsh/Japanese *see Welsh onions*

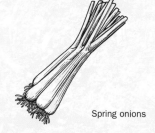
Spring onions

Globe onion

15cm (6in) tall. Harvest alternate plants, leaving others to continue growing. Pickling onions are harvested when the foliage has died back or used fresh.

Pak choi

Brassica rapa var. *chinensis*
BRASSICACEAE

Pak choi leaves have a wide mid-rib and form a loose head. A close relative of Chinese cabbage, to eat raw or lightly cooked at any stage from seedling to mature plant. Leaves, stems and flowering shoots all edible. Grow spring sowings as seedling crops as early sowings run to seed quickly. Will stand light frost.

SEED TO HARVEST Mature plants: 5–8 weeks; seedling crops: 2–3 weeks.
CROP DIVERSITY White-, green- and purple-stemmed cultivars in varying sizes. Some are more resistant to bolting.
SITE Humus-rich, moisture-retentive soil to ensure the fast growth needed for a good crop. This quick growth makes it good for intercropping between slower plants. Suitable for growing as a late-season crop in an unheated greenhouse or polytunnel.
SOIL TREATMENT Apply a medium-fertility soil improver or a low-fertility one with organic fertiliser before planting.
IDEAL PH RANGE 6.5–7

Sowing
MINIMUM GERMINATION TEMPERATURE 10°C (50°F)
UNDER COVER Sow in modules for transplanting June–August.

Some cultivars can be sown earlier. The latest sowings can be planted under cover.
OUTSIDE Sow June–August.

Spacing
For harvesting young leaves: 13–15cm (5–6in). For medium-sized plants: 18–23cm (7–9in). Large plants: 45cm (18in). As a seedling cutting crop – broadcast thinly. Spacing will also depend to some extent on cultivar.

Plant care
Water if needed in dry weather. If flea beetle is a problem, grow under fleece or fine mesh netting.
PROBLEMS Flea beetle; slugs; clubroot.

Parsnip

Pastinaca sativa APIACEAE

Long white parsnip roots make a deliciously sweet winter staple. They are utterly hardy and easy to grow, but do need a long growing season. Germination is slow and fresh seed must be used every year. Harvest in the late autumn and winter. Leave a parsnip in the ground over winter and it will produce a majestic flower spike the following year; a magnet for beneficial insects. Parsnip seed is notoriously slow to germinate – it may take three weeks or so. Sow parsnips mixed with radish seed to mark the area. The radish is ready to harvest when the parsnips are just starting to emerge.

SEED TO HARVEST 16 weeks.
CROP DIVERSITY Long- and short-rooted cultivars, but

otherwise little variety. Modern cultivars tend to be smaller and faster-growing. May also be grown as a mini-vegetable.
SITE For good roots, parsnips need a well-worked, stone-free soil, in an open, sunny position.
SOIL TREATMENT Parsnips do best on soil manured or composted for a previous crop. They will benefit from a low-fertility organic mulch, applied in the winter before sowing.
IDEAL PH RANGE 6.5–8

Sowing
Sow outdoors for preference.
UNDER COVER Sow in biodegradable tubes, to plant out without disturbing the roots.
OUTSIDE First sowings can be made from February, but as they germinate slowly later sowings in warmer soil (until May) may be more successful. Fluid-sowing can improve the germination rate. Sow thinly in shallow drills, or station-sow, 3 seeds per station, thinned to 1 per station.
MINIMUM GERMINATION TEMPERATURE 1.5°C (35°F); maximum 17.5°C (63°F).

Spacing
Root size depends on spacing.
ROWS For small roots: 10 x 20cm (4 x 8in). For larger roots: 15 x 30cm (6in x 12in).
BLOCK PLANTING 15–20cm (6–8in).

Plant care
Keep seedlings weed-free until established.
PROBLEMS Carrot fly; violet root rot; parsnip canker. Canker is more of a problem in nitrogen-rich and acid soils. Early sowings are most prone to attack.

Harvesting
Flavour improves after a frost. Lift as required when leaves start to die. Can be left in the ground over winter, but harvest by late winter as older roots will develop a hard woody core.

Peas

Pisum sativum PAPILIONACEAE

Peas are well suited to cooler climates. By growing a range of types and varieties, peas can be harvested from May to September. The climbing, edible-podded types are easy to fit into almost any garden, producing attractive flowers and tasty pods. Pea roots fix nitrogen, boosting soil fertility. In cool climates peas are more reliable than beans when grown for drying.

SEED TO HARVEST Early cultivars: 11–12 weeks. Maincrops: 13–14 weeks.
CROP DIVERSITY
Shelling peas: Early maincrops and maincrops: mostly 45–120cm (18–48in) tall, but old cultivars, to 2.5m (8ft) tall or more, are still available. Pods usually green, some purple. Round-seeded peas are hardier but less productive and not so sweet-tasting as wrinkle-seeded types. Petit-pois are selected smaller pea cultivars.
Edible-podded peas: Mangetout ("eat-all") peas are eaten when immature pods are flat. Sugar, or snap pod, peas are picked when pods are thick-walled and plump. Both may grow 0.6–1.5m (2–5ft) tall.
SITE Soil that does not dry out in summer, but is not waterlogged

Pak choi

Parsnips

Peas

Parsley see p.288

in winter. Summer crops tolerate some shade. Tall peas make an attractive screen. The leafless types look decorative in small clumps or containers.

SOIL TREATMENT Apply a low-fertility soil improver before sowing.

IDEAL pH RANGE 6–6.8

Sowing

Grow a range of varieties for a regular crop through summer. Use quick, early varieties for early and late sowings, which are less likely to be attacked by pea moth.

MINIMUM GERMINATION TEMPERATURE 10° C (50°F)

UNDER COVER Start the earliest crops in deep modules or pots under protection from March. Harden off and transplant when about 10cm (4in) tall.

OUTSIDE Peas do not germinate well in cold, wet soil, so delay spring sowings until the soil is warm, or sow under cloches. Sow until early July; summer sowings only thrive if the soil does not dry out. Sow round-seeded cultivars in November in mild districts.

Spacing

ROWS Sow in broad drills, 23cm (9in) wide, or in double rows of two drills 5cm (2in) wide and 23cm (9in) apart, spacing seed 5cm (2in) apart each way in the drill. Leave 60–90cm (24–36in) between drills, depending on height of cultivar.

BLOCK PLANTING Suitable for semi-leafless and shorter cultivars: 5–7cm (2–3in) apart.

Plant care

Provide supports for plants early on. Peas have tendrils that cling to twiggy sticks, wire mesh, or pea netting. Leafless and semi-leafless types need little support if grown in a block. Mulch to keep soil moist. Water regularly in dry conditions from when flowers first open. Watering before will not improve the crop, but just encourage lots of leafy growth.

PROBLEMS Birds (pigeons, pheasants, jays); mice; pea and bean weevil; pea moth; pea thrips; foot and root rots.

Harvesting

Pick mangetout peas as soon as of convenient size. Keep picking to encourage production. Harvest sugar peas when pods are plump. Pick shelling peas when the peas can be felt through the pod, before they get too large. Fresh peas freeze well. Peas for drying should be left to hang on plants until rattling dry. Shell peas to finish drying. Keep in airtight jars.

Peppers

Capsicum annuum Grossum Group (sweet) and Longum Group (chilli)
SOLANACEAE

Sweet and chilli peppers are very different in flavour, but grow in the same way. These tropical and sub-tropical plants need warmth (more so than tomatoes) and good light levels to crop well; they are only suitable for outdoors in a sunny, sheltered site in mild areas. Chillies grown in a cool climate can still be very hot, but the hotter the chilli, the longer the growing season it requires.

SEED TO HARVEST 20–28 weeks.

CROP DIVERSITY Sweet peppers: mature fruits may be green, red, yellow or purple; oblong or tapered in shape. Some have thicker walls and are slower to mature. Compact cultivars grow well in containers. Chilli peppers vary in heat, shape and colour. Orange-, red- and purple-fruited cultivars are available.

SITE Peppers need a minimum temperature of 21°C (70°F) to crop well. In temperate climates, this means peppers are normally grown in a cool greenhouse or polytunnel or in a very warm, sheltered site in milder regions. A fertile soil that warms up early is essential.

SOIL TREATMENT Apply a medium-fertility soil improver.

IDEAL pH RANGE 6–6.5

Sowing

MINIMUM GERMINATION TEMPERATURE 20°C (70°F). Sow seed in gentle heat in pots or modules, in April or May. Transplant into 8–9cm (3–3½in) pots; as soon as the roots have filled the pots, move the plants into 10–13cm (4–5in) pots. Keep temperatures at 12–16°C (54–61°F) during this period.

Planting out

Plant out into greenhouse soil or large pots or growing bags when first flowers appear. Plant outside only after the last frost. Protect plants as necessary to maintain them at a temperature of at least 15°C (59°F), and no higher than 30°C (86°F).

Spacing

30–45cm (12–18in) depending on the cultivar.

Plant care

Support taller plants with a cane. Water regularly in dry weather, and feed plants in pots with a high-potash liquid fertiliser. Maintain high humidity in the greenhouse by damping down when necessary, which may mean up to twice a day in hot weather.

PROBLEMS Aphids; glasshouse red spider mite; glasshouse whitefly; blossom end rot.

Harvesting

Pick sweet peppers when still green to encourage more fruits to form, or leave for 2–3 weeks to develop a mature colour and a sweeter flavour. At the end of the season, when frost is forecast, pull up all the plants whole and hang them up upside-down in a frost-free shed. The fruits will continue to ripen. Chillis should be left to ripen on the plant. They can be stored dry, preferably in an airtight jar, in the dark.

Potatoes

Solanum tuberosum SOLANACEAE

Potatoes are easy to grow. They require a fair amount of space but can give a good return. The work involved is a rewarding way of clearing ground. Frost-tender, potatoes are usually planted in spring for an early and late summer crop, or in summer for a late autumn crop. Potatoes are usually grown from small tubers called "seed" potatoes. Always buy certified seed potatoes, grown to a strict standard to ensure they are

---

Cultivar choice

Peas Peas in the pod: 'Feltham First'; 'Meteor' – early, round-seeded; 'Douce Provence' – very early, wrinkle-seeded; 'Little Marvel'; 'Gradus'; 'Early Onward' – early maincrop, first introduced in 1890 and 1908; 'Greenshaft' – one of the best, resistant to downy mildew and fusarium wilt; 'Alderman' – one of last tall maincrop cultivars; 'Kelvedon Wonder' – a mildew-resistant maincrop; 'Markana' – semi-leafless maincrop.
Mangetout: 'Carouby de Maussane' – purple flowers and long wide pods. Snap pod: 'Sugar Snap'; 'Sugar Rae'.
Drying peas: 'Carlin' – tall, brown seeded. May only be available from heritage collections.
Peppers Sweet peppers: 'Yolo Wonder'; 'Long Red Macaroni'; 'Redskin' F1 – compact plants for pots. Hot peppers: 'Habenero' – very hot; 'Hungarian Wax' – long pointed yellow fruit, quite sweet when young, getting hotter as they mature.

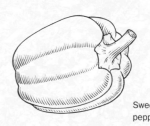

Sweet pepper

healthy. Reject shrivelled, soft or damaged tubers. They can also be grown from micro-propagated plants – usually old or scarce cultivars. The flavour of potatoes can vary widely depending on where grown, so try a selection to discover what suits you and your soil.

Seed to harvest 13–20 weeks from planting.

Crop diversity There are over 100 cultivars of seed potato available in the UK. Early, second early and maincrop cultivars are classified by the time taken to mature. Earlies are the quickest, but lowest-yielding. Maincrops store well. Skin colours include pink, yellow, purple and red, and flesh colours are usually yellow or white, but there are purple-fleshed cultivars. Textures vary from floury, high dry-matter cultivars (good for roasting and chips) to waxy salad potatoes. Cultivars with resistance to blight, blackleg, slugs and eelworm are available, and well worth choosing to help combat these problems.

Site Open, sunny, site, though will tolerate a little shade. The ideal soil is deep, fertile, humus-rich and, preferably, acid. Avoid poorly drained sites. Can be grown in large containers. An extra early crop to harvest in late April or May can be grown in an unheated greenhouse/polytunnel or under cloches if adequate frost protection can be given.

Soil treatment Apply a high-fertility soil improver to the soil or planting trenches, or use a low- or medium-fertility soil improver, depending on the soil, with a nitrogen-rich organic fertiliser.

Ideal pH range 5–6

Planting

Seed potatoes are sprouted or "chitted" before planting to help them grow quickly. To produce sturdy short shoots, put potatoes in trays or egg-boxes, rose end (the end with most eyes) upwards, in late winter or very early spring. Put in a light, warm place, 18° C (64°F), out of direct sunlight until shoots have just started to grow. Move to a cooler position for about 6 weeks before planting outside. Pot micro-propagated plants into 10cm (4in) pots of loam-based compost. Harden off before planting outside when the danger of frost has passed.

Growing under cover Plant mid-February. Protect from frost.

Growing outside Plant into trenches or individual holes, 7–15cm (3–6in) deep, and cover with at least 3cm (a generous inch) of soil. Potatoes can also be grown on the soil surface under a mulch using the no-dig technique (see p.327). Plant mid-March–May. Tubers suffer if planted into cold wet soil; if weather conditions are uncertain, delay planting. Protect early plantings from frost if necessary.

It is now possible to buy cold-stored potato tubers for planting in June and July for a late autumn/early winter crop. These are more likely to be attacked by blight, and the plants will need frost protection with fleece or cloches at the end of the growing season.

Spacing

Rows Early cultivars: 28–36cm (11–14in) apart, with 38–50cm (15–20in) between rows. Second earlies and maincrop cultivars: 36–45cm (14–18in) apart, with 65–75cm (26–30in) between rows. Space larger tubers further apart and smaller ones closer.

Block planting Early cultivars: 30cm (12in). Second earlies and maincrop cultivars: 35cm (16in).

Plant care

Frost protection Early potatoes are most at risk. Cover foliage with soil, straw, newspaper or fleece overnight if frost is likely.

Earthing up Earth up potatoes as they grow, bringing the soil up around the shoots. This helps control weeds, prevents the tubers turning green, and gives some protection against tuber blight. Start when plants are 15cm (6in) tall, leaving a small amount of foliage showing. Earth up again just before the foliage meets across the rows. Earthing up is not possible with closer spacing, but the plants shade themselves. Alternatively, plants can be mulched with a thick layer of hay, straw, leafmould or grass mowings, which also helps to conserve moisture.

Soil moisture and watering For the highest yield of good-sized tubers, keep the soil moist throughout the season. The most effective stage for watering, where necessary, is when tubers are the size of marbles (which usually coincides with flowering). Water the soil rather than the foliage.

Problems Slugs (mainly tubers); potato cyst eelworm (tubers); wireworm (tubers); potato blight (foliage and tubers); scab (tubers); potato blackleg (stems); black-heart and hollow heart (tubers); internal browning (tubers); rust spot (tubers); magnesium and potassium deficiencies (foliage).

Harvesting

Start harvesting early varieties in late June and July. Flowering is an indication that tubers will be large enough, but not all cultivars flower. Maincrops should be dug as the foliage dies down, usually in September. Harvest as soon as possible if slug attack is likely. Second earlies usually mature somewhere between the two. If in doubt scrape some of the soil away from a plant to investigate. All tubers must be removed when harvesting to reduce the risk of disease. Only store disease-free, undamaged tubers. Harvest on a dry day, if possible, and rub off excess soil before storing in paper or hessian sacks. Keep them cool, between 7–10°C (45–50°F), frost-free and dark. Allow slight humidity and air to circulate.

Pumpkins and squashes

Cucurbita maxima, C. moschata, C. pepo CUCURBITACEAE

Large and often very vigorous half-hardy plants, with a diversity of shapes, colours and sizes of fruit. Undemanding and very rewarding to grow. Heat-tolerant.

Seed to harvest Summer squash: 7–8 weeks after planting. Pumpkins and winter squashes: 12–20 weeks after planting.

Crop diversity Summer squashes: soft-skinned and smooth fruits, available in all shapes, from round "patty pan" or "custard" squashes to the crookneck types. Usually eaten fresh; they do not store well.

Potato

Often trailing habit. **Pumpkins and winter squashes:** May be bushy or trailing in habit. Fruit size, shape, colour and eating quality varies widely. Fruits may be several to the kilo, or weigh in at tens of kilos. Colour ranges from orange to green and grey; skin may be smooth or warty. The flesh may be watery, or dense and sweet. All store well.
SITE Sheltered, in full sun. Small-fruited varieties look good trained up a pergola or archway.
SOIL TREATMENT Apply a low or medium fertility soil improver, depending on soil condition. Rich feeding can produce a lot of foliage at the expense of the fruit. Can be grown on a compost trench (see p.48).
IDEAL pH RANGE 5.5–6.8

Sowing

MINIMUM GERMINATION TEMPERATURE 13°C (55°F).
UNDER COVER Sow in late spring, 3–4 weeks before the end of the last frosts. Push 2 seeds into 9cm (3in) pots; remove the weaker seedling. Harden off well before planting outside after the danger of frosts passes. Transplant without disturbing the roots.
OUTSIDE Sow direct in early summer in mild areas. Protect with bottle cloches for extra warmth at the start.

Spacing

Plants will grow to fill all available space; when transplanting, mark the centre of each plant with a cane so you know where to water if necessary. They will grow happily beneath runner beans or sweetcorn.

ROWS Bush cultivars: 60–90cm x 90–120cm (24–36in x 36–48in) Trailing cultivars: 1.2–1.8m x 1.8m (4–6ft x 6ft).
BLOCK PLANTING Bush: 90cm (36in); trailing: 1.2–1.8m (4–6ft).

Plant care

Trailing varieties can be trained up a strong support, or pegged out into a circle to keep them under control. Keep weed-free until established. Water only until established. Plants root deeply and need little further watering. When growing well, mulch with straw, hay or low fertility soil improver. Allow only 3–4 fruits per plant to mature on larger pumpkin cultivars. Push a tile or board underneath large fruits. In wet seasons they may rot if in contact with the soil.
PROBLEMS Slugs, especially on young plants in cold and wet weather; powdery mildew.

Harvesting

Shoots, young leaves, flowers, fruits and seeds can be eaten. Harvest summer squashes as soon as an edible size. They will keep in the fridge for 2–3 weeks. Winter squashes and pumpkins to be stored should be left on the plant as long as possible to develop a hard skin before the first frosts. When fruits feel hard and sound hollow if tapped, pick and expose the underside to the sun for 10 days or so to complete the ripening process. Well-ripened fruit will store for 6–12 months in an airy place at 7–10°C (45–50°F). All types lend themselves to making chutney, pickles, and wine.

Purslane, summer

Portulaca oleracea
PORTULACACEAE

An attractive, half-hardy plant with succulent bright green or golden leaves and stems, for summer salads. Needs warm conditions, so grow in a warm sheltered spot with light, well-drained soil. Sow direct in May and June. Can also be sown in modules in April to plant out. Space 15cm (6in) between plants. Earlier and later seedling crops can be grown under cover. Pick young leafy shoots after 4–8 weeks, leaving at least 2 leaves on the plant, which should resprout.

Radish

Raphanus sativus, Raphanus sativus Longipinnatus Group
BRASSICACEAE

A diverse crop, suited to cool climates. Typical salad radishes crop in as little as 4 weeks in summer. Hardy autumn and winter radishes have substantial roots that can be harvested over a long period and eaten raw or cooked. If the roots are left to produce a flowering stem, the immature seed pods can be eaten too. They are crisp and hot. Radish can also be grown as a seedling cutting crop (see p.332). Leave a radish to go to seed. A single plant will provide a good supply of seed.

SEED TO HARVEST Summer types: 4 weeks. Mooli types: 7–8

weeks. Autumn and winter types: from 20 weeks.
CROP DIVERSITY Summer cultivars: small pink, red, white or bicoloured roots, round, elongated or long. Mooli or Daikon: large, long, hot white roots, grown to crop in late summer/autumn. Autumn and winter cultivars: large, round or elongated roots, with black, pink or red skins. Autumn and winter radishes are frost-tolerant.
SITE Open site generally, but prefers light shade in summer. Avoid soil prone to drought. Summer types are good for intercropping, growing in containers, and as early and late crops under cover.
SOIL TREATMENT Prefer a soil that has already been improved for a previous crop. Apply a low-fertility soil improver to light soil.
IDEAL pH RANGE 6.5–7.5

Sowing

Not suitable for transplanting.
MINIMUM GERMINATION TEMPERATURE 5°C (41°F).
UNDER COVER For early and late crops, sow summer cultivars under cloches or fleece, or in the soil in a cool greenhouse or polytunnel. Sow February–March and September–October. Sow mooli types in August for a winter crop.
OUTSIDE Summer cultivars: sow thinly in rows, or broadcast. For succession, sow in late February–September at 10-day intervals. Avoid hot, dry months. Mooli cultivars: midsummer onwards. Winter cultivars: July–August.

Spacing

ROWS Summer cultivars: 2–2.5 x 10–15cm (¾–1 x 4–6in). Mooli:

Cultivar choice
Pumpkins and squashes Summer squash: 'Custard White'; 'Long Green Trailing'; 'Vegetable Spaghetti'; 'Tromboncino'. Winter squash and pumpkins: 'Golden Nugget' – bush; 'Blue Kuri', 'Pompeon'; 'Turk's Turban'; 'Early Acorn' F1; 'Gemstore' F1.
Radishes Summer cultivars: 'French Breakfast'; 'Icicle' – long and white; 'Red Meat' – red-fleshed; 'Sirri' RZ – good under cover; 'Scarlet Globe' – first introduced in 1896. Mooli: 'April Cross' F1. Autumn and winter cultivars: 'Black Spanish Round'; 'Black Spanish Long' – introduced in 1783; 'Belrosa' RZ; 'China Rose'; 'Munchen Bier' – said to produce the most succulent pods.

Radicchio *see Chicory*

Summer purslane

10 x 25cm (4 x 10in). Winter cultivars 20 x 30cm (8 x 12in). **BLOCK PLANTING** Summer cultivars: broadcast thinly; thin to 10cm (4in). Mooli cultivars: 22.5–25cm (9–10in). Winter cultivars: 20–30cm (8–12in).

Plant care

Do not allow to dry out, but avoid over-watering, which encourages leafy growth.

Harvesting

SUMMER CULTIVARS Harvest as soon as roots are large enough. They go woody and run to seed quickly.

MOOLI CULTIVARS Harvest when large enough in mid–late summer. Will stand for several weeks.

WINTER CULTIVARS Harvest in autumn–early spring. Protect from frost with straw or store in sand in a frost-free shed. Leave a large root in the soil to flower and produce pods the next year. Pick pods when young and juicy.

Red orache

Atriplex hortensis
CHENOPODIACEAE

Also known as mountain spinach, this is a tall decorative annual. It self-seeds at will. Sow in spring and summer, leaving 20cm (8in) between plants. Eat the mild-flavoured leaves lightly cooked.

Rhubarb

Rheum x cultorum POLYGONACEAE

One rhubarb plant can take up a lot of space, but it is usually all a family needs. It is simple and trouble-free to grow, well-suited to cool temperate climates. As it is the young, pinky-red stalks that are eaten, botanically this fruit is classed as a vegetable. It makes an attractive ornamental. Rhubarb leaves are poisonous to eat, but quite safe to compost. The toxic oxalic acid they contain breaks down harmlessly during the composting process.

CROP DIVERSITY Some cultivars are more suited to forcing and early cropping than others.
SITE Fertile, fairly heavy soil in sun or light shade. Tolerant of all soils except waterlogged soils.
SOIL TREATMENT Dig soil deeply. Apply a medium to high fertility soil improver before planting. Mulch with a low fertility soil improver after planting.
IDEAL pH RANGE 5–6

Sowing and planting

Most easily grown from "sets" or crowns, but can be raised from seed – although the results will be variable and take some time.
MINIMUM GERMINATION TEMPERATURE 13°C (55°F). Sow under cover in February, 2–3 seeds in 9cm (3½in) pots. Harden off and plant out once frosts have passed. Sow outside in spring, 2.5cm (1in) deep in rows 30cm (12in) apart. Thin to 15cm (6in). Plant in permanent position in the autumn.
PLANTING Buy virus-free plants or divide existing plants that are at least 3 years old, in winter. Plant sets in October–November and February–March. The bud should be just below the soil surface. Firm soil well after planting. Sets may be grown on in pots for a few months before planting to give them a better start. Pot-grown plants can be planted at any time if the soil conditions are suitable.

Spacing

At least 90cm (36in) each way.

Plant care

Water until established. Remove flower stems as they appear. Clear up leaves after foliage has died down. Mulch in late winter or early spring with a medium- to high-fertility soil improver.
PROBLEMS Usually trouble-free. May suffer from crown rot or viruses for which there is no cure. Remove infected plants and do not replant on the same site.

Forcing

Established plants can be forced in early spring for pale pink, delicately flavoured stems. Plants can be dug up and brought under cover, or blanched *in situ*.
UNDER COVER Lift crowns over 2 years old in November or December and leave on the soil surface to expose them to the cold. In January, place crowns close together in deep boxes or pots packed with soil. Keep in a warm dark shed or garage, or under greenhouse staging. Keep moist and warm, covering with an upturned bucket to exclude light. Discard after cropping.
IN SITU From February, cover crowns with a bucket or blanching pot. To speed up the process, pile fresh manure mixed with leaves or half-made compost around the blanching cover. Harvest after 6 weeks or so. Do not take another crop from forced plants for at least 2 years.

Harvesting

Harvest 12–18 months after planting. Take only a few stems in the second year. From then on, harvest until June or July. If you sow seed early enough there is often enough to harvest from surplus seedlings from a late winter sowing. Twist off, rather than cut, stalks. Harvest lightly in autumn if you have not taken a crop in spring.

Salad rocket

Eruca vesicaria BRASSICACEAE

Also called rucola and arugula, a fast-growing crop of spicy salad leaves that can be cut as little as 3 weeks after sowing. The flowers are also edible. It makes a good quick catch crop, and grows well in containers. Rocket can be grown for most of the year. Early and late sowings can be made under cloches or in a tunnel or greenhouse. It likes moisture-retentive soil and partial shade. No special treatment is needed on most soils. Apply a low-fertility soil improver on light soils. Make regular sowings direct into soil February–June and late August–October. Plants sown in high summer tend to bolt. Broadcast thinly in wide rows or blocks for a seedling crop for cutting. Space at 15 x 15cm (6 x 6in) for larger leaves. Pick or cut leaves as required. Water in dry weather. Flea beetle is often a problem, but plants can be grown under mesh or fleece. As a brassica, rocket is also vulnerable to clubroot and must be included in a crop rotation.

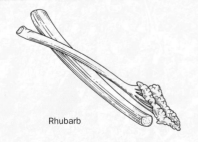

Rhubarb

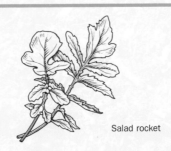

Salad rocket

Cultivar choice
Rhubarb 'Glaskin's Perpetual' – raised from seed easily; 'Timperley Early' – best for early forcing, thin pink stalks; 'Victoria' – latest to crop; 'Stockbridge Arrow' – extra-long cropping season.
Salad rocket 'Salad Rocket'; 'Turkish Rocket'; 'Sylvetta'.

Salsify

Tragopogon porrifolius
ASTERACEAE

An easy-to-grow root vegetable that is also known as vegetable oyster. It needs a long growing season but can be harvested all winter and takes up relatively little space. Can be blanched to give a spring crop.

SEED TO HARVEST 20 weeks
CROP DIVERSITY Little
SITE Well-cultivated soil free of stones in open, sunny position. Makes compact clumps to fit amongst other crops or in a border. Unharvested plants will bear glorious mauve dandelion flowers in their second year – a favourite of hoverflies.
SOIL TREATMENT No additional feeding needed on reasonable soil that has been improved for a previous crop.
IDEAL pH RANGE 6–7.5

Sowing
MINIMUM GERMINATION TEMPERATURE 7°C (45°F). Sow outside in April. Use fresh seed every year. The large seeds are easy to station sow, 2–3 seeds per station at 1cm (½in) deep. A second sowing can be made 1 month later. Germination may be erratic, but it usually takes about 20 days.

Spacing
ROWS 20 x 30cm (8 x 12in)
BLOCK PLANTING 23cm (9in)

Plant care
Little needed. Hand-weed or mulch for weed control. Hoeing can damage the roots.

Harvesting
ROOTS Lift in autumn when the leaves have died. The long roots are brittle, so dig carefully. Keeps for a week in the fridge. Survives most winters left in the soil.
SHOOTS Roots left in the soil sprout in late spring. Remove dead leaves and mound up the soil around shoots to a depth of 15–20cm (6–8in) or cover with straw or leaves. Cover with an upturned bucket if you only have one or two plants. Blanched shoots taste similar to chicory and re-sprout for 2–3 cuttings.

Scorzonera

Scorzonera hispanica ASTERACEAE

An uncommon, hardy perennial root crop, usually grown as an annual. The edible roots are black-skinned with white flesh.

SEED TO HARVEST 18 weeks.
CROP DIVERSITY Little.
SITE Deep, light soil is essential for long roots to develop.
SOIL TREATMENT No additional feeding is needed on reasonable soil improved for a previous crop.
IDEAL pH RANGE 6–7.5

Sowing
MINIMUM GERMINATION TEMPERATURE 7°C (45°F). Sow direct in April and May as soon as the soil warms up.

Spacing
10 x 20cm (4 x 8in)

Plant care
Hand-weed or mulch for weed control. Hoeing can damage the roots. Generally trouble free.

Harvesting
Allow roots to grow for at least 4 months. Harvest from autumn to spring. Roots that have not reached a reasonable size can be left *in situ* for another year. Cover with straw or leaves in early spring to produce fresh greens. This blanches emerging leaves, which can be cut when 10cm (4in) tall. Scorzonera produces flowers in its second season, and the flower buds can be eaten.

Seakale

Crambe maritima BRASSICACEAE

This Victorian favourite is a perennial vegetable that can be grown in a demanding or relaxed fashion. The blanched shoots are harvested in mid- to late winter. With its large grey leaves and sweet-scented fountains of white flowers, seakale is an attractive ornamental and should crop well for 7 years.

SEED TO HARVEST 2 years.
CROP DIVERSITY Little.
SITE Open, permanent site in reasonably fertile soil. A deep, well-drained, slightly alkaline soil rich in organic matter is best.
SOIL TREATMENT Clear all weeds, especially perennials, and apply a medium-fertility soil improver. Lime the previous autumn if soil is acid.
IDEAL pH RANGE 6.5–8

Sowing
Plants from seed tend to be more vigorous than those propagated from "thongs" *(see below)*.
MINIMUM GERMINATION TEMPERATURE 7°C (45°F)

UNDER COVER Seed can be slow to germinate; sandpaper it lightly to get it started. Sow in early spring in 9cm (3in) pots or in soil in a cold frame. Select the strongest-looking plants, harden off, and transplant to final position when they have 3–4 leaves.
OUTSIDE Sow in seedbed in mid-March, 2.5cm (1in) deep in rows 30cm (12in) apart. Thin to 15–20cm (6–8in).

Planting thongs
Seakale is often raised from offsets or "thongs"(root cuttings). These are sometimes offered for sale. Root cuttings can be taken from plants that are at least 3 years old. Cut lateral root branches off in 7.5–15cm (3–6in) lengths in winter. Buds grow from the end nearest the main root. Cut that end square, and the other slanted, so you know which is which. Stand bunches of thongs, square cut upwards, in moist sand in a cool shed and plant in late March, by which time buds should have appeared. Rub out all but the strongest bud, plant in a dibber hole with the buds 2.5cm (1in) below the soil surface.

Spacing
30–38cm x 46–60cm
(12–15in x 18–24in)

Plant care
Apply an annual top-dressing of medium-fertility soil improver or seaweed meal to permanent plants in late spring once stems are cut. Remove yellowing foliage and flowering shoots so the plant's energy goes into the roots.
PROBLEMS Slugs on young shoots; clubroot; violet root rot.

Cultivar choice
Salsify 'Mammoth White'; 'Sandwich Island'.
Scorzonera 'Maxima'; 'Russian Giant'.
Seakale 'Lily White'; 'Angers'.

Seakale

Forcing to harvest

Allow plants to grow for at least one full year before harvesting.

OUTSIDE METHOD In February or March, clear away leaf debris from plants and cover them with a large, upturned bucket (at least 38cm/15in deep) or seakale forcing pot. Cover with leaves or straw to protect young shoots from cold. Cut blanched pale stems low down, with a little piece of root attached, when 10–20cm (4–8in) long. Stop cutting in May. Take 3–4 cuttings of shoots from each established plant – this can be repeated annually.

FORCING INSIDE Forcing indoors allows a prolonged cutting season. Lift plants over 18 months old in early winter after the first frosts. Remove any side roots of pencil thickness from crowns to make thongs for replanting in spring. Store the crowns (plants) in sand until required for forcing over the winter. Force a few at 2–3 week intervals. Plant 3 crowns in a 27cm (9in) flowerpot, with the tops just showing, in a mixture of leafmould and loam. Cover with an upturned bucket or flowerpot with the hole obscured. Keep in a cool shed or cellar no less than 10°C (50°F); in 5 or 6 weeks the shoots will be ready to cut. After forcing, plants are exhausted so discard. Seakale does not store.

Shallot

Allium cepa Aggregatum Group
ALLIACEAE

A hardy, easy crop, less demanding than onions. Shallots raised from sets form a clump of small bulbs. Plants raised from seed produce a single bulb. Ready from July, they may keep in store for up to a year.

SEED TO HARVEST From seed: 20 weeks; from sets: 20–24 weeks.
CROP DIVERSITY A range of shapes, sizes and skin colours.
SITE Open, sunny situation preferred, but tolerates a little shade.
SOIL TREATMENT No treatment needed if soil was improved for a previous crop. If not, apply a low- to medium-fertility soil improver, depending on soil condition.
IDEAL pH RANGE 6–7

Sowing

Shallots are usually planted as sets (*see below*) but a few cultivars can be raised from seed. Sow in March and April. Broadcast seed thinly in wide drills, aiming for 2.5–5cm (1–2in) around each plant. Thin if necessary.
MINIMUM GERMINATION TEMPERATURE 7°C (45°F)

Growing from sets

Plant in February and March when soil conditions are suitable. Can be planted in November and December for an earlier crop in mild areas with well-drained soil. Push sets gently into a light soil. Otherwise make a small hole or take out a drill. The tip of the set should be at soil level. Cultivars such as 'Sante' dislike cold soil and are best planted later, in April.

Spacing

ROWS 15cm x 20cm (6 x 8in)
BLOCK PLANTING 20cm (8in). Plant small sets 2.5cm (1in) apart in autumn for an early crop used as spring onions.

Plant care

Little attention needed. Water in dry weather when bulbs swell.
PROBLEMS Onion problems may also affect shallots, but they are usually trouble-free. They often bolt if weather conditions fluctuate. Either pull the plants up, or enjoy the flowers! Some cultivars are less prone to bolting; choose these for early planting.

Harvesting

Harvest when leaves are dying back, usually from July onwards. Lift bulbs and leave them to dry. Once totally dry, separate individual bulbs and store in nets or on slatted trays in a cool, dry place.

Sorrel

Rumex acetosa POLYGONACEAE

Hardy perennial with sharp, lemony leaves to harvest early in the season. May stay green throughout the winter. Sow in spring or autumn, either direct or in trays for transplanting, leaving 30cm (12in) between plants. Remove flower spikes to encourage leaf production. Renew plants every 3–4 years. Sorrel has such a sharp flavour that the leaves are best mixed with something milder.

Spinach

Spinacia oleracea
CHENOPODIACEAE

A quick-growing, leafy crop, best grown in cool temperatures. Runs to seed rapidly in hot weather.

SEED TO HARVEST 5–10 weeks.
CROP DIVERSITY Some cultivars are suited to spring and autumn sowing, while others, more resistant to bolting, can also be grown in summer.
SITE Prefers light shade in summer, making it a useful intercrop. Or grow in an open site on a fertile soil that does not easily dry out. Can be grown in containers in light shade, and in an unheated greenhouse or polytunnel for an early or late crop.
SOIL TREATMENT Apply a low-fertility soil improver or a medium-fertility soil improver on poor soil.
IDEAL pH 6.5–7.5

Sowing

Successional sowing of suitable cultivars can give a crop over a long period. Sow when previous crop is just coming through.
MINIMUM GERMINATION TEMPERATURE 7°C (35°F). Will not germinate above 30°C (86°F).
UNDER COVER Sow direct in early spring and early autumn under cloches or in an unheated greenhouse or polytunnel.
OUTSIDE Sow thinly in drills in early and late spring, then again in late summer and early autumn.

Spacing

ROWS 7–15cm x 30cm (3–6in x 12in)
BLOCK PLANTING 15cm (6in)

Plant care

Water in dry weather. Can be prone to downy mildew.

Harvesting

As soon as plants are over 5cm (2in) tall, start picking individual

Shallots

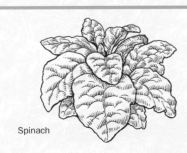

Spinach

Cultivar choice

Shallots From sets: 'Pikant' – bolt resistant; Hative di Niort' – a favourite for shows; 'Golden Gourmet' – plant from February; 'Sante' – plant from late April. From seed: 'Creation' F1; 'Matador' F1; 'Atlas' F1 – pink skin and violet flesh.

Spinach 'Avanti' F1 – for outside and under cover cropping, resistant to downy mildew; 'Medania' – spring to late autumn sowing, resistant to bolting; 'Monnopa' – spring- and autumn-sowing.

leaves. Pull whole plants when 15–20cm (6–8in), or cut 2.5cm (1in) above ground; they may re-sprout. Rapidly goes to seed. Use fresh, or freeze. Mainly problem-free as it grows so quickly.

Swede

Brassica napus Napobrassica Group
BRASSICACEAE

A very hardy root crop with a long growing season. It needs cool, damp conditions to do well. Roots can be left in the ground until the end of the year for autumn and early winter harvest. Delicious, sweet-flavoured orange flesh.

SEED TO HARVEST 26 weeks.
CROP DIVERSITY Flesh colour is usually yellow, though may be white. Skin colour is purple or creamy brown, or a combination of both. Some cultivars are resistant to mildew and clubroot.
SITE Open site. Fertile soil that does not dry out, nor suffer from poor drainage.
SOIL TREATMENT Apply a low-fertility soil improver if soil has been manured or composted for a previous crop. If not, treat also with a general organic fertiliser or use a medium-fertility soil improver. Do this in good time to let soil settle before sowing. Firm seedbed first if soil is still loose.
IDEAL pH RANGE 5.5–7

Sowing
MINIMUM GERMINATION TEMPERATURE 5°C (40°F)
UNDER COVER Sow suitable cultivars under fleece in February for an early crop of small-to-medium roots. Can be grown in root trainers and bio-degradable tubes for transplanting.
OUTSIDE Sow outside in early May in cooler areas, late May and early June in warmer regions. Sow thinly in drills 2cm (¾in) deep. Thin seedlings when small, no more than 2.5cm (1in) high. Sow under fleece or fine mesh cover to protect against flea beetle and cabbage root fly where necessary.

Spacing
ROWS 23 x 38cm (9 x 15in)
BLOCK PLANTING Early crops 15cm (6in); main crops 30cm (12in).

Plant care
Water regularly in dry weather, or may turn woody. Roots are also likely to split if watered suddenly after a dry period.
PROBLEMS Cabbage root fly; flea beetle; boron deficiency; violet root rot; clubroot; downy mildew; powdery mildew.

Harvesting
Harvesting can start as soon as roots are large enough, usually in early to mid-autumn. They can be left in the ground and dug as needed, but tend to go woody after December. Swedes can be stored in boxes (see p.335) in a cool location.

Sweetcorn

Zea mays POACEAE

A grain crop, unrelated to any other usually grown in the garden. Half-hardy, it is easy to grow in a good summer, less successful in a cold or wet year. Grows up to 1.7m (5½ft), each plant producing one or two cobs. Eaten within a few minutes of picking, their flavour is unrivalled by anything you can buy.

SEED TO HARVEST 10–15 weeks.
CROP DIVERSITY The fresh kernels of traditional sweetcorn cultivars store carbohydrate as sugar, not starch. Once cut, the sugar changes to starch, which is why sweetcorn should be eaten as fresh as possible. Supersweet varieties are specially selected to produce sugar-enhanced kernels, which take longer to loose their sweetness but which can be too sweet for some tastes. They are less hardy than the usual sweet-corn. The two types should not be planted together, as the super-sweetness is lost if the plants are cross-pollinated. Mini-corn is grown by close planting of selected, early cultivars.
SITE Warm, sheltered, sunny, with well-drained soil. Avoid very dry or cold, heavy soils. Can also be grown under cover if there is sufficient headroom. Mini-corn can be grown in pots.
SOIL TREATMENT Grow on soil that has been improved for a previous crop or apply a medium-fertility soil improver.
IDEAL pH RANGE 5.5–7

Sowing
MINIMUM GERMINATION TEMPERATURE 10°C (50°F). Sweetcorn needs to germinate in warm temperatures to do well.
UNDER COVER Sow in April. Sweetcorn resents root disturb-ance, so raise transplants in root trainers or biodegradable tubes. Harden off well before planting out when the soil has warmed up and danger of frost is past.
Planting out through black or clear plastic, which warms the soil, will speed up growth and cropping considerably.
OUTSIDE In warm areas, sow direct into warm soil. Warm soil under cloches or black plastic before sowing if necessary. Station sow 2–3 seeds, 2.5–4cm (1–1½in) deep. Thin to one seedling.

Spacing
Sweetcorn is wind-pollinated, so plant in blocks rather than rows, with 35cm (14in) between plants. For mini-corn, leave 15cm (6in) between plants, or grow 4 plants in a 30cm (12in) pot. Grow supersweet cultivars at least 8m (25ft) from other types to avoid cross-pollination.

Plant care
May need support on exposed sites. Stems can be earthed up to encourage more rooting for extra support. If necessary, water when corn starts to swell. Hand-weed or mulch for weed control – do not hoe. Sweetcorn has shallow roots, which are easily damaged.
PROBLEMS Mice; birds; slugs.

Harvesting
Corn is ripe when "silks" turn brown. Press a thumbnail into a corn grain – a milky juice means it is ripe. Can be frozen or pickled. Pick mini-corn when cobs are 7cm (3in) long.

Tomato

Lycopersicon esculentum SOLANACEAE

A popular vegetable, grown by many people who do not have a

Cultivar choice
Swede 'Acme Purple Top'; 'Joan' – for early sowing, moderate resistance to clubroot and powdery mildew; 'Marian' – has some resistance to clubroot and powdery mildew.
Sweetcorn 'Sundance' F1; 'Kelvedon Glory' F1; 'Earlivee' F1, – normal sweetness; 'Northern Extra Sweet' F1 – supersweet; 'Minisweet' F1 – good for mini-corn; 'Sweet Nugget' F1

Squash *see Pumpkins and squashes*

Sweetcorn

vegetable garden. A short-season half-hardy summer crop, relatively easy to grow without a greenhouse anywhere that has a reasonable summer. For earlier cropping, and/or higher yields per plant, use a greenhouse or polytunnel (for more information on growing tomatoes under cover, see p.224).

There are literally hundreds of cultivars. Disease-resistant cultivars are good for greenhouse growing where a long crop rotation is not practical. Yellow cultivars may be more resistant to potato blight than others. Those listed here are suited to growing both outside, in warmer regions, and under cover unless otherwise stated.

SEED TO HARVEST 7–12 weeks.
CROP DIVERSITY From the gardener's viewpoint there are 2 main types of tomato:
Indeterminate (sometimes called cordon or tall) varieties produce a single main shoot which grows indefinitely in warm conditions and is normally trained up a central support. Sideshoots are pinched out. Most cultivars of this type are for the greenhouse, but some grow outdoors.
Determinate or bush varieties have no leading shoot but develop many side branches, forming a sprawling bush – the commonest form of outdoor tomato. Trailing or extra dwarf types are selections of this type especially chosen for containers. There are also cultivars that are semi-determinate.

Tomato fruits can be round, plum-shaped, or ribbed, from cherry size to fruits that weigh 450g (16oz) or more. Colour is even more variable, including red, white, yellow, orange, green, purple and striped. The larger-fruited beefsteak and plum cultivars tend to ripen later. Plum cultivars are thick-walled and good for making sauces. Cultivars resistant to various pests, diseases and ripening disorders are available.
SITE Warm, sheltered, in full sun with fertile, well-drained soil. Under cover, tomatoes are easiest to manage in soil beds but can also be grown in large containers, indoors or out. Bush varieties can even be grown in a hanging basket.
SOIL TREATMENT Apply a medium-fertility soil improver, or a low-fertility soil improver combined with a general organic fertiliser.
IDEAL pH RANGE 5.5–7

Sowing
MINIMUM GERMINATION TEMPERATURE 16°C (60°F). Seedlings can withstand cooler temperatures. Sowing under cover, in gentle heat, is the best method of getting consistently successful crops in the UK. For growing in a heated greenhouse, start sowing in January. For an unheated greenhouse/polytunnel, or growing outside, sow 6–8 weeks before the last frost. Sow in trays (pricking out into pots), modules or in 9cm (3in) pots. Plants may need potting up again before transplanting outside. Harden off once danger of frost has passed. Move into bigger pots only when plants become pot bound. Plants are often offered for sale as an alternative to raising your own.

Tomato cuttings
Sideshoots are easily rooted as cuttings to provide several plants from a single seed. Cut off sideshoots when 15cm (6in) long. Insert into 8cm (3in) pots filled with equal parts of leafmould or coir and sharp sand. Cover with a plastic bag or bottle. Provide bottom heat 15–16°C (60–62°F) early in the season. Cuttings root in 10–14 days. Pot up or plant out as appropriate. Remove first truss of flowers if plant is not growing strongly.

Planting out
Plant out when first flowers show. To crop well, tomatoes need temperatures of around 21–24°C (70–75°F). If these temperatures are unlikely in summer, plant in a greenhouse/polytunnel. Leggy plants can be planted slightly deeper than in a pot. Under cover, interplant with French marigolds to reduce the risk of whitefly attack.
PLANTING OUTSIDE Harden off and transplant once all danger of frost has passed. Soil temperature should be at least 10°C (50°F) and air temperature a minimum of 7°C (45°F). Protect with fleece or cloches if necessary. To warm the soil and encourage fruit to ripen earlier in cooler regions, plant through a black plastic mulch.

Spacing
ROWS Tall, indeterminate, and semi-determinate types: 38–45 x 45cm (15–18 x 18in); allow 90cm (36in) between each pair of rows. Train as cordons with single stem. Bush types: 45–48 x 45–60cm (18–20 x 18–24in). Extra-dwarf bush types: 25–30 x 30–35cm (10–12 x 12–14in). Bush types are usually left to sprawl over the ground without support.
BLOCK PLANTING 45cm (18in)

Plant care
Protect from low temperatures and frost, but remember to allow access for pollinating insects once flowers open. Mulch for moisture retention. Once fruit has formed, water plants in very dry weather. Plants in containers need regular watering, even twice a day in hot weather, and supplementary feeding with a high-potash organic liquid fertiliser. Plants grown in a well-managed soil should not need additional feeding. Mulch with a medium-fertility soil improver, or cut comfrey leaves, if necessary. Overwatering or overfeeding reduces the flavour of a crop. Train indeterminate types up a string or sturdy support. Pinch out sideshoots. In late summer or earlier in cooler regions, pinch out the growing tip to prevent further growth and encourage development and ripening of the fruit. Do not pinch out sideshoots of bush cultivars. To keep the crop clean, support plants with pea-sticks or similar, or mulch with straw. Shade greenhouse in summer.
PROBLEMS Potato and tomato blight. **Under cover:** aphids; glasshouse whitefly; glasshouse red spider mite; tomato moth; fusarium wilt; grey mould (botrytis); tobacco mosaic virus; tomato leaf mould; verticillium wilt; blossom end rot; magnesium deficiency; tomato greenback.

Harvesting
Pick fruits as they ripen fully, reaching the colour appropriate to the cultivar. Cut the fruit stalk,

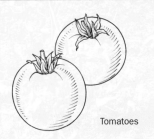
Tomatoes

leaving the calyx attached to the fruit. Towards the end of the season, pull up outdoor plants still cropping and hang by their roots in a frost-free shed or garage. The fruit will continue to ripen. Alternatively, when frost threatens, pick all fruit and place green ones in a single layer in a drawer or box in a cool place to ripen. Healthy fruits continue to ripen until the New Year. They can also be bottled, frozen, or made into jams and chutneys.

Turnip

Brassica rapa Rapifera Group
BRASSICACEAE

A root vegetable in the cabbage family, turnips are suited to moist, cool conditions and tolerate mild frosts. Young turnip leaves are excellent as a spicy spring green.

SEED TO HARVEST Early cultivars 5 weeks; maincrops 6–10 weeks.
CROP DIVERSITY Flesh can be white or yellow, the skins white, yellow, pink or red. Early cultivars are small and white, fast growing for spring and summer crops. Maincrop cultivars are hardier; used fresh in summer and winter; also for winter storage.
SITE Need moist, cool soil; can take some shade. Quick-maturing cultivars useful for catch-cropping.
SOIL TREATMENT Apply a low-fertility soil improver if soil has been improved for a previous crop. Otherwise a medium-fertility soil improver, or low-fertility soil improver with a general organic fertiliser.
IDEAL pH RANGE 5.5–7.5

Sowing

Not suitable for transplanting.
MINIMUM GERMINATION TEMPERATURE 5°C (42°F)
UNDER COVER The earliest sowings of quick cultivars can be made under fleece or cloches in early March, as soon as the soil is workable. Sow thinly in drills 2–2.5cm (¾–1in) deep, or station sow. Sowing under fleece or fine mesh netting will protect against flea beetle and cabbage root fly.
OUTSIDE Early/quick cultivars – sow in March and April every 3 weeks in shallow drills 2cm (½in) deep for successional cropping. May/June sowings are possible if weather is cool and wet. Maincrop cultivars – sow in July and August. To ensure good root formation, thin to required spacing as soon as possible, before seedlings are more than 2.5cm (1in) high.

Spacing

ROWS Quick cultivars: 10 x 23cm (4 x 9in); maincrop cultivars: 15 x 30cm (6 x 12in).
BLOCK PLANTING 15cm (6in).

Plant care

Water regularly in hot, dry weather or plants may bolt.
PROBLEMS Turnip gall weevil; cabbage root fly; flea beetle (seedlings); clubroot; downy mildew; powdery mildew; violet root rot; boron deficiency.

Harvesting

Early turnips: pull when 4–5cm (1½–2in) across. Maincrop turnips: harvest at tennis-ball size; will keep in the ground until New Year. Any still growing can be used for greens; cut tops at 10–15cm (4–6in) high. Usually tops will crop several times.

Welsh onions, bunching onions

Allium fistulosum
ALLIACEAE

Perennial Welsh onions grow in clumps like chives, with hollow leaves up to 45cm (18in) tall. The base of the leaf is thickened at and below ground level. A useful winter vegetable, eaten raw or cooked, surviving temperatures as low as –10°C (14°F). Developed from the Welsh onion, the Japanese or Oriental bunching onion is a ubiquitous Chinese vegetable. A perennial usually grown as an annual or biennial, the plants are harvested at any stage from seedling to fully grown. They tend to be more vigorous and productive than Welsh onions.

CROP DIVERSITY Japanese bunching onions: multi-stemmed and single-stemmed, white or red.
SITE See Onions, globe and bulb. Will grow in containers. Flowering forms of Welsh onion look good in large pot, and make attractive green edging to a vegetable patch. Japanese bunching onions are a useful intercrop between other plants.
IDEAL pH RANGE 6–7.5

Sowing

MINIMUM GERMINATION TEMPERATURE 5°C (45°F)
Oriental bunching onions can be sown in modules for transplanting, or sown direct.
UNDER COVER Sow Welsh onions in modules in April; harden off and transplant about 6 weeks later.
OUTSIDE Sow in spring or summer. Sow in shallow drills, a pinch of 3–4 seeds every 5cm (1in), allowing 20cm (10in) between rows. Transplant to rows 23 x 30cm (9 x 12in), in blocks 20cm (8in). Divide established clumps and replant younger outer sections.

Harvesting

To harvest as small leafy shoots, sow all year round under cover; from spring to autumn outside. Sow thickly in wide drills. Harvest when around 15cm (6in), 30–40 days after sowing.

To harvest as larger scallions/ small bunching onions, sow all year round under cover; from spring to early autumn outside. Sow thinly in wide rows, thinning to 4cm (1½in), or multi-sow, 6 seeds per module, to transplant. Harvest when 30cm (12in) tall, after 60–80 days.

To harvest as larger bunching onions, sow in modules in spring and early summer. Transplant after 4–8 weeks for a late summer/autumn harvest. Sow late summer to transplant in early autumn, for harvesting the following spring. Row spacing 7.5cm x 30cm (3 x 12in), in blocks 20cm (8in). Ready to harvest in 3–4 months. Use the thickened white stem and the green leaves.

Plant care

For winter harvests in cold areas, protect Welsh onions with cloches or frames. Divide established clumps every 4–5 years. Remove spent flower heads from cultivars which flower.
PROBLEMS Thrips; stem and bulb eelworm; downy mildew; onion white rot.

Cultivar choice
Turnip Quick, early: 'Snowball' – first introduced in 1869; 'Market Cross' F1 – also suitable for growing under cover. Maincrop: 'Golden Ball'; 'Veitch Red Globe' – introduced in 1882.

Watercress *see p.226*
Zucchini *see Courgettes and marrows*

Turnip

A–Z of Plant Problems

THE FOLLOWING REFERENCE SECTION, while it cannot be completely comprehensive, covers the majority of plant problems that you may encounter in the garden, and under cover, in greenhouses and polytunnels. It may also help in diagnosing and dealing with similar problems on conservatory and houseplants too.

Entries are arranged by common name: additional common names may be cross-referred at the base of each page. For pests and diseases, to avoid any confusion, scientific name(s) are also given. Each entry briefly describes the problem, whether a cultural disorder, a disease, or a pest. Plants susceptible to the problem are then listed; in some cases, these are quite specific, but in others, groups of related plants, or any plant growing under similar conditions, may be affected. The most commonly seen symptoms are described.

For each problem, measures for prevention and control are then given – if any are necessary. This latter point cannot be overstresssed. Above all, never use sprays, even "organic" ones, unless essential.

Best practice for healthy plants

Use the following general measures to encourage healthy, problem-free plant growth and reduce the need to use controls.

• Provide appropriate food and shelter to encourage natural predators (see Gardening for Wildlife, pp.186–201)
• Create a good soil structure (see Soil and Soil Care, pp.33–39).
• Feed the soil with composted organic soil improvers (see also Soil and Soil Care, pp.40–61)
• Grow plants that suit the site.
• Do not sow or plant when temperatures are too low.
• Practise good hygiene – clear away pest-ridden and diseased foliage and plants, both in the garden and under cover (see also Management Tips Under Cover, pp.228–229).
• Encourage good airflow around plants, by thinning out and pruning.
• Do not overfeed, particularly with nitrogen, which causes lush growth, attractive to pests.
• Use a crop rotation when growing vegetables (see pp.301–303).
• Pick off pests and diseases as they appear.
• Grow resistant cultivars where there is a known problem.

Spraying – best practice
Never:
• Spray if another method is available.
• Mix different sprays together.
• Spray on a windy day.
Always:
• Identify the problem correctly, so the right spray is used.
• Check that the product is legally, and organically, approved for the job. Regulations are frequently updated.
• Spray at dusk to avoid harming bees.
• Follow the instructions on the bottle or packet.
• Wear protective clothing and use a good-quality sprayer.
• Avoid spraying predators.

Other useful references

Most of the techniques and materials listed here for prevention and control are given fuller descriptions, and often pictured, in the chapter on Plant Health, pp.84–103 – including biological controls, traps and barriers, and "organic" sprays. Other useful references are:
• Crop covers – fleece and mesh, pp.230–233.
• Mineral (nutrient) deficiencies and soil pH: pp.36–37 and p.61.
• Soil testing and analysis pp.33–37.

Getting more help

If you cannot find a specific problem, or you are unsure as to the diagnosis of your problem, the HDRA offers its members a diagnostic and advice service for plant problems, and keeps them up-to-date on the latest advances in keeping plants healthy. It also publishes a series of leaflets and factsheets on common problems, available to all. Some of the most popular can be accessed at the HDRA website, www.hdra.org.uk, along with details of all other publications that can be obtained by mail (see also p.402). Techniques and materials for pest and disease control can be seen in use at the HDRA's three garden sites (see p.403), together with new methods on trial. The gardens also host a selection of open days, events and short courses throughout the year on specific topics, where much detailed advice can be obtained.

Acer tar spot

Rhytisma acerinum

This fungal disease overwinters on fallen leaves and infects the new season's growth in spring. Different strains exist that infect particular species of *Acer*.

SUSCEPTIBLE PLANTS Common on sycamore, but also affects many ornamental *Acer* species.
SYMPTOMS Yellowish patches first appear on upper leaf surfaces. These darken into large tar-like black blotches with yellow edges from midsummer onwards. The disease rarely affects vigour, although appearance is severely affected.
PREVENTION AND CONTROL Ornamental maples – clear away any diseased plant leaves and other debris. No action is practical for large trees.

Ants

Lasius and *Myrmica* spp.
These red, browny-yellow or black insects have a distinct head, thorax and abdomen. They live in colonies in flower beds, lawns, compost heaps and plant pots. Ants are generally a nuisance rather than a pest.

SUSCEPTIBLE PLANTS None.
SYMPTOMS Ants rarely damage plants directly, but their activities can disturb growth, and increase damage caused by other pests. Tunnelling can interfere with root activity, causing wilting and death. Some ants build mounds over their nests in lawns, spoiling the appearance and making mowing difficult. Ants may steal seeds, especially those with a high oil content. Many feed on the sticky honeydew excreted by aphids and scale insects. They may "farm" these pests – moving them around a plant, and protecting them from predators.
PREVENTION AND CONTROL Ants are almost impossible to eliminate, so it is only worth trying to control them where specific damage is being caused. Grease bands, or a band of fruit tree grease, can prevent ants moving up into a tree, shrub or greenhouse bench. Douse troublesome outdoor colonies thoroughly with cold or boiling water. Flooding pot plants with water may flush out a nest.
Pesticide spray: Pyrethrum; plant oil-based product.

Aphids

Small, soft-bodied, sap-feeding insects 1–5mm in length. Often called greenfly or blackfly, depending on their colour; they may be winged or wingless, with long legs and antennae, and prominent tube-like structures at the end of the abdomen. Body colour is red, orange, yellow, green, brown or black, depending on species. In favourable conditions, females when only a week old give birth to live young so colonies can build up rapidly.

SUSCEPTIBLE PLANTS Most plants may be attacked by aphids. Many aphid species are plant-specific, such as the lupin aphid (q.v.), while others, such as the peach potato aphid, will attack hundreds of different types of plant. Aphids may spend the summer on certain plants, moving to a different host species for the winter.
SYMPTOMS Tender young growth is most prone to attack, but aphids will also colonise leaves, stems and, in some cases, roots. Leaves and shoots become distorted. Heavy infestation can kill a plant. Leaves are often coated with honeydew, a sticky substance produced by aphids. Black sooty moulds (q.v.) grow on the honeydew, inhibiting photosynthesis and spoiling appearance. Root aphids can cause plants to wilt. Aphids also transmit viruses.
PREVENTION AND CONTROL Tolerate aphid colonies where they are not causing damage. They will act as a "nursery" for aphid predators and parasites to feed and breed on. To control aphids, rub them off or pick off infested shoots. Grow attractant flowers and create suitable habitats for birds, earwigs, lady-birds, hoverflies, spiders, ground beetles, parasitic wasps, lace-wings and other natural enemies of the aphid. Allow natural predators time to work. Do not overfeed plants with nitrogen; soft, sappy growth is a magnet to aphids. Keep containers adequately fed and watered, and pot up plants as necessary. Use crop rotation to avoid build-up of root aphids. Grow resistant cultivars. **Biological controls:** Under cover, *Aphidius* and *Aphidoletes* – both need a minimum temperature of 10°C (50°F) and at least two hours at 18°C (64°F) every day to stimulate activity. Lacewing larvae are ideal trouble-shooters when an aphid infestation has got out of control. Use them to reduce the pest population to manageable levels, then introduce the other controls. They need a minimum temperature of 10°C (50°F). They may be used outside from early May; or use ladybird larvae from April.
Pesticide sprays: Insecticidal soap; pyrethrum; rapeseed oil. All of these must hit the aphids to work. Once leaf curling has occurred and pests are concealed a spray is unlikely to be effective.
See also Black bean aphid; Cherry blackfly; Currant blister aphid; Lettuce root aphid; Lupin aphid; Mealy cabbage aphid; Plum leaf-curling aphid; Woolly aphid.

Apple and pear canker

Nectria galligena

This fungal disease is spread by wind and rain-splash, and enters the plant through cracks in the bark, leaf scars or pruning cuts. Diseased fruit left on trees can also be a source of infection.

SUSCEPTIBLE PLANTS Apple, pear, hawthorn and poplar. Some apples, such as 'Cox's Orange Pippin', 'Elstar' and 'Gala', are particularly susceptible. More resistant cultivars include 'Bramley's Seedling', 'Lane's Prince Albert' and 'Newton Wonder'. Canker is a particular problem on wet

---

Apple bitter pit *see Calcium deficiency*

Apple capsid *see Capsid bugs*

Never mix different pesticide sprays together.

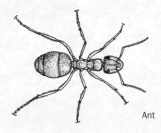
Ant

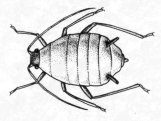
Honeysuckle aphid
Actual length 2mm

sites where soil is poorly drained.

SYMPTOMS Tree bark shrinks and cracks, often in concentric rings with the central piece of bark falling away. Deep lesions develop on the branches. Swelling can occur around the canker, and young twigs may die back. Cream-coloured pustules may be seen in summer; red spots are more common in autumn. Papery bark can result. Uncontrolled canker can ring an entire stem. Fruit skins crack; some fruits dry and can remain, "mummified", on the tree.

PREVENTION AND CONTROL Do not grow trees on wet sites or badly drained clay soil. Improve drainage. If a young tree becomes affected, it may be advisable to remove it. Once a tree is established, sow a grass seed mixture up to the main stem, to reduce the risk of infection by rain-splash. Cut out cankers and diseased branches. Do not use poplar or hawthorn as a windbreak near apple orchards.

Apple powdery mildew

Podosphaera leucotricha

Fungal disease that overwinters in buds. Infected buds open later than healthy ones. *See also* Powdery mildews.

SUSCEPTIBLE PLANTS Apple; also pear, quince, peach, *Photinia* and medlar.

SYMPTOMS A powdery white coating on buds, leaves and

stems. Flowers drop; leaves distort, wither and fall. Early infections cause web-like russetting on fruit.

PREVENTION AND CONTROL Grow resistant cultivars. Mulch under trees to stop soil drying out. Water trees in dry weather. In winter, cut out infected shoots. In spring, remove infected leaves and shoots. Spray with seaweed extract to promote strong growth.

Fungicide spray: Sulphur, although it can harm some apple cultivars. Check the label before use.

Apple sawfly

Hoplocampa testudinea

The small white, brown-headed larvae of this insect hatch from eggs laid on embryo fruit at blossom time. They burrow into developing fruit to feed and may visit several fruits before dropping to the soil as the fruit falls prematurely in midsummer. Sawflies overwinter in the soil and hatch the following spring. *See also* Sawflies.

SUSCEPTIBLE PLANTS Apple.

SYMPTOMS Fruits fall early, and may have a hole where the larva has emerged. Fruit is tunnelled and filled with brown "frass" or excrement. Fruits on tree may be distorted, with characteristic ribbon scarring.

PREVENTION AND CONTROL Pick up fallen fruit immediately and compost it. Remove mulches during winter. Gently dig over the soil in winter to expose the cocoons to birds.

Apple scab

Venturia inaequalis

This fungal disease overwinters in leaf debris and is spread to new leaves in spring by wind and rain. In severe cases the disease can overwinter in twig lesions. Apple scab is worse when the weather is cool, wet or overcast in spring and early summer, especially at flowering time.

SUSCEPTIBLE PLANTS Apple.

SYMPTOMS Dark brown/green blotches appear on the leaves; these may expand along the veins and run into each other. Leaves may drop prematurely. Dark spots, which develop into corky patches, appear on the fruit skin. Fruit may crack, but does not rot. In severe cases, twigs blister, swell and burst to produce brown-green pustules in spring.

PREVENTION AND CONTROL Grow resistant cultivars such as 'Ellison's Orange' and 'Court Pendu Plat'. In autumn, water fallen leaves on the ground with diluted urine, or any other high-nitrogen liquid (nettle brew, manure tea), as this will help to kill spores and decompose leaves. Mow the ground below trees to shred leaves and speed decomposition, or collect leaves and compost them. Cut out and burn diseased twigs. Prune apple trees to maintain good air circulation.

Apple sucker

Psylla mali

Nymphs (the young) of this pest are orange-brown or green

with prominent red eyes. Eggs overwinter on fruit spurs and hatch in early to mid-spring. Nymphs feed and mature in opening buds from May onwards. Adults feed in the trees until winter, when they die. *See also* Suckers.

SUSCEPTIBLE PLANTS Apple.

SYMPTOMS Buds damaged by nymphs. Blossom is distorted, and may fail to develop. Similar symptoms to frost damage (q.v.).

PREVENTION AND CONTROL Check fruit buds in early spring. Squash any eggs. If damage is not extensive, remove and burn affected buds and leaves at once. Grow flowers such as corn marigold, corn chamomile and cornflower to attract predators.

Asparagus beetle

Crioceris asparagi

The adult beetles are up to 6mm (¼in) long, with distinctive yellow and black wing cases. Larvae are grey-black with a humped back. Adults hibernate under stones, in soil and in plant debris, emerging in spring to feed on asparagus foliage. Eggs are laid in June. There may be two or three generations in a year.

SUSCEPTIBLE PLANTS Asparagus.

SYMPTOMS Foliage eaten. Growth may be checked.

PREVENTION AND CONTROL Pick off larvae and adults. Clear plant debris where beetles may overwinter. **Pesticide spray:** Derris.

Apple replant disease *see Replant disease*

Asparagus beetle
Actual length 6mm

Apple sucker
Actual length 2mm

Grow resistant cultivars if possible where there is a known problem.

Bacterial canker

Pseudomonas mors-prunorum

In autumn and winter canker bacteria, spread by rain-splash from the leaves, enter twigs through leaf scars to cause canker lesions. In spring and summer the foliage is attacked, but no new cankers are formed.

SUSCEPTIBLE PLANTS Plum and cherry.
SYMPTOMS Dark brown spots appear on leaves in the late spring. These drop out leaving a "shot hole" appearance. Cankers usually occur on plum tree trunks and cherry branches. Initially, amber-coloured gum exudes from a slight depression. Leaves become yellow and stems die back.
PREVENTION AND CONTROL Not an easy disease to control. There are no fully resistant plum or cherry cultivars, but the plum cultivars 'Marjorie's Seedling' and 'Warwickshire Drooper' are rarely seriously affected. 'Victoria' and 'Early Laxton' are very susceptible. Try to avoid damaging the bark of trees. Make sure trunks will not rub on any supporting stake, take care when cutting surrounding grass, and do not leave rough pruning cuts.

Bacterial soft rot

Erwinia carotovora

A common disease caused by a soil-dwelling bacteria. It does not appear to survive in the soil, but can survive on plant debris. Infection enters through wounds such as those caused by slugs or carrot root fly.

SUSCEPTIBLE PLANTS Brassicas, especially turnip and swede; also celery, cucurbits, leeks, lettuce, onion, parsnip, potato, tomato and cyclamen.
SYMPTOMS Water-soaked lesions around a wound that rapidly enlarges. The infected stem, leaf base or storage organ disintegrates into a foul-smelling, slimy, brownish rotting mass. The skin of most storage organs is not affected, although cracks may appear through which the slimy interior may seep.
PREVENTION AND CONTROL Ensure that land is well-drained. When growing vegetables use a strict crop rotation – minimum three years, but preferably four or five. Control wound-forming pests like wireworms, slugs, and root-damaging larvae. Once rot has started there is no cure. Dispose of or bury infected plant material.

Bay sucker

Trioza alacris

Adults of this pest overwinter in curled bay leaves, and in debris at the base of the plant. They feed on young shoots in spring. One or two generations a year.

SUSCEPTIBLE PLANTS Sweet bay (bay laurel), especially plants over five years old.
SYMPTOMS Leaf edges curl, then become pale, thickened and "blistered". If infestation is severe, leaves may shrivel and fall, and shoots die. Copious sticky honeydew is produced, and black sooty moulds develop.

PREVENTION AND CONTROL Pick off, prune out and collect up infected leaves.

Beet leaf spot

Cercospora beticola, Ramularia beticola

This fungal disease overwinters in residue from diseased plants or on seed. It is spread by rain-splash, wind, insects, tools and by hand. High humidity and warm temperatures encourage disease development.

SUSCEPTIBLE PLANTS Red beet, spinach beet; also sugar beet.
SYMPTOMS Small, more or less circular spots with a pale ashen centre and brown-purple margins appear on leaves.
PREVENTION AND CONTROL Clear up crop debris; use fresh seed. Damage is rarely significant.

Big bud mite

Cecidophyopsis ribis

Minute pest also known as the blackcurrant gall mite. Adults and young feed within black-currant buds. They overwinter and breed in the buds, leaving when they open in the spring. Mites are dispersed widely by wind, rain and on larger pests, to invade healthy young buds.

SUSCEPTIBLE PLANTS Blackcurrant.
SYMPTOMS An infestation is also known as "big bud" – the infested buds becoming swollen and rounded from June to September. The swollen buds, which are easiest to spot in winter and early spring, fail to develop normally. This damage is usually less of a problem than the effects of blackcurrant reversion virus (q.v.), which this mite transmits.
PREVENTION AND CONTROL Always buy certified planting stock. Remove and destroy swollen buds in the autumn and winter. Destroy all infected plants before planting new stock on a new site as far away as possible from the previous one.

Black bean aphid

Aphis fabae

Small, black winged aphids, forming dense colonies.
See also Aphids.

SUSCEPTIBLE PLANTS Beans, leaf beet and chard, poppy, nasturtium and other ornamentals. Winter hosts are *Euonymus* (spindle tree), *Philadelphus* and *Viburnum*.
SYMPTOMS *See* Aphids.
PREVENTION AND CONTROL Earlier sowings of broad beans are less susceptible to attack. Pinch out tips of broad bean plants in May or early June, or when pests are seen. Remove heavily infested plants.
See also Aphids.

Blackcurrant reversion virus

Big bud mite (q.v.) is thought to spread this common virus.
See also Viruses.

SUSCEPTIBLE PLANTS Blackcurrant.

Bean rust *see Broad bean rust*
Beet leaf miner *see Leaf miners, also p.310*
Blackcurrant gall mite *see Big bud mite*

Pick off or prune out pests and diseases as they appear.

Bacterial canker

SYMPTOMS A healthy leaf is deeply indented at four distinct points, with five main veins running from the top of the leaf stalk to the tips of leaf lobes. Diseased leaves are darker and narrower, and have fewer indentations. Sometimes there are only one or two main veins. Fruit yield is significantly reduced but as this disease is widespread there may be no "ideal" to compare this to; it may therefore go unnoticed in the early stages.
PREVENTION AND CONTROL Buy plants from a reputable source. Check leaves each season for signs of reversion. Reduce big bud mite levels by removing any over-large, round, swollen buds that differ in shape from the ordinary buds on the bush, before they burst into leaf in early spring. Remove and dispose of infected bushes. Where big bud is common, renew blackcurrant bushes every seven to eight years, planting in a new site.

Blossom wilt

Sclerotinia laxa

Fungal disease that also causes wither tip. Spores, spread by wind or insects, infect flowers and leaves. The disease overwinters in cankers in tree branches or on mummified fruit. Often associated with brown rot (*Sclerotinia fructigena*) and aphid infestations.

SUSCEPTIBLE PLANTS Apple, pear, plum, cherry, nectarine, peach and apricot; also ornamental *Prunus* spp.

SYMPTOMS Flowers and leaves on spurs wilt, normally a couple of weeks after flowering. Cankers may develop on spurs where blossoms have wilted or where fruit is infected with brown rot. Branches may be girdled and subsequently die. Spur tips of plum, almond and cherry may wilt.
PREVENTION AND CONTROL Cut out cankers and diseased spurs during normal winter pruning. Remove all mummified fruit from the tree and the ground. Do not compost infected material. The apple 'Bramley's Seedling' is resistant to blossom wilt.
See also Brown rot.

Boron deficiency

Root crops are most susceptible to this disorder; also cabbages, cauliflowers, celery, pears, strawberries and carnations.

SYMPTOMS Growing tips die, plants are bushy and stunted. Beetroot – rough, cankered patches appear on roots; may cause a brown rot internally. Cabbage – leaves distorted; hollow areas in stems. Cauliflower – curds develop poorly, and may develop brown patches. Stem, leafstalks and midribs roughened. Celery – leaf stalks develop cracks on the outer surface; inner tissue is reddish-brown. Pears – fruits develop hard, brown flecks in the flesh; may be distorted. New shoots may die back in spring. Strawberries – plants stunted. Leaves small, yellow and puckered at tips. Fruits small and pale, developing a "waist" close to the stem end. Swede and turnip – brown or grey areas, often in concentric rings, develop internally in the lower parts of the root.
CAUSES A true soil deficiency is fairly rare; it may occur when the bedrock contains granite, which is low in boron. Leaching from light soils in heavy rainfall, excess liming/high pH, and very dry soils may also be the cause.
PREVENTION AND TREATMENT Improve moisture-retention of light soils. Measure pH before liming; keep pH below 7. Rake borax into the soil at 35g/sq m (1oz/sq yd). Use a foliar spray on pears (70g in 22 litres of water (2oz in 5 gal).

Box sucker

Psylla buxi

This insect lays its eggs in late summer in slits in leaf axils and twigs. They hatch in mid-spring. Nymphs (the young) feed on growing points and young shoots from late spring onwards. There is one generation each year.

SUSCEPTIBLE PLANTS Box.
SYMPTOMS The leaves at the tip of infected shoots arch inwards to form tight cabbage-like clusters. Growth can be checked if infestation is severe. Sticky honeydew and black sooty moulds may be present.
PREVENTION AND CONTROL Control is only necessary on young plants if they become stunted. Clip regularly, particularly in early spring, to remove infested shoot tips.

Brassica white blister

Albugo candida

Fungal disease spread by wind, insects and rain-splash. It can remain dormant in the soil for several months, where it overwinters.

SUSCEPTIBLE PLANTS Vegetable and ornamental brassicas; the annual weed shepherd's purse.
SYMPTOMS Small, smooth white blotches resembling white paint spots appear on leaves and stems. These spots later become powdery. Distortion of affected areas or the entire plant follows. Commonly associated with brassica downy mildew.
PREVENTION AND CONTROL Destroy diseased plants. Use a strict crop rotation – minimum three years but preferably four or five years.

Broad bean chocolate spot

Botrytis fabae

This fungal disease thrives in damp and overcrowded conditions. Spores can overwinter on infected plants and plant debris. The disease is more likely to be a problem where soil is short in potassium.

SUSCEPTIBLE PLANTS Broad bean, field bean.
SYMPTOMS Round, chocolate-brown spots develop on leaves, stems, pods and seed coats. These may merge until totally blackened parts of the plant die.

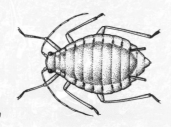

Black bean aphid
Actual length 2mm

PREVENTION AND CONTROL
Provide ample spacing between plants. Grow in well-drained soil. Avoid autumn sowing if this disease is a regular problem. Spring-sown beans are more likely to recover than plants infected later in the season. Improve potassium levels if low.

Broad bean rust

Uromyces viciae-fabae

Fungal disease that proliferates in warm damp weather; spread by rain-splash, insects, animals and wind. It can overwinter on plant debris.

SUSCEPTIBLE PLANTS Broad beans and peas.
SYMPTOMS Undersides of leaves and stems develop rusty-brown pustules. Symptoms spectacular but rarely damaging to the plant.
PREVENTION AND CONTROL Remove and compost all plant debris. To prevent spore germination, avoid wetting leaves when irrigating.

Brown rot

Sclerotinia fructigena, S. laxa

Airborne fungal disease that infects plants through wounded bark. Caterpillars, birds, support stakes or hailstones can cause the initial damage. It spreads quickly throughout the plant and cankers may develop. The fungus overwinters on infected fruit and cankers.
See also Blossom wilt.

SUSCEPTIBLE PLANTS Apple, peach, almond, nectarine, cherry, quince, plum and pear.
SYMPTOMS A very common fungal problem which produces soft, brown patches on fruit (see p.91). Concentric circles of white fluffy growth also develop on these areas while fruit is on the tree or in storage. Fruit may turn black. Some fruit on the tree will shrivel, become "mummified", and remain attached throughout the winter.
PREVENTION AND CONTROL Prune out affected branches and remove fruit from the tree. Pick up windfalls. Do not compost any of this material. Take care not to damage fruit that is to be stored. Do not store any diseased fruit. Cut out cankers and diseased spurs during normal winter pruning.

Cabbage caterpillars

There are two butterfly caterpillars that are pests of cabbages. The cabbage white or large white butterfly (*Pieris brassicae*) is a creamy-white, with a broad black tip to the forewing, appearing in April and May. Clusters of bright orange eggs are laid on and under leaves of susceptible plants. The distinctive yellow and black caterpillars, often found in large clusters, grow up to 5cm (2in) long, feeding for a month or so (see p.304). There are two or three generations a year. The spring brood of the small cabbage white butterfly (*Pieris rapae*) is white, with slightly clouded, black tips on forewings. The summer brood have darker tips and black markings on the wings. Eggs are laid singly, under leaves. The caterpillars, which grow up to 3.5cm (1½in) long, are velvety green, making them difficult to spot, especially when lying along the vein of a leaf. They are often found feeding in the heart of a plant.There can be three generations in a year, with the severest attacks in late summer.

SUSCEPTIBLE PLANTS Brassicas; large whites may also attack nasturtiums (*Tropaeolum* spp.).
SYMPTOMS Foliage eaten. A plant may be quickly stripped to a skeleton.
PREVENTION AND CONTROL Examine plants regularly when the butterflies have been seen. Squash eggs, pick off caterpillars. Wasps are particularly effective at controlling this pest. Grow crops under fine mesh netting to exclude the butterflies.
Biological control: Apply *Bacillus thuringiensis* (Bt) as a spray to infested plants.

Cabbage root fly

Delia radicum

Adults of this flying insect are 6mm (¼in) long and resemble small horseflies. They lay eggs in soil near, or occasionally on, host plants. Legless white larvae, up to 8mm (⅜in) long, feed on roots. Pupae overwinter in the soil. Damage is usually worse in late spring and early summer, but a second and even third generation may continue to damage plants into autumn. Transplants raised in seed beds, pots and modules are also prone to attack.

SUSCEPTIBLE PLANTS Brassicas; also related ornamentals such as wallflowers and stocks.
SYMPTOMS Young plants wilt or grow poorly, and are easily pulled out of the ground. Established plants may show no obvious symptoms. Damage to root crops (radish, turnip, swede) may make them inedible. Larvae occasionally found inside Brussels sprouts.
PREVENTION AND CONTROL Cover with non-woven fleece or fine mesh netting immediately after sowing or planting. Or, protect individual plants with a cabbage root fly mat (see p.304) – a 12cm (5in) square of soft woven material or rubber carpet underlay, or purchased equivalent. Plant into a slight hollow; in the event of an attack, earth up to encourage new root growth. Intercrop with French or dwarf broad beans.

Cabbage whitefly

Aleyrodes proletella

Adult whitefly readily fly up when the plants are disturbed. Immature nymphs (the young) are flat, oval scale-like insects that remain immobile on the lower leaf surface. Heavy infestations make the foliage sticky with honeydew produced by the whitefly, and sooty moulds (q.v.) may grow on this substance. *See also* Whiteflies.

SUSCEPTIBLE PLANTS Brassicas.
SYMPTOMS See Whiteflies. Eggs are laid on the undersides of leaves from mid-May.

Bud blast *see Rhododendron bud blast*

Barriers and crop covers can protect many crops from pest damage. See p.101, and also pp.230–233.

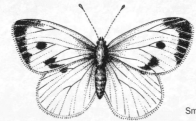
Small cabbage white butterfly

Development to adults takes about four weeks. Reproduction continues until autumn. Eggs and adults overwinter on host plants.
PREVENTION AND CONTROL Break the cycle of infestation by removing remains of all winter brassicas as soon as cropping has finished. Bury them in a compost trench or compost heap before planting out new brassica plants. Remove lower leaves infested with immobile young whitefly scales. Brushing plants to disturb the whitefly will disrupt the adults' feeding pattern. Wash off whitefly, honeydew and sooty mould with a jet of water. **Pesticide spray:** Insecticidal soap. Apply the spray directly onto the pests in the early morning when temperatures are low and adults less mobile. Apply weekly for 3–4 weeks for best results.

Calcium deficiency

A disorder common on acidic soils, and on plants growing in containers where the water supply is erratic.

SYMPTOMS Curling of young leaves or shoot tips, poor growth. Apple – "bitter pit". Fruit skins pitted; brown spots in flesh, which tastes bitter. Large fruits, such as Bramley, particularly susceptible. Symptoms may develop in store.
Brussels sprouts and cabbage – internal browning.
Carrot – "cavity spot". Oval spots on roots develop into cracks and craters. Organisms

may invade, causing rapid root rotting.
Celery – central leaves blackened, plants stunted. Tomatoes, sweet peppers – "blossom end rot" (see picture, p.88). A dark brown/ black patch appears on blossom end of developing fruit. Not all fruit on a truss, or all trusses on a plant need be affected.
PREVENTION AND TREATMENT A true calcium deficiency is rare, though it can occur on some acid soils. Symptoms are more commonly the result of disruption in the supply of calcium. This may be caused by a shortage of water, which slows the transport of calcium to the plant, and also by excessive use of potassium or magnesium-rich fertilisers. Add lime to acid soils, where appropriate, up to a pH of 6.5. Apply organic matter to soil to maintain conditions that allow a steady water supply throughout the season. Never let container-grown plants dry out.

Capsid bugs

Small, active, sap-feeding winged creatures, up to 6mm (¼in) long. Nymphs (the young) are similar to adults but without wings. Colour varies with species. These creatures are rarely seen as they quickly drop to the ground or fly away when disturbed.

SUSCEPTIBLE PLANTS A wide range of wild and cultivated plants, including runner bean, black- and redcurrants, apple, chrysanthemum, dahlia, fuchsia and rose.

SYMPTOMS Most species feed on plants, causing small ragged holes in leaves, particularly at shoot tips. The damage is distinctive. Leaves develop a characteristic tattered appearance as they grow. Buds and shoots may be killed; flowers and fruit deformed. Apple fruits develop raised bumps and scabby patches. Some capsids are useful predators of small pests, particularly on fruit.
PREVENTION AND CONTROL Encourage birds to feed near apple, pear, plum and hawthorn trees in winter by hanging fat and bags of nuts from branches. If damage is extensive, tidy up under hedges over winter, raking out leaf litter and clearing away any plant debris. Control is not always easy as adults are elusive, but damage is not usually severe.

Carnation tortrix moth

Cacoecimorpha pronubana
Adult moths are small, pale grey-brown with coppery hind-wings. Caterpillars are small, about 1.8mm long, and pale green. When disturbed they wriggle backwards and drop on a silk thread. There are several generations a year, and the caterpillars may be found at any season under cover. They pupate within webbed leaves.

SUSCEPTIBLE PLANTS A wide range of shrubs and herbaceous plants, both outdoors and inside.
SYMPTOMS The caterpillars can be found feeding between leaves bound together by silk webbing.

They graze the leaf surfaces, causing the leaf to dry up and turn brown. Buds and flowers may be damaged.
PREVENTION AND CONTROL Squash caterpillars or pick off webbed leaves.

Carrot fly

Psila rosae

Small, shiny black flies lay eggs in small clusters near host plants, starting in late spring. The larvae are creamy-white, up to 1cm (½in) long. Pupae, and sometimes larvae, overwinter in soil and roots of carrot and parsnip. There are two or three generations per year, the first causing most damage.

SUSCEPTIBLE PLANTS Carrot, celery, chervil, parsley and parsnip.
SYMPTOMS Young seedlings can be killed. The first sign of attack on mature plants is often a reddening of the foliage and stunted growth. The roots have rusty-brown irregular tunnels eaten away just below the skin. Larvae may be visible.
PREVENTION AND CONTROL Avoid growing carrots in sheltered sites, the preferred areas of weak-flying carrot flies. Delay sowing until June to avoid first generation attack. Harvest crops by late autumn. Some cultivars such as 'Sytan' and 'Flyaway' are said to be less susceptible; 'Autumn King' types tend to be very susceptible. Sow seed thinly to avoid the need for thinning; the fly can be attracted by the smell of bruised foliage. If thinning is necessary, remove all thinnings immediately and water

Capsid bug
Actual length 6mm

Canker, apple and pear *see Apple and pear canker*
Canker, cherry and plum *see Bacterial canker*
Canker, parsnip *see Parsnip canker*
Carrot cavity spot *see Calcium deficiency*

Avoid spraying unless essential.

to consolidate the soil. Grow one row of carrots between four rows of onions to mask the smell of carrots. This is only effective before the onions begin to form bulbs in early to midsummer, and may not be effective on a small scale. Cover with horticultural fleece or a fine mesh netting immediately after sowing. Grow under the cover throughout the life of the crop. Can also be grown within a topless enclosure of fine mesh netting, max. 90cm x 3m x 75cm high (3ft x 10ft x 30in high). Dig over soil in winter where damage has occurred, to expose overwintering larvae.

Caterpillars

Caterpillars are the larvae of butterflies and moths. Their bodies are segmented. The first three segments behind the head carry a pair of jointed legs, making up the thorax, while the remaining ten segments makes up the abdomen, which may have up to five pairs of fleshy legs. Sawfly larvae, similar in appearance but not related, have at least six pairs of legs on the abdominal segments.
See Cabbage caterpillars; Carnation tortrix moth; Codling moth; Cutworm; Winter moths. *See also* Sawflies, for comparison.

Celery crown rot

Mycocentrospora acerina
This fungal disease lives in damp soils rich in organic matter. Infection always enters through wounds. It can survive without a suitable host for several years.

SUSCEPTIBLE PLANTS Celery.
SYMPTOMS Plants become yellow and stunted. Dark lesions develop on roots, crown and leaf stalks. Plants in store develop tinged red leaves. Severe basal rot may develop even after two months in store and cause the crown to fall away.
PREVENTION AND CONTROL Grow celery in a well-drained soil. Use a crop rotation. Harvest when slightly immature and store in cool conditions and low humidity. Crown rot does not spread once plants are lifted.

Celery fly

Euleia heraclei (Philophylla heraclei)
Also known as celery leaf miner. Adult insects, up to 5mm (¼in) long, emerge between April and June, from pupae overwintering in the soil. Eggs are laid in leaves. The legless, white or pale green larvae, up to 8mm (⅜in) long, feed within leaves for a month, before pupating in leaves or in the soil. There may be three generations a year.

SUSCEPTIBLE PLANTS Celery, celeriac, parsley, lovage and related plants.
SYMPTOMS Yellow-brown blotches on leaves. The larvae may be seen feeding in the leaf mines. Plant growth may be checked and eating quality impaired.
PREVENTION AND CONTROL Immediately after sowing or planting, cover crops with fleece or fine mesh netting. Grow under cover throughout the life of the crop. Pick off infested leaves when seen and squash all larvae within.

Celery leaf spot

Septoria apiicola
Seed is the main source of infection by this fungal disease. The germinating seedlings are infected; the disease spreads to other plants by rain-splash.

SUSCEPTIBLE PLANTS Celery; also celeriac.
SYMPTOMS Brown spots with a lighter or darker border develop on older leaves. These soon spread to other foliage and occasionally to leaf stalks. Spots can be numerous and may merge causing leaf death.
PREVENTION AND CONTROL Clear away diseased leaves and other debris. Never save seed from infected plants.

Chafer beetles

Pests of various species including the cockchafer (*Melolontha melolontha*), garden chafer (*Phyllopertha horticola*) and rose chafer (*Centonia aurata*). Both adults and larvae attack plants. The major damage is caused by the soil-living larvae – soft-bodied white grubs, up to 4cm (1½in) long, with an obvious brown head and three pairs of legs. Eggs are laid in the soil in summer, particularly on overgrown land. Larvae feed for up to five years.

SUSCEPTIBLE PLANTS Herbaceous ornamentals, lawns, lettuce, potato, raspberries and strawberries are very susceptible.
SYMPTOMS Chafer grubs feed on roots, bulbs, corms, tubers and stems. Plants may suddenly wilt and die. Infested lawns can be further damaged by birds and badgers which dig up the turf to eat the larvae. Similar symptoms can be caused by leatherjackets and vine weevil larvae (q.v.). Adult beetles can damage leaves, buds, flowers and fruit of apples, roses and some other plants.
PREVENTION AND CONTROL Cultivation and weed control should clear the pest from overgrown land. Roll lawns in late spring to kill pupae and emerging adults.
Biological control: Apply *Heterorhabditis megidis* (a parasitic nematode) from mid–July to mid–August. The soil must be moist, with a minimum temperature of 12°C (54°F).

Cherry blackfly

Myzus cerasi
A small, shiny, browny-black aphid that infests cherry leaves in early spring. It moves on to a range of weed hosts in late spring, returning to the cherry to lay eggs in the autumn.

SUSCEPTIBLE PLANTS *Prunus avium* and *P. cerasus* are especially prone; *P. serrulata* and *P. x yedoensis* are less susceptible.
SYMPTOMS Leaves tightly curled and distorted, covered in dark sooty moulds and honeydew.
PREVENTION AND CONTROL *See* Aphids.

Celery leaf miner *see Celery fly*
Cherry bacterial canker *see Bacterial canker*

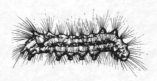

Yellow-tailed moth caterpillar

For more information on biological controls, see p.100.

Chrysanthemum leaf miner

Chromatomyia syngenesiae (Phytomyza syngenesiae)

Small inconspicuous dark flies lay up to 100 eggs in small incisions in leaves during summer months from which larvae hatch and feed within the leaves; most damage occurs in late spring to mid-summer. In heated greenhouses breeding continues for most of the year.

SUSCEPTIBLE PLANTS
Chrysanthemum, cineraria, calendula, lettuce, groundsel, sow-thistle and other related members of the Asteraceae family – indoors and outside.
SYMPTOMS First symptoms are a white spotting of leaves caused by the feeding of adult females. Narrow white tunnels appear between the upper and lower leaf surface. These later widen and meander towards the leaf midrib. After approximately two to three weeks small dark bumps can be seen on the lower leaf surface.
PREVENTION AND CONTROL Examine plants regularly. Pick off and destroy infected leaves. Control weeds, especially groundsel and thistle, as these can support populations of chrysanthemum leaf miner.

Chrysanthemum white rust

Puccinia horiana

This fungus is encouraged by a moist, humid atmosphere. It may persist from year to year on overwintering plants and stools.

SUSCEPTIBLE PLANTS
Chrysanthemums, in greenhouses and outdoors.
SYMPTOMS Yellow to pale green spots on upper leaf surfaces, corresponding to pustules on lower leaf surface, initially dirty buff in colour, later white. Leaf spots gradually turn brown and dead in the centre.
PREVENTION AND CONTROL Choose less susceptible cultivars, and destroy affected plants immediately. Do not propagate from diseased plants.

Clematis wilt

Ascochyta clematidina

This fungal disease originates from the soil or other plants. It is thought infection occurs in conditions of high humidity. Infection enters through small wounds caused, for example, by birds, insects and bruising by plant ties.

SUSCEPTIBLE PLANTS Clematis.
SYMPTOMS Sudden drooping of young growth. Affected leaves next to the stalks blacken, then wither and die. Dark lesions may be seen on the stem at or near ground level. Patchy blackening can occur on otherwise healthy leaves. Large-flowered hybrids are most susceptible to this disease, especially those with *Clematis lanuginosa* in their parentage.
PREVENTION AND CONTROL Plant newly purchased clematis 15cm (6in) deeper than originally grown. *Clematis viticella* cultivars are said to be much less susceptible. Avoid mechanical damage to stems particularly when securing ties. Cut back infected growth to soil level or below. New healthy growth should emerge from ground level. If symptoms recur, remove the soil to a depth of 30cm (12in) and destroy the infected plant. Replace with fresh soil and replant.

Clubroot

Plasmodiophora brassicae

This soil-borne fungal disease can survive in the soil for up to 20 years in the absence of a suitable host. Clubroot thrives in damp acid conditions. It is less of a problem in alkaline soils, in hot dry seasons and in spring-maturing crops. The disease is spread on infected plant material and contaminated soil. It is easily carried in soil on tools, machinery, footwear and on infected transplants, which may not show symptoms.

SUSCEPTIBLE PLANTS Brassicas; wallflower, stocks and candytuft.
SYMPTOMS Plants wilt on hot sunny days but may recover at night; they may become stunted and develop red tints on foliage. Roots develop swollen galls – either a single large gall, known as "clubroot" or several smaller swellings, known as "fingers and toes". Plant growth and crop yields are severely reduced.
PREVENTION AND CONTROL This disease is very difficult to control, so avoidance is very important Buy transplants from a reliable source, or raise your own. Build up good soil fertility and improve drainage. Lime acid soils. Where clubroot is present, liming to a pH of at least 7.0 may help. Remove all infected roots from the soil as soon as possible, preferably before the galls disintegrate; do not compost. Earth up crops which have been attacked with fresh compost to encourage new healthy roots. If clubroot is present on your land, raise plants in pots using disease-free potting mix. Grow brassica crop cultivars that show resistance such as swede 'Marian', kale 'Tall Green Curled', Chinese cabbage 'Harmony' and calabrese 'Trixie'.

Codling moth

Cydia pomonella

The adult moth, 8mm (⅜in) long, mottled grey-brown in colour, lays its eggs on fruits and leaves in early and midsummer. Single caterpillars tunnel into a fruit, often through the eye, leaving no obvious signs. The caterpillar, pinkish-white with a black or brown head, grows to 2cm (¾in) in length, as it eats its way to the core of the fruit. After a month or so it leaves the fruit, to pupate under loose bark, tree ties and similar locations. In a hot summer there may be two generations.

SUSCEPTIBLE PLANTS Apple; less frequently pear and quince.
SYMPTOMS Caterpillars cause extensive tunnels through fruit, spoiling it. Damaged fruit may ripen and drop prematurely. *See also* Apple sawfly.

Chafer grub *Actual size 4cm*

Chocolate spot *see Broad bean chocolate spot*

Practise good garden hygiene – clear away pest-ridden and diseased foliage and plants.

PREVENTION AND CONTROL
Hang sticky pheromone traps in trees from mid–May to the end of July, or early September in a hot year. Traps alone may reduce damage on isolated trees – or can be used to monitor the presence of the moth, so a spray can be timed accurately, before the caterpillars move into the safety of the fruit. Earwigs and bluetits are predators. **Pesticide sprays:** *Bacillus thuringiensis* is partially effective. Derris will work but is a contact killer and needs to hit the codling larvae before they burrow into fruit.

Coral spot

Nectria cinnabarina

This fungal disease normally invades diseased or dying wood. Plants that have suffered frost damage, have damaged bark, or that stand in damp conditions such as long grass in spring, are more vulnerable.

SUSCEPTIBLE PLANTS Most deciduous trees and shrubs.
SYMPTOMS Initial symptoms appear in spring. Wilting and bark death occurs above an entry point where coffee-coloured pinhead-sized pustules can be seen. Individual stems or multiple branches may die back. Pink or red pustules (shown on p.157) occur on dead or dying branches.
PREVENTION AND CONTROL Prune woody plants and clip hedges only in dry weather. Cut out all diseased branches as soon as seen, and burn all prunings. Disinfect equipment. Remove badly infected soft fruit bushes.

Cucumber mosaic virus

Viral disease spread primarily by aphids; it may also be spread by handling diseased plants, and on contaminated tools. Infection usually occurs when plants are about six weeks old.
See also Viruses.

SUSCEPTIBLE PLANTS
Cucumber, courgette, melon; also celery, beans and peppers. Ornamentals include anemone, aquilegia, begonias, campanula, dahlia, lily and primula.
SYMPTOMS Vary according to plant affected. In cucurbits, the virus causes mottling or mosaic patterns (shown on p.91) and distortion on the leaves. Flowering is reduced; plants are stunted and may die. The fruits will be small, dark and pitted, and may develop bright yellow blotches.
PREVENTION AND CONTROL Grow resistant cultivars. Remove infected plants as soon as symptoms are identified. There is no cure.

Currant blister aphid

Cryptomyzus ribis

Pale yellow aphids that are found on the underside of leaves in spring and early summer. They overwinter as shiny black eggs on currant and gooseberry bushes, hatching as the buds break. They migrate in summer to hedge woundwort.
SUSCEPTIBLE PLANTS Red- and whitecurrants; less frequently, blackcurrant and gooseberry.
SYMPTOMS Leaves develop blisters in spring and early summer; red on red- and whitecurrants, yellow on blackcurrants. Symptoms remain after aphids have moved on.
PREVENTION AND CONTROL *See* Aphids.

Cutworm

Noctuidae

Various nocturnal moth caterpillars are grouped under the general name of cutworm. These soil-living larvae tend to be fat, and will curl up as a "C" when disturbed. They may be brown, yellow or green with dark markings. Cutworm feed at night, and can be found at almost any time of year, both outdoors and in the greenhouse.

SUSCEPTIBLE PLANTS Young vegetable plants, especially lettuce and brassicas; also carrot, celery, beetroot, potato, strawberries and many ornamentals.
SYMPTOMS Stems of seedlings and young plants eaten through at ground level. Roots, corms, tubers and leaves may also be damaged.
PREVENTION AND CONTROL Cultivate infested soil in winter to expose caterpillars to predators, or allow chickens to scratch it over. Keep ground weed-free, as weeds provide sites for egg-laying. In the greenhouse, soak the soil thoroughly, then cover and leave overnight. This will bring cutworm to the surface, where they can be picked up. On a small scale, locate caterpillars in soil, or feeding on plants at night, and destroy. Protect susceptible transplants with a collar – such as a cardboard or plastic tube, or tin can with the base removed – pushed down into the soil around the plant.

Damping off

Rhizoctonia solani and *Pythium* spp.

There is a wide range of these troublesome soil-dwelling fungal diseases. Some survive on decaying plant debris, others exist as spores in the soil. They will multiply rapidly in cool, wet, poorly ventilated situations.

SUSCEPTIBLE PLANTS Seeds, seedlings, cuttings, roots, and vegetable parts at or below soil level, such as carrot and celery. Will spread rapidly through trays of seedlings, e.g. of bedding.
SYMPTOMS Seeds fail to germinate. Seedlings are attacked at soil level or below; stems become water-soaked, blackened and thin. Seedlings collapse and die. Reddish-brown root lesions form on seedlings and mature plants, initially just below the soil surface. Rootlets of older plants die. Vegetables such as potatoes, cucurbits and beans may become infected during extended wet periods. This results in a cottony fungal growth followed by the disintegration of the vegetable interior into a soft watery mass. *Rhizoctonia* also causes brown patches on lawns and fine turf.
PREVENTION AND CONTROL Always ensure pots and trays are scrubbed clean before sowing

---

Common green capsid *see Capsid bugs*

Common scab *see Potato common scab*

Cuckoo spit *see Froghopper, common*

Identify problems correctly so that the right spray, if necessary, is used.

Earwig

seed or taking cuttings. Use a sterile medium for seed sowing. Ensure drainage is good – waterlogged plants are more prone to pest and disease attack. Do not overcrowd seedlings, cuttings or older plants – good ventilation is essential to reduce humidity, which will encourage disease. Sow when soil has warmed up well in the spring. This will encourage plants to grow quickly and without check.
See also Phytophthora root and stem rots.

Downy mildew

Disease caused by a range of related fungi which attack specific plants, or groups of plants. These include *Peronospora destructor* on onion; *Bremia lactuca* on lettuce; *Peronospora sparsa* on rose; *Plasmopara viticola* on grape vines and *Peronospora violae* on pansies. These fungi survive in the soil, in crop debris, and on infected plants, not all of which will show symptoms.

SUSCEPTIBLE PLANTS Many plants, particularly when young.
SYMPTOMS Yellow patches on upper leaf surface, with corresponding patches of mould beneath in damp weather. Large areas of a leaf may be infected and the leaf may die. Onions rot in store. The disease is most common in damp and humid growing situations.
PREVENTION AND CONTROL Grow resistant lettuces such as 'Saladin' or 'Avoncrisp'. Use a

five-year rotation for onions where downy mildew has occurred. Improve ventilation and air flow. Remove infected leaves or individually affected plants. If it continues, remove and destroy all infected plants.
See also Onion downy mildew.

Earwigs

Forficula auricularia

The earwig can be a pest in some situations, but it is also a useful predator, particularly of apple pests such as codling moth and aphids, feeding at night. It has an elongated reddish-brown body, 2.5cm (1in) long, with pincers at tip of the abdomen. Earwigs lay eggs in the soil in late winter, which hatch in early spring. There may be a second generation.

SUSCEPTIBLE PLANTS Dahlia, clematis, chrysanthemum, delphinium, and other flowers.
SYMPTOMS Young shoots and flowers are eaten, leaving large ragged holes. Earwigs are often found in cavities in damaged tree fruits, but do not usually initiate the damage.
PREVENTION AND CONTROL Earwigs do not usually travel far, so clearing up debris where they might hide, and trapping, can make a local difference. Trap in upturned flower pots stuffed with straw and placed on top of a cane, or in lengths of dry broad bean stalk, or in a "lacewing hotel" (*see* p.192) Shake traps into a bucket of soapy water to kill the creatures, or liberate the earwigs on fruit trees.

Eelworm

Microscopic nematode worms, invisible to the naked eye. Some attack plants, while others are beneficial, attacking slugs and larvae of weevils and other pests. *See also* Potato cyst eelworm.

Flea beetle

Phyllotreta spp.

Small shiny black beetles, around 3mm (⅛in) long, that jump when disturbed. They hibernate in mulches and plant debris. Feeding starts in spring. Eggs are laid in soil near susceptible plants in late spring and early summer. There is one generation a year.

SUSCEPTIBLE PLANTS Brassicas, such as radish, swede, turnip, rocket and Oriental brassicas, particularly when seedlings. Also ornamentals such as nasturtium, alyssum, anemone and godetia.
SYMPTOMS During spring and summer, adult beetles eat small holes in leaves and stems. A severe attack will check growth and kill young plants. Damage is always more severe in dry weather. Larvae feed on plant roots, or in leaf mines.
PREVENTION AND CONTROL Encourage quick, vigorous seedling growth. Sow at the right time, prepare the site well, and never let plants go short of water. Sow under fleece or ultra-fine mesh netting (0.8mm mesh). Some crops can be uncovered once established; others such as

Chinese cabbage, radish and rocket, may need to be covered until harvest. Japanese radish may tolerate some flea beetle attack, and divert the pest away from other more sensitive crops.

Froghopper, common

Philaenus spumarius

Also called the "spittlebug", this sap-feeding pest ranges in colour from yellow to greeny-brown. It grows up to 6mm (¼in) long, with a blunt, wedge-like appearance with large eyes. Adults jump when disturbed. Young nymphs on plant stems cover themselves with a distinctive froth – "cuckoo spit" – for protection.

SUSCEPTIBLE PLANTS Roses and rosemary; also numerous outdoor and undercover plants.
SYMPTOMS Young shoots may become distorted and wilt. Flowers may be damaged. The white "cuckoo spit" if extensive may be disfiguring.
PREVENTION AND CONTROL Damage is rarely a problem. Spittle and nymphs can be removed by spraying with a high-pressure jet of water.

Frost damage

Tender plants are the most susceptible to this disorder. Normally hardy plants can also be damaged if a hard frost follows a period of warm weather that has encouraged new growth, or if a frost occurs

Flea beetle
Actual length 3mm

Encourage good airflow in and around plants by thinning out and pruning. It can reduce the risk of some diseases.

in the summer, for example. Plants that receive early morning sun, which melts the frost rapidly, are also vulnerable.

SYMPTOMS Frost symptoms appear overnight, and may affect many unrelated plants. Flowers and buds are discoloured, usually brown. Frosted blooms may not produce fruit. Leaves and stems turn brown or black; young growth towards the outside of the plant will be most affected. Apple skins may be russetted, usually at the flowering end of the fruit opposite the stalk. Damage may not be noticed until the fruit has developed.
PREVENTION AND CONTROL Protect susceptible plants with horticultural fleece, sheets of newspaper or other cover during risk periods. Harden off plants before planting out. Keep tender plants indoors until risk of frost is past. Select later-flowering cultivars. Avoid planting susceptible plants in frost pockets, or where they will receive the early morning sun.

Fruit tree red spider mite

Panonychus ulmi

Tiny, sap-sucking creatures, oval in shape. Their tiny, round, red-brown eggs (0.15mm across) overwinter on host plants in clusters and hatch from April to June. There may be five more generations in a season.

SUSCEPTIBLE PLANTS Apple and plum; also cotoneaster, damson, hawthorn, pear and rowan.

SYMPTOMS Leaves become speckled and dull green, then bronze, and may fall prematurely. Severe attacks in June or July can reduce fruit bud formation.
PREVENTION AND CONTROL Encourage natural predators. Do not overfeed plants.
Pesticide spray: Insecticidal soap.

Glasshouse mealybugs

Pseudococcus and *Planococcus* spp.

The adult female of this pest is small, up to 4mm long, and powdery grey. Eggs are laid in batches of 100–150, with a protective covering of woolly wax. Newly hatched mealybugs crawl over plants for a few days then settle down to feed. Adult males have wings and can appear in large numbers during the breeding season. Populations are usually highest in the autumn and early winter. In colder areas they are restricted to greenhouses but in warmer areas they may spread outdoors. Breeding can be continuous in greenhouses and in the home.

SUSCEPTIBLE PLANTS Sprouting potatoes; cacti, succulents, plus many tender indoor plants; glasshouse plants such as jasmine, asparagus fern and oleander.
SYMPTOMS Severe infestations on young growing shoots can weaken plants. Wax-covered colonies are often found in leaf axils and on cacti spines. Leaves may be covered in sticky honeydew. This may in turn be covered in black sooty mould.

PREVENTION AND CONTROL Cut out and burn severely infested shoots and branches. Wash out inaccessible colonies with a powerful jet of water or remove with a paintbrush as appropriate. Repeat inspection and removal of mealybugs two or three times at twice-weekly intervals. Examine all new plant introductions; ideally, quarantine new plants for a month.
Biological control: The predatory ladybird *Cryptolaemus montrouzieri*; optimum temperature 20-25°C (68-77°F).
Pesticide spray: Insecticidal soap. Disturb the waxy coating covering colonies before spraying.

Glasshouse red spider mite

Tetranychus urticae

"Red" can be misleading as these tiny pests, up to 0.5mm long, only become red during autumn and winter. They are also known as the two-spotted mite; for most of the year, they are pale green/yellow with two dark spots. They thrive in hot, dry conditions, reproducing in as little as eight days at 26°C (80°F). The mites hibernate in cracks and crevices, leaf litter, garden canes. In the greenhouse they may breed all year round if the temperature remains above 12°C (54°F).

SUSCEPTIBLE PLANTS A wide range of plants in greenhouses and indoors. May also attack outdoor plants in a hot dry season: strawberries, peach, grape vine, cucumber, French and runner beans, aubergine, carnation, fuchsia, busy Lizzies.
SYMPTOMS Leaves initially show a fine speckling. As the attack continues, they take on a bronzed appearance and may wither and die. A fine webbing is produced, strung between parts of the plant or under the leaves. Using a magnifying glass, mites and their tiny eggs can be seen on the undersides of leaves. In an unheated greenhouse the most severe attacks occur from June to September, but mites can be active all year round.
PREVENTION AND CONTROL Spray plants, if appropriate, with a fine mist of water, twice daily. Ensure all plants have the best growing conditions possible. Red spider mite can be severe on plants that are pot-bound or overcrowded, or growing poorly in hot and dry conditions. Discard badly infested plants. In spring clean out the greenhouse, and scrub down staging. Use a high-pressure hose on cracks and crevices.
Biological control: Under cover, and in warm areas outside, use *Phytoseiulus persimilis*, a predatory mite; optimum temperature 18–24°C (64–75°F). **Pesticide sprays:** Insecticidal soap; rape seed oil.

Glasshouse thrips

Heliothrips haemorrhoidalis
See Thrips

SUSCEPTIBLE PLANTS Azalea, citrus, ferns, fuchsia, orchids and zantedeschia; also other

---

Fungus gnat *see Sciarid fly*
Fusarium wilt *see Wilt diseases*

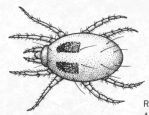
Red spider mite
Actual length 0.5mm

Never spray on a windy day.

greenhouse and house plants.
SYMPTOMS Infested plants may be marked with globules of red/brown liquid caused by feeding thrips.
PREVENTION AND CONTROL Maintain a humid atmosphere. Damp down regularly. Examine new plants for thrips before introducing into the house or greenhouse. Tap plant over a sheet of white paper; thrips will fall onto the paper.
Biological control: The predatory mite *Amblyseius cucumeris*; optimum temperature 25°C (77°F).

Glasshouse whitefly

Trialeurodes vaporariorum

These insects will breed all year round in a greenhouse if plants are present. They may move out into the garden in the summer, but will not survive winter outdoors. Can transmit viruses. *See also* Whiteflies.

SUSCEPTIBLE PLANTS Tomato, cucumber and many other greenhouse and house plants.
SYMPTOMS Leaves may develop yellow spots and other discolorations. The plant may become sticky and stunted. In bright sunlight the leaves can wither and die.
PREVENTION AND CONTROL Hang yellow sticky traps near plants to control small infestations, and for monitoring the appearance of whitefly where biological control agents are to be used. Remove sticky traps before introducing

biological control agents. Dispose of badly infested plants. Clean greenhouses thoroughly in early spring. Wash down all surfaces, including staging.
Biological control: Under cover, use *Encarsia formosa*, a parasitic wasp (works best at 18-25°C/64-77°F; not recommended below 10°C/50°F); or *Delphastus*, a predatory beetle; optimum temperature 21-28°C (70–82°F).
Pesticide spray: Insecticidal soap. Spray directly onto whiteflies in early morning when temperatures are low and adults less mobile. Apply once a week for 3–4 weeks for best results.

Gooseberry sawfly

Nematus ribesii

Larvae of this pest are green with black spots and a shiny black head, reaching 3cm (1¼in) long when fully grown. Eggs are pale green/white, about 1mm long, laid on the underside of leaves along the main veins, usually low down in the middle of a bush. There are two or three generations a year, with damage starting in April or May. Larvae of the third generation overwinter as cocoons in the soil.

SUSCEPTIBLE PLANTS Gooseberries, and red- and whitecurrants.
SYMPTOMS The first symptoms are tiny holes in the leaves made by the young larvae. Newly hatched larvae feed at the centre of a bush for one to two weeks then progress outwards. They can

quickly strip a whole bush of foliage leaving only a skeleton of leaf veins. Repeated defoliation may reduce cropping.
PREVENTION AND CONTROL Grow plants as a cordon or fan to make location and removal of larvae easier. Inspect bushes carefully for pinhole size holes in mid-spring, early to midsummer and early autumn. Destroy any eggs or larvae found. If infestation is heavy remove the whole leaf. Daily inspection is advisable. Remove mulches in late autumn/winter and cultivate lightly around bushes. *See also* Sawflies.

Grey mould

Botrytis cinerea

This fungus survives on plant debris, and in the soil. Spores are spread by air currents, and rain or water splash. Infection is usually through a wound of some sort.

SUSCEPTIBLE PLANTS Most living or dead plant material including fruits, flowers and leaves.
SYMPTOMS Fluffy, greyish-white mould grows on infected areas (see p.90). Where stems are infected, growth above the infection will yellow and wilt. Flowers, for example of strawberries, may be infected, but no symptoms may show until the fruit starts to ripen.
PREVENTION AND CURE Good general hygiene. Remove all dead and dying plants, or plant parts, as soon as infection is noticed. Ensure good ventilation around plants. *See also* Peony wilt/blight; lettuce grey mould; onion neck rot.

Holly leaf miner

Phytomyza ilicis

Adults of this pest are small inconspicuous flies. Eggs are laid from late spring onwards on the underside of holly leaves near the mid-rib. Larvae hatch and tunnel into leaves, remaining there until the following spring. One generation each year.

SUSCEPTIBLE PLANTS Holly.
SYMPTOMS Not a serious pest but the damage it causes can be unsightly. First symptoms show as straight, narrow, light green tunnels burrowed between the upper and lower leaf surface. These develop into blotches, or "mines" as the larvae continue feeding between leaf layers.
PREVENTION AND CONTROL Where infestation is light, pick off and destroy affected leaves.

Honey fungus

Armillaria spp.

Honey fungus lives primarily on dead tree stumps. It spreads to living trees mainly by means of bootlace-like growths, although infection by root contact is also possible. Infection by spores produced by the toadstools (shown on p.91) is rare. There are many strains of this fungus; not all harm plants.

SUSCEPTIBLE PLANTS Many trees, all tree fruit, shrubs and woody climbers. Particularly susceptible plants include birch, cotoneaster, currants, lilac, pine, privet, willow and wisteria.

Holly leaf miner damage

Greenfly *see Aphids*

For tips on reducing pest and disease problems in the greenhouse, see pp.228–229.

SYMPTOMS Initial symptoms include dying back of leafy branches or failure of leaves to appear in spring. Death can be rapid, or can take several years. When the bark is peeled back from roots or the base of the trunk of an infected plant, thin sheets of creamy fungal growth, smelling of mushrooms, will be found. Long black bootlace-like growths will be visible under the bark and in the soil around the base of the plant. Honey-coloured toadstools may appear in clumps between July and December. Young trees are more prone to attack.

PREVENTION AND CONTROL On a site known to have had honey fungus, try to use plants with some resistance: bamboos, chaenomeles, clematis, cotinus, hebe, passion flower, yew, beech, oak and catalpa. Plants growing strongly are less vulnerable. Remove infected plants with as much root as possible.

Iron deficiency

Also known as lime-induced chlorosis. Has very similar symptoms to and often occurs with manganese deficiency (q.v.).

SUSCEPTIBLE PLANTS Pears, raspberries; acid soil-lovers such as camellias and azaleas growing on alkaline soils, but any type of plant can be affected.
SYMPTOMS Leaves turn yellow or brown around the margins. This extends between the veins (se p.89). Young leaves may be totally yellow, or bleached white, with no green showing. Fruit quantity and quality poor.

CAUSES Soil pH too high for acid-loving plants. Waterlogging. Excessive use of phosphates.
PREVENTION AND CURE Choose plants to suit the soil type. Apply well-rotted manure or compost.

Leaf-cutter bee

Megachile centuncularis
A small solitary bee, pale brown to black, 1cm (½in) long.

SUSCEPTIBLE PLANTS Roses, laburnum, rhododendron, lilac, privet and other ornamentals.
PLANT SYMPTOMS Oval, semicircular sections are cut from edges of leaves.
PREVENTION AND CONTROL No action is necessary. Damage is rarely severe, and does not seriously affect the plant.

Leaf miners

Larval pests that tunnel around feeding within leaves, creating characteristic maze patterns. They can be squashed in their "mines" between finger and thumb, or leaves can be picked off. Damage tends to be more unsightly than harmful, except on leafy crops. See Celery fly, Chrysanthemum leaf miner, Holly leaf miner.

Leatherjackets

Tipula and *Nephrotoma* spp
The larvae of the crane fly or "daddy-long-legs": legless, brown to greyish-black, fat, soft-bodied, up to 5cm (2in) long, with no distinct head. In late summer, adult flies lay up to 300 eggs in grassland or in soil near plants. Eggs hatch approximately two weeks later. Larvae feed on roots during the autumn and the following spring and summer. Adults emerge in late summer to early autumn.

SUSCEPTIBLE PLANTS Lawns; also brassicas, strawberries, lettuce and various ornamentals.
SYMPTOMS Yellowing patches on lawns in dry weather. Starlings may be seen probing lawns in search of leatherjackets. Larvae also feed on roots of young plants in spring. Plants turn yellow, wilt and may die. Symptoms can be confused with cutworm damage and also root-infecting fungi; it is important to confirm the presence of leatherjackets before taking action.
PREVENTION AND CONTROL Raise plants in pots to produce a vigorous root system. Do not plant susceptible plants on newly cleared land. Trap leatherjackets on lawns by thoroughly watering yellow areas and covering overnight with sacking, tarpaulin or a similar material. Larvae will come to the surface under the covering. Pick off and destroy the following morning. This method can be used on cultivated land, by placing a layer of grass mowings under the cover. Leave for one or two days then pick off and destroy any leatherjackets that surface. Repeat, then fork the soil lightly to expose larvae that remain.
Biological control: Outdoors, use *Steinernema feltiae*, a parasitic nematode. Apply mid-September, to moist soil.

Leek rust

Puccinia allii
Fungal disease that survives on crop debris and wild *Allium* species. May be worse on nitrogen-rich soil or where potassium levels are low.

SUSCEPTIBLE PLANTS Leeks, onions, chives, garlic and other *Allium* species; ornamental alliums are less susceptible.
PLANT SYMPTOMS Dusty reddish-orange pustules appear on leaves and stems during summer. In a severe attack the leaves may turn yellow and die. Plant size and therefore crop yield may be reduced. Later growth may be disease-free as infection declines in the cooler weather of autumn. In mild autumns, the disease may continue to develop.
PREVENTION AND CONTROL Check nitrogen and potassium levels in soil. Improve the drainage of soil, if necessary. Use a crop rotation – minimum three years but preferably four or five years. Grow more resistant leek cultivars such as 'Poristo' and 'Poribleu'. Do not overcrowd seedlings. Clear away and compost any diseased plant debris.

Lettuce grey mould

Botrytis cinerea
Spores of this fungal disease are seed- and soil-borne and survive in the soil between crops. The disease also survives on decaying plant matter. It

Feed the soil with composted organic soil improvers (see pp.40–41).

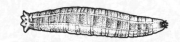

Leatherjacket (cranefly larva) *Actual length 5cm*

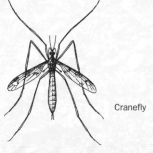

Cranefly

spreads quickly in wet summers.

SUSCEPTIBLE PLANTS Lettuce.
SYMPTOMS Fluffy grey mould develops on leaves followed by slimy, orangy-brown stem rot. Plants collapse as the stem is severed. Seedlings turn yellow, wilt and die.
PREVENTION AND CONTROL Do not overcrowd plants. Remove all plant debris. Avoid stress or damage to plants. Downy mildew infection (shown on p.311) often precedes lettuce grey mould. In a greenhouse, avoid overhead watering; space plants widely to ensure good air circulation.

Lettuce root aphid

Pemphigus bursarius

Small, yellow-white, wingless, waxy aphid pests with small dark spots on abdomen, found among lettuce roots during summer. Overwinters mainly on Lombardy poplar, moving in June to lettuce and sow-thistle. Root colonies can persist into the winter, and may survive in the soil until the next season. *See also* Aphids.

SUSCEPTIBLE PLANTS Lettuce, sowthistle. Lombardy poplar is a winter host.
SYMPTOMS A severe infestation will cause lettuce plants to wilt suddenly, then die.
PREVENTION AND CONTROL Grow root aphid-resistant cultivars, such as 'Avondefiance', 'Musette' and 'Beatrice'. Rotate crops.

Lily beetle

Lilioceris lilii

The adult beetles are bright red and up to 8mm (⅜in) long. Their larvae are reddish/yellow, hump-backed and covered with black slime. Adults overwinter in the soil and move onto plants from early spring. Over several months each female can lay 200–300 eggs on leaves and stems. Larvae hatch ten days or so after the eggs were laid, then feed for a month before returning to the soil to pupate. There is only one generation each year.

SUSCEPTIBLE PLANTS Lily, particularly Madonna lily; also fritillary and Solomon's seal.
SYMPTOMS Both adults and larvae feed on leaves, stems, and seedpods, and can decimate plants. Damage can occur from April to September.
PREVENTION AND CONTROL Check plants regularly from mid-spring onwards. Remove and destroy any beetles, eggs or larvae as seen.

Lupin aphid

Macrosiphum albifrons

Large pale grey-blue aphid, up to 5mm (¼in) long with a waxy appearance. It overwinters on mature lupins. *See also* Aphids.

SUSCEPTIBLE PLANTS Herbaceous and tree lupins.
SYMPTOMS Dense colonies develop in late spring and summer on flower spikes and on the undersides of leaves. Flower spikes are distorted

and whole plants may be killed.
PREVENTION AND CONTROL Check plants regularly in late spring and summer. Remove infested stems or squash aphids.

Magnesium deficiency

Disorder particularly affecting potato, tomato, blackcurrant, apple, gooseberry, raspberry, rose and chrysanthemum.

SYMPTOMS Symptoms develop first on older leaves, spreading to young leaves later. Leaves turn yellow (or sometimes red, purple or brown) between the veins and around the margins, while veins remain green.
CAUSES Acid soil. Magnesium is easily washed out of light soils by heavy rain. Overuse of high-potash fertilisers can make magnesium unavailable to plants.
PREVENTION AND CONTROL For immediate effect, foliar-feed fortnightly with Epsom salts diluted at the rate of 200g per 10 litres of water (8oz per 2½ gal) after flowering. Reduce the use of potash fertiliser if appropriate. Treat with dolomitic limestone (if pH is too acidic) or other magnesium-containing rocks such as Kieserite.

Manganese deficiency

Disorder particularly affecting French bean, pea, onion, apple, cherry and raspberry. *See also* Iron deficiency.

SYMPTOMS Leaves become yellow, with the smallest leaf veins remaining green to produce a chequered effect. Youngest leaves affected first, though the plant may grow away from the problem so that new leaves may seem least affected. Brown spots appear scattered over the leaf surface. Severely affected leaves turn brown and wither.
CAUSES Most common on soils with a pH of over 7.5, and also those with poor drainage and high organic matter levels.
PREVENTION AND CONTROL Grow plants suited to the soil type. Improve soil structure.

Mealy cabbage aphid

Brevicoryne brassicae

Adults of this pest are grey-green in colour and are covered in a powdery white mealy wax. Overwintering eggs, laid on stems and leaves of brassicas, hatch in spring. Infestations occur from midsummer onwards reaching a peak in early to mid-autumn.
See also Aphids.

SUSCEPTIBLE PLANTS Brassicas.
SYMPTOMS Dense colonies of aphids cause distortion and discoloration of leaves. A severe infestation can check growth and can kill shoot tips and young plants.
PREVENTION AND CONTROL Remove overwintering brassica plants as soon as they have finished cropping. This should be done by mid-spring. Bury

Lily beetle
Actual length 8mm

Grow plants that suit the site.

plant debris deep in a compost heap, or in a compost trench. Examine young plants regularly from early summer to early autumn and squash any colonies of eggs or young.

Pesticide sprays: Insecticidal soap; pyrethrum; rape seed oil.

Mineral deficiencies

It is unwise to treat soil for a deficiency unless you are sure that it really is deficient in that particular element, as this may simply exacerbate the condition. Deficiency symptoms often occur as a result of over-liming, excessive fertiliser use or poor soil structure – rather than a true shortage in the soil. Cold weather, drought and water-logging can also cause a temporary deficiency in a plant. True shortages of elements are much less common. A soil, or plant, analysis may be necessary to identify a deficiency accurately. *See also* Boron, Calcium, Iron, Potassium, Phosphorus, Nitrogen, Magnesium and Manganese Deficiencies.

Moles

Talpa europea

Adult moles are about 15cm (6in) long, with dense, dark brown fur. Females raise a litter of four or so per year. They do not feed on plants, but their activities can undermine them, disrupting growth, and make lawn mowing difficult.

SYMPTOMS Moles create mounds of loose soil ("mole hills") on cultivated land, lawns and rough ground. Light, well-drained soils are most affected. Damage is usually greatest in late winter and early spring.

PREVENTION AND CONTROL Trapping is the only certain way to control this pest. The best time to trap moles is in late winter and early spring when runs can be more easily located. First locate permanent mole runs by careful observation, probing and excavation. Place a mole trap in the run choosing a straight length of run within 15–20cm (6–8in) of the soil surface. Examine the trap at least once a day; if it fails to catch a mole within four days, move it to another run. It may be possible to deter moles for a brief length of time by using repellents that create strong smells or by using a device to produce a vibration in the run.

Nitrogen deficiency

All vegetables except nitrogen-fixing legumes are prone to this disorder, as are apples, plums, currants and many other plants.

SYMPTOMS Plants grow poorly; leaves are pale green or in some cases, such as brassicas, with yellow, red or purplish tints. Lower leaves show symptoms first. Flowering and fruiting may be reduced and delayed.

CAUSES Shortage of available nitrogen in the soil. This can occur on any soil, but is more likely on light soils, low in organic matter, where rainfall is heavy. Cold weather, especially early in the season, can cause a temporary shortage. Adding wood shavings and similar woody material to the soil can cause "nitrogen robbery" – where soil organisms are mopping up any available nitrogen to help them break down the woody material.

PREVENTION AND CONTROL Build up organic matter levels in the soil. Grow a green manure, such as grazing rye, over winter to reduce leaching of nitrogen from the soil. Grow nitrogen-fixing green manures such as winter tares. Apply composted green waste and animal manures. Mulch plants with grass clippings. Apply nitrogen-rich organic fertilisers.

Oedema

Disorder affecting a wide range of plants, particularly glass-house plants such as begonias, brassicas, cacti and succulents, solanum, tomato, pelargonium, camellia, capsicum (peppers and ornamental winter cherries), peperomia and grape vines.

SYMPTOMS Small wart-like growths on the undersides of leaves and sometimes on stems. Upper leaf surface has pale blotches. At first greenish-white, the swellings become rusty and have a corky texture.

CAUSES Caused by overwatering during cloudy, humid weather, when the plant takes up more water than it can lose through the leaves.

PREVENTION AND CONTROL Reduce watering. Improve drainage and air circulation. Do not remove affected plant parts; this will just make the symptoms worse. The condition is not infectious.

Onion downy mildew

Peronospora destructor

A fungal disease that survives in the soil for up to five years, and in crop debris and on infected plants, not all of which will show symptoms. It can, for example, overwinter in seemingly healthy autumn-planted onions, acting as a source of infection for the spring-planted crop.

SUSCEPTIBLE PLANTS Onion, Egyptian onion and shallot.
SYMPTOMS Leaves turn dark grey, wither and collapse. Bulbs may rot in store. The disease is worst in cool wet seasons.
PREVENTION AND CONTROL Use a five-year rotation where onion downy mildew has occurred. Do not save seed from infected onions. Break the cycle – give up growing both autumn- and spring-planted onions for a year or two. Remove infected plants as soon as they are noticed. Remove weeds to encourage good air flow around plants.

Onion fly

Delia antiqua

Adults of this pest emerge in May from pupae overwintering in

---

Mice *see Wood mouse*

Mildew, downy *see Downy mildew*

Mildew, powdery *see Powdery mildew*

Mushroom fly *see Sciarid fly*

Nutrient deficiencies *see Mineral deficiencies*

the soil. Eggs are laid on young leaves, stems, or soil near plants. White larvae, up to 8mm (⅜in) long, feed in stems and on roots and bulbs for two or three weeks before pupating. There may be three or four generations in a single year.

SUSCEPTIBLE PLANTS Onion; also shallot, garlic and leeks.
SYMPTOMS Young plants wilt and die; leaves and stems of more established plants become soft and rotten. Larvae bore into onion bulbs, which then tend to rot. Attacks are most severe in early to midsummer. May be confused with stem eelworm and onion white rot.
PREVENTION AND CONTROL Grow under fleece or fine mesh netting, put in place immediately after sowing or planting. Remove infested plants as soon as onion fly is discovered. Use a crop rotation and cultivate the soil in winter to expose pupae to predators.

Onion neck rot

Botrytis allii

Fungal disease favoured by wet, cool summers. The main source is infected seed. The fungus also survives in soil and crop debris for three to four years. Infection does not spread between bulbs in store, but symptoms do not all develop at the same time.

SUSCEPTIBLE PLANTS Onion.
SYMPTOMS Onions appear healthy when growing, but bulb scales become soft after 8–12 weeks in store. Brown sunken

lesions and a fluffy grey mould develop in the neck. The upper part of the bulb is soft when pressed, with brownish-black discoloration under the dry outer leaves. The fungus spreads downwards through the bulb, which in severe cases may decay completely and be covered with fluffy, grey mould. Sides and base of bulbs are rarely affected unless outer scales have been damaged before or during harvest.
PREVENTION AND CONTROL Buy seed and sets from reputable suppliers. Use wide spacing during growth to allow air movement around the crops. Avoid damage before or during harvest, and allow tops to fall over naturally. Dry well in an airy, warm dry atmosphere until the onion skins rustle. Do not store damaged bulbs. Store in cool, dry airy conditions and remove bulbs that develop symptoms as they occur. Use a crop rotation of at least four years.

Onion thrips

Thrips tabaci
See Thrips

SUSCEPTIBLE PLANTS Onion and leeks; mainly a pest of plants under cover in Britain and northern Europe.
SYMPTOMS *See* Thrips.
PREVENTION AND CONTROL Outdoors, crops can withstand a light infestation. Water plants well during dry spells. Remove and destroy crop debris after harvest. **Pesticide sprays:** Rape seed oil, derris.

Onion white rot

Sclerotium cepivorum

Onion white rot is caused by a highly persistent soil-living fungus. The resting bodies (sclerotia) can survive for 15 years in the soil without a suitable host plant. The fungus is active when the soil temperature is around 10–20°C (50–68°F). Autumn-planted garlic and winter onions are particularly susceptible in mid- to late spring when soil temperatures are ideal. By this time they have a well-developed root system, extensive enough to stimulate the sclerotia into germination.

SUSCEPTIBLE PLANTS Bulb onions and garlic; also spring onions, leeks, chives and shallots.
SYMPTOMS Plants suddenly start to die. Older leaves turn yellow, roots become stunted or rotten. Seedlings keel over; larger plants can easily be pulled out of the ground, and garlic stems pull away easily from the bulb. A few plants in a small patch may be affected at first, and then a whole row may show signs as the disease spreads. As the disease progresses, a white, cottony-looking fungal growth will be seen around the base and up the side of bulbs, with tiny black globules, like poppy seeds, among the fungus. These are the fungal resting bodies of white rot, known as sclerotia.
PREVENTION AND CONTROL Grow onions from seed, not sets, so the root system will be small when disease activity is at its highest. Grow garlic purchased

from a reputable source, and avoid infecting clean ground. Clean tools and boots well after cultivating contaminated soil or after use in another garden. Use a strict crop rotation, ideally at least 8 years if onion white rot is present. Space plants widely; when stimulated by nearby plants, white rot can spread sideways through the soil and intertwined roots will also move infection along a row. Clumps of multi-sown onions should be 30cm (12in) apart. If the area of infection is small, remove and dispose of affected and adjacent plants, and the surrounding soil. In areas known to be infected with white rot, try growing garlic in 10cm (4in)-diameter holes filled with uncontaminated soil. Leeks are worth trying, even on badly infected ground.

Parsnip canker

Itersonilia pastinacae, Myco-centrospora acerina and Phoma spp.

There are three main types of parsnip canker: black, orange-brown, and purple. All cause damage to the root. Wet sites exacerbate them. Black canker is spread by rain-splash from diseased spots on the leaves. Spores then enter through damaged roots. Carrot fly wounds may create entry points. Orange-brown canker is possibly caused by soil-inhabiting organisms. Purple canker occurs in black fen soil, high in organic matter.

SUSCEPTIBLE PLANTS Parsnip.
PLANT SYMPTOMS Black canker produces dark lesions, often on lateral roots. Orange-brown

Onion fly larva *Actual length 8mm*

Provide appropriate food and shelter to encourage natural predators (see pp.186–202).

canker produces a brown coloration on the skin, initially on the shoulder of the main root. Purple canker produces a purple lesion with brown water-soaked margins.

PREVENTION AND CONTROL
Grow in a well-drained site. Grow a resistant variety such as 'Avonresister'. Earth up in summer to stop the spores of black canker from reaching the roots. Use close spacing to produce uniformly smaller roots that may be less susceptible to some forms of canker. Control carrot fly. Use a crop rotation.

Pea and bean weevil

Sitona lineatus

Adults, brown-grey and 5–6mm (¼in) long, overwinter in plant debris and vegetation, moving on to plants to feed in early spring. Eggs are laid in the soil, and the larvae feed on root nodules for a few weeks, pupating in the soil. Adults emerge in June or July. There is one generation a year. *See also* Weevils.

SUSCEPTIBLE PLANTS Peas, broad bean; also related plants.
SYMPTOMS Characteristic scalloped holes are eaten out of the edges of leaves in spring and summer. Young plants may be severely damaged early in the season when growth is slow. Otherwise healthy plants can usually tolerate the damage.
PREVENTION AND CONTROL
Avoid using vetch/winter tares as an overwintering green manure. Prepare ground well

before sowing to encourage strong, fast growth. Protect young plants by placing a barrier of fleece or mesh over the area immediately after sowing.

Pea moth

Cydia nigricana

Caterpillars of this moth live in pea pods and feed on the peas. Up to 6mm long, they have black heads and creamy-white bodies, often with small dark spots.

SUSCEPTIBLE PLANTS Peas.
SYMPTOMS Often only seen once pods are opened: the peas are damaged and "wormy", usually with the larvae and their excrement evident.
PREVENTION AND CONTROL
The moth lays its eggs when peas are in flower, so early and late sowings that flower outside the moth's flight period, from early to late summer, will escape damage. Cover peas in flower during the flight period, especially in early July, with fine mesh. Dig over plots where infested plants have grown thoroughly in winter. **Pesticide spray:** Derris, as a last resort.

Pea thrips

Kakothrips pisivorus (*K. robustus*)

Adult pea thrips, yellow-brown and about 2mm long, are active from late spring to midsummer in hot, dry weather. Population peak is midsummer. The larvae are yellow. *See also* Thrips.

SUSCEPTIBLE PLANTS Peas; occasionally broad bean.

SYMPTOMS Pea and bean pods become silvered and distorted; they may have brown scarring. Peas may fail to develop in pods.
PREVENTION AND CONTROL
Sow peas and broad beans early to avoid severe infestation. Winter-dig plots where infested plants have been growing.
Pesticide sprays: Rape seed oil, derris.

Peach leaf curl

Taphrina deformans

Spores of this fungal disease are spread by rain. The disease is worse following cold, wet springs and in cool, damp areas.

SUSCEPTIBLE PLANTS Peach; also almond, nectarine, and rarely apricot. Both edible and ornamental types may be affected.
SYMPTOMS In early spring new leaves thicken and start to twist and curl, becoming yellow or orange-red in colour. Red blisters appear on leaves in early summer. Infected leaves develop a pale bloom, turn brown and fall prematurely. Regular attacks will reduce vigour and the production of fruit, and spoil the appearance of the tree.
PREVENTION AND CONTROL
Cover wall-grown specimens from mid-winter to mid-spring to prevent rain-splash spreading the disease to developing buds and young foliage. Construct a lean-to frame of wood and clear plastic sheeting, rather like a rectangular cold frame light, but make the vertical pieces long enough so that they can be inserted in the soil. This cover

can be attached to a wall or fence and secured in the ground. Do not plant susceptible trees in cool, damp situations. Avoid sites near ponds. Pick off diseased leaves on sight. Keep trees well fed and watered to encourage the development of new healthy growth. **Fungicide spray:** Spray with Bordeaux mixture just after autumn leaf-fall, and again as buds begin to swell in late winter or early spring.

Pear scab

Venturia pirina

Fungal disease similar to apple scab (q.v.) but infection also occurs frequently on bud scales. Scab is worse in cool, wet periods in spring and early summer.

SUSCEPTIBLE PLANTS Pear.
PLANT SYMPTOMS Dark scabby spots, similar to apple scab symptoms, appear on shoots, leaves, fruit and buds. Fruit spotting can be more severe than on apples, causing fruit to become deformed with deep clefts. Twigs develop conspicuous swellings which later burst.
PREVENTION AND CONTROL
See Apple scab.

Pear sucker

Psylla pyricola

Adults of this pest overwinter on twigs and branches. Their eggs are laid in April on spurs and shoots, and hatch a few weeks later. Nymphs (the young) are pink to orange, with pink/red

Never spray when bees are working – the evening is usually the safest time.

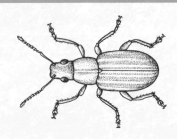

Pea and bean weevil
Actual length 5-6mm

eyes. They feed on young buds and leaves. There are three generations a year.

SUSCEPTIBLE PLANTS Pear, plus a wide range of trees and shrubs.
SYMPTOMS Leaf and blossom buds are damaged in spring. Summer feeding results in large deposits of honeydew, and the growth of sooty mould. Damage to fruit buds forming in late summer reduces the next year's fruit crop. Severe infestation causes premature leaf fall.
PREVENTION AND CONTROL Prune off and burn the most severely infested shoots. Grow flowers such as corn marigold, corn chamomile and cornflower to attract predators.

Peony wilt

Botrytis paeoniae

Also known as peony blight, this fungal disease persists in the soil and can survive on infected plant debris. It thrives in humid conditions.

SUSCEPTIBLE PLANTS Peony and lily-of-the-valley.
SYMPTOMS Stems develop dark brown coloration at soil level. Grey mould develops on young buds and flowers, which darken. Stems wilt and collapse. Flowers may fail to open.
PREVENTION AND CONTROL Space plants widely to promote good air flow. Plants that are infected should be cut down to ground level in the autumn. Clear away all diseased plant debris. Carefully remove a layer of topsoil around infected plants and replace with fresh soil.

Phosphorus deficiency

All plants may be prone to this disorder, but it is not common.

SYMPTOMS Poor growth. Leaves turn bluish-green with purple tints, but not yellow. Fruits small and green, with acid taste. Not easy to diagnose, and can be confused with drought, root damage or nitrogen deficiency.
CAUSES Soil may be naturally deficient in phosphorus – particularly acid soils, poor chalk soils and in areas of high rainfall. Cold weather can cause a temporary deficiency.
PREVENTION AND CONTROL Apply organic sources of phosphorus like rock phosphate, or meat and bone meals.

Phytophthora root & stem rots

Phytophthora spp.

Various species of these soil-borne fungi cause root and stem rots in plants. Plants in wet soils are more likely to be infected. Some strains of the fungus are host-specific, others attack a range of plants.

SUSCEPTIBLE PLANTS Azalea, rhododendron, Lawson cypress, beech, heather, apple, raspberry, yew, lime, ornamental *Prunus* spp., planes, sweet chestnut coppice and other woody plants.
SYMPTOMS Sparse yellowing foliage, partial dieback of twigs, whole branches or one side of a shrub or tree. On fruit-bearing

trees, fruit becomes smaller and sparser. Infected trees increase little in height or diameter and die within three to ten years of initial infection. Tongues of dead bark can extend up the stem from soil level. On examination, roots at that point will be dead. On smaller specimens lower leaves may drop and the entire plant wilts. Difficult to diagnose. Can be confused with other, less severe problems.
PREVENTION AND CONTROL Never plant in land known to have *Phytophthora*; replace the soil. Avoid transferring contaminated soil on boots and equipment. Make sure land is well-drained. Some plants are less susceptible: crab apples and *Quercus robur* (common oak) seem to be resistant. There is no cure.

Plum leaf-curling aphid

Brachycaudus helichrysi

A green aphid, up to 2mm (1⁄16in) in length. It hatches from overwintering eggs and starts feeding as early as mid-January. From May it moves on to a range of herbaceous plants, returning to its woody hosts in the autumn. *See also* Aphids.

SUSCEPTIBLE PLANTS Plum, damson and gage.
PLANT SYMPTOMS Foliage is tightly curled and crinkled in early spring. May be blackened and sticky with sooty mould growing on honeydew.
PREVENTION AND CONTROL *See* Aphids.

Pollen or blossom beetle

Meligethes aeneus

Adults of this pest are small green/bronze or shiny black beetles, 2–3mm (1⁄16–1⁄8in) long. Found in spring and in midsummer on flowers, and on calabrese and cauliflower heads. They tend to appear in gardens in large numbers in midsummer, arriving from oilseed rape crops.

SUSCEPTIBLE PLANTS Many ornamental and vegetable flowers; calabrese and cauliflower heads.
SYMPTOMS Adult beetles feed on pollen. In the garden they are mainly a nuisance, especially on flowers for cutting. They may also damage calabrese and cauliflower heads.
PREVENTION AND CONTROL Place cut flowers, such as sweet peas, in a dark location a short distance away from a bright window or lamp. Beetles will leave flowers and move towards the light. Grow calabrese and cauliflowers under fleece or ultra-fine mesh netting (0.8mm/1⁄32in mesh) if damage by pollen beetles is common.

Poor/no fruit set

Disorder especially affecting fruit, courgettes and runner beans.

SYMPTOMS Plants fail to fruit, or fruit poorly. Raspberry and strawberry fruits may be distorted, or have dry areas. Plants otherwise growing well.
CAUSES Frost at flowering time. Lack of suitable pollinator in

Pear sucker *Actual length 2mm*

Peony blight *see Peony wilt*

For more information on organically approved fertilisers, see p.61.

the vicinity (apples and pears). Lack of flowers as a result of inappropriate pruning. Male flowers not open at same time as female flowers (cucurbits). Poor weather at flowering time, hindering pollinating insects. Dry soil.
PREVENTION AND CONTROL Identify the cause and then remedy if possible.

Potassium deficiency

Disorder also known as potash deficiency, caused by a shortage of potassium in the soil. Most common on light sandy soils, and those with a low clay, or high chalk or peat, content.

SUSCEPTIBLE PLANTS Potato, tomato, apple, currants, pear and other edible and ornamental fruiting plants.
SYMPTOMS Brown scorching on leaf tips and margins, which may curl up. Purply-brown spots may appear on the underside. Poor flowering and fruit set. Plants may be more prone to frost damage and disease.
PREVENTION AND CONTROL Improve soil structure. Plant-based potash fertilisers, composted bracken, seaweed meal, comfrey leaves and comfrey liquid can all be used to supply potassium. Apply well-rotted manure that has been stacked undercover, or compost. Add wood ash, which has a good potash content, to the compost heap. Do not add it directly to the soil as it is very soluble.

Potato blackleg

Erwinia carotovora

The bacteria that cause this disease overwinter in potato tubers, plant debris and soil. Tubers are invaded through damaged skin. Poor drainage, potassium deficiency or excess nitrogen exacerbate the condition.

SUSCEPTIBLE PLANTS Potato.
SYMPTOMS First seen as small water-soaked lesions on stems. Stems turn brown or black 10cm (4in) above and below soil level, becoming mushy. Leaves roll, wrinkle and blister. Lower stem disintegrates and can be foul-smelling. Tubers can also be attacked, resulting in a grey slimy rot. This disease can affect isolated individual plants and even isolated stems on one plant. It is more likely during prolonged wet conditions.
PREVENTION AND CONTROL Plant in well-drained soil. Less susceptible cultivars include 'Wilja', 'Cara' and 'Pentland Crown'. Lift crops during dry weather if possible, to prevent cross-infection of healthy tubers at harvest. Avoid wounding tubers. Never save tubers from infected plants for seed. Maintain storage temperatures at 4°C (39°F) to inhibit new infections.

Potato common scab

Streptomyces spp.
A widespread bacterial disease, common on light, sandy, alkaline soils and encouraged by hot dry weather. Serious attacks can

occur on newly cleared grassland. Following initial infection the scab lesions produce further spores, which persist in the soil. The disease is usually present in most soils but is only active given the correct conditions.

SUSCEPTIBLE PLANTS Potato.
SYMPTOMS Scabby, angular spots of corky tissue appear on the skin of the tuber (shown on p.91). Spots can almost cover the skin surface and may be either superficial or form deep pits. Yield is seldom affected but wastage is increased with the extra peeling needed.
PREVENTION AND CONTROL Do not apply lime as this will increase scab incidence. Water potato crops in dry weather, especially when in flower. Add organic soil improvers to increase the water-holding capacity of the soil. Grow resistant cultivars. Do not grow susceptible varieties such as 'Desiree', 'Majestic' and 'Maris Piper'.

Potato cyst eelworm

Heterodera spp.
The golden cyst eelworm (*H. rostochiensis*) and the white cyst eelworm (*H. pallida*) are microscopic nematode worms, which feed in the roots of tomatoes and potatoes. They survive in the soil in the form of pinhead-sized cysts, each containing hundreds of eggs. Cysts can remain dormant for ten years or more, hatching in the presence of exudates from

the roots of potatoes and related plants. New cysts – which can be white, yellow or brown – may be seen on roots from late June to August. A hand lens is usually needed to see the cysts. Common on allotments and other plots where vegetables have been grown for many years.

SUSCEPTIBLE PLANTS Potato and tomato.
SYMPTOMS Plants yellow and die back prematurely, sometimes in patches. Crop yields reduced. In severe cases, growth may be poor and the crop minimal.
PREVENTION AND CONTROL Plant certified seed potatoes. Avoid bringing in soil on plants or tools from sites that may harbour the pest. Grow resistant potato cultivars. Most are only resistant to the golden form, though some, including 'Cromwell', 'Kestrel' and 'Sante' also have some tolerance of the white form. Use as long a crop rotation as possible. Feed the soil with bulky organic soil-improvers to encourage natural predators. On infested land, the no-dig technique (see p.327) may give a better yield. Early cultivars may produce a reasonable crop before the pest attack takes effect.

Potato and tomato blight

Phytophthora infestans
This fungal disease overwinters on infected potato tubers and surviving plants. Plants growing from volunteer tubers (potatoes

---

Potash deficiency *see Potassium deficiency*

Use a crop rotation when growing vegetables.

left in the ground at harvest time) are a common source of infection. It spreads rapidly to new crops in warm, damp weather. Spores are washed from leaves down into the soil by rain to infect potato tubers. Resistant spores which can survive in the soil may also be produced – but it is not known yet how commonly they occur.

SUSCEPTIBLE PLANTS Potato and tomato.
SYMPTOMS A common and serious fungal problem in warm, wet seasons when it spreads rapidly. Less frequent in dry conditions. Potato – dark blotches on leaves, mainly tips and edges, and on stems. White mould develops under leaves in humid conditions. The whole plant may collapse quickly. Infected tubers develop dark sunken lesions, which become firm and dry. Tubers may decay to a foul-smelling mush as a result of invasion by bacterial soft rots. Tomato – foliage symptoms similar to potato but less severe. Green fruit and stems show dark markings, mature fruit quickly develop a dry, leathery rot. This may only become evident days after harvest. A whitish-grey mould may also develop over the rot.
PREVENTION AND CONTROL Plant good-quality seed potatoes from a reputable source. Grow resistant potato cultivars such as 'Stirling', 'Cara' and 'Teena'. Avoid highly susceptible ones such as 'Arran Comet', 'King Edward' and 'Ulster Chieftain'. Destroy volunteer plants including self-set tomatoes and potatoes growing on

compost heaps and similar sites. Earth up potatoes or mulch them to reduce the likelihood of spores being washing down onto tubers. Smooth the sides of the ridges to prevent spores being washed into the soil through cracks. If blight appears on the foliage, remove all affected leaves immediately. Cut off all foliage and stems in a bad case. Compost only in a hot heap. Do not harvest the potato crop for at least 3 weeks to avoid infecting tubers with spores during lifting. Harvest all tubers and do not save tubers for seed from blighted potatoes or seed from infected tomatoes.

Powdery mildew

Erysiphe, *Sphaerotheca* and *Podosphaera* spp.

The distinctive symptoms of powdery mildew can be caused by a range of related fungi. Each mildew species only affects a specific group of plants. Most common when conditions are warm and dry during the day and cold at night, and on dry soils.

SUSCEPTIBLE PLANTS Almost any: specific mildews attack apple, apricot, cherry and plum; brassicas, cucurbits, gooseberry and blackcurrant, grapes, roses, strawberry and raspberry.
SYMPTOMS A white to grey powdery-like coating may develop on almost any part of a plant.
PREVENTION AND CONTROL Prune out any infected shoots of perennials in spring and late summer. Make sure plants are supplied with correct amounts

of water and nutrients at all times. Prepare the ground well before planting. Mulch plants to retain moisture. Do not overdo nitrogen-rich fertilisers as this can encourage soft growth more easily infected by the fungus. New cultivars that show some degree of resistance to mildew are constantly being developed. *See also* Apple powdery mildew, Vine powdery mildew.
Fungicide spray: Sulphur. This may harm young leaves, and some gooseberry and apple cultivars. Check the label before use.

Rabbits

Oryctolagus cuniculus

Burrowing animals that live in tunnels excavated in hedge banks and similar situations. They feed at night or during the early morning and late afternoon on a wide range of plants. A rabbit can eat 0.5kg (1lb) of vegetation per day, so a large colony can cause extensive damage.

SUSCEPTIBLE PLANTS A wide variety of fruits, vegetables, grasses and flowers.
SYMPTOMS Rabbits graze on young shoots. Plants can be eaten to ground level and bark stripped from trees. Most damage is done in spring and early summer.
PREVENTION AND CONTROL If rabbit numbers are high, erect a rabbit-proof fence around important plants. Use a mesh size of 2.5–3cm (1–1¼in). The fence should be 1–1.2m (3–4ft) high with a further 30cm (1ft) buried below ground level and

angled outwards. It should be well supported by posts and straining wires and should be inspected regularly for holes. If the local rabbit population is small, protect individual plants with netting or tree-protectors. Surrounding plants with spiky plant clippings will also deter grazing rabbits. Electric fencing may also be used. Some plants are said to be less attractive to rabbits (see pp.157 and 172).

Raspberry beetle

Byturus tomentosus

Yellow-brown larvae, 6–8mm (¼–⅜ in) long, found in ripening fruit. The adults, small brown beetles 3–4mm (⅛–⅛in) long, overwinter in the soil near host plants. In spring they emerge to feed on flowers of apple and hawthorn and other members of the Rosaceae family, moving on to raspberry, loganberry and blackberry flowers as they open. Eggs are laid on flowers in summer; larvae feed for about a month before pupating in the soil. There is only one generation a year.

SUSCEPTIBLE PLANTS Tayberry, raspberry, blackberry, loganberry and related hybrid berries.
SYMPTOMS Larvae feed on developing fruit causing segments of the berry to become shrivelled and hardened.
PREVENTION AND CONTROL If larvae have been found in fruit, at the end of the season remove mulches and gently fork over the soil around canes. If grown in a fruit cage, remove netting after fruiting to allow

If you have to spray, always read the label first and follow the instructions carefully.

birds access, or put in chickens. Cut all canes to the ground at the end of the year. This should kill off the pest, although one year's crop will usually be lost.

Raspberry cane blight

Leptosphaeria coniothyrium

Soil-borne fungal disease, which enters through cracks in bark, or wounds caused by the raspberry midge. It is spread by rain-splash and on tools.

SUSCEPTIBLE PLANTS Raspberry; also blackberry, hybrid berries and strawberry.
SYMPTOMS Leaves shrivel and die. Dark patches and cracked bark develop on canes just above the soil. Within the patches, masses of pinhead-sized pustules develop. Canes become brittle. 'Lloyd George' and 'Norfolk Giant' are particularly susceptible.
PREVENTION AND CONTROL Handle canes with care to avoid damage. If the canes are infected, cut back to below soil level. Burn all infected material. Disinfect tools after use.

Raspberry cane and leaf spot

Elsinoe veneta

From late spring to early summer this fungal disease infects young canes. Spores overwinter on host plants. Fruiting canes develop lesions from infection the previous year.

SUSCEPTIBLE PLANTS Raspberry; blackberry, loganberry and other hybrid berries.
SYMPTOMS Attacks young growth. Purple spots are found on canes, leaves, blossom and stalks. Leaves may drop, bark can split and small cankers form. Fruit yield is reduced. Severe infection will cause distortion and death.
PREVENTION AND CONTROL Cut out and burn infected canes.
Fungicide spray: Bordeaux mixture when buds on fruiting canes open, and again 10 days later.

Raspberry spur blight

Didymella applanata

This fungal disease is spread in wet conditions by rain and wind, especially in a damp spring.

SUSCEPTIBLE PLANTS Raspberry and loganberry.
SYMPTOMS Leaves may develop dark brown lesions in early summer. In late summer, purplish blotches appear on stems around buds, turning brown-black to silver in winter. Diseased canes become dotted with tiny black fruiting bodies. Plants rarely die as a result of this disease but fruit yield is reduced. A dry summer can cause the canes to become dry and shrivelled.
PREVENTION AND CONTROL Cut out and burn diseased canes. In spring, thin canes to reduce overcrowding. Cultivars 'Leo' and 'Malling Admiral' have some resistance to this disease.

Fungicide spray: Where this disease has been a problem, spray with Bordeaux mixture at 14-day intervals in spring when the buds are 1cm (½in) long.

Replant disease

Exact causes are still not known. Soil-dwelling nematodes and fungal diseases are probably responsible. It is thought that the level of these organisms increases in proportion to the size or age of the plant, and that they can co-exist with the strong woody roots of mature plants., but new plants with soft root tissue are overwhelmed by the level of these organisms in the soil.

SUSCEPTIBLE PLANTS Cherry, rose, viola, China aster, apple, and peach; pear, plum and strawberry.
SYMPTOMS Effects occur when a new plant is placed in a site once inhabited by a related plant. In the first year, the new plant grows poorly. Root systems are weak and may become blackened. Plants may fail to establish.
PREVENTION AND CONTROL Avoid planting susceptible plants where the same or a related plant has recently been removed. If you must replant in the same spot, dig out a large hole, remove the soil and replace it with fresh soil from a site where susceptible plants have not been grown. Plants grown in large containers, with a large root ball at planting-out time, may have more chance of survival.

Rhododendron bud blast

Pycnostysanus azaleae

Fungal disease that can survive on dead buds for up to three years. Transmission is often associated with a leafhopper that lays eggs in slits on buds.

SUSCEPTIBLE PLANTS Azalea and rhododendron.
SYMPTOMS Flower buds become silvery-grey in early autumn and fail to open. In spring the dried-up buds are covered with small, black pinhead-sized fruiting bodies. Buds and twigs may die.
PREVENTION AND CONTROL Remove and destroy diseased buds. Encourage beneficial insects into the vicinity to prey on the leafhopper by growing attractant flowers such as convolvulus or candytuft (see pp.198-9). No cultivars can be guaranteed as resistant.

Rose black spot

Diplocarpon rosae

Fungal disease spread by rain-splash, on hands and on tools. Attacks are worst in warm, moist conditions. Overwinters on stems, fallen leaves and in soil.

SUSCEPTIBLE PLANTS Rose.
SYMPTOMS Small to large black spots develop on the leaves. Eventually they merge to produce large irregular patches. Affects both leaf surfaces. Edges of leaf spots may turn yellow. Leaves fall prematurely. Bushes become weak if disease is severe.

Red spider mite *see Fruit tree red spider mite; Glasshouse red spider mite*

Reversion virus *see Blackcurrant reversion virus*

Root aphids *see Aphids*

Root rots *see Damping off, Phytophthora root and stem rots*

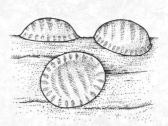

Scale
Actual length 1–5mm

PREVENTION AND CONTROL
Clear up fallen leaves. Prune infected stems hard back in spring. Grow resistant cultivars such as 'Veilchenblau', 'New Dawn' and 'Little Rambler'. Mulch plants with compost or leafmould before buds burst in spring, to reduce the risk of overwintering spores splashing up from the ground.
Fungicide spray: Sulphur. This may harm some young leaves. Check the label before use.

Rose rust

Phragmidium spp.

Spores of this fungal disease overwinter on fallen leaves. They germinate in spring, re-infecting bushes through wind and rain-splash. Spores also survive on the soil surface, on plant stems, fences, stakes and plant debris.

SUSCEPTIBLE PLANTS Rose.
SYMPTOMS Initially, bright orange pustules appear on leaf stalks, branches, lower leaf surfaces, especially along veins, and on any hips persisting from the previous year. During summer, yellow–orange pustules develop on lower leaf surfaces away from leaf veins. Later pustules become speckled with black spores, the overwintering stage of the disease. *Rosa pimpinellifolia* is particularly susceptible.
PREVENTION AND CONTROL
Grow healthy plants, in well-drained soil. Keep well pruned to encourage good air circulation. Grow resistant cultivars. Clear away any diseased plant leaves and other debris. Prune out stems showing symptoms immediately they are seen in spring. Cut well back beyond the point of infection.

Sawflies

Adults sawflies are small, inconspicuous, dark-bodied flies up to 1cm (½in) long. The larvae, which are what damage plants, vary in colour from cream to green and brown and resemble moth or butterfly caterpillars. They range in size from 1.5–3cm (½–1¼in) long. (*See also* Caterpillars, for comparison.) The larvae feed on leaves, stems and fruit of a wide range of wild and cultivated plants. If infestation is severe the plant is often reduced to a skeleton. *See also* Apple sawfly, Gooseberry sawfly, Solomon's seal sawfly.

Scale insects

Sap-feeding pests that move only when newly hatched, when they crawl about looking for a suitable feeding site. These young "crawlers" settle to feed near the leaf veins or stem of the affected plant, developing a waxy shell (scale). Adults resemble tiny limpet shells and when young can be mistaken for small brown flecks.
There are two species most likely to be found on plants in the greenhouse, conservatory and house. Hemispherical scale (*Saissetia coffeae*) is dark brown in colour, dome-shaped, 3mm (⅛in) long. Soft scale (*Coccus hesperidum*) is light green/brown in colour with a darker centre spot; oval and flat in shape, about 5mm (¼in) long. Breeding can take place all year round if temperatures are suitable.

SUSCEPTIBLE PLANTS A wide range of plants, particularly under glass and indoors.
SYMPTOMS Plants are weakened by the feeding scales and leaves may fall. Scale insects excrete a sticky substance, known as honeydew, which drops from the feeding area onto leaves below. Black sooty moulds may grow on it. Appearance is marred, and growth inhibited.
PREVENTION AND CONTROL
Check plants regularly, especially the undersides of the leaves, for the presence of scale. Where an infestation is light, individual scales can be removed easily with a fingernail or a cotton bud. Check new plants carefully for signs of scale before introducing them into the house or greenhouse.
Biological control: In warm, sunny conservatories and greenhouses use *Metaphycus helvolus*, a parasitic wasp. Optimum temperature 20–30°C (68–86°F). Needs high levels of sunshine to be really effective.
Pesticide spray: Insecticidal soap

Sciarid fly

Bradysia spp.

Also known as mushroom fly and fungus gnat. Adult flies, dark brown, midge-like, up to 4mm long, are found on the surface of moist potting composts, running quickly and vibrating their wings rapidly. They fly up when disturbed. Eggs are laid in the compost. Transparent white larvae, up to 1cm (½in) long with shiny black or brown heads, hatch a week later. They feed on plant roots. The whole life cycle can be completed within four weeks at a temperature of 20°C (68°F). Breeding can continue all year round in suitable temperatures.

SUSCEPTIBLE PLANTS Pot plants under cover; also mushrooms. Seedlings, cuttings and young plants most at risk.
SYMPTOMS Seedlings and young plants may collapse and die. Mature plants will grow poorly where infestation is high. Plants in growing media based on high levels of coir, peat or other types of organic matter are more prone to attack.
PREVENTION AND CONTROL
Always water from below, and keep watering to a minimum without allowing plants to dry out. Pot up plants as necessary, using a loam-based growing medium. Cover the compost surface with a 1cm (⅓in) layer of sand or grit to discourage infestation. Yellow sticky traps and insectivorous plants, such as Mexican butterwort (*Pinguicula caudate*), will trap flying adults. Check new plants for presence of sciarid fly before introducing into house or greenhouse. Remove severely infested plants.
Biological controls: Use the predatory mite *Hypoaspis miles* at temperatures above 11°C (52°F). *Steinernema feltiae*, a parasitic nematode, needs moist soil and a lower minimum temperature, 14°C (57°F).

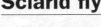

Sciarid fly larvae
Actual length 5mm

Avoid spraying predators.

Scorch

Disorder affecting soft and hairy-leaved plants.

SYMPTOMS Bleached-looking or pale brown patches on leaves. Damaged areas may crisp.
CAUSES Strong sunlight. Made worse by water droplets on foliage, concentrating the rays.
PREVENTION AND CONTROL Avoid wetting foliage in strong sunlight. Always water susceptible plants from below. Provide shading.

Shanking

Disorder of grapes.

SYMPTOMS Odd berries, or groups of berries, do not colour and develop, shrivelling and turning watery. Black grapes turn red; white grapes remain translucent. Fruit tastes sour.
CAUSES Under- or overwatering is the most likely cause; also shortage of nutrients.
PREVENTION AND CONTROL Do not overcrop vines as this will put a strain on the root system. Water well but do not overwater. Improve soil conditions if appropriate. If spotted early in the season cut out withered berries and foliar-feed with an organic liquid feed.

Silverleaf

Chondrostereum purpureum
Infection with this fungal disease normally occurs between early autumn and late spring when growth is slow. Fungal spores enter through bark wounds.

SUSCEPTIBLE PLANTS Plum and trees in the Rosaceae family such as almond, apple, apricot, cherry, hawthorn and rose; also currants, gooseberry, laburnum, poplar, rhododendron and willow.
SYMPTOMS Leaves develop a silvery sheen, which may initially be confined to a single branch. Leaves can split and become brown along the margins and around the midrib. Branches may die back and if cut through will show a brownish ring of stain running through the wood. From late summer small bracket-shaped or flat crust-like fungi may grow from dead branches. They may be soft and leathery when wet, and crisp and shrivelled when dry. This disease can be confused with false silver leaf, a nutritional disorder which produces the same foliage symptoms but no staining in the wood. Not all plants listed will develop the foliage symptoms.
PREVENTION AND CONTROL Prune plums and related species from early to late summer only. Vigorous growth during this period prevents the disease from gaining entry through pruning cuts. Natural recovery is quite common. If the disease persists cut out infected wood well beyond staining. Burn all infected wood.

Slugs

Soft-bodied, slimy pests, which move on a slimy, muscular foot and leave a characteristic slime trail. They can vary in colour from pink to black, and in size from a few millimetres to several centimetres. Some, like the grey-brown field slug, live and feed mainly above ground; others such as the keeled slug, a major potato pest, inhabit the soil. In the daytime slugs may be found in cracks and crevices and under any shelter where it is cool and damp. At night, especially when damp, slugs will be found feeding and crawling over plants. Slug eggs are laid in clusters in soil cavities. They are spherical, opaque or translucent and colourless.

SUSCEPTIBLE PLANTS A huge range of plants are liable to be attacked, particularly seedlings and young plants, annuals and herbaceous perennials. Slugs will also attack tubers and fruit.
SYMPTOMS Irregular holes eaten in roots, stems, bulbs, tubers, buds, flowers, fruit and leaves of a wide range of plants. Seedlings fail to come up or are eaten off. Most damage occurs at night. Tell-tale slime trails may be seen.
PREVENTION AND CONTROL There is no one single, simple method of controlling slugs. Use a range of techniques to protect susceptible plants, especially when young. When sowing seeds, water the bottom of the drill then cover with dry soil. Encourage quick germination and growth of seedlings and young plants. Plant out sturdy, module-grown transplants rather than sowing directly. Water in the morning; damp soil and plants in the evening encourage slugs and snails. Do not mulch young plants. Protect individual young plants with plastic bottle cloches. Hoe regularly to disturb slime trails that may be used by other slugs and snails to locate edible plants. Dig in winter to expose slugs and eggs to weather and predators. Grow varieties of potato less susceptible to slugs; harvest all potato tubers by early autumn. Hand-pick slugs at night and destroy. Use traps baited with beer, milk or grape juice; ensure the lip is raised 2–3cm (¾–1¼in) above the soil surface to avoid trapping beetles. Surround susceptible plants with bran; remove slugs found in it. Lay a ring of comfrey leaves around any susceptible plants. This will act a decoy, but is ineffective after midsummer. Provide alternative food – such as lettuce leaves (preferably under bricks or slates to keep them moist) – when transplanting into an empty bed. Plant sacrificial plants, such as French marigolds. Use a Butcombe box (see p.101). Protect pots and larger plants with copper-coated tape. Encourage natural enemies such as frogs, hedgehogs, beetles and centipedes. Hens can help to clear slugs from empty ground, or in a greenhouse.
Biological control: Outdoors and under cover, use *Heterorhabditis megidis*, a parasitic nematode; min. soil/compost temperature 12°C (54°F).

Snails

These creatures have a conspicuous hard shell which they withdraw into when threatened. They move on a

Do not overfeed plants, especially with nitrogen, which causes lush growth attractive to pests.

Slug

large, slimy, muscular foot and leave a characteristic slime trail. Active from spring to autumn, snails usually hide under hedges and in cool damp places during the day. They feed at night, especially during damp weather. The garden snail (*Helix aspersa*) is the most common pest, with a grey-brown shell up to 3cm (1¼in) across. Banded snails (*Cepaea nemoralis, C. hortensis*) are not normally a serious pest. Their shells have white, yellow, grey or pink bands with darker stripes, or are sometimes entirely pale yellow.

SUSCEPTIBLE PLANTS A wide range of plants.
SYMPTOMS Irregular holes eaten in roots, stems, bulbs, tubers, buds, flowers, fruit and leaves. Seeds fail to come up and seedlings are eaten. Most damage occurs at night.
PREVENTION AND CONTROL Some of the methods suggested for slugs (q.v.) may also work for snails. Do not grow very susceptible plants near locations like rockeries, walls and wood piles, where snails hide.

Solomon's seal sawfly

Phymatocera aterrima
Larvae of this pest are light grey, wrinkled, with black heads, and up to 2cm (¾in) long. Young larvae a greyish-yellow. Eggs are laid on plants in late spring and early summer. Larvae feed on both sides of the leaves. When fully grown they move into the soil to overwinter as cocoons.

SUSCEPTIBLE PLANTS Solomon's seal and other *Polygonatum* spp.
SYMPTOMS Foliage is quickly shredded leaving only the main leaf vein.
PREVENTION AND CONTROL Pick off and destroy eggs and larvae. Cultivate around plants in winter to expose cocoons.

Sooty moulds

Cladosporium spp. and others
Sooty mould fungi grow on sugary honeydew excreted by sap-feeding insects. They do not directly damage plants but are unsightly and block out light needed for photosynthesis. Leaves may fall; in severe cases the plant may be weakened.

SUSCEPTIBLE PLANTS Camellia, bay laurel, birch, ornamental citrus, lime, oak, plum, rose, tomato, vines, willows and many others, outdoors and under glass.
SYMPTOMS Black or brown soot-like deposits appear on upper leaf surfaces and other plant parts. Plants will also be infested with sap-feeding pests such as aphids, whiteflies, scale insects or mealybugs.
PREVENTION AND CONTROL Control the pests that are producing the honeydew. Spray or sponge leaves with water. When cleaned of mould, fruit will still be edible.

Splitting

Disorder affecting cabbage, carrot, cherries, onion, parsnip, plum, potato, swede and tomatoes.

SYMPTOMS Fruits, heads, roots and stems split lengthways. This can allow organisms that cause dieback or rotting to enter. Apple fruits may become hollow.
CAUSES Rapid growth, especially when rain or watering follows a very dry period. Wide fluctuations in temperature can also be responsible.
PREVENTION AND CONTROL Improve waterholding capacity of soil. Mulch soil.

Strawberry crown rot

Phytophthora cactorum
Fungal disease, soil-borne and spread by rain-splash onto the fruit. Spores also enter through damaged plant parts.

SUSCEPTIBLE PLANTS Strawberry.
SYMPTOMS Drought-like effects. Young leaves wilt, older leaves develop a red coloration. Plants die. When cut through, the crown is brown and dead.
PREVENTION AND CONTROL Remove infected plants. Apply a good layer of straw or other protection to keep fruit off the soil surface. Plant new crops far from the previous growing site.

Strawberry red core

Phytophthora fragariae var. *fragariae*
Spores of this fungal disease are released into the soil from the decaying roots of infected plants. The spores can lie dormant for at least 12 years. Infection of healthy roots occurs in wet conditions. It is spread on contaminated plants and on soil on tools and boots.

SUSCEPTIBLE PLANTS Strawberry.
SYMPTOMS Leaves develop a brownish-purplish tinge. A reddish band appears around the leaf edges; this may colour the whole of the central leaf area. Growth can be patchy with individual plants becoming weak and stunted. Roots are stunted and dark brown or black in colour, and the outer layers are easily peeled off. When the root is split open, the classic symptom is a red core running down the centre. It is most noticeable in spring and autumn but less defined during summer.
PREVENTION AND CONTROL Always plant certified, healthy planting stock. Make sure the growing site is well-drained. Grow cultivars with resistance to particular strains of red core. Check with a reputable fruit nursery for suitable cultivars. Avoid growing varieties such as 'Royal Sovereign', which is particularly susceptible. Burn affected plants. Do not grow strawberries on the same land again; spores can lie dormant in the soil for many years.

Suckers

Small, sap-feeding pests that feed on flowers, leaves, young buds and shoots of plants, causing distorted growth. Plants may be covered in sticky honeydew leading to black sooty

Snail

Spittlebug *see Froghopper, common*
Stem and foot rots *see Damping off*

For more information on watering problems, see pp.63–64.

mould growth. It is the young nymphs that cause most damage. They have wide, flattened bodies, with prominent wing buds and eyes. Adults, 2–3mm (¹⁄₁₆–¹⁄₈in) long, resemble winged aphids; they can jump and fly. *See also* Apple sucker; Bay sucker; Box sucker; Pear sucker.

Thrips

Insect pests that attack a wide range of plants, indoors and out. They are small, elongated, cylindrical insects, up to 4mm (¹⁄₈in) long, sometimes referred to as "thunder flies". Colour ranges from white/yellow to brown/black. Larvae resemble adults but without wings. There are over 150 species in Britain and northern Europe. They feed in large numbers on the upper side of leaves, and on flowers and buds of a wide range of plants, indoors and out, causing a characteristic silvery mottling and some distortion. They can reproduce in as little as a month, eggs being laid on plants. Adults and young stages overwinter in soil, leaf litter and plant debris.
See also Glasshouse thrips; Onion thrips; Pea thrips.

Tomato ghost spot

Botrytis cinerea

Fungal disease common when short periods of high moisture occur. Often seen in cool greenhouses towards the end of the growing season. It is spread from tomato leaves by rain-splash or on hands, tools and boots, and overwinters in plant debris and related weeds. It may also be seed-borne.

SUSCEPTIBLE PLANTS Tomato.
SYMPTOMS Tiny pale rings, with raised brown dots in the centre, form on the skin of tomato fruits. Leaves can be affected by beige, wrinkled spots, which move inwards from the leaf edge. They are flame-shaped. If humidity persists, grey mould fruit rot may set in.
PREVENTION AND CONTROL Reduce humidity in greenhouses by increasing ventilation and heat. Clear away plant debris. Do not save seed from infected plants. Avoid damp sites.

Tomato greenback

Disorder affecting greenhouse-grown tomatoes. Usually caused by excessive heat. Shortage of potassium and phosphorus may be a contributing factor.

SYMPTOMS A hard leathery ring, or partial ring, of flesh develops around the stalk. The fruit does not ripen properly, remaining green or yellow.
PREVENTION AND CONTROL Keep the greenhouse well-aired, and shade plants in hot weather. Grow resistant cultivars such as 'Golden Sunrise', 'Shirley' or 'Totem'. Check details in seed catalogues before buying, as resistance seems to be failing in some formerly resistant cultivars.

Vine powdery mildew

Uncinula necator

This fungus overwinters in bud scales and twigs. Developing buds become heavily mildewed in spring. Most prevalent when soil is dry and air is humid around the top growth. Spores are carried by the wind.

SUSCEPTIBLE PLANT Grapevine.
SYMPTOMS White powdery fungal growth develops on young shoots, which become stunted and whitened. The mildew is also seen on the underside of leaves. Grapes show brown dead patches and grey discoloration. They may burst during ripening, then dry up and rot. Some cultivars such as 'Cabernet Sauvignon' and 'Carignan' are highly susceptible.
PREVENTION AND CONTROL Scrape and peel old bark off vine stems, exposing clean new bark. Use a blunt knife and take care not to damage the new surface. Scrub down greenhouses in winter, using hot soapy water. Rinse with clean water. Allow to dry before closing vents. Ensure good ventilation (this may entail installing heating) and moisture supply, both outside and in the greenhouse. Keep wall-grown vines well watered until the grapes start to ripen. Remove overcrowded branches to promote good air flow.
Fungicide spray: Sulphur dust. Care must be taken when using sulphur as many cultivars are "sulphur shy". Apply to one or two lower leaves, and wait for 24 hours to see if leaves fall.

Vine weevil

Otiorhynchus sulcatus

The adults of this pest are wingless, dull dark brown-black, about 9mm (³⁄₈in) long, covered in small buff-yellow specks. They emerge in May and June, feeding by night. Virtually all are female and each lays several hundred eggs in soil or compost around host plants from late July. The larvae are a characteristic creamy-white "C" shape with a brown head and can be up to 1cm (½in) long. They feed on plant roots until the following spring, when they pupate in the soil. Most adults die at the end of the season, but some will survive the winter. In the warmer conditions of a house or greenhouse, adult weevils may emerge in the autumn, and eggs will be laid over a longer period.
See also Weevils.

SUSCEPTIBLE PLANTS A wide range of plants in the garden, greenhouse and house. Plants in pots are particularly at risk.
SYMPTOMS Adult weevils eat irregular holes around the edges of leaves. This damage is more cosmetic than life-threatening. Larvae are the main problem as they feed on plant roots. If a plant is growing poorly, or suddenly wilts and dies, check in and around the root ball for this pest. It may show no leaf symptoms.
PREVENTION AND CONTROL Inspect plants regularly for adult weevils, particularly at night. Inspect newly purchased plants for adults and larvae before

---

Tar spot *see Acer tar spot*
Tomato blight *see Potato and tomato blight*
Two-spotted mite *see Glasshouse red spider mite*
Verticillium wilt *see Wilt diseases*

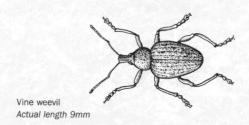

Vine weevil
Actual length 9mm

planting out. Protect individual pots, and greenhouse staging legs, with sticky tape smeared with non-drying glue. Check regularly that barriers have not been breached.
Biological control: Outdoors and under cover, use *Heterorhabditis megidis*, a parasitic nematode; min. soil/compost temperature 12°C (54°F). Under cover it may be used year-round as long as soil temperatures are adequate. Outside it is best applied in April/May, and August/early September.

Violet root rot

Helicobasidion purpureum
A fungal disease which can persist in soil without host plants for many years. It also persists on the roots of many wild plants. Acid soils and temperatures of around 15°C (59°F) favour development of the disease.

SUSCEPTIBLE PLANTS Beetroot, carrot, parsnip, potato, swede and turnip; also causes serious root rot of asparagus, celery, seakale and many ornamental plants. Can affect vegetables stored in clamps or pits.
SYMPTOMS Common and widespread throughout Europe, less serious in cooler northern areas and rare in Scotland. Dark purple strands containing dark spots cover roots and tubers. A felty mass, to which soil adheres, may also be present. Roots may rot. The upper part of the plant may become stunted and yellow.
PREVENTION AND CONTROL Remove plants before they

disintegrate and release diseased fruiting bodies into the soil. Burn diseased roots. Do not compost infected plant material. Improve drainage. Avoid growing all root crops on the site for at least 4 years.

Viruses

Viruses, invisible to the naked eye, exist in living plant material, where they do not necessarily cause symptoms. They are spread by sap-sucking insects, such as aphids, by contact (on hands and on tools, especially cutting tools such as secateurs), by birds and by propagation from contaminated plants. Some viruses are plant-specific while others will infect a number of unrelated plants.

SUSCEPTIBLE PLANTS A huge range of plants are vulnerable to some form of virus.
SYMPTOMS Many and varied, including stunting, mottled and mosaic-patterned leaves, distorted fruits and even death. Yield of perennial crops will decline.
PREVENTION AND CONTROL Control the agent that transmits the virus. Grow resistant cultivars. Plant certified virus-free planting material. Use a crop rotation for viruses transmitted by soil living organisms. Once a plant is infected there is no cure. Dig up infected plants. Burn woody plants.
See also Blackcurrant reversion virus, Cucumber mosaic virus and Zucchini yellow mosaic virus.

Wasps

Paravespula vulgaris and *P. germanica*
Adults of this pest are winged, with conspicuous yellow and black markings, up to 2cm (¾in) long. They construct large, papery nests in cavities in soil, walls, buildings and compost heaps. Early in the year, wasps are valuable predators, feeding their young on small caterpillars and other pests. Most wasps are killed by frosts in autumn. Queen wasps overwinter in dry protected areas such as outbuildings, sheds and under loose bark of trees.

PLANTS ATTACKED Ripening fruits of apples, pears, grapes, damsons and plums.
SYMPTOMS Holes eaten in ripening fruit in summer and early autumn, usually extending damage caused by other factors. The stems of dahlias may be damaged and in dry weather the pods of runner beans may be damaged by the wasps scraping at them with their mouthparts.
PREVENTION AND CONTROL Tolerate wasps where possible. Protect fruits with bags made of muslin, nylon tights or similar. If absolutely necessary, accessible nests can be destroyed. This is best done after dark and should not be considered if you are allergic to wasps. Pay very strict attention to safety; keep not only children but also pets well away. Full protective clothing must be worn, to cover every part of the body. Knock an aerial nest into a plastic bag. Tie tightly then place in freezer to kill the wasps. Nests in the

ground or in compost heaps can be sealed by placing a glass bowl over the entrance, pushing it down into the earth to seal it. Wasps will starve in a few weeks. The safest option is to call in a pest-control expert. Ask them to use a soap or synthetic pyrethroid spray, rather than carbamate or organophosphate compounds.

Waterlogging

This is a common disorder of houseplants and other pot-grown plants; also plants in poorly drained soils.

SYMPTOMS Yellowing of leaves, dry angular blotches on leaves, general stunting of growth. Root-rotting diseases may also be encouraged.
CAUSES Overwatering, especially when growth is slow. Poor drainage.
PREVENTION AND CONTROL Adjust watering according to plant species and time of year. Improve drainage of soil; ensure that pots can drain well. Grow plants that thrive in waterlogged soils.

Weevils

Beetles with a characteristic snout and clubbed antennae. They range in size from 2mm (¹⁄₁₆in) to 2.5cm (1in), depending on species. The larvae have a soft white body and obvious head; they are otherwise featureless.
See also Pea and bean weevil, Vine weevil.

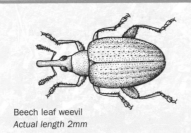

Beech leaf weevil
Actual length 2mm

For more information on improving soil structure and drainage, see pp.38–41.

Whiteflies

Adults of this pest, 2mm long with white wings, fly up from plants when disturbed. Eggs, laid on host plants, hatch into "scales" – oval, immobile creatures found on the undersides of leaves. Both scales and adults are sap-feeders and excrete sticky honeydew, which drops on to the upper surface of leaves below. Sooty moulds (q.v.) develop on this. A severe infestation may stunt growth.
See also Cabbage whitefly; Glasshouse whitefly.

Willow anthracnose

Marssonina salicicola
The spores of this fungal disease overwinter in stem lesions and on fallen leaves. Wet conditions encourage spread.

SUSCEPTIBLE PLANTS Willow.
SYMPTOMS Small pale brown lesions on the stems; reddish spots on leaves. Leaves drop off and shoot tips die back. In serious cases weeping willow no longer displays its weeping habit.
PREVENTION AND CONTROL Prune out infected stems. If the disease is serious, replace with resistant weeping Peking willow (*Salix babylonica* var. *pekinensis*), *Salix* 'Pendula' or the hybrid *Salix x sepulcralis* var. *sepulcrali*.
Fungicide spray: Bordeaux mixture, before bud burst in early spring.

Wilt diseases

Fusarium and *Verticillium* spp.
A common and widespread group of diseases with similar symptoms. Damage is usually caused by a blockage of the water-conducting tissues of the stem, starving the leaves of water. The disease may persist in the soil for several years, depending on the particular causal organism, and can enter plants through wounds. Commonly associated with eelworm attack. Some wilts such as those affecting China asters and peas, are host-specific, while others will attack a wide range of plants.

SUSCEPTIBLE PLANTS Fruit, vegetables (especially legumes, tomato, cucurbits), ornamentals.
SYMPTOMS Wilting, which often starts on lower leaves, with some recovery at night initially. A dark discoloration can be seen in the middle of the stem when cut open well above soil level.
PREVENTION AND CONTROL Earth up infected plants. If infection is severe remove all infected plants and associated soil. Do not compost any of the plant material. Do not grow susceptible plants on the same site for at least six years.
See also Clematis wilt, Peony wilt.

Wind rock

Disorder that often affects young trees and shrubs and also herbaceous plants that have a large amount of foliage compared to root growth.

SYMPTOMS Plants are rocked to and fro but not completely uprooted. This produces a hollow around the base of the stem which can fill with rainwater that may freeze. This will damage the base of the stem and allow access to disease.
CAUSES Strong winds.
PREVENTION AND CONTROL Firm in any wind-rocked plants as soon as possible. Stake plants if appropriate.

Wind scorch

Disorder affecting many plants.

PLANT SYMPTOMS Browning of foliage on the side of a plant facing the prevailing wind. Individual leaf margins or tips may be markedly browner than the leaf centres. Apples and other fruit may show a red/brown russetting on the skin surface.
CAUSES Severe winds, especially salt laden. Buildings can create a wind tunnel or a particularly draughty spot in a garden.
PREVENTION AND CONTROL Grow plants suitable for windy positions – usually, plants for coastal areas are suitable but check the hardiness of these for inland and northern areas. Grow or erect a windbreak.

Winter moths

"Looper" caterpillars of three moth species are included under this pest heading – winter moth (*Operophtera brumata*), March moth (*Alsophila aescularira*) and mottled umber moth (*Erannis defoliaria*). Winter moth caterpillars are green with three yellow longitudinal stripes. Mottled umber moth caterpillars are dark brown with yellow lateral longitudinal bands. March moth caterpillars are green with light-coloured stripes. Wingless female moths emerge from the soil in winter and early spring, mate, then crawl up host plants to lay their eggs. The March moth lays a distinctive ring of eggs around twigs; the others lay eggs singly or in small groups by buds or in bark crevices. Caterpillars feed from March to the end of June, then drop down to the soil on a silken thread to pupate. There is one generation a year.

SUSCEPTIBLE PLANTS Apple, pear, plum, cherry, cotoneaster, dogwood, hawthorn, hazel, roses and many other ornamentals.
SYMPTOMS Irregular holes eaten in leaves, often before they have expanded from the bud. The main attack is in spring and early summer, though symptoms will persist through the season. Extensive damage to fruit blossom may reduce crops; persistent attacks weaken plants.
PREVENTION AND CONTROL Place grease bands, or a band of fruit tree grease, around the stems, trunks and stakes of susceptible plants, from October to March. Check regularly that the band has not been breached.

Wireworms

Wireworms are the larvae of click beetles, the two main species being the garden click beetle (*Athous haemorrhoidalis*) and the common click beetle (*Agriotes lineatus*). Wireworm are tough-skinned, slender, cylindrical, 25mm (1in) in length and golden/yellow to orange/brown in colour. They have three pairs of legs at the head end of the body. Eggs are laid in grassland and weedy soil from early to midsummer and larvae may feed for up to five years. Because they dislike disturbance, they are usually found on grassland and newly cleared ground.

SUSCEPTIBLE PLANTS Potato, strawberry, brassicas, beans, beetroot, carrot, lettuce, onion, and tomato; also ornamentals including anemone, carnation, dahlia, gladioli and primula.
SYMPTOMS The roots, corms, tubers and stems of many plants are attacked, most severely in the spring and autumn, but damage can occur thorough the year. Potatoes show small entry holes 2–3mm (1/16–1/8in) across and when cut open a network of tunnels run through the tuber. Later these holes may be enlarged by slugs or millipedes.
PREVENTION AND CONTROL Damage is most severe on newly cultivated land. Cultivate the soil during winter to expose larvae to birds and other predators. Lift potatoes in early autumn to limit damage. In greenhouses trap wireworms on spiked pieces of potato or carrot buried in the soil. Remove regularly and destroy. Expose home-made compost to birds and other predators before use if it is infested with wireworm. Grow the green manure mustard on the area. It is said to speed up the life cycle.

Woodlice

Armadillidium vulgare, Oniscus asellus, Porcellio scaber and other spp.

Mid- to dark grey, hard-bodied, jointed, terrestrial crustaceans up to 2cm (¾in) long. Young woodlice are lighter in colour, depending on age, and much smaller. They hide during daylight under seed boxes, pots, stones and other debris, emerging at night to feed. Batches of 20 or more eggs are laid and held in brood pouches by the adult female. The young disperse and feed for a year or so before they mature.

SUSCEPTIBLE PLANTS Seedlings and young plants.
SYMPTOMS The main source of food for the woodlouse is dead or decaying plant matter, not living plants. They can, however, eat off seedlings at soil level.
PREVENTION AND CONTROL Woodlice are such ubiquitous creatures that trying to eliminate them would be impossible, and is rarely necessary, except perhaps in greenhouses and garden frames in spring where seed-raising is going on. Destroy large colonies by pouring boiling water over them. Control survivors by setting baits of bran, dried blood, boiled potato, grated cheese or sugar, under a plank of wood, a box or other dark location. Collect and destroy. Keep greenhouses clear of decaying plant debris. Do not mulch susceptible young plants.

Wood mouse

Apodemus sylvaticus
Also known as the long-tailed field mouse. The adult mouse is brown with grey/white underparts. Its tail is long relative to body size. Breeding takes place from mid-spring to late autumn. The wood mouse does not hibernate but remains active throughout the winter.

SUSCEPTIBLE PLANTS Pea and bean seeds; bulbs and corms.
SYMPTOMS Damage is worse in autumn to early spring, especially to bulbs and corms of lilies, narcissus and tulips. Seeds, particularly of peas and beans, are dug up and eaten after sowing. Seed can also be eaten after germination – leaving only the shoot remaining. Small holes may appear in seed beds where mice have tunnelled down to the seed. Sweetcorn seed and cobs may also be eaten. During autumn and winter stored fruit and vegetables and packaged seed can be damaged.
PREVENTION AND CONTROL Traps and barriers can give some protection. Humane traps are available, but you must release the mouse a considerable distance away. Bait traps with carrot, apple, potato or melon seeds. Cover traps with cloches or other protection to prevent birds and pets being harmed. Protect seed beds and bulbs with fine mesh wire fencing laid over the soil. Raise early sowings of peas and beans indoors in pots, boxes or guttering and transplant to final growing positions when ground has warmed up. Avoid autumn and early spring sowings.

Woolly aphid

Eriosoma lanigerum
This small brown aphid lives in colonies on stems and branches, protected by a white waxy substance which looks rather like cotton wool. They are most conspicious in late spring and early summer, but present all year. Young aphids overwinter in cracks in bark, and in galls.

SUSCEPTIBLE PLANTS Apple, cotoneaster, hawthorn, ornamental *Malus*, pyracantha and other related plants.
SYMPTOMS Leaves and fruit become disfigured; galls may develop on twigs and branches. Canker may enter through cracks in the bark and dieback may result.
PREVENTION AND CONTROL Use a stiff brush to remove woolly colonies. Cut out and burn badly infested branches. *See also* Aphids.

Zucchini yellow mosaic virus

Viral disease transmitted by aphids.

SUSCEPTIBLE PLANTS Courgette, marrow and squash.
SYMPTOMS Bright yellow mosaic pattern on leaves. Plants stunted and distorted. Fruits knobbly and distorted.
PREVENTION AND CONTROL Remove infected plants as soon as symptoms are noticed. There is no cure.

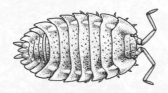
Woodlouse

If spraying, check that the product is legally and organically approved for the job. Regulations may have changed since this information was compiled.

Gardening and the law

Regulations and byelaws in the UK

Depending on the type, scale and extent of your proposals for your garden project, they may require planning permission and Building Regulation approval. To ensure that regulations and byelaws are not breached, consult the planning or development control section of your local council office at an early stage of planning, or carrying out improvements to, a garden. Alternatively, contact an architect, landscape architect or surveyor who can advise you.

Planning permission is necessary for developments which may affect your neighbours or the area surrounding your garden and is granted by the local planning authority (LPA) following your application for approval. Not all development requires an application, and many proposals for a garden scheme would not be applicable, although the siting or height of a wall or fence may be restricted. The table below illustrates various developments, and whether there is a need for planning consent. It is wise to check for local variations with the LPA at the outset of your designs.

Building Regulation approval is necessary to protect standards of design, construction and materials in order to safeguard public health and safety and, although most garden structures will be exempt from the regulations, it is advisable to check with the Building Control section at your local council office.

Another regulation that may affect your gardening aspirations is a Tree Preservation Order (TPO). This is made by the local planning authority in respect of trees, groups of trees and woodlands. A TPO prohibits the cutting down, uprooting, lopping, topping, wilful damage or destruction of trees without the consent of the LPA. If you consider that a tree is dead, dying or diseased, or is causing damage to a property but is covered by a TPO, the council will normally grant consent to fell if you apply to do so.

The information below, on other aspects of legislation that may be applicable to gardeners, has been summarised, so it is advisable to seek professional advice on these matters.

Boundary lines

Where there is ambiguity or disputes with neighbours regarding boundary ownerships, these can usually be resolved by consulting the deeds of the property. A description or plan of the extent and limits of the property can usually be found. Other potential restrictions, which may affect your garden project may be listed, so these documents should be consulted at an early stage of your project to avoid additional costs and disappointments.

As a rough rule of thumb to determine your property line, the structural supports of fences and piers within walls are usually erected on the land of the owner allowing the face of the wall or fence to be installed up to the boundary line.

Trespass would occur if the supports for the fence or the wall projected into the neighbours land and consequently the owner could be made to remove them.

Similarly when vegetation from a neighbouring garden overhangs a boundary line, you have the right to remove this if you wish, but the lopped boughs, clippings or fruit should be returned to the owner.

High hedges

The UK government is considering legislation to allow local authorities to specify height restrictions on tall hedges where neighbours consider these as nuisances. If this legislation goes through parliament, local authorities would be able to impose fines if heights were not adhered to, and to instruct contractors to carry out the work.

DEVELOPMENT IN THE GARDEN: THE NEED FOR CONSENT

Type of Work	Planning permission	Building regulation	Notes regarding planning
Constructing a conservatory	YES	NO	Similar to house extensions so contact the LPA for possible restrictions
Constructing a garden fence or wall	YES	NO	Permission needed if it is greater than 2m (6ft) high, or more than 1m (3ft) high and forms a boundary enclosure adjoining a highway
Constructing a path or driveway	NO	NO	Unless it forms the access to a main road
Constructing a hard standing for vehicles	NO	NO	Provided it is within your property boundary and not for use by commercial vehicles
Constructing a shed, greenhouse or outbuilding	NO	NO	If within the boundary of your property or for the benefit of the householder only, and no part is greater than 3m (10ft) high, or 4m (12ft) for a pitched roof
Constructing a pond	NO	NO	Unless the structure is to be located within a Conservation Area where planning restrictions will be applicable
Felling/lopping/topping trees	NO	NO	Unless protected by a TPO or the tree is within a Conservation Area
Planting a hedge	NO	NO	See "High hedges" above

HDRA Organic Guidelines for Gardeners

HDRA supports whole-heartedly the concept of a common organic standard. The HDRA Organic Guidelines for Gardeners follow closely the organic standards set for commercial organic growers by the British organic movement, by the UK government and the EU. The HDRA Guidelines have been produced because the existing commercial standards are not always applicable and do not cover all aspects of gardening. In almost all cases, HDRA Guidelines match EU organic standards.

These Guidelines are not set in stone. As knowledge changes and grows they will be adjusted accordingly. The HDRA Organic Guidelines have no legal standing. They are purely advisory, to be used by anyone interested in organic gardening methods. They are designed for all types and sizes of garden.

The Guidelines divide gardening practices and materials into four categories:

Best practice
Recommended for organic gardening – the ideal to aim towards.

Acceptable
Acceptable for use in an organic garden but not as ideal as those above.

Qualified acceptance
Less acceptable for regular use in an organic garden.

Not recommended
Not considered suitable for use in an organic garden.

For footnotes, see p.401.

Soil management

A healthy fertile soil is the basis of all effective organic growing. The soil should be managed in ways that develop and protect its structure, its fertility and also the millions of tiny creatures for which it is home.

Caring for the soil organically involves the use of organic residues, in the form of animal manures and plant and animal remains. This is to improve soil structure and maintain humus levels; to feed the soil life, whose activities are essential for soil health; and to provide plant nutrients. Attention is paid to drainage and maintenance of appropriate pH. Green manure cover crops are grown to protect and feed the soil. Cultivations are kept to a minimum and timed to avoid damage to soil structure.

Best practice
• Keep the soil covered with a protective covering of vegetation, such as a green manure or other plants, or a surface mulch.
• Apply manures and plant wastes only as detailed in other sets of Guidelines.
• Loosen subsoil to break up compaction if present.
• Improve drainage as necessary.
• Keep pH at appropriate level. Use a rotation system for annual plants.

Acceptable
• Soil cultivations, where necessary. These should be carried out only when the soil conditions are neither too wet nor too dry. Do not mix subsoil layers with topsoil. Keep soil cultivations to a minimum to avoid damaging soil structure.

Qualified acceptance
• Rotovating[1].

Not recommended
• All other practices.

Manures and waste plant materials

Organic materials should be recycled within the garden, producing compost and leafmould to feed the soil where necessary. These can be augmented with materials brought in such as manures and other "waste" materials and proprietary gardening products. Ideally these inputs should be from organic growing systems, but where this is not possible, materials from non-organic sources can be used.

Manures from intensive production systems should never be used. They may contain unwanted contaminants, and there are ethical considerations concerning the way in which the animals are kept.

Fresh manures and other waste products should be composted or otherwise processed before use.

Best practice
• Plant and animal wastes[2] from the house and garden, after being composted[3] or, if autumn leaves, made into leafmould.

Acceptable
• Composted or well-rotted[4] strawy farmyard, horse and poultry manures from organic sources.
• Plant waste materials and byproducts from organic food processing industries.
• Proprietary manures and composts carrying an HDRA or other organic symbol.
• Straw and hay from organic sources.
• Sawdust, shavings and bark from timber untreated after harvest.
• Microbial and plant extract compost activators.
• Autumn leaves collected from parks and other public areas not adjacent to busy roads.
• Organic mushroom compost.
• Wool products not containing organophosphate residues.
• Feathers from acceptable production systems[5].

Qualified acceptance
• Straw, hay and farmyard and horse manures from non-organic sources after being composted for three months or stockpiled for six months[6].
• Composted green and household waste from centralised composting plants, not containing unacceptable levels of PTEs (see footnote 12).
• Poultry manure and deep litter from less intensive, non-organic systems[7] after being composted for six months or stockpiled under cover for twelve months.
• Seaweed from unpolluted beaches[8].
• Manures from non-organic straw-based pig production systems after being properly composted for six months or stacked for 12 months[9].
• Plant wastes and byproducts from non-organic food processing industries, after being properly composted.
• Mushroom and worm composts made from non-organic animal manures, except those from unacceptable intensive systems (see footnote 17).
• Proprietary gardening products such as bagged manures and garden composts from non-organic sources except those from unacceptable production systems (see footnote 17) and

those containing peat[10].
• Processed animal products from slaughterhouses, except where cattle or sheep are likely to graze.
• Processed waste products from the fishing industry.
• Sewage sludge, effluent and sludge-based composts, suitably treated and free of potentially toxic elements[11,12].

Not recommended
• Any materials containing levels of potentially toxic elements (PTEs) greater than those permitted[12].
• Leaves and leafmould collected from woodland[13].
• Leaves collected from busy roadsides[14].
• Peat and coir[15] as a soil conditioner[16].
• Proprietary manure and garden compost products containing coir or peat.
• The use of animal residues and manures (other than processed animal products from slaughterhouses and fish industries) from intensive livestock systems[17].

Storage and application of manures and composts

Manures, composts and other materials containing plant foods should be stored, and applied, in ways that avoid leaching out of plant foods. Leaching both wastes nutrients and pollutes watercourses and groundwater.

Best practice
• Store and compost manures, and other materials that contain plant foods, indoors or under a waterproof cover[18].
• Apply no more than one wheelbarrow-full of well-rotted strawy manure, or two of compost, per 5 square metres of ground each year[19] (the equivalent of, approximately, 50 litres/11 gal of manure or 100 litres/22 gal of compost per square foot).
• Apply manures and compost only to growing plants, or to soil where plants are soon to be grown.

Acceptable
• Autumn/early winter applications of composted manures to an actively growing green manure crop.
• Applications of composts and composted manures to greenhouse soils at any time.

Qualified acceptance
• None.

Not recommended
• Storage systems and practices which result in the pollution of watercourses.
• Autumn application of manure to bare soil intended to be left fallow over winter.

Fertilisers and liquid feeds

Organic fertilisers may be of plant, animal or mineral origin. They should be regarded as a supplement to, and not as a replacement for, recycling of nutrients within the garden – through a compost heap for example – and the use of other bought/brought-in bulky organic materials. They should only be applied if adequate supplies are not available from other sources.

Liquid feeds should only be used on plants growing in a restricted environment such as a pot, growing bag or greenhouse border.

In the absence of more acceptable materials, restricted use of soluble fertilisers to treat severe trace element deficiencies may be allowed. A soil analysis is recommended to identify, or confirm, a particular deficiency.

The products listed below may not all be readily available to the gardener.

Best practice
• None.

Acceptable
• Homemade liquid feeds, made from plants or animal manures.

Qualified acceptance
• **Nitrogen (N)** Blood meal, in growing media and on overwintered crops in spring only; hoof and horn meals.
• **Phosphorus (P) (as phosphate, P_2O_5)** Natural rock phosphate; basic slag; calcined aluminium phosphate rock; meat and bone meals. Cadmium levels in rock phosphates should not exceed 90mg/kg P_2O_5.
• **Potassium (K) (potash)** Wood ash, added to a compost or manure heap only[20]; plant extracts such as vinasse and sugar beet waste; sulphate of potash, only where soil analysis shows exchangeable potassium (K) levels are below index 2[21] and clay content is less than 20%.
• **Compound fertilisers** Fish, blood and bone meals (supplying N, P, Ca[22]), free from nonpermitted substances; fish meals (N)[23]; meat and bone meals (P, Ca, N); seaweed meal (K,N, trace elements).
• **Liming materials** Dolomitic limestone; ground limestone; ground chalk.
• **Minor minerals** Calcareous magnesium rock, or dolomitic limestone (supplying Mg[22] and Ca); gypsum, or calcium sulphate (Ca); ground chalk and limestone (Ca); Epsom salts (Mg), for acute deficiency only; magnesium rock, including Kieserite (Mg); sulphur; calcium chloride, for bitter pit in apples.
• **Trace elements** Dried seaweed meal; seaweed extract; limestone and chalk; rock dusts.

Trace elements boron; copper; iron; manganese; molybdenum; cobalt; selenium and zinc, following soil analysis or other evidence of deficiency.
• Commercially available liquid feeds, made from plants or animal manures, preferably with an HDRA or other organic symbol.

Not recommended
• Fresh blood
• All other synthetic and natural fertilisers including nitrochalk, Chilean nitrate, urea, muriate of potash, superphosphates, kainite.
• Slaked lime, quicklime.
• The use of slaughterhouse by-products (bone meal, hoof and horn meal etc) where cattle or sheep are likely to graze.

Rotation

An essential aspect of soil management and weed, pest and disease control. When growing annual plants, such as vegetables, herbs and flowers, or replanting fruit, shrubs and other perennials, it is unwise to reuse the same site for the same type of plant. As far as possible the position should be varied, returning to the first site only after a period of years. This practice, known as rotation, helps in the control of pests, diseases and weeds, and in the maintenance of soil fertility, organic matter levels and structure.

Best practice
• Plants with similar pest and disease susceptibility are separated by an appropriate time interval[24].
• A balance between fertility building and exploitative cropping.
• A nitrogen-fixing leguminous crop or green manure included in the rotation to add nitrogen where appropriate.
• Varying weed-suppressing with

weed-susceptible crops.
• Rotations that minimise the time that the soil is left uncovered.
• Perennials, especially fruit and roses, not planted where a closely related plant has recently grown.

Acceptable
• Shorter rotations where space is limited, for example in a greenhouse, as long as attention is paid to keeping the soil healthy.

Qualified acceptance
• None.

Not recommended
• Growing the same annual crop in the same location year after year.

For information on soil management and compost-making, see Soil and Soil Care, pp.32–61.

Pest and disease management

Prevention is the mainstay of an organic strategy for pest and disease management. Work with nature, rather than trying to dominate it. Encourage healthy growth by providing plants with a well-structured soil and a balanced diet, by matching site and plants, and by growing pest- and disease-resistant varieties. Natural predators and parasites help to keep pests and diseases in check. The organic garden should be designed and managed to provide a mixed environment to favour these beneficial creatures. Organic gardeners should also be aware that the presence of a pest or a disease-causing organism does not necessarily require any action. The use of killing sprays should be kept to a minimum.

Good growing practice, hygiene, barriers, traps and scarers complete the range of pest and disease management techniques.

The following products and practices are for use both outdoors and in a greenhouse or polytunnel.

Best practice
• Build soil with good structure which supplies plants with a balanced diet.
• Maintain good hygiene to minimise carry-over of pests and diseases.
• Monitor plants regularly to catch potential problems early.
• Use healthy seed and planting material, certified virus-free where applicable.
• Pest- and disease-resisting varieties.
• Suit plants to site and soil.
• Provide habitats to encourage natural predators and parasites.
• Grow plants and flowers to feed predators and parasites.
• Use a crop rotation.
• Select sowing/planting dates to avoid specific pests and diseases.
• Scaring devices.
• Good ventilation, around and within plants.
• Balanced watering.
• Mixed and companion planting; avoid monoculture.
• Biodegradable barriers.
• Give in gracefully when necessary!
(See also Conservation Guidelines, p.401.)

Acceptable
• Introduced biological control agents.
• Non-biodegradable barriers, reused where possible.
• Steam sterilisation of buildings and equipment.

Qualified acceptance
• Sticky barriers and traps, including those with pheromone lure.
• Steam sterilisation of soils.
• Plant oils.

• Disinfectants based on citric acid (from natural sources) or peroxyacetic acid for disinfection of pots, trays, equipment and glasshouses.
• For controlling pests where there is a threat to the plant: potassium soap (soft soap) and soaps containing plant fatty acids, *Bacillus thuringiensis*, derris/rotenone, pyrethrum[25], insecticidal soap; also neem, quassia and granulosis virus where permitted[26].
• For controlling diseases where there is a threat to the plant: Bordeaux mixture, copper sulphate, copper oxychloride and copper ammonium carbonate; sulphur.

Not recommended
• All other pesticides, including nicotine, phenols, aluminium sulphate and metaldehyde.

Wood preservatives

Wood preservatives are, by their very nature, persistent and toxic. In the organic garden they should be avoided where possible. Their use should be restricted to structural timbers, where decay could prove a safety hazard. Wood that is in contact with both soil and air is at most risk.

Best practice
• Untreated timber.
• Timber from trees such as oak, larch and sweet chestnut, which has more resistance to decay. Check that it is from a well-managed, sustainable source.
• Concrete posts.

Acceptable
• Synthetic wood made from recycled polystyrene.
• Treating wood not in contact with the soil (such as fence panels) with linseed oil or similar water-repellent product

that allows the wood to breathe.

Qualified acceptance
• Boron compounds (water-based).

Not recommended
• Creosote.
• Timber treated with CCA (copper chrome arsenic)[27], often sold as "pressure-treated".

Weed control and ground clearance

Weeds provide food and shelter for a multitude of natural creatures, and provide a useful source of material for the compost heap. They should be allowed to grow where possible, eliminating them only where they interfere with chosen plants. There is a range of cultural techniques that can be used to clear ground and keep the garden weed-free. There are no weed-killing sprays for use in an organic garden.

Best practice
• Crop rotation.
• Varying weed-suppressing and weed-susceptible crops.
• Hoeing, hand-pulling, using the stale seed bed technique.
• Close spacing; ground-cover plants and cover crops.
• Creating a good, solid foundation for paths.
• Biodegradable mulches of organic origin.

Acceptable
• Digging in, or out.
• Biodegradable mulches not of organic origin.
• Pointing joints between pavers, slabs, bricks etc.

Qualified acceptance
• Rotovating[1].
• Non-biodegradable mulches, preferably those that are water-permeable, and that can be

reused several times.
• Permeable, non-biodegradable mulches under path surfaces or around perennial plants.
• Flame-weeding.

Not recommended
• Any weedkillers, including those based on glyphosate and natural fatty acids.

For more information on organic weed control, see Weeds and Weed Control, pp.73–83.

Weed control in lawns

A lawn of one or two species of grass only, which is tantamount to monoculture, does not fit well with organic principles. A mixture of grasses and broad-leaved species is much more likely to provide a healthy lawn that will stay green all year round. Clover will also help to feed the grass. Follow a good programme of lawn maintenance. If grass is encouraged to grow strongly, weed problems are minimised.

Best practice
• Cut regularly, but only when required. Do not cut lower than 1.25cm (½in) for a fine lawn, 2.5cm (1in) for an all-purpose lawn.
• Leave mowings on the lawn whenever possible, but not when soil is cold and wet, or when mowings are long.
• Scarify and aerate as necessary.
• Adjust pH and drainage and remove shade as necessary if a lawn is not thriving.
• Feed only if growth is poor and/or yellow, and drought or waterlogging is not the cause. Use an organic manure, compost or fertiliser.
• Top-dress in autumn.

Acceptable
• None.

Qualified acceptance
• None.

Not recommended
• Worm killers.
• All chemical fertilisers and pesticides.

For more information on organic lawns, see Lawns and Lawn Care, pp.174–185.

Planting material, growing media and container-growing

The ideal is to grow your own plants from organically grown seed, using organic growing media when growing in containers. Organically grown seeds, tubers, corms, bulbs and other planting material should be used where available. As a minimum, use seed not treated with chemicals after harvest. When buying wild flower seeds, ensure that they are indigenous, not imported from another country. Bulbs and other planting material should never be taken from the wild. There are some suppliers of organic vegetable, fruit, and ornamental plants. Use these where available, or raise your own plants.

Wherever possible, grow plants directly in the ground. Growing conditions in a pot or growing bag are inevitably restricted, requiring additional attention and feeding with soluble nutrients. An organic growing medium, preferably peat-free, should be used when raising plants and growing in containers. Purchased growing media should, ideally, carry the HDRA organic symbol. Homemade mixtures should only contain ingredients listed in the Guidelines that follow.

For more information on growing media and making seed and potting composts, see Raising Plants, pp.114–115.

Sowing and planting material

Best practice
• Plants grown to organic standards.
• Organically grown seed, tubers and other planting material.

Acceptable
• Conventionally grown seed, tubers and other planting material not treated with chemicals after harvest.

Qualified acceptance
• Plants and planting material grown using non-organic methods.
• Rooting powders not containing fungicide.

Not recommended
• Rooting powders with fungicides.
• Plants and material from the wild.
• Seed treated after harvest.
• Seeds or plants of genetically modified (GM) cultivars, produced using genetic engineering.

Growing media

Best practice
• Homemade growing media consisting only of materials listed in these Guidelines.
• Proprietary growing media, peat-free and carrying an HDRA or other recognised organic symbol.

Acceptable
• Organic growing media containing recycled peat, preferably with an HDRA or other recognised organic symbol.

Qualified acceptance
• Perlite, vermiculite, bentonite and zeolites which have not undergone chemical treatment with prohibited materials.
• Organic growing media containing peat, preferably with recognised organic symbol.

Not recommended
• Growing media containing materials not listed in these Guidelines.

Growing in containers

The same principles should be applied to plants grown in pots, baskets, planters and other containers as are applied in the organic garden.

Best practice
• Organic growing media with recycled organic waste as the major source of fertility.
• Plants and seeds as above.
• Hanging basket liners made of wool or other recycled materials.
• Pots and containers of appropriate size.
• Additional feeding, where necessary, by top-dressing with composts, manures or proprietary products made of the same.

Acceptable
• Organic growing media with organic fertilisers as the main source of plant foods.
• Additional feeding with organic fertilisers.
• Additional feeding with homemade liquid feeds made from plants, or animal manures.

Qualified acceptance
• Commercially available organic liquid feeds, preferably with a recognised organic symbol.

Not recommended
- Moss lining for hanging baskets.
- Other liquid feeds.

Conservation and the environment

Conservation and organic gardening are inextricably linked. Human activities pollute the world; habitats, and wildlife, are disappearing fast. Loss of diversity has particular consequences for organic gardeners, who rely on natural pest/predator networks to keep pests in check. Conservation and creation of a diverse environment, both in the garden and further afield, is essential. Diverse planting, including the use of native species and less highly bred varieties where appropriate, is also recommended. Activities that pollute, such as bonfires, dumping of organic wastes, or excessive use of non-renewable resources, have no place in an organic garden.

Best practice
- Retention and creation of traditional boundaries such as hedges, stone walls and ditches.
- Retention and creation of habitats such as hedges, ponds and uncut grassy areas to feed and protect wildlife.
- Native species of plants.
- Non-native species with particular features for wildlife.
- Creating wildlife corridors – linked habitats to allow safe passage for wildlife.
- Using a hedge–cutting regime, if any, that avoids disturbing nesting birds, and, where appropriate, allows the hedge to flower and produce fruit.
- Use of timber from renewable sources.
- Recycling and reuse.

Acceptable
- None.

Qualified acceptance
- Hot, dry bonfires for disposal of diseased plant material.

Not recommended
- Bonfires other than as above.
- Clearing away all plant debris from under hedges, shrubs etc, unless for disease control purposes.
- Storage of manures uncovered.
- Timber from non-renewable sources.
- Plants taken from the wild; wild flower seed from overseas sources.
- Use of materials transported over long distances, when a suitable, more local, alternative can be used.

Notes

1 Rotovating can destroy soil structure; it can also create an impermeable "pan" or hard layer of soil.
2 Manures from rabbits, hens, gerbils and most other vegetarian pets should be safe to compost. Those from cats and dogs can contain parasites harmful to humans. If the latter are to be composted, particular attention to hygiene is essential when handling; their use is not advised where children could come into contact with fresh or composted material.
3 Composting is an aerobic process, converting plant and animal wastes to dark, soil-like material known as compost. Ideally the compost heap should be turned several times to keep the process aerobic. Composting converts the material into a more stable form and may also kill weed seeds and diseases.
4 "Well-rotted" means manure which has been stockpiled under a waterproof cover and left to mature for a month or more. This process converts the free nitrogen and potassium that fresh manure contains into forms which are less likely to be washed out by the rain and which cannot damage plants.
5 See note 7.
6 The extra time is to allow some breakdown of any chemical residues that might be present.
7 Poultry systems from which manure can be used in an organic garden:
a) Egg production systems (defined by EU Regulation No. 1274/91): free-range (max. 400 birds/acre); semi-intensive (max. 1600 birds/acre); deep litter (max. 7 birds/sq m).
b) Deep litter pullet rearing systems (max. housing density of birds 17kg/sq m).
c) Meat-producing systems (defined by EEC Regulation No. 1538/91): free-range, traditional free-range; extensive indoor barn reared (max. housing density of mature birds: 12 hens or 17–25kg/sq m).

8 Fresh seaweed should be treated as a resource for local use only. Loose seaweed may be collected from the shoreline – growing seaweed should not be removed from rocks. Stripping of resources, even those that are renewable, is not recommended.
9 Regular use of non-organic pig manure is not advised; these manures can contain copper and other contaminants that can accumulate in the soil.
10 The use of peat as a soil improver is not acceptable in the organic garden. Its extraction destroys invaluable natural habitats.
11 Sewage is not allowed under EU or UK organic standards. HDRA regards sewage as a wasted resource and so has included it in these Guidelines – as long as it meets the required standards. There may not be any suitable uncontaminated sewage products available at present.
12 Potentially Toxic Elements (PTEs) include heavy metals and other elements, many of which are naturally present in the soil. Some are essential to plants and animals in trace amounts but can be toxic at higher levels. There are many different standards setting maximum permissible levels in soil and materials added to the soil. The variation in these standards shows that no one really knows the answer. For these Guidelines we have chosen the Soil Association figures for permitted levels in the soil. For levels in materials added to the soil, and the quantity of such materials that can be applied, we have taken those set by the EU Ecolabelling board* (see table below). These are stricter than those set by the EU organic standards, but as these Guidelines are for gardeners, who come into closer contact with the soil than many farmers, and where materials are likely to be applied to the top few centimetres of soil, we felt these were more appropriate.
*Anon (1993): Ecolabelling criteria: Soil improvers. UK Ecolabelling Board, London.
13 These are part of the natural cycle of fertility in the woodland and as such should not be removed from it.
14 These are likely to be contaminated with lead and cadmium.
15 Coconut fibre.
16 For peat, see note 10. As there are many organic materials of local origin available, often recycling waste materials, the use of coir – a material that is transported across the world – as a soil conditioner is not seen as appropriate in an organic garden.

17 Including poultry battery systems and broiler units with stocking rates over 25kg/sq m; indoor tethered sow breeding units; other systems where stock are not freely allowed to turn through 360°, where they are permanently in the dark, or are permanently kept without bedding.
18 To prevent washing out of nutrients by rain.
19 Excessive application of manure or compost can contribute to pollution of watercourses. On a large scale, the maximum application recommended is 50 tonnes per hectare. This translates into approximately one builder's wheelbarrow full of manure per 10 square metres of ground. Obviously this figure can only be a guideline as composts and manures vary in their composition. It is included here to make the point that it is not good practice to apply excessive quantities of nutrient-supplying material to the soil. The maximum rate recommended is lower than many gardeners use.
20 The nutrients in wood ash are very soluble and quickly wash out if applied directly to soil.
21 This figure refers to results given in a soil analysis.
22 Ca = calcium; Mg = magnesium.
23 Fishmeal that is a waste product from the fishing industry is acceptable; meal from fish caught directly for the purpose is not.
24 For vegetables, a 3- to 4-year rotation is usually recommended. Where particular problems such as persistent soil-borne pests and diseases occur, a longer period may be appropriate. For more specific recommendations, look at the life cycle of the particular pest or disease.
25 Ideally pure pyrethrum of plant origin should be used. Currently the only pyrethrum available contains a synergist, piperonyl butoxide, to make it more effective. This synergist also has insecticidal properties. Synthetic permethrins are not recommended.
26 The use of quassia, neem and granulosis virus is illegal in the UK, as they are not registered for use as pesticides.
27 Highly toxic chemicals such as copper chrome arsenate are used in this treatment, which raises the question of danger to the processor and of safe disposal. The treatment process is said to render the wood safe to use, but there is evidence to show that this may not be the case. Use of this type of timber is restricted in other countries. If burnt, fumes and ash are toxic.

POTENTIALLY TOXIC ELEMENTS (PTES)

	zinc	chromium	copper	lead	nickel	cadmium	mercury
Maximum permitted levels in the top soil (mg/kg dry matter)	150	150	50	100	50	2	1
Maximum permitted levels in material (mg/kg dry matter)	300	140	75	140	50	1.5	1
Loading rate averaged over a 10-year period (kg/ha/year)	7.5	7	3.8	7	1.5	0.08	0.05

Resources

ORGANISATIONS

Agroforestry Research Trust
46 Hunters Moon, Dartington,
Totnes, Devon TQ9 6JT
Tel: 01803 840776
Email: mail@agroforestry.co.uk
www.agroforestry.co.uk
Non-profit-making charity; researches into temperate agroforestry and all aspects of plant cropping and uses, with a focus on tree, shrub and perennial crops. Publications, journal; plants and seeds.

Architectural Salvage® Index,
Hutton and Rostron, Netley House,
Gomshall, Guildford, Surrey GU5 9QA
Tel: 01483 203221
Email: admin@handr.co.uk
www.handr.co.uk
Register of all types of re-usable building materials available throughout the UK.

Association for Environmentally Conscious Builders
PO Box 32, Llandysul, Wales SA44 5EJ
Tel: 01559 370908
Email: admin@aecb.net
www.aecb.net
The leading independent environmental building trade organisation.

B&Q
B&Q have an independently verified organic gardening range audited and endorsed by HDRA and are at the forefront of sourcing timber products from independently certified well-managed sources. For information telephone their environmental helpline: 0800 09266556. More details and information on local branches are available at www.diy.com.

Biodynamic Agricultural Association
Painswick Inn Project, Gloucester Street,
Stroud, Gloucestershire GL5 1QG
Tel: 01453 759501
Email: bdaa@biodynamic.freeserve.co.uk
www.anth.org.uk/biodynamic

British Trust for Conservation Volunteers
36 St Mary's Street, Wallingford, Oxford
OX10 0EU
Tel: 01491 839766
Email: information@btcv.org.uk
www.btcv.org.uk

Community Composting Network
67 Alexandra Road, Sheffield S2 3EE
Tel: 0114 258 0483
Email: ccn@gn.apc.org.
www.othas.org.uk/ccn/
Providing advice and support to existing and would-be community composting projects across the UK.

The Community Recycling Network
Trelawny House, Surrey Street,
Bristol BS2 8PS
Tel: 0117 942 0142
Email: info@crn.org.uk
www.crn.org.uk
Promotes community waste management. Provides support for local groups and a national voice for community recyclers.

Ecological Design Association
The British School, Slad Road, Stroud,
Gloucester GL5 1QW
Tel: 01453 765575
www.edaweb.org
Membership organisation promoting the design and use of ecologically friendly materials and products.

Education
For a list of colleges running organic courses, contact HDRA – the organic organisation.

Elm Farm Research Centre
Hamstead Marshall,
nr Newbury RG15 0HR
Tel: 01488 658298
Email: elmfarm@efrc.com
Organic agriculture research and development. Soil analysis services, developed specifically for organic growers.

Federation of City Farms and Community Gardens
The Greenhouse, Hereford Street,
Bedminster, Bristol BS3 4NA
Tel: 0117 923 1800
Email: FarmGarden@internet.com
www.farmgarden.org.uk
Promotes, supports and represents groups engaged in community-led development of open space through locally managed farming and gardening.

Forest Stewardship Council (FSC)
Unit D, Old Station Building, Llanidloes,
Powys SY18 6EB
Tel: 01686 413916
Email: Fsc-uk@fsc-uk.demon.co.uk
www.fsc-uk.demon.co.uk
International, independent organisation promoting environmentally appropriate, socially beneficial and economically viable management of the world's forests. Its logo on timber and wood products means that the wood is from a well-managed forest.

Froglife
Mansion House, 27/28 Market Place,
Halesworth, Suffolk IP19 8AY
Tel: 01986 873733
Email: froglife@froglife.org
www.froglife.org
Charity working to conserve reptiles and amphibians. Free helpline; pond doctors.

HDRA – the organic organisation
Ryton Organic Gardens, Coventry CV8 3LG
Tel: 024 7630 2517
Email: enquiry@hdra.or.uk
www.hdra.org.uk

The Herb Society (UK)
Deddington Hill Farm, Warmington,
Banbury OX17 1XB
Tel: 01295 692000
www.herbsociety.co.uk
Aims to increase the understanding and use of herbs and their benefits to health.

Heritage Seed Library
HDRA, Ryton on Dunsmore,
Coventry CV8 3LG
www.hdra.org.uk/hsl
Set up by HDRA to promote and conserve genetic diversity in vegetable crop plants. Annual seed catalogue for its members.

Humungus Fungus
Penrhiw House, Llanddeusant, Llangadog,
Carmarthenshire SA19 9YW
Tel: 01550 740306
Email: mushrooms.jac@virgin.net
www.jac-by-the-stowl.co.uk
Mushroom-growing supplies.

National Society of Allotment and Leisure Gardeners (NSALG)
Odell House, Hunters Road, Corby,
Northants NN17 5JE
Tel: 01536 266576
Email: webmaster@nsalg.demon.co.uk
www.nsalg.co.uk
National representative body for allotment holders and vegetable growers in the UK.

The Organic Gardening Catalogue
Riverdene Business Park, Molesey Road,
Hersham, Surrey KT12 4RG
Tel: 01932 253666
Email: chaseorg@aol.com
www.OrganicCatalog.com
The official catalogue of HDRA: organic seeds, sundries and publications.

PAN UK (formerly Pesticides Trust)
Eurolink Centre, 49 Effra Road, London
SW2 1BZ UK
Tel: 020 7274 8895
Email: admin@pan-uk.org
www.pan-uk.org
Environmental charity, providing information about pesticides and their usage. Promotes less pesticide-dependent methods of agriculture. Advice/leaflets on woodworm treatments, how to remove wasps and fleas and related subjects.

Permaculture Association (Britain)
London WC1N 3XX
Tel: 07041 390170/0113 2621718
Email: office@permaculture.org.uk
www.permaculture.org.uk
Working to make permaculture accessible to all people in Britain.

Permanent Publications
The Sustainability Centre
East Meon, Hants GU32 1HR
Tel:01730823311
info@permaculture.co.uk
www.permaculture.co.uk
Publishers of *Permaculture Magazine* and the *Earth Repair Catalogue* – a resource for environmental books, including ecological architecture and permaculture.

Plantlife
21 Elizabeth Street, London SW1W 9RP
Tel: 020 7808 0100
Email: enquiries@plantlife.org.uk
www.plantlife.org.uk
Britain's only national membership charity dedicated exclusively to conserving all forms of plant life in its natural habitat: the nation's champion of wild plants.

Plants for a Future
The Field, Higher Penpol, Lostwitheil,
Cornwall PL22 0NG
Tel: 01208 972963
Email: pfaf@scs.leeds.ac.uk
www.scs.leeds.ac.uk/pfaf
Resource centre for rare and unusual plants, particularly those with edible, medicinal or other uses. Vegan-organic permaculture. Database of useful plants which contains over 7000 species, with details on edible, medicinal and other uses and cultivation advice.

Reed bed water treatment
For sources of advice and information, contact HDRA – the organic organisation for factsheet FR5.

Royal Society for the Protection of Birds
The Lodge, Sandy, Bedfordshire SG19 2DL
Tel: 01767 680551
www.rspb.org.uk
Works for a healthy environment rich in birds and wildlife.

Salvo
PO Box 333, Cornhill on Tweed TD12 4YJ,
Northumberland
Tel: 01890 820333
Email: tk@salvoweb.com
www.salvo.co.uk
Architectural salvage, reclaimed building
materials.

Soil analysis services
Contact HDRA – the organic organisation,
for their fact sheet GG21 Soil Analysis
Services. See also Elm Farm research
Centre.

The Soil Association
Bristol House, 40–56 Victoria Street,
Bristol BS1 6BY
Tel: 0117 929 0661
Email: info@soilassociation.org
www.soilassociation.org
Membership charity campaigning for
organic food and farming and responsible
forestry. Its sister company, Soil
Association Certification Ltd, is the UK's
leading certification body.

**Straw Bale Building Association
(SBBA)**
PO Box 17, Todmorden OL14 8FD
www.strawbalefutures.org.uk
An organisation for those interested in
straw bale building in the UK.

Sustain
94 White Lion Street, London N1 9PF
Tel: 0207 8371288
Email: sustain@sustainweb.org
www.sustainweb.org
The alliance for better food and farming.
Represents around 100 national public
interest organisations working at
international, national, regional and local
level.

The Vegan Organic Network
58 High Lane, Chorlton, Manchester
M21 9DZ
Tel: 0161 860 4869
Email: veganorganic@supanet.com
www.veganvillage.co.uk/vohan
Researching and promoting vegan-organic
methods of agriculture and horticulture.

Waste Watch
Europa House, Ground Floor, 13–17
Ironmonger Row, London EC1V 3QG
Tel: 020 7253 6266
Email: info@wastewatch.org.uk
www.wastewatch.org.uk
Promoting action on waste reduction,
reuse and recycling. Produces a UK
recycled products guide.

Wessex Coppice Group
Vale Farm, Smugglers Lane, Marchwood,
nr Alresford, Hants SO24 0HD

Tel: 01962 772030
Email: linda.glynn@coppice.org.uk
www.coppice.org.uk
Information on coppice woods, coppice
products and related items throughout
the UK.

**The Wholesome Food
Association WFAUK**
Ball Cottage, East Ball Hill, Hartland,
Devon EX39 6BU
Tel: 01237 441118
Email: skymccain@btconnect.com
www.wfa.org.uk
Dedicated to the needs of smaller-scale
farmers and growers who want to supply
naturally grown produce in their local area.

**The Wildlife Trusts
UK Office**
The Kiln, Waterside, Mather Road, Newark
NG24 1WT
www.wildlifetrusts.org
The Wildlife Trusts partnership is the UK's
leading conservation charity exclusively
dedicated to wildlife.

Women's Environmental Network
PO Box 30626, London E1 1TZ
Tel: 020 7481 9004
Email: info@wen.org.uk
www.wen.org.uk
Tackles environmental issues of the
greatest concern to women, as well as
many which affect everyone.

**WWOOF (Willing Workers on
Organic Farms) UK**
PO Box 2675, Lewes, East Sussex
BN7 1RB
Tel: 01273 476286
www.phdcc.com/wwoof
Dedicated to helping those who would like
to work as volunteers on organic farms.

Woodnet
Email: info@woodnet.org.uk
www.woodnet.org.uk
An online network of UK producers and
users of wood.

FURTHER READING

Bartholomew, Mel
Square Foot Gardening (Rodale Press)

Cherfas, Jeremy & Fanton, Michel and Jude
The Seed Savers' Handbook (Grover
Books)

Fern, Ken
Plants for a Future (Permanent
Publications)

Green, Charlotte
Gardening Without Water (HDRA and

Search Press)
Guerra, Michael
*The Edible Container Garden – Fresh Food
from Tiny Spaces* (Gaia Books)

Hamilton, Geoff
The Organic Garden Book (Dorling
Kindersley)

Lampkin, Nicholas
Organic Farming (Farming Press)

Larkcom, Joy
The Vegetable Garden Displayed (RHS)

Larkcom, Joy
Creative Vegetable Gardening (Mitchell
Beazley)

Pears, Pauline
*Beds – Labour-saving, Space-saving, More
Productive Gardening* (HDRA and Search
Press)

Pears, Pauline & Green, Charlotte
All About Compost (HDRA and Search
Press Ltd)

Pears, Pauline & Sherman, Bob
Healthy Fruit and Vegetables (HDRA and
Search Press)

Pears, Pauline & Sherman, Bob
*Pests – How to Control them on Fruit and
Vegetables* (HDRA and Search Press)

Pears, Pauline & Stickland, Sue
RHS Organic Gardening (Mitchell Beazley)

Readman, Jo
Muck and Magic (HDRA and Search Press)

Readman, Jo
Soil Care and Management (HDRA and
Search Press)

Readman, Jo
Weeds – How to Control and Love Them
(HDRA and Search Press)

Steineck, Hellmut
Mushrooms in the Garden (Mad River
Press)

Stickland, Sue
Greenhouses (HDRA and Search Press)

Stickland, Sue
Heritage Vegetables (Gaia Books)

Stickland, Sue
The Small Ecological Garden
(HDRA and Search Press)

Stickland, Sue
*Back Garden Seed Saving – keeping our
vegetable heritage alive* (eco-logic books)

Salt, Bernard
Gardening Under Plastic (BT Batsford)

FACTSHEETS

HDRA produce over 100 factsheets on
various aspects of organic gardening.
Contact them for a list.

PLANT AND SEED DIRECTORIES

RHS Plant Finder
Editor Tony Lord. (Dorling Kindersley)
Also available at www.rhs.org.uk
The 2001–2002 edition lists 70,000
plants and directs you to over 800
nurseries where they are available.

The Seed Search
Karen Platt (Karen Platt 2000)
www.seedsearch.demon.co.uk
Over 40,000 seeds and where to buy
them worldwide. All types of flowering
plants and over 7,500 vegetables.

ORGANIC GARDENS TO VISIT

**Audley End Organic Kitchen
Garden**
Saffron Walden, Essex CB11 4JF
Tel: 01799 522399

Barnsdale Plants and Gardens
The Avenue, Exton, Oakham, Rutland
LE15 8AH.
Tel: 01572 813200

Hatfield House
Hatfield, Hertfordshire AL9 5NQ
Tel: 01707 262823
Open March to September, phone for
details.

Ryton Organic Gardens
Coventry CV8 3LG
Tel: 024 7630 8211
Email: enquiry@hdra.org.uk
www.hdra.org.uk

Yalding Organic Gardens
Benover Road, Yalding, nr Maidstone,
Kent ME18 6EX
Tel: 01622 814650

Index

Page numbers in *italic* indicate
illustrations

D

Acknowledgments

This book is dedicated to Lawrence Hills, one of the pioneers of the organic movement, who founded HDRA.

The Editor-in-chief would like to thank HDRA staff, and, in particular, colleagues in HDRA's Information and Education department for their forbearance, and hard work, during the production of this book. Also Kate Brown and Ned Litton.

Pauline Pears
June 2001

Dorling Kindersley would like to thank:

Pam Brown, Simon Maughan, Sue Stickland and Joanna Chisholm for editorial assistance; Katie Butler, Nick Robinson, Ben Rafkin, David Pierson, Julian Goodfrey and Glen Pierce for their help and support during photography sessions at Yalding, and Mike Thurloe at Audley End.

Text credits

Introduction to Organic Gardening
Alan Gear, Jackie Gear, Pauline Pears

Organic by Design
Dr Isabelle Van Groeningen
(Garden plans: Kathleen Askew
pp.27, 28 and 29; Andrew Miller
pp.21, 22–23 and 24–25)

Soil and Soil Care
Colin Shaw

Water and Watering
Owen Smith

Weeds and Weed Control
Pauline Pears

Plant Health
Dr Martin Warnes

Raising Plants
Owen Smith

The Garden Framework
Kathleen Askew

Woody Plants and Climbers
Dr Isabelle Van Groeningen

Herbaceous Plants
Dr Isabelle Van Groeningen

Lawns and Lawn Care
Adam Pasco

Gardening for Wildlife
Sally Cunningham

Container Gardening
Bernard Salt and Pauline Pears

Gardening Under Cover
Bernard Salt

Growing Fruit
Bob Sherman

Growing Herbs
Anna Corbett

Growing Vegetables
Anna Corbett and John Walker

A–Z of Vegetable and Salad Crops
Sally Cunningham, Pauline Pears

A–Z of Plant Problems
Patsy Dyer and Janet Walker,
with Pauline Pears, Rebecca
Potts and Maggi Brown

Gardening and the Law
Andrew Miller

Index

Hilary Bird

Picture credits

The publisher would like to thank the following for their kind permission to reproduce their photographs:
(t=top, b=bottom, r=right, l=left, c=centre, f=far)

Peter Anderson: 63b.
Charlotte De La Bedoyere: 12bfl, 13bfl, 14br, 47tl, 47tr, 47cla, 47cra, 47bl, 47br, 48tl, 55tr, 68cl, 68c, 70b, 70t, 71t, 295bl, 303tr, 304bc, 304br, 305tr, 305bl, 305br, 307br, 310br, 311tr, 313bl, 318tl, 318bl, 319bc.
Flowform sequence at Ruskin Mill designed by John Wilkes, photo by Laurence Snook: 71b.
Garden Picture Library: A. I. Lord 204bc; Brian Carter 218; Christopher Gallagher 8; Friedrich Strauss 211; Howard Rice 278; Janet Sorrell 204br; Jerry Pavia 219tl; Juliet Greene 66b; Juliette Wade 9b, 209tr; Mayer/Le Scanff 216; Philippe Bonduel 91tr; Steven Wooster 232tc; Sunniva Harte 186cl.
Holt Studios International: 231l, 307tr; Gordon Roberts 59b; Nigel Cattlin 35tc, 74bc, 86cl, 86cr, 86bl, 88bc, 89cl, 89cr, 89br, 89bfl, 89cfl, 93bl, 98tl, 98tr, 98cla, 98cra, 98crb, 99tl, 99tr, 99cla, 99cra, 99clb, 99crb, 186clb, 186bl, 225tr, 303cr, 304bl, 304bfl; Peter Wilson 98br, 198br; Phil McLean 198bl; Rosemary Mayer 98clb, 217; Sarah Rowland 88br.
Stephen Josland: 144t, 163tr, 167t, 189.
Andrew Lawson: 14bfl.
Joy Michaud/Sea Spring Photos: 99br, 99br, 219tr, 220, 225br, 227bc, 228b, 293bc, 295c, 302tl, 308tl, 312cl.
Natural History Museum, London: 195cr.
Oxford Scientific Films: D. G. Fox 195b; David Fox 98bl; Geoff Kidd 335bl; Gordon Maclean 314b; John McCammon 296b; Terry Heathcote 192tr.
Photos Horticultural: 80br, 81cra, 81clb, 87tr, 87cr, 198bc, 204cl, 208, 209tl, 212bl, 219b, 225bl, 226br, 230b, 232tr; Arends Nursery, Germany 203b; Wisley RHS Garden 212tl.
S & O Mathews Photography: 42bl.
Harry Smith Collection: 42br.

All other images © Dorling Kindersley.
For further information see:
www.dkimages.com